THE
GOLF COURSE GUIDE

TO THE BRITISH ISLES
BY DONALD STEEL OF THE
SUNDAY TELEGRAPH

PUBLISHED BY COLLINS WITH
The Daily Telegraph

First published 1968
Sixth revised edition 1982

© The Daily Telegraph and Sunday Telegraph
© 1977, 1982 maps by William Collins Sons & Co Ltd

Cover photograph: Hermitage Golf Course, Dublin; courtesy of the Irish Tourist Board
Maps drawn by Kazia Kram and Michael Shand and reproduced by John Gerrard

ISBN 000 434179 1

Contents

Publisher's Note

For easy reference the country has been divided into 28 areas and each area has been given an identifying letter from A to Z, then AA and BB. Within each area the courses are arranged alphabetically and numbered, starting from 1 in each new area. There is a map at the start of each section which shows the location of each of the golf courses within that section identified by the number given to each course. The outline map on page 6 shows the 28 areas within the book and the index at the back of the book lists each golf course and gives its identifying letter and number for any reference in case of doubt.

   All the information in this book has been compiled with the help of Club Secretaries. Information on subjects such as green fees is liable to change quickly and the Publishers would welcome letters from Club Secretaries or golfers finding any discrepancy between details given in the guide and their own experiences. It should be noted that many green fees are subject to V.A.T. and that weekend rates usually apply on public holidays also.

   The distribution of golf courses into grouped county areas has generally been done on the basis of the address of courses. This has resulted in some courses, particularly around London and other major cities, being included in other areas. Reference to the index will clear up any confusion and show the identifying letter and number under which each course is located.

Foreword

The theme of the sixth edition of the *Golf Course Guide* is no different to the first. It is a register of the courses of the British Isles compiled in order to help golfers in their unique choice of places to play.

In no other game and in no other country (we can count them as one for the purposes of this exercise) is there such a freedom of choice and, whilst many go in search of courses to tackle from the same back tees as Jack Nicklaus, the vast majority are content with a pleasant course for a good day out where the priorities may be more on the lunch and the setting.

Whatever your taste, the Guide holds all the answers as well as information round which holidays and short tours can be planned. No two courses in the world are the same but the opportunity for exploring is enormous and never one to be missed. Where shall we start?

The Sunday Telegraph,   Donald Steel 1982
Fleet Street,
London EC 4.

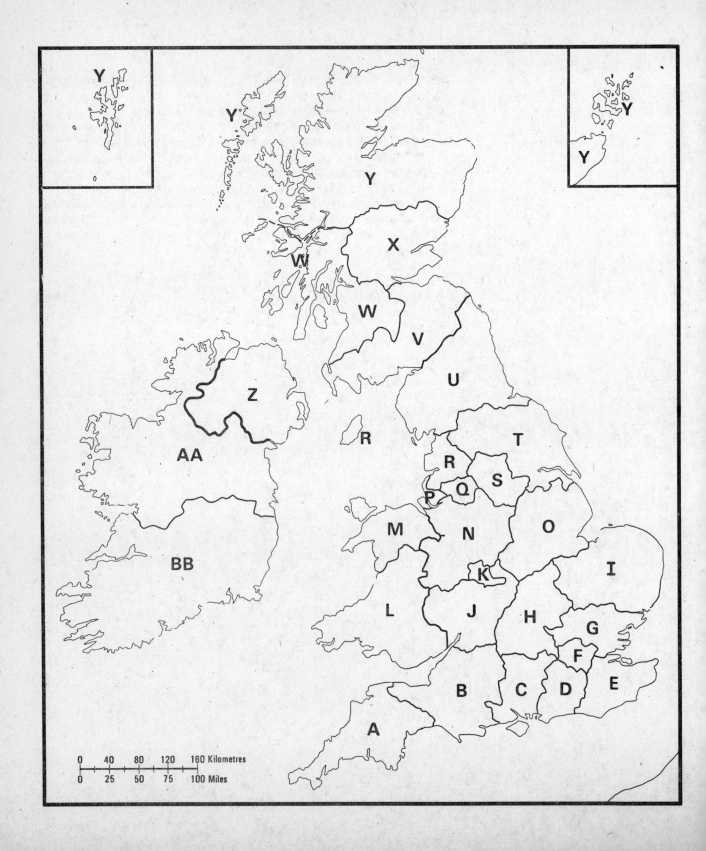

A Cornwall, Devon, Channel Islands

A 1 Alderney

Tel. Alderney (048 182) 2835
Route des Carrieres, Alderney, Channel
Islands.
1 mile E of St. Annes
Seaside course.

9 holes, 2498 yds. S.S.S. 67
Visitors welcome.
Green Fees. £4.00 per day Monday to
Friday; £5.00 per day Saturday, Sunday and
public holidays; weekly £20.00; fortnightly
£30.00; three-weekly £40.00; four-weekly
£45.00.
Snacks served. Meals only for matches or
visiting societies.

A 2 Axe Cliff

Tel. Seaton (0297) 20499
Axmouth, Seaton, Devon EX12 4AB.
A35, ¼ mile from Seaton.
Undulating seaside course.
18 holes, 4888 yds. S.S.S. 64
Visitors welcome.
Green Fees. Monday to Friday £3.50
(£2.00 with member); weekends and bank
holidays £4.00 (£2.00 with member).
Juniors: £2.50 anytime.

Society Meetings welcome on weekdays.
Hotels: Anchor; Beach House, Beer,
Seaton.
Lunches, teas and dinners served except
Tues.

A 3 Bigbury

Tel. Bigbury on Sea 207
Bigbury, Kingsbridge, Devon TQ7 4BB.
Off main Plymouth to Kingsbridge road, turn
right at Harraton Cross.
Undulating seaside course.
18 holes, 6007 yds. S.S.S. 69
Visitors welcome with members or club
membership certificate.
Green Fees. Weekdays £4.00; weekends
£5.00, after 5 p.m. £2.75.
Society Meetings by arrangement.
Hotels: Seagulls, Bigbury on Sea;
Thurlestone Hotel, Thurlestone.
Meals served.

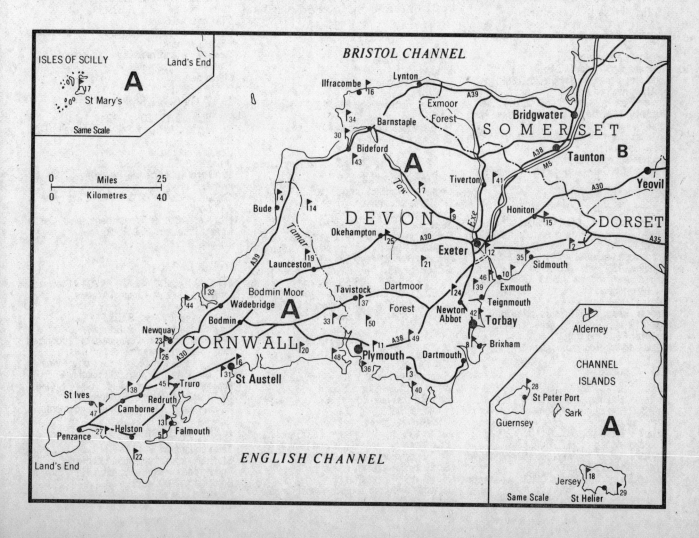

A 4 Bude & North Cornwall

Tel. Bude (0288) 2006
Burn View, Bude, Cornwall EX23 8DA.
1 minute from town centre.
Seaside course.
18 holes, 6202 yds. S.S.S. 70
Course designed by Tom Dunn (1890).
Visitors welcome.
Green Fees. Weekdays £5.00; Sundays
£6.00; weekly £18; fortnightly £26.
Society Meetings welcome on weekdays.
Hotels: in Bude.
Meals served except Mon.

A 5 Budock Vean

Tel. Mawnan Smith 281
Falmouth, Cornwall.
On main road between Falmouth and Helston.
Undulating parkland course.
9 holes, 3100 yds. S.S.S. 67
Course designed by James Braid.
Visitors welcome.
Green Fees. Weekdays £2.30; weekends
£3.45.
Society Meetings by arrangement.
Hotels: Budock Vean; Muedon Vean;
Nansidwell.

A 6 Carlyon Bay

Tel. Par 4250
Carlyon Bay, St. Austell, Cornwall PL25 3RG.
On main Plymouth to Truro road 1 mile W of
St. Blazey.
Seaside/parkland course.
18 holes, 6463 yds. S.S.S. 71
Course designed by J. Hamilton Stutt.
Visitors welcome.
Green Fees. £6.00 (£3.50 with member).
Society Meetings by arrangement with
hotel management
Hotels: Carlyon Bay Hotel; Porth Avallen
Hotel, Carlyon Bay.
Lunches served except Mon.
Free golf for Carlyon Bay Hotel residents.

A 7 Chulmleigh

Tel. 076 98 248
Tresco, Leigh Rd., Chulmleigh, N. Devon.
Midway between Exeter and Barnstaple 1
mile off A377.
Meadowland course.
18 holes, 1311 yds. S.S.S. 54
Course designed by J.W.D. Goodban and
W.G. Mortimer.
Visitors welcome.
Green Fees. £1.50 per round or day.
Society Meetings by arrangement.
Hotels: Red Lion Hotel.
Meals served. Accommodation.

A 8 Churston

Tel. Churston 842218
Churston, Brixham, Devon.
On A379 3 miles from Paignton.
Downland course.
18 holes, 6243 yds. S.S.S. 70
Course designed by H.S. Colt.
Visitors welcome with proof of membership
to recognized golf club.
Green Fees. Weekdays £6.00; weekends
and bank holidays £7.00.
Society Meetings by arrangement.

Hotels: Broadsands Links Hotel, Churston.
Snacks and lunches served.

A 9 Crediton Downes

Tel. Crediton 3991
Hookway, Crediton, Devon EX17 2DH.
8 miles from Exeter.
Parkland course.
18 holes, 6003 yds. S.S.S. 70
Visitors welcome.
Green Fees. £5.00 (£2.50 with member).
Hotels: in Exeter.
Lunch and dinner served.

A 10 East Devon

Tel. Budleigh Salterton 2018
North View Rd., Budleigh Salterton, Devon.
5 miles from Exmouth, 12 miles from Exeter;
7 miles from M5, junction 30 to A377.
Heathland course.
18 holes, 6217 yds. S.S.S. 70
Visitors welcome with letter of introduction.
Green Fees. Weekdays £6.50; weekends
£7.50.
Hotels: Rosemullion, Budleigh; Devoncourt,
Royal Beacon, Exmouth.
Meals served except Mon.

A 11 Elfordleigh Hotel & Golf Club.

Tel. Plymouth (0752) 336428
Plympton, Plymouth, Devon.
A38.
Parkland course.
9 holes, 5481 yds. S.S.S. 67
Course designed by J.H. Taylor.
Visitors welcome.
Green Fees. Weekdays £3.00; weekends
£3.50.
Hotel: attached to course.
Bar snacks served.

A 12 Exeter Golf & Country Club

Tel. Topsham 4139
Countess Wear, Exeter, Devon.
On A377 to Exmouth.
Parkland course.
18 holes, 6048 yds. S.S.S. 69
Course designed by James Braid.
Visitors welcome, weekends restricted
during summer; ladies' day Tues.
Green Fees. Weekdays £5.00 per round
(guests £3.50), £6.50 per day (guests
£4.50); weekends £6.50 per round (guests
£5.00), £9.00 per day (guests £7.00).
Society Meetings welcome.

A 13 Falmouth

Tel. Falmouth 311262
Swanpool Rd., Falmouth, Cornwall.
½ mile W of Swanpool Beach.
Seaside parkland course.
18 holes, 5581 yds. S.S.S. 67
Visitors welcome.
Green Fees. Weekdays £5.00 per round,
£6.00 per day; weekends and bank holidays
£6.00 per round, £7.00 per day.
Society Meetings welcome.
Hotels: in Falmouth.
Lunches and teas served; evening meals by
arrangement.

A 14 Holsworthy

Tel. 0409 253177
Killatree, Holsworthy, N. Devon.
A3072 from Holsworthy, 2 miles on left.
Parkland course.
18 holes, 5904 yds. S.S.S. 68
Visitors welcome.
Green Fees. £4.00.
Hotels: many in area.
Snacks served.

A 15 Honiton

Tel. Honiton 2943
Middlehills, Honiton, Devon.
2 miles S of town.
Parkland course.
18 holes, 5239 yds. S.S.S. 66
Visitors welcome.
Green Fees. Weekdays £4.50 per round;
weekends £6.00.
Society Meetings by arrangement.
Hotels: Deer Park Hotel; Coombe House.
Lunches, teas and suppers served.

A 16 Ilfracombe

Tel. Ilfracombe 62176
Hele Bay, Ilfracombe, N. Devon.
On A399 Ilfracombe to Combe Martin road.
Undulating downland course.
18 holes, 5841 yds. S.S.S. 68
Visitors welcome.
Green Fees. Weekdays £5.00; weekends
£6.00 per day.
Society Meetings by arrangement.
Hotels: in Ilfracombe.
Meals served.

A 17 Isles of Scilly

Tel. Scillonia (07204) 692
St. Mary's, Isles of Scilly, Cornwall TR21
0NF.
Seaside course.
9 holes, 3033 yds. S.S.S. 69
Visitors welcome on weekdays, Sun. by
invitation only.
Green Fees. £4.00 per day; weekly
£11.50.
Hotels: Atlantic; Tregarthens; Star Castle
Hotel; Godolphin; Bell Rock.
Snacks served.

A 18 La Moye

Tel. 0534 43401 (Sec.); 42701 (Steward)
La Moye, Jersey, Channel Islands.
Seaside course.
18 holes, 6589 yds. S.S.S. 71
Course designed by G. Boomer.
Visitors welcome if members of recognized
club, weekends restricted.
Green Fees. £8.00 per day; weekly
£30.00; fortnightly £45.00; monthly £55.00.
Hotels: Atlantic, La Pulente; Silver Springs,
St. Brelade; Mermaid, St. Peter.
Snacks served; lunches by arrangement.

A 19 Launceston

Tel. Launceston 3442
St. Stephens, Launceston, Cornwall.
Bude road from Launceston, left turn to
Egloskerry, 200 yards.
Parkland course.
18 holes, 6385 yds. S.S.S. 71

Unique setting at Moretonhampstead

It is no denouncement of hotel courses that they conjure up ideas of miniature golf where the greens are small, the hazards unusual and local knowledge is an asset.

For many they provide pleasant recreation in leisurely surroundings with no thought of keeping a score but, generally speaking in England, they do not attract the good player anxious to try his hand at something a little more stern.

The exception, to the best of my knowledge, is Moretonhampstead where in its own grounds 700 feet up on the north-east fringe of Dartmoor, the Manor House Hotel offers 18 holes of intriguing and testing quality that once seen are not readily forgotten.

For many years its length remained at a modest 5600 yards but gradually it became obvious that if it were to fulfil its proper function as a first-rate course, it required a few adjustments to bring it in line.

The increase to 6260 yards was carried out without giving the occasional golfer the impression that he was now attempting something impossible, but simply as a means of making better use of some fascinating golfing country in a glorious setting.

One is aware of something special even before stopping in the town for final directions delivered in rich Devon tones by a local constable. There are distant views of Dartmoor and the course comes in sight through the lodge gates, but first impressions of the fairly straightforward holes beside the drive can be misleading.

The first eight holes, planned with just the right blend of malice and cunning along the tortuous path of the fast flowing River Bovey, in which the trout obviously thrive on golf balls, represent by far the hardest part of the course where even the gifted player is thankful to keep his ball above water level.

From the elevated 1st tee, from which one is almost afraid to play for fear of spoiling the groundsman's work, the stream is an immediate threat having to be crossed with a thunderous drive or, more likely, a delicate second. A thumping good second is needed to make the carry to the 2nd and 5th greens while in between come two splendid holes of widely differing lengths that are not easily mastered either.

The 3rd ('Waters Meet') is only 160 yards, but the green, set in a picturesque alcove of rhododendrons, is bordered on the right by the ubiquitous river into which, at that point, it is particularly easy to stray. At the excellent 4th (530 yds) trouble lies to worry the hooker in the form of a grey stone boundary wall.

It is just as well that the 6th offers the chance of a three, for the 7th (390 yds, and aptly named 'The Styx') most probably will not. The drive should be slightly to the left away from the Bovey which also restricts the entrance to the green farther up; but the 8th mercifully sees it flow away to the hills, its work done, and as the climb is made to the 9th tee, pausing to let the mind and eye wander, the remaining holes offer more scope for opening the shoulders.

This is the more congenial part for a family foursome although the 9th to a punchbowl green and 11th require two big shots to get home and the 12th is a difficult one-shotter from the back marker.

The 14th poses a tricky pitch through a funnel of trees but the 16th and 17th take us up and back over the brow of Manor Tor before the 18th, with its blind second, suddenly leaves us happily within a safe pitch of the hotel's front door.

This fine, beautifully weathered stone building completes an air of intimacy rare on most courses. And as one relaxes with a drink, looking out from the terrace at the peaceful, moorland scene, the reminder that the Manor House, being a British Transport hotel, is something in which I suppose we all technically have an interest, makes the desire for another round that little bit stronger and, when it comes, that much more enjoyable.

Course designed by Hamilton Stutt.
Visitors welcome.
Green Fees. Weekdays £4.00 per round or day; weekends and bank holidays £5.00; weekly £15.00.
Society Meetings welcome.
Hotels: Eagle House; White Hart, Launceston; Arundell Arms, Lifton.
Meals served by arrangement.

A 20 Looe Bin Down

Tel. Widegates (05034) 247
Looe, Cornwall.
3 miles E of Looe.
Undulating heathland course.
18 holes, 5875 yds. S.S.S. 68
Visitors welcome.
Green Fees. Weekdays £5.50; weekends £6.50.
Hotels: Looe; Hannafore Point; Boscain.
Lunches and teas served.

A 21 Manor House Hotel

Tel. Moretonhampstead 355
Manor House Hotel, Moretonhampstead, Devon.
Leave A382, join B3212 to Moretonhampstead (16 miles) straight through village (2½ miles).
Parkland, moorland course.
18 holes, 6016 yds. S.S.S. 69
Visitors welcome.
Green Fees. Weekdays £4.50 per round, £7.00 per day; weekends £5.00 per round, £7.50 per day.
Society Meetings welcome, packages available - please contact Golf Manager.
Hotels: Manor House Hotel.
Bar and snacks Apr. to Dec.

A 22 Mullion

Tel. Mullion 240685
Cury, Helston, Cornwall.
5 miles from Helston on Lizard road.
Undulating course.
18 holes, 5610 yds. S.S.S. 67
Visitors welcome with handicap certificate.
Green Fees. Weekdays £4.00 per round, £5.50 per day; weekends £6.50 per day.
Society Meetings by arrangement.
Hotels: Poldhu Cove; Polurrian, Mullion.
Meals served except Tues.

A 23 Newquay

Tel. Newquay 3454; Professional 4830
Tower Rd., Newquay, Cornwall TR7 1LT.
1 mile from town centre, adjacent to Fistral Beach.
Seaside course.
18 holes, 6140 yds. S.S.S. 69
Course designed by H.S. Colt.
Visitors welcome Mon. to Sat., Sun. with member only.
Green Fees. Weekdays £5.50 per round; Sun. £7.00.
Society Meetings welcome weekdays only.
Hotels: Bredon Court; Hotel Riviera; Kilbirnie; Headland.
Lunches and snacks served except Mon.

A 24 Newton Abbot (Stover)

Tel. Newton Abbot 2460
Newton Abbot, S. Devon.
On main road between Newton Abbot and Bovey Tracey (A382).
Parkland course.
18 holes, 5724 yds. S.S.S. 68.
Visitors welcome if members of recognized club.
Green Fees. Weekdays £6.00 per round or day; weekends £7.00 per round or day; weekly £25.00.
Society Meetings by arrangement.
Hotels: Coombe Cross Hotel; Edgemoor Hotel, Bovey Tracey; Bel-Alp, Haytor.
Lunches and teas served.

A 25 Okehampton

Tel. Okehampton 2113
Okehampton, Devon.
A30 to Okehampton, then clearly signposted.
Moorland course.
18 holes, 5272 yds. S.S.S. 67
Visitors welcome.
Green Fees. £5.00.
Society Meetings welcome.
Hotels: White Hart; Plume of Feathers; Fountain.
Bar snacks between 12 noon and 2 p.m.
Meals booked at the club for groups of 12 or more.

Jersey's link with history

For all the thousands of people who take up golf each year, it is unlikely that more than a handful come to show any great interest in the game's history. But even those with only a sparing knowledge of days long ago will probably be aware of the remarkable number of famous players who have emerged from the Channel Islands.

Harry Vardon, son of a gardener, and Ted Ray, until Tony Jacklin the only English professionals to have won the United States Open championship, were born not far from the links of Royal Jersey; Vardon actually in a cottage that stood on the edge of the course at Grouville. The Boomers, the Chevaliers, the Renoufs, the Gaudins and Tommy Horton all learned their golf either there or at La Moye, the other 18-hole course on the island. Guernsey, for its part, can claim Herbert Jolly and Henry Cotton's mother, who almost certainly gave the great man his first sight of golf from his pram at the home of the Royal Guernsey club.

Regrettably my travels have not yet allowed the chance of a round at Guernsey, an omission I hope may be rectified soon, but happily I am familiar with both Royal Jersey and La Moye, which provide a pleasant contrast to each other and offer the thriving community of Jersey golfers two delightful places to play.

Royal Jersey, founded in 1878 and the senior of the two clubs by nearly a quarter of a century, is, to my mind, the more difficult, occupying a quiet position along the shores of Grouville Bay which curves gently away towards the picturesque harbour at Gorey under the imposing walls of the historic castle of Mont Orgueil. The 2nd, 3rd, 4th and 5th, an area used partly for gun sites during the German occupation of the last war, follow this same path, but thereafter the holes move inland.

The 8th (406 yards, with gorse on either hand) is a fearsome prospect; the 10th is a genuine par five of over 500 yards and the remainder of the inward half cuts to and fro across the broader reaches of the course, culminating in two consecutive short holes (the 16th and 17th) and an 18th that takes us back past the shadow of Fort Henry to a green raised up surveying the scene.

Royal Jersey's overall length of just over 6,000 yards is not a true indication of its many qualities, and the same could be said of La Moye; but La Moye enjoys, in the beauty of its setting, a blessing that few courses in the world surpass and, whatever the shortcomings of one's own play, it is always admirable consolation.

The lighthouse on its lonely tip at Corbiere; mile after mile of sea, sand and rock, and a distant glimpse of the other islands make a memorable picture from the clubs elevated perch, but the golf is entertaining too, and, in winds from which there is no escape, rarely straightforward.

Various improvements have been made to the course, but some new holes in the best of the neighbouring dune country have transformed the test which the professionals took in their stride.

The combination of fairways that tumble among these dunes, a smaller quota of blind shots than hitherto and a good finish have raised La Moye to a new pitch; but countless visitors to the island each summer are not in search of courses that would test Nicklaus. Golf for the vast majority is, thank goodness, a game to be enjoyed in nice, friendly surroundings, and in that light, more than any other, Royal Jersey and La Moye fit the bill to perfection.

A 26 Perranporth

Tel. Perranporth 2454
Budnick Hill, Perranporth, Cornwall.
B3285 off A3075 S of Newquay.
Seaside course.
18 holes, 6078 yds. S.S.S. 70
Course designed by James Braid.
Visitors welcome.
Green Fees. Weekdays £5.00; weekends £6.00; weekly £25.00; fortnightly £35.00.
Society Meetings by arrangement.
Hotels: Droskyn House Hotel, Perranporth.
Meals served by arrangement.

A 27 Praa Sands

Tel. Germoe (073 676) 3445
Germoe Crossroads, Penzance, Cornwall TR20 9RB.
Off A394, 7 miles Helston, 7 miles Penzance.
Undulating seaside course.
9 holes, 2018 yds. S.S.S. 60
Visitors welcome at all times except Sun. a.m. and during competitions.
Green Fees. £4.00 per day, £2.50 after 5 p.m. (£1.50 with member). Holiday membership available.
Society Meetings welcome on weekdays.
Hotels: Lesceave Cliff; Praa Sands.
Bar snacks, lunches; evening meals by arrangement.

A 28 Royal Guernsey

Tel. Guernsey (0481) 46523
L'Ancresse, Vale, Guernsey, Channel Islands.
3 miles from St. Peter Port.
Undulating seaside course.
18 holes, 6141 yds. S.S.S. 70
Visitors welcome except Thurs. and Sat. afternoons and all day Sun.
Green Fees. £8.00 per day; weekly £30.00; fortnightly £45.00; monthly £55.00.
Hotels: L'Ancresse Lodge Hotel; Pembroke Bay Hotel, L'Ancresse.
Lunches and evening meals served by arrangement.

A 29 Royal Jersey

Tel. Jersey Central (0534) 54416
Grouville, Jersey, Channel Islands.
4 miles E of St. Helier.
Seaside course.
18 holes, 6106 yds. S.S.S. 69
Visitors welcome if members of recognized club.
Green Fees. £8.00 per day; weekly £35.00; fortnightly £65.00.
Hotels: Grouville Bay Hotel; Beachcomber, Grouville; Moorings Hotel, Gorey.
Meals served.

A 30 Royal North Devon

Tel. Bideford 3817
Westward Ho!, N. Devon.
Northam road from Bideford, right by Post Office in Northam (¼ mile).
Seaside course.
(Championship) 18 holes, 6639 yds. S.S.S. 72
(Winter) 18 holes, 5960 yds. S.S.S. 69
Course designed by Tom Morris.

Visitors welcome.
Green Fees. Weekdays £4.00 per round or day; weekends £4.50 per round or day.
Society Meetings welcome.
Hotels: Durrant House; Yeolden House, Northam, Bideford.
Snacks and afternoon teas served; lunches by arrangement.

A 31 St. Austell

Tel. St. Austell 2649
Tregongeeves Lane, Tregongeeves, St. Austell, Cornwall PL26 7DS.
On main St. Austell to Truro road 1 mile W of St. Austell.
Undulating parkland/moorland course.
18 holes, 5363 yds. S.S.S. 66
Visitors welcome.
Green Fees. Weekdays £5.00 per round or day; weekends £6.00 per round or day.
Reduced rates when playing with member.
Meals served by arrangement except Mon.

A 32 St. Enodoc

Tel. Trebetherick 3216
Rock, Wadebridge, Cornwall.
From Wadebridge follow Port Isaac road for 3 miles, then turn left to Rock.
Seaside course.
18 holes, 6188 yds. S.S.S. 70
9 holes, 2061 yds. S.S.S. 59
Visitors welcome. Handicap certificate requested for 18 hole course.
Green Fees. 18 hole, £4.50-£7.00 seasonal; weekly £18.00-£28.00 seasonal;

St. Enodoc—remoteness and beauty

It is perhaps its remoteness and the fact that progress along West Country roads can, at times, be discouragingly slow that makes St. Enodoc form a gap in the education of far too many golfers.

Yet, as I discovered not long ago on a special journey of my own, traffic is not always a problem and the delights of motoring in Devon and Cornwall have an added attraction when one's destination is the charming village of Rock, nestling on the quiet estuary of the River Camel opposite Padstow.

There, at the top of a short, steep lane, a white clubhouse stands looking out on one of the finest settings in golf, and it is quite likely that the visitor will be thinking more of his surroundings and what is in store, than the task of hitting his second to the 1st hole between a narrow entrance of dunes.

It is more than likely, too, that the stroke will have to be played from an uneven stance, for this opening hole, the longest on the course, is part of a piece of rolling, broken ground that could only be found at the seaside; but beyond the guide post lies the promise of rich enjoyment, and once the pitch to a fine natural green has been negotiated it is immediately evident why St. Enodoc's fame has spread so far. There are few places where it is greater fun to play.

Those who go on a golfing holiday will probably not feel inclined to keep their score unless it turns out to be good, and by the time they reach the 4th, an innocent looking hole from a distance, they may be thankful that they are not. The 2nd and 3rd are splendid holes and it is not until the 4th (274 yds) that the first real chance of a three arises, but like all good short par fours, it can easily cost five or six to the unwary.

With the Himalaya bunker now in sight at the 6th there is the danger that things may quickly get out of hand. This giant sandhill—certainly the highest in my experience—has to be cleared with the second shot, as has its half-brother with the drive at the 7th.

But that is the last of the dunes for a while and the 10th, full of adventure, marks a definite change in the terrain as well as offering the first sight of the famous little church which the raging winds once covered up with sand. It strikes a note of timelessness to consider that it stood for centuries before ever golf came to Cornwall, or anywhere else, and during the playing of the holes that encircle it, one's thoughts may understandably be transported from golf to less mundane matters.

Still, the 12th has its tee close to Daymer Bay's beautiful beach and though the 13th and 14th, with a hint of downland about them,

are not severe in normal conditions, they are no doubt a different story in the good old sea breezes that frequently blow.

The 18 holes measure only a fraction over 6,000 yards and in days when everyone seems bent on stretching courses to their limit, this may not sound particularly formidable; but there is not overmuch run to be had on pleasant spring turf, and the would-be Palmers may be suprised to find how much stout hitting there is to be done, especially on the last three holes, which return to the shadow of the glorious dune country.

The 16th, where my second with a spoon finished way out in the sunlit waters—partly because I had not done sufficient reconnaissance—is a genuine par five, and after a grand long one-shotter at the 17th, it needs two hefty blows at the last to bring players home to a Cornish tea and a pause for reflection.

Missed putts, a lost ball or a skirmish with the Himalayas may have cast an air of gloom, but looking out on the peacefulness of the estuary with the little boats and strips of sand running away towards the open sea, it is impossible to be downcast for long. The feeling that St. Enodoc is a delightful place for a day's golf is exceeded only by the desire to return at the first opportunity.

---

9 hole, £2.25-£3.50 seasonal; weekly £9.00-£14.00 seasonal.
Society Meetings by arrangement.
Hotels: St. Moritz; St. Enodoc.
Lunches served except Fri.

A 33   St. Mellion Golf & Country Club

Tel. St. Dominick 50101
St. Mellion, Saltash, Cornwall.
3 miles S of Callington on A388.
Parkland meadowland course.
18 holes, 6604 yds. S.S.S. 72
6162 yds. S.S.S. 69
Course designed by Hamilton Stutt.
Visitors welcome if members of recognized club.
Green Fees. Weekdays £5.50; weekends £6.50.
Society Meetings by arrangement.
Hotels: St. Mellion Hotel, adjacent to golf course.
Restaurant and buttery.
Meals available each day.

A 34   Saunton

Tel. Braunton (0271) 812436
Saunton, Braunton, N. Devon EX33 1LG.
B3231 off A361 from Barnstaple at Braunton.
Seaside course.

East 18 holes, 6703 yds. S.S.S. 73
West 18 holes, 6322 yds. S.S.S. 70
Course designed by (East) Herbert Fowler, (West) Frank Pennink.
Visitors welcome with letter of introduction from own club.
Green Fees. (East) weekdays £7.00 per round or day (juniors £3.50); weekends £8.00 per round or day (juniors £4.00); weekly £35.00 (juniors £17.50); (West) weekdays £6.00 per round or day (juniors £3.00); weekends £7.00 per round or day (juniors £3.50).
Society Meetings by arrangement.
Hotels: Saunton Sands Hotel; Preston House Hotel, Saunton; Imperial, Barnstaple; Croyde Bay House Hotel, Croyde.

A 35   Sidmouth

Tel. Sidmouth 3451 and 3023
Cotmaton Rd., Peak Hill, Sidmouth, Devon.
Easy distance from town.
Undulating parkland course.
18 holes, 5188 yds. S.S.S. 65
Course designed by J.H. Taylor.
Visitors welcome.
Green Fees. Weekdays £4.00; weekends £4.50.
Society Meetings welcome on weekdays, by arrangement with Secretary.
Hotels: in Sidmouth.
Meals served except Tues.

A 36   Staddon Heights

Tel. Plymouth 42475
Staddon Heights, Plymstock, Plymouth, Devon.
5 miles from Plymouth by coast road to Turnchapel.
Undulating seaside course.
18 holes, 5584 yds. S.S.S. 67
Visitors welcome if members of recognized club.
Green Fees. Weekdays (summer) £5.00, (winter) £3.00; weekends (summer) £5.00, (winter) £3.50.
Society Meetings welcome on weekdays.
Hotels: in Plymouth.
Meals served except Mon.

A 37   Tavistock

Tel. Tavistock (0822) 2344
Down Rd., Tavistock, Devon.
On Whitchurch Down.
Moorland course.
18 holes, 6250 yds. S.S.S. 70
Visitors welcome.
Green Fees. Weekdays £4.50 per day; weekends £6.00.
Hotels: Bedford.
Meals served.

Trevose—Cornish holiday haven

As a golfing crow might fly, Trevose and St. Enodoc are something under five miles apart. They lie on either side of the peaceful Camel estuary which slips quietly into Cornwall between Rock and Padstow, and to an increasing number of visitors each summer, provide a twin attraction that is not willingly missed.

Yet for all their proximity their link by road is far from straightforward, and a good deal of careful negotiating of typical Cornish lanes is necessary after leaving St. Enodoc, before one arrives at Trevose's broad and pleasant links.

Outside the south west, Trevose's reputation is based primarily on its undoubted quality in fulfilling the requirements of golfers intent on enjoying themselves on a course that would not make Ben Hogan scratch his head. This suggests something of medium length, plenty of room to manoeuvre without the constant threat of searching for balls, and the chance for the average player to play above himself.

But for those who set their sights higher there is also just the right blend of challenge. At full stretch Trevose measures 6516 yards, the air is rarely still and the task of breaking par can be unexpectedly formidable.

The first four holes make a stern beginning with two attractive par fours—a splendid seaside hole across a grassy valley where the line is slightly left and a fine swinging dogleg between the dunes to the 4th green set above Booby's sandy bay.

This offers a stimulating sight of Atlantic rollers pounding to their reluctant halt, and with the distant view of forbidding rock islands beyond Trevose Head, it seems almost a pity to turn away up the 5th. Here a demanding second dominates the hole, as it does at the 7th—and the short 8th may well hold terrors for the slicer.

Some of the golf in the middle of the course is a shade less interesting, but the 10th has a distinctive saucer-shaped green unguarded on all sides; one would always be glad of a four at the 12th; out of bounds at the long

13th (510 yds) awaits the pulled stroke all the way down the left, and then the last three holes, together with the first four, make the round.

The 16th (204 yds) is full of character, the 17th calls for a more accurate drive and second shot than most, and finally, after a glimpse of the ruins of the original church named after the first Christian emperor of Rome, St. Constantine, the 18th takes us back up the hill with a shot which, well executed and controlled, makes a most satisfying ending.

Away to the left the short par three course presents a less rigorous, though no less amusing, test, and a line of chalets—available under certain stipulations to anyone—underlines that Trevose is essentially a holiday centre.

The clubhouse offers many other amenities to take the mind off golf; a general air of friendliness and helpfulness abounds, and always the glory of Cornwall's coastline and countryside puts the visitor at his ease.

A 38 Tehidy Park

Tel. Portreath 842208
Camborne, Cornwall TR14 0HH.
On A30.
Parkland course.
18 holes, 6356 yds. S.S.S. 70
Visitors welcome with handicap certificate if members of recognized club.
Green Fees. Weekdays £6.00 per round or day; weekends £9.00 per round or day.
Society Meetings by arrangement.
Hotels: Tregenna, Tyacks, Camborne; Glenfeadon, Portreath.
Light lunches, evening a la carte.

A 39 Teignmouth

Tel. Teignmouth 4194
Teignmouth, S. Devon TQ14 9NY.
2 miles from Teignmouth on B3102.
Moorland course.
18 holes, 6142 yds. S.S.S. 69
Visitors welcome with handicap certificate.
Green Fees. Weekdays £5.75 (£3.75 with member); weekends £7.50 (£5.50 with member).
Society Meetings welcome on weekdays.
Hotels: Royal; London, Teignmouth; Murley Grange; Cockhaven Manor, Bishopsteignton.
Lunches and bar snacks daily. Evening meals by prior arrangement except Mon. and Fri.

A 40 Thurlestone

Tel. Thurlestone 405
Thurlestone, Kingsbridge, S. Devon TQ7 3NZ.
Off A379, 4 miles S. of Kingsbridge.
Downland course by the sea.

18 holes, 6337 yds. S.S.S. 70
Visitors welcome with handicap certificate.
Green Fees. From £5.00 per day; weekly tickets available.
Hotels: Thurlestone Hotel, Thurlestone.
Lunches and teas served.

A 41 Tiverton

Tel. Tiverton (0884) 252187
Post Hill, Tiverton, Devon EX16 4NE.
5 miles from Junction 27 on M5, towards Tiverton on A373.
Parkland/meadowland course.
18 holes, 6227 yds. S.S.S. 70
Course designed by James Braid.
Visitors welcome with letter of introduction or with handicap certificate.
Green Fees. Weekdays £5.00 (£2.50 with member); weekends £6.50 (£3.00 with member).
Society Meetings Restricted to those who already have an association with the Club.
Hotels: Merrimeade, Sampford Peverell; St. George's House Hotel; Tiverton Motel, Tiverton; Green Headland Hotel, Sampford Peverell.
Lunches and teas served daily.

A 42 Torquay

Tel. Torquay (0803) 37471
Petitor Rd., St. Marychurch, Torquay TQ1 4QF.
Coast road from Teignmouth.
Undulating parkland course.
18 holes, 6251 yds. S.S.S. 70
Visitors welcome.

Green Fees. Weekdays £5.00; weekends £6.00.
Society Meetings welcome on weekdays.
Hotels: Palace Hotel; Toorak; Maidencombe House.
Lunches and teas served except Fri.

A 43 Torrington

Tel. Bideford 2792
Furzebeam Hill, Weare Trees, Torrington, Devon.
1 mile out of Torrington on Torrington to Weare Giffard road.
Undulating commonland course.
9 holes, 4582 yds. S.S.S. 63
Visitors welcome on weekdays.
Green Fees. Weekdays £2.00 per round or day; weekends £3.00 per round or day; juniors, £1.00 per round or day at all times.
Society Meetings by arrangement.
Hotels: Black Horse Hotel, Torrington.

A 44 Trevose Golf & Country Club

Tel. 520208
Constantine Bay, Padstow, Cornwall PL28 8JB.
4 miles W of Padstow off B3276.
Seaside course.
18 holes, 6461 yds. S.S.S. 71
9 holes, 1357 yds.
Course designed by H.S. Colt (1924).
Visitors welcome, handicap certificate required. No 3 or 4 ball matches 1 July to 1 October, restricted remainder of year.
Green Fees. £5.00 to £8.00 per day; weekly £20.00 to £35.00.
Society Meetings welcome Nov. to Apr.

Remote splendour of Lelant

The West Cornwall Golf Club, familiarly known as Lelant, first became famous through its connection with Jim Barnes who, born in the little village beside the links, began his golfing life there as a caddie and later went on to become British and American Open champion.

Situated within a very few miles of Land's End, Lelant has the geographical distinction of being the most westerly course on the mainland of England, Scotland and Wales but it also occupies one of the most spectacular settings and deservedly earns the respect of golfers on account of its own special merits.

At first, it catches you unawares. A stranger driving across Bodmin Moor and on past the tin mines to Redruth, Camborne and Hayle, cannot possibly suspect what lies at the rainbow's end. The approach is long and the surroundings a trifle bleak, but the turning to St. Ives is the signal that all is changing and, by the time that the course comes into sight round the corner by the church, all else except golf is quickly forgotten.

If Lelant's beauty is not fully unfurled from the clubhouse, the course imposes immediate demands with an opening short hole of 238 yards. It is comparable in length to the 1st at Royal Mid Surrey and certainly only a shot ruled on the church tower will fit the bill. The second shot to the 2nd green, perched between imposing sandhills with the sea beyond, is another test of judgment and control but thereafter the holes are not all designed to kill although, with a strong wind off the sea, scoring is no light task.

The 3rd doubles back and the 4th continues with a drive near the corner of the churchyard, dropping down towards the Saltings Estuary and the little triangle of ground on the other side of the little railway which houses the 5th, 6th and 7th. From here, the town of Hayle is no more than a stone's throw across the estuary which, though fringed with industry, is imposing none the less; but, as we leave the 8th, climb the hill to the 9th—invariably dropping a stroke as we go—and drive away from the beach huts over the hill to the 10th, the splendour of the setting is by now overwhelmingly distracting.

This, in one sense, is a pity because the 11th, bordered on the right by the railway which serves the quaintly Cornish town of St. Ives (very much a feature of Lelant's superb view), is a magnificent hole. It is dominated by another fine second between sandhills to a green nestling at the bottom of a gorse clad hill and, equally important, leads on to the long 12th where the miles of beach and vast expanse of ocean are seen at their best from the tee.

The prospect should be enough to inspire something extra from the drive but though the 13th is another shortish par four, the finish can be formidable. The 14th, returning to the dune country, is the longest par four on the course; the 16th is the second and longer of the two par fives; the 17th completes a batch of five short holes, four of which are over 190 yards, and the 18th, downhill to a smallish green, rounds things off well.

Lelant would probably have no championship pretensions beyond the county even if it were not such a remote spot but, as a delightful place to play, there are few better. With Trevose and St. Enodoc, it forms a notable trinity of courses which enrich the coast of north Cornwall and, between them, must provide thousands each year with the mixture of escape and pleasure that makes golf unique in this respect.

Hotels: Self-catering accommodation available at club for 100 in bungalows, chalets and flats.
Lunches and dinners served by arrangement except during Nov.

A 45 Truro

Tel. Truro (0872) 2640
Treliske, Truro, Cornwall.
2 miles W of Truro on A390.
Undulating parkland course.
18 holes, 5300 yds. S.S.S. 66
Visitors welcome.
Green Fees. Weekdays £5.00 per round or day; weekends and bank holidays £6.00 per round or day; weekly £15.00; monthly £25.00.
Society Meetings welcome on weekdays.
Hotels: Brookdale; Carlton, Truro.
Lunches, teas and evening meals served except Mon.

A 46 Warren

Tel. Dawlish (0626) 862255 (Sec.), 862738 (Members)
Dawlish, Devon EX7 0NF.
From Exeter take A379 to Dawlish Warren.
Seaside links course.
18 holes, 5926 yds. S.S.S. 68
Visitors welcome weekdays, summer and winter.
Green Fees. Weekdays £5.50 per round or day (£4.00 with member); weekends £7.00 per round or day (£5.50 with member).
Society Meetings welcome weekdays except Mon.
Hotels: Langstone; Rockstone.
Meals served except Mon.

A 47 West Cornwall

Tel. Hayle (0736) 753401
Lelant, St. Ives, Cornwall TR26 3DZ.
On A3074 2 miles from Lelant.
Seaside course.
18 holes, 6070 yds. S.S.S. 69
Visitors welcome if members of recognized club.
Green Fees. Weekdays £5.00; weekends £6.00; weekly £20.00.
Hotels: in St. Ives.
Snacks served; meals served except Mon.

A 48 Whitsand Bay Hotel

Tel. St. Germans (050 33) 276
Portwrinkle, Crafthole, Torpoint, Cornwall.
On coast 3 miles from A374 Torpoint Liskeard road.
Seaside course.
18 holes, 5466 yds. S.S.S. 67
Course designed by Fernie of Troon.
Visitors welcome except Sun.
Green Fees. £4.50.
Society Meetings by arrangement.
Hotels: Whitsand Bay Hotel.

A 49 Wrangaton

Tel. South Brent 3229
South Brent S. Devon.
Turn off A38 between South Brent and Bittaford at Wrangaton Post Office.
Moorland course.
9 holes, 5790 yds. S.S.S. 68
Visitors welcome.
Green Fees. Weekdays £3.00; weekends £4.00; weekly (Mon.-Fri.) £10.00.
Hotels: Carew Arms.
Snacks available.

A 50 Yelverton

Tel. Yelverton 2824
Golf Links Rd., Yelverton, S. Devon PL20 6BN.
8 miles N of Plymouth, 5 miles S of Tavistock on A386.
Moorland course.
18 holes, 6316 yds. S.S.S. 70
Course designed by Herbert Fowler.
Visitors welcome if members of recognized club.
Green Fees. Weekdays £4.00 per round or day (£3.00 with member); weekends £5.00 per round or day (£4.00 with member), plus V.A.T.
Society Meetings welcome on weekdays.
Hotels: Moorland Links Hotel, Roborough; Devon Tors, Yelverton.
Snacks and meals served by arrangement.

B Somerset, Dorset, Wiltshire, Avon

B 1 Ashley Wood

Tel. Blandford 2253
Tarrant Rawston, Blandford Forum, Dorset.
B3082 Blandford to Wimborne road.
Undulating downland course.
9 holes, 6010 yds. S.S.S. 69 (redesigned)
Visitors welcome.
Green Fees. Weekdays £4.00 per day;
weekends and bank holidays £6.00 per day.
Society Meetings by arrangement.
Meals by arrangement.

B 2 Bath

Tel. Bath 63834
Sham Castle, Bath, Avon BA2 6JG.
1½ miles SE of city centre off A36.
Undulating inland course.
18 holes, 6285 yds. S.S.S. 70
Vistors welcome, handicap certificate
required.
Green Fees. Weekdays £6.00 (£3.00 with
member); weekends and bank holidays
£7.00 (£3.00 with member); weekly
£17.00; monthly £35.00.
Society Meetings welcome Wed. and Fri.
Ladies' day Tues.
Hotels: Beaufort; Francis; Royal Crescent;
Redcar.
Meals served every day.

B 3 Bournemouth (Private Club)

Tel. Bournemouth 20307
Meyrick Park, Bournemouth, Dorset.
5 minutes from town centre.
Parkland course.
18 holes, 5865 yds.
Visitors welcome with letter of introduction.

B 4 Brean

Tel. Brean Down (027 875) 467 or 359
Brean Leisure Centre, Coast Rd., Brean,
Burnham-on-Sea, Somerset TA8 2RF.
4½ miles from M5, junction 22; follow signs for
Brean, Leisure Centre on right.
Meadowland course.
9 holes, 5532 yds. S.S.S. 66
Course designed by A.H. Clarke.
Visitors welcome weekdays, except Sat.
morning, Sun. afternoon and during
competitions.
Green Fees. Weekdays £3.50; weekends
£4.50.
Society Meetings welcome weekdays.
Hotels: Royal Clarence; Dunstan House,
Burnham-on-Sea.
Snacks, lunches, dinners.

B 5 Bridport & West Dorset

Tel. Bridport 22597
West Bay, Bridport, Dorset.
B3157 off A35, 1½ miles S of Bridport.
Seaside course.
18 holes, 5203 yds. S.S.S. 65
Course designed by J. Braid.
Visitors welcome.
Green Fees. Weekdays £5.50; weekends
£6.50.
Society Meetings welcome weekdays
only.
Hotels: George; West Bay Hotel; Bridport
Arms.
Meals served by arrangement.

B 6 Bristol & Clifton

Tel. Long Ashton (027 580) 3474
Beggar Bush Lane, Failand, Bristol BS8 3TH.
1 mile over Clifton suspension bridge.
Undulating parkland course.
18 holes, 6294 yds. S.S.S. 70
Visitors welcome on weekdays, weekends
11.00 a.m. to 12.15 p.m. and after 5.00 p.m.
Green Fees. On application to Secretary.
Society Meetings welcome on weekdays.
Hotels: Birkdale; Rock View; Redwood
Lodge Motel.
Lunches and teas served except Mon.

B 7 Broadstone

Tel. Broadstone 692595
27, Lower Links Rd., Broadstone, Dorset
BH18 8BQ.
Off A349 half way between Wimborne and
Poole.
Moorland course.
18 holes, 6115 yds. S.S.S. 70
Course designed by T. Dunn (1898); Largely
redesigned H.S. Colt (1920).
Visitors welcome with reservation.
Green Fees. Weekdays £5.00 per round,
£7.00 per day; weekends £6.00 per round,
£8.00 per day.
Society Meetings by arrangement.
Hotels: King's Head, Wimborne; Antelope;
Dolphin, Poole.
Meals served.

B 8 Broome Manor

Tel. Swindon 32403
Pipers Way, Swindon, Wiltshire.
On M4 take exit 15 to Swindon. At Coate
take Marlborough Road and turn left at Pipers
Roundabout into Pipers Way.
Parkland course.
18 holes, 6906 yds. S.S.S. 73
9 holes, 3192 yds.
Visitors welcome.
Green Fees. 18 hole, weekdays £2.50 per
round; weekends £3.30 per round; 9 hole,
weekdays £1.40; weekends £1.80.
Society Meetings weekdays by
arrangement.
Hotels: King's Arms; Post House.
Meals served.

B 9 Burnham & Berrow

Tel. Burnham-on-Sea (0278) 783137
Burnham-on-Sea, Somerset TA8 2PE.
M5 leave at junction 22 for Burnham-on-Sea
one mile N of Burnham on Berrow Road.
Seaside course.
18 holes, 6608 yds. S.S.S. 73
Visitors welcome if members of recognized
club.
Green Fees. £6.00 (half fee with
member); weekends £7.00.
Society Meetings by arrangement.
Hotels: Richmond; Dunstan House Hotel;
Sundowner.
Lunches served.

B 10 Came Down

Tel. Upwey 2531
Dorchester, Dorset.
Off A354 2 miles S (signposted).
Downland course.
18 holes, 6214 yds. S.S.S. 71
Visitors welcome with reservation except
Sun. morning.
Green Fees. Weekdays £5.00 per round
or day (£4.00 with member); weekends
£6.50 per round or day (£5.00 with
member); weekly £15.00.
Society Meetings weekdays by
arrangement.
Hotels: King's Arms, Dorchester; Royal,
Weymouth.
Snacks served; meals by arrangement
except Fri.

B 11 Chippenham

Tel. Chippenham (0249) 2040
Malmesbury Rd., Chippenham, Wilts. SN15
5LT.
Off A429 and off junction 17 M4 2 miles.
Meadowland course.
18 holes, 5540 yds. S.S.S. 67
Visitors welcome on weekdays.
Green Fees. Weekdays £4.00; weekends
£6.50.
Society Meetings welcome weekdays
only.
Hotels: Angel, Chippenham; Bell House,
Sutton Benger; King's Arms, Malmesbury.
Meals served.

B 12 Chipping Sodbury

Tel. Chipping Sodbury 319042 Secretary.
Chipping Sodbury, Bristol BS17 6PU.
Leave M4 at Exit 18, M5 at Exit 14.
Parkland course.
New Course, 18 holes, 6912 yds. S.S.S. 73
Old Course, for beginners, 9 holes, 3076
yds.
New Course designed by Fred Hawtree.
Visitors welcome (Sun. after 12 noon).
Green Fees. 18 hole, weekdays £4.00;
weekends £5.00 (reduction with member). 9
hole, weekdays £1.00; weekends £1.25
(reduction with member).
Society Meetings welcome.
Hotels: Moda, Cross Hands, Petty France.
Meals served.

B 13 Clevedon

Tel. Clevedon 874057
Walton St. Mary, Clevedon, Avon BS21.
B3124 off A369.
Undulating course.
18 holes, 5835 yds. S.S.S. 68

Course designed by J.H. Taylor (1907).
Visitors welcome on weekdays; weekends if members of recognized club.
Green Fees. Weekdays £5.00; weekends £7.00.
Society Meetings Mon. only.
Hotels: Walton Park Hotel; Highcliffe, Clevedon.
Meals and Bar snacks served.

B 14   Enmore Park

Tel. Spaxton 481 Secretary Manager; Steward, Spaxton 244
Enmore, Bridgwater, Somerset.
On Spaxton road off A39 W of town.
Parkland course.
18 holes, 6444 yds. S.S.S. 71
Course designed by Fred Hawtree & Co.
Green Fees. Weekdays £5.00 per day; weekends £6.00 per day, plus V.A.T.
Society Meetings welcome weekdays only.
Hotels: Clarence, North Petherton; County, Taunton.
Meals served. Caravan park for golfers.

B 15   Ferndown

Tel. Ferndown 874602
119 Golf Links Rd., Ferndown, Wimborne, Dorset BH22 8BU.
Off A31.
Heathland course.
(Old) 18 holes, 6469 yds. S.S.S. 71
(New) 9 holes, 5604 yds. S.S.S. 68
Old course designed by H. Hilton (1912), new course by Hamilton Stutt (1971).
Visitors welcome if members of recognized club, with letter of introduction.
Green Fees. Weekdays £8.00 per day; weekends and bank holidays £8.50.
Society Meetings welcome Mon. Wed. and Fri. only.
Hotels: Dormy Hotel.
Lunch and tea served.

B 16   Filton

Tel. 0272 694169
Golf Course Lane, Filton, Bristol BS12 7QS.
Off A38 N of Bristol.
Parkland course.
18 holes.
Visitors welcome on weekdays; weekends with member only.
Green Fees. Weekdays £6.00 (£5.00 with member); weekends £5.00 with member.
Society Meetings by arrangement.
Hotels: in Bristol.
Meals served.

B 17   Fosseway Country Club

Tel. Midsomer Norton (0761) 412214
Charlton Lane, Midsomer Norton, Bath, Somerset BA3 4BD.
Just off A367, 10 miles from Bath.
Parkland course.
9 holes, 4194 yds. S.S.S. 61
Visitors welcome except Wed. after 5 p.m., Sun. morning.
Green Fees. Weekdays £2.00; weekends £3.00 all day.
Society Meetings welcome.
Hotels: Court, Emborough; Swan, Wells.
Restaurant open at all times except Sat. morning and Sun. evening.

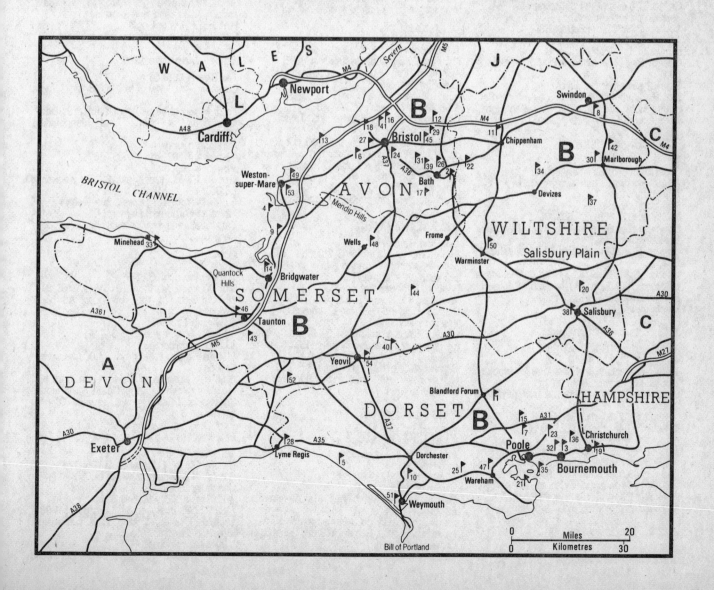

B 18 Henbury

Tel. Bristol (0272) 500660
Henbury Hill, Westbury-on-Trym, Bristol BS10 7QB.
3 miles N of city centre; signposted Westbury-on-Trym from all directions. M5 Junction 17.
Parkland course.
18 holes, 6039 yds. S.S.S. 70
Course alterations by Hawtree and Son.
Visitors welcome on weekdays, weekends with member only.
Green Fees. Weekdays £5.00 per round or day; weekends £5.50 per round or day.
Society Meetings Tues. and Fri. by arrangement.
Hotels: St. Vincent Rocks; Grand Spa, Clifton.
Meals served; dinner by arrangement.

B 19 Highcliffe Castle

Tel. Highcliffe (04253) 72953; Secretary, Highcliffe 72210
Lymington Rd., Highcliffe, Christchurch, Dorset.
On A337 2 miles E of Christchurch.
Seaside parkland course.
18 holes, 4655 yds. S.S.S. 63
Visitors welcome if members of recognized club, with handicap certificate.
Green Fees. Weekdays £6.00; weekends £8.00.
Society Meetings welcome.
Hotels: Avonmouth Hotel, Somerford; Red House Hotel, Barton; Chewton Glen Hotel, Christchurch Road, New Milton.

B 20 High Post

Tel. 0722 73 231
Great Durnford, Salisbury, Wilts.
A345 midway between Salisbury and Amesbury.
Parkland course.
18 holes, 6267 yds. S.S.S. 70
Course designed by Hawtree and Taylor.
Visitors welcome.
Green Fees. Weekdays £5.00; weekends £5.00.
Society Meetings welcome weekdays.
Hotels: Red Lion; White Hart; Cathedral Hotel; Rose and Crown, Salisbury.
Meals served.

B 21 Isle of Purbeck

Tel. Studland (092 944) 361
Swanage, Dorset BH19 3AB.
Between Studland and Swanage, overlooking Poole Harbour and Bournemouth.
18 hole undulating course; 9 hole downland course.
18 holes, 6248 yds. S.S.S. 71
9 holes, 4044 yds. S.S.S. 60
Visitors welcome.
Green Fees. 18 hole course Mon.-Sat. £6.50 per day; Sun. and bank holidays £7.50 per day. 9 hole course £3.00 per day.
Society Meetings welcome except Sun.
Hotels: Pines; Corrie; Knoll House.
Lunches and evening meals served.

B 22 Kingsdown

Tel. Box (0225 74) 2530
Kingsdown, Corsham, Wilts. SN14 9BS.
Turn off A4 onto A363, turn left at Crown Inn, uphill for 2 miles.
Heathland course.
18 holes, 6235 yds. S.S.S. 70
Visitors welcome.
Green Fees. Weekdays £4.50 per day; weekends £6.50 per day.
Society Meetings by arrangement.
Hotels: Stagecoach Motel, Corsham; Beaufort, Bath.
Meals served, Wed. to Sat.

B 23 Knighton Heath

Tel. Northbourne 2633
Francis Ave., Bournemouth, Dorset.
A348 from Ferndown or Poole or B3061 from Bournemouth. At Wallisdown Rd. Roundabout take road marked 'no exit'.
Heathland course.
18 holes, 6206 yds. S.S.S. 70
Visitors welcome on weekdays.
Green Fees. Weekdays £5.00; weekends £6.00.
Society Meetings weekdays by arrangement.
Hotels: in Bournemouth and Poole.
Lunches, evening meals served except Mon.

B 24 Knowle

Tel. Bristol (0272) 770660
Fairway, Brislington, Bristol BS4 5DF.
A37 from Bristol for 3 miles, left at Happy Landings for ½ mile.
Parkland course.
18 holes, 6016 yds. S.S.S. 69
Course designed by Hawtree and Taylor.
Visitors welcome.
Green Fees. Weekdays £5.00 per round or day (£2.50 with member); weekends £6.00 (£3.00 with member).
Society Meetings Thurs. only.
Hotels: Grange, Keynsham.
Snacks served; meals by arrangement.

B 25 Lakey Hill

Tel. Bere Regis 776
Hyde, Wareham, Dorset BH20 7NT.
3 miles W of Wareham. Worgret Heath signpost, off Worgret Rd.
Parkland/wooded flat course.
18 holes, 6137 yds. S.S.S. 69
Course designed by Brian Bramford.
Visitors welcome.
Green Fees. Weekdays £5.00 (£3.00 with member); weekends £7.00 (£5.00 with member).
Society Meetings welcome.
Hotels: Worgret Manor; Woolbridge Manor.
Lunches served.

B 26 Lansdown

Tel. Bath 22138
Lansdown, Bath, Avon BA1 9BT.
Adjoining Bath racecourse, Exit 18 off M4.
Parkland course.
18 holes, 6228 yds. S.S.S. 70
Visitors welcome.
Green Fees. Weekdays £4.00; weekends £6.75.
Society Meetings by arrangement.
Hotels: Francis; Beaufort, Bath; Lansdown Grove, Lansdown.
Meals served except Mon.

B 27 Long Ashton

Tel. Long Ashton (027 580) 2316
The Clubhouse, Long Ashton, Bristol BS18 9DW.
On B3129, 3 miles SW of Bristol.
Moorland, parkland course.
18 holes, 6219 yds. S.S.S. 70
Visitors welcome on weekdays, weekends with member only.
Green Fees. Weekdays £6.00; weekends £7.00.
Society Meetings Wed. only.
Hotels: Grand; Dragonara, Bristol.
Meals served.

B 28 Lyme Regis

Tel. Lyme Regis 2043
Timber Hill, Lyme Regis, Dorset DT7 3HQ.
Off A35 1 mile N of Lyme Regis.
Undulating downland course.
18 holes, 6010 yds. S.S.S. 69
Visitors welcome.
Green Fees. Weekdays and weekends £6.00 (£3.00 with member); weekly £25.00.
Society Meetings welcome weekdays except Thurs. and Sun. morning.
Hotels: in Lyme Regis.
Snacks served; meals by arrangement.

B 29 Mangotsfield

Tel. Bristol 565501
Carsons Rd., Mangotsfield, Bristol, Avon BS17 3LW.
From M4 junction 18, 1 mile towards Bath; turn right for Hinton and Mangotsfield (B4465).
Parkland course.
18 holes, 5297 yds. S.S.S. 66
Visitors welcome.
Green Fees. Weekdays £3.50; weekends £5.00.
Society Meetings welcome weekdays.
Hotels: Eurocrest, Hambrook.
Bar; meals and snacks available every day. Caravan site.

B 30 Marlborough

Tel. Marlborough 52147
The Common, Marlborough, Wilts. SN8 1DU.
On outskirts of the town, on A345 to Swindon.
Downland course.
18 holes, 6434 yds. S.S.S. 71
Visitors welcome.
Green Fees. Weekdays £4.00; weekends £6.00.
Society Meetings welcome on Tues.
Hotels: Ailesbury Arms; Castle & Ball Hotel.
Snacks and light meals served, Dinners served on Sat.

B 31 Mendip

Tel. Oakhill 840570
Gurney Slade, Bath, Avon BA3 4UT.
3 miles N of Shepton Mallet on A37.
Undulating downland, inland course.
18 holes, 5958 yds. S.S.S. 69
First 9 holes designed by A. Vardon (1908), second 9 holes, Cotton (C.K.), Pennink, Lawrie & Partners (1965).
Visitors welcome.
Green Fees. Weekdays £4.50 per round

or day (£3.00 with member); weekends £6.00 per round or day (£3.50 with member); juniors under 18, half above fees.
Society Meetings welcome weekdays
Hotels: Crown, Swan, Wells; Charlton House, Shrubbery, Stagecoach, Shepton Mallet; Red Lion, Somerton.
Full catering daily (Mon. bar snacks only).

B 32 Meyrick Park

Tel. Bournemouth (0202) 20871
Meyrick Park, Bournemouth, Dorset.
Correspondence to Recreation Officer, Town Hall, Bournemouth, Dorset BH2 6DY Tel. (0202) 22066 ext. 576.
½ mile from town centre.
Undulating parkland, seaside course.
18 holes, 5865 yds. S.S.S. 69
Course designed by Tom Dunn (1894).
Visitors welcome.
Green Fees. £3.50 per round, £4.50 per day.
Society Meetings welcome.
Hotels: in Bournemouth.
Lunches served.

B 33 Minehead & West Somerset

Tel. Minehead (0643) 2057
The Warren, Minehead, Somerset.
At eastern end of seafront.
Seaside course.
18 holes, 6131 yds. S.S.S. 69
Visitors welcome, wide wheel trolleys only.
Green Fees. Weekdays £5.00 (£2.50 with member); weekends £6.30 (£3.15 with member).
Society Meetings welcome by arrangement.
Hotels: Beach; Benares; Wyndcott; York.
Lunches, evening meals and teas served.

B 34 North Wilts

Tel. Cannings (038086) 627
Bishop's Canning's, Devizes, Wilts. SN10 2LP.
1 mile from A4 at Quemerford, Calne; 4 miles from Devizes.
Downland course.
18 holes, 6451 yds. S.S.S. 71
Visitors welcome.
Green Fees. Weekdays £4.50 (£2.50 with member); weekends £6.50 (£4.00 with member).
Society Meetings by arrangement.
Hotels: Bear; Castle Hotel, Devizes; Lansdowne, Calne.
Lunches, teas and evening meals served.

B 35 Parkstone

Tel. Canford Cliffs 708025
Links Rd., Parkstone, Poole, Dorset BH14 98U.
A338. Turn S at St. Osmunds Church, St. Osmunds Rd., Parkstone.
Undulating heathland course.
18 holes, 6250 yds. S.S.S. 70
Course designed by W. Park.
Visitors welcome if members of recognized club, with handicap certificate, between 9.30 a.m. and 12.30 p.m. and after 2 p.m. Book starting time.
Green Fees. Weekdays £7.00 per round or day; weekends £8.50 per round or day.

Society Meetings by arrangement.
Lunches and teas served.

B 36 Queen's Park

Tel. Bournemouth (0202) 36198
Queen's Park, Bournemouth, Dorset.
Correspondence to Recreation Officer, Town Hall, Bournemouth, Dorset BH2 6DY. Tel (0202) 2206 ext. 576.
3 miles N of town centre, adjacent to Bournemouth Ringwood spur road.
Undulating parkland, seaside course.
18 holes, 6505 yds. S.S.S. 72
Course designed by J.H. Taylor (1905).
Visitors welcome.
Green Fees. From £2.30 per round.
Society Meetings welcome.
Hotels: in Bournemouth.
Lunches served.

B 37 R.A.F. Upavon

Pewsey, Wilts.
14 miles S of Marlborough on A342.
Green Fees. £2.00.
Hotels: Ship; Antelope.

B 38 Salisbury & South Wilts.

Tel. Wilton (0722 74) 2645 (Sec.), 2929 (Pro.), 2131 (Steward and members).
Netherhampton, Salisbury, Wilts. SP2 8PB.
A3094, 2 miles from Salisbury, 2 miles from Wilton.
Downland course.
18 holes, 6146 yds. S.S.S. 70
9 holes, 4848 yds. S.S.S. 64
Visitors welcome.
Green Fees. Weekdays £5.00 (£3.50 with member); weekends £6.00 (£4.50 with member); juniors £2.50. Reduced rates for societies.
Society Meetings welcome weekdays, weekends by arrangement.
Hotels: Rose & Crown, Salisbury; Pembroke Arms, Wilton.
Full catering.

B 39 Saltford

Tel. Saltford 3220
Saltford, Bristol.
Off the A4 between Bath and Bristol.
Meadowland course.
18 holes, 6081 yds. S.S.S. 69
Visitors welcome.
Green Fees. Weekdays £4.00 per round or day; weekends £5.00 per round or day.
Reduced rates when playing with member.
Society Meetings Thurs. by arrangement.
Hotels: Grange, Keynsham; Crown, Saltford.
Meals served every day.

B 40 Sherborne

Tel. Sherborne 4431
Clatcombe, Sherborne, Dorset.
1½ miles N of Sherborne on B3145 to Wincanton.
Parkland course.
18 holes, 5776 yds. S.S.S. 68
Course designed by J. Braid.
Visitors welcome.
Green Fees. Weekdays £5.75 per day; weekends £6.80 per day.
Society Meetings welcome weekdays

Hotels: Holbrook House, Wincanton; Half Moon, Post House, Sherborne.
Meals, snack lunches; teas and high teas served.

B 41 Shirehampton Park

Tel. Avonmouth 823059
Shirehampton Park, Shirehampton, Bristol BS11 0UL.
1½ miles from Exit 18 (Avonmouth) on M5.
Parkland course.
18 holes, 5493 yds. S.S.S. 67
Course designed by A.N. Andrews.
Visitors welcome on weekdays.
Green Fees. £5.00 per day or round.
Society Meetings Mon. only.
Hotels: Eurocrest Motel, Hambrook; Ship Motel, Olveston; St. Vincent Rocks, Clifton.
Meals served.

B 42 Swindon

Tel. 067 284 327
Ogbourne St. George, Marlborough, Wilts.
A345, junction 15, M4.
Undulating downland course.
18 holes, 6226 yds. S.S.S. 70
Visitors welcome.
Green Fees. Weekdays £4.00 per round, £6.50 per day; weekends £8.50 per round or day.
Society Meetings welcome weekdays, Sun. after 2 p.m. £5.00 per round.
Hotels: Aylesbury Arms, Marlborough; Post House, Swindon.
Meals served except Mon., snacks available every day.

B 43 Taunton & Pickeridge

Tel. Blagdon Hill 537
Corfe, Taunton, Somerset TA3 7BY.
B3170, 4 miles S of Taunton, first left.
Parkland course, fine views.
18 holes, 5917 yds. S.S.S. 68
Visitors welcome.
Green Fees. Weekdays £4.50 (£3.00 with member); weekends £6.00 (£4.50 with member).
Society Meetings welcome weekdays only.
Hotels: Castle Hotel; County; Creech Castle Hotel, Taunton.
Lunches, teas and light meals served by arrangement.

B 44 Tower Hill

Tel. 074981 3233
Tower Hill, Bruton, Somerset BA10 0BA.
On A359. Edge of town, 5 miles N of Wincanton.
Parkland course.
9 holes, 4366 yds. S.S.S. 63
Course designed by Sam Chisholm & Associates.
Visitors welcome.
Green Fees. Weekdays £3.00 (£2.00 with member); weekends and bank holidays £4.00 (£3.00 with member).
Society Meetings weekdays by arrangement.
Hotels: George; Castle Cary Hotel; Glen; Evercreech Hotel.
Bar snacks served. First class Bed & Breakfast accommodation at clubhouse.

B 45   Tracy Park Golf & Country Club

Tel. Abson (027582) 2251
Tracy Park, Wick, Bristol BS15 5RM.
M4 Junction 18, S on A46 for 4 miles, turn right onto A420 for 2 miles.
Undulating parkland course.
18 holes, 7120 yds. S.S.S. 74 or 6601 yds. S.S.S. 72 or 6188 yds. S.S.S. 69
Course designed by G. Aitken.
Visitors welcome on weekdays, weekends with reservation.
Green Fees. Weekdays £5.00 per round, £6.00 per day; weekends £6.00 per round, £7.00 per day.
Society Meetings welcome.
Hotels: Holiday Inn, Bristol; Lansdown Grove, Bath; Bath Priory, Bath.
Meals served daily, lunch and evening.

B 46   Vivary

Tel. 0823 3875
Vivary Park, Taunton, Somerset.
In centre of Taunton.
Meadowland parkland course.
18 holes, 4256 yds. S.S.S. 62
Visitors welcome with reservation.
Green Fees. Weekdays £1.07; weekends £1.60.
Hotels: Castle Hotel; County.

B 47   Wareham

Tel. Wareham 2658
Sandford Rd., Wareham, Dorset BH20 4DH.
A351 from Poole.
Heathland course.
9 holes, 4906 yds. S.S.S. 64
Visitors welcome on weekdays, weekends with member only.
Green Fees. £2.00 per round.
Hotels: Black Bear; Red Lion.

B 48   Wells (Somerset)

Tel. Wells (0749) 72868
East Horrington Rd., Wells, Somerset BA5 3DS.
1 mile from city centre.
Parkland course.
9 holes, 6255 yds. S.S.S. 70
Visitors welcome.
Green Fees. Weekdays £3.50; weekends £4.00.
Society Meetings welcome.
Hotels: Star; Swan; White Hart, Wells; Court, Emborough.
Lunches, snacks and teas served.

B 49   Weston-super-Mare

Tel. Weston-super-Mare 26968
Uphill Road North, Weston-super-Mare, Avon BS23 4NQ.
M5 or A370 from Bristol.
Seaside course.
18 holes, 6279 yds. S.S.S. 70
Course designed by T. Dunn.
Visitors welcome.
Green Fees. Weekdays £5.00; weekends £6.50.
Society Meetings by arrangement.
Hotels: Grand Atlantic; Royal Pier; Beachlands.
Lunches and teas served except Mon.

B 50   West Wiltshire

Tel. Warminster 213133 (Secretary) 212110 (Pro.)
Elm Hill, Warminster, Wilts.
On A350 towards Westbury.
Downland course.
18 holes, 5701 yds. S.S.S. 68
Course designed by J. H. Taylor (1898), redesigned by Huggett & Coles (1972).
Visitors welcome on weekdays.
Green Fees. Weekdays £5.00 per round or day; weekends £6.00 per round or day.
Society Meetings welcome Wed, Thurs. Fri.
Hotels: Cedars, Westbury; Farmers, Warminster.
Meals served except Tues.

B 51   Weymouth

Tel. Weymouth 784994
Links Rd., Westham, Weymouth, Dorset DT4 0PF.
Off main Dorchester road via Radipole Lane.
Seaside course.
18 holes, 5962 yds. S.S.S. 69
Visitors welcome.
Green Fees. Weekdays £4.50; weekends £6.00 per round.
Society Meetings welcome.
Hotels: Lupins; Burlington; Gresham.
Snacks and meals served.

B 52   Windwhistle

Tel. Winsham 231
Cricket St. Thomas, Chard, Somerset.
A30 3 miles from Chard, 5 miles from Crewverne.
12 holes, 6299 yds. S.S.S. 70
Visitors welcome with reservation.
Green Fees. On application to Secretary.
Society Meetings by arrangement.
Hotels: George, Chard.

B 53   Worlebury

Tel. Weston-super-Mare 23214 and 25789
Worlebury Hill Rd., Weston-super-Mare, Avon BS22 9SX.
A370 from Bristol, turn right at Baytree Rd.
Course 2 miles from sea front.
Seaside course.
18 holes, 5909 yds. S.S.S. 68
Visitors welcome.
Green Fees. Weekdays £5.00 (£3.00 with member); weekends £8.00 (£4.00 with member), plus V.A.T.
Society Meetings welcome.
Hotels: in Weston-super-Mare.
Meals served.

B 54   Yeovil

Tel. Yeovil 5949 or 22965 (Sec.)
Sherborne Rd., Yeovil, Somerset.
A30 E of town on A30.
Parkland course.
18 holes, 6139 yds. S.S.S. 69
Visitors welcome.
Green Fees. Weekdays £5.00 per round or day; weekends £6.00 per round or day.
Society Meetings by arrangement.
Lunches served except Mon. by arrangement.

C Hampshire, Berkshire, Isle of Wight

C 1   Alresford

Tel. Alresford (096 273) 3746
Cheriton Rd., Alresford, Hants. SO24 0PN.
1 mile S of A31, 2 miles N of A272.
Undulating parkland course.
9 holes, 5931 yds. S.S.S. 68
Visitors welcome.
Green Fees. Weekdays £4.00 per round (£2.50 per round, £3.50 per day with member); weekends £6.00 per round (£3.00 with member).
Society Meetings by arrangement.
Hotels: Bell; Swan.
Meals served except Mon.

C 2   Alton

Tel. Alton (0420) 82042
Old Odiham Rd., Alton, Hants.
1½ miles N of Alton on A32.
Undulating course.
9 holes, 5699 yds. S.S.S. 67
Visitors welcome.
Green Fees. Weekdays £2.87; weekends £4.60 (18 holes).
Society Meetings weekdays by arrangement.
Hotels: Swan, Alton.

C 3   Ampfield Par Three Golf & Country Club

Tel. Braishfield 68480, 68750 (Professional)
Ampfield, Romsey, Hants. SO5 9BQ.
On A31, 2½ miles E of Romsey.
Parkland course.
18 holes, 2478 yds. S.S.S. 53
Course designed by Henry Cotton.
Visitors welcome.
Green Fees. Weekdays £2.25 per round, £3.50 per day; weekends £4.00 per round, £6.00 per day.
Society Meetings welcome, max. 60.
Hotels: Potters Heron Motel, Hursley; White Horse, Romsey.
Snacks and light meals served except Tues.

C 4   Andover

Tel. Andover (0264) 3980
51 Winchester Rd., Andover, Hants.
1 mile from town centre on Winchester road.
Undulating moorland / meadowland course.
9 holes, 5896 yds. S.S.S. 68
Visitors welcome on weekdays and Sun. afternoon.
Green Fees. Weekdays £3.00 per round;

weekends £6.00 per round.
Society Meetings by arrangement.
Hotels: Star & Garter; White Hart.
Snacks served.

C 5   Army

Tel. Farnborough (0252) 41104
Laffans Rd., Aldershot, Hants. GU11 2HF.
A325 to Queens Hotel roundabout; signpost
to club.
Tree-lined parkland course.
18 holes, 6553 yds. S.S.S. 71
Visitors welcome on weekdays.
Green Fees. £7.50 per day (reduced fees
for H.M. forces).
Society Meetings welcome Wed., Thurs.,
Fri.
Hotels: Queens, Farnborough.
Catering 11 a.m. to 5 p.m. (limited Mon.).

C 6   Barton on Sea

Tel. New Milton 615308
Marine Drive, Barton on Sea, Hants. BH25
2DY.
Off A337, 11 miles E of Bournemouth.
Seaside course.
18 holes, 5650 yds. S.S.S. 67

Course designed by H.S. Colt.
Visitors welcome if members of recognized
club.
Green Fees. Weekdays £6.00; weekends
£8.00.
Society Meetings by arrangement.
Hotels: Chewton Glen, New Milton; Red
House Hotel; Coastguard, Barton on Sea.
Light meals only.

C 7   Basingstoke

Tel. Basingstoke 65990
Kempshott Park, Basingstoke, Hants.
Off M3 at Exit 7, or A30, 3 miles S of
Basingstoke.
Parkland course.
18 holes, 6253 yds. S.S.S. 70
Course designed by James Braid.
Visitors welcome if members of recognized
club. Weekends with member only.
Green Fees. £5.00-£7.00 all day (£3.00-
£5.00 with member).
Society Meetings welcome Wed., Thurs.
and Fri.
Hotels: Hampshire House Hotel; Golden
Lion.
Meals served except Mon.

C 8   Berkshire

Tel. Ascot 21495/6
Swinley Road, Ascot, Berks.
On A332 between Ascot and Bagshot.
Heathland course.
Red 18 holes, 6356 yds. S.S.S. 70
Blue 18 holes, 6258 yds. S.S.S. 70
Visitors welcome, with reservation.
Green Fees. £11.50 per day.
Society Meetings welcome Tues.-Fri.
Hotels: Berystede; Royal Foresters, Ascot;
Pennyhill Park Hotel; Cricketers, Bagshot.
Lunch served except Mon.

C 9   Bishopswood

Tel. Tadley (07356) 5213
Bishopswood Lane, Tadley, Basingstoke,
Hants.
Off A340, 6 miles N of Basingstoke.
9 holes, 6338 yds. S.S.S. 70
Visitors welcome.
Green Fees. Weekdays £1.75 per 9 holes;
weekends £2.30.
Society Meetings by arrangement.
Snacks served.

C 10   Blackmoor

Tel. Bordon 2775
Whitehill, Bordon, Hants. GU35 9EH.
½ mile W of only crossroads at Whitehill on
A325.
Heathland course.
18 holes, 6202 yds. S.S.S. 70
Course designed by H.S. Colt.
Visitors welcome with letter of introduction.
Green Fees. Weekdays £7.50; weekends
by arrangement.
Society Meetings by arrangement.
Hotels: Queens, Selborne.
Meals served until 6.15 p.m.

C 11   Bramshaw

Tel. Cadnam (042 127) 3433
Brook, Lyndhurst, Hants. SO4 7HE.
B3079 near Cadnam roundabout.
Manor course, parkland; Forest course,
undulating.
Manor 18 holes, 5634 yds. S.S.S. 67 (1982
S.S.S. 70)
Forest 18 holes, 5753 yds. S.S.S. 68
Visitors welcome.
Green Fees. Weekdays £5.00 (£3.50 with
member); weekends £7.00 (£4.50 with
member).
Society Meetings by arrangement.

C 12   Bramshott Hill Public Course

Tel. Hythe (0703) 845596
Bramshott Hill, Dibden, Hythe, Southampton.
Turn off A326 at Dibden roundabout;
signposted Hythe; ½ mile right-hand side.
Undulating meadowland course..
18 holes, 6223 yds. S.S.S. 70
Course designed by J.Hamilton Stutt.
Visitors welcome.
Green Fees. Weekdays £2.80 per round;
weekends £3.50 per round. Reduced rates
for juniors and O.A.P.s.
Society Meetings weekdays by
arrangement.
Hotels: Montagu Arms, Beaulieu; West Cliff
Hall Hotel; Stewart Lodge Hotel, Hythe.
Meals and snacks served.

C 13   Brokenhurst Manor

Tel. Lymington 23332
Sway Rd., Brockenhurst, Hants. SO4 7SG.
On A337, 1 mile S of Brockenhurst.
Undulating parkland course.
18 holes, 6216 yds. S.S.S. 70
Course designed by H. S. Colt.
Visitors welcome after 9.30 a.m. Mon. to Sat. and on Sun. afternoons. Must be members of recognized club.
Green Fees. Weekdays £6.50; weekends £8.50.
Society Meetings by arrangement.
Hotels: Balmer Lawn Hotel; Forest Park Hotel; Rose and Crown; Carey's Manor; The Brockenhurst.
Snacks served; lunches and dinners by arrangement.

C 14   Burley

Tel. Burley (042 53) 2431
Burley, Ringwood, Hants. BH24 4RR.
A31 from Ringwood and right at Picket Post.
Undulating moorland course.
9 holes, 6140 yds. S.S.S. 69
Visitors welcome.
Green Fees. Weekdays £3.00; weekends £4.00; weekly £12.00.
Hotels: Burley Manor Hotel; White Buck; Moorhill House Hotel; Woods End Hotel.

C 15   Calcot Park

Tel. Reading (0734) 27124
Bath Rd., Calcot, Reading, Berks. RG3 5RN.
3 miles W of Reading on A4. 1 mile E of junction 12 on M4.
Parkland course.
18 holes, 6257 yds. S.S.S. 70
Visitors welcome on weekdays.
Green Fees. £8.00 per round or day.
Society Meetings weekdays by arrangement.
Hotels: Copper Inn, Pangbourne; George, Reading.
Lunches and teas served.

C 16   Corhampton

Tel. Droxford 279
Sheeps Pond Lane, Droxford, Southampton SO3 1QZ.
Right off A32 at Corhampton on to B3057 for 1 mile.
Downland course (Estd. 1890) Private.
18 holes, 6088 yds. S.S.S. 69
Course redesigned by Charles Lawrie.
Visitors welcome.
Green Fees. Weekdays £5.75; weekends £4.60 (with member only).
Society Meetings Mon. and Thurs. only by arrangement.
Hotels: 3 residential inns Droxford (The White Horse; Bakers Arms; The Hurdles).
Lunches served; dinners by arrangement

C 17   Cowes

Tel. Cowes (098 382) 3529
Baring Rd., Cowes, Isle of Wight.
Parkland course.
9 holes, 5569 yds. S.S.S. 67
Visitors welcome.
Green Fees. Weekdays £3.00 per round; weekly £12.
Hotels: Fountain Hotel; Holmwood Hotel

C 18   Downshire

Tel. Bracknell 24066
Easthampstead Park, Wokingham, Berks. RG11 3DH.
M3 or M4 to Bracknell, then follow signs.
Parkland course.
18 holes, 6395 yds. S.S.S. 70
Course designed by F.W. Hawtree.
Visitors welcome.
Green Fees. Summer £3.25 per round; winter £2.15 per round; juniors and O.A.P.s, summer £1.80 per round; winter £1.30 per round.
Society Meetings welcome.
Hotels: Cricketers, Bagshot; Waterloo, Crowthorne.
Snacks served. Private parties catered for.

C 19   Dunwood Manor

Tel. Lockerley 40549
Danes Rd., Awbridge, Romsey, Hants.
Off A27, 3 miles W of Romsey.
Parkland course.
18 holes, 6021 yds. S.S.S. 69
Visitors welcome.
Green Fees. Weekdays £4.60; weekends £5.75.
Society Meetings welcome.
Hotels: White Horse, Romsey; New Forest Lodge Motel, Ower. Special Green Fee rates from these hotels.
Food available to order. All day golf, lunch, evening meal £10.35.

C 20   East Berkshire

Tel. Crowthorne (03 466) 2041
Ravenswood Avenue, Crowthorne, Berks. RG11 6BD.
M4 Exit 10 or M3 Exit 3 or 4. On A3095, 4 miles S of Wokingham, 1½ miles W of Crowthorne.
Heathland course.
18 holes, 6315 yds. S.S.S. 70
Course designed by Peter Paxton.
Visitors welcome on weekdays with reservation if member of recognized club.
Green Fees. Weekdays one round £8.00 (£4.00 with member); all day £8.00 (£4.00 with member); weekends £4.00 with member only.
Society Meetings Thurs. and Fri. only.
Hotels: Waterloo, Crowthorne; Berystede; Royal Berkshire, Ascot.
Bar snacks served; meals by arrangement.

C 21   Fleming Park (Eastleigh)

Tel. Southampton (0703) 612797
Magpie Lane, Eastleigh, Hampshire.
5 miles N of Southampton.
Parkland course.
18 holes, 4494 yds. S.S.S. 62
Visitors welcome.
Green Fees. Weekdays £2.00; weekends £3.00.
Society Meetings welcome.
Hotels: in Southampton.
Lunches, snacks and teas served.

C 22   Freshwater Bay

Tel. Freshwater (0983) 752955
Afton Down, Freshwater Bay, Isle of Wight.
2½ miles from Yarmouth, on military road overlooking Freshwater Bay.
Downland course with extensive views of Solent and Channel.
18 holes, 5538 yds. S.S.S. 68
Visitors welcome.
Green Fees. £4.00 per day; weekly £17.00.
Hotels: Golf holidays in conjunction with Sentrymead, Country Garden and Nodes Hotels, Totland.
Licensed bar - no food.
Separate pitch and putt course, 18 holes.

C 23   Goring & Streatley

Tel. Goring on Thames 873229 (Sec.) 872688 (Club House)
Rectory Rd., Streatley on Thames.
On A329, 10 miles NW of Reading.
Parkland, moorland course.
18 holes, 6232 yds. S.S.S. 70
Visitors welcome on weekdays, with handicap certificate (non-competition days); weekends with members only.
Green Fees. £7.00 (£3.50 with member).
Society Meetings weekdays only.
Hotels: Bull Hotel, Streatley; Miller of Mansfield, Swan Hotel, Goring.
Meals served by arrangement.

C 24   Gosport & Stokes Bay

Tel. Gosport 81625/27941 (Sec.)
Hasler, Gosport, Hants.
On A32, 6 miles from Fareham.
Seaside course.
9 holes, 5918 yds. S.S.S. 68
Visitors welcome weekdays, Sats. and Sun. afternoons.
Green Fees. Weekdays £3.00; weekends £4.00.
Hotels: Anglesea Hotel, Old Lodge Hotel, Alverstoke.
Meals and snacks served.

C 25   Hartley Wintney

Tel. Hartley Wintney 2214
London Rd., Hartley Wintney, Hants.
On A30, 8 miles NE of Basingstoke.
Parkland course.
9 holes, 6034 yds. S.S.S. 69
Visitors welcome, but must be introduced by member at weekends.
Green Fees. Weekdays £3.50 per 18 holes (£2.00 with member); £6.00 per 36 holes (£3.60 with member); weekends £5.00 per 18 holes (£2.75 with member); juniors £1.30 per 18 holes (75p with member).
Society Meetings welcome.
Meals served except Tues.

C 26   Hayling

Tel. Hayling Island (070 16) 4446
Ferry Rd., Hayling Island, Hants. PO11 0BX.
On A3023, 5 miles S of Havant.
Seaside course.
18 holes, 6489 yds. S.S.S. 71
Visitors welcome if members of recognized club.
Green Fees. Weekdays £5.50; weekends £7.50. Period by arrangement with Secretary.
Society Meetings weekdays by arrangement.
Hotels: Newton House Hotel.
Lunches and teas served except Mon.

C 27   Hockley

Tel. Twyford 713165
Twyford, Winchester, Hants. SO21 1PL.
On A333, 300 yards from Winchester by-pass.
Downland course.
18 holes, 6260 yds. S.S.S. 70
Visitors welcome on weekdays, weekends with member or by permission of Secretary only.
Green Fees. Weekdays and weekends £6.50 per round or day (£3.00 with member).
Society Meetings welcome on weekdays.
Hotels: Winchester Hotel; Wessex Hotel, Winchester.
Light meals served.

C 28   Leckford

Tel. Stockbridge 710
Leckford, Stockbridge, Hants.
On A3057, 5½ miles S of Andover.
Undulating meadowland course.
9 holes, 3222 yds. S.S.S. 71
Course designed by Colt and Morrison.
Visitors with member only.
Green Fees. Weekdays £1.75.
Society Meetings by arrangement, max. 12.
Hotels: Star and Garter; White Hart, Andover.

C 29   Lee-on-the-Solent

Tel. Lee-on-the-Solent 551170
Brune Lane, Lee-on-the-Solent, Hants. PO13 9PB.
3 miles S of Fareham on B3385.
Parkland course.
18 holes, 6022 yds. S.S.S. 69
Visitors welcome on weekdays, weekends with members only.
Green Fees. £5.00 per round (£2.50 with member), £6.00 per day (£5.00 with member).
Society Meetings Thurs. only.
Hotels: Belle Vue, Lee-on-the-Solent; Red Lion, Fareham.
Bar snacks, lunches and afternoon teas served; dinner by arrangement.

C 30   Liphook

Tel. Liphook 723271
Wheatsheaf Enclosure, Liphook, Hants. GU30 7EH.
On A3, 1 mile S of Liphook.
Heathland course.
18 holes, 6207 yds. S.S.S. 70
Visitors welcome with member or with letter of introduction, except Sun. morning.
Green Fees. Weekdays £5.00 per round, £8.00 per day; weekends £10.00.
Society Meetings by arrangement.
Hotels: Southdown Hotel, Rogate; Lythe Hill Hotel, Haslemere.

C 31   Maidenhead

Tel. Maidenhead (0628) 24693
Shoppenhangers Rd., Maidenhead, Berks. SL6 2PZ.
Right under railway off A308 going S; top of hill on left.
Parkland course.
18 holes, 6028 yds. S.S.S. 70

Visitors welcome weekdays with handicap certificate, weekends with member only.
Green Fees. £8.00 per day or round.
Society Meetings by arrangement.
Hotels: Aldingham House Hotel; Esso Motel.
Meals served by arrangement.

C 32   Meon Valley Hotel, Golf & Country Club

Tel. Wickham (0329) 833455
Sandy Lane, Shedfield, Southampton.
On A334, 8 miles E of Southampton.
Woodland parkland course.
18 holes, 6523 yds. S.S.S. 71
Course designed by Hamilton Stutt.
Visitors welcome on weekdays.
Green Fees. Weekdays £5.00 per round, £6.50 per day.
Society Meetings welcome weekdays. Meals served. Residential accommodation available.

C 33   Newbury & Crookham

Tel. Newbury (0635) 40035
Bury's Bank Rd., Greenham, Newbury, Berks. RG15 8BZ.
2 miles SE of Newbury off A34.
Undulating parkland course.
18 holes, 5843 yds. S.S.S. 68
Visitors welcome weekdays, weekends with member only.
Green Fees. £7.00 per round or day if member of recognized club.
Society Meetings welcome weekdays by arrangement.
Hotels: Chequers; Queens, Newbury.
Meals served except Mon.

C 34   New Forest

Tel. Lyndhurst 2450
Southampton Rd., Lyndhurst, Hants. SO4 7BU.
On A35, on Southampton side of Lyndhurst.
Heathland course.
18 holes, 5833 yds. S.S.S. 68
Course designed by Peter Swann.
Visitors welcome except Sun. before noon.
Green Fees. £3.00 per day.
Society Meetings by arrangement.
Hotels: Lyndhurst Park Hotel; Crown; Evergreens; Forest Park Hotel.
Meals served.

C 35   Newport

Tel. Newport (098 381) 5076
St. George's Down, Newport, Isle of Wight.
1 mile SE of Newport. St. George's Lane leads to course.
Downland course.
9 holes, 5712 yds. S.S.S. 68
Visitors welcome.
Green Fees. Weekdays £4.00; weekends and bank holidays £5.00.
Hotels: Wheatsheaf; Bugle, Newport.
Meals served by arrangement.

C 36   North Hants.

Tel. Fleet 6443
Minley Rd., Fleet, Aldershot, Hants.
400 yards from railway station.
Heathland course.
18 holes, 6257 yds. S.S.S. 70

Green Fees. Weekdays £5.50 (£2.50 with member); weekends £3.00 with members only.
Society Meetings Tues. and Wed.
Hotels: Fleet Hotel; Lismoyne Hotel.
Snacks served; lunches except Mon.

C 37   Osborne

Tel. Cowes (0983) 295421
Osborne, East Cowes, Isle of Wight.
On A3027, one mile from East Cowes.
Parkland course.
9 holes, 3143 yds. S.S.S. 70
Visitors welcome on weekdays.
Green Fees. Weekdays 9 or 18 holes £5.00, all day £6.00; weekends 9 or 18 holes £6.00, all day £7.00.

C 38   Petersfield

Tel. Petersfield (0730) 3725
The Heath, Petersfield, Hants.
A3 to town centre, then Heath Rd. to course.
Heath and parkland course.
18 holes, 5681 yds. S.S.S. 68
Visitors welcome except Sun. morning.
Green Fees. Weekdays £4.00 per round; weekends £5.00 per round.
Hotels: Red Lion; Southdown Hotel; Concord Hotel.
Snacks served.

C 39   Portsmouth

Tel. Cosham 72210
Crookhorn Lane, Portsmouth, Hants.
Lies on slopes of Portsdown Hill.
Parkland course.
18 holes, 6200 yds. S.S.S. 70
Visitors welcome.
Green Fees. Weekdays £2.00 per round; weekends £2.75 per round.

C 40   Portsmouth Municipal

Tel. Cosham 72210
Crookhorn Lane, Portsmouth, Hants.
⅔ mile from junction of B2177 and A3.
Downland course.
18 holes, 6200 yds. S.S.S. 70
Lunches served.

C 41   Reading

Tel. Reading (0734) 472909
Kidmore End Rd., Emmer Green, Reading, Berks. RG4 8SG.
2 miles N of Reading off Peppard Road.
Meadowland course.
18 holes, 6025 yds. S.S.S. 69
Visitors welcome on weekdays; weekends with member only.
Green Fees. £6.00 per round or day.
Society Meetings weekdays by arrangement.
Lunches and teas served, except Mon.

C 42   Romsey

Tel. Southampton (0703) 732218
Nursling, Southampton SO1 9XW.
At junction of M271 and A3057, N of Southampton.
Undulating parkland and woodland course.
18 holes, 5704 yds. S.S.S. 68
Course designed by Charles Lawrie.
Visitors welcome on weekdays, weekends with member only.

Green Fees. Weekdays £3.50 (£2.50 with member); weekends £4.00 with member only.
Society Meetings welcome weekdays.
Hotels: White Horse, Romsey.
Meals served except Thurs.

C 43   Rowlands Castle

Tel. Rowlands Castle 2784
Links Lane, Rowlands Castle, Hants.
Off B2149, 3 miles N of Havant, and B2149 off A3(M).
Parkland course.
18 holes, 6675 yds. S.S.S. 72
Course designed by H.S. Colt (1902).
Visitors welcome.
Green Fees. Weekdays, £4.50 per round, £6.50 per day; weekends, £6.00 per round, £8.00 per day, half above rates if playing with member.
Society Meetings welcome.
Hotels: Albany Inn.
Full catering except Mon.

C 44   Royal Ascot

Tel. Ascot (0990) 22923/25175
Winkfield Rd., Ascot, Berks.
In centre of Royal Ascot racecourse.
Heathland course.
18 holes, 5530 yds. S.S.S. 67
Course designed by J.H. Taylor (1905).
Visitors welcome, weekends with member only.
Green Fees. £5.20, £2.65 with member.
Society Meetings welcome.
Hotels: Foresters, Ascot; Berystede, Sunninghill.
Meals by arrangement.

C 45   Royal Winchester

Tel. Winchester (0962) 2462
Sarum Rd., Winchester, Hants. SO22 5QE.
Leave Winchester on Romsey road. After hospital (on left), fork right up Sarum Rd. for ¾ mile.
Downland course.
18 holes, 6206 yds. S.S.S. 70
Visitors welcome on weekdays.
Green Fees. £5.50.
Society Meetings limited to two per week, max. 50.
Hotels: in Winchester.
Meals served by arrangement except Thurs. afternoon and Tues.

C 46   Ryde

Tel. Ryde 62088
Ryde House Park, Ryde, Isle of Wight.
On A3054 close to town.
Parkland course.
9 holes, 5220 yds. S.S.S. 65
Visitors welcome.
Green Fees. Weekdays £2.90; weekends £3.45; weekly £9.80.

C 47   Shanklin & Sandown

Tel. Sandown 403217
Fairway, Lake, Sandown, Isle of Wight.
On A3055 near Sandown station.
Seaside course.
18 holes, 5950 yds. S.S.S. 68
Visitors welcome.
Green Fees. Weekdays £5.50 per round

or day; weekends £7.50 per round or day.
Society Meetings weekdays by arrangement.
Lunches (except Mon.) and teas served.

C 48   Sonning

Tel. Reading (0734) 693332
Duffield Rd., Sonning, Reading, Berks. RG5 4RJ.
A4 to Sonning/Woodley Roundabout. Turn left towards Woodley, then first left again.
Parkland course.
18 holes, 6321 yds. S.S.S. 70
Visitors welcome on weekdays if members of recognized club; weekends with member only.
Green Fees. Weekdays £7.00 (£3.50 with member); weekends £3.50 with member only.
Society Meetings welcome weekdays.
Hotels: White Hart; French Horn.
Lunches served by arrangement except Mon.

C 49   Southampton

Tel. Southampton 760472
Municipal Golf Course Pavilion, Bassett, Southampton.
Northern outskirts of Southampton, via Golf Course Rd., Bassett Avenue. Turn left at footbridge.
Municipal parkland course, fast in summer, slow in winter.
18 holes, 6218 yds. S.S.S. 70
Also 9 hole course.
Visitors welcome.
Green Fees. Weekdays £2.30 18 hole course, £1.15 9 hole course; weekends £3.60 18 hole course, £1.80 9 hole course.
Meals served. Parties catered for.

C 50   Southsea

Tel. Portsmouth (0705) 660945
The Mansion House, Great Salterns, Eastern Rd., Portsmouth, Hants. PO3 6QZ.
Directly off E access road into Portsmouth from A3(M).
Meadowland municipal course.
18 holes, 5950 yds. S.S.S. 68
Visitors welcome.
Green Fees. Weekdays £1.90; weekends £2.50.
Society Meetings by arrangement.

C 51   Southwick Park (Royal Navy)

Tel. Portsmouth (0705) 380131
Pinsley Drive, Southwick, Hants. PO17 6EL.
A27 or A3 to junction with A333 to Southwick village; follow signs to HMS Dryad. 7 miles from Portsmouth.
Parkland course with 8 acre lake.
White 18 holes, 6035 yds. S.S.S. 69
Yellow 18 holes, 5526 yds. S.S.S. 68
Course designed by Henry Cotton; modified by Charles Lawry.
Visitors welcome Tues. by arrangement or with member.
Green Fees. Servicemen £1.90; civilians guest rate.
Society Meetings welcome Tues. by arrangement.
Hotels: George Inn; in Portsmouth and Wickham.
Limited menu; order in advance.

C 52   Southwood

Tel. Farnborough (Hants) 48700
Ively Rd., Farnborough, Hants.
1 mile W of Farnborough town centre.
Parkland course.
9 holes, 2263 yds. S.S.S. 62
Course designed by John D. Harris.
Visitors welcome.
Green Fees. Weekdays adults 18 holes £2.50, 9 holes £1.50; weekends 18 holes £3.00, 9 holes £1.75; weekdays before 4.30 p.m., juniors and O.A.P.s 18 holes £1.30, 9 holes 75p.
Society Meetings by arrangement.
Lunches and snacks served.

C 53   Stoneham

Tel. Southampton (0703) 68151
Bassett Green Rd., Southampton SO2 3NE.
N of Southampton. At Chilworth roundabout take road marked 'to Airport'. Club is ½ mile on left.
Heather, parkland course.
18 holes, 6295 yds. S.S.S. 70
Course designed by Willie Park (1906).
Visitors welcome.
Green Fees. Weekdays £5.00 per round, £7.00 per day; weekends £9.00 per round or day.
Society Meetings Welcome Mon., Thurs. and Fri.
Hotels: Polygon; Wessex Motel.
Meals served except Sun. Tea only.

C 54   Sunningdale

Tel. Ascot (0990) 21681
Ridgemount Rd., Sunningdale, Ascot, Berks.
A30, first left going W from level crossing, then 350 yards on left.
Heather and woodland course.
Old 18 holes, 6336 yds. S.S.S. 70
New 18 holes, 6601 yds. S.S.S. 72
Course designed by Willie Park (Old), H. S.Colt (New).
Visitors welcome on weekdays with member or advance letter of introduction; weekends with member only.
Green Fees. Weekdays £13.00 (£5.00 with member).
Society Meetings welcome Tues., Wed. and Thurs.
Hotels: Berystede, South Ascot.
Lunches served except Mon.

C 55   Sunningdale Ladies'

Tel. Ascot (0990) 20507
Cross Rd., Sunningdale, Ascot, Berks. SL5 9RX.
A30, second left going W from level crossing.
Heathland course specially designed for ladies' golf.
18 holes, 3624 yds. S.S.S. 60
Visitors welcome with letter of introduction except on bank holidays.
Green Fees. Weekdays ladies £4.60 per round, men £6.00; weekends ladies £5.25, men £6.90.
Society Meetings (ladies) by arrangement.
Hotels: Berystede, South Ascot.
Snacks served.

C 56   Swinley Forest

Tel. Ascot (0990) 20197
Coronation Rd., Ascot, Berks. SL5 9LE.
N off A30 at Windmill Inn, then signed; or from High St., through South Ascot, Coronation Rd., third on right.
Undulating heather course.
18 holes, 6001 yds.
Course designed by H.S. Colt.
Visitors welcome with member only.
Society Meetings Tues. and Thurs. March to October.
Hotels: Cricketers, Bagshot; Berystede, South Ascot; Royal Foresters, Ascot.
Lunches and teas except Mon. and Fri.

C 57   Temple

Tel. Littlewick Green 4248
Henley Rd., Hurley, Maidenhead, Berks. SL6 5LH.
Off M4 at Junction 8/9, on A423 between Maidenhead and Henley.
Parkland course.
18 holes, 6200 yds. S.S.S. 69
Course designed by Willie Park and J. Hepburn (1909).
Visitors welcome on weekdays with letter of introduction or handicap certificate.
Green Fees. £9.00 (£7.00 in afternoon), £3.50 with member.
Society Meetings welcome Tues. to Fri. only.
Hotels: Ye Olde Bell, Hurley; The Compleat Angler, Marlow.
Snacks served; meals except Mon.

C 58   Tidworth Garrison

Tel. Tidworth 2301
Tidworth, Hants.
1 mile W of Tidworth on Bulford road.
Downland course.
18 holes, 6072 yds. S.S.S. 69
Visitors welcome on weekdays.
Green Fees. Weekdays £4.00 per round, £5.00 per day; weekends £5.00 per round, £6.00 per day.
Society Meetings weekdays by arrangement.
Hotels: Antrobus Arms, Amesbury; Savernake Forest, Burbage.
Meals served except Mon.

C 59   Tylney Park

Tel. Hook 2079
Rotherwick, Basingstoke, Hants.
Off A30 at Nately Scures follow signs for Rotherwick; approx. 1½ miles.
Parkland course.
18 holes, 5300 yds. S.S.S. 66
Course designed by W. Wiltshire.
Visitors welcome on weekdays with handicap certificate, at weekends with members only.
Green Fees. Weekdays £4.00 per round, £5.00 per day; weekends £6.00 per round.
Society Meetings welcome Mon. to Fri.
Hotels: Raven Hook Hotel.
Meals served.

C 60   Ventnor

Tel. Ventnor 853326
Steephill Down Rd., Upper Ventnor, Isle of Wight.

Left at Post Office in Upper Ventnor into Steephill Down Rd. to end, then follow private road for 600 yards.
Downland course.
9 holes, 5869 yds. S.S.S. 68
Visitors welcome.
Hotels: Royal; Ventnor Towers Hotel; Old Park Hotel.
Green Fees. Daily £2.50; weekly £10.00; fortnightly £15.00.

C 61   Waterlooville

Tel. Waterlooville (0714) 3388
Idsworth Rd., Cowplain, Portsmouth, Hants. PO8 8BD.
Off A3 in Cowplain, 5 miles N of Portsmouth.
Parkland course.
18 holes, 6629 yds. S.S.S. 72
Visitors welcome on weekdays.
Green Fees. £5.50 per round or day (£2.75 with member).
Society Meetings Thurs. only.
Hotels: in Havant, Portsmouth and Southsea.
Snacks, lunches and teas served; book for large numbers.

C 62   West Berks

Tel. Chaddleworth (04882) 574
Chaddleworth, Newbury, Berks.
On M4, exit 14 through Gt. Shefford, first right turn for 1 mile.
Downland course.
18 holes, 7053 yds. S.S.S. 74
Visitors welcome.
Green Fees. Weekdays £5.75; weekends £6.75.
Society Meetings welcome.
Hotels: in Newbury.
Snacks available.

C 63   Wexham Park

Tel. Fulmer (028 16) 3271
Wexham St., Stoke Poges, Slough, SL3 6ND.
2 miles from Slough towards Gerrards Cross.
Parkland course.
18 holes, 5480 yds. S.S.S. 67
Course designed by Emil Lawrence (first 9 holes).
Visitors welcome at any time.
Green Fees. Weekdays £2.20; weekends £3.00.
Society Meetings welcome by arrangement.
Hotels: The Bull, Gerrards Cross; Holiday Inn, Langley.
Snacks available; meals by arrangement.

C 64   Winter Hill

Tel. Bourne End (062 85) 27613
Grange Lane, Cookham, Maidenhead, Berkshire SL6 9RP.
Parkland course.
18 holes, 6432 yds. S.S.S. 71
Course designed by Cotton (C.K.), Pennink, Lawrie & Partners.
Visitors welcome on weekdays.
Green Fees. Weekdays £6.00; weekends £7.00.
Hotels: The Compleat Angler, Marlow.
Lunches and snacks served.

D Surrey, West Sussex

D 1   Addington

Tel. 01-777 1055
205 Shirley Church Rd., Addington, Croydon, Surrey CR0 5AB.
2½ miles from E Croydon station.
Heathland, woodland course.
18 holes, 6245 yds. S.S.S. 70
Course designed by J.F. Abercromby.
Visitors welcome with letter of introduction, or club membership card.
Green Fees. Weekdays £7.50; weekends £9.00, only by arrangement.
Society Meetings by arrangement.
Hotels: Selsdon Park Hotel, Selsdon.
Lunches served.

D 2   Addington Court Public Courses

Tel. 01-657 0281
Featherbed Lane, Addington, Croydon, Surrey CR0 9AA.
2 miles E of Croydon. Leave B281 at Addington Village.
Old 18 holes, 5604 yds. S.S.S. 67
New 18 holes, 5515 yds. S.S.S. 67
Lower 9 holes, 4610 yds. S.S.S. 63
Course designed by F.W. Hawtree.
Visitors welcome.
Green Fees. Per 18 holes, weekdays and weekends: April - September Old Course £3.00, New Course £2.50, Lower Course £1.50; October - March Old Course £2.00, New Course £1.75, Lower Course £1.50.
Society Meetings weekdays by arrangement.
Hotels: Selsdon Park Hotel, Selsdon.
Snacks and meals served all day.

D 3   Addington Palace

Tel. 01-654 3061
Addington Park, Gravel Hill, Croydon, Surrey CR0 5BB.
2 miles E of Croydon on A212.
Parkland course.
18 holes, 6410 yds. S.S.S. 71
Visitors welcome on weekdays, weekends with member only.
Green Fees. Weekdays £8.00 (£3.50 with member); weekends £4.00.

D 4   Banstead Downs

Tel. 01-642 2284
Burdon Lane, Belmont, Sutton, Surrey SM2 7DD.
100 yds. E of junction of A216 and B2230.

Downland course.
18 holes, 6150 yds. S.S.S. 69
Visitors welcome with letter of introduction.
Green Fees. Weekdays all day £7.00; afternoon £4.50; weekends with member only.
Society Meetings by arrangement.
Hotels: Thatched House Hotel, Cheam; Drift Bridge Hotel, Epsom.
Lunches and teas served except Mon.

D 5 Betchworth Park

Tel. Dorking (0306) 882052
Reigate Rd., Dorking, Surrey RH4 1NZ.
On A25, 1 mile E of Dorking.
Parkland course.
18 holes, 6247 yds. S.S.S. 70
Visitors welcome on weekdays except Tues. and Wed. a.m.
Green Fees. Weekdays £6.50 per round, £7.00 per day (with member £3.25 and £3.50 respectively); weekends £10.00 per round or day. When permitted, with member £5.00.
Society Meetings by arrangement on Mon., Thurs. and Fri.
Hotels: White Horse; Punch Bowl Motel.
Lunches and bar snacks served.

D 6 Bognor Regis

Tel. Bognor Regis (024 33) 21929
Downview Rd., Felpham, Bognor Regis, W. Sussex PO22 8JD.
2 miles NE of Bognor Regis on A259. Turn left at traffic lights at Felpham Junction.
Parkland course.
18 holes, 6219 yds. S.S.S. 70
Course designed by James Braid.
Visitors welcome weekdays, weekends from April to October with member only. Ladies' day Tues.
Green Fees. Weekdays £5.00 per round or day; weekends £6.00 per round or day.
Society Meetings welcome weekdays, max. 24.
Hotels: Royal Norfolk; Royal, Bognor Regis; Old Manor House Hotel, Middleton-on-Sea.
Meals served by arrangement.

D 7 Bramley

Tel. 0483 892696
Gosden Hill, Bramley, Guildford, Surrey.
3 miles S of Guildford on Horsham road.
Undulating parkland course.
18 holes, 5910 yds. S.S.S. 68
Course designed by Charles Mayo (1913), redesigned by James Braid.

Visitors welcome on weekdays, weekends with member only.
Green Fees. £5.00 per round (£2.00 with member), £7.00 per day (£3.00 with member).
Society Meetings welcome Wed., Thurs. and Fri.
Hotels: in Guildford.
Meals served.

D 8 Burhill

Tel. Walton-on-Thames 27345
Walton-on-Thames, Surrey KT12 4BL.
Off A3 at A245, Seven Hills Rd., then Burwood Rd.
Parkland course.
18 holes, 6213 yds. S.S.S. 70
Visitors welcome on weekdays.
Green Fees. £12.00 (£8.00 after 12 noon).
Society Meetings welcome Wed., Thurs. and Fri.
Hotels: Seven Hills Motel, Cobham.
Lunches and snacks served.

D 9 Camberley Heath

Tel. Camberley (0276) 23258
Golf Rd., Camberley, Surrey GU15 1JG.
On A325 S of Camberley, near M3 Exit 4.
Heathland course.
18 holes, 6253 yds. S.S.S. 70
Course designed by H.S. Colt.
Visitors welcome with letter of introduction.
Green Fees. £10.00 per round or day.
Society Meetings by arrangement.
Hotels: Frimley Hall Hotel; Pennyhill Park Hotel.
Meals served.

D 10 Chipstead

Tel. Downland 55781
How Lane, Chipstead, Surrey.
Off A23, 6 miles S of Croydon.
Undulating meadowland course.
18 holes, 5418 yds. S.S.S. 66
Visitors welcome on weekdays, weekends with members only.
Green Fees. £6.00 (£3.00 with member).
Society Meetings by arrangement.
Meals served by arrangement except Mon.

D 11 Coombe Hill

Tel. 01-942 2284/5
Golf Club Dr., Kingston Hill, Surrey KT2 7DF.
3 miles S of Putney off A3 near New Malden.
Undulating woodland course.
18 holes, 6256 yds. S.S.S. 71
Course designed by Abercromby.
Visitors welcome.
Green Fees. £12.00 per day.
Meals served.

D 12 Coombe Wood

Tel. 01-942 0388
George Rd., Kingston Hill, Kingston-upon-Thames, Surrey KT2 7NS.
On A307, N of Kingston-upon-Thames.
Parkland course.
18 holes, 5200 yds. S.S.S. 66
Visitors welcome on weekdays, weekends with member only.

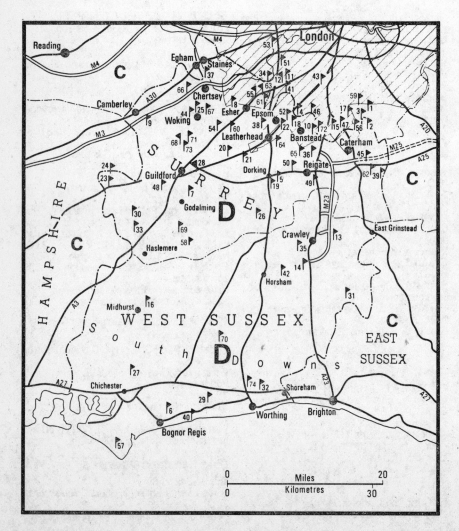

Green Fees. Weekdays £7.00 per day; weekends £4.50 per day with member.
Society Meetings welcome Wed. and Thurs.
Hotels: Warwick House Hotel, Surbiton.
Meals served.

D 13 Copthorne

Tel. Copthorne 2033
Borers Arms Rd., Copthorne, Crawley, W. Sussex RH10 3LL.
On A264, 4 miles W of Crawley.
Heathland course.
18 holes, 5738 yds. S.S.S. 70
Course designed by James Braid.
Visitors welcome weekdays, weekends afternoons only.
Green Fees. Weekdays £4.00 per round, £5.00 per day; weekends £6.00.
Society Meetings by arrangement.
Hotels: Copthorne Hotel.
Meals served by arrangement.

D 14 Cottesmore

Tel. Crawley 28256
Pease Pottage, Crawley, W. Sussex.
At end of M23, 3 miles S of Crawley.
Undulating meadowland course.
36 holes
Old Course, 6097 yds. S.S.S. 70
New Course, 5321 yds. S.S.S. 68
Course designed by M.D. Rogerson.
Visitors welcome.
Green Fees. Weekdays £5.00; weekends £8.00.
Society Meetings welcome.
Hotels: George, Crawley; Airport Hotel, Gatwick; King's Head, Horsham.
Snacks served; meals by arrangement.

D 15 Coulsdon Court

Tel. 01-660 0468
Coulsdon Rd., Coulsdon, Surrey CR3 2LL.
Off A23 at Coulsdon.
Parkland course.
18 holes, 6045 yds. S.S.S. 68
Visitors welcome on weekdays, mornings at weekends with reservation.
Green Fees. Weekdays £2.75 per round, £4.25 per day; weekends £4.90 mornings, £3.90 afternoons.
Hotels: Aerodrome Hotel.
Lunches and snacks served.

D 16 Cowdray Park

Tel. Midhurst 2088
Midhurst, W. Sussex GU29 0BB.
On A272, 1 mile E of Midhurst.
Undulating meadowland course.
18 holes, 6204 yds. S.S.S. 70
Visitors welcome.
Green Fees. Weekdays £5.00 (£2.50 with member); weekends £6.00 (£3.00 with member).
Society Meetings by arrangement.
Hotels: Spread Eagle; Angel.
Meals served.

D 17 Croham Hurst

Tel. 01-657 2075
Croham Rd., South Croydon, Surrey CR2 7HJ.

On A23 from London, ½ mile from South Croydon station, on road to Selsdon.
Parkland course.
18 holes, 6274 yds. S.S.S. 70
Visitors welcome on weekdays, weekends with member only.
Green Fees. £9.50 daily.
Society Meetings welcome.
Hotels: Selsdon Park Hotel.
Meals served.

D 18 Cuddington

Tel. 01-393 0952
Banstead Rd., Banstead, Surrey.
200 yards from Banstead railway station.
Parkland course.
18 holes, 6282 yds. S.S.S. 70
Course designed by H.S. Colt.
Visitors welcome with reservation, or with letter of introduction.
Green Fees. Weekdays £7.50; weekends £9.00.
Society Meetings Thurs. only, max. 60.
Hotels: Pickard Motor Hotel.
Snacks served; lunches by arrangement.

D 19 Dorking

Tel. Dorking 86917
Chart Park, Dorking, Surrey RH5 4BX.
On A24, 1 mile S of Dorking.
Undulating parkland course.
9 holes, 5106 yds. S.S.S. 65
Course designed by James Braid.
Visitors welcome.
Green Fees. Weekdays £5.00 per round or day; weekends and bank holidays £3.00 (with member only).
Society Meetings by arrangement.
Hotels: Burford Bridge Hotel; White Horse; Punch Bowl Hotel and Motel.
Snacks served weekdays, meals weekends only.

D 20 Drift Golf & Country Club

Tel. East Horsley (04865) 4641 & 2
The Drift, East Horsley, Surrey.
2 miles from A3, turning off at signs for East Horsley onto B2039.
Woodland course - four starting points.
18 holes, 6469 yds. S.S.S. 71
Visitors welcome weekdays, weekends by appointment.
Green Fees. Weekdays £7.00 per day, £5.00 after 2 p.m.; weekends £10.00.
Societies weekdays only.
Hotels: Thatchers, East Horsley; Seven Hills Hotel, Cobham; Bookham Grange Hotel, Bookham.
Meals served.

D 21 Effingham

Tel. Bookham (0372) 52203
Guildford Rd., Effingham, Surrey.
Off A246, 8 miles E of Guildford.
Downland course.
18 holes, 6488 yds. S.S.S. 71
Course designed by H.S. Colt (1927).
Visitors welcome on weekdays. Ladies' day Tues.
Green Fees. £7.50 per day (£3.50 with member); £5.00 after 12.00 a.m. (£3.00 with member).

Society Meetings welcome Wed., Thurs. and Fri.
Hotels: Bookham Grange Hotel, Preston Cross Hotel, Bookham.
Meals served.

D 22 Epsom

Tel. Epsom (037 27) 21666
Longdown Lane South, Epsom Downs, Epsom, Surrey KT17 4JR.
On A241, 300 yards from Epsom Downs station.
Undulating downland course.
18 holes, 5656 yds. Par 69. S.S.S. 67
Visitors welcome on weekdays, Tues. Sat., Sun. after 11.00 a.m.
Green Fees. £4.00 per day (£2.50 with member).
Society Meetings welcome Wed. and Fri., small societies up to 30.
Hotels: Chalk Lane Hotel, Epsom; Drift Bridge Hotel, Burgh Heath.
Bar snacks served; meals by arrangement.

D 23 Farnham

Tel. Runfold 2109
The Sands, Farnham, Surrey GU10 1PX.
Off A31, 2 miles E of Farnham.
Parkland, heathland course.
18 holes, 6221 yds. S.S.S. 70
Visitors welcome if members of recognized club.
Green Fees. £7.50 per round or day.
Society Meetings welcome weekdays only.
Hotels: Hog's Back, Runfold; Frensham Ponds Hotel, Frensham; Bush, Farnham; Queen's, Farnborough.
Meals served.

D 24 Farnham Park

Tel. Farnham 713319
Folly Hill, Farnham, Surrey.
¾ mile N of Farnham.
Undulating parkland course.
9 holes, 2200 yds. S.S.S. 54
Course designed by H. Cotton.
Visitors welcome.
Green Fees. 70p per 9 holes (80p weekends).
Hotels: Bush Hotel.

D 25 Foxhills

Tel. Ottershaw 2050
Stonehill Rd., Ottershaw, Surrey.
On A320, M3 Exit 2, M25 take exit for Woking (A320), continue until Otter Public House, turn R into Foxhills Road.
Heathland courses.
(1) 18 holes, 6880 yds. S.S.S. 73
(2) 18 holes, 6747 yds. S.S.S. 72
Course designed by F.W. Hawtree.
Visitors welcome.
Green Fees. Weekdays £6.00 per round, £9.00 per day; weekends £12.00 per round or day.
Society Meetings welcome.
Hotels: Ship Hotel, Weybridge; Seven Hills Motel, Cobham.
Meals served until 4.30p.m.; snacks served after 4.30p.m.

D 26   Gatton Manor

Tel. Oakwood Hill 555
Ockley, Dorking, Surrey RH5 5PQ.
On A29, 7 miles S of Dorking.
18 holes, 6903 yds. S.S.S. 72
Visitors welcome.
Green Fees. Weekdays £4.25 per day;
weekends £5.50 per day.
Society Meetings welcome weekdays
only.

D 27   Goodwood

Tel. Chichester (0243) 527491
Goodwood, Chichester, W. Sussex PO18
OPN.
On A286, 5 miles N of Chichester.
Downland parkland course.
18 holes, 6370 yds. S.S.S. 70
Visitors welcome on weekdays.
Green Fees. Weekdays £5.00; weekends
£7.00.
Society Meetings by arrangement.
Hotels: Dolphin & Anchor, Chichester;
Richmond Arms, Goodwood.
Light meals and snacks served.

D 28   Guildford

Tel. Guildford 63941
High Path Rd., Merrow, Guildford, Surrey
GU1 2HI.
2 miles E of Guildford on A246.
Parkland course.
18 holes, 6080 yds. S.S.S. 70
Visitors welcome on weekdays, weekends
with member only.
Green Fees. £6.50 per round or day,
juniors £2.50 per round or day.
Society Meetings welcome.
Hotels: Angel; White Horse, Guildford.
Lunches, snacks and evening meals served
by arrangement.

D 29   Ham Manor

Tel. Rustington 3288
Angmering, Littlehampton, W. Sussex BN16
4JE.
On A259, 6 miles W of Worthing.
Parkland course.
18 holes, 6216 yds. S.S.S. 70
Visitors welcome on weekdays.
Green Fees. On application to Secretary.
Society Meetings welcome weekdays
only.
Hotels: Broadmark, Rustington; Beach
Hotel, Littlehampton; Lamb Inn, Angmering.
Lunch, morning coffee and afternoon tea
served.

D 30   Hankley Common

Tel. Frensham 2493
Tilford, Farnham, Surrey GU10 2DD.
4 miles SW of Farnham.
Heathland course.
18 holes, 6515 yds. S.S.S. 71
Course designed by J. Braid.
Visitors must be members of a recognized
golf club and have a bona fide handicap. No
visitors at weekends or on bank holidays
unless cleared in advance by the Secretary.
Society Meetings welcome Tues. and
Wed.
Hotels: Pride of the Valley Hotel, Hindhead.
No catering on Fri.

D 31   Haywards Heath

Tel. Haywards Heath 414457
High Beech Lane, Haywards Heath, W.
Sussex BH16 186.
1 Mile from Haywards Heath station.
Parkland course.
18 holes, 5900 yds. S.S.S. 68
Visitors welcome on weekdays with
reservation, weekends after 12.00 a.m.
Green Fees. Weekdays £6.00 per round
or day; weekends £8.00 per round or day.
Society Meetings by arrangement.
Hotels: Hayworthe, Haywards Heath; Bent
Arms, Lindfield.
Bar food available; main meals by
arrangement.

D 32   Hill Barn

Tel. Worthing 33918 (Club house), 37301
(Professional)
Hill Barn Lane, Worthing, W. Sussex BN14
9QF.
NE Worthing off Upper Brighton road at
Excess roundabout.
Downland course.
18 holes, 6224 yds. S.S.S. 70
Visitors welcome.
Green Fees. Weekdays £3.00 per round;
weekends and bank holidays £3.80 per
round.
Society Meetings weekdays by
arrangement; none in August.
Hotels: Chatsworth; Warnes; Eardley;
Beach.

D 33   Hindhead

Tel. Hindhead (042 873) 4614
Churt Rd., Hindhead, Surrey GU26 6HX.
On A287, 7 miles S of Farnham.
Heathland course.
18 holes, 6364 yds. S.S.S. 70
Visitors welcome if members of recognized
club.
Green Fees. Weekdays £6.00 (£3.00 with
member); weekends £10.00 (£5.00 with
member).
Society Meetings welcome weekdays.
Hotels: Frensham Ponds Hotel, Frensham;
Lythe Hill Hotel; Georgian, Haslemere.
Snacks served; full lunches if ordered before
9 a.m.

D 34   Home Park

Tel. 01-977 6645, Sec. 01-977 2423,
Professional 01-977 2658
Hampton Wick, Kingston-upon-Thames,
Surrey KT1 4AD.
Between Hampton Court and Kingston
Bridge.
Parkland course.
18 holes, 6496 yds. S.S.S. 71
Visitors by arrangement with professional.
Green Fees. Weekdays £4.25 per round,
£6.25 per day; weekends £6.00 per round,
£8.25 per day.
Society Meetings by arrangement.
Hotels: Greyhound; Griffin.
Meals served except Fri.

D 35   Ifield Golf & Country Club

Tel. Crawley (0293) 20222
Rusper Rd., Ifield, Crawley, W. Sussex RH11
0LW.
3 miles from Ifield roundabout on the outskirts
of Crawley.
Parkland course.
18 holes, 6268 yds. S.S.S. 70
Course designed by F. Hawtree & J.H. Taylor
Ltd.
Visitors welcome on weekdays, weekends
with member only.
Green Fees. Weekdays £5.50 per round
(£3.00 with member), £7.50 per day
(£5.00 with member); Sat. with member
£4.50 per round, £6.00 per day; Sun. with
member £5.00 per round (p.m.).
Society Meetings welcome weekdays.
Hotels: George, Crawley; Ifield Court Hotel,
Ifield.
Lunches, snacks and high teas served.

D 36   Kingswood

Tel. Mogador 832188
Sandy Lane, Kingswood, Surrey KT20 6NE.
5 miles S of Sutton (Surrey) off A217.
Parkland course.
18 holes, 6501 yds. S.S.S. 71
Course designed by James Braid.
Visitors welcome with reservation.
Green Fees. Weekdays £8.50 (£6.00 with
member), after 1.00 p.m. £6.00 (£4.50 with
member), after 4.00 p.m. £4.50 (£3.00 with
member); weekends £10.00 (£7.50 with
member); after 2.00 p.m. £8.00 (£6.00 with
member).
Society Meetings by arrangement.
Hotels: in Reigate and Banstead area.
Meals served.
Squash Courts - by prior arrangement.

D 37   Laleham

Tel. Chertsey 62188
Laleham Reach, Chertsey, Surrey KT16
8AP.
2 miles from Staines along Staines Lane turn
in at Penton Hook Yacht Basin, Mixnams
Lane.
Flat meadowland course.
18 holes, 6049 yds. S.S.S. 69
Visitors welcome on weekdays.
Green Fees. £5.00 per round, £7.00 per
day.
Society Meetings welcome Mon., Tues.
and Wed.
Hotels: Packhorse, Staines.
Meals served.

D 38   Leatherhead

Tel. Leatherhead 74348 or 72013
Oxshott Rd., Leatherhead, Surrey KT22
0EE.
On A244 beside junction with A243.
Undulating parkland course.
18 holes, 6209 yds. S.S.S. 70
Visitors welcome.
Green Fees. Weekdays £8.00 per round,
£9.50 per day; weekends £10.00 per round
or day.
Society Meetings welcome weekdays
except Thurs. a.m.
Hotels: New Bull, Leatherhead.
Meals served.

D 39   Limpsfield Chart

Tel. Limpsfield Chart 2106
Limpsfield, Oxted, Surrey RH8 0SL.
On A25, 7 miles W of Sevenoaks.

Historical courses around London

Golf courses around London in late Victorian days were more or less confined to two main groups. There were a few famous courses on public commons such as Blackheath and Wimbledon, and a number of others that broadly fitted the description of field and parkland, but round the turn of the century a whole new generation of courses—the generation of sand and heather—began to arise out of the mists.

Most of this now familiar golfing country is to be found south of the river in Surrey and Berkshire, and though it was never intended to make up for seaside golf which has always come first in this country, it did show that the best inland golf could no longer be reproached as being a bad second.

Of these clubs still in existence, Woking was the first and Sunningdale one of the next, but close behind in 1904 came Walton Heath which rapidly became acknowledged as ranking at the very top of the long list of inland courses in Britain, a position that has never wavered.

It was Herbert Fowler who first saw the possibilities of golf on the grand scale on Walton Heath, and it is a lasting tribute to his skill as an architect that most of it remains unaltered even in an age when tampering has become a sort of disease. In area the heath is not all that large, but it stands very high, almost 700 feet above sea level, and, being so exposed, the lightest wind affects the golfer and anything stronger can blow him off his feet.

The turf is also wonderfully dry and with the ball liable to run freely, the control needed to escape the profusion of heather, bracken or the many bunkers that Fowler arranged so mercilessly, is considerable.

The professionals soon recognized its merits and in 1905 the News of the World matchplay Championship—the oldest professional event in the world—adopted it as its most popular home; but undoubtedly the most famous and most romantic link with the club came when its name appeared in brackets after that of the beloved James Braid.

Originally there was only one course known as the Old; then nine more holes were added and in due time made up to eighteen holes to form the present New course; but though the Old generally comes first to mind, not just for reasons of seniority, the New has equal charm and underlines that there are few more pleasant spots when the blessings of summer are at hand and the wandering public are not invading the golfer's privacy.

The fact is that golf is permitted there under an Act of Parliament and that the public have a righ of way provided only that they do not interfere in any way with the members and their guests at play. Yet any such interference to the casual golfing visitor is a minor complaint.

His concern is solely enjoyment, and no pair of courses provide him with more fun or a greater challenge. At all times there is plenty of hard hitting to be faced and the last six holes on the Old comprise as difficult a finish as could be imagined—but the greens, with their many subtle borrows, are sleek and fast and always there is the knowledge and thrill of following in the stud marks of Braid, Cotton and countless other masters of the past. Is there anyone who could ask for more than that from a course?

Private course.
9 holes, 5718 yds. S.S.S. 68
Visitors welcome. Ladies' day Thurs.
Green Fees. Weekdays £4.00; weekends £6.00.
Society Meetings by arrangement.
Hotels: Hoskins, Oxted.
Snacks and lunches served by arrangement.

D 40 Littlehampton

Tel. Littlehampton 7170
Riverside West, Littlehampton, W. Sussex.
Off A259, 1 mile W of Littlehampton.
Seaside course.
18 holes, 6104 yds. S.S.S. 69
Course designed by Hawtree & Taylor.
Visitors welcome.
Green Fees. Weekdays £5.00; weekends £7.00.
Society Meetings by arrangement.
Hotels: Birers, Clymping; Beach Hotel, Littlehampton.
Snacks served; lunches served except Mon. and Tues.

D 41 Malden

Tel. 01-942 0654
Traps Lane, New Malden, Surrey KT3 4RS.
Off Kingston by-pass (A3) at Malden roundabout. Through town, ½ mile beyond station.
Parkland course.
18 holes, 6314 yds. S.S.S. 70
Visitors welcome on weekdays.
Green Fees. Weekdays £7.50 (£3.00 with member); weekends between 11.30 a.m. and 12.30 p.m. £12.00 (£5.00 with member).
Society Meetings welcome weekdays only, max 60.

Hotels: Griffin, Kingston-upon-Thames.
Meals served.

D 42 Mannings Heath

Tel. Horsham 65224 (Club), 66217 (Sec.)
Goldings Lane, Mannings Heath, Horsham, W. Sussex RH13 6JU.
Off A281, 2 miles SE of Horsham.
Heathland course.
18 holes, 6402 yds. S.S.S. 72
Visitors welcome on weekdays with reservation, weekends with letter of introduction. No weekend visitors during winter months except with a member.
Green Fees. Weekdays £5.50 (£4.50 after 2.30 p.m.); weekends £6.50.
Society Meetings by arrangement on weekdays only.
Hotels: Old King's Head, Horsham; George, Crawley.
Meals served.

D 43 Mitcham

Tel. 01-648 1508
Mitcham Junction, Surrey.
A237 off A23, by Mitcham Junction station.
Commonland course.
18 holes, 5931 yds. S.S.S. 68
Visitors welcome on weekdays, weekends with reservation.
Green Fees. Weekdays £2.00 per round, £3.00 per day; weekends £3.00 per round.
Snacks served.

D 44 New Zealand

Tel. Byfleet 45049
Woodham Lane, Woodham, Weybridge, Surrey KT15 3QD.
On A245 N of Woking, 1 mile from West Byfleet.
Heather, woodland course.
18 holes, 6012 yds. S.S.S. 69
Visitors welcome on weekdays, weekends with member only.
Green Fees. Weekdays £8.50 per round, £11.00 per day (£4.00 with member).
Society Meetings welcome weekdays except Mon.
Hotels: Ship Hotel, Weybridge.
Lunches served by arrangement except Mon.

D 45 North Downs

Tel. Woldingham (905) 3298
Northdown Rd., Woldingham, Caterham, Surrey CR3 7AA.
Off A22 at Caterham roundabout on to Woldingham Rd. 2 miles.
Downland course.
18 holes, 5745 yds. S.S.S. 68
Visitors welcome on weekdays with reservation.
Green Fees. £9.00 per day, £7.00 after 2.30 p.m.
Society Meetings by arrangement.

D 46 Oaks Park

Tel. 01-643 8363
Woodmansterne Rd., Carshalton, Surrey.
Off B280 S of Carshalton.
Meadowland course.
18 holes, 5845 yds. S.S.S. 68
Visitors welcome.
Green Fees. Weekdays £2.00; juniors and O.A.Ps £1.25; weekends £3.10 before 11 a.m., £2.50 after 11 a.m. 9 hole pitch and putt 65p.
Society Meetings by arrangement.
Hotels: Greyhound; Hotel Carshalton.
Meals served.

D 47   Purley Downs

Tel. 01-657 8347
106 Purley Downs Rd., Purley, Surrey CR2 0RB.
Off A233 between Purley and Croydon stations.
Downland course.
18 holes, 6237 yds. S.S.S. 70
Visitors welcome on weekdays.
Green Fees. Weekdays £9.00 per round or day.
Society Meetings welcome by arrangement.
Bar snacks served; lunches by arrangement.

D 48   Puttenham

Tel. Guildford 810498
Puttenham Heath, Guildford, Surrey.
600 yards S of Hog's Back (A31), 4 miles S of Guildford.
Heathland course.
18 holes, 5362 yds. S.S.S. 66
Visitors welcome weekdays (weekends with member only).
Green Fees. Weekdays £6.00 (£3.00 with member); weekends £4.00 (only with member).
Society Meetings welcome.
Hotels: Angel, Guildford.
Lunches and teas served by arrangement.

D 49   Redhill & Reigate

Tel. Reigate 44626, Hon. Sec. Reigate 40777
Clarence Lodge, Pendleton Road, Redhill, Surrey RH2 7NT.
1 mile S of Redhill.
Moorland course.
18 holes, 5360 yds. S.S.S. 65
Visitors welcome on weekdays, weekends after 10.30a.m., Sun. until 2.00p.m.
Green Fees. Weekdays £2.25 per round, £4.50 per day; weekends £2.50 per round.
Society Meetings by arrangement.
Hotels: Lakers Hill Hotel, Redhill.
Lunches served.

D 50   Reigate Heath

Tel. Reigate 42610
Flanchford Rd., Reigate, Surrey RH2 8QR.
½ mile S of A25 on Western boundary of Reigate.
Heathland course.
9 holes, 5554 yds. S.S.S. 67
Visitors welcome with reservation. Sun. with member only.
Green Fees. Weekdays £4.50 per round, £5.50 per day; Sat. £5.50 per round, £7.00 per day.
Society Meetings welcome Wed. and Thurs., max. 30.
Lunches served by arrangement except Mon.

D 51   Richmond

Tel. 01-940 1463
Sudbrook Park, Richmond, Surrey TW10 7AS.
On A307 2 miles S of Richmond, look for Sudbrook Lane, on left.
Wooded parkland course.
18 holes, 6040 yds. S.S.S. 69
Course designed by T. Dunn (1891).
Visitors welcome on weekdays, weekends with reservation.

Green Fees. Weekdays £9.00 per round; weekends £10.00 per round.
Society Meetings by arrangement.
Lunches and teas served except Mon.

D 52   R.A.C. Country Club

Tel. Ashtead 76311
Woodcote Park, Wilmerhatch Lane, Epsom, Surrey.
A24 1½ miles from Epsom station.
Parkland courses.
Old 18 holes, 6672 yds. S.S.S. 72
Coronation 18 holes, 5548 yds. S.S.S. 67
Visitors welcome, with member only.
Green Fees. Weekdays Old course £7.00, Coronation course £6.00; weekends Old course £9.00, Coronation course £6.50.
Society Meetings welcome weekdays only.
Hotels: Accommodation available at clubhouse.
Meals served.

D 53   Royal Mid-Surrey

Tel. 01-940 1894
Old Deer Park, Twickenham Rd., Richmond, Surrey TW9 2SB.
250 yards from Richmond roundabout on A316.
Parkland course.
Outer 18 holes, S.S.S. 70
Inner 18 holes, S.S.S. 68
Course designed by J.H. Taylor.
Visitors welcome weekdays by introduction, weekends with member.
Green Fees. Weekdays £8.00 per round, £10.00 per day.
Society Meetings welcome.
Hotels: Richmond Hill Hotel; Quinns Hotel; Richmond Gate Hotel; Bishops Hotel.
Snacks served; lunch except Mon.

D 54   St. George's Hill

Tel. Weybridge 42406
St. George's Hill, Weybridge, Surrey.
B374 from station towards Cobham, ½ mile on left.
Heathland, woodland course.
18 holes, 6492 yds. S.S.S. 71
9 holes, 2360 yds. S.S.S. 36
Course designed by H.S. Colt.
Visitors 18 hole course: welcome with letter of introduction and reservation, weekends with member only. 9 hole course: welcome any time.
Green Fees. Weekdays 18 hole course: £6.90 per round, £10.90 per day; 9 hole course: weekdays £3.00 per round, weekends £4.00 per round.
Society Meetings by arrangement on weekdays.
Hotels: Ship Hotel, Weybridge; Seven Hills Motel.
Lunches and teas served by arrangement.

D 55   Sandown Park

Tel. Esher 65921
Sandown Park Racecourse, More Lane, Esher, Surrey KT10 8AN.
A3 from Kingston by-pass, first right into Station Rd., then first left.
Meadowland course.
9 holes, 2829 yds. S.S.S. 67
Course designed by J. Jacobs and J. Corby.

Visitors welcome.
Green Fees. Weekdays £1.70; weekends £2.25.
Hotels: Haven, Esher; Seven Hills Motel, Cobham.
Snacks and lunches served.

D 56   Selsdon Park Hotel

Tel. 01-657 8811, Telex 945003
Addington Rd., Sanderstead, S. Croydon, Surrey CR2 8YA.
B275 from Croydon, B268 at Selsdon.
Undulating parkland course. Championship status.
18 holes, 6402 yds. S.S.S. 71
Course designed by J.H. Taylor.
Visitors welcome except Sat. and Sun. mornings from Mar. to Oct.
Green Fees. Weekdays £6.50; Sat. £8.50; Sun. £9.50.
Society Meetings by arrangement.
Hotels: Selsdon Park Hotel.
Meals served.

D 57   Selsey

Tel. Selsey (024361) 2203
Golf Links Lane, Selsey, Chichester, W. Sussex PO20 9DR.
On B2145, 7 miles S of Chichester.
Seaside course.
9 holes, 5730 yds. S.S.S. 67
Visitors welcome if members of recognized club.
Green Fees. Weekdays £3.50 per day; weekends £4.50 per day.
Society Meetings small societies welcome.
Lunches and snacks served.

D 58   Shillinglee Park

Tel. Haslemere (0428) 53237
Chiddington, Godalming, Surrey.
Off A283, 2 miles S of Chiddingfold.
Parkland course.
9 holes, 1907 yds.
Visitors welcome.
Green Fees. £1.50 per round (juniors and O.A.P.s £1.00).
Society Meetings welcome.
Hotels: Crown; Winterton Arms, Chiddingfold.
Bar; snacks served.

D 59   Shirley Park

Tel. 01-654 1143
Addiscombe Rd., Croydon, Surrey CR0 7LB.
1 mile E of Croydon Station.
Parkland course.
18 holes, 6300 yds. S.S.S. 70
Visitors welcome weekdays, weekends with member only.
Green Fees. £6.50 per round or day.
Society Meetings welcome.
Hotels: Queens, Upper Norwood; Greyhound, E. Croydon.
Meals served.

D 60   Silvermere

Tel. Cobham 7275 or 4988
Redhill Rd., Cobham, Surrey.
Redhill Rd. leaves A245 midway between Cobham and Byfleet to join A3.
Woodland, parkland, meadowland course.

Pulborough, a perfect haven

The West Sussex Golf Club, on the edge of the little town of Pulborough, has the sort of course against which it is impossible to level any serious criticism. Set amid the glories of a county renowned for its beauty, it is one of the most attractive of all our inland courses and possesses in its sandy soil the true foundation for golf.

In addition to being sandy, Pulborough is also heathery and the combination of the two is irresistible. Not least of its many charms is the fact that, like Woodhall Spa in Lincolnshire, it is the only piece of ground for miles around possessing these admirable qualities—a veritable oasis in a desert of clay.

How long it would have taken a man less knowledgeable about golf than Commander Hillyard to discover the possibilities of the site is hard to say. When the Commander came to live in Pulborough, he immediately realized what could be done. He subsequently engaged Major C.K. Hutchison and Sir Guy Campbell to design the course, and was himself much involved in the work carried out.

Both the designers did notable work in golf course architecture, but it is doubtful whether they ever had a better piece of land with which to work or made better use of any which they were given. Pulborough is a reminder of their expertise and, even with its relatively modest length, a fine test for the golfer.

It has never been a club with a great desire for the big occasions, but it is a course which everyone loves to play and it never disappoints. Its surroundings, of course, play a large part in this and they attract almost as much as the golf. From the moment you turn off the road after an approach that bears no hint of what is in store, the pines, the birch, the heather and the glorious white sand unfold their patterns and colours. In the distance the romantic grove of Chanctonbury Ring looks down approvingly, and the simple beauty of a typically English scene is complete. However, if this all unmistakably portrays a picture of rural peace, the fineness of the turf suggests more the character of a seaside links. This is undoubtedly its most appealing quality, particularly to those more used to courses around London which can be villainously muddy in winter.

Pulborough, rather like Rye, possesses an unusual number of long par fours and two of the hardest start us off. However, though the outward half measures less than 3,000 yards from the Medal Tees, not many can do it in the 33 strokes which the card tells us is par, or help reflecting that length in golf is not everything. Control along the heather lined fairways is the essence of success even on the picturesque dogleg 4th, which, properly played, is no more than a drive and short iron.

Pulborough also has a rare variety in its five short holes, three of which come in four holes from the 5th; but if two short holes in a row is an uncommon enough feature of the golf courses of the world to come as a surprise, the 6th in particular can leave a trail of destruction. It demands a long iron or wood to a fiendishly protected green with the threat of out of bounds lurking to the left, and it is no moment for the betrayal of positive thoughts. But neither is the drive up over the great ridge at the 7th, or the tee shot across a slight valley to the short 8th.

The 9th is fairly straightforward at 350 yards, but, starting with the 10th and its curving swing to the left, the homeward half abounds with excellent golf. The 11th, 13th and 14th are wonderful holes; the 15th is a tantalizingly short hole across a pond while the 16th requires a firm second over a deep gully.

Two more holes of over four hundred yards complete a round played without a single par five, a rarity in itself on a course of over 6,200 yards (although the 1st from the back tee is now measured at 476 yards); yet Pulborough's delights do not stop there. The South Downs make a soothing background and the Club, which Commander Hillyard also helped to form, always keeps a hospitable welcome.

---

18 holes, 6608 yds. S.S.S. 72
Visitors welcome weekdays, weekends with member only.
Green Fees. Weekdays £7.00; weekends (with member) £5.00.
Society Meetings welcome on weekdays, max. 100.
Hotels: Seven Hills Hotel.
Meals served.

D 61   Surbiton

Tel. 01-398 3101
Woodstock Lane, Chessington, Surrey KT9 1UG.
Off A3 (Kingston by-pass) at Hook roundabout on to A243 (Leatherhead Rd.) turning right towards Claygate.
Undulating course.
18 holes, 6211 yds. S.S.S. 70
Visitors welcome on weekdays, weekends with member only.
Green Fees. £7.50 per round or day.
Reduced rates when playing with member.
Society Meetings by arrangement.
Hotels: Haven Hotel, Esher.
Lunches; snacks and teas served every day.

D 62   Tandridge

Tel. Oxted 2274
Oxted, Surrey.
Off A25, 2 miles E of Godstone.
Parkland course.
18 holes, 6429 yds. S.S.S. 70
Course designed by H.S. Colt.

Visitors welcome with reservation.
Green Fees. £10.00 per day, £8.00 after 1.30 p.m.
Society Meetings by arrangement, 2 years in advance.
Lunches and teas served.

D 63   Thames Ditton & Esher

Tel. 01-398 1551
'Marquis of Granby', Portsmouth Rd., Esher, Surrey.
On A3 by Scilly Isles roundabout.
Common land course.
9 holes, 5415 yds. S.S.S. 64
Visitors welcome except Sun. morning.
Green Fees. Weekdays £1.50; weekends £2.50.

D 64   Tyrrells Wood

Tel. Leatherhead (03723) 73687
Tyrrells Wood, Leatherhead, Surrey KT22 8QP.
Off A24 Leatherhead by-pass, 1½ miles SE of Leatherhead.
Undulating parkland course.
18 holes, 6219 yds. S.S.S. 70
Visitors welcome weekdays, weekends after 12 noon if members of recognized club.
Green Fees. Weekdays and Sat. £7.50; Sun. £10.00.
Society Meetings welcome on weekdays.
Hotels: Bull, Leatherhead; Burford Bridge Hotel, Dorking.
Lunches served except Mon.

D 65   Walton Heath

Tel. Tadworth 2380
Deans Lane, Tadworth, Surrey.
From Dorking take A25 Reigate road for 2 miles. At roundabout turn on to B2032, up Pebblecombe Hill. After 2 miles turn left into Deans Lane. From London take A217 (Sutton by-pass). Turn on to B2032 at roundabout. After 1 mile turn R into Deans Lane.
Heathland courses.
Old 18 holes, 6859 yds. S.S.S. 73
New 18 holes, 6742 yds. S.S.S. 72
Course designed by H.W. Fowler.
Visitors welcome on weekdays with reservation.
Green Fees. Weekdays £11.50 (£8.50 after 11.30 a.m.).
Society Meetings welcome weekdays only.
Hotels: Copthorne Hotel, Gatwick; Burford Bridge Hotel, Dorking; Pickard Motor Hotel, Burgh Heath.

D 66   Wentworth

Tel. Wentworth 2201
Virginia Water, Surrey GU25 4LF.
On A30 at junction with A329.
Wooded heathland course.
East 18 holes, S.S.S. 70
West 18 holes, S.S.S. 74
Also 9 hole course
Visitors welcome on weekdays with reservation.

Green Fees. Weekdays £12.00 (£4.00 with member).
Society Meetings welcome Tues., Wed., Thurs. only.
Hotels: Royal Berkshire; Berystede, Ascot, Berkshire; Great Fosters, Egham, Surrey.
Lunches served; also snack bar.

D 67   West Byfleet

Tel. Byfleet 45230
Sheerwater Rd., West Byfleet, Surrey.
On A245.
Parkland course.
18 holes, S.S.S. 70
Visitors who are members of recognized golf clubs welcome on weekdays with letter of introduction.
Meals served.

D 68   West Hill

Tel. Brookwood 2110 & 4365
Brookwood, Surrey GU24 0BH.
On A322 midway between Bagshot and Guildford.
Heath and woodland course.
18 holes, 6309 yds. S.S.S. 70
Visitors welcome on weekdays with letter of introduction.
Green Fees. Weekdays £7.00 per round (£4.00 with member), £10.00 per day (£6.00 with member).
Society Meetings welcome weekdays except Mon. and Fri.
Hotels: Worplesdon Place, Worplesdon; Mayford Manor, Woking.
Lunches served.

D 69   West Surrey

Tel. Godalming 21275
Enton Green, Godalming, Surrey GU8 5AF.
Off A3, ½ mile E of Milford.
Parkland course.
18 holes, 6204 yds. S.S.S. 70
Course designed by Herbert Fowler (1909).
Visitors welcome on weekdays, weekends with letter of introduction.
Green Fees. Weekdays £6.33 per round, £8.63 per day; weekends £11.05.
Society Meetings by arrangement.
Hotels: Manor Hotel, Farncombe; Lake Hotel, Godalming.
Meals by arrangement; snacks on Mon. only.

D 70   West Sussex

Tel. Pulborough 2563
Pulborough, W. Sussex RH20 2EN.
On A283 between Pulborough and Storrington.
Heathland course.
18 holes, 6131 yds. S.S.S. 70
Course designed by Major C.K. Hutchison and Sir Guy Campbell.
Visitors welcome with reservation and letter of introduction.
Green Fees. £8.00 per day.
Society Meetings by arrangement.
Hotels: Roundabout Hotel, West Chiltington; Abingworth Hall Hotel, Pulborough.
Lunches and teas served.

D 71   Woking

Tel. Woking 60053
Pond Rd., Hook Heath, Woking, Surrey.
At end of Golf Club Rd. which is turning off Hook Heath Ave., just S of first bridge over Woking-Southampton railway, to W of Woking.
Heathland course.
18 holes, 6365 yds. S.S.S. 70
Visitors welcome on weekdays with prior reservation.
Green Fees. £7.00 per round; £11.00 per day.
Society Meetings by arrangement.
Hotels: Mayford Manor, Woking; Worplesdon Place, Worplesdon.
Lunches and teas served to prior order except Mon.

D 72   Woodcote Park

Tel. 01-668 2788
Bridle Way, Meadow Hill, Coulsdon, Surrey CR3 2QQ.
A23 to Purley, take Wallington Rd. to crossroads, turn left then 4th right.
Parkland course.
18 holes, 6592 yds. S.S.S. 71
Visitors welcome on weekdays.
Green Fees. £7.00 per round or day.
Society Meetings weekdays by arrangement.
Meals served.

D 73   Worplesdon

Tel. Brookwood 2277 (Sec.) & 3287 (Pro.)
Heath House Rd., Woking, Surrey GU22 0RA.
A322.
Wooded heathland course.
18 holes, 6422 yds. S.S.S. 71
Course designed by F.J. Abercromby.
Visitors welcome on weekdays with reservation.
Society Meetings by arrangement.
Hotels: Worplesdon Place, Worplesdon; Mayford Manor, Mayford.
Lunches served.

D 74   Worthing

Tel. Worthing 60801
Links Rd., Worthing, W. Sussex BN14 9QZ.
On A27, 1½ miles from Worthing Central railway station.
Downland courses.
Lower 18 holes, 6274 yds. S.S.S. 70
Upper 18 holes, 5127 yds. S.S.S. 65
Courses designed by H.S. Colt.
Visitors welcome.
Green Fees. Weekdays £6.00 (£3.00 with member); weekends (starting time 10 a.m.) £9.00 (£4.50 with member).
Society Meetings welcome Tues. and Fri.
Hotels: Downland Hotel; Thomas a Becket Hotel.
Meals served.

E Kent, East Sussex

E 1   Ashdown Forest Hotel

Tel. Forest Row 2010
Chapel Lane, Forest Row, E. Sussex RH18 5BB.
Off A22 London to Eastbourne road.
Woodland course.
18 holes, 6025 yds. S.S.S. 69
Visitors welcome.
Green Fees. £5.50 per day, £3.50 after 4.00 p.m.
Society Meetings welcome.
Hotels: Ashdown Forest Hotel.
Meals served.

E 2   Ashford (Kent)

Tel. Ashford 0233 20180
Sandyhurst Lane, Ashford, Kent TN25 4NT.
Off A20, 1½ miles N of Ashford.
Parkland course.
18 holes, 6442 yds. S.S.S. 70
Visitors welcome weekdays, weekends after 11.30a.m. except when playing with a member.
Green Fees. Weekdays £6.00; weekends £8.00.
Society Meetings welcome weekdays only.
Hotels: Spierpoint; Kempton Manor Hotel.
Meals served except Mon.

E 3   Barnehurst

Tel. Crayford 523746
Mayplace Rd. East, Barnehurst, Bexleyheath, Kent DA7 6JU.
From Erith Rd., about 750 yards on left, near Bexleyheath clock tower.
Undulating parkland course.
Course designed by James Braid.
Visitors welcome Mon., Wed., Fri.
Green Fees. Weekdays £1.90 per round plus V.A.T.; weekends £3.15 per round plus V.A.T.
Meals served by arrangement.

E 4   Bearsted

Tel. Maidstone (0622) 38389
Ware St., Bearsted, Maidstone, Kent.
3 miles E of Maidstone on A2011, near Bearsted station.
Parkland course.
18 holes, 6232 yds. S.S.S. 70
Visitors welcome on weekdays.
Green Fees. £5.00 per round (£4.00 with member); £7.00 per day (£5.00 with member).

Society Meetings welcome on weekdays by arrangement.
Hotels: Great Danes, Hollingborne.
Lunches served except Mon.

E 5 Beckenham Place Park

Tel. 01-650 2292
Beckenham Place Park, Beckenham, Kent.
1 mile NE of Beckenham.
Parkland course.
18 holes, 5672 yds. S.S.S. 67
Visitors welcome.
Green Fees. Weekdays £1.30 per round; weekends £1.90 per round.
Hotels: Bromley Court Hotel, Bromley Hill.
Meals and snacks served.

E 6 Bexleyheath

Tel. 01-303 4232
Mount Rd., Bexleyheath, Kent DA6 8JS.
1 mile from Bexleyheath railway station.
Undulating course.
9 holes, 5239 yds. S.S.S. 66
Visitors welcome on weekdays if member of recognized club.
Green Fees. Weekdays £4.50 (£2.00 with member); weekends £2.00; Sat. all day, Sun. p.m. with member only.
Society Meetings by arrangement.

Hotels: Eltham Private Hotel.
Snacks served except Mon.; lunches by arrangement except Mon.

E 7 Brighton & Hove

Tel. Brighton (0273) 556482
Dyke Rd., Brighton, E. Sussex BN1 8YJ.
S from A27 at Patcham traffic lights, turn right and right again at crossroads, 2 miles on left.
Downland course.
9 holes, 5535 yds. S.S.S. 67
Course designed by James Braid (1910).
Visitors welcome, Sun. after 12.00 a.m.
Green Fees. Weekdays £4.00 18 holes, £6.00 per day; weekends £5.00 18 holes.
Reduced rates with member.
Society Meetings by arrangement.
Hotels: Dudley Hotel, Hove.
Meals served except Mon.

E 8 Bromley

Tel. 01-462 7014
Magpie Hall Lane, Bromley, Kent BR2 8JF.
A21 2 miles S of Bromley.
Parkland course.
9 holes, 2745 yds. S.S.S. 69
Visitors welcome.

Green Fees. Weekdays 65p (O.A.P.'s 50p); weekends £1.15.
Meals served.

E 9 Broome Park and Country Club

Tel. Barham (022 782) 512
Broome Park Estate, Barham, Canterbury, Kent.
A2 Canterbury-Dover; ¼ mile from Folkestone turn-off (A260).
Parkland course.
18 holes, 6606 yds. S.S.S. 72
Course designed by D. Steel.
Visitors by appointment.
Green Fees. £5.00 per round; £8.00 per day.
Society Meetings by arrangement.
Hotels: County, Canterbury.
Two restaurants and bars.

E 10 Canterbury

Tel. Canterbury 63586
Littlebourne Rd., Canterbury, Kent CT1 1TW.
On A257 Sandwich road, 1½ miles from city centre.
Undulating parkland course.
18 holes, 6222 yds. S.S.S. 70
Visitors welcome on weekdays, weekends.

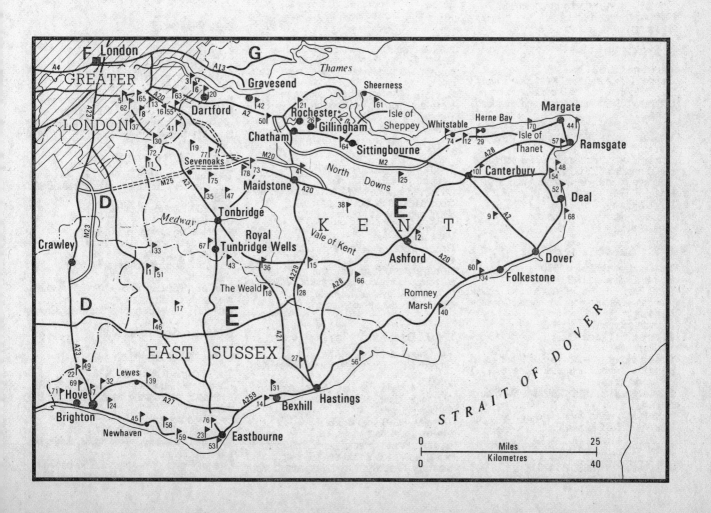

Green Fees. Weekdays £5.00 per round, £7.00 per day; Sunday p.m. £5.50.
Society Meetings by arrangement.
Hotels: Chaucer; County; Barton Court; Falstaff.
Snacks served; meals by arrangement.

E 11   Cherry Lodge

Tel. Biggin Hill 29 72250
Jail Lane, Biggin Hill, Kent TN16 3AX.
Off A233 S of R.A.F. Station.
Undulating parkland course.
18 holes, 7028 yds. S.S.S. 74
Course designed by John Day.
Visitors welcome on weekdays.
Green Fees. £4.00 per round, £5.60 per day.
Society Meetings welcome on weekdays.
Hotels: Kings Arms, Westerham.
Meals served to members and guests only.

E 12   Chestfield (Whitstable)

Tel. Chestfield 2243
Chestfield Rd., Whitstable, Kent.
A299 from London, turn right at roundabout by Chestfield railway station.
Undulating seaside course.
18 holes, 6068 yds. S.S.S. 69
Visitors welcome.
Green Fees. Weekdays £4.50 per round, £5.50 per day; weekends £7.00.
Society Meetings by arrangement.
Hotels: Marine, Tankerton.
Meals served.

E 13   Chislehurst

Tel. 01-467 2782
Camden Pl., Chislehurst, Kent BR7 5HJ.
On A222, 2 miles E of Bromley.
Undulating heathland, moorland, parkland course.
18 holes, 5200 yds. S.S.S. 65
Visitors welcome on weekdays, weekends with member only.
Green Fees. Weekdays £6.00 per round, £8.00 per day (£3.00 with member).
Society Meetings welcome, max. 40.
Hotels: Bull, Chislehurst; Bromley Court Hotel, Bromley.
Lunches served; afternoon tea by arrangement.

E 14   Cooden Beach

Tel. Cooden (042 43) 2040
Bexhill, E. Sussex TN39 4TR.
A259 Eastbourne to Hastings road. Follow 'Cooden Beach' sign at Little Common roundabout.
Seaside course.
20 holes, 6411 yds. S.S.S. 71
Visitors welcome.
Green Fees. Weekdays £6.00 per round or day; weekends and bank holidays £7.00 per round or day.
Society Meetings welcome weekdays only.
Hotels: Cooden Beach Hotel adjacent.
Lunches served except Fri.

E 15   Cranbrook

Tel. Cranbrook (0580) 712833
Benenden Rd., Cranbrook, Kent TN17 4AL.
Between Sissinghurst and Benenden.
Parkland course.
18 holes, 6000 yds. S.S.S. 69
Course designed by Cdr. J.D. Harris.
Visitors welcome.
Green Fees. Weekdays £4.25 per round, £7.20 per day; weekends £6.00 per round, £9.60 per day.
Society Meetings by arrangement.
Hotels: Willsley; George; Kennel Holt.
Meals served except Tues.

E 16   Cray Valley

Tel. Orpington 31927 / 37909 (Pro. shop)
Sandy Lane, Orpington, Kent.
Off A20 at Ruxley roundabout, 1 mile down Sandy Lane.
Open parkland course.
18 holes, 6112 yds. S.S.S. 69
Further 9 holes under construction.
Visitors welcome on weekdays.
Green Fees. £4.00 per round.
Society Meetings welcome on weekdays by arrangement.
Hotels: Bull, Birchwood, Swanley.
Lunches served 7 days; clubhouse available for functions.

E 17   Crowborough Beacon

Tel. Crowborough 61511
Beacon Rd., Crowborough, E. Sussex.
1 mile S of Crowborough on A26.
Heathland course.
18 holes, 6255 yds. S.S.S. 71
Visitors welcome with reservation.
Green Fees. Weekdays £6.50 per round or day; weekends £6.50 per round (p.m. only).
Society Meetings by arrangement.
Hotels: Crest, Crowborough; Spa, Tunbridge Wells.
Meals and bar snacks served.

E 18   Dale Hill

Tel. Ticehurst (0580) 200112
Ticehurst, Wadhurst, E. Sussex TN5 7DQ.
Off A21 London to Hastings road at Flimwell crossroads on to Ticehurst road.
Undulating parkland course.
18 holes, 6075 yds. S.S.S. 69
Visitors welcome.
Green Fees. Weekdays £5.00; weekends £7.00.
Society Meetings welcome.
Hotels: Sandlewood, Ticehurst; Willsley, Cranbrook; Royal Oak, Hawkhurst.
Meals available at most times.

E 19   Darenth Valley

Tel. Otford (9932) 2944
Station Rd., Shoreham, Sevenoaks, Kent TN14 7SA.
A225, 4 miles N of Sevenoaks, near Shoreham station.
Parkland course.
18 holes, 6356 yds. S.S.S. 70
Visitors welcome.
Green Fees. Weekdays £2.50 per 18 holes; weekends £4.00 per 18 holes.
Society Meetings by arrangement, Mon. to Sat.

Hotels: White Hart, Brasted; Donnington Manor, Dunton Green, Sevenoaks.
Lunches served except Mon.

E 20   Dartford

Tel. Dartford 26455
Dartford Heath, Dartford, Kent DA1 2TN.
1 mile from town centre.
Parkland / heathland course.
18 holes, 5907 yds. S.S.S. 68
Visitors welcome weekdays with letter of introduction.
Green Fees. Weekdays £6.50 (£3.00 with member); weekends £3.00 with member only.
Society Meetings welcome Fri. only.
Light meals served; lunch and dinner by arrangement.

E 21   Deangate Ridge

Tel. Medway 251180
Hoo, Rochester, Kent.
Off A228, 4 miles NE of Rochester.
Downland course.
18 holes, 6300 yds. S.S.S. 70
Visitors welcome.
Green Fees. Weekdays £1.80; weekends £2.23.
Society Meetings by arrangement.
Hotels: Inn on the Lake (A2), Shorne.
Meals served.

E 22   Dyke

Tel. Poynings 230
Dyke Rd., Brighton, E. Sussex.
4 miles N of Brighton.
Undulating moorland course.
18 holes, 6519 yds. S.S.S. 72
Visitors welcome except Sun. morning.
Green Fees. Weekdays £6.00 per day; weekends and bank holidays £8.00 per day.
Society Meetings welcome.

E 23   Eastbourne Downs

Tel. Eastbourne 20827
East Dean Rd., Eastbourne, E. Sussex BN20 8ES.
On A259 W of Eastbourne.
Downland course.
18 holes, 6623 yds. S.S.S. 72
Course designed by J.H. Taylor.
Visitors welcome.
Green Fees. Weekdays £4.50 per day; weekends £5.50.
Society Meetings welcome weekdays, weekends by arrangement.
Hotels: Cavendish; Lansdowne; Grand; Queens.
Lunches served except Mon.

E 24   East Brighton

Tel. Brighton (0273) 604838
Roedean Rd., Brighton, E. Sussex BN2 5RA.
2 miles E of Brighton on A259 behind the marina.
Downland course.
18 holes, 6291 yds. S.S.S. 70
Visitors welcome weekdays, weekends after 11.00a.m.
Green Fees. Weekdays £5.00 per round or day; weekends and bank holidays £6.50

per round or day. Reduced rates when playing with member.
Society Meetings by arrangement.
Hotels: Bedford, The Old Ship, Brighton; Sackville, Hove.
Morning coffee, lunches and teas served.

E 25 Faversham

Tel. Eastling 561 (Sec.)
Belmont Park, Faversham, Kent.
Off A2 at Belmont Rd. sign, W of Faversham.
Parkland course.
18 holes, 5965 yds. S.S.S. 69
Visitors welcome if members of recognized club, Mon. to Fri.
Green Fees. Weekdays £4.70 per round, £7.80 per day.
Society Meetings by arrangement Tues. to Fri.
Hotels: Ship Hotel.
Meals served by arrangement.

E 26 Gillingham

Tel. Medway 53017, 50999, 55862
Woodlands Rd., Gillingham, Kent.
On A2.
Parkland course.
18 holes, 5911 yds. S.S.S. 68
Visitors welcome on weekdays.
Green Fees. £4.00 per round, £5.00 per day.
Society Meetings welcome weekdays only by arrangement.
Hotels: Park Hotel.
Meals served.

E 27 Hastings

Tel. Hastings (0424) 52977
Battle Rd., St. Leonards-on-Sea, E. Sussex.
On A2100, 3 miles NW of Hastings.
Undulating parkland course.
18 holes, 6325 yds. S.S.S. 70
Course designed by J.J.F. Pennink.
Visitors welcome.
Green Fees. Weekdays £2.30; weekends £3.00.
Society Meetings welcome weekdays only.
Hotels: Beauport Park Hotel; Highbeech.
Lunches and snacks served; meals by arrangement.

E 28 Hawkhurst

Tel. Hawkhurst 2396
High St., Hawkhurst, Kent.
On A268, 1 mile W of Hawkhurst.
Parkland course.
9 holes, 5791 yds. S.S.S. 70
Visitors welcome.
Green Fees. Weekdays £3.00 (£2.00 with member); weekends £6.00 (£4.00 with member).
Society Meetings welcome weekdays only.
Hotels: Royal Oak; Tudor Arms.
Bar snacks and meals by arrangement.

E 29 Herne Bay

Tel. Herne Bay 4097
Thanet Way, Herne Bay, Kent.
Parkland course.
18 holes, 5364 yds. S.S.S. 66

Visitors welcome on weekdays, Sat. and Sun. mornings restricted.
Green Fees. Weekdays £5.00 per round; weekends £6.00 per round.
Society Meetings weekdays by arrangement.
Lunches served except Mon., ordered in advance.

E 30 High Elms

Tel. Farnborough (Kent) 58175
High Elms Rd., Downe, Kent.
Off A21, 4 miles S of Bromley.
Undulating parkland course.
18 holes, 6170 yds. S.S.S. 70
Course designed by Hawtree & Son.
Visitors welcome.
Green Fees. Weekdays £1.80; weekends £2.75. Half price after 5 p.m. during summer, and after 2 p.m. during winter.
Society Meetings welcome weekdays.
Meals served.

E 31 Highwoods

Tel. 0424 212625
Ellerslie Lane, Bexhill-on-Sea, E. Sussex TB39 4LJ.
On A259 W of Bexhill.
Undulating course.
18 holes, 6215 yds. S.S.S. 70
Course designed by J.H. Taylor.
Visitors welcome, Sun. with member only.
Green Fees. £6.00 per day.
Hotels: Cooden Beach Hotel; Whydown; Granville.
Meals served.

E 32 Hollingbury Park

Tel. Brighton 552010
Ditchling Rd., Brighton, E. Sussex.
Off A23.
Downland course.
18 holes, 6394 yds. S.S.S. 70
Visitors welcome.
Green Fees. £3.00 per round, £3.70 per day.
Society Meetings welcome on weekdays.
Hotels: Royal Pavilion Hotel; Clarence Hotel.
Lunches and teas served by arrangement.

E 33 Holtye

Tel. Cowden 635
Holtye Common, Cowden, Edenbridge, Kent TN8 7ED.
On A264, 7½ miles W of Tunbridge Wells.
Heathland course.
9 holes, 5265 yds. S.S.S. 67
Visitors welcome on weekdays: Sun. a.m. with member only.
Green Fees. Weekdays £3.75 (£2.50 with member); weekends £5.75 (£3.50 with member).
Society Meetings welcome weekdays only (small societies).
Hotels: in East Grinstead and Tunbridge Wells.

E 34 Hythe Imperial

Tel. Hythe 60659
Princes Parade, Hythe, Kent.
On A259, 4 miles W of Folkestone.

Seaside course.
9 holes, 5575 yds. S.S.S. 67
Visitors welcome.
Green Fees. Weekdays £4.00 (£3.00 with member); weekends £5.00.
Hotels: Hotel Imperial.

E 35 Knole Park

Tel. Sevenoaks 52150
Seal Hollow Rd., Sevenoaks, Kent.
Fork right at lower end of Sevenoaks High St., follow road down hill for ½ mile.
Parkland course.
18 holes, 6249 yds. S.S.S. 70
Course designed by Abercromby.
Visitors welcome weekdays with reservation.
Green Fees. £7.50 per round, £10.00 per day.
Society Meetings welcome weekdays only, max. 32.
Hotels: Moorings, Sevenoaks Park.
Lunches, snacks, teas and supper served.

E 36 Lamberhurst

Tel. Lamberhurst 890591
Church Rd., Lamberhurst, Tunbridge Wells, Kent.
On A21, 6 miles W of Tunbridge Wells.
Parkland course.
18 holes, 6249 yds. S.S.S. 70
Course designed by Cotton (C.K.), Pennink, Lawrie and Partners.
Visitors welcome weekdays, weekends after 12.00 a.m.
Green Fees. Weekdays £5.00 per day; weekends £7.00.
Society Meetings by arrangement.
Hotels: George & Dragon; Horse & Groom.
Meals served by arrangement.

E 37 Langley Park

Tel. 01-650 6849
Barnfield Wood Rd., Beckenham, Kent.
A214 to West Wickham station, then Red Lodge Road, or A21 to bottom of Bromley High St.; at lights turn into Westmoreland Rd. then straight into Barnfield Wood Rd.
Parkland course.
18 holes, 6488 yds. S.S.S. 71
Visitors welcome weekdays with letter of introduction, weekends with member only.
Green Fees. Weekdays £6.50 per round, £8.50 per day.
Society Meetings Wed. by arrangement.
Hotels: Bromley Court Hotel, Bromley.
Lunches and teas served.

E 38 Leeds Castle

Tel. Hollingbourne 467
Maidstone, Kent.
Turn off from A20 at Broomfield and Kingwood.
Parkland course.
18 holes, 6018 yds. S.S.S. 70
Visitors welcome.
Green Fees. Mon. £2.75 per day, Tues-Fri. £3.25 per day; Sat. £4.35 per day, Sun. £4.95 per day.
Society Meetings welcome.
Hotels: Great Danes, Hollingbourne.
Meals served by arrangement.

E 39 Lewes

Tel. Lewes 3074/3245
Chapel Hill, Lewes, E. Sussex.
On A27 Lewes to Eastbourne road opposite junction of Cliffe High St./South St.
Downland course.
18 holes, 5818 yds. S.S.S. 69
Visitors welcome.
Green Fees. Weekdays £3.50; weekends £4.25 per day.
Society Meetings welcome.
Hotels: Shelleys; White Hart.
Meals served except Mon.

E 40 Littlestone

Tel. New Romney (067 93) 3355, 2310
St. Andrews Rd., Littlestone, New Romney, Kent TN28 8RB.
1½ miles E of New Romney on B2071.
Links course.
18 holes, 6338 yds. S.S.S. 70
9 holes, 1998 yds. S.S.S. 32
Course designed by W. Laidlaw Purves (1888).
Visitors welcome on 9 hole course, welcome on 18 hole course if members of recognized club.
Green Fees. Weekdays £6.00 per round; weekends £7.50.
Society Meetings welcome weekdays except Tues.
Hotels: Hotel Windacre, Littlestone; Broadacre, New Romney.
Meals served except Tues.

E 41 Lullingstone Park

Tel. Badgers Mount 542
Park Gate, Chelsfield, Orpington, Kent.
A20 to Swanley, then B258, Daltons Rd. to Park gate.
Parkland, meadowland, woodland course.
18 holes, 6742 yds. S.S.S. 72
9 holes, 4886 yds. S.S.S. 66
Course designed by F.W. Hawtree.
Visitors welcome.
Green Fees. 18 hole course £2.20; 9 hole course £1.25.
Society Meetings welcome.
Hotels: Chelsfield Park Hotel, Chelsfield; Lion, Farningham.
Lunches served weekdays, weekends snacks only.

E 42 Mid-Kent

Tel. Gravesend 68035
Singlewell Rd., Gravesend, Kent.
On A2, S of Gravesend.
Meadowland course.
18 holes, 6103 yds. S.S.S. 69
Visitors welcome on weekdays, weekends with member only. Handicap certificate of 18 or under required.
Green Fees. Weekdays £8.50 per day (£4.25 with member); weekends £4.50.
Society Meetings Tues. only.
Hotels: Inn on the Lake; Toll Gate Motel.
Lunches and snacks served; meals by arrangement.

E 43 Nevill

Tel. Tunbridge Wells 25818
Benhall Mill Rd., Tunbridge Wells, Kent TN2 5JW.
Off Forest Rd., S side of Tunbridge Wells, follow signs.
Parkland/heathland course.
18 holes, 6336 yds. S.S.S. 71
Visitors welcome with letter of introduction and handicap certificate.
Green Fees. Weekdays £6.00 per day (£3.00 with member); weekends £8.00 per day (£4.00 with member).
Society Meetings welcome Mon., Wed., and Fri.
Hotels: Spa Hotel.
Lunches served.

E 44 North Foreland

Tel. Thanet (0843) 62140
Convent Rd., Kingsgate, Broadstairs, Kent CT10 3PU.
On B2052 1 mile N of Broadstairs.
Seaside course.
18 holes, 6378 yds. S.S.S. 70
Course designed by Fowler & Simpson, J.S.F. Morrison.
Visitors welcome weekdays, Sat. and Sun. p.m. if members of recognized club, with handicap certificate.
Green Fees. Summer, weekdays £5.50 per round, £8.50 per day, weekends £6.50 per round, £10.00 per day; winter, weekdays £4.50 per round, £8.50 per day, weekends £5.50 per round, £10.00 per day.
Society Meetings welcome weekdays only, subject to the same requirements as visitors.
Hotels: Castle Keep; Fayreness.
Meals served.

E 45 Peacehaven

Tel. Newhaven 4049
Brighton Rd., Newhaven, E. Sussex BN9 9UH.
On A259, 2½ miles W of Newhaven.
Downland course.
9 holes, 5473 yds. S.S.S. 67
Visitors welcome.
Green Fees. Weekdays £1.50 per round; weekends £2.50 (£1.75 with member).
Society Meetings welcome, max. 20.
Hotels: Peacehaven Hotel, Peacehaven.
Light lunches served except Tues. and Thurs.; meals by arrangement.

E 46 Piltdown

Tel. Newick 2033
Uckfield, E. Sussex TN22 3XB.
2½ miles W of Uckfield, between A272 and B2102.
Undulating moorland course.
18 holes, 6108 yds. S.S.S. 69
Visitors welcome if members of recognized club. After 12.00 a.m. on Sun.
Green Fees. £6.00 per round or day. Reduced rates when playing with member.
Society Meetings welcome on weekdays.
Lunch and tea served by arrangement except Thurs.

E 47 Poult Wood

Tel. Tonbridge 364039
Higham Lane, Tonbridge, Kent.
200 yds. off A227, 3 miles N of Tonbridge town centre.
Wooded parkland course.
18 holes, 5569 yds. S.S.S. 67
Course designed by F.W. Hawtree.
Visitors welcome weekdays, weekends.
Green Fees. Weekdays £2.15; weekends £2.55.
Society Meetings by arrangement.
Hotels: Rose & Crown.
Snacks served; lunches and dinners by arrangement.

E 48 Prince's

Tel. Sandwich 612000
Prince's Dr., Sandwich Bay, Sandwich, Kent.
3 miles from Sandwich via St. George's Rd., next to Sandwich Station.
Seaside course.
18 holes, 7083 yds. S.S.S. 74
9 holes, 3034 yds. S.S.S. 35
Course redesigned by J.S.F. Morrison and Sir Guy Campbell (1948).
Visitors welcome.
Green Fees. Weekdays £6.00 per round, £8.00 per day; Sat. £7.00 per round, £9 per day; Sun. £8.00 per round, £10.00 per day.
Society Meetings welcome.
Hotels: Accommodation available at club (18 bedrooms).
Snacks; lunch and dinner served by arrangement.

E 49 Pyecombe

Tel. Hassocks (07918) 4176
Clayton Hill, Pyecombe, Brighton, E. Sussex BN4 7FF.
On A273, 4 miles N of Brighton.
Undulating downland course.
18 holes, 6707 yds. S.S.S. 68
Visitors welcome.
Green Fees. Weekdays £6.00 (£3.00 with member); weekends £8.00 (£4.00 with member).
Society Meetings welcome weekdays only.
Teas served, lunches served except Thurs.

E 50 Rochester & Cobham Park

Tel. Shorne 3412
Park Pale, by Rochester, Kent ME2 3UL.
On A2, between Rochester and Gravesend.
Undulating parkland course.
18 holes, 6467 yds. S.S.S. 71
Visitors with credited handicap certificate welcome on weekdays, weekends with member only, except after 5.00 p.m.
Green Fees. £7.50 per round (£3.75 with member), £10.00 per day (£5.00 with member.)
Society Meetings welcome Tues. and Thurs.
Hotels: Inn on the Lake, Shorne.
Snacks and teas served; lunches and evening meals served by arrangement.

Rye's desolate marshlands

There is no doubt that the most romantic approach to Rye is by means of the little train gliding gently across the surrounding expanse of flat marshland. The town, huddled round the ancient church, looks down from its hill as it has done for centuries, and with its narrow gateway and cobbled streets, makes a memorable introduction before the mind strays towards the links out by Camber.

In days gone by the journey to the club used to be memorable too, but though an eccentrically twisting road has long since replaced the old steam tram which, according to Bernard Darwin, indulged in a prodigious amount of panting and snorting, golf at Rye still has a singular charm.

All, of course, is not quite as our fathers or grandfathers would remember, and much hot debate has centred around the changing of some of the holes. The Germans, too, apparently showed excellent judgment in the clubbing of one of their last flying bombs, for it virtually destroyed the clubhouse, which was a somewhat basic structure. But anyone of this generation unfamiliar with Rye at any other period cannot imagine there was ever a better layout than the existing one or that there is now a nicer clubhouse in the land.

At a time when modern artificial fertilizers are altering the character of so many of our seaside courses, it is well worth recording that Rye has not fallen victim and that the whole course, can become alarmingly fast; well-judged scuffles usually prove more effective than an armoury of wedges.

The other special features of the golf are the behaviour of the wind, which normally makes a flanking attack; the variety of stances to be had at a number of the long holes; the excellence of five short holes, which in a medal almost certainly decide the quality of the score; and, even more remarkably, a bunkering system that is kept to an absolute minimum. Nearly all Rye's defences are natural.

Is there, for instance, a more difficult shelf of fairway to hit in a gusty crosswind than the 4th on its elevated perch, or two more demanding strokes than those at the short 7th and 14th? Rye is as far removed as could be from watered American pastures, but though it is only a dream, how Hogan would have loved to have shown his mastery of control there and what a joy it would have been to see.

Not that the challenge made upon him would have been confined to these few holes. From the time that the round begins alongside the Camber road—which, before the invasion of holiday-makers and their cars, used to be crossed by the golfers—until just about the best 18th hole in Britain is reached, there is hardly a bad or unenjoyable shot to be played.

It is, in fact, invidious to distinguish between them, but what could be better than the second up the slope to the 3rd green by the little row of cottages or the thrill of the 6th with an angled drive over a great ridge of dunes and the ensuing decision for the young and strong of what to do with the second. Then there is the new 10th—the most recent of the alterations—with its green set amidst an avenue of gorse; the 12th down by the disused railway—the famous Sea hole with its blind second, which can be so awesome; and finally the 15th and 16th, two of the best of the 11 holes of 430 yards or more.

This is as much as any advanced student could wish for, but Rye's delights go further than the golf and on a fine, crisp winter's day there is nothing comparable anywhere. The course, so easy for spectators, is characteristic of all that seaside golf means to us.

The brooding background of sandhills and sea, the picturesque harbour with its little boats, the desolate beauty of vast acres of marsh inhabited only by sheep, and always the distant view of the walled town—the true symbol of Rye's appeal.

E 51   Royal Ashdown Forest

Tel. Forest Row (034 282) 2018
Forest Row, E. Sussex RH18 5LR.
On A22, 4½ miles S of East Grinstead.
Undulating moorland course.
Yellow 18 holes, 6406 yds. S.S.S. 71
White 6168 yds. S.S.S. 70
Visitors welcome with reservation.
Green Fees. Weekdays £7.50 (£3.75 with member); weekends £8.50 (£4.25 with member).
Society Meetings by arrangement.
Hotels: Roebuck, Wych Cross; Ashdown Forest Hotel, Forest Row.
Lunches served by arrangement except Mon.

E 52   Royal Cinque Ports

Tel. Deal 4007
Golf Rd., Deal, Kent CT14 6RF.
Off A258 N of Deal.
Seaside course.
18 holes, Medal 6393 yds. Championship 6653 yds. S.S.S. 72
Visitors welcome if members of recognized club, with letter of introduction.
Green Fees. Weekdays £5.00 per round, £8.00 per day; weekends £7.00 per round, £10.00 per day.
Society Meetings by arrangement.
Hotels: Royal.
Snacks served Mon. to Sat.; lunches served Sun. and for visiting societies.

E 53   Royal Eastbourne

Tel. Eastbourne (0323) 30412 (Mem.), 29738 (Sec.), 36986 (Pro.)
Paradise Dr., Eastbourne, E. Sussex BN20 8BP.
1 mile from town centre, via Meads Road and Comptom Place Road.
Undulating downland course.
18 holes, 6084 yds. S.S.S. 70
9 holes, 4300 yds. S.S.S. 61
Visitors welcome.
Green Fees. 18 hole course: weekdays £5.75; Sat., Sun., bank holidays £6.35. 9 hole course: weekdays £4.50; Sat., Sun., bank holidays £5.00.
Society Meetings welcome weekdays.
Hotels: Grand; Cavendish; Burlington; Lansdowne; Queens; Princes.
Full catering available except Mon.

E 54   Royal St. George's

Tel. Sandwich 613090
Sandwich, Kent CT13 9PB.
1 mile from Sandwich on road to Sandwich Bay.
Links course.
18 holes, Medal 6539 yds. S.S.S. 72; Championship 6841 yds. S.S.S. 73
Visitors welcome on weekdays with reservation.
Green Fees. £12.00.

Society Meetings weekdays by arrangement.
Hotels: Bell; King's Arms.
Snacks and meals served.

E 55   Ruxley

Tel. Orpington 71490
Sandy Lane, St. Paul's Cray, Orpington, Kent.
Off A20 at Ruxley roundabout.
Undulating course.
18 holes, 5017 yds. S.S.S. 65
Visitors welcome.
Green Fees. Weekdays £3.00; weekends £4.00 (£2.00 per 9 holes).
Society Meetings welcome.
Hotels: Lion, Farningham.
Meals served.
Floodlit driving range; golf tuition.

E 56   Rye

Tel. Camber 241
Camber, Rye, E. Sussex.
A259 from Rye then Camber Rd. to Lydd.
Links course.
18 holes, 6301 yds. S.S.S. 72
Course designed by H.S. Colt.
Visitors welcome if introduced by, or playing with member.
Green Fees. Weekdays £3.00 per round; £4.00 per day; Sat., Sun. £5.00 per round, £6.00 per day (all playing with a member);

weekdays £7.00 per day; Sat., Sun. £10.00 per day (introduced by a member).
Society Meetings by arrangement.
Hotels: in Rye.
Lunch and tea served.

E 57   St. Augustine's

Tel. Thanet (0843) 821346
Cottington Rd., Cliffsend, Ramsgate, Kent.
1 mile from Ramsgate, turn right opposite Hoverport.
Parkland seaside course.
18 holes, 5081 yds. S.S.S. 65
Visitors welcome with handicap certificate from a recognized golf club.
Green Fees. Weekdays £5.00; weekends £7.50.
Society Meetings weekdays by arrangement.
Hotels: Viking Motel, Pegwell Bay; Savoy; San Clu, Ramsgate.
Meals served except Mon.

E 58   Seaford

Tel. Seaford 892442
East Blatchington, Seaford, E. Sussex.
Off A259 N of Seaford.
Downland course.
18 holes, 6645 yds. S.S.S. 72
18 holes, 6330 yds. S.S.S. 71
Visitors welcome with reservation.
Green Fees. £7.00 per round or day.
Society Meetings weekdays by arrangement.
Hotels: Dormy House Hotel.
Meals served.

E 59   Seaford Head

Tel. Seaford 894843
Southdown Rd., Seaford, E. Sussex BN 25.
Off A259 SE of Seaford.
Undulating seaside course.
18 holes, 5812 yds. S.S.S. 68
Course designed by Thompson of Felixstowe (1887).
Visitors welcome.
Green Fees. Weekdays £2.00 per round, £3.00 per day; weekends £2.50 per round, £3.40 per day.
Society Meetings by arrangement.
Hotels: Sea Hotel; Wellington.
Meals served by arrangement.

E 60   Sene Valley, Folkestone & Hythe

Tel. Folkestone 66726
Sene, Folkestone, Kent.
A20 or A259 from Folkestone, then B2065.
Downland course.
18 holes, 6673 yds. S.S.S. 72
Course designed by H. Cotton (1960).
Visitors welcome.
Green Fees. Weekdays £6.00; weekends £8.00; weekly (Mon. to Fri.) £18.00.
Society Meetings welcome weekdays only.
Hotels: Hotel Imperial, Hythe; Burlington, Folkestone.
Snacks served; meals served except Mon.

E 61   Sheerness

Tel. Sheerness 662585
Power Station Rd., Sheerness, Kent ME12 3AE.
On A249 1½ miles SE of Sheerness.
Seaside marshland course.
18 holes, 6448 yds. S.S.S. 71
Visitors welcome.
Green Fees. £4.00 per round; Sat. £5.00.
Society Meetings welcome.
Hotels: Royal, Victoriana.
Meals served except Mon.

E 62   Shortlands

Tel. 01-460 2471
Meadow Rd., Shortlands, Bromley, Kent BR2 0PB.
On A222, 1 mile W of Bromley.
Meadowland course.
9 holes, 5261 yds. S.S.S. 66
Visitors welcome weekdays if members of recognized club. Ladies' Day Tues.
Green Fees. £5.00 per round (£3.00 with member).
Hotels: Bromley Court Hotel; Crest, Bromley.
Meals served by arrangement except Mon.

E 63   Sidcup

Tel. 01-300 2150
Hurst Rd., Sidcup, Kent DA15 9AE.
A222 off A2. Three minutes' walk from Sidcup station.
Undulating parkland course.
9 holes, 5692 yds. S.S.S. 68
Visitors welcome on weekdays.
Green Fees. £4.00 for 18 holes (£2.00 with member).
Society Meetings by arrangement.
Lunches and bar snacks served; meals by arrangement.

E 64   Sittingbourne & Milton Regis

Tel. Newington (0795) 842261
Wormdale, Newington, Sittingbourne, Kent ME9 7PX.
800 yards N of M2 at Sittingbourne exit (exit 5).
Undulating downland course.
18 holes, 6077 yds. S.S.S. 69
Visitors welcome, Sun. with member only.
Green Fees. Weekdays £6.50 per day; Sat. £7.50 per day.
Society Meetings welcome Tues., Thurs., Fri. by arrangement.
Hotels: Coniston, Sittingbourne; Great Danes, Hollingbourne.
Meals served.

E 65   Sundridge Park

Tel. 01-460 0278
Garden Rd., Bromley, Kent.
Off Plaistow Lane.
East, parkland course; West, undulating parkland, moorland course.
East 18 holes, 6334 yds. S.S.S. 70
West 18 holes, 6027 yds. S.S.S. 69
Visitors welcome by arrangement if members of recognized club.
Green Fees. Weekdays £8.50 per round (£4.00 with member), £11.50 per day (£5.50 with member).

Society Meetings welcome weekdays, max. 60.
Hotels: Bromley Court Hotel; New Hackwood.
Lunches and teas served.

E 66   Tenterden

Tel. Tenterden 3987
Woodchurch Rd., Tenterden, Kent.
1 mile E of Tenterden on B2067.
Parkland course.
9 holes, 5119 yds. S.S.S. 65
Visitors welcome except Sun. before 12.00a.m. Juniors not permitted weekends.
Hotels: White Lion, Woolpack, The Vine.

E 67   Tunbridge Wells

Tel. Tunbridge Wells 23034
Langton Rd., Tunbridge Wells, Kent.
Adjacent to Spa Garage and Hotel.
Parkland course.
9 holes, 4684 yds. S.S.S. 62
Visitors welcome weekdays except Wed. p.m., weekends with member only.
Green Fees. £4.50 per round plus V.A.T.
Society Meetings by arrangement.
Hotels: Spa Hotel.
Meals served by arrangement.

E 68   Walmer & Kingsdown

Tel. Deal (03045) 3256
Kingsdown, Deal, Kent CT14 8ER.
Off A258, 2½ miles S of Deal.
Seaside course.
18 holes, 6488 yds. S.S.S. 71
Visitors welcome if members of recognized club.
Green Fees. Weekdays £5.50; weekends £6.50.
Society Meetings by arrangement.
Hotels: in Deal and Dover.
Snack lunches served; evening meals and lunches by arrangement.

E 69   Waterhall

Tel. Brighton 508658
Mill Rd., Brighton, E. Sussex BN1 8YN.
5 miles from centre of Brighton. Devil's Dyke Rd., turn right to Saddlescombe.
Downland course.
18 holes, 5615 yds. S.S.S. 67
Visitors welcome with reservation except Sun. morning.
Green Fees. Weekdays £3.00 per round (£2.00 after 4 p.m.), £3.70 per day; weekends £3.70 per round (£2.30 after 4 p.m.).
Society Meetings welcome weekdays except Tues. by arrangement.
Hotels: in Brighton.

E 70   Westgate & Birchington

Tel. Thanet (0843) 31115
Domneva Rd., Westgate-on-Sea, Kent.
On A28, ½ mile from Westgate station.
Seaside course.
18 holes, 4926 yds. S.S.S. 65
Visitors welcome if members of recognized club.
Green Fees. Weekdays £3.50 (£2.50 with member); weekends £5.00 (£4.00 with member)

Society Meetings by arrangement.
Hotels: Bungalow Hotel, Birchington.
Meals served by arrangement.

E 71   West Hove

Tel. Brighton 419738
369 Old Shoreham Rd., Hove, E. Sussex.
Off A27.
Downland course.
18 holes, 6130 yds. S.S.S. 69
Course designed by James Braid (1910).
Visitors welcome.
Green Fees. Weekdays £5.00 per round
or day; weekends £6.50 per round or day.
Society Meetings welcome weekdays.
Hotels: in Brighton and Hove.
Snacks; light lunches and tea served; meals
by arrangement.

E 72   West Kent

Tel. Farnborough (Kent) 51323
West Hill, Downe, Orpington, Kent.
4 miles S of Orpington Station.
Undulating course.
18 holes, 6375 yds. S.S.S. 70
Visitors welcome on weekdays.
Green Fees. £6.50 per round, £10.00 per
day.
Society Meetings by arrangement.
Hotels: Bromley Court Hotel, Bromley.
Snacks served; lunch and tea by
arrangement.

E 73   West Malling

Tel. 0732 844785
Addington, Nr. Maidstone, Kent.
On A20, 8 miles N.W. of Maidstone, 2
minutes from M25.
Parkland course.
18 holes, 7250 yds. S.S.S. 74
Course designed by Faulkner and Lyons.
Visitors welcome on weekdays.
Green Fees. £6.50 (£4.00 with member).
Society Meetings by arrangement.
Hotels: Swan, Challis Court, Greenways,
West Malling; Hunting Lodge, Larkfield.
Meals served.

E 74   Whitstable & Seasalter

Tel. Whitstable (0227) 272020
Collingwood Rd., Whitstable, Kent.
M2 and Thanet Way; turn off at roundabout to
Whitstable; 2nd left after town traffic lights.
Seaside course.
9 holes, 5284 yds. S.S.S. 63
Visitors weekdays only, accompanied by
member.
Green Fees. £4.00 (£2.00 with member).
Hotels: Marine.
Bar snacks.

E 75   Wildernesse

Tel. Sevenoaks 61199
Park Lane, Seal, Sevenoaks, Kent.
S off A25 at Seal, E of Sevenoaks.
Parkland course.
18 holes, 6448 yds. S.S.S. 72
Visitors welcome weekdays with
reservation; weekends with member only.
Green Fees. £7.00 per round, £10.00 per
day.
Society Meetings by arrangement.

E 76   Willingdon

Tel. Eastbourne (0323) 32383
Southdown Rd., Eastbourne, E. Sussex.
½ mile N of Eastbourne off A22.
Downland course.
18 holes, 6049 yds. S.S.S. 69
Course designed by J.H. Taylor; modernized
by Dr. Mackenzie (1924).
Visitors welcome on weekdays.
Green Fees. Weekdays £5.75 (£2.75 with
member); weekends £6.35 (£3.00 with
member).
Society Meetings welcome weekdays
except Mon.
Hotels: Grand; Cavendish; Cumberland,
Eastbourne; Chalk Farm Hotel, Willingdon.
Lunches by arrangement.

E 77   Woodlands Manor

Tel. Otford (095 92) 3806
Woodlands, Sevenoaks, Kent TN15 6AB.
Off A20 at Portobello Inn, West Kingsdown,
or A225, 4 miles NE of Sevenoaks.
Undulating parkland course.
18 holes, 6180 yds. S.S.S. 68
Visitors welcome weekdays, weekends
after 12.00a.m. with handicap certificate.
Green Fees. Weekdays £5.00 per round
or day; weekends £5.50 per round or day.
Society Meetings welcome.
Hotels: Brands Hatch Place, Fawkham.
Meals served.

E 78   Wrotham Heath

Tel. Borough Green 884800
Seven Mile Lane, Wrotham Heath, Kent.
Off A20, 1 mile S of Wrotham Heath.
Heathland course.
9 holes, 5823 yds. S.S.S. 68
Visitors welcome on weekdays if members
of recognized club, at weekends only with
member.
Green Fees. £4.00 per round, £5.00 per
day.
Hotels: Bull, Wrotham.
Lunches served by arrangement.

F Greater London

F 1   Aquarius

Tel. 01-693 1626
Beachcroft Reservoir, Marmora Rd., Honor
Oak, London SE22.
9 holes, 2584 yds. S.S.S. 64 (18 holes).
Visitors welcome with member.
Green Fees. £1.50 per round.
Limited catering.

F 2   Ashford Manor

Tel. Ashford (69) 52049
Fordbridge Rd., Ashford, Middx. TW15 3RT.
On A308 2 miles E of Staines.
Parkland course.
18 holes, 6348 yds. S.S.S. 70
Visitors welcome on weekdays with letter
of introduction.
Green Fees. £8.00 per round or day.
Society Meetings welcome on weekdays.
Hotels: at London Airport.
Teas served. Lunches served except Mon.

F 3   Brent Valley

Tel. 01-567 1287
Church Rd., Hanwell, London W.7.
S of A40.
Parkland course.
18 holes, 5426 yds. S.S.S. 66
Visitors welcome.
Green Fees. Weekdays £1.70; weekends
£2.10.
Meals served.

F 4   Bush Hill Park

Tel. 01-360 5738
Bush Hill, Winchmore Hill, London N21 2BU.
Off main Enfield to London road.
Parkland course.
18 holes, Yellow 5720 yds. S.S.S. 68
White 5394 yds. S.S.S. 66
Visitors welcome on weekdays.
Green Fees. Weekdays £5.50 per round
(£4.00 with member), £8.00 per day
(£5.00 with member); weekends (with
member only) £4.00 per round.
Society Meetings Tues., Thurs., Fri. only.
Hotels: Royal Chase; Enfield Hotel, Enfield.
Meals served. Catering facilities available.

F 5   Crews Hill

Tel. 01-363 6674
Cattlegate Rd., Crews Hill, Enfield, Middx.
A10 to Bullsmore Lane, Enfield; signposted.
A1005 thence East Lodge Lane.

Undulating course.
18 holes, 6230 yds. S.S.S. 70
Visitors welcome weekdays if members of recognized club.
Green Fees. £6.35 per round, £8.00 per day.
Society Meetings by arrangement.
Hotels: Royal Chase, Enfield.
Lunches served except Mon.

F 6   Dulwich & Sydenham Hill

Tel. 01-693 3961
Grange Lane, College Rd., Dulwich, London, SE21.
Off S circular road.

Undulating parkland course.
18 holes, S.S.S. 69
Visitors welcome if members of recognized club.
Green Fees. £5.50 per round, £7.00 per day.
Society Meetings welcome, max. 30.
Hotels: Queens Hotel.
Lunches served.

F 7   Ealing

Tel. 01-997 0937
Perivale Lane, Greenford, Middx. UB6 8SS.
On A40 1 mile W of Hanger Lane underpass.
Parkland course.
18 holes, 6118 yds. S.S.S. 69

Visitors welcome weekdays if members of recognized club, preferably by introduction. Weekends by arrangement.
Green Fees. Weekdays £5.00 per round, £7.50 per day (£3.50 with member).
Society Meetings by arrangement.
Hotels: Carnarvon, Ealing Common.
Meals served.

F 8   Eltham Warren

Tel. 01-850 4477
Bexley Rd., Eltham, London SE9.
5 minutes' walk Eltham Park Station.
Parkland course.
9 holes, 5820 yds. S.S.S. 68
Visitors welcome on weekdays.

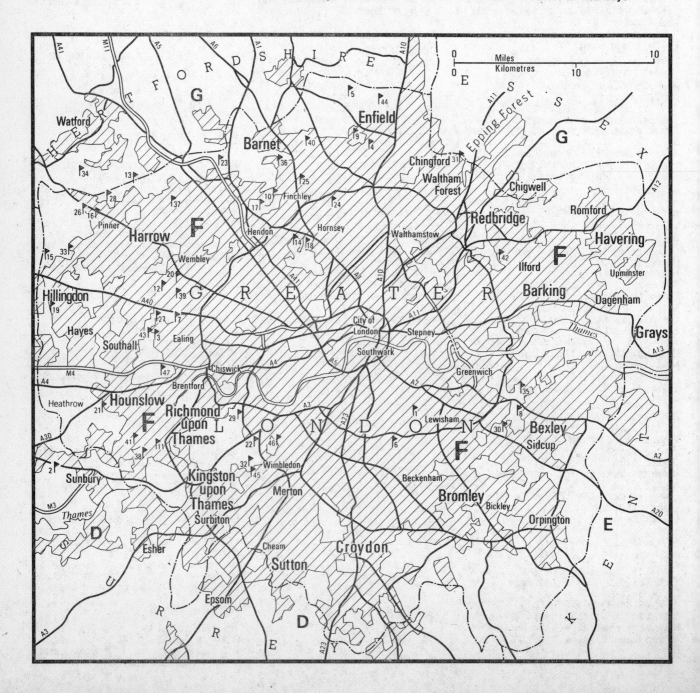

Green Fees. £4.60 per round, £5.60 per day.
Society Meetings welcome, max. 25.
Snacks served; meals by arrangement.

F 9   Enfield

Tel. 01-363 3970
Old Park Rd., Windmill Hill, Enfield, Middx.
About 1 mile from Enfield Chase railway station.
Parkland course.
18 holes, 6137 yds. S.S.S. 70
Course designed by James Braid.
Visitors welcome on weekdays with reservation if members of recognized club.
Green Fees. £5.00 per round, £7.00 per day.
Society Meetings welcome on weekdays.
Hotels: Old Park Heights Hotel; Enfield Hotel, Enfield.
Lunches and teas served.

F 10   Finchley

Tel. 01-346 2436 Secretary
Nether Court, Frith Lane, London NW7 1PU.
Mill Hill East station 1 mile.
Undulating parkland course.
18 holes, 6411 yds. S.S.S. 71
Course designed by James Braid.
Visitors welcome on weekdays, weekends after 12.15p.m.
Green Fees. Weekdays £5.00 per round, £8.00 per day; weekends £9.00 after 12.00.
Society Meetings by arrangement on Wed. and Fri.
Hotels: Hendon Hall Hotel.
Meals served except Mon.

F 11   Fulwell

Tel. 01-977 2733
Wellington Rd., Hampton Hill, Middx. TW12 1JY.
2 miles S of Twickenham on A311.
Parkland course.
18 holes, 6490 yds. S.S.S. 71
Course designed by J.S.F. Morrison.
Visitors by introduction only.
Green Fees. Weekdays £8.50 (£4.50 with member); weekends £10.00 (£5.50 with member).
Society Meetings welcome Wed., Thurs. and Fri.
Hotels: Richmond Hill Hotel, Richmond; The Cardinal Wolsey, Hampton Court.
Lunches and teas or high teas served except Mon.

F 12   Greenford

Tel. 01-578 3949
Rockware Ave., Greenford, Middx. 0AA UB6.
Between A40 and Sudbury Hill.
Meadowland course.
9 holes, 4412 yds. S.S.S. 62
Visitors welcome on weekdays.
Green Fees. £2.60.
Meals served.

F 13   Grim's Dyke

Tel. 01-428 4539
Oxhey Lane, Hatch End, Pinner, Middx. HA5 4AL.
On A4008 between Harrow and Watford.

Parkland course.
18 holes, 5598 yds. S.S.S. 67
Visitors welcome on weekdays, Sat. with reservation.
Green Fees. Weekdays £5.75 per round, £7.50 per day.
Society Meetings welcome.
Hotels: in NW London.
Snacks, lunches, teas and high teas served.

F 14   Hampstead

Tel. 01-455 0203
Winnington Rd., London N2 0TU.
A41 from Highgate Village, 1 mile down Hampstead Lane.
Parkland course.
9 holes, 5812 yds. S.S.S. 68
Visitors welcome.
Green Fees. Weekdays £6.00 per round; weekends £9.00 per round.
Society Meetings by arrangement.
Meals served.

F 15   Harefield Place

Tel. Uxbridge 31169
The Drive, Harefield Place, Uxbridge, Middx. UB10 8PA.
2 miles N of Uxbridge (A40).
Parkland course.
18 holes, 5660 yds. S.S.S. 67
Visitors welcome.
Green Fees. Weekdays £2.60; weekends and bank holidays £3.00.
Hotels: Master Brewer Motel, Hillingdon.
Bar, snacks.

F 16   Haste Hill

Tel. Northwood (65) 26485
The Drive, Northwood, Middx.
On A404.
Parkland course.
Visitors welcome.
Green Fees. Weekdays £2.20; weekends £3.00.
Society Meetings by arrangement with Hillingdon Borough Council.
Snacks served, dinners by arrangement.

F 17   Hendon

Tel. 01-346 6023
Sanders Lane, Hendon, London NW7 1DG.
Finchley Rd. to Golders Green then left through Hendon to roundabout, first left.
Parkland course.
18 holes, 6230 yds. S.S.S. 70
Course designed by Harry Colt.
Visitors welcome weekdays, weekends with reservation (tel. 01-346 8990).
Green Fees. Weekdays £6.00 per round, £8.00 per day; weekends £10.00 per round.
Society Meetings welcome weekdays except Mon.
Hotels: Hendon Hall Hotel.
Meals served except Mon.

F 18   Highgate

Tel. 01-340 3745
Denewood Rd., Highgate N6.
18 holes, 6005 yds. S.S.S. 69
Visitors welcome on weekdays.

Green Fees. £4.25 per round, £6.40 per 2 rounds.
Society Meetings welcome.
Lunches served.

F 19   Hillingdon

Tel. Uxbridge 33956 (Sec.), 39810 (Clubhouse), 51980 (Pro.)
Dorset Way, Hillingdon, Middx.
Turn off Uxbridge Rd. 1½ miles from Uxbridge centre towards Hayes at Vine public house into Vine Lane. Club ¼ mile on left.
Parkland course.
9 holes Men, 5404 yds. S.S.S. 66; Ladies, 4897 yds. S.S.S. 67
Visitors welcome on weekdays, Sat., Sun. p.m. with member only.
Green Fees. £5.00 (£2.00 with member).
Society Meetings weekdays by arrangement.
Hotels: Cottage Hotel.
Lunch and tea served.

F 20   Horsenden Hill

Tel. 01-902 4555
Woodlands Rise, Greenford, Middx.
Off Whitton Ave.
Undulating parkland course.
9 holes, 3150 yds. S.S.S. 54
Visitors welcome.
Green Fees. Weekday 60p per 9 holes; weekends 80p per 9 holes.
Meals served.

F 21   Hounslow Heath

Staines Rd., Hounslow, Middx.
Heathland course.
18 holes, 5941 yds. S.S.S. 69
Course designed by F.M. Middleton.
Visitors welcome.
Green Fees. Weekdays £2.00 (O.A.P.s and juniors £1.00 weekdays only); weekends £2.50.

F 22   London Scottish

Tel. 01-788 0135
Windmill Enclosure, Windmill Rd., Wimbledon Common, London SW19 5NQ.
2 miles from Wimbledon Railway Station.
Parkland course.
18 holes, 5846 yds. S.S.S. 67
Course redesigned by T. Dunn (1901).
Visitors welcome on weekdays, weekends with member only. All players must wear a red upper garment.
Green Fees. £3.00 (£2.00 with member).
Snacks served; meals by arrangement.

F 23   Mill Hill

Tel. 01-959 2282
Barnet Way, Mill Hill, London NW7.
Off A1. Signposted via Marsh Lane from Apex Corner.
Parkland course.
18 holes, 6309 yds. S.S.S. 70
Visitors welcome on weekdays, weekends after 12.00 noon.
Green Fees. Weekdays £6.00 one round, £8.50 two rounds; weekends £10.00 (after 12.00).
Hotels: Spiders Webb, Elstree; Hendon Hall Hotel, Hendon.
Snacks and lunches served.

F 24 Muswell Hill

Tel. 01-888 2044 (Club House), 01-888 1764 (Sec.)
Rhodes Ave., Wood Green, London N22 4UT.
Off Durnsford Rd., off A109 (Bounds Green).
Parkland course.
18 holes, 6446 yds. S.S.S. 71
Visitors welcome weekdays, weekends with member only. Ladies day Tues. morning.
Green Fees. £8.00.
Society Meetings welcome on Wed., Thurs.
Lunches served except Mon

F 25 North Middlesex

Tel. 01-445 1604
Friern Barnet Lane, Whetstone, London N20.
A1000 5 miles N of Finchley.
Undulating parkland course.
18 holes, 5611 yds. S.S.S. 67
Visitors welcome on weekdays if members of recognized club, weekends with member only.
Green Fees. £3.50 (£2.00 with member).
Society Meetings welcome except Mon.
Lunches served except Mon.

F 26 Northwood

Tel. Northwood (65) 25329
Rickmansworth Rd., Northwood, Middx. HA6 2QW.
A404 3 miles E of Rickmansworth.
Parkland course.
18 holes, 6459 yds. S.S.S. 71
Visitors welcome on weekdays.
Green Fees. Weekdays £6.00 per round (£3.00 with member), £7.50 per 2 rounds (£4.00 with member).
Society Meetings welcome Mon., Thurs. and Fri.
Snacks and lunches served.

F 27 Perivale Park

Tel. 01-578 1693
Ruislip Rd. East, Greenford, Middx.
On Ruislip Rd. East between Greenford and Perivale.
Parkland course.
9 holes, 2667 yds. S.S.S. for ladies 67, S.S.S. for men 65
Visitors welcome.
Green Fees. Weekdays £1.00; weekends £1.50.
Hotels: Kenton Hotel, Hanger Hill.
Snacks served.

F 28 Pinner Hill

Tel. 01-866 0963
South View Rd., Pinner Hill, Middx. HA5 3YA.
Off A404 at Northwood Hills roundabout.
Parkland course.
18 holes, 6293 yds. S.S.S. 70
Visitors welcome on weekdays.
Green Fees. Mon., Tues. and Fri. £7.00; Sat. £8.00; Wed. and Thurs. £2.20.
Society Meetings welcome except Wed., Thurs.
Snacks served.

F 29 Roehampton

Tel. 01-876 5505
Roehampton Lane, London SW15 5LR.
Off A306 bottom of Roehampton Lane.
Parkland course.
18 holes, 6067 yds. S.S.S. 69
Visitors welcome with member.
Green Fees. Weekdays £3.50; weekends £5.00.
Hotels: Richmond Hill Hotel, Richmond; Lodge Hotel, Putney.
Lunch and tea served.

F 30 Royal Blackheath

Tel. 01-850 1795
Court Rd., Eltham SE9 5AF.
Parkland course.
18 holes, 6024 yds. S.S.S. 69
Course designed by J. Braid.
Visitors welcome.
Green Fees. Weekdays £5.35 per day; weekends £4.25 per day, with member only.
Society Meetings welcome Wed. and Thurs.
Hotels: Bromley Court Hotel, Bromley.
Lunches and teas served except Mon.

F 31 Royal Epping Forest

Tel. 01-529 1039; Course 01-529 5708
Forest Approach, Chingford, London E4.
100 yards E of Chingford railway station.
Woodland course.
18 holes, 6135 yds. S.S.S. 69
Green Fees. Weekdays £2.30; weekends £3.45; O.A.P.s £1.15 between 10.00 a.m. and 3.00 p.m. Mon. to Fri.

F 32 Royal Wimbledon

Tel. 01-946 2125
29 Camp Rd., Wimbledon Common, London SW19 4UW.
¾ mile W of War Memorial in Wimbledon Village.
Parkland course.
18 holes, 6300 yds. S.S.S. 70
Course designed by H.S. Colt (modified by C.D. Lawrie).
Visitors welcome weekdays with letter of introduction, weekends with member only.
Green Fees. £10.00 (£6.00 with member).
Society Meetings welcome weekdays only.
Lunches served except Mon. and Sat.

F 33 Ruislip

Tel. Ruislip 32004
Ickenham Rd., Ruislip, Middx.
300 yards from W. Ruislip station.
Parkland course.
18 holes, 5126 yds. S.S.S. 65
Visitors welcome.
Green Fees. Weekdays £2.20 per round; Weekends £3.00.
Hotels: Orchard Hotel.
Snacks and meals served. Licensed bar.

F 34 Sandy Lodge

Tel. Northwood 25429
Sandy Lodge Lane, Northwood, Middx. HA6 2JD

Between Northwood and Bushey Arches.
Sandy heathland course.
18 holes, 6361 yds. S.S.S. 71
Visitors welcome on weekdays.
Green Fees. £7.50 per round; £10.00 per day.
Society Meetings welcome.
Hotels: Clarendon, Watford; Victoria, Rickmansworth.
Meals served.

F 35 Shooters Hill

Tel. 01-854 6368
Eaglesfield Rd., Shooters Hill, SE18 3DA.
Off Shooters Hill.
Undulating parkland course.
18 holes, 5645 yds. S.S.S. 67
Course designed by W. Park.
Visitors must be introduced by and playing with a member, or be members of other clubs (Mon. to Fri. only).
Green Fees. Introduced by member: weekdays £2.00 per round or day; weekends £4.00 per round or day. Members of other clubs: £4.00 per round, £5.00 per day (weekdays only).
Society Meetings welcome, max. 40.
Hotels: Clarendon, Blackheath.
Meals served by arrangement except Mon.

F 36 South Herts

Tel. 01-445 2035
Links Dr., Totteridge, London N20.
High Rd. from Whetstone to Barnet, left into Totteridge Lane, 3rd right.
Undulating parkland course.
18 holes, 6432 yds. S.S.S. 71
Course designed by Harry Vardon.
Visitors welcome on weekdays if members of recognized club.
Green Fees. Weekdays £4.70 and £5.85.
Society Meetings Wed., Thurs. and Fri. only.
Hotels: Royal Chase, Enfield; Totteridge Hotel, Totteridge.
Lunches, teas and high teas served except Mon.; lunches by arrangement.

F 37 Stanmore

Tel. 01-954 4661
Gordon Ave., Stanmore, Middx. HA7 2RL.
To Stanmore from Harrow turn right at Stanmore Church, then first right.
Undulating parkland course.
18 holes, 5925 yds. S.S.S. 68
Visitors welcome weekdays, weekends with member only.
Green Fees. £6.00.
Society Meetings welcome.
Meals served.

F 38 Strawberry Hill

Tel. 01-894 1246
Wellesley Rd., Strawberry Hill, Twickenham, Middx.
Parkland course.
9 holes, 4690 yds. S.S.S. 62
Visitors welcome on weekdays.

F 39   Sudbury

Tel. 01-902 3713 (Sec.), 01-902 7910 (Pro.)
Bridgewater Rd., Wembley, Middx. HA0 1AL.
Junction of A4005 and A4090.
Woodland course.
18 holes, 6282 yds. S.S.S. 70
Visitors welcome on weekdays; check weekends.
Green Fees. Weekdays £8.50 per day (£3.50 with member).
Society Meetings by arrangement.
Hotels: Eurocrest.
Lunches, teas and snacks except Mon.

F 40   Trent Park

Tel. 01-366 7432
Bramley Rd., Southgate, London N14.
Opposite Oakwood Tube Station.
Parkland course.
18 holes, 5971 yds. S.S.S. 69
Visitors welcome.
Green Fees. Weekdays £2.20 per round; weekends £2.50 per round.
Society Meetings by arrangement.
Hotels: Royal Chase.
Meals served.

F 41   Twickenham

Tel. 01-979 0032
Staines Rd., Twickenham, Middx.
On A305 near Hope and Anchor roundabout.
Parkland course.
9 holes, 3180 yds. S.S.S. 36
Course designed by Cotton (C.K.), Pennink, Lawrie and Partners.
Visitors welcome.
Green Fees. Weekdays £1.10 per 9 holes, £2.20 per 18 holes; weekends and bank holidays £1.90 per 9 holes, £3.80 per 18 holes. Before 10.30 a.m. Tues. and Thurs. 80p per 9 holes.
Hotels: in Richmond.
Meals served.

F 42   Wanstead

Tel. 01-989 3938
Overton Dr., Wanstead, London E11 2LW.
Off A12 at Wanstead station, right into 'The Green', into St. Mary's Ave., left at T-junction at St. Mary's Church.
Parkland course.
18 holes, 6203 yds. S.S.S. 70
Visitors welcome with reservation.
Green Fees. On application to Secretary.
Society Meetings welcome on weekdays.
Meals served.

F 43   West Middlesex

Tel. 01-574 3450
Greenford Rd., Southall, Middx.
Off A4020 to Greenford at Iron Bridge.
Parkland course.
18 holes, 6221 yds. S.S.S. 70
Visitors welcome on weekdays, weekends after 3p.m. only.
Green Fees. Mon. and Wed. £3.00 per round; Tues., Thurs. and Fri. £4.50 per round; weekends £5.00 per round.
Society Meetings welcome on weekdays.

Hotels: Carnarvon, Ealing. Osterley Motel, Osterley.
Lunches and teas served except Mon.

F 44   Whitewebbs

Tel. 01-363 3454
Beggars Hollow, Clay Hill, Enfield, Middx.
1 mile N of Enfield.
Parkland course.
18 holes, 5881 yds. S.S.S. 68
Visitors welcome.
Green Fees. Weekdays £2.50; weekends £3.30.
Hotels: West Lodge Hotel; Royal Chace.
Meals served.

F 45   Wimbledon Common

Tel. 01-946 0294, Sec. 01-946 7571
Camp Rd., Wimbledon Common, London SW19 4UW.
Off Wimbledon Parkside at War Memorial, ½ mile to club.
Common land course.
18 holes, 5486 yds. S.S.S. 67
Visitors welcome on weekdays, weekends with member only except Sun. afternoon. All players must wear red upper garment.
Green Fees. £3.00 per round.
Snacks served.

F 46   Wimbledon Park

Tel. 01-946 1250
Home Park Rd., Wimbledon, London SW19 7HR.
300 yards from Wimbledon Park District Line Station.
Parkland course.
18 holes, 5450 yds. S.S.S. 66
Visitors welcome weekdays with reservation.
Green Fees. £8.50 per day; £6.50 after 3 p.m.
Society Meetings by arrangement.
Lunch and tea served weekdays except Mon. and Fri.

F 47   Wyke Green

Tel. 01-560 8777
Syon Lane, Isleworth, Middx. TW7 5PT.
Off A4, ½ mile from Gillette's Clock Tower.
Parkland course.
18 holes, 6233 yds. S.S.S. 70
Visitors welcome on weekdays, Sun. after 3p.m. only.
Green Fees. Weekdays £7.00 (£3.50 with member); weekends £10.00 (£5.00 with member).
Society Meetings by arrangement.
Hotels: Osterley Motel.
Meals served except Mon.

G Essex, Hertfordshire

G 1   Abridge Golf & Country Club

Tel. Stapleford (04028) 396
Stapleford Tawney, Romford, Essex RM4 1ST.
M11 from London exit 5 via Abridge; from N, M11 exit 7 via Epping.
Parkland course.
18 holes, 6609 yds. S.S.S. 71
Course designed by Henry Cotton.
Visitors welcome except Sun.
Green Fees. £7.50.
Society Meetings welcome.
Hotels: Tree Tops; Bell Motel; The Cock, Epping.
Meals served.

G 2   Aldenham

Tel. Radlett 7775
Radlett Rd., Aldenham, Herts.
Watford to Radlett Road.
Parkland course.
18 holes, 6400 yds. S.S.S. 71
Visitors welcome.
Green Fees. Weekdays £6.00; weekends after 12 noon £7.00.
Society Meetings by arrangement.

G 3   Arkley

Tel. 01-449 0394
Rowley Green Rd., Barnet, Herts. EN5 5HL.
A1000 from London to Barnet, turn left on to A411 to Arkley.
Undulating parkland course.
9 holes, 6016 yds. S.S.S. 69
Visitors welcome Wed., Thurs. and Fri. Weekends with member only.
Green Fees. £4.00 per round, £6.00 per day (£1.50 with member).
Snacks and light lunches served.

G 4   Ashridge

Tel. Little Gaddesden (044284) 2244
Little Gaddesden, Berkhamsted, Herts. HP4 1LY.
A41 to Berkhamsted, turn right at Northchurch on B4506.
Parkland course.
18 holes, 6508 yds. S.S.S. 71
Course designed by Sir Guy Campbell and T. Simpson.
Visitors welcome with reservation.
Green Fees. On application.
Society Meetings by arrangement.
Hotels: Bell Inn, Aston Clinton; Royal, Tring.
Meals served by arrangement.

G 5   Basildon

Tel. Basildon (0268) 3532
Kings Wood, Bellshill Rd., Basildon, Essex.
Off A13 at Nethermayn exit.
Undulating meadowland course.
18 holes, 6225 yds. S.S.S. 70
Course designed by Basildon Development
Corporation.
Visitors welcome.
Green Fees. Weekdays £1.17; weekends
£2.35.
Hotels: Essex Centre Hotel.

G 6   Batchwood Hall

Tel. St. Albans 52101
Batchwood Dr., St. Albans, Herts.
Parkland course.
18 holes, Ladies 5811 yds. S.S.S. 74
Gents 6465 yds. S.S.S. 71
Course designed by Hawtree and Taylor
(1934-36).
Visitors welcome.
Green Fees. Weekdays £2.00; weekends
£2.80.
Society Meetings by arrangement.
Hotels: in St. Albans.
Meals served.

G 7   Belfairs Park

Tel. Southend (0702) 525345
Eastwood Rd., Leigh-on-Sea, Essex.
Parkland course.
18 holes, 5871 yds. S.S.S. 68
Visitors welcome.

G 8   Belhus Park

Tel. South Ockendon (04025) 4260
Belhus Park, South Ockendon, Essex.
A13 to Aveley, Essex.
Parkland course.
18 holes, 5501 yds. S.S.S. 65
Course designed by Cotton (C.K.), Pennink,
Lawrie and Partners.
Visitors welcome.
Green Fees. Weekdays 90p, juniors and
O.A.P.'s 45p; weekends £1.45.
Society Meetings welcome.
Hotels: Royal, Purfleet; Europa, North
Stifford; Old Plough House Hotel, Bulphan.
Light meals served.

G 9   Bentley Golf & Country Club

Tel. Coxtie Green 73179
Ongar Rd., Brentwood, Essex.
On A128 about 4 miles from Wilson Corner,
Brentwood.
Parkland course.
18 holes, 6550 yds. S.S.S. 72
Course designed by Golf Landscapes Ltd.
Visitors welcome on weekdays, weekends
with member only.
Green Fees. Weekdays £5.00, juniors and
O.A.P.s £3.00.
Society Meetings welcome on weekdays.
Hotels: Post House; Moat House.
Meals served.

G 10   Berkhamsted

Tel. Berkhamsted (04427) 5832
The Common, Berkhamsted, Herts. HP4
2QB.
A41 to Berkhamsted or M1 to Hemel
Hempstead, 1½ miles from town towards
Potten End.
Heathland course.
18 holes, 6545 yds. S.S.S. 72
Course designed by C. J. Gilbert, partly
redesigned by James Braid (1920).

Visitors welcome with reservation, but may
not start play until after 11.30 a.m. at
weekends.
Green Fees. Weekdays £8.00 per round
or day (£2.50 with member); weekends
£11.00 (£3.50 with member).
Society Meetings welcome Wed. and Fri.
Hotels: Swan.
Snacks served, lunches by arrangement
except Mon.

G 11   Bishop's Stortford

Tel. Bishop's Stortford (0279) 54715
Dunmow Rd., Bishop's Stortford, Herts.
CM23 5HP.
½ mile from M11 on A120.
Parkland course.
18 holes, 6417 yds. S.S.S. 71
Visitors welcome weekdays if members of
recognized club.
Green Fees. £4.00 per round, £5.00 per
day.
Society Meetings welcome, min. 12, max.
40.
Hotels: Nags Head.
Snacks and lunches served.

G 12   Boxmoor

Tel. Hemel Hempstead 42434
Box Lane, Boxmoor, Hemel Hempstead,
Herts.
On A41 1½ miles from town centre.
Undulating moorland course.
9 holes, 4770 yds. S.S.S. 64
Visitors welcome Mon. to Sat.
Green Fees. Weekdays £2.00 (£1.00 with
member); Sat. £3.00 (£1.50 with member).
Society Meetings welcome on weekdays
except Tues.
Snacks served except Tues.

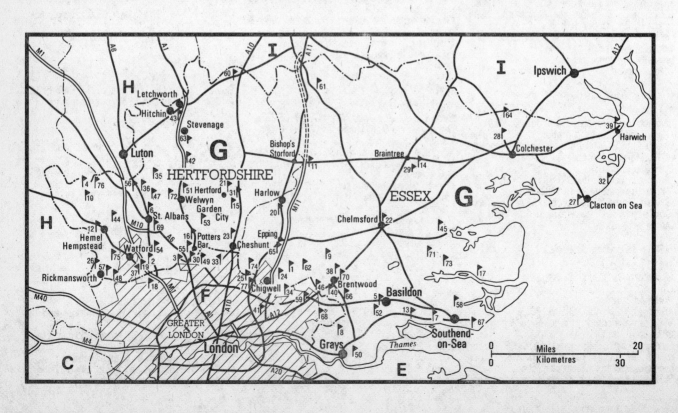

G 13   Boyce Hill

Tel. South Benfleet (03745) 3625
Vicarage Hill, Benfleet, Essex SS7 1PD.
7 miles W of Southend-on-Sea. A127 to
Rayleigh Weir (3 miles from course); A13 to
Victoria House Corner (1 mile from course).
Undulating parkland course.
18 holes, 5882 yds. S.S.S. 68
Visitors welcome on weekdays, weekends
after 12 noon with member only.
Green Fees. £5.50 per round (£3.50 with
member), £7.00 per day (£3.50 with
member).
Society Meetings Thurs. only.
Hotels: in Southend.
Lunches served except Tues.

G 14   Braintree

Tel. Braintree 24117
Kings Lane, Stisted, Braintree, Essex.
1½ miles NE of Braintree on A120.
Parkland course.
18 holes, 6026 yds. S.S.S. 69
Course designed by Hawtree & Sons.
Visitors welcome except Sun.; Sat. with
handicap certificate.
Green Fees. Weekdays £5.00; weekends
£6.50 per round.
Society Meetings welcome.
Hotels: White Hart, Braintree.
Meals served.

G 15   Brickendon Grange Golf & Country Club

Tel. Bayford 228
Brickendon, Hertford SG13 8PD.
From A10 turn off at Broxbourne on to A1170
then take Bell Lane to Brickendon Green.
Parkland course.
18 holes, 6325 yds. S.S.S. 71
Course designed by Cotton (C.K.) Pennink,
Lawrie and Partners.
Visitors welcome except Sun.
Green Fees. Weekdays £7.50 (£3.75 with
member); Sat. £9.00 (£4.50 with member).
Society Meetings welcome.
Meals served.

G 16   Brookmans Park

Tel. Potters Bar 52487
Hatfield, Herts. AL9 7AT.
From A1000 Potters Bar to Hatfield road turn
left into Mymms Dr.
Parkland course.
18 holes, 6436 yds. S.S.S. 71
Visitors welcome on weekdays, weekends
with member only.
Green Fees. £7.00 per day.
Society Meetings welcome on weekdays.
Hotels: Crest Motel, South Mimms;
Salisbury Hotel; Hatfield Lodge Hotel,
Hatfield.

G 17   Burnham-on-Crouch

Tel. Maldon (0621) 782282
Ferry Lane, Creeksea, Burnham-on-Crouch,
Essex CM0 8PQ.
1¼ miles W of Creeksea.
Undulating meadowland course.
9 holes, 5810 yds. S.S.S. 68
Visitors welcome on weekdays, after 12.00
a.m. at weekends.

Green Fees. Weekdays £4.00 per round
or day (£2.00 with member); weekends
£5.00 (£2.50 with member).
Society Meetings Wed. and Fri. only.
Hotels: White Harte; Quay Hotel, Burnham-
on-Crouch.
Snacks and lunches served except Mon.

G 18   Bushey Golf & Squash Club

Tel. 01-950 2283
High St., Bushey, Herts.
On A411 - ½ mile M1/A41.
Private parkland course.
9 holes, 3000 yds. S.S.S. 69
Course designed by Donald Steel, Cotton
(C.K.), Pennink, Lawrie & Partners Ltd.
Visitors welcome by arrangement.
Green Fees. Weekdays £4.00; weekends
£5.00.
Society Meetings by arrangement, limited
numbers only.
Hotels: Ladbrokes; Spiders Web.
Meals served.

G 19   Bushey Hall

Tel. Watford 25802
Bushey Hall Rd., Bushey, Herts.
1 mile S of Watford.
Parkland course.
18 holes, 6055 yds. S.S.S. 69
Visitors welcome on weekdays, weekends
with member only.
Green Fees. Weekdays £6.50 per round
(£4.50 with member), £8.50 per day
(£6.00 with member).
Society Meetings welcome weekdays
except Wed.
Full catering facilities.

G 20   Canons Brook

Tel. Harlow (0279) 21482
Elizabeth Way, Harlow, Essex CM19 5BE.
On A11.
Parkland course.
18 holes, 6745 yds. S.S.S. 73
Course designed by Henry Cotton.
Visitors welcome on weekdays.
Green Fees. £6.00 per round or day.
Society Meetings welcome on weekdays.
Hotels: Saxon Inn Motel, Harlow;
Churchgate, Old Harlow.
Meals served except Sun. and Mon.

G 21   Chadwell Springs

Tel. Ware 3647
Hertford Rd., Ware, Herts. SG13 7HB.
On the main A119 halfway between Hertford
and Ware.
Parkland course.
9 holes, 3209 yds. S.S.S. 71
Course designed by J.H. Taylor.
Visitors welcome on weekdays, weekends
after 12.00 a.m. (subject to competition
times).
Green Fees. Weekdays 18 holes £3.50;
weekends £5.00.
Society Meetings welcome weekdays
only.
Hotels: Cannons Hotel, Ware; Salisbury
Arms Hotel, Hertford.
Meals served.

G 22   Channels

Tel. Chelmsford (0245) 440005
Belsteads Farm Lane, Little Waltham,
Chelmsford.
A12. Turn off N Springfield, Pump Lane,
Broomfield.
18 holes, 6200 yds. S.S.S. 69
Visitors welcome.
Green Fees. Weekdays £5.25; weekends
£6.50 with member only.
Society Meetings on application to
secretary.
Hotels: County, Chelmsford.

G 23   Cheshunt Park

Tel. Waltham Cross (0992) 24009
Park Lane, Cheshunt, Herts.
A10 London Cambridge, turn off W at junction
with College Rd., proceed along Churchgate
travelling N.
Meadowland course.
18 holes, 6500 yds. S.S.S. 71
Course designed by F.W. Hawtree B.A.
(Oxon).
Visitors welcome by arrangement in person
only.
Green Fees. Weekdays £1.95 per round,
jun. and O.A.P.s £1.00; weekends £3.15.
Snacks served.

G 24   Chigwell

Tel. 01-500 2059
High Rd., Chigwell, Essex.
On A113 13¼ miles NE of London.
Parkland course.
18 holes, 6283 yds. S.S.S. 70
Visitors welcome weekdays with
reservation and letter of introduction.
Green Fees. £7.50 per day, £6.00 per
round (£3.00 with member).
Society Meetings by arrangement.
Hotels: Roebuck, Buckhurst Hill.
Lunches and teas served.

G 25   Chingford

Tel. 01-529 2107 Public course Tel. 01-529
5708
158 Station Road, Chingford E.4.
18 holes, 6220 yds. S.S.S. 70
Visitors welcome. Red coats must be worn.
Green Fees. Weekdays £1.60 per round;
weekends £2.30 per round.

G 26   Chorleywood

Tel. 01-260 2009
Common Rd., Chorleywood, Herts.
Off A404 at Common Rd.
9 holes, 5676 yds. S.S.S. 67
Visitors welcome on weekdays, weekends
with member only.
Green Fees. Weekdays £3.50 per day;
weekends £4.50.
Society Meetings restricted.
Hotels: Sportsman.
Meals by arrangement.

G 27   Clacton-on-Sea

Tel. Clacton-on-Sea (0255) 21919/26304
(Pro)
West Rd., Clacton-on-Sea, Essex CO15 1AJ.
A133 Colchester to Clacton.
18 holes, 6217 yds. S.S.S. 70

Course designed by Jack White.
Visitors welcome on weekdays and after 11am. at weekends if members of recognized club.
Green Fees. Weekdays £6.00 per round or day (juniors £3.00); weekends and bank holidays £7.00 per round or day (juniors £4.00; times restricted). Special rates apply for Societies by arrangement.
Society Meetings welcome weekdays by arrangement.
Hotels: Royal; Kingscliff; Waverly; Westcliffe.
Meals by arrangement except Mon.

G 28   Colchester

Tel. Colchester (0206) 74296
Braiswick, Colchester, Essex CO4 5AU.
From A12 fork left at signpost Harwich then ½ mile on Bakers Lane. Signpost Braiswick to club.
Undulating parkland course.
18 holes, S.S.S. 70
Course designed by James Braid.
Visitors welcome weekdays by introduction.
Green Fees. £6.00 per round, £9.00 per day.
Society Meetings by arrangement.
Hotels: George, Colchester.
Meals served.

G 29   Courtauld & Crittall-Hope

Tel. Braintree (0376) 20019
Chapel Hill, Braintree, Essex.
SE edge of Braintree.
Undulating meadowland course.
9 holes, 5579 yds. S.S.S. 67
Visitors welcome weekdays.
Green Fees. Weekdays £3.00; weekends and bank holidays £5.00.
Hotels: White Hart.
No catering facilities.

G 30   Dyrham Park

Tel. 01-440 3361
Galley Lane, Barnet, Herts.
2 miles outside Barnet near Arkley and A1.
Parkland course.
18 holes, 6369 yds. S.S.S. 70
Society Meetings by arrangement.

G 31   East Herts

Tel. Ware 821978
Hamels Park, Buntingford, Herts. SG9 9NA.
½ mile N of Puckeridge By-pass on A10.
Parkland course.
18 holes, 6416 yds. S.S.S. 71
Course designed by D. Lewis and D. Hunt.
Visitors welcome weekdays if members of recognized club.
Green Fees. £6.00 per round, £7.50 per day.
Society Meetings welcome weekdays by arrangement.
Hotels: Cannons, Ware; Salisbury Hotel, Hertford.
Meals by arrangement except Tues.

G 32   Frinton

Tel. Frinton (025 56) 4618
The Esplanade, Frinton-on-Sea, Essex CO13 9EP.

B1033 to Frinton and turn right at sea front.
Seaside course.
9 holes, 1370 yds. S.S.S. 33
18 holes, 6259 yds. S.S.S. 70
Course designed by Willie Park.
Visitors welcome.
Green Fees. Weekdays £5.00 per round, £6.50 per day; weekends £6.50 per round.
Society Meetings weekdays by arrangement.
Hotels: Maplin; Grand; Frinton Lodge Hotel.
Meals served.

G 33   Hadley Wood

Tel. 01-449 4328/4486
Beech Hill, Barnet, Herts.
Off A111 between Cockfosters and Potters Bar.
Parkland course.
18 holes, 6444 yds. S.S.S. 71
Course designed by Dr. Alastair Mackenzie (1921).
Visitors welcome on weekdays.
Green Fees. £8.50 per round, £12.00 per day.
Society Meetings Wed., Thurs. and Fri. Apr. to Oct.
Hotels: West Lodge Park Hotel, Hadley Wood; Royal Chase Hotel, Enfield.
Meals served.

G 34   Hainault Forest

Tel. 01-500 2097
Chigwell Row, Hainault, Essex.
On A127 12 miles from central London.
Undulating parkland course.
(1) 18 holes, 5754 yds. S.S.S. 67
(2) 18 holes, 6479 yds. S.S.S. 71
Visitors welcome.
Green Fees. Weekdays £2.20; weekends £3.50. Season ticket operating for 2 years at £155.00 per year; 5 day ticket £50.00 per year.
Meals served to members and guests only.

G 35   Harpenden

Tel. Harpenden 2580
Hammonds End, Redbourn Lane, Harpenden, Herts.
Turn off A6 4 miles after St. Albans on B487.
Undulating parkland course.
18 holes, 6267 yds. S.S.S. 70
Course designed by Hawtree and Taylor.
Visitors welcome with reservation.
Green Fees. Weekdays £4.00 per round (£2.00 with member), £5.00 per day (£2.00 with member); weekends £2.50 per round with member only.
Society Meetings by arrangement.
Hotels: Moat House; Glen Eagle, Harpenden; Aubrey Park Hotel, Redbourn.
Light lunches and teas served.

G 36   Harpenden Common

Tel. Harpenden 5959
East Common, Harpenden, Herts.
A6 between Luton and St. Albans.
Parkland course.
18 holes, 5613 yds. S.S.S. 67
Visitors welcome weekdays, weekends with member only.
Green Fees. £5.75 per round or day (£2.90 with member).

Society Meetings welcome Wed., Thurs. and Fri.
Meals served except Mon.

G 37   Hartsbourne Country Club

Tel. 01-950 1133
Hartsbourne Ave., Bushey Heath, Herts. WD2 1JW.
Turn S off A411 at entrance to Bushey Heath Village.
Parkland course.
18 holes, 6286 yds. S.S.S. 70
9 holes, 4968 yds. S.S.S. 66
Visitors welcome weekdays by arrangement.
Green Fees. £9.00.
Society Meetings Mon., Wed. and Fri. by arrangement.
Hotels: Ladbroke Mercury Motel.
Meals served.

G 38   Hartswood

Tel. Brentwood (0277) 218850 (Sec.)
King George's Playing Fields, Ingrave Rd., Brentwood, Essex.
1 mile S of Brentwood on A128.
Municipal parkland course.
18 holes, 6238 yds. S.S.S. 70
Visitors welcome.
Green Fees. Weekdays £2.20; weekends £3.50.
Society Meetings welcome weekdays by arrangement.
Hotels: Post House, Brentwood.
Full catering every day.

G 39   Harwich & Parkeston

Tel. Harwich 3616
Parkeston Rd., Dovercourt, Essex.
A604 from Colchester to Parkeston Quay.
Course on left after leaving Parkeston Rd. roundabout.
Meadowland course.
9 holes, 5862 yds. S.S.S. 68
Visitors welcome on weekdays, weekends with member only.
Green Fees. On application.
Society Meetings by arrangement.
Hotels: Cliff Hotel, Dovercourt; Pier Hotel, Harwich.
Meals by arrangement.

G 40   Havering Municipal

Tel. Romford 41429
Risebridge Chase, Lower Bedfords Rd., Romford, Essex.
2 miles from Gallows Corner and Romford station.
18 holes, S.S.S. 70
Green Fees. Weekdays £2.04, juniors £1.02; weekends £3.12, juniors (after 3.00 p.m.) £1.55; 9 holes weekdays £1.32, juniors 66p; weekends adults £2.04.

G 41   Ilford

Tel. 01-554 2930
Wanstead Park Rd., Ilford, Essex IG1 3TR.
½ mile from Ilford railway station.
Meadowland course.
18 holes, 5687 yds. S.S.S. 67
Visitors welcome on weekdays, weekends restricted.

Green Fees. Weekdays £5.00 per round; weekends £6.50 per round.
Society Meetings welcome on weekdays.

G 42   Knebworth

Tel. Stevenage 812752
Deards End Lane, Knebworth, Herts. SG3 6NL.
A1 to Stevenage.
Undulating course.
18 holes, 6440 yds. S.S.S. 71
Visitors welcome weekdays, weekends with member only.
Green Fees. £5.75 per round, £7.50 per day.
Society Meetings welcome Mon. Tues. and Thurs. only.
Hotels: Roebuck Motel.
Meals served.

G 43   Letchworth

Tel. Letchworth 3203
Letchworth Lane, Letchworth, Herts. SG6 3NQ.
Off A505 at Letchworth.
Parkland course.
18 holes, 6057 yds. S.S.S. 69
Course designed by Harry Vardon.
Visitors welcome on weekdays, weekends with member only.
Green Fees. £5.75 per round, £8.50 per day.
Society Meetings welcome on weekdays.
Hotels: Letchworth Hall Hotel.
Lunches and teas served except Mon.
Snacks at the bar daily.

G 44   Little Hay Golf Course

Tel. Hemel Hempstead 833798
Hemel Hempstead, Herts.
Off A41 at Box Lane traffic lights.
Meadowland course.
18 holes, 6610 yds. S.S.S. 72
Course designed by Hawtree and Son.
Hotels: Post House; Watermill, Hemel Hempstead; Albury Park Hotel, Redbourn.
9 hole pitch and putt; 18 hole public putting green.

G 45   Maldon

Tel. Maldon 53212
Beeleigh, Langford, Maldon, Essex CM9 7SS.
B1019 from Maldon, turn left by Old Waterworks in Langford.
Parkland course.
9 holes, 6077 yds. S.S.S. 69
Visitors welcome on weekdays, Sun. with member only.
Green Fees. Weekdays £4.00 per round, £5.00 per day; weekends £5.00 per round.
Society Meetings by arrangement.
Hotels: Blue Boar; Kings Head, Maldon.
Light lunches served; meals by arrangement.

G 46   Maylands

Tel. Ingrebourne 42055
Colchester Rd., Harold Park, Romford, Essex RM3 0AZ.
On A12 between Romford and Brentwood.
Undulating meadowland course.
18 holes, 6101 yds. S.S.S. 70

Visitors welcome if members of recognized club.
Green Fees. 18 holes £6.00; 36 holes £8.00.
Society Meetings weekdays by arrangement.
Hotels: Post House; Moat House, Brentwood.
Meals served.

G 47   Mid-Herts

Tel. Wheathampstead 2242
Gustard Wood, Wheathampstead, Herts.
B651 or A6129 to Wheathampstead, 1 mile N on B651.
Heathland/parkland course.
18 holes, 6094 yds. S.S.S. 69
Visitors welcome weekdays with reservation, weekends with member only.
Green Fees. £5.00 per round, £7.00 per day.
Society Meetings weekdays only by arrangement.
Hotels: St. Michaels Manor Hotel, St. Albans; Glen Eagle; Moat House, Harpenden.
Meals by arrangement.

G 48   Moor Park

Tel. Rickmansworth 73146
Moor Park, Rickmansworth, Herts. WD3 1QN.
A404.
Parkland courses.
High course 18 holes, 6663 yds. S.S.S. 72
West course 18 holes, 5815 yds. S.S.S. 68
Visitors welcome on weekdays with reservation.
Green Fees. Weekdays £12.00.
Society Meetings welcome on weekdays.
Hotels: Bedford Arms, Chenies; Victoria, Rickmansworth.
Lunches served; dinners by arrangement.

G 49   Old Fold Manor

Tel. 01-449 2266 Secretary 01-440 9185
Old Fold Lane, Hadley Green, Barnet, Herts. EN5 4Q(.
On Potters Bar road, ½ mile from Barnet.
Parkland course.
18 holes, 6449 yds. S.S.S. 71
Visitors welcome on weekdays, weekends with member or with reservation.
Green Fees. Weekdays £6.00 per round, £8.00 per day.
Society Meetings Thurs. only.
Meals served except Mon. and Wed.

G 50   Orsett

Tel. 0375 891 352
Brentwood Rd., Orsett, Essex.
On A128 400 yds. from the A13.
Heathland course.
18 holes, 6622 yds. S.S.S. 72
Course designed by James Braid.
Visitors welcome by arrangement.
Green Fees. £6.00-£9.00.
Society Meetings by arrangement.
Meals served every day.

G 51   Panshanger

Tel. Welwyn Garden City 33350
Herns Lane, Welwyn Garden City, Herts.
Adjacent to B1000. 1 mile NE of town centre.

Parkland course.
18 holes, 6200 yds. S.S.S. 70
Course designed by John D. Harris Associates.
Visitors welcome.
Green Fees. Weekdays £1.85; juniors 65p; weekends £2.90.
Society Meetings welcome on weekdays.
Hotels: Clock Motel; Treetops; Crest, Welwyn.
Meals and snacks served.

G 52   Pipps Hill Country Club

Tel. Basildon (0268) 27278/9
Aquatels Recreation Centre, Cranes Farm Rd., Basildon, Essex.
On A127 or A13.
Meadowland course.
9 holes, 2829 yds. S.S.S. 67
Course designed by Golf Landscapes Ltd.
Visitors welcome.
Green Fees. £2.00 per round.
Society Meetings welcome on weekdays.
Hotels: Essex Centre Hotel.
Meals served.

G 53   P.L. London

Tel. Potters Bar 42624
Bedwell Park, Essendon, Hatfield, Herts. AL9 6JA.
2 miles along B158 off A1000.
Undulating parkland course.
18 holes, 6878 yds. S.S.S. 72
Course designed by F.W. Hawtree & Son.
Visitors welcome.
Green Fees. On application to Secretary.
Society Meetings welcome.
Hotels: in area.
Light lunches served.

G 54   Porters Park

Tel. Radlett 4127
Shenley Hill, Radlett, Herts. WD7 7A2.
Turn off A5 to Shenley road at railway station, ½ mile.
Parkland course.
18 holes, 6253 yds. S.S.S. 70
Visitors welcome on weekdays with reservation except Tues.
Green Fees. £5.50 per round, £7.50 per day.
Society Meetings Wed. and Thurs. only.
Hotels: Red Lion, Radlett; Sopwell House Hotel, St. Albans.
Lunches and teas served.

G 55   Potters Bar

Tel. Potters Bar (77) 52020
Darkes Lane, Potters Bar, Herts. EN6 1DF.
A1000 N of Barnet.
Parkland course.
18 holes, 6273 yds. S.S.S. 70
Visitors welcome weekdays, weekends with member only.
Green Fees. Weekdays £7.00.
Meals served.

G 56   Redbourn

Tel. 058-285 3493
Kinsbourne Green Lane, Redbourn, Herts. AL3 7QA.
S off M1 at junction 9 on to A5, take first left

turning after 1 mile down Luton Lane.
Parkland course.
18 holes, 6381 yds. S.S.S. 70
9 holes, 1361 yds. Par 27 (public course)
Visitors welcome except Sat. and Sun. mornings with reservation.
Green Fees. 18 hole course weekdays £3.25. 9 hole public course £1.50 juniors, £2.00 adults.
Society Meetings by arrangement.
Hotels: Aubrey Park Hotel.
Snacks served; meals by arrangement.

G 57   Rickmansworth Public

Tel. Rickmansworth 73163
Moor Lane, Rickmansworth, Herts.
B4504 off A404 at waterworks, then first on right.
Undulating parkland course.
Ladies 18 holes, 3937 yds. S.S.S. 66
Gents 18 holes, 4412 yds. S.S.S. 63
Visitors welcome.
Green Fees. Weekdays £1.75 per round, juniors £1.10 per round; weekends £3.00 per round. Juniors not permitted at weekends.
Society Meetings by arrangement.
Hotels: Victoria, Rickmansworth; Bedford Arms, Chenies.
Meals served.

G 58   Rochford Hundred

Tel. 0702-544302
Hall Rd., Rochford, Essex SS4 1NW.
B1013 4 miles N of Southend-on-Sea.
Parkland course.
18 holes, 6170 yds. S.S.S. 69
Visitors welcome on weekdays except Tues. a.m. if members of recognized club.
Green Fees. £8.00 per round or day.
Society Meetings Wed. and Thurs. by arrangement.
Hotels: Airport Hotel, Southend.
Lunches served by arrangement Tues. to Fri.

G 59   Romford

Tel. Romford 40986
Heath Dr., Gidea Park, Romford, Essex RM2 5QB.
1 mile E of Romford.
Parkland course.
18 holes, 6378 yds. S.S.S. 70
Course designed by James Braid.
Visitors welcome on weekdays except Wed.
Green Fees. Weekdays £4.25 per round, £6.25 per day.
Society Meetings Tues., Thurs. and Fri.
Hotels: Moat House; Post House, Brentwood.
Meals served.

G 60   Royston

Tel. Royston (0763) 42177
Baldock Rd., Royston, Herts. SG8 5BG.
On A505 between Royston and Baldock.
Undulating heathland course.
18 holes, 6032 yds. S.S.S. 69
Visitors welcome on weekdays, at weekends must be members of recognized club. Sun. after 11a.m. only.

Green Fees. Weekdays £4.50; weekends £6.00.
Society Meetings by arrangement.
Hotels: Banyers Hotel.
Snacks served; meals by arrangement.

G 61   Saffron Walden

Tel. Saffron Walden 22788
Windmill Hill, Saffron Walden, Essex.
10 miles from Bishop's Stortford.
Parkland course.
18 holes, 6450 yds. S.S.S. 71
Course designed by Harry Vardon.
Visitors welcome on weekdays; advisable to phone.
Green Fees. £6.50.
Society Meetings by arrangement.
Hotels: Saffron Hotel, Saffron Walden; University Arms; Garden House Hotel, Cambridge.

G 62   Skips

Tel. Ingrebourne 48234
Horsemanside, Tysea Hill, Stapleford Abbotts, Essex RM4 1JU.
B175 to Stapleford Abbots, left up Tysea Hill.
Meadowland course.
18 holes, 6146 yds. S.S.S. 71
Course designed by C.K. Cotton, Pennink, Lawrie and Partners.
Visitors welcome.
Green Fees. Weekdays 9 holes £1.00, 18 holes £1.50; weekends 9 holes £1.50, 18 holes £2.50.
Society Meetings except Sun. by arrangement.
Hotels: in area.

G 63   Stevenage

Tel. (0438) 88424
Aston Lane, Bragbury End, Aston, Stevenage.
From A1(M) Stevenage South take A602 to Hertford; course signposted approx. 1½ miles.
Municipal meadowland course.
18 holes, 6560 yds. S.S.S. 71
Course designed by John Jacobs.
Visitors welcome.
Green Fees. On application.
Society Meetings welcome.
Hotels: Roebuck Motel.
Bar and snacks.

G 64   Stoke by Nayland

Tel. Nayland (0206) 262836
Keepers Lane, Leavenheath, Colchester, Essex CO6 4PZ.
Off A134 from Colchester onto B1068 at Levenheath.
Undulating countryside courses.
Constable Course 18 holes, 6461 yds. S.S.S. 71
Gainsborough Course 18 holes, 6471 yds. S.S.S. 71
Visitors welcome on weekdays.
Green Fees. £5.50 per round, £8.00 per day.
Society Meetings welcome on weekdays.
Hotels: White Hart, Nayland; Swan, Lavenham; Sun, Dedham.
Meals served by arrangement.

G 65   Theydon Bois

Tel. Theydon Bois 3054
Theydon Rd., Theydon Bois, Epping, Essex CM16 4EH.
On A11, turn right just before Epping at the Bell Motel.
Woodland / parkland course.
18 holes, 5506 yds. S.S.S. 68
Old nine holes designed by James Braid (1897), new nine holes by Hawtree (1971).
Visitors welcome weekdays and after 12.30p.m. at weekends if members of recognized club.
Green Fees. £6.50 per round or day (£3.25 with member).
Society Meetings Mon., Tues. and Wed., max. 40.
Hotels: Tree Tops; Bell Motel, Epping.
Meals served by arrangement.

G 66   Thorndon Park

Tel. Brentwood 81 1666/81 0345 (Sec.)
Thorndon Park, Ingrave, Brentwood, Essex CM13 3RH.
Parkland course.
18 holes, 6403 yds. S.S.S. 71
Visitors from other clubs welcome on weekdays with reservation.
Lunches served except Mon.

G 67   Thorpe Hall

Tel. Southend (0702) 582205
Thorpe Hall Ave., Thorpe Bay, Essex SS1 3AT.
East of town, off front.
Parkland course.
18 holes, 6259 yds. S.S.S. 70
Visitors welcome if members of recognized club.
Green Fees. On application.
Society Meetings welcome.
Hotels: Roslin Hotel.
Meals served.

G 68   Upminster

Tel. Upminster (86) 22788
114 Hall Lane, Upminster, Essex.
A127 towards Southend.
Parkland.
18 holes, 5926 yds. S.S.S. 68
Visitors welcome on weekdays if member of recognized club.
Green Fees. £6.00 per round; £10.00 per day.
Society Meetings by arrangement.
Hotels: Fairlane Motor Inn, Upminster; Post House, Brentwood.
Meals served except Mon.

G 69   Verulam

Tel. St. Albans (0727) 53327
London Rd., St. Albans, Herts. AL1 1JG.
A6 to St. Albans.
Parkland course.
18 holes, 6386 yds. S.S.S. 70
Visitors welcome weekdays, weekends with member only.
Green Fees. Weekdays £5.50 per round, £7.50 per day.
Society Meetings by arrangement.

Hotels: Sopwell House; Red Lion; Peahen; St. Michaels Manor Hotel; The Haven.
Meals by arrangement except Mon.

G 70 Warley Park (Brett Essex)

Tel. Brentwood (0277) 224891
Magpie Lane, Little Warley, Brentwood, Essex.
Off A127 at Brentwood.
Undulating parkland course.
27 holes.
Visitors welcome weekdays if members of recognized club.
Green Fees. £6.00 per round, £7.50 per day.
Society Meetings welcome weekdays only.
Hotels: Post House; Moat House, Brentwood.
Meals served.

G 71 Warren

Tel. Danbury 3258
Woodham Walter, Maldon, Essex CM9 6RW.
A414 towards Maldon, left at road to Woodham Walter, ½ mile.
Parkland course.
18 holes, 6152 yds. S.S.S. 69
Visitors welcome on weekdays, weekends with member only.
Green Fees. £7.50 per round, £9.50 per day.
Society Meetings welcome weekdays except Wed.
Hotels: Blue Boar, Maldon.
Meals served.

G 72 Welwyn Garden City

Tel. Welwyn Garden City 25243
Mannicotts, Welwyn Garden City, Herts. AL8 7BP.
Off A1 at Stanborough. Follow B197 to town centre.
Parkland course.
18 holes, 6152 yds. S.S.S. 69
Course designed by Hawtree & Son.
Visitors welcome on weekdays.
Green Fees. £5.00 per round, £6.50 per day.
Society Meetings welcome on weekdays.
Hotels: Tree Tops, Welwyn Garden City.
Lunches served except Mon.

G 73 Westcliff Country Club

Tel. Maldon 828631
Stow Rd., Purleigh, Chelmsford, Essex CM3 6RR.
On B1012 from Wickford.
Parkland course.
18 holes, 6625 yds. S.S.S. 72
Visitors welcome on weekdays, weekends with member only.
Green Fees. Weekdays £4.50 per round; weekends £5.50 per round.
Society Meetings welcome Tues. and Thurs.
Hotels: Accomodation available at club.
Meals served except Sun. evening.

G 74 West Essex

Tel. 01-529 7558
Bury Road, Stewardstonebury, London E4 7QL.
Off A11 ¾ mile from Chingford Station.
Parkland course.
18 holes, 6325 yds. S.S.S. 70
Visitors welcome on weekdays.
Green Fees. £5.00 per round, £7.50 per day.
Society Meetings Mon., Wed. and Fri. by arrangement.
Meals served by arrangement.

G 75 West Herts

Tel. Watford (0923) 36484
Cassiobury Park, Watford, Herts. WD1 7SL.
2 miles from Watford on A412.
Parkland course.
18 holes, 6488 yds. S.S.S. 71
Course designed by Tom Morris and Harry Vardon.
Visitors welcome on weekdays, weekends with member only.
Green Fees. £7.00 per round, £9.50 per day (£3.00 with member).
Society Meetings Wed. and Fri. only.
Hotels: Caledonian; Southern Cross.
Lunches and teas served except Mon.

G 76 Whipsnade Park

Tel. Little Gaddesden 2330/2331
Studham Lane, Dagnall, Nr. Berkhamsted, Herts.
Off A4146 between Dagnall and Studham.
Parkland course.
18 holes, 6800 yds. S.S.S. 72
Visitors welcome.
Green Fees. Weekdays £5.00.
Society Meetings welcome on weekdays.
Hotels: Post House, Hemel Hempstead; Moat House.
Meals served except Mon.

G 77 Woodford

Tel. 01-504 0553
Sunset Ave., Woodford Green, Essex IG8 0ST.
A11 to Woodford Green.
Parkland course.
9 holes, 5741 yds. S.S.S. 68
Visitors welcome on weekdays except Tues. and Thurs. mornings, weekends with member only.
Green Fees. Weekdays £3.50.
Snacks served.

H Buckinghamshire, Bedfordshire, Oxfordshire, Northamptonshire

H 1 Abbey Hill

Tel. Milton Keynes (0908) 563845
Monks Way, Stony Stratford, Milton Keynes.
One mile S of Stony Stratford.
Meadowland course.
18 holes, 6505 yds. S.S.S. 71
Visitors welcome on weekdays, weekends with reservation.
Green Fees. Weekdays £1.20 a.m., £2.10 p.m.; weekends £3.20.
Society Meetings by arrangement.

H 2 Aspley Guise & Woburn Sands

Tel. Woburn Sands 583596
West Hill, Aspley Guise, Milton Keynes, Bucks MK17 8DK.
On A5140, Bletchley 5 miles, Milton Keynes 6 miles. 3 miles from M1, junction 13.
Undulating parkland course.
18 holes, 6115 yds. S.S.S. 70
Course designed by Charles Willmott and Sandy Herd.
Visitors welcome.
Green Fees. £5.00 per round, £6.00 per day.
Society Meetings Wed. and Fri. by arrangement.
Hotels: Swan, Woburn Sands; Bedford Arms, Woburn.
Meals and snacks served except all day Mon. and Tues. lunch.

H 3 Badgemore Park Country Club

Tel. Henley-on-Thames 2206 (Sec.)/4175 (Pro).
Henley-on-Thames, Oxon. RG9 4NR.
1 mile W of Henley traffic lights on B290.
Parkland course.
18 holes, 6112 yds. S.S.S. 69
Visitors welcome on weekdays, weekends with reservation.
Green Fees. Weekdays £6.00 (£3.00 with member); weekends £7.50 (£4.00 with member); evenings Mon.-Fri. £4.00.
Society Meetings welcome.
Hotels: Little White Hart; Red Lion; Sidney House Hotel.
Meals served.

H 4 Beaconsfield

Tel. Beaconsfield 6545
Seer Green, Beaconsfield, Bucks.
M40, then A355 for one mile. Turn right at sign Seer Green/Jordans. Club adjoins Seer Green Railway Station.

Parkland course.
18 holes, 6450 yds. S.S.S. 71
Visitors welcome on weekdays with letter of introduction; weekends with member only.
Green Fees. £9.00.
Society Meetings Tues. and Wed. only, min. 30.
Hotels: Bell House Hotel; Royal White Hart. Meals and snacks served.

H 5 Beadlow Manor Golf & Country Club

Tel. Silsoe (0525) 60800
Beadlow, Shefford, Beds.
On A507 between Silsoe and Shefford.
Parkland course.
9 holes, 5918 yds.
18 holes, 6472 yds. S.S.S. 71
Visitors welcome.
Green Fees. 9 hole course: weekdays £2.50; weekends £3.75. 18 hole course: weekdays £4.00; weekends £6.00.
Society Meetings welcome.
Hotels: Accommodation available at club. Meals served.

H 6 Bedford & County

Tel. Bedford 52617
Green Lane, Clapham, Bedford.
A6 N from Bedford for 2 miles; turn right before Clapham.
Undulating parkland course.
18 holes, 6347 yds. S.S.S. 70
Visitors welcome on weekdays, weekends with members only.
Green Fees. Weekdays £4.50 per round, £5.50 per day.
Society Meetings weekdays by arrangement.
Hotels: Woodlands Manor Hotel. Full catering.

H 7 Bedfordshire

Tel. Bedford 61669
Biddenham, Bedford.
A428, one mile outside Bedford.
Parkland course.
18 holes, 6196 yds. S.S.S. 69
Green Fees. Weekdays £5.00; weekends £6.00.
Society Meetings by arrangement.

Hotels: Swan; County; De Parys. Lunches and teas served.

H 8 Bremhill Park

Tel. Shrivenham 782946
Shrivenham, Swindon, Wilts.
On A420 between Shrivenham and Watchfield.
Parkland course.
18 holes, 4823 yds. S.S.S. 63
Visitors welcome.
Green Fees. Weekdays £3.00 (£2.50 with member); weekends £5.00.
Society Meetings by arrangement.
Hotels: Swindon Motel.
Snacks served.

H 9 Buckingham

Tel. Buckingham 3282
Radclive, Buckingham.
1½ miles on Oxford road.
18 holes, 6135 yds.
Visitors welcome on weekdays.
Green Fees. £6.00.

H 10 Burford

Tel. Burford 2149
Burford, Oxon.
19 miles W of Oxford at junction of A40 and A361.
Meadowland course.
18 holes, 6425 yds. S.S.S. 71
Visitors welcome with reservation.
Green Fees. Weekdays £6.50; weekends £7.50.
Society Meetings Mon., Wed. and Thurs. by arrangement.
Hotels: in Burford.
Meals served.

H 11 Burnham Beeches

Tel. Burnham 61150
Green Lane, Burnham, Bucks. SL1 8EG.
4 miles W of Slough.
Parkland course.
18 holes, 6387 yds. S.S.S. 70
Visitors welcome on weekdays with letter of introduction, weekends with member only.
Green Fees. £7.50 per round, £9.00 per day.
Society Meetings Wed., Thurs., and Fri.
Hotels: Burnham Beeches Hotel.

H 12 Cherwell Edge

Tel. Banbury (0295) 711591
Chacombe, Banbury, Oxon.
4 miles from Banbury, A422/A4525
Public meadowland course.
9 holes, 2566 yds. S.S.S. 33
Visitors welcome every day.
Green Fees. Weekdays 9 holes £1.30 (juniors and O.A.P.s 65p); weekends 9 holes £1.85.
Society Meetings welcome by arrangement.
Hotels: Crest; Moat House; Whatley, Banbury.
No catering facilities.

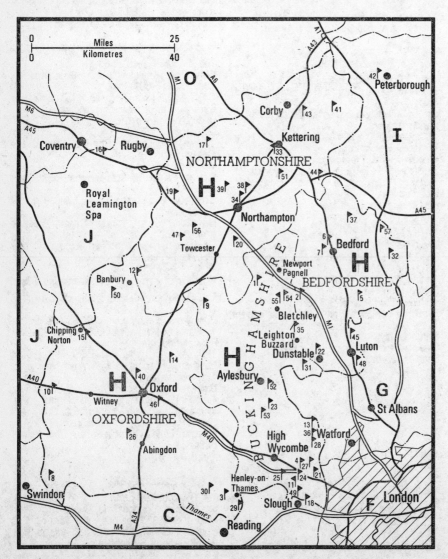

H 13　Chesham & Ley Hill

Tel. Chesham 784541
Ley Hill, Chesham, Bucks. HP5 1UZ.
Heathland course.
9 holes, 5147 yds. S.S.S. 65
Visitors welcome weekdays except Tues. and Fri. after 1p.m., weekends with member only.
Green Fees. £3.50 per round or day (£2.00 with member).
Light meals and snacks except Mon.

H 14　Chesterton Golf and Country Club

Tel. Bicester (08692) 41204
Chesterton, Bicester, Oxon.
From Oxford take Northampton Road, turn right after Weston-on-the-Green airport.
Parkland course.
18 holes, 6542 yds. S.S.S. 71
Visitors welcome on weekdays, weekends with handicap certificate.
Green Fees. Weekdays £4.00 per round or day; weekends £5.00 per round or day.
Society Meetings weekdays by arrangement.
Hotels: Weston Manor.

H 15　Chipping Norton

Tel. Chipping Norton (0608) 2383
Southcombe, Chipping Norton, Oxon. OX7 5QQ.
At junction of A34/A44 2 miles from Chipping Norton.
Undulating course.
9 holes, 6137 yds. S.S.S. 69
Visitors welcome on weekdays; weekends and after 3.30 p.m. May to September with member only.
Green Fees. Weekdays £4.00 per round or day (£2.50 with member); weekends £4.00.
Hotels: Crown and Cushion; White Hart, Chipping Norton.

H 16　City of Coventry (Brandon Woods)

Tel. Coventry 543141
Brandon Lane, Wolston, Nr. Coventry.
A45 6 miles S of Coventry.
Meadowland course.
18 holes, 6500 yds. S.S.S. 71
Visitors welcome.
Green Fees. £2.50, juniors and O.A.P.s 90p.
Society Meetings by arrangement.
Hotels: Brandon Hall, Wolston.
Meals served every day.

H 17　Cold Ashby

Tel. Northampton (0604) 740548
Cold Ashby, Northampton.
Off A50 N of Northampton 5 miles M1 (junction 18 Crick). From M1 follow A428 bear left West Haddon to Cold Ashby.
Undulating course.
Visitors welcome.

Green Fees. Weekdays £3.50 per round (£2.50 with member), £5.00 per day (£3.50 with member); weekends £4.25 per round (£3.25 with member), £6.00 per day (£4.25 with member).
Society Meetings welcome on weekdays, weekends limited.
Hotels: Pytchley Hotel, West Haddon; Royal Cavendish, Long Buckby.
Meals and snacks served.

H 18　Datchet

Tel. Slough 43887
Buccleuch Rd., Datchet, Slough, Berks.
Turn off Slough to Windsor road at level crossing 2 miles from Slough.
Meadowland course.
9 holes, 5901 yds. S.S.S. 68
Visitors welcome on weekdays before 3 p.m., weekends with member only.
Green Fees. £4.50 (£2.00 with member).
Society Meetings welcome.
Hotels: Manor Hotel.
Snacks served.

H 19　Daventry & District

Tel. Daventry 2829
Norton Rd., Daventry, Northants.
9 holes, 5742 yds. S.S.S. 68
Visitors welcome.
Green Fees. Weekdays £2.00 (£1.50 with member); weekends £3.00 (£2.00 with member).
Hotels: Wheatshead Hotel; Abercorn Hotel; John O'Gaunt Hotel.

H 20　Delapre Golf Complex

Tel. Northampton (0604) 64036
Eagle Dr. Nene Valley Way, Northampton NN4 0DU.
Junction 15 on M1. Turn off on A508 to Bedford for 2½ miles.
Parkland course. 9 hole par 3, 9 hole pitch & putt, floodlit driving range.
18 holes, S.S.S. 70
Course managed by John Jacobs Golf Ltd.
Visitors welcome.
Green Fees. Weekdays 18 holes £2.55, 9 holes £1.75; weekends 18 holes £3.25, 9 holes £2.25; 9 holes par 3 weekdays £1.10, weekends £1.20; pitch & putt 50p.
Society Meetings welcome on weekdays.
Hotels: Saxon; Grand; Westone; Angel.
Meals and snacks served. Full bar facilities.

H 21　Denham

Tel. Denham 832022
Tilehouse Lane, Denham, Bucks. UB9 59E.
A40 to Denham, then A412 for ½ mile. Turn left up Tilehouse Lane.
Parkland course.
18 holes, 6439 yds. S.S.S. 71
Visitors welcome on weekdays, weekends with member only.
Green Fees. £7.00, £10.00 per day.
Society Meetings Tues., Wed. and Thurs.
Hotels: Ethorpe; Bull, Gerrards Cross.
Meals served.

H 22　Dunstable Downs

Tel. Dunstable 63634
Whipsnade Rd., Dunstable, Beds.

2 miles from Dunstable on Whipsnade road.
Downland course.
18 holes, 6184 yds. S.S.S. 70
Visitors welcome on weekdays, weekends with member only.
Green Fees. Weekdays £6.00 per round or day (£3.00 with member).
Society Meetings welcome weekdays except Mon. and Wed.
Meals served except Mon.

H 23　Ellesborough

Tel. Wendover 622114
Butlers Cross, Aylesbury, Bucks. HP17 0TZ.
On B4010 1 mile W of Wendover.
Downland course.
Visitors welcome on weekdays, must have handicap certificate or letter of introduction unless with member; weekends with member only.
Green Fees. Weekdays £7.50 per round or day.
Society Meetings Wed., Thurs. by arrangement.
Hotels: Red Lion, Wendover; Bernard Arms, Kimble.
Meals served except Mon.

H 24　Farnham Park

Tel. Farnham Common 3335
Park Rd., Stoke Poges, Bucks.
Opposite Stoke Poges Golf Club.
Parkland course.
9 holes, 2904 yds. S.S.S. 34
Visitors welcome.
Green Fees. Weekdays £2.00 per round (18 holes); weekends £2.75 per round; O.A.P.s before 12.00 noon £1.15 per round; juniors £1.25.
Hotels: Burnham Beeches Hotel, Burnham.
Meals served.

H 25　Flackwell Heath

Tel. Bourne End 20929
High Wycombe, Bucks. HP10 9PE.
Off A40 High Wycombe to Beaconsfield, at Loudwater.
Undulating course.
18 holes, 6129 yds. S.S.S. 69
Visitors welcome on weekdays, weekends with member only.
Green Fees. Weekdays £7.00 per round or day.
Society Meetings by arrangement.
Hotels: Falcon, High Wycombe; Bellhouse, Beaconsfield.
Meals served.

H 26　Frilford Heath

Tel. Frilford Heath 390428
Abingdon, Oxon. OX13 5NW.
On A338, 3 miles W of Abingdon.
Wooded heathland courses.
Red 18 holes, 6768 yds. S.S.S. 73
Green 18 holes, 6006 yds. S.S.S. 69
Course redesigned by Cotton (C.K.) Pennink, Lawrie and Partners.
Visitors welcome weekdays if members of recognized club; weekends with reservation.
Green Fees. Weekdays £8.00 (£5.00 with member); weekends £10.50 (£7.00 with member).

Society Meetings weekdays by arrangement.
Hotels: Dog House, Frilford Heath; Upper Reaches, Abingdon; Rose Revived, Standlake.
Morning coffee, lunch and tea served; evening meals by arrangement.

H 27 Gerrards Cross

Tel. Gerrards Cross 83263
Chalfont Park, Gerrards Cross, Bucks. SL9 0QA.
A40, then A413 for 1 mile. Club is on right hand side, next to British Aluminium offices.
Parkland course.
18 holes, 6305 yds. S.S.S. 70
Visitors welcome on weekdays, except Tues., Sat., Sun. before 3 p.m., with letter of introduction or handicap certificate. Advisable telephone in advance.
Green Fees. Weekdays £9.00 per round or day, £5.00 after 3 p.m.; weekends and bank holidays, after 3 p.m. £12.00 per round.
Society Meetings by arrangement.
Hotels: Bell; Ethorpe; Bellhouse.
Meals served.

H 28 Harewood Downs

Tel. Little Chalfont 2184
Cokes Lane, Chalfont St. Giles, Bucks. HP8 4TA.
Off A413 between Chalfont St. Giles and Amersham.
Undulating parkland course.
18 holes, 5871 yds. S.S.S. 69
Visitors welcome on weekdays, ladies day Tues.
Green Fees. £7.50 per round or day (£3.75 with member).
Society Meetings Wed. and Thurs.
Hotels: The Greyhound, Chalfont St. Peter; King's Arms, Amersham.
Meals served by arrangement except Mon.

H 29 Henley

Tel. Henley 3304
Harpsden, Henley-on-Thames, Oxon. RG9 4HG.
From Henley-on-Thames take Reading road for ½ mile. Fork right at 'Three Horseshoes' onto Harpsden Way. Follow to club.
Parkland course.
18 holes, 6157 yds. S.S.S. 69
Course designed by James Braid.
Visitors welcome on weekdays, weekends with member only.
Green Fees. £6.00 per round, per day (£3.00 with member).
Society Meetings welcome on weekdays.
Hotels: Imperial, Henley-on-Thames.
Meals served every day.

H 30 Huntercombe

Tel. Nettlebed 641207
Nuffield, Henley-on-Thames, Oxon. RG9 5SL.
On A423, 7 miles W of Henley-on-Thames.
Woodland, heathland course.
18 holes, 6249 yds. S.S.S. 70
Course designed by Willie Park jnr. (1901).
Visitors welcome.
Green Fees. Weekdays £7.50; Sat. £10.00; Sun. £15.00; juniors £1.75.
Society Meetings welcome on weekdays.

Hotels: Shillingford Bridge Hotel, Shillingford; Beetle and Wedge, Moulsford; White Hart, Nettlebed.
Meals served by arrangement.

H 31 Ivinghoe

Tel. Cheddington 668696
Ivinghoe, Leighton Buzzard, Beds.
In Ivinghoe village, Bucks., 5 miles from Leighton Buzzard.
Undulating meadowland course.
9 holes, 4602 yds. S.S.S. 61
Course designed by R. Garrad and Sons.
Visitors welcome seven days per week.
Green Fees. Weekdays £2.00 per day; weekends £3.00 per day.
Hotels: Royal; Rose and Crown, Tring.
Meals served.

H 32 John O' Gaunt

Tel. Potton 260252
Sutton Park, Sandy, Beds. SG19 2LY.
2 miles N of Biggleswade on B1040.
Parkland course.
John O'Gaunt Course 18 holes, 6505 yds. S.S.S. 71
Carthagena Course 18 holes, 5882 yds. S.S.S. 69
Visitors welcome with reservation.
Green Fees. Weekdays £6.50; weekends £8.00. Handicap certificate required at weekends.
Society Meetings welcome Mon. to Thurs.
Hotels: Rose and Crown, Potton.
Meals served.

H 33 Kettering

Tel. Kettering (0536) 512074
Headlands, Kettering, Northants.
From town centre follow Headlands to club.
Meadowland course.
18 holes, 6035 yds. S.S.S. 69
Visitors welcome on weekdays, weekends with member only.
Green Fees. £5.75 per day (£3.00 with member).
Society Meetings Wed. by arrangement.
Hotels: George Hotel; Royal Hotel.
Meals served by arrangement.

H 34 Kingsthorpe

Tel. Northampton (0604) 711173 (Members), 719602 (Professional)
Kingsley Rd., Northampton NN2 7BU.
Situated in town.
Parkland course.
18 holes, 5880 yds. S.S.S. 68
Course designed by C. H. Allison.
Visitors welcome on weekdays, weekends with member only.
Green Fees. Weekdays £3.00 per round £4.00 per day (£1.75 with member).
Society Meetings by arrangement.
Hotels: Westone; Saxon.
Snacks served; lunches by arrangement.

H 35 Leighton Buzzard

Tel. Leighton Buzzard 373811
Plantation Rd., Leighton Buzzard, Beds.
2 miles NE of station.
Parkland course.

18 holes, 5359 yds. S.S.S. 68
Visitors welcome on weekdays with letter of introduction, weekends with member only.
Green Fees. Weekdays £4.00 per round (£3.00 with member).
Society Meetings by arrangement.
Hotels: Bedford Arms, Woburn.
Meals served except Mon.

H 36 Little Chalfont

Tel. Little Chalfont 4877 (Pro 4863)
Lodge Lane, Little Chalfont, Amersham, Bucks.
Off A404 Amersham-Watford; course 1½ miles from London underground Metropolitan Line station Chalfont and Latimer.
Undulating meadowland course, opened 1981.
9 holes, 5852 yds. S.S.S. 68
Course designed by Reg. Garrad & Sons.
Visitors welcome weekdays, restricted at weekends and bank holidays.
Green Fees. Weekdays £5.00; weekends and bank holidays £7.00.
Society Meetings welcome weekdays.
Full catering facilities in new clubhouse.

H 37 Mowsbury

Tel. Bedford (0234) 771041
Cleat Hill, Bedford MK41 8DQ.
On B660, 2 miles N of city centre.
Parkland course.
18 holes, 6514 yds. S.S.S. 71
Course designed by F.W. Hawtree.
Visitors welcome.
Green Fees. Weekdays £1.70; weekends £3.40.
Society Meetings weekdays by arrangement with dept. of amenities, Town Hall, Bedford. Tel. (0234) 67422 ext. 258.
Hotels: Bedford Swan; County; De Parys.
Snacks served, meals by arrangement for society meetings.

H 38 Northampton

Tel. Northampton 711054 (Club) / 719453 (Sec.)
Kettering Rd., Northampton NN3 1AA.
On A43 on N outskirts of town.
Parkland course.
18 holes, 6002 yds. S.S.S. 69
Visitors welcome weekdays, weekends with member only. Handicap certificate must be produced.
Green Fees. Weekdays £6.00 per round or day; weekends £2.00 with member only.
Society Meetings welcome.
Hotels: Westone; Grand; Saxon.
Catering by arrangement except Tues.

H 39 Northamptonshire County

Tel. Northampton (0604) 843025
Church Brampton, Northampton, NN6 8AZ.
Off A50, 4 miles NW of Northampton.
Heathland course.
18 holes, 6460 yds. S.S.S. 71
Course designed by H.S. Colt.
Visitors welcome on weekdays, weekends with or introduced by member.
Green Fees. Weekdays £6.00 per round or day (£3.00 with member); weekends £7.50 per round or day (£3.00 with member).

Northampton's quality par fours

Motorway travel has made quite a difference in setting golfers' sights farther afield for simple excursions and, having driven over 60 miles in about the same time that it can take to cross London, I was waiting to play at the Northamptonshire County Club at Church Brampton little more than an hour and a half after setting out.

It is possible, to those unfamiliar with these parts, that the nearness of Northampton suggests a course overlooking a predominantly urban scene, but Church Brampton, in keeping with its delightful name, enjoys a fine rural setting and offers, as well as an escape, a test of inland golf that, of its type, is as good as any.

At a glance, a length of 6,290 yards does not appear too formidable, but the staging of the English Golf Union's county champions meeting there in 1966 and the Youths' Championship in 1971 reflect its merits. Though there is only one par five—the 18th—the strength of several excellent par fours give it its enjoyment and quality.

James Braid, who with J.H. Taylor, Ben Sayers and Tom Ball, opened the course in 1910, returned after the last war to bring it up to date. But, broadly speaking, there have been few major alterations since H.S. Colt designed the layout on a site acquired from Earl Spencer over half a century ago.

The first two holes, both over 450 yards, immediately give an indication of its pleasant character, a fringe of light woodland bordering the left. The width of the fairways is not alarming, but the approach to the first green is particularly well protected and, a little later, out-of-bounds awaits if the drive is held too far left at the 4th, an inviting 300-yard hole curving across the corner of a boundary hedge.

The 5th, turning at right angles, takes us down over the brook and is the last of the holes before crossing the busy railway line which divides the course. From the golfing point of view, the railway is not readily accessible, the drives at the 6th and 7th being angled away from the fence on the right, but each has a most satisfying second when executed properly and anyone would be glad to attempt the next three holes alongside the deep pine woods of Harlestone Firs with the encouragement of two fours.

Back under the railway again, the short 11th re-introduces us to the brook which, running diagonally this time, is far more of a threat, and takes us on to the 12th (440 yds) which the handicapper deems as the first stroke hole—a decision no doubt influenced by the shape of an unusually undulating green.

The surroundings are now fairly thickly dotted with crops of gorse and broom and the drive at the 13th (321 yds) over a low wall of such bushes is perhaps the narrowest of all. Thereafter, apart from the 16th with its strategically-placed hidden bunker beside the green, the gorse should be decorative rather than destructive, but the finish is nicely testing for all that.

The second at the 14th must carry another attracting bunker. The short 15th between guardian oaks rewards the truly hit stroke better than most short holes, and finally the 17th and 18th, especially with the wind from a westerly quarter, can mean two fives or maybe worse.

If that is so, it is unlikely that the par of 69 will have been broken but, be that as it may, it should have no effect on the fun and, as the visitor slips quietly away down the drive and makes for Northampton and beyond, Northamptonshire County will assuredly join a list of clubs that provide him with a splendid day out. In a part of England that is not always renowned for its golf courses, Church Brampton is certainly one that stands apart.

Society Meetings Wed. min. 24, Mon. and Thurs. max. 24.
Hotels: Westone, Weston Favell; Saxon Inn Motel, Northampton; Rugby Post House, Crick.
Lunches and teas served.

H 40   North Oxford

Oxford 54924.
Banbury Rd., Oxford OX2 8EZ.
2½ miles N of city centre, just past roundabout on A40 towards Banbury on A423.
Parkland course.
18 holes, 5805 yds. S.S.S. 67
Visitors welcome.
Green Fees. Weekdays £5.00; weekends £7.00.
Society Meetings by arrangement.
Snacks and meals served except Mon.

H 41   Oundle

Tel. Oundle 3267
Benefield Rd., Oundle, Peterborough.
On A427 1 mile W of Oundle.
Undulating parkland course.
18 holes, 5271 yds. S.S.S. 66
Visitors welcome weekdays, weekends restricted.

Green Fees. Weekdays £3.50; weekends £4.50.
Society Meetings weekdays by arrangement.
Hotels: Talbot Hotel.
Meals served by arrangement.

H 42   Peterborough Milton

Tel. Castor (073 121) 489 and 204.
Milton Ferry, Peterborough PE6 7AG.
On A47 4 miles W of Peterborough. Leave A1 at Wansford turn-off 4 miles E on A47.
Parkland course.
18 holes, 6441 yds. S.S.S. 71
Course designed by James Braid.
Visitors welcome.
Green Fees. Weekdays £5.00 (£2.50 with member); weekends £7.50 (£4.00 with member).
Society Meetings welcome on weekdays except Mon.
Hotels: Haycock, Wansford; Saxon Inn, Peterborough.
Meals served except Mon.

H 43   Priors Hall

Tel. Corby (05366) 4922
Stamford Rd., Weldon, Corby, Northants.

1 mile E of Weldon village on A43.
Parkland course.
18 holes, 6677 yds. S.S.S. 72
Visitors welcome.
Green Fees. Weekdays £2.00 per round; weekends and bank holidays £3.00 per round.
Society Meetings by arrangement.
Hotels: Strathclyde; Raven, Corby.
Snacks served; meals served except Tues.

H 44   Rushden & District

Tel. Rushden 2581
Chelveston, Wellingborough, Northants.
On A45, 2 miles from Higham Ferrers E towards St. Neots.
Parkland course.
10 holes, 6200 yds. S.S.S. 70
Course designed by C. Catlow.
Visitors welcome on weekdays except Wed. p.m.
Green Fees. Weekdays £5.00 (£3.00 with member).
Society Meetings welcome on weekdays except Wed. Numbers restricted.
Hotels: Green Dragon, Higham Ferrers; Westward, Rushden.
Meals served by arrangement.

Tadmarton, a testing time in the gorse

It is natural, I suppose, that golf clubs should develop a more strongly individual character or atmosphere than clubs of other kinds, and in this country where there is such a variety of courses it is not surprising that this impression is more marked than anywhere else in the world.

At the older championship links—St. Andrews, Prestwick, Royal St. George's, Westward Ho! and so on—there is an atmosphere that is at once distinguishable from all the others, but the same applies to many less celebrated clubs upon which the public gaze is seldom directed. When I was invited to play at Tadmarton Heath in North Oxfordshire, this fact was quickly confirmed.

Perhaps my feelings were influenced by having achieved the perfect escape from the general confusion of Christmas week; or maybe the drive from Banbury Cross through the neighbouring countryside formed an unusually romantic introduction to the golf, but much respected opinion had told me that Tadmarton Heath—one of only seven clubs in the county—had many fine qualities. If it was a course that Roger Wethered saw fit to play as often as he could, it is surely one that is good enough for most of us.

In an age when there is so much emphasis on power and stretching holes to limits for which they were not designed, it was encouraging to see from a glance at the card that Tadmarton measured well below 6,000 yards, but in this case bare details were deceptive. In winds that never miss those exposed parts it must frequently seem to play about twice its normal length.

As a course it has what may conveniently be described as a split personality, the first nine holes being fairly open and the second nine possessing a characteristic commonly associated with heathland golf —a profusion of gorse which makes some of the fairways alarmingly narrow.

As this tests a player's nerve at a critical point in the round, it is as well that there should have been temptation earlier to open the shoulders, but for all the latitude that may be allowed, there are many splendidly demanding second shots—particularly those at the 1st, 2nd, 4th, 6th and 9th—which can only be negotiated successfully from drives that have been strategically placed.

The first seven holes do not stray far from the clubhouse, the short 7th—with its attractive shot over the waters of the Holy Well which are said to provide a cure for rheumatism—bringing some danger to its walls and windows. But the fun really begins when the 9th turns away alongside the road by the gate and the short 10th (114 yds) induces a tremble or two at the prospect of seeing more of the prominent bunker and the intervening gorse than of the freely undulating green.

Gorse again dominates the drive over the distant ridge at the 11th and the cleverly angled second at the 14th, where a slice off the tee is not to be recommended, but the 15th (288 yds) and the 17th (365 yds), despite their innocent length, are the two holes where the slightest deviation from the fairway inevitably decrees a prickly fate.

Although the 18th immediately provides relief on the right, the staunchest of hopes may already have been destroyed, though even that need be no cause for discontent.

All around the scene is one of simple beauty and tranquillity. The whirl of traffic is far away, and ahead, in the warmth of the old Cotswold stone clubhouse that was converted from a farmhouse, lies the assurance that all thoughts of golf can, if necessary, be dulled—though not, let me hasten to add, the urge to try again.

H 45   South Bedfordshire

Tel. Luton (0582) 591500
Warden Hill, Luton, Beds. LU2 7AA.
3 miles N of town on A6 to Bedford.
2 well-drained courses.
Galley Course 18 holes, 6362 yds. S.S.S. 70
Warden Course 9 holes, 5190 yds. S.S.S.65
Visitors welcome on weekdays.
Green Fees. Weekdays £4.00 per round, £5.00 per day; weekends £6.00 per round, £7.00 per day.
Society Meetings welcome.
Meals, snacks available at most times.

H 46   Southfield

Tel. Oxford 42158
Hill Top Rd., Oxford OX4 1PF.
Cowley Rd., Southfield Rd., then right into Hill Top Rd.
Undulating parkland course.
18 holes, 6236 yds. S.S.S. 70
Visitors welcome on weekdays; weekends with member only.
Green Fees. £5.00.
Society Meetings by arrangement, max. 40.
Hotels: Eastgate Hotel.
Meals served daily except Mon.

H 47   Staverton Park

Tel. Daventry (032 72) 5911
Staverton, Daventry, Northants. NN11 6JB
Exit J16 on M1, A425.
Parkland course.
18 holes, 6507 yds. S.S.S. 71
Course designed by Commander John D. Harris.
Visitors welcome weekdays; 18 handicap limit at weekends.
Green Fees. Weekdays £5.00 per day; weekends and bank holidays £7.00 per day.
Society Meetings catered for Mon. to Sat.
Restaurant, grill room, bar snacks. Accommodation within club.

H 48   Stockwood Park

Tel. Luton (0582) 413704
Stockwood Park, Luton, Beds.
1 mile S of city centre on A6. 2 miles from M1 junction 10.
Parkland course.
18 holes, 6276 yds. S.S.S. 70
Visitors welcome.
Green Fees. Weekdays £2.10; weekends £3.15. O.A.P.s £1 weekdays.

Society Meetings weekdays by arrangement.
Hotels: Strathmore; Esso Motel; Crest Motel.
Meals served.

H 49   Stoke Poges

Tel. Slough 26385
Park Rd., Stoke Poges, Slough, Bucks. SL2 4PG.
Turn N off A4 at Slough into Stoke Poges Lane, club is 1½ miles on left.
Parkland, woodland course.
18 holes, 6646 yds. S.S.S. 72
Course designed by H.S. Colt (1908).
Visitors welcome on weekdays with handicap certificate.
Green Fees. £10.50 per day.
Society Meetings welcome Wed., Thurs. and Fri.
Hotels: Bellhouse, Beaconsfield; Bull, Gerrards Cross.
Snacks served; lunches except Mon.

H 50   Tadmarton Heath

Tel. Hook Norton 737278 (0608) STD
Wiggington, Banbury, Oxon. OX15 5HL.
5 miles from Banbury on B4035.

The Duchess takes her bow

When the idea of golf at Woburn was first conceived, the Duke's and Duchess courses were planned and cleared together. As events turned out, the Duchess was delayed while the Duke's earned immediate praise, but now the Duchess forms a twin attraction that has few equals anywhere.

In terms of character, the two courses have much in common, arising from the same dense forest in which it was virtually impossible six or seven years ago to see more than ten yards ahead. The massive tree felling operation was the biggest ever undertaken on a new course in Britain but from the moment in the summer of 1979 when 18 holes on the Duchess were open for play, a remarkable story was complete.

The story of the Duchess was remarkable in itself. Work only began on its construction in the summer of 1978, and in May 1979, after the severest winter for many years, half of it was not yet sown. Yet by October of that year all 18 holes were being played. No praise therefore can be too great for Woburn's greenkeeping staff who, in addition to preparing the Duke's for the Dunlop Masters, undertook the work themselves under the guiding hand of Derek Green, the Head Greenkeeper.

Having been entrusted with the privilege of interpreting the wishes of the late Charles Lawrie who designed both courses, it was stimulating for me to be involved in such an exercise. Harmonious dealings with the Club Director, Oliver Green, and frequent inspections of the site meant that the closest possible understanding was achieved. Adjustments to the shape and levels of greens were made entirely to mould with the natural contours, thus avoiding the regular

patterns which appear althogether more artificial.

At the end, it was impossible for any of us to believe that we would ever find a finer piece of land for an inland golf course in Britain, or that you could improve on the arrangement whereby a course is built by those who subsequently have to look after it.

One possible disadvantage of such a close connection with its creation is that it might blur judgement. However, it is something I must risk in a description of a course which forms a nice contrast to its neighbour. The Duchess is not as long; nor does it have the spectacular rises and falls that mark the beginning of the Duke's but it is a supreme test of the art of control, manoeuvrability and varied shotmaking.

There is always one place on almost every fairway from which the second shot is easier, and the feeling of escape which the beauty of the surroundings engenders is overwhelming. With the sun piercing the trees, highlighting the colours of beech, birch and pine, many a care will be forgotten; yet the fact remains that Woburn's courses are only a tiny, elevated backwater. All around, Bedfordshire and Buckinghamshire offer an example of how quickly things change and only just across the fields, a busy motorway is submerged in noise.

The enjoyment of the Duchess lies in an ideal balance of its holes. There is contrast in the par fives; the short holes vary nicely in length and there is a good mixture of par fours from a drive and pitch to two full shots. The 1st gives a good first impression, the distant green on an elusive plateau being reached only with a well struck second from a tumbling fairway.

In four holes, in fact, there is all the variation you can have. The 2nd, a par 3, needs a shot through the eye of a needle; the 3rd calls for a straight drive and well judged pitch over a belt of heather and the 4th, a left hand dogleg, is a par 5 where there are plenty of ways of taking six.

The 5th green in its alcove of giant beech is the first on the other side of the lane leading down to Bow Brickhill Church while the 6th, changing direction yet again, rewards positional play more than most par fives.

It is a rare feature that no two consecutive holes follow the same direction and the short 7th twists back over the ancient earthworks that make an excellent golfing landmark. Next comes the 8th, a ciassic dogleg to a three level green and then the turn is reached by way of the 9th green which, like the 10th tee, needed enormous build-up.

Over the brow at the 10th, the chief hazard is the angled green but the 11th, 12th and 13th all have distinctive markings, the 13th occupying a natural, little punchbowl. From there it is over the road again with two spanking two shot holes for the experts and two three shot holes for the rest.

There is no doubt that the finish is demanding but the 16th and 17th offer scenic relief, if nothing else; and by then the 18th is the only obstacle, though a tough one, between you and the non-golfing delights which Woburn has to offer. Swimming, tennis and squash await those with the fitness and energy to tackle them but a relaxing drink will be the comfort that most seek. In which case, you can look out on a sylvan setting of peace and tranquility; and ponder whether golf has anything better to offer.

Heathland course.
18 holes, 5917 yds. S.S.S. 69
Course designed by Maj. C.K. Hutchinson and Harry Vardon.
Visitors welcome on weekdays, weekends with member or with reservation.
Green Fees. On application.
Society Meetings welcome.
Hotels: Whateley Hall Hotel; Manor Hotel, Banbury; Wroxton Hotel, Wroxton; Manor House Hotel, Morton-in-Marsh.
Meals served except Mon.

H 51   Wellingborough

Tel. Wellingborough (0933) 677234
Great Harrowden Hall, Wellingborough, Northants. NN9 5AD.
On A509, 2 miles from Wellingborough.
Parkland course.

18 holes, 6421 yds. S.S.S. 71
Course designed by F.W. Hawtree and Son.
Visitors welcome weekdays only.
Green Fees. £5.00.
Society Meetings Wed., Thurs. and Fri.
Hotels: Hind Hotel.
Lunches, teas, evening meals served.

H 52   Weston Turville

Tel. Aylesbury (0296) 24084
New Rd., Weston Turville, Nr. Aylesbury, Bucks. HP22 5QT.
2½ miles from Aylesbury towards London, between A41 and A413; follow signs to Weston Turville village.
Parkland course.
9 holes, 6027 yds. S.S.S. 69
Visitors welcome.
Green Fees. Weekdays £3.00 per day;

weekends £4.00 per 18 holes.
Society Meetings by arrangement.
Hotels: Red Lion, Wendover.
Bar snacks and meals served.

H 53   Whiteleaf

Tel. Princes Risborough 3097
Whiteleaf, Princes Risborough, Aylesbury, Bucks.
1 mile from Princes Risborough on Aylesbury Rd. turn right for Whiteleaf.
Parkland course.
9 holes, 5359 yds. S.S.S. 66
Visitors welcome on weekdays; weekends with member only.
Green Fees. £5.00 per 18 holes, £7.00 per day.
Hotels: George & Dragon, Princes Risborough.
Meals served by arrangement.

H 54   Windmill Hill

Tel. Milton Keynes (0908) 78623
Tattenhoe Lane, Bletchley, Milton Keynes, Bucks.
Meadowland course.
18 holes, 6869 yds. S.S.S. 73
Course designed by Henry Cotton.
Visitors welcome.
Green Fees. Weekdays £2.10; weekends £3.20.
Society Meetings by arrangement.
Snacks, grills served; meals for parties by arrangement.

H 55   Woburn Golf & Country Club

Tel. Milton Keynes 70756
Bow Brickhill, Milton Keynes MK17 9LJ.
A5 to Little Brickhill, E at Woburn signposts for ½ mile, left at fork.
Heathland courses.
18 holes, 6861 yds. S.S.S. 74
18 holes, 6616 yds. S.S.S. 72
Course designed by Cotton (C.K.) Pennink, Lawrie and Partners.
Visitors welcome on weekdays by arrangement.
Green Fees. On application to Secretary.
Society Meetings welcome on weekdays.
Hotels: in Milton Keynes, Luton and Woburn.
Meals served.

H 56   Woodlands

Tel. Preston Capes (023736) 291
Farthingstone, Towcester, Northants NN12 8MA.
Junction 16 M1. W of A5 between Weedon and Towcester.
Undulating woodland.
18 holes, 6125 yds. S.S.S. 70
Visitors welcome on weekdays, weekends with reservation.
Green Fees. Weekdays £3.50 per day, £2.50 after 3.00 p.m.; weekends £5.00 per day, £3.00 after 3.00 p.m.
Society Meetings welcome on weekdays, some Sats. by arrangement.
Hotels: Saraccins, Towcester; Crossroads, Weedon.
Meals and snacks served.

H 57   Wyboston Lakes

Tel. Huntingdon (0480) 212501
Wyboston, Beds.
A428 2 miles S of St. Neots adjacent to junction with A1.
New meadowland course with water hazards.
18 holes, S.S.S. 68.
Course designed by Hoveringham Leisure and Estates Ltd.
Visitors welcome weekdays and weekends.
Green Fees. Weekdays £2.70; weekends £3.50.
Society Meetings welcome at any time by arrangement.
Hotels: Brampton; Bridge, Huntingdon.
No catering facilities at present; clubhouse under construction.

Suffolk, Norfolk, Cambridgeshire

I 1   Aldeburgh

Tel. Aldeburgh (072885) 2890
Aldeburgh, Suffolk.
On A1094 1 mile from town centre.
Seaside courses.
18 holes, 6344 yds. S.S.S. 71
9 holes, 4228 yds. S.S.S. 62
Visitors welcome.
Green Fees. Weekdays £5.00 per round, £7.20 per day; weekends £6.50 per round, £8.20 per day. Reductions in winter. River course (9 holes): weekdays £2.00 per day; weekends £2.50 per day.
Society Meetings welcome.
Hotels: Brudenell; Wentworth; White Lion; Uplands.
Lunches served during summer, snack lunches only during winter.

I 2   Barnham Broom Golf & Country Club

Tel. 060 545 393
Norwich, Norfolk NR9 4DD.
Off A47 7 miles SW of Norwich.
Meadowland course.
18 holes, 6603 yds. S.S.S. 72
Course designed by Cotton (C.K.), Pennink, Lawrie and Partners.
Visitors welcome.
Green Fees. Weekdays £5.00 (£3.00 with member); weekends £5.00 with member. Special rates for parties over 10.
Society Meetings welcome on weekdays. Special arrangements for hotel guests on breakaway weekends.
Hotel: adjacent to course.
Meals and snacks served.

I 3   Beccles

Tel. Beccles 712244
The Common, Beccles, Suffolk.
1 mile off A146, 9 miles W of Lowestoft.
Heathland course.
9 holes, 5392 yds. S.S.S. 66
Visitors welcome on weekdays, weekends with member only.
Green Fees. Weekdays £3.00 (£2.50 with member); weekends £3.50 (£3.00 with member).
Hotels: Kings Head; Waveney House Hotel.
Snacks served.

I 4   Bungay & Waveney Valley

Tel. Bungay (0986) 2337
Outney Common, Bungay, Suffolk NR35 1DS.
¼ mile from town centre, 14 miles W of Lowestoft.
Moorland course.
18 holes, 5901 yds. S.S.S. 68
Visitors welcome on weekdays, weekends with member only.
Green Fees. £5.00 (£2.50 with member).
Society Meetings by arrangement.
Hotels: Swan; Magpie, Harleston; King's Head, Beccles; King's Head, Bungay.
Snack lunches served by arrangement.

I 5   Bury St. Edmunds

Tel. Bury St. Edmunds (0284) 5979
Tut Hill, Bury St. Edmunds, Suffolk.
On A45 from Newmarket turn left at roundabout W of Bury on B1106.
Parkland course.
18 holes, 6615 yds. S.S.S. 72
Course designed by Ted Ray.
Visitors welcome on weekdays, after 10 a.m. on Sat. and Sun. unless playing with member.
Green Fees. Weekdays £6.00 per day (£3.00 with member); weekends £8.00 (£4.00 with member).
Society Meetings welcome on weekdays.
Hotels: Angel; Suffolk; Grange.
Meals served.

I 6   Cambridgeshire Hotel

Tel. Crafts Hill (0954) 80555
Bar Hill, Cambs.
Off A604, 4 miles NW of Cambridge.
Undulating parkland course.
18 holes, 6734 yds. S.S.S. 72
Course designed by Fraser Middleton.
Visitors welcome with reservation.
Green Fees. Weekdays £6.00; weekends £7.50.
Society Meetings welcome by arrangement.
Hotels: Cambridgeshire Hotel.
Meals served.

I 7   Dereham

Tel. Dereham (0362) 3122/5900 (Sec.)
Quebec Rd., Dereham, Norfolk NR19 2DS.
½ mile from town centre on B1135, 16 miles W of Norwich.
Parkland course.
9 holes, 6133 yds. S.S.S. 69
Visitors welcome with letter of introduction.
Green Fees. £4.00, £5.50.
Society Meetings by arrangement.
Hotels: Phoenix; Kings Head; George.
Meals available by arrangement.

I 8   Diss

Tel. Diss 2847
Stuston, Diss, Norfolk.
B1077 off A140.
Commonland course.
9 holes, 5824 yds. S.S.S. 68
Visitors welcome.
Hotels: Park Hotel; Kings Head, Diss.
Green Fees. £4.00 (£2.00 with member).
Meals served.

I 9 Eaton

Tel. Norwich 52881
Newmarket Rd., Norwich NR4 6SF.
Parkland course.
18 holes, 6076 yds. S.S.S. 69
Visitors welcome on weekdays.
Green Fees. Weekdays £4.60; weekends £5.75.
Lunches served Mon. to Thurs.

I 10 Ely City

Tel. Ely 2751
Cambridge Rd., Ely, Cambs. CB7 4HX.
On A10 15 miles N of Cambridge.
Meadowland course.
18 holes, 6686 yds. S.S.S. 72
Course designed by Henry Cotton.
Visitors welcome.
Green Fees. Weekdays £5.00 (£2.00 with member); weekends £6.50 (£3.50 with member).
Society Meetings by arrangement.
Hotels: Lamb Hotel; Knighton House Guest House.
Full catering service.

I 11 Fakenham

Tel. Fakenham (0328) 2867
Sports Centre, The Race Course, Fakenham, Norfolk.
B1146 from Dereham or A1067 from Norwich.
Parkland course.
9 holes, 5636 yds. S.S.S. 67
Visitors welcome.
Green Fees. Weekdays £3.00 (£1.50 with member); weekends £4.00 (£2.00 with member).
Hotels: Crown; Limes.

I 12 Felixstowe Ferry

Tel. Felixstowe (03942) 6834 mornings only.
Felixstowe, Suffolk IP11.
A45 from Ipswich.
Seaside course.
18 holes, 6308 yds. S.S.S. 70
Course redesigned by Henry Cotton.
Visitors welcome.
Green Fees. £5.00 per round, £7.00 per day; weekends £6.00 per round, £8.00 per day.
Society Meetings welcome on weekdays.

Hotels: Orwell Moat House Hotel; Highcliff; Fludyers.
Lunches and teas served. Evening meals by arrangement.

I 13 Flempton

Tel. Culford 291
Flempton, Bury St. Edmunds, Suffolk 1P28 6EQ.
On A1101, 5 miles NE of Bury St. Edmunds.
Meadowland course.
9 holes, 6050 yds. S.S.S. 69
Visitors welcome on weekdays with reservation, weekends with member only.
Green Fees. Weekdays £5.50 (£3.00 with member); weekends and bank holidays £6.00 (£3.00 with member).
Society Meetings weekdays by arrangement.
Bar snacks available; lunches by arrangement.

I 14 Girton

Tel. Cambridge (0223) 276169
Dodford Lane, Girton, Cambs. CB3 0QE.
3 miles N of Cambridge.
18 holes, 5728 yds. S.S.S. 68

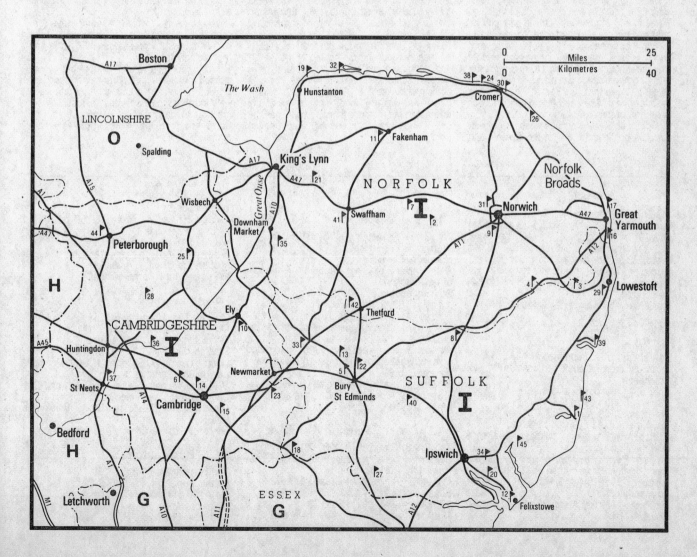

Brancaster, where time stands still

Hunstanton and the Royal West Norfolk club at Brancaster are two of several courses throughout the British Isles which naturally divide themselves into groups of neighbours and about which there is considerable diversity of feeling.

For a long time, I had been unable to take part in the discussion because I had never been to Brancaster, and clearly this was a terrible confession; but one grey morning when the golfers of Oxford and Cambridge were beginning their match at Hunstanton in 1966 I set off along the coast road to put things right.

Hunstanton's staging of English women's and men's championships is proof of its many qualities, and I shall always associate it happily with my very first match for Cambridge, and the accompanying realization that success on occasions of that kind came in learning one's lunchtime capacity for port and barley wine, and never exceeding it.

For these reasons, I will not hear a word against Hunstanton, but from the moment that one turns by the old church in Brancaster village down through the marsh to the club, it is easy to see that little has changed since it was formed in 1891 and that in consequence it has an appeal all of its own.

Golf, with a very definite seaside character, has continued in one of the quietest and most remote spots in England, and, except for one or two minor alterations, time has virtually stood still. The clubhouse, on the edge of the strand, stands at one end of the course, which like many seaside links goes straight out and straight back, and is flanked on the inland side by a great expanse of flat saltmarsh.

This creeps down through channels from the harbour at Brancaster Staithe and when the tide is unusually high, these deserted wastes and the little lane, the club's only link by car, become flooded.

The clubhouse can be cut off for hours and the course is an island, but this is an added charm and excitement. There is a grandeur to the golf, particularly at the far end by the 8th and 9th, a distant point which offers one of the most peaceful views in the world—a foreground of small boats, river and marsh and a background of sandy wilderness by Scolt Head.

The prospect from the 8th tee is not quite so friendly, because the course of the marsh and its tributaries, which are treated as a hazard, splits the hole into three. There is nothing quite like it anywhere else that I know but, flood or no flood, golfers invariably attempt to cut off more than they can manage and if they are unsuccessful, then heaven help them.

The 9th is another magnificent hole in which the marsh plays its sinister part from the tee, and when that is surmounted there is a huge dark, sleepered bunker to be cleared before the green in among the dunes and the turn are reached. Sleepers are not a weapon of the modern architect but they are still menacing and one is glad to be turning for home with a short hole, though like all those at the seaside, it can vary enormously according to prevailing conditions.

Coming home that day in March, a cold wind was against us and there was a lot of honest hitting to be done. The short 13th was almost out of range; the 14th (430 yds) was two mighty strokes to its green in a sandy dell by the beach; the 15th was another difficult three, and the 16th, 17th and 18th, though all well under 400 yards, are never easy fours.

The fairways, which in early days are reported to have been a little rough, were excellent, and the greens beautifully true and frighteningly fast.

Many courses pose longer and more difficult problems than Brancaster, but few provide as much fun and, as my companion —who retired to Norfolk and seldom allows a morning to pass without a round or a few holes—assured me, it never grows wearisome.

Visitors welcome on weekdays.
Green Fees. Weekdays £5.00 per round (£2.50 with member), £6.00 per day (£3.00 with member); weekends £2.50 per round, £3.00 per day with member only.
Society Meetings welcome on weekdays.
Hotels: University Arms; Garden House, Cambridge.
Meals served by arrangement except Mon.

I 15   Gog Magog

Tel. Cambridge (0223) 47626
Babraham Rd., Cambridge CB2 4AB.
3 miles from Cambridge on A604 to Colchester.
Undulating meadowland course.
9 holes, 5850 yds. S.S.S. 68
18 holes, 6263 yds. S.S.S. 70
Course designed by F.W. Hawtree.
Visitors welcome on weekdays, weekends with member only.
Green Fees. 18 hole course £7.50 per round or day; 9 hole course £5.00 per round.
Society Meetings Tues. and Thurs. by arrangement.
Hotels: University Arms; Blue Boar; Garden House Hotel.
Meals served.

I 16   Gorleston

Tel. Great Yarmouth (0493) 61082
Warren Rd., Gorleston, Great Yarmouth, Norfolk NR31 6JT.
A12 3 miles S of Great Yarmouth, 7 miles N of Lowestoft.
Seaside course.
18 holes, 6279 yds. S.S.S. 70
Course designed by J.H. Taylor.
Visitors welcome if members of recognized club.
Green Fees. Weekdays £4.50 per round or day; weekends £5.50 per round or day; weekly £15.00.
Society Meetings welcome on weekdays.
Hotels: St. Edmunds; Cliff; Links.
Meals served except Mon.

I 17   Great Yarmouth & Caister

Tel. Great Yarmouth (0493) 728699
Beach House, Caister-on-Sea, Great Yarmouth, Norfolk NR30 5TD.
On A149, 2 miles N of Great Yarmouth.
Seaside course.
18 holes, 6254 yds. S.S.S. 70
Visitors welcome on weekdays and Sun. after 11.30. Proof of club membership must be produced.
Green Fees. Weekdays £5.50 per round or day; weekends £6.00 per round or day; weekly £16.00; fortnightly £26.00.
Society Meetings by arrangement.
Hotels: in Great Yarmouth.
Meals served by arrangement.

I 18   Haverhill

Coupals Rd., Haverhill, Suffolk.
On A604, ½ mile SE of Haverhill.
Undulating meadowland course.
9 holes, 5470 yds. S.S.S. 68
Course designed by Cotton (C.K.), Pennink, Lawrie and Partners.
Visitors welcome except 1st Sat. and 3rd Sun. mornings each month.
Green Fees. Weekdays £1.85; weekends £2.65.
Hotels: Rose & Crown; Australian Arms.

I 19   Hunstanton

Tel. Hunstanton (04853) 2811
Hunstanton, Norfolk PE36 6JQ.
On A149, 17 miles N of Kings Lynn.
Links course.
18 holes, 6670 yds. S.S.S. 72
Visitors welcome.

Green Fees. Nov. to Feb.: £6.00 per day. Mar. to Oct.: weekdays £6.00 per day; weekends £7.50. Half rates for juniors or visitors with members.
Society Meetings welcome.
Hotels: Le Strange Arms; Golden Lion; Neptune; Linksway.
Lunches and teas served.

I 20   Ipswich

Tel. Ipswich 78941
Purdis Heath, Ipswich, Suffolk IP3 8UQ.
3miles E of town centre. A45, turn left at St. Augustines Church roundabout into Bucklesham Rd., ¼ mile on left.
Heathland course.
18 holes, 6405 yds. S.S.S. 71
9 holes, 3900 yds. Par 62
Course designed by James Braid (1927).
Visitors welcome. For 18 hole course letter of introduction or handicap certificate required.
Green Fees. On application.
Society Meetings welcome on weekdays.
Hotels: Great White Horse; Marlborough; Copdock; The Post House.
Full catering service.

I 21   King's Lynn

Tel. Castle Rising (0553 87) 654
Castle Rising, Norfolk PE31 6BD.
4 miles NE of King's Lynn between South Wootton and Castle Rising.
Woodland course.
18 holes, 6514 yds. S.S.S. 71
Visitors welcome if members of recognized club.
Green Fees. Weekdays £6.90 per round or day; weekends £8.00 per round or day.
Society Meetings welcome on weekdays by arrangement.
Hotels: Dukes Head, King's Lynn.
Snacks, lunches and teas served.

I 22   Lark Valley Country Club

Tel. Bury St. Edmunds 63426
Fornham St. Martin, Bury St. Edmunds, Suffolk.
Off A45 at Bury St. Edmunds (A1101 turn-off Mildenhall), or off A134 Bury-Thetford at Culford Rd., Fornham St. Martin.
18 holes, 6241 yds. S.S.S. 70
Visitors welcome.
Green Fees. Weekdays £3.00; weekends £4.00.
Society Meetings welcome.
Hotels: Suffolk Hotel; Angel Hotel, Bury St. Edmunds.
Lunches served; dinners served Tues. to Sat.

I 23   Links

Tel. Newmarket 3000 (Sec.)
Cambridge Rd., Newmarket, Suffolk.
1 mile from centre of town opposite racecourse.
Parkland course.
18 holes, 6402 yds. S.S.S. 71
Course designed by Col. Hotchkin.
Visitors welcome on weekdays, after 11 a.m. at weekends.
Green Fees. Weekdays £5.00 per round, £7.00 per day; weekends £7.00 per round, £8.00 per day.

Society Meetings by arrangement.
Hotels: Rutland Arms; White Hart; Bedford Lodge.
Meals served.

I 24   Links Country Park

Tel. West Runton (026 375) 691
West Runton, Cromer, Norfolk.
A148 Holt-Cromer, turn left 6 miles from Holt by Roman Camp public house, signposted West Runton; course ½ mile on right.
Seaside downland course.
9 holes, 4902 yds. S.S.S. 64
Visitors welcome.
Green Fees. Weekdays £3.50 (£2.50 with member); weekends £4.00 (£3.00).
Society Meetings welcome weekdays.
Hotels: Links Country Park Hotel adjacent to course.
Buffet lunch and dinner; full meals in evening.

I 25   March

Tel. March 2364
Frogs Abbey, Grange Rd., March, Cambs.
W off bypass.
Parkland course.
9 holes, 6278 yds. S.S.S. 70
Visitors welcome if members of recognized club.
Green Fees. Weekdays £4.00; weekends £5.00.
Hotels: Men of March; White Horse.

I 26   Mundesley

Tel. Mundesley 720095
Links Rd., Mundesley, Norwich NR11 8ES.
On A148, 7 miles SE of Cromer.
Seaside course.
9 holes, 5376 yds. S.S.S. 66
Visitors welcome except Wed. 12.30 p.m. to 3.30 p.m. and Sun. 8 a.m. to 11.30 a.m.
Green Fees. Weekdays £4.00 per day; weekends and bank holidays £5.00 per day.
Hotels: Manor Hotel; Royal.
Meals served by arrangement.

I 27   Newton Green

Tel. Sudbury 77501
Newton Green, Sudbury, Suffolk.
On A134, 3 miles E of Sudbury.
Moorland course.
9 holes, 5442 yds. S.S.S. 66
Visitors welcome on weekdays, weekends with member only.
Green Fees. £4.00 (£2.00 with member).
Hotels: Saracen's Head.

I 28   Ramsey

Tel. Ramsey (0487) 812600/813573
Abbey Terrace, Ramsey, Huntingdon, Cambs. PE17 1DD.
Off B1040, 11 miles SE of Peterborough.
Parkland course.
18 holes, 6041 yds. S.S.S. 70
Course designed by J. Hamilton Stutt.
Visitors welcome.
Green Fees. Weekdays £6.00 per day (£3.00 with member); weekends £8.50 per day (£4.50 with member).
Society Meetings welcome on weekdays.
Bar snacks served; lunches weekdays by arrangement.

I 29   Rookery Park

Tel. Lowestoft 60380 or 4009
Carlton Colville, Lowestoft, Suffolk NR33 8HJ.
On A146 W of Lowestoft.
Parkland course.
18 holes, 6645 yds. S.S.S. 72
Course designed by C.D. Lawrie.
Visitors welcome weekdays, weekends with reservation.
Green Fees. Weekdays £5.00; weekends £6.00.
Society Meetings welcome on weekdays.
Meals served except Mon.

I 30   Royal Cromer

Tel. Cromer (0263) 512219
Overstrand Rd., Cromer, Norfolk NR27 0JH.
On B1159, ½ mile SE of Cromer.
Seaside course.
18 holes, 6636 yds. S.S.S. 72
Course designed by James Braid.
Visitors welcome on weekdays and Sat.
Green Fees. Weekdays £5.00 per day; Sat. £6.50 per day.
Society Meetings welcome on weekdays, max. 28.
Hotels: Cliff House Hotel; Cliftonville; Red Lion.
Meals served except Tues.

I 31   Royal Norwich

Tel. Norwich 45712 or 49928 (Sec.)
Drayton Rd., Hellesdon, Norwich, Norfolk NR6 5AH.
Centre of city and then by A1067 Fakenham or via Ring Rd., then 500 yds along A1067.
Parkland course.
18 holes, 6603 yds. S.S.S. 72
Visitors welcome with club membership card, weekends with member only.
Green Fees. Weekdays £6.00 per round, £9.00 per day; weekends £7.50 per round, £10.00 per day.
Lunches and teas served.

I 32   Royal West Norfolk

Tel. Brancaster 223
Brancaster, King's Lynn, Norfolk PE31 8AX.
On A149, 7 miles E of Hunstanton.
Seaside course.
Course designed by Horace Hutchinson (1891).
Visitors welcome; weekends Jul. to Sept. with member only.
Green Fees. Weekdays £7.00 per round or day; weekends £8.50 per round or day.
Society Meetings by arrangement.
Hotels: Ship, Brancaster; Manor, Titchwell.
Snacks served; lunches served at weekends, weekdays by arrangement.

I 33   Royal Worlington & New-market

Tel. Mildenhall (0638) 712216
Worlington, Bury St. Edmunds, Suffolk.
A11, 7 miles NE of Newmarket.
9 holes, 6218 yds. S.S.S. 70
Visitors welcome.
Society Meetings welcome, max. 30.
Hotels: Bull Hotel, Barton Mills.
Lunches and teas served.

Worlington, best nine holes in the world

Most of us, at some time or another, have whiled away a nostalgic half-hour compiling a list of all the golf courses on which we have played, and have then perhaps been moved to wonder which we would choose if the remainder of our golfing lifetime were restricted to one alone.

It is a heart-rending task but if, for various reasons, the choice is eased by the introduction of two categories—seaside and inland—my ideal inland retreat would, without any doubt, be Royal Worlington and Newmarket.

This has been described as the best nine-hole course in the world, a claim I make no attempt to dispute or confirm, but having played round the tiny, triangular oasis between Newmarket and Thetford a good many times, it would be hard to imagine any course—of any length—where the pleasures of the golf and the peacefulness of a rural setting blend more naturally.

Rather like St. Andrews, at first sight it may not quite measure up to all the tributes paid to it but the more familiar it becomes the more the special quality of the golf becomes evident and never for a moment is one deterred by the prospect of playing the same holes eight times in a weekend. Rather the opposite.

Generations of Cambridge golfers have been blessed by being allowed to adopt it as their golfing home and, for this reason, they are one up on Oxford every March before they start. In the early days the under-graduate's journey ended with the guard producing a special pair of steps for his descent from the train at Worlington Halt, but for some years, even before the line was declared unplayable by Dr. Beeching, the fashionable means of transport has been a varied assortment of cars which, depending on their vintage, take between seventeen and thirty-five minutes for the twenty-three odd miles.

To them, the club to which they refer affectionately—though wrongly—as Mildenhall has great warmth and atmosphere, but though atmosphere can make a club, it cannot make a course and there is nowhere in Britain, especially in winter, where conditions for golf are more pleasant. This is because the sandy soil lends a seaside character and provides greens, prepared what is more with the minimum of artificial aids, which are unbelievably fast and true.

The short game in fact holds the secret of scoring at Worlington, but the course is full of excellent long shots and each hole offers something different, rather, it is said, like Beethoven's symphonies.

The nine begins with a splendid par five and is followed by a long short hole whose green is about as hard to stay on as a policeman's helmet; then comes a glorious hole that in the days of the gutty ball must have held even more menace than it does today, and later, with two more short holes in between, come the 4th, 6th and 8th that are sometimes in range of two shots and sometimes not.

The 6th offers a superb second to a green set in the gap at the end of a majestic line of pine trees; and the 8th another over a row of good old-fashioned cross-bunkers before turning for home with one of the best short par fours in the country.

The scratch man is expected to be out in about 35 but it is doubtful whether he will be, and though one of the beauties of a nine-hole course is that scores should not vary much in view of knowing exactly what to expect the second time round, this seldom applies at Worlington, where each round is different.

The celebrated short 5th with its long, glassy hog's back green, where tee shots can be in sight of a two one minute and doomed for a five the next, is no respecter of the law of averages; indeed one of the favourite local stories is of the wretched fellow who was once on the green in one and off in ten.

This may sound a slight exaggeration but anyone aware of its tortuous charm will know how readily it can happen, and I can only suggest to any further doubters that they would do well to go and see for themselves.

I 34 Rushmere

Tel. Ipswich 75648
Rushmere Heath, Ipswich, Suffolk IP4 5SS.
Off A12 just E of Ipswich.
Heathland course.
18 holes, 6287 yds. S.S.S. 70
Visitors welcome on weekdays, after 10.30a.m. at weekends.
Green Fees. On application to secretary.
Society Meetings welcome on weekdays.
Hotels: Post House; Seckford Hall Hotel.
Meals served by arrangement.

I 35 Ryston Park

Tel. Downham Market (036 63) 2133
Ely Rd., Denver, Downham Market, Norfolk PE38 0HH.
On A10 1 mile S of Downham Market.
Parkland course.
9 holes, 6292 yds. S.S.S. 70
Visitors welcome on weekdays.
Green Fees. £4.00 (£3.00 with member).
Society Meetings by arrangement.

Hotels: Castle Hotel; Crown.
Light meals served by arrangement except Thurs.

I 36 St. Ives

Tel. St. Ives (0480) 68392
High Leys, St. Ives, Huntingdon, Cambs. PE17 4RS.
Off A604, 5 miles E of Huntingdon.
Parkland course.
9 holes, 6052 yds. S.S.S. 69
Visitors welcome weekends after 11.00a.m.
Green Fees. Weekdays £5.00 per round or day (£2.50 with member); weekends and bank holidays £6.00 (£3.00 with member).
Society Meetings by arrangement.
Hotels: Slepe Hall Hotel; Golden Lion; St. Ives Motel.
Lunches served except Mon.

I 37 St. Neots

Tel. Huntingdon 72363
Crosshall Rd., St. Neots, Huntingdon, Cambs. PE19 1PJ.

Off A1, ½ mile W of St. Neots.
Wooded parkland course.
18 holes, 6005 yds. S.S.S. 69
Visitors welcome.
Green Fees. Weekdays £7.00 (£3.50 with member); weekends and bank holidays £9.00 (£4.50 with member).
Society Meetings by arrangement.
Hotels: in Huntingdon.
Meals served except Mon.

I 38 Sheringham

Tel. Sheringham (0263) 823488
Weybourne Rd., Sheringham, Norfolk NR26 8HG.
On A149, ½ mile W of town centre.
Seaside course.
18 holes, 6430 yds. S.S.S. 71
Course designed by G. Dunn.
Visitors welcome if members of recognized clubs with handicap certificate.
Green Fees. Weekdays £6.50; weekends £8.50; winter weekdays £5.00; weekends £6.50.
Society Meetings welcome Tues., Thurs.

and Fri. Weekends from May to Sept. excepted.
Hotels: Southlands, Sheringham; Cliftonville, Cromer; Maltings, Weybourne; Links, West Runton.
Meals served.

I 39 Southwold

Tel. Southwold 723234
The Common, Southwold, Suffolk.
Off A12 on A1093.
Seaside course.
9 holes, 5983 yds. S.S.S. 68
Visitors welcome with reservation.
Hotels: Swan; Crown.

I 40 Stowmarket

Tel. Rattlesden 473 (Pro 392)
Lower Rd., Onehouse, Stowmarket, Suffolk IP14 3DA.
Off B115, 3 miles W of Stowmarket.
Parkland course.
18 holes, 6119 yds. S.S.S. 69
Visitors welcome with reservation and letter of introduction.
Green Fees. Weekdays £5.00 per round, £7.00 per day; weekends £6.00 per round.
Society Meetings welcome Tues., Thurs. and Fri.
Hotels: Cedars; Fox, Stowmarket; Limes, Needham Market.
Lunches, snacks and teas served; dinners and suppers by arrangement. No meals on Mon.

I 41 Swaffham

Tel. Swaffham (0760) 21611
Cley Rd., Swaffham, Norfolk PE37 7EY.
2 miles S of Swaffham.
Moorland course.
9 holes, 6216 yds. S.S.S. 70
Visitors welcome on weekdays, Sat. and after 12.00 noon on Sun. with member only.
Green Fees. £4.00 (£2.00 with member).
Society Meetings weekdays by arrangement.
Hotels: George.
Lunches served except Mon.; evening meals served except Mon. and Thurs.

I 42 Thetford

Tel. Thetford 2258
Brandon Rd., Thetford, Norfolk IP24 3ND.
Off A11, 1½ miles W of Thetford.
Moorland, parkland course.
18 holes, 6468 yds. S.S.S. 71
Course designed by C.H. Mayo (1912).
Visitors welcome.
Green Fees. Weekdays £5.00; weekends £6.00.
Society Meetings welcome on weekdays.
Hotels: Bell Hotel; Sir Thomas Paine Hotel.
Snacks served; lunches and dinners by arrangement.

I 43 Thorpeness

Tel. Aldeburgh (0278 85) 2176
Thorpeness, Leiston, Suffolk.
On Coast road, 3 miles N of Aldeburgh.
Moorland course.
18 holes, 6241 yds. S.S.S. 71
Course designed by James Braid.

Visitors welcome with reservation.
Green Fees. Weekdays £4.50 per round, £6.50 per day; weekends and bank holidays £6.00 per round, £7.50 per day.
Society Meetings by arrangement.
Hotels: Dolphin Inn, Thorpeness; Uplands; Wentworth; Brudenall, Aldeburgh.
Snacks served; lunches except Mon. and Tues.

I 44 Thorpe Wood

Tel. Peterborough (0733) 267701, Sec. (0733) 43737
Thorpe Wood, Peterborough, Cambs. PE3 6SE.
Off A47, 2 miles W of Peterborough.
Parkland course.
18 holes, 6810 yds. S.S.S. 73
Course designed by P. Aliss, D. Thomas Ltd.
Visitors welcome.
Green Fees. Ladies and gents. Weekdays £1.90; weekends £3.30.
Society Meetings by arrangement with Professional.
Hotels: Saxon (opposite course).

I 45 Woodbridge

Tel. Woodbridge (039 43) 2038
Bromeswell Heath, Woodbridge, Suffolk.
Off A1152, 2 miles E of Woodbridge.
Heathland course.
18 holes, 6314 yds. S.S.S. 70
9 holes, 2243 yds. S.S.S. 31
Visitors welcome.
Green Fees. Weekdays £6.00 per round, £8.00 per day; weekends £7.00 per round, £9.50 per day.
Society Meetings welcome on weekdays.
Hotels: Melton Grange Hotel; Melton; Seckford Hall Hotel; Bull Hotel; Crown, Woodbridge.
Snacks served; lunches served except Mon.

J Warwickshire, Hereford & Worcester, Gloucestershire

J 1 Atherstone

Tel. Atherstone 3110
The Outwoods, Atherstone, Warwicks.
A5 to town centre then ½ mile up Coleshill Rd.
Undulating course.
9 holes, 6208 yds. S.S.S. 70
Visitors welcome.
Green Fees. £4.00 per day (£2.00 with member); Sat. £2.50 (with member only); no Sun. Green Fees.
Hotels: Red Lion.
Meals by arrangement.

J 2 Blackwell

Tel. 021-445 1470
Blackwell, Bromsgrove, Worcs.
Parkland course.
18 holes, 6105 yds. S.S.S. 70
Visitors welcome on weekdays.
Green Fees. Weekdays £8.00 (£2.50 with member).
Society Meetings welcome Wed. and Thurs. and after 4p.m. Tues. and Fri.
Meals served by arrangement.

J 3 Broadway

Tel. Broadway 3683
Willersey Hill, Broadway, Worcs. WR12 7LG.
1 mile N of A44; turn off at 'picnic area' at top of Fish Hill, Broadway.
Downland course.
18 holes, 6211 yds. S.S.S. 70
Visitors welcome if members of recognized clubs.
Green Fees. Weekdays £6.00 (£2.50 with member); weekends £8.50 (£3.50 with member).
Society Meetings by arrangement.
Hotels: Dormy House Hotel.
Meals served except Mon.

J 4 Churchill & Blakedown

Tel. Kidderminster 700200
Churchill Lane, Blakedown, Kidderminster, Worcs.
Off A456, 3 miles NE of Kidderminster.
Hilly meadowland course.
9 holes, 5399 yds. S.S.S. 67
Visitors welcome on weekdays, weekends with member only.
Green Fees. £4.00 (£2.00 with member).
Society Meetings by arrangement.
Hotels: Gainsborough; Stone Manor Hotel, Kidderminster.
Meals served except Mon.

J 5 Cirencester

Tel. Cirencester 3939
Cheltenham Rd., Bagendon, Cirencester, Glos. GL7 7BH.
On A435, 1½ miles N of Cirencester.
Parkland course.
18 holes, 6008 yds. S.S.S. 69
Visitors welcome.
Green Fees. Weekdays £5.00 (£2.50 with member); weekends £6.00 (£3.00).
Society Meetings weekdays by arrangement.
Snacks served; meals by arrangement.

J 6 Cleeve Hill Municipal

Tel. Bishop Cleeve (0242 67) 2592
Cleeve Hill, Cheltenham, Gloucestershire GL52 3PW.
Course is situated approximately 6 miles from the M5, 4 miles N of Cheltenham off the A46.
Undulating heathland course.
18 holes, 6055 yds. (Mens) 5240 yds. (Ladies) S.S.S. 70 (Mens) S.S.S. 72 (Ladies)
Visitors welcome.
Green Fees. Weekdays £2.00; weekends £2.75; O.A.P.s and juniors (weekdays only) £1.20.
Society Meetings by arrangement.
Hotels: Malvern View; De la Bere, Cleave Hill.
Meals served.

J 7 Coleford

Tel. Dean 32583
Coalway Rd., Coleford, Gloucestershire.
½ mile on right on Parkend Road from Coleford.
Parkland course.
18 holes, 5519 yds. S.S.S. 66
Visitors welcome.
Green Fees. Weekdays £3.00 per round, £4.00 per day; weekends £4.00 per round, £5.00 per day.
Society Meetings welcome.
Hotel: adjacent to course.
Meals served. Tennis courts, bowling green, swimming (summer).

J 8 Cotswold Hills

Tel. Cheltenham (0242) 515264
Ullenwood, Cheltenham, Glos. GL53 9QT.
3 miles S of Cheltenham, between A436 and B4070.
Undulating meadowland course.
18 holes, 6650 yds. S.S.S. 72
Course designed by M.D. Little.
Visitors welcome if members of recognized

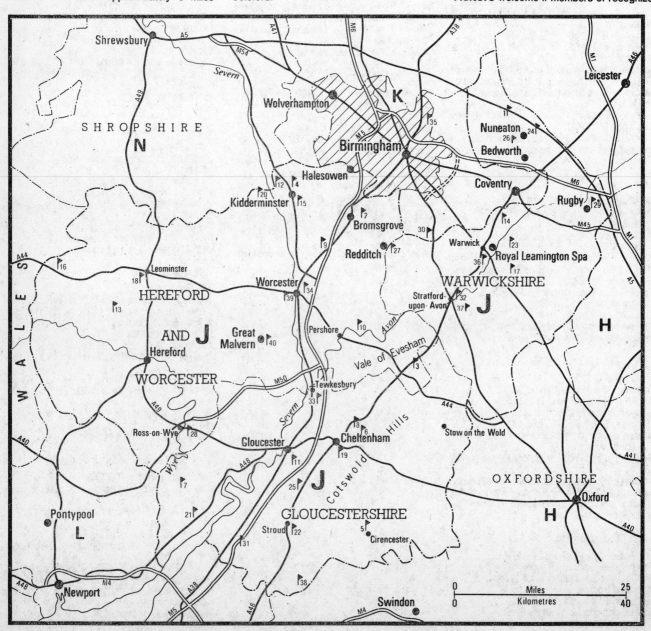

club; weekends with reservation.
Green Fees. Weekdays £3.50 per round (£2.50 with member), £4.50 per day (£2.50 with member); weekends and bank holidays £5.00 per round (£2.50 with member), £6.00 per day (£2.50 with member).
Society Meetings weekdays by arrangement.
Hotels: Lilley Brook; Golden Valley, Cheltenham.
Lunches served except Mon.; evening meals by arrangement.

J 9   Droitwich Golf & Country Club

Tel. Droitwich (0905) 770129
Ford Lane, Droitwich, Worcs. WR9 0BH.
Off A38, ¾ mile from Droitwich North, down lane marked Elmbridge.
Meadowland course.
18 holes, 5955 yds. S.S.S. 69
Visitors welcome on weekdays.
Green Fees. £6.00 per day.
Society Meetings Wed. and Fri.
Hotels: Chateau Impney; Raven; Worcestershire; St Andrews.
Meals served.

J 10   Evesham

Tel. Evesham 860395
Craycombe Links, Fladbury, Pershore, Worcs.
On B4084, 3 miles from Evesham.
Parkland course.
9 holes, 6228 yds. S.S.S. 70
Visitors welcome on weekdays, weekends with member only. Visitors not allowed on Competition or Match days until after 4.30p.m.
Green Fees. Weekdays £5.00 (£1.50 with member); weekends £1.50 (with member).
Society Meetings weekdays by arrangement 3 weeks in advance.
Hotels: in Evesham and Pershore.
Lunches and snacks served; dinners by arrangement.

J 11   Gloucester Hotel and Country Club

Tel. Gloucester 25653
Robinswood Hill, Gloucester.
2 miles S of Gloucester city centre on B4073 to Painswick.
Parkland, undulating, woodland course.
18 holes, 6127 yds. S.S.S. 69; 9 hole Par 3 and 12 bay floodlit driving range.
Visitors welcome at all times.
Green Fees. Weekdays £4.00 per round; weekends £5.00.
Society Meetings welcome.
Hotels: Own hotel; 20 rooms.

J 12   Habberley

Tel. Kidderminster 745756
Habberley, Kidderminster, Worcs.
2 miles W of Kidderminster on Trimpley road.
Undulating parkland course.
9 holes, 5432 yds. S.S.S. 67
Visitors welcome on weekdays.
Green Fees. £4.00 (£1.75 with member).
Hotels: in Kidderminster.
Meals served by arrangement.

J 13   Herefordshire

Tel. Canon Pyon (043 271) 219
Ravens Causeway, Wormsley, Hereford.
6 miles NW of Hereford on road to Weobley.
Undulating parkland, meadowland course.
18 holes, 6100 yds. S.S.S. 69
Visitors welcome.
Green Fees. Weekdays £5.00 (£2.50 with member); weekends £6.00 (£3.50 with member).
Society Meetings welcome on weekdays.
Hotels: Green Dragon, Hereford; Red Lion, Weobley.
Meals served except Mon.

J 14   Kenilworth

Tel. Kenilworth 58517
Crew Lane, Kenilworth, Warwicks. CV8 2EA.
On Knowle Hill, 1 mile E of Kenilworth.
Undulating course.
18 holes, 6251 yds. S.S.S. 70
Course designed by Roger Dyer Associates.
Visitors welcome.
Green Fees. Mon. to Fri. £5.50 (£2.50 with member); Sat. and Sun. £7.50 (£3.50 with member).
Society Meetings Wed. only.
Hotels: Clarendon, Leamington Spa; Hilton, Stratford-upon-Avon.
Meals served.

J 15   Kidderminster

Tel. Kidderminster 2303
Russell Rd., Kidderminster, Worcs.
Off A449 Chester road S.
Parkland course.
18 holes, 6069 yds. S.S.S. 69
Visitors welcome if members of recognized club, weekends with member only.
Green Fees. £5.75.
Society Meetings will be considered on application.
Meals served except Mon.

J 16   Kington Herefordshire

Tel. Kington 230340
Bradnor Hill, Kington, Herefordshire.
On B4355, 1 mile N of Kington.
Undulating course; highest 18 hole course in England and Wales.
18 holes, 5820 yds. S.S.S. 68
Course designed by C.K. Hutchison.
Visitors welcome.
Green Fees. Weekdays £3.50; weekends £5.00.
Society Meetings welcome, weekends max. 24.
Hotels: Burton; Oxford; Swan, Kington.
Meals served.

J 17   Leamington & County

Tel. Leamington Spa 20298
Golf Lane, Whitnash, Leamington Spa, Warwicks.
Off A452, 2½ miles S of Leamington Spa.
Parkland course.
18 holes, 6452 yds. S.S.S. 71
Course designed by H.S. Colt.
Visitors welcome.
Green Fees. Weekdays £5.00; weekends £7.00; plus V.A.T.
Society Meetings welcome Wed., Thurs. and Fri.
Hotels: Manor House Hotel; Regent,

Leamington Spa; Lord Leycester, Warwick.
Meals served except Mon.

J 18   Leominster

Tel. Leominster 2863
Ford Bridge, Leominster, Herefordshire.
On A49, 2½ miles S of Leominster.
Meadowland course.
9 holes, 5314 yds. S.S.S. 66
Visitors welcome.
Green Fees. Weekdays £4.00 (£1.50 with member); weekends £5.50 (£2.50 with member).
Hotels: Talbot; Royal Oak, Leominster.
Meals served.

J 19   Lilley Brook

Tel. Cheltenham (0242) 26785
Cirencester Rd., Charlton Kings, Cheltenham GL53 8EG.
On A435, 2 miles S of Cheltenham.
Undulating parkland course.
18 holes, 6226 yds. S.S.S. 70
Visitors welcome on weekdays, weekends with letter of introduction.
Green Fees. Weekdays £4.50; weekends £6.75.
Society Meetings Tues. - Fri. by arrangement.
Hotels: Lilley Brook Hotel.
Lunches and teas served except Mon.; Dinners by arrangement.

J 20   Little Lakes

Tel. 0299 266137
Lye Head, Bewdley, Worcs. DY12 2UU.
2 miles W of Bewdley. Turn left off the A456 and follow signposts to Little Lakes.
Undulating course.
9 holes, 3200 yds. S.S.S. 71
Course designed by Michael Cooksey.
Visitors welcome.
Green Fees. Weekdays £3.00; weekends £4.50.
Society Meetings by arrangement.
Hotels: George Hotel; Black Boy Hotel, Bewdley; Gainsborough House Hotel, Kidderminster.
Meals served.

J 21   Lydney

Tel. Dean 42614
Off Lakeside Ave., Lydney, Glos.
Correspondence and enquiries to: Hon. Secretary, K.J. Mullan, 21 High St., Lydney, Glos. GL15 5DP. (Tel. Dean 42436).
A48 from Gloucester, left at bottom of Highfield Hill, Lydney, left again into Lakeside Ave., about ½ mile.
Parkland, meadowland course.
9 holes, 5442 yds. S.S.S. 66
Visitors welcome weekdays.
Green Fees. Weekdays £3.00 (£2.50 with member); weekends £3.00 (with member only).
Society Meetings by arrangement.
Hotels: Feathers; Swan.

J 22   Minchinhampton

Tel. Nailsworth 3866
The New Course, Minchinhampton, Stroud, Glos. GL6 9BE.
Meadowland courses.
New 18 holes, 6675 yds. S.S.S. 72

Old 18 holes, 6495 yds. S.S.S. 70
New Course designed by F.W. Hawtree.
Visitors welcome on weekdays both courses, and Sat. on Old Course.
Green Fees. Weekdays New Course £5.00 per day (£3.50 with member); weekends £6.00. Old Course £2.50 per day (£2.00 with member).
Society Meetings by arrangement.
Hotels: Amberley Inn, Amberley; Bear of Rodborough, Burleigh Court.
Meals served.

J 23   Newbold Comyn

Tel. Leamington Spa (0926) 21157
Newbold Terrace East, Leamington Spa, Warwicks.
Location central, off Willes Rd. (B4099).
Parkland course.
18 holes, 6221 yds. S.S.S. 70
Course designed by Frederick Gibberd and Partners.
Visitors welcome.
Green Fees. Weekdays £1.10 per 9 holes, £1.80 per round; weekends £1.50 per 9 holes, £2.40 per round.
Society Meetings by arrangement.
Hotels: Regent; Clarendon; Berni Inn; Manor House.
Bar and restaurant.

J 24   Nuneaton

Tel. Nuneaton 383281, Sec. 347810
Whitestone, Nuneaton, Warwicks.
2 miles S of Nuneaton.
18 holes, 6368 yds. S.S.S. 70
Green Fees. Weekdays £5.75 (£3.45 with member), weekends with members only.

J 25   Painswick

Tel. Painswick 2180
Painswick, Stroud, Glos.
3 miles NE of Stroud on A46.
Commonland course.
18 holes, 4800 yds. S.S.S. 64
Visitors welcome on weekdays and Sat. mornings, Sat. afternoons and Sun. mornings.
Green Fees. Weekdays £2.00; Sats. £3.00 (£2.00 with member).
Society Meetings by arrangement.
Hotels: Royal William; Falcon; Cranham Wood Hotel, Painswick.
Lunches served by arrangement.

J 26   Purley Chase

Tel. Nuneaton (0203) 393118
Ridge Lane, Nuneaton, Warwicks.
Ridge Lane is signposted off A47 (Coleshill-Nuneaton) and B4116 (Coleshill-Atherstone).
Meadowland course.
18 holes, 6604 yds. S.S.S. 69
Course designed by J.B. Tomlinson.
Visitors welcome at any time.
Green Fees. £3.00.
Society Meetings most welcome.
Hotels: Red Lion, Atherstone; Chase, Nuneaton; Metropole, N.E.C. Birmingham.
Full catering facilities.

J 27   Redditch

Tel. Redditch 43309
Lower Grinsty, Green Lane, Callow Hill,

Redditch, Worcs. B97 5PJ.
On A441.
Parkland course.
18 holes, 6671 yds. S.S.S. 72
Visitors welcome on weekdays, weekends with member only.
Green Fees. £6.90.
Society Meetings weekdays by arrangement.
Meals served except Mon.

J 28   Ross-on-Wye

Tel. Gorsley 267
Two Park, Gorsley, Ross-on-Wye, Herefordshire HR9 7UT.
On B4221, adjacent to M50 Exit 3.
Undulating woodland course.
18 holes, 6491 yds. S.S.S. 73
Course designed by Cotton (C.K.), Pennink, Lawrie and Partners.
Visitors welcome if members of recognized club.
Green Fees. Weekdays £6.00; weekends £7.00.
Society Meetings Wed., Thurs. and Fri., max. 60.
Hotels: Wye; Chase; Pengethley.
Snacks and meals available except Mon.

J 29   Rugby

Tel. Rugby 2306
Clifton Rd., Rugby, Warwicks.
On Rugby-Market Harborough road.
18 holes, 5457 yds. S.S.S. 67
Visitors welcome, weekends and bank holidays with member only.
Green Fees. Weekdays £4.00.

J 30   Shirley

Tel. 021-744 7024/6001
Stratford Rd., Shirley, Solihull, West Midlands.
On A34, 7 miles S of Birmingham.
Parkland course.
18 holes, 6445 yds. S.S.S. 71
Visitors welcome on weekdays.
Green Fees. Weekdays £6.00; Sat. £9.00.
Society Meetings by arrangement.
Hotels: St. John's; George, Solihull.
Meals served except Mon.

J 31   Stinchcombe

Tel. Dursley 2015
Dursley, Glos. GL11 6AQ.
Off A38, 13 miles SW of Gloucester.
Downland course.
18 holes, 5910 yds. S.S.S. 68
Course designed by James Braid.
Visitors welcome.
Green Fees. Weekdays £5.00; Sat. £6.00; Sun. £7.00.
Society Meetings Wed. by arrangement.
Hotels: Hare and Hounds, Westonbirt; Swan, Wotton-under-Edge.
Snacks served; meals by arrangement.

J 32   Stratford-upon-Avon

Tel. Stratford-upon-Avon 5749
Tiddington Rd., Stratford-upon-Avon, Warwicks.
Parkland course.
18 holes, 6309 yds. S.S.S. 70

Visitors welcome on weekdays.
Green Fees. Weekdays £6.00 (£3.00 with member); weekends £8.50 (£3.50 with member).
Hotels: in area.
Lunches served by arrangement.

J 33   Tewkesbury Park Hotel Golf & Country Club

Tel. Tewkesbury (0684) 295405 Telex 43563
Lincoln Green Lane, Tewkesbury, Glos. GL20 7DN.
On A38, 1 mile S of Tewkesbury; 3 miles from junction 9 M5.
Parkland course.
18 holes, 6606 yds. S.S.S. 72
Course designed by Cotton (C.K.), Pennink, Lawrie and Partners.
Visitors welcome with handicap certificate.
Green Fees. Weekdays £5.00 per day; weekends £6.00 per day.
Society Meetings welcome on weekdays.
Hotels: Accomodation available at club.
Meals served.

J 34   Tolladine

Tel. Worcester 21074
Tolladine Rd., Worcester.
Leave M5 at Exit 6. Course is 1 mile from city centre off Tolladine Rd.
Meadowland course.
9 holes, 2578 yds. S.S.S. 66
Visitors welcome on weekdays, weekends and bank holidays with member only.
Green Fees. Weekdays £5.00 per round or day (£2.00 with member); weekends £2.70.
Hotels: Star; Gifford.
Snacks served, meals by arrangement.

J 35   Walmley

Tel. 021-373 0029
Brooks Rd., Wylde Green, Sutton Coldfield, West Midlands B72 1HR.
On Birmingham to Sutton Coldfield road. In Wylde Green turn up Greenhill Rd. which leads into Brooks Rd.
Parkland course.
18 holes, 6381 yds. S.S.S. 70
Visitors welcome on weekdays, weekends with member only.
Green Fees. Weekdays £7.50 per day (£2.00 with member).
Society Meetings by arrangement.
Hotels: Penns Hall Hotel; Royal, Sutton Coldfield.
Meals served except Mon.

J 36   Warwick Golf Centre

Tel. Warwick 44316
The Racecourse, Warwick.
In centre of Warwick Racecourse.
Meadowland course.
9 holes, 5224 yds. S.S.S. 66
Course designed by D.G. Dunkley.
Visitors welcome.
Green Fees. Weekdays 85p per 9 holes; weekends £1.10 per 9 holes.
Society Meetings welcome.
Hotels: Westgate Arms; Woolpack; Warwick Arms.
Snacks served.

J 37   Welcombe Hotel Avon

Stratford-upon-Avon (0789) 295252
Welcombe Hotel, Warwick Rd., Stratford-upon-Avon, Warwicks. CV37 0NR.
1½ miles outside Stratford-upon-Avon on A46 (Stratford-Warwick).
Mature wooded parkland course with lake.
18 holes, 6202 yds. S.S.S. 70
Course designed by T.J. McAuley.
Visitors welcome, preferably with handicap certificate. Phone bookings advisable, especially weekends.
Green Fees. Weekdays £6.50 per day (hotel residents £4.50); weekends and bank holidays £7.50 per day (hotel residents £5.50).
Society Meetings welcome.
Hotels: Welcombe adjacent to course; others in Stratford.
Lunches and dinners served; special rates for societies.

J 38   Westonbirt

Tel. 06 666 242
Westonbirt, Tetbury, Glos. GL8 8QP.
Turn off A433 3 miles SW of Tetbury; through Westonbirt village; take turning opposite Westonbirt Arboretum entrance.
Parkland course.
9 holes, 4504 yds. S.S.S. 62
Course designed by Monty Hearn.
Visitors welcome.
Green Fees. Weekdays £2.00 per round or day; weekends £2.00 per round.
Hotels: Holford Arms, Knockdown; Hare and Hounds, Westonbirt.

J 39   Worcester Golf & Country Club

Tel. Worcester 422555
Broughton Park, Worcester WR2 4EZ.
2 miles from Worcester city centre on Bransford Rd.
Parkland course.
18 holes, 6015 yds. S.S.S. 68
Course designed by Dr. MacKenzie.
Visitors welcome on weekdays, weekends with member only.
Green Fees. £7.00.
Society Meetings by arrangement.
Hotels: Gifford; Star.
Meals served except Mon.

J 40   Worcestershire

Tel. Malvern (06845) 5992
Wood Farm, Malvern Wells, Worcs. WR14 4PP.
From Great Malvern take A449 to Malvern Wells; then take B4209 for 200 yards and turn left.
Meadowland course.
18 holes, 6430 yds. S.S.S. 71
Course designed by Dr. McKenzie.
Visitors welcome if members of recognized club.
Green Fees. Weekdays £5.00 (£2.00 with member); weekends £7.00 (£2.00 with member).
Society Meetings by arrangement.
Hotels: Essington, Malvern Wells; Abbey; Foley Arms; Tudor, Great Malvern.
Snacks served; lunches by arrangement.

K Birmingham, West Midlands

K 1   Belfry

Tel. Curdworth (0675) 70301
Lichfield Rd., Wishaw, Nr. Sutton Coldfield, W. Midlands B76 8BR.
Apex A4091/A446, 9 miles from Birmingham.
Parkland courses. Championship courses.
Brabazon 18 holes, 7182 yds.
Derby 18 holes, 6082 yds.
Course designed by Peter Alliss, D. Thomas Ltd.
Visitors welcome.
Society Meetings by arrangement.
Bargain facilities.
Hotels: The Belfry.
Meals served.

K 2   Bloxwich

Tel. Bloxwich 405724
Stafford Rd., Bloxwich, Walsall, W. Midlands.
Main Walsall to Stafford road.
Undulating parkland course.
18 holes, 6286 yds. S.S.S. 70
Course designed by J. Sixsmith.
Visitors welcome on weekdays, weekends with member only.
Green Fees. £6.00.
Society Meetings by arrangement.
Hotels: Crest Motel; County; Royal.
Meals served.

K 3   Boldmere

Tel. 021-354 2324
Monmouth Dr., Sutton Coldfield, W. Midlands.
On A34, 7 miles from centre of Birmingham.
Parkland course.
18 holes, 4391 yds. S.S.S. 61
Course designed by Carl Bretherston.
Visitors welcome.
Green Fees. Weekdays 80p (O.A.P.'s 45p).
Hotels: Penns Hall Hotel; Royal.
Snacks served.

K 4   Cocks Moor Woods

Tel. 021-444 3584
Alcester Rd. South, Kings Heath, Birmingham B14 6ER.
On A435, near city boundary.
Parkland course.
18 holes, 5888 yds. S.S.S. 68
Visitors welcome.
Green Fees. 75p per 9 holes, £1.35 per 18 holes.
Hotels: in Birmingham.
Snacks served.

K 5   Copt Heath

Tel. Knowle 2650
Warwick Rd., Knowle, Solihull, W. Midlands.
On A41 midway between Knowle and Solihull.
Parkland course.
18 holes, 6505 yds. S.S.S. 71
Visitors welcome on weekdays, weekends with member only.
Society Meetings welcome.
Hotels: George, Solihull; Greswolde Arms, Knowle.
Lunches served by arrangement.

K 6   Coventry

Tel. Coventry 411298
Finham Park, Coventry, CV3 6PJ.
Parkland course.
18 holes, 6525 yds. S.S.S. 72
Course designed by J. H. Taylor.
Visitors welcome on weekdays only.
Green Fees. £8.00 per day.
Society Meetings Wed. and Thurs. only.
Hotels: Hotel Leofric; Godiva, Coventry; de Montfort, Kenilworth.
Snacks served; meals except Mon.

K 7   Dartmouth

Tel. 021-588 2131
Vale St., West Bromwich, W. Midlands.
West Bromwich to Walsall road, right at Churchfields.
Undulating meadowland course.
9 holes, 3152 yds. S.S.S. 70 (18 holes)
Visitors welcome on weekdays, weekends with member only.
Green Fees. Weekdays £4.60 (£2.30 with member); weekends £3.45 with member only.
Society Meetings by arrangement.
Hotels: Barr Hotel, Gt. Barr; Europa Lodge.
Meals served by arrangement with steward.

K 8   Druids Heath

Tel. Aldridge 55595
Stonnall Rd., Aldridge, W. Midlands.
Off A452 6 miles NW of Sutton Coldfield.
Undulating, heathland course.
18 holes, 6914 yds. S.S.S. 73
Visitors welcome on weekdays, weekends with member only.
Green Fees. Weekdays £2.50; weekends £4.00.
Society Meetings welcome on weekdays.
Hotels: Fairlawns.
Meals served on Fri. and Sat. nights.

K 9   Dudley

Tel. Dudley 53719
Turners Hill, Rowley Regis, Warley, W. Midlands B65 9DP.
1 mile S of town centre.
Undulating course.
18 holes, 5715 yds. S.S.S. 67
Visitors welcome.
Green Fees. Weekdays £2.95 per round, £3.75 per day.
Society Meetings by arrangement.
Hotels: Station, Dudley.
Meals served.

K 10 Edgbaston

Tel. 021-454 1736
Church Rd., Edgbaston, Birmingham B15 3TB.
A38 from city centre. At second traffic lights turn right into Priory Rd. then left into Church Rd. Club entrance is 100 yards on left immediately beyond church.
Parkland course.
18 holes, 6118 yds. S.S.S. 69
Course designed by H.S. Colt.
Visitors welcome with reservation.
Green Fees. Weekdays £8.00; weekends £10.00.
Society Meetings welcome particularly Tues. and Fri.
Hotels: in Birmingham.
Lunches and teas served except Sun., evening meals by arrangement.

K 11 Forest of Arden Golf & Country Club

Tel. Meriden (0676) 22118
Maxstoke Lane, Meriden, Coventry CV7 7HR.
Off A45, 9 miles from Coventry, 11 miles from Birmingham.
Parkland course.
9 holes, 1890 yds. S.S.S. 29
18 holes, 6872 yds. S.S.S. 73
Course designed by B. Tomlinson.
Visitors welcome weekdays, 9 hole course only weekends.
Green Fees. 9 hole weekdays £2.00; weekends £2.50. 18 hole weekdays £5.50.
Society Meetings weekdays only.
Hotels: Manor Hotel, Meriden; Post House, Allesley.
Food available 7 days a week.

K 12 Fulford Heath

Tel. 0564 822806
Tanners Green Lane, Wythall, Birmingham.
Off A435, ½ mile up Tanners Green Lane.
Meadowland course.
18 holes, 6256 yds. S.S.S. 70
Course designed by James Braid.
Visitors welcome on weekdays, weekends with member only.
Green Fees. Weekdays £5.50 (£2.00 with member); weekends with member only.
Society Meetings Tues. and Thurs. by arrangement.
Meals served except Mon.

K 13 Gay Hill

Tel. 021-430 8544
Alcester Rd., Hollywood, Birmingham.
On A435, 7 miles from city centre.
Meadowland course.
18 holes, 6238 yds. S.S.S. 70
Visitors welcome on weekdays.
Green Fees. £7.00 per round or day.
Society Meetings welcome on Thurs.
Hotels: in Birmingham and Solihull.
Lunches served except Mon. and Sat.

K 14 Grange

Tel. 0203 451465
Copsewood, Binley Rd., Coventry, W. Midlands CV3 1HS.
On A427/A428, 3 miles from city centre.
Parkland course.

9 holes, 6002 yds. S.S.S. 69
Visitors Members' guests only 1981/2 due to course reconstruction.
Hotels: Brandon Hall Hotel, Brandon.

K 15 Great Barr

Tel. 021-357 1232
Chapel Lane, Great Barr, Birmingham B43 7BA.
6 miles NW of Birmingham, exit 7, M6.
Meadowland course.
18 holes, 6517 yds. S.S.S. 71
Visitors welcome. Members of recognized clubs only at weekends (Max. handicap 18).
Green Fees. Weekdays £5.00 (£2.00 with member); weekends £6.00.
Society Meetings by arrangement.
Hotels: Post House; Walsall Crest Motel.
Meals served by arrangement.

K 16 Halesowen

Tel. 021-550 1041
The Leasowes, Halesowen, W. Midlands B62 8QF.
M5, turning to Kidderminster, then to Halesowen.
Parkland course.
18 holes, 5646 yds. S.S.S. 68
Visitors welcome weekdays only.
Green Fees. £5.00 per day.
Society Meetings by arrangement.
Hotels: in Halesowen.
Meals served by arrangement.

K 17 Handsworth

Tel. 021-554 0599
Sunningdale Close, Handsworth Wood, Birmingham B20 1NP.
3 miles W of city centre. 1 mile from M6.
Undulating meadowland course.
18 holes, 6312 yds. S.S.S. 70
Visitors welcome. Sat., Sun., bank holidays and proscribed days with member only.
Green Fees. £6.50 (£2.00 with member).

Society Meetings by arrangement.
Hotels: Post House, Great Barr.
Lunch and dinner served.

K 18 Harborne

Tel. 021-427 1728
40 Tennal Rd., Harborne, Birmingham B32 2JE.
W Birmingham, via Harborne Rd. and War Lane.
Undulating course.
18 holes, 6240 yds. S.S.S. 70
Course designed by H. S. Colt.
Visitors welcome on weekdays; weekends with member only.
Green Fees. Weekdays £6.50 (£2.50 with member).
Society Meetings welcome Wed. and Thurs.
Hotels: in Birmingham.
Meals served by arrangement except Mon.

K 19 Harborne Church Farm

Tel. 021-427 1204
Vicarage Rd., Harborne, Birmingham 17.
From Birmingham, via Broad St., Harborne Rd., and War Lane to Vicarage Rd.
Parkland course.
9 holes, 4514 yds. S.S.S. 62
Visitors welcome.
Green Fees. £2.00 per 18 holes; £1.20 per 9 holes.
Hotels: in Birmingham.
Meals served.

K 20 Hatchford Brook

Tel. 021-743 9823
Coventry Rd., Sheldon, Birmingham 26.
On A45, adjacent to National Exhibition Centre.
Parkland course.
18 holes, 6157 yds. S.S.S. 69
Visitors welcome.

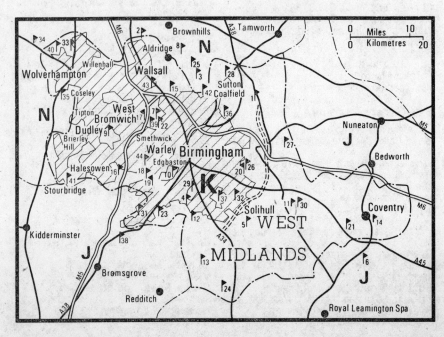

Green Fees. £1.35 per 9 holes; £2.20 per round.
Society Meetings welcome.
Hotels: Excelsior, Birmingham Airport; Metropole, National Exhibition Centre.
Snacks served.

K 21   Hearsall

Tel. Coventry 713470
Beechwood Ave., Earlsdon, Coventry CV5 6DF.
Off A46, 1 mile S of Coventry.
Parkland course.
18 holes, 5951 yds. S.S.S. 69
Visitors welcome Mon. to Sat., Sun. with member only.
Green Fees. Mon.-Thurs. £6.00; Fri., Sat. and bank holidays £8.00.
Hotels: Hyland Hotel.
Lunches served except Tues.

K 22   Hill Top

Park Lane, Handsworth Wood, Birmingham 20.
Parkland course.
18 holes
Details on application to Secretary.

K 23   Kings Norton

Tel. Wythall (0564) 826706
Brockhill Lane, Weatheroak, Alvechurch, Birmingham B48 7ED.
8 miles from Birmingham between A435 and A441.
Parkland course (3 loops of 9) 27 holes.
Blue 9 holes, 3567 yds.
Red 9 holes, 3518 yds.
Yellow 9 holes, 3290 yds.
Also 12 hole, Par 3 course.
Course designed by Fred Hawtrey & Son.
Visitors welcome on weekdays, weekends with member only.
Green Fees. £7.00 per day (£3.00 with member).
Society Meetings welcome Mon. to Fri. (£6.00 per day).
Hotels: St. John's; St. George, Solihull; Chateau Impney, Droitwich.
Meals served except Mon.

K 24   Ladbrook Park

Tel. Tanworth in Arden 2264
Poolhead Lane, Tanworth in Arden, W. Midlands B94 5ED.
7 miles from Solihull.
Undulating parkland course.
18 holes, 6411 yds. S.S.S. 71
Visitors welcome on weekdays if members of recognized club, weekends with member only.
Green Fees. Weekdays £8.00 per round or day; weekends £3.00.
Society Meetings by arrangement.
Hotels: in Solihull.
Meals served except Mon.

K 25   Little Aston

Tel. 021-353 2066
Streetly, Sutton Coldfield, W. Midlands B74 3AN.
Off A454.
Parkland course.
18 holes, 6711 yds. S.S.S. 72

Course designed by J. Colt.
Visitors welcome on weekdays, weekends with reservation only.
Green Fees. £10.00.
Society Meetings by arrangement.
Hotels: Penns Hall Hotel, Walmley.
Meals served by arrangement.

K 26   Marston Green

Tel. 021-779 2449
Elmdon Lane, Marston Green, Birmingham B37.
Meadowland course.
9 holes, 4776 yds. S.S.S. 63
Course designed by Carl Bretherton.
Visitors welcome with reservation.
Green Fees. £1.35 per round.
Snacks served.

K 27   Maxstoke Park

Tel. Coleshill 62158
Castle Lane, Coleshill, Birmingham B46 2RD.
Off A47, 3 miles from Coleshill.
Parkland course.
18 holes, 6597 yds. S.S.S. 71
Visitors welcome on weekdays, weekends with member only.
Green Fees. Weekdays £7.00 per round, £10.00 per day. Special rates for societies.
Society Meetings Tues. and Thurs. by arrangement in January for date in that year.
Hotels: Swan.
Meals served except Mon.

K 28   Moor Hall

Tel. 021-308 6130 and 0103
Moor Hall Park, Sutton Coldfield, W. Midlands B75 6LN.
9 miles NE of Birmingham, 5 miles from Tamworth.
Parkland course.
18 holes, 6249 yds. S.S.S. 70
Visitors welcome on weekdays (Thurs. after 12.30 p.m.), weekends and bank holidays with member only.
Green Fees. £7.00 (£2.00 with member).
Society Meetings Tues. and Wed. by arrangement.
Hotels: Moor Hall Hotel; Penns Hall Hotel, Walmley.
Meals served by arrangement.

K 29   Moseley

Tel. 021-444 2115
Springfield Rd., Kings Heath, Birmingham B14 7DX.
4 miles S of city centre.
Parkland course.
18 holes, 6245 yds. S.S.S. 70
Visitors welcome by prior arrangement, or when introduced by and playing with a member.
Green Fees. Weekdays £8.50 (£2.50 with member); Sun. £8.50 (£3.00 with member).
Society Meetings Thurs. mainly.
Meals served on weekdays except Mon.

K 30   North Warwickshire

Tel. Meriden (0676) 22259
Hampton Lane, Meriden, Coventry, W. Midlands CV7 7LL.
A45 from Birmingham or Coventry to Meriden.

Meadowland course.
9 holes, 6276 yds. S.S.S. 70
Visitors welcome on weekdays, weekends with member only.
Green Fees. Weekdays £4.50 (£1.50 with member); weekends £3.00.
Society Meetings by arrangement.
Hotels: Post House; Leofric, Coventry; Manor Hotel, Meriden.
Meals served by arrangement one week in advance.

K 31   North Worcestershire

Tel. 021-475 1047
Hanging Lane, Northfield, Birmingham B31 5LP.
On A38, 1 mile from Northfield station.
Meadowland course.
18 holes, 5907 yds. S.S.S. 69
Course designed by James Braid.
Visitors welcome on weekdays, weekends with member only.
Green Fees. £4.60 per day.
Society Meetings Mon. or Thurs. by arrangement.
Hotels: on Bristol Rd. South.
Meals served.

K 32   Olton

Tel. 021-705 1083
Mirfield Rd., Solihull, W. Midlands B91 1JH.
1 mile from centre of Solihull along Warwick Rd. towards Birmingham.
Parkland course.
18 holes, 6229 yds. S.S.S. 71
Visitors welcome on weekdays, weekends and bank holidays with member only.
Green Fees. £7.50.
Society Meetings by arrangement.
Hotels: St. John's; George.
Meals served by arrangement.

K 33   Oxley Park

Tel. Wolverhampton 20506
Bushbury, Wolverhampton WV10 6DE.
Off A449 1½ miles N of Wolverhampton.
Parkland course.
18 holes, 6146 yds. S.S.S. 69
Visitors welcome.
Green Fees. Weekdays £4.40 per round, £5.50 per day; weekends £5.75.
Society Meetings Wed. only.
Hotels: Mount Hotel; Ravensholt; Park Hall.
Meals by arrangement.

K 34   Patshull Park

Tel. Wolverhampton (0902) 700100
Burnhill Green, Wolverhampton WV6 7HR.
A41 from Wolverhampton towards Shifnal, Patshull signposted near Albrighton.
Parkland course.
18 holes, 6460 yds. S.S.S. 71
Course designed by John Jacobs.
Visitors welcome 7 days a week.
Green Fees. £6.00 per round, £8.50 per day (Eurogolf members 20 per cent discount).
Society Meetings welcome. Telephone Golf Professional.
Hotels: Own hotel adjacent; 28 bedrooms. Restaurant; snack bar; lounge bar.

K 35 Penn

Tel. Wolverhampton 341142
Penn Common, Penn, Wolverhampton, W. Midlands.
3 miles from Wolverhampton.
Heathland course.
18 holes, 6449 yds. S.S.S. 71
Visitors welcome on weekdays, weekends with member only.
Green Fees. £5.00 (£3.00 with member).
Society Meetings by arrangement.
Hotels: Park Hall Hotel, Wolverhampton.
Meals served except Mon.

K 36 Pype Hayes

Tel. 021-351 1014
Eachelhurst Rd., Walmley, Sutton Coldfield, B76 8EP, W. Midlands.
Off A453.
Parkland course.
18 holes, 5790 yds. S.S.S. 67
Visitors welcome.
Green Fees. 18 holes £2.20, 9 holes £1.50.
Hotels: in area.
Meals served.

K 37 Robin Hood

Tel. 021-706 0061
St. Bernard's Rd., Solihull, W. Midlands B92 7DJ.
8 miles S of Birmingham on A41.
Parkland course.
18 holes, 6609 yds. S.S.S. 72
Course designed by H. S. Colt.
Visitors welcome on weekdays.
Green Fees. £7.00.
Society Meetings Tues., Thurs. and Fri.
Hotels: St. John's; George, Solihull; Metropole, National Exhibition Centre.
Lunches served except Mon.; dinners by arrangement.

K 38 Rose Hill

Tel. 021-453 3159 (Pro), 021-453 2846 (club)
Lickey Hills, Rednal, Birmingham.
M5 Exit 4, on city boundary.
Parkland course.
18 holes, 6010 yds. S.S.S. 69
Course designed by Carl Bretherton.
Visitors welcome.
Green Fees. £1.35 per 9 holes, £2.20 per 18 holes.
Society Meetings welcome.
Hotels: Rose and Crown.
Snacks served.

K 39 Sandwell Park

Tel. 021-553 4637
Birmingham Rd., West Bromwich, W. Midlands B71 4JJ.
400 yds. from exit 1 of M5, on left of A41 towards Birmingham.
Undulating parkland course.
18 holes, 6422 yds. S.S.S. 72
Course designed by Colt.
Visitors welcome weekdays only.
Green Fees. £6.50 (£2.50 with member).
Society Meetings welcome weekdays by arrangement.
Hotels: Europa Lodge Motel.
Meals served except Mon.

K 40 South Staffordshire

Tel. Wolverhampton 751065
Danescourt Rd., Tettenhall, Wolverhampton, W. Midlands.
2½ miles from Wolverhampton on A41 to Shrewsbury.
Parkland course.
18 holes, 6604 yds. S.S.S. 71
Visitors welcome weekdays only.
Green Fees. £6.00.
Society Meetings welcome.
Hotels: Mount Hotel, Tettenhall Wood.

K 41 Stourbridge

Tel. Stourbridge 3062 & 5566
Worcester Lane, Pedmore, Stourbridge, W. Midlands DY8 2RB.
Stourbridge to Hagley.
Parkland course.
18 holes, 6178 yds. S.S.S. 69
Visitors welcome.
Green Fees. £6.50.
Society Meetings Tues. by arrangement.
Hotels: Talbot; Bell, Stourbridge.
Lunches and evening meals served by arrangement except Mon.

K 42 Sutton Coldfield

Tel. 021-353 2014
Thornhill Rd., Streetly, Sutton Coldfield, W. Midlands B74 3ER.
½ mile from A452 at Streetly, 7 miles from Birmingham.
Parkland course.
18 holes, 6491 yds. S.S.S. 71
Visitors welcome.
Green Fees. Weekdays £6.50; weekends £8.00.
Society Meetings by arrangement.
Hotels: Parson and Clerk Motel, Streetly; Royal, Sutton Coldfield; Post House, Great Barr.
Meals served by arrangement.

K 43 Walsall

Tel. Walsall 22710
The Broadway, Walsall, W. Midlands W51 3EY.
1 mile NW of junction 7 on M6.
Parkland course.
18 holes, 6424 yds. S.S.S. 70
Course designed by Dr. Mackenzie.
Visitors welcome on weekdays.
Green Fees. £6.50 per round or day.
Society Meetings by arrangement.
Hotels: Royal; Walsall Crest; Post House; County.
Meals served by arrangement except Mon.

K 44 Warley

Tel. 021-429 2440
Lightwoods Hill, Warley, Birmingham.
Off A456, 3½ miles from city centre.
Parkland course.
9 holes, 5212 yds. S.S.S. 64
Visitors welcome.
Green Fees. £1.20 per 9 holes, £2.00 per round.
Hotels: in Birmingham.
Snacks served.

L South Wales

L 1 Aberdare

Tel. Aberdare (0685) 871188
Aberdare, Mid Glam.
½ mile from town centre.
18 holes, 5875 yds. S.S.S. 68
Visitors welcome.
Society Meetings by arrangement.
Hotels: Boot Hotel; Black Lion; Ysguborwen Country Club; Baverstocks.
Lunches served except Mon.

L 2 Aberystwyth

Tel. Aberystwyth (0970) 615104
Bryn-y-mor, Aberystwyth, Dyfed.
1 mile from town centre.
Undulating meadowland course.
18 holes, 5735 yds. S.S.S. 68
Course designed by Harry Vardon.
Visitors welcome.
Green Fees. High season: weekdays £4.00, weekends and bank holidays £5.75; weekly £13.80. Low season: weekdays £2.25.
Society Meetings by arrangement.
Hotels: Marine; Central; Cambrian, Aberystwyth.
Meals served.

L 3 Ashburnham

Tel. Burry Port 2269
Cliff Terr., Burry Port, Dyfed.
5 miles W of Llanelli. Turn left off A484 after sign for Ashburnham Hotel.
Seaside course.
18 holes, 6814 yds. S.S.S. 74
First 9 holes designed by C. Gibson (1894), further 9 holes by Wm. Tate (1902). Redesigned by C.K. Cotton (1948).
Visitors welcome if members of recognized club.
Green Fees. Weekdays £5.75 (£4.00 with member); weekends £9.20 (£6.90 with member).
Society Meetings welcome on weekdays.
Hotels: Stradey Park Hotel; Stepney Hotel, Llanelli; Ashburnham Hotel, Pembrey.
Meals served except Mon.

L 4 Bargoed

Tel. Bargoed (0443) 830143
Heolddu, Bargoed, Mid Glam.
15 miles from Cardiff on A469. Turn left opposite Gwerthonor Hotel; 2nd left after Heolddu Leisure Centre.
Undulating parkland course.
18 holes, 6012 yds. S.S.S. 70
Visitors welcome on weekdays, weekends and bank holidays with member only.
Green Fees. Weekdays £3.50 (£2.50 with

member); weekends and bank holidays £2.50 (with member only).
Society Meetings weekdays by arrangement.
Hotels: Maes Manor Hotel, Blackwood. Snacks and meals served.

L 5 Blackwood

Tel. Blackwood (0495) 223152
Cwmgelli, Blackwood, Gwent.
Off A494 ½ mile N of Blackwood.
Undulating course.
9 holes, 5352 yds. S.S.S. 66
Visitors welcome if members of recognized club.

Green Fees. Weekdays £3.00 per day (£2.50 with member).
Society Meetings by arrangement.

L 6 Borth & Ynyslas

Tel. Borth 202
Borth, Dyfed SY24 5JS.
7 miles N of Aberystwyth.
Seaside course.
18 holes, 5992 yds. S.S.S. 70
Course redesigned by H.S. Colt.
Visitors welcome if members of recognized club.
Green Fees. £5.00 per day; July and Aug. £6.00 per day.

Society Meetings by arrangement.
Hotels: Grand; Golf Hotel.
Limited catering.

L 7 Brecon

Tel. Brecon 0874 2004
Newton Park, Brecon, Powys LD3 8PA.
1 mile W of town centre on A40.
Meadowland course.
9 holes.
Visitors welcome.
Green Fees. Weekdays £1.50 per round, juniors £1.00; weekends £2.00 per round.
Hotels: Wellington; Castle of Brecon Hotel.

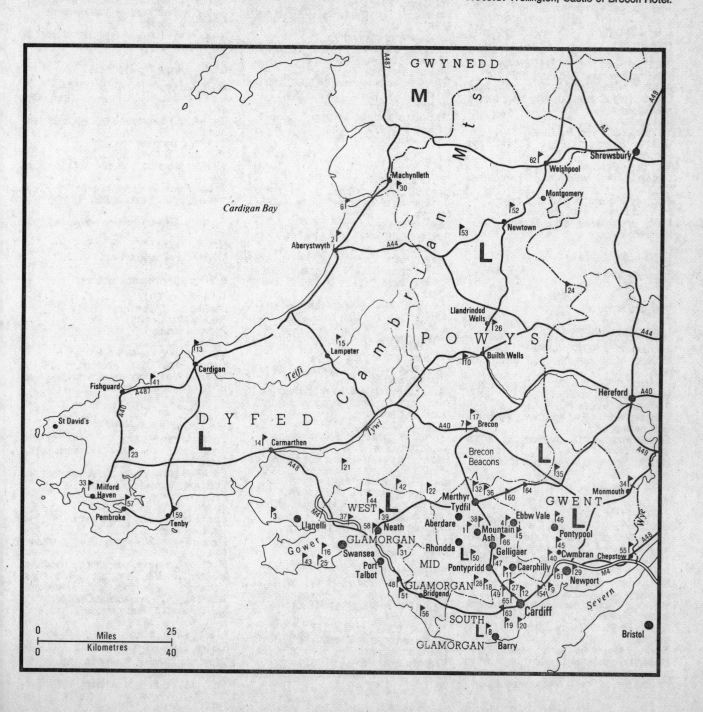

L 8 Brynhill

Tel. Barry 735061
Port Rd., Barry, S. Glam. CF6 7PN.
Off M4 at Cardiff, right at first roundabout,
left at first roundabout on to Wenvoe Rd., 4
miles on right.
Undulating meadowland course.
18 holes, 6029 yds. S.S.S. 69
Course designed by C.K. Cotton.
Visitors welcome.
Green Fees. Weekdays £4.60 (£3.45 with
member); weekends £6.40 (£5.00 with
member).
Society Meetings by arrangement.
Hotels: Barry; Mont Sorrel; Waters Edge.
Meals served except Mon.

L 9 Bryn Meadows Golf & Country Club

Tel. Blackwood (0495) 225590/227276
The Bryn, Hengoed, Mid Glam. CF8 7SN.
A472 11 miles from Newport, 14 miles from
Cardiff. Turn up lane opposite filling station
near Crown Hotel.
Parkland course.
18 holes, 6300 yds. S.S.S. 69
Course designed by Edgar Jefferies and
Partners.
Visitors welcome.
Green Fees. Weekdays £3.00; weekends
£4.00.
Society Meetings weekdays only.
Hotels: Maes Manor, Blackwood.
Meals and snacks available every day.
Functions catered for.

L 10 Builth Wells

Tel. Builth Wells 553296
Builth Wells, Powys.
9 holes, 5530 yds. S.S.S. 66
Visitors welcome.

L 11 Caerphilly

Tel. Caerphilly (0222) 883481
Mountain Rd., Caerphilly, Mid Glam. CF8
1HJ.
7 miles N of Cardiff.
Undulating course.
13 holes, 6218 yds. S.S.S. 72
Visitors welcome on weekdays, weekends
with member only.
Green Fees. £4.00 per round, £5.00 per
day (£1.50 with member).
Hotels: Greenhill; Mount Guest House.

L 12 Cardiff

Tel. Cardiff (0222) 753067, 753320 (Mgr),
754772 (Pro)
Sherborne Ave., Cyncoed, Cardiff CF2 6SJ.
3 miles N of city centre. From M4, A48(M)
to Post House Hotel; leave at Pentwyn
junction; take Pentwyn Industrial Estate road
to Cyncoed.
Parkland course.
18 holes, 6016 yds. S.S.S. 70
Visitors welcome on weekdays, weekends
with member only.
Green Fees. Weekdays £6.50 (£3.00 with
member).
Society Meetings Thurs. by arrangement.
Hotels: Post House, Inn on the Avenue;
others in Cardiff.
Snacks served; meals served except Mon.

L 13 Cardigan

Tel. Cardigan 612035
Gwbert-on-Sea, Cardigan, Dyfed SA43 1PR.
2½ miles NW of Cardigan.
Seaside meadowland course.
18 holes, 6258 yds. S.S.S. 71
Visitors welcome.
Green Fees. Weekdays £4.50 per day;
weekends £5.00; weekly £18.00.
Society Meetings welcome.
Hotels: Cliff Hotel; Anchor Hotel, Gwbert-
on-Sea; Castle Malgwyn, Llechryd.

L 14 Carmarthen

Tel. Conwyl Elfed 214
Blaenycoed Rd., Carmarthen, Dyfed SA33
6EH.
4 miles NW of Carmarthen.
Undulating course.
18 holes, 6212 yds. S.S.S. 71
Visitors welcome.
Green Fees. weekdays £4.50 (£3.50 with
members); weekends £5.50 (£4.50 with
member).
Society Meetings welcome.
Hotels: Ivy Bush.
Meals served except Wed.

L 15 Cilgwyn

Tel. Llangybi 286
Llangybi, Lampeter, Dyfed.
4 miles NE of Lampeter off the A485 at
Llangybi.
Parkland course.
9 holes, 5318 yds. S.S.S. 67
Visitors welcome.
Green Fees. Weekdays £3.00; weekends
£4.50. Reduced rates if playing with member.
Society Meetings by arrangement well in
advance.
Hotels: Black Lion Royal Hotel; Royal Oak
Hotel, Lampeter; Talbot Hotel, Tregaron.

L 16 Clyne

Tel. Swansea 401989
Owls Lodge Lane, Mayals, Blackpyl,
Swansea SA3 5DR.
Coast road from Swansea to Blackpyl (3
miles); turn right into Mayals Rd.
Moorland course.
18 holes, 6267 yds. S.S.S. 71
Course designed by H.S. Colt.
Visitors welcome.
Green Fees. Weekdays £4.50 per day
(£3.00 with member); weekends £5.00 per
day (£3.50 with member).
Society Meetings Wed. and Fri.
Hotels: Dragon, Swansea; Osborne,
Langland Bay.
Meals served except Mon.

L 17 Cradoc

Tel. Brecon (0874) 3658
Penoyre Park, Brecon, Powys, Wales LD3
9LP.
2 miles NW of Brecon on B4520.
Parkland course.
18 holes, 6300 yds. S.S.S. 71
Course designed by Cotton (C.K.), Pennink,
Lawrie and Partners.
Visitors welcome.
Green Fees. Weekdays £4.00; weekends
£6.00.

Society Meetings welcome.
Hotels: Nythfa House Hotel; Wellington
Hotel, Brecon.
Meals available except Mon.

L 18 Creigiau

Tel. Cardiff (0202) 890263
Creigiau, Cardiff CF4 8NN.
Off Cardiff to Llantrisant road.
Meadowland course.
11 holes, 5873 yds. S.S.S. 69
Visitors welcome on weekdays, weekends
with member only.
Green Fees. Weekdays £4.00 (£2.00 with
member); weekends £3.50 (with member).
Society Meetings by arrangement.
Hotels: in Cardiff.
Meals served by arrangement 1 day in
advance.

L 19 Dinas Powis

Tel. Dinas Powis (0222) 512727
Old Highwalls, Dinas Powis, S.Glam. CF6
4AJ.
On A4055 midway between Cardiff and
Barry.
Undulating parkland course.
18 holes, 5377 yds. S.S.S. 66
Visitors welcome if members of recognized
club.
Green Fees. Weekdays £4.00 (£2.00 with
member); weekends £5.00 (£2.00 with
member).
Society Meetings Mon., Wed. and Fri.
only.
Hotels: in Cardiff, Barry and Penarth.
Meals served except Thurs.

L 20 Glamorganshire

Tel. Penarth 701185
Lavernock Rd., Penarth, S. Glam.
5 miles W of Cardiff.
Parkland course.
18 holes, S.S.S. 70
Visitors welcome on weekdays.
Green Fees. £5.00; weekends £6.00.
Society Meetings welcome on weekdays.
Hotels: in Cardiff and Barry.
Meals served except Mon.

L 21 Glynhir (Llandeilo)

Tel. Llandybie 850472
Glynhir Rd., Llandybie, Nr. Ammanford,
Dyfed SA18 2JF.
Off A483 halfway between Ammanford and
Llandybie; 1½ miles from Glynhir Rd. end.
Parkland course.
18 holes, 6036 yds. S.S.S. 70
Course designed by F.W. Hawtree.
Visitors welcome.
Green Fees. Weekdays £3.45; weekends
£4.60; weekly £11.50.
Society Meetings welcome on weekdays.
Hotels: The Mill, Llandybie; Cawdor Arms,
Llandeilo; Wernolau, Ammanford;
Accommodation available at Clubhouse.
Meals served by arrangement.

L 22 Glynneath

Tel. Glynneath 720452
Penycraig, Pontneathvaughan, Neath, W.
Glam. SA11 5UG.
On A4109 10 miles N of Neath.

Hillside course.
9 holes, 5472 yds. S.S.S. 68
Visitors welcome.
Green Fees. Weekdays £3.00; weekends £4.00.
Society Meetings welcome on weekdays.
Hotels: Plas-y-Felin, Pontwalby, Glynneath.

L 23   Haverfordwest

Tel. Haverfordwest (0437) 3565
Arnold's Down, Haverfordwest, Dyfed.
1 mile E of Haverfordwest.
Meadowland course.
9 holes, 6258 yds. S.S.S. 70
Visitors welcome on weekdays before 3.00 p.m., weekends with member only.
Green Fees. £4.00 (£2.50 with member).
Society Meetings by arrangement with Hon. Sec.
Hotels: in Haverfordwest.
Meals served by arrangement.

L 24   Knighton

Tel. Knighton 500
Golf Links, Knighton, Powys.
Correspondence to R.P. Evans, 8 Underhill Cres., Knighton, Powys LD7 1DG.
½ mile S of Knighton.
Undulating course.
9 holes, 5320 yds. S.S.S. 66
Course designed by H. Vardon.
Visitors welcome.
Green Fees. Mon. to Fri. £2.00; Sat. and Sun. £3.00.
Hotels: Norton Arms; Swan.

L 25   Langland Bay

Tel. Swansea (0792) 61721
Mumbles, Swansea SA3 4QR.
6 miles W of Swansea.
Seaside parkland course.
18 holes, 5812 yds. S.S.S. 69
Visitors welcome.
Green Fees. Weekdays £4.00; weekends £4.50.
Hotels: Osborne; Brynfield, Langland; Caswell Bay Hotel, Caswell.
Meals served.

L 26   Llandrindod Wells

Tel. Llandrindod Wells (0597) 2010
Llandrindod Wells, Powys.
Signposted from A483.
Moorland course.
18 holes, 5687 yds. S.S.S. 68
Course designed by H. Vardon.
Visitors welcome.
Green Fees. Weekdays £3.00 per round or day (£1.50 with member); Sat. £4.00 (£2.00 with member); Sun. £4.50 (£2.25 with member).
Society Meetings by arrangement.
Hotels: Metropole; Commodore; Barcourt.
Meals served except Tues.

L 27   Llanishen

Tel. Cardiff 755078
Cwm, Lisrane, Cardiff.
1½ miles N of Llanishen church via Heol Hir.
Undulating parkland course.
18 holes, 5303 yds. S.S.S. 66
Visitors welcome on weekdays, weekends with member only.

Green Fees. Weekdays £5.00 (£2.50 with member); weekends £5.00.
Society Meetings Thurs. only.
Hotels: Cedars; Phoenix, Llanishen.
Meals served except Mon.

L 28   Llantrisant & Pontyclun

Tel. Llantrisant (0443) 222148
Talbot Green, Pontyclun, Mid Glam. CF7 8HZ.
On A4119 10 miles from Cardiff.
Undulating meadowland course.
12 holes, 5613 yds. S.S.S. 67
Visitors welcome on weekdays, weekends with member only.
Green Fees. Weekdays £3.00 (£1.50 with member); weekends (with member only) £3.00.
Society Meetings weekdays by arrangement.
Hotels: Centre Hotel; Angel, Cardiff; New Inn, Pontypridd; Bear, Cowbridge.
Lunches and teas served.

L 29   Llanwern

Tel. Newport 412029
The Clubhouse, Llanwern, Newport, Gwent NP6 2DW.
Meadowland course.
18 holes, 6298 yds. S.S.S. 72
9 holes, 5674 yds. S.S.S. 72
Visitors welcome weekdays.
Green Fees. Weekdays £4.50 (£2.00 with member); weekends £5.00 (with member); societies £3.50 per player.
Society Meetings by arrangement.
Hotels: Ladbroke Mercury; Westgate; Kings Head, Newport.
Meals served.

L 30   Machynlleth

Tel. Machynlleth (0654) 2000
Newtown Rd., Machynlleth, Powys.
½ mile from Machynlleth on A489 to Newtown.
Undulating course.
9 holes, 5726 yds. S.S.S. 68
Course designed by James Braid (1905).
Visitors welcome on weekdays.
Green Fees. £3.00; weekends and bank holidays £3.50.
Society Meetings welcome.
Hotels: Wynnstay Arms.
Lunches served except Tues.

L 31   Maesteg

Tel. Maesteg 73 2037
Mount Pleasant, Maesteg, Bridgend, Mid Glam.
Off Maesteg to Bryn road 50 yards past Maesteg General Hospital.
Moorland course.
18 holes.
Visitors welcome.
Green Fees. On application to secretary.
Hotels: in Bridgend.
Snacks and meals served except Thurs.

L 32   Merthyr Tydfil Cilsanws

Tel. Merthyr Tydfil 3308, 3063 (Sec.)
Cilsanws, Cefn Coed, Merthyr Tydfil, Mid Glam.
Near junction of A470-A465.

Mountain course.
9 holes, 6360 yds. S.S.S. 70
Visitors welcome.
Green Fees. Weekdays £1.00; weekends £2.00.
Hotels: Baverstocks.
Meals served by arrangement.

L 33   Milford Haven

Tel. Milford Haven 2368
Woodbine House, Milford Haven, Dyfed.
1 mile from Milford on Dale road.
Parkland course.
18 holes, 6174 yds. S.S.S. 71
Visitors welcome.
Green Fees. £3.00 plus V.A.T.
Meals served by arrangement.

L 34   Monmouth

Tel. Monmouth 2212
Leasebrook Lane, Monmouth, Gwent.
1 mile along A40 Monmouth-Ross.
Parkland course.
9 holes, 5424 yds. S.S.S. 66
Visitors welcome.
Society Meetings welcome on weekdays except Mon.
Hotels: White Swan; Kings Head; Beaufort Arms.
Meals served except Mon.

L 35   Monmouthshire

Tel. Abergavenny (1873) 3171
Llanfoist, Abergavenny, Gwent.
2 miles from Abergavenny, between Llanfoist and Llanellen.
Parkland course.
18 holes, 6045 yds. S.S.S. 69
Course designed by James Braid.
Visitors welcome.
Green Fees. Weekdays £5.00; weekends £7.00.
Society Meetings Mon. and Fri. only.
Hotels: Angel; Swan, Abergavenny.
Meals served except Tues.

L 36   Morlais Castle

Tel. Merthyr 2822
Pant, Dowlais, Merthyr Tydfil, Mid Glam.
Mountain course.
9 holes, 6072 yds. S.S.S. 69
Visitors welcome on weekdays, Sat. morning and Sun. afternoon if members of recognized club.
Green Fees. £3.00.
Hotels: New Inn; Castle Hotel, Merthyr.
Snacks served when bar is open.

L 37   Morriston

Tel. Swansea 71079
160 Clasemont Rd., Morriston, Swansea, W. Glam.
3 miles N of Swansea on A4067, then W along A40 ½ mile.
Parkland course.
18 holes, 5672 yds. S.S.S. 68
Visitors welcome.
Society Meetings by arrangement.
Hotels: Dragon; Dolphin, Swansea.
Lunches served.

L 38 Mountain Ash

Tel. Mountain Ash 2265
Cefnpennar, Mountain Ash, Mid Glam.
On A4052.
Mountain course.
18 holes, 5575 yds. S.S.S. 68
Visitors welcome.
Green Fees. Weekdays £2.00; weekends £3.00.
Society Meetings by arrangement.
Meals served.

L 39 Neath

Tel. Neath 3615
Cadoxton, Neath, W. Glam.
3 miles from Neath.
Undulating course.
18 holes, 6436 yds. S.S.S. 72
Visitors welcome.
Green Fees. Weekdays £4.00; weekends £5.00.
Society Meetings weekdays by arrangement.
Hotels: Castle Hotel; Cambrian, Neath.
Meals served except Mon.

L 40 Newport

Tel. Rhiwderin 2643
Rogerstone, Newport, Gwent NP1 9FX.
A467, 4 miles from Newport; turn off at Vixen Service Station.
Undulating parkland course.
18 holes, summer 6370 yds. S.S.S. 71
winter 5815 yds. S.S.S. 70
Visitors welcome.
Green Fees. Weekdays £6.00 (£3.00 with member); weekends £8.00 (£4.00 with member).
Society Meetings weekdays by arrangement.
Hotels: Gateway Motel; King's Head; Westgate, Newport.
Meals served.

L 41 Newport (Pembs)

Tel. Newport (0239) 820244
Newport, Dyfed SA42 0NR.
Follow signs to Newport Sands from Newport.
Seaside course.
9 holes, S.S.S. 69
Visitors welcome.
Green Fees. £3.50.
Society Meetings by arrangement.
Hotels: Golden Lion Hotel, Newport; Fishguard Bay Hotel, Fishguard.
Snacks served.

L 42 Palleg

Tel. Glantawe 842193
Ystradgynlais, Swansea, W. Glam. (Club in Brecon).
Off A4067 N of Swansea.
Moorland course.
9 holes, 6510 yds. S.S.S. 72
Visitors welcome.
Society Meetings welcome except Mon.
Hotels: Copper Beech Hotel, Abercrave.
Lunches served.

L 43 Pennard

Tel. Bishopton (044 128) 3131
Southgate Rd., Southgate, Swansea, W. Glam. SA3 2BT.
10 miles W of Swansea on B4436.
Undulating seaside course.
18 holes, 6266 yds. S.S.S. 71
Visitors welcome.
Green Fees. Weekdays £4.25 (£3.00 with member); weekends £5.00 (£3.75 with member).
Society Meetings welcome on weekdays.
Hotels: Dowdswell's, Bishopston; Nicholaston House, Gower; Heatherslade, Southgate.
Meals served by arrangement except Mon.

L 44 Pontardawe

Tel. Pontardawe (0792) 863118
Cefn Llan, Pontardawe, Swansea, W. Glam.
4 miles N of M4 on A4067.
Meadowland course.
18 holes, 6061 yds. S.S.S. 69
Visitors welcome.
Green Fees. Weekdays £3.00; weekends £5.00.
Society Meetings weekdays and Sun. by arrangement.
Hotels: Glanafon County Hotel, Pontardawe.
Meals served except Mon.

L 45 Pontnewydd

Tel. Cwmbran 06333 2170
Maesgwyn Farm, Upper Cwmbran, Cwmbran, Gwent NP4 4AR.
2 miles N of Cwmbran, which is 5 miles N of Newport.
Meadowland course.
10 holes, 5367 yds. S.S.S. 67
Visitors welcome on weekdays, weekends with member only.
Green Fees. £4.00.
Society Meetings by arrangement.
Hotels: Commodore; The Conifers, Cwmbran.
Meals served by arrangement.

L 46 Pontypool

Tel. Pontypool 3655
Trevethin, Pontypool, Gwent NP4 8TR.
1 mile N of Pontypool.
Undulating parkland, moorland course.
18 holes, 6070 yds. S.S.S. 69
Visitors welcome.
Green Fees. Weekdays £5.00; weekends £6.00.
Society Meetings welcome on weekdays.
Hotels: Clarence.
Meals served.

L 47 Pontypridd

Tel. Pontypridd 402742
Ty-Gwyn, Pontypridd, Mid Glam.
11 miles from Cardiff on A470.
18 holes, 5650 yds. S.S.S. 68
Visitors welcome.
Green Fees. Weekdays £2.87; weekends £3.45.
Society Meetings welcome on weekdays.
Hotels: New Inn, Pontypridd.
Snacks served; meals by arrangement.

L 48 Pyle & Kenfig

Tel. Porthcawl 3093
Waun-y-mer, Pyle, Mid Glam. CF33 4PU.
M4 to Pyle, then B4283 to Nottage.
Seaside course.
18 holes, 6655 yds. S.S.S. 73
Course designed by H.S. Colt, extended by P. Mackenzie Ross.
Visitors welcome on weekdays if members of recognized club or with handicap certificate.
Green Fees. £5.50.
Society Meetings welcome on weekdays.
Hotels: Seabank; Esplanade; Fairways; Atlantic, Porthcawl.
Lunches served except Mon; dinners by arrangement except Mon.

L 49 Radyr

Tel. Radyr (0222) 842408
Drysgol Rd., Radyr, Cardiff CF4 8BS.
Off A470 at Taffs Well.
Undulating parkland course.
18 holes, 6031 yds. S.S.S. 70
Visitors welcome.
Green Fees. Weekdays £5.00 (£2.50 with member); weekends £7.50.
Society Meetings Wed., Thurs., Fri.
Hotels: Post House, Pentwyn; Churchills, Llandaff; Avon, Cardiff.
Meals served except Sun. evening and Thurs.

L 50 Rhondda

Tel. Tonypandy 433204
Pontygwaith, Ferndale, Mid Glam. CF43 3PW.
On Cardiff to Rhondda road 1 mile from Porth.
Mountain top course.
18 holes, 6403 yds. S.S.S. 70
Visitors welcome.
Green Fees. Weekdays £3.00; weekends £5.00. Reduced rates if playing with member.
Society Meetings by arrangement.
Hotels: Dunraven, Trenerbert.
Meals served except Mon.

L 51 Royal Porthcawl

Tel. Porthcawl (065 671) 2251
Porthcawl, Mid Glam.
On A48 Cardiff to Swansea road 25 miles from Cardiff, 8 miles E of Bridgend.
Seaside course.
18 holes, 6605 yds. S.S.S. 74
Course designed by James Braid.
Visitors welcome with member or letter of introduction.
Green Fees. Weekdays £8.00; weekends £10.00; weekly £33.00.
Society Meetings by arrangement.
Hotels: Seabank; Esplanade; Fairways; Atlantic.
Lunches and teas served; dinners and suppers by arrangement.

L 52 St. Giles

Tel. Newtown (0686) 25844
Pool Rd., Newtown, Powys.
¾ mile from Newtown on A483 to Welshpool.
Undulating parkland course.
9 holes, 5864 yds. S.S.S. 68
Visitors welcome on weekdays, restricted at weekends.

Glad to shelter in a gorse bush

This is the time of year when golfers look back. The putts they have holed at vital moments grow in length, the good shots become great and all rounds seem to the listener to have been played when conditions were vile. The only difference is that in the following case they undoubtedly were!

You always know when it is going to blow and be rough at Porthcawl; there is an ominous calm followed two days later by the sea cascading over the esplanade, eroding the paint-work of your car quicker than salt on winter roads.

The night before the Home Internationals in September 1970, this theory was blossoming nicely and by morning the wireless by my bed was issuing the worst-sounding weather forecast I have ever heard. I am never quite sure of the whereabouts of Fisher, Dogger and German Bight, but Lundy and Bristol Channel were outside my window and the promised gale force ten sounded a conservative estimate.

Just the conditions, maybe, that a Welsh prop forward hopes for his baptism in the January mud at the Arms Park, but hardly ideal for the grooved swing I like to think I had spent most of the summer perfecting. Timing and finesse were as much good as they are to a demolition worker; survival was the only keyword.

Down at the club an anxious committee, having contacted every R.A.F. and coastguard station for miles in the hope the B.B.C. might be wrong, stoically gave the go-ahead, muttering something about a nice fresh morning and a good, testing day for

golf. The starter did his best to instil the right sense of occasion by announcing the players to the crowd of 14, but they were upwind of him and, in any case, hadn't left the club-house with the notable exception of Tony Duncan, who is well accustomed to such weather for his Duncan Putter at Easter.

Footballers have been known to sprain ankles running on to the field, and in a first international it was therefore reassuring to know that one had made it. The drives were hit and off we went in the vicious crosswind, using our umbrellas like a shield at Agincourt; an experience I remember as vividly as the putt of six feet I worked in on the first green, although the conscious act of taking the putter back remains a blur.

One of the charms of Porthcawl, so I was once assured, is that the start runs beside the sea, but this was not the morning to appreciate it, particularly without a caddie. Sharing the habit with Gene Sarazen (the only one, incidentally) of never wearing a waterproof jacket, my cashmere sweater, which an hour or two earlier had looked so nice in its cellophane wrapper, was soaked by the time we reached the second tee by one of the horizontal squalls that practically took you with them. I never thought I would ever seek refuge in a gorse bush and, waiting to drive, I confess for the first time that my old university tutor had a point in saying that 'golf is not a game but a disease.'

A minute or two later, things were temporarily impossible. We sheltered in a tiny stone hut like guerrillas on a windswept mountain. Contrary to some reports, the

Welsh captain would have called a halt there and then if the English captain could have been summoned from a similar huddle two holes ahead, but the squall passed, a walk-out was averted and the ordeal continued.

I was momentarily encouraged by the thought that someone had once written that 'Steel's rotundity is proof against the wind,' but either Steel's rotundity has diminished, which I doubt, or else nothing was proof against that wind.

All stories tend to become distorted with time and in years to come the survivors of Porthcawl will be linking the battle with Mons and Vimy Ridge. It wasn't that bad—quite— but for two days the only consolation seemed to be that we weren't keeping our scores with the big ball, as the professionals were in the quieter waters of Lytham, although last week at Turnberry there arose another amusing aftermath.

Renewing his partnership as caddie with his brother, Roddy, who made his first appearance for Ireland this year, Jody Carr was asked on the fierce final morning whether conditions were as bad as at Porthcawl, "Good Lord, nothing like," he replied indignantly. "At Porthcawl we broke five umbrellas."

Editor's footnote. Any suggestion that Porthcawl is always like that must be immediately refuted. It has always been one of my favourite courses and offers a great treat whatever the weather.

Reprinted from The Sunday Telegraph *8th November 1970.*

Green Fees. Weekdays £3.50 per round or day; weekends £4.50.
Society Meetings by arrangement.
Hotels: Elephant & Castle; Bear; Maesmawr Hall.
Meals served by arrangement except Mon.

L 53 St. Idloes

Tel. Llanidloes (055 12) 2299
Penrhallt, Llanidloes, Powys.
Off A492 on to A407 for 1 mile.
Undulating course.
9 holes, 5210 yds. S.S.S. 66
Visitors welcome.
Green Fees. Weekdays £2.00 per day; weekends £3.00 per day; weekly £6.00.
Hotels: Lloyd's; Lion Hotel.

L 54 St. Mellons

Tel. Castleton (063 680408)
St. Mellons, Cardiff CF3 8XS.
Midway between Newport and Cardiff.
Parkland course.

18 holes, 6225 yds. S.S.S. 70
Course designed by H.S. Colt and J.S. Morrison in conjunction with Henry Cotton (1937).
Visitors welcome with member or letter of introduction.
Green Fees. Weekdays £5.50 per day; weekends with member only.
Society Meetings welcome on weekdays except Wed.
Hotels: St. Mellons County Hotel, Castleton; Post House, Cardiff.
Morning coffees, lunches and evening meals served.

L 55 St. Pierre Golf & Country Club

Tel. Chepstow (02912) 5261
St. Pierre Park, Chepstow, Gwent NP6 6YA.
On A48, 1 mile from Chepstow roundabout.
Old course. parkland; new course, meadowland.
Old 18 holes, 6619 yds. S.S.S. 72
New 18 holes, 5757 yds. S.S.S. 69
Old course designed by Ken Cotton, new course by Bill Cox.

Visitors welcome with reservation.
Green Fees. Weekdays £8.00 per round, £10.00 per day; weekends £9.00 per round, £11.00 per day.
Society Meetings welcome on weekdays.
Hotels: Accommodation available for 144 at club. Conference facilities.
Meals served. Swimming pool, sauna, squash, badminton.

L 56 Southerndown

Tel. Southerndown 880 326
Ewenny, Bridgend, Mid Glam. CF35 5BT.
4 miles from Bridgend on A48 from Cardiff to Swansea; turn off at Pelican Hotel, Ogmore by Sea.
Downland course.
18 holes, 6707 yds. S.S.S. 73
Course designed by H.S. Colt.
Visitors welcome if members of recognized club, Sun. with member only.
Green Fees. Weekdays £4.50 (£3.00 with member); weekends £6.00 (£4.00 with member) Sun. with member only.
Society Meetings Tues. and Thurs. only.

Hotels: Brig y Don, Ogmore by Sea; Seabank, Porthcawl.
Meals served.

L 57   South Pembrokeshire

Tel. Pembroke 3817
Defensible Barracks, Pembroke Dock, Dyfed.
2 miles from Pembroke.
Meadowland course.
9 holes, 5804 yds. S.S.S. 69
Visitors welcome.
Green Fees. £3.00 per day (£1.50 with member).
Society Meetings by arrangement.
Hotels: Kings Arms, Pembroke.
Light meals served.

L 58   Swansea Bay

Tel. Skewen 812198
Jersey Marine, Neath, W. Glam SA1 7DQ.
4 miles from Neath on road to Swansea.
Seaside course.
18 holes, 6417 yds. S.S.S. 71
Visitors welcome if members of recognized club.
Green Fees. Weekdays £4.00 per day; weekends £5.50 per day.
Hotels: Cimla Court Hotel; Castle Hotel, Neath; Dragon, Swansea.
Meals served except Wed.

L 59   Tenby

Tel. Tenby 2978 (Sec.), 2787 (Steward), 4447 (Pro)
The Burrows, Tenby, Dyfed SA70 7NP.
A40 from Carmarthen to St. Clears, then A477.
Seaside course.
18 holes, 6450 yds. S.S.S. 71
Visitors welcome.
Green Fees. Jan.-Sept. Weekdays £4.50 per day; weekends £5.50; weekly £22.50. Oct.-Mar. Weekdays & weekends £3.50 per day; weekly £17.50.
Society Meetings welcome.
Hotels: in Tenby.
Meals served except Tues.

L 60   Tredegar & Rhymney

Tel. Rhymney 840743
Cymtyssyg, Rhymney, Gwent.
At junction of A4048 and A465.
Moorland course.
9 holes, 5564 yds. S.S.S. 68
Visitors welcome.
Green Fees. £2.00.
Hotels: Castle Hotel, Tredegar.

L 61   Tredegar Park

Bassaleg Rd., Newport, Gwent NPT 3PX.
Leave M4 at Exit 26.
Parkland course.
18 holes, 6044 yds. S.S.S. 70
Visitors welcome.
Green Fees. Weekdays £5.00; weekends £6.50 plus V.A.T.
Society Meetings welcome on weekdays.
Hotels: in Newport.
Meals served except Mon.

L 62   Welshpool

Tel. Castle Caereinion 249, Sec. Welshpool 3377
Y Golfa, Welshpool, Powys.
4 miles from Welshpool on A458.
Mountain course.
18 holes, 5708 yds. S.S.S. 69
Course designed by James Braid.
Visitors welcome.
Green Fees. Weekdays £3.00; weekends £4.00.
Society Meetings by arrangement with Sec.
Hotels: Royal Oak.
Meals served except Mon.

L 63   Wenvoe Castle

Tel. Cardiff 594371
Wenvoe, Cardiff, S. Glam.
3½ miles from Cardiff on Barry road.
Undulating parkland course.
18 holes, 6411 yds. S.S.S. 71
Visitors welcome.
Green Fees. Weekdays £5.00 (£3.50 with member); weekends £6.50 (£5.00 with member). Societies £4.00 per player.
Society Meetings Mon. and Thurs. only.
Hotels: in Cardiff, Barry and Penarth.
Lunches served by arrangement.

L 64   West Monmouthshire

Tel. Brynmawr 310233, 312746 (Sec.)
Pond Rd., Nantyglo, Gwent.
Turn off A467 at Dunlop Semtex Ltd., signposted.
Moorland course.
18 holes, 6132 yds. S.S.S. 69
Visitors welcome.
Green Fees. Weekdays £2.00; weekends £3.00.
Society Meetings welcome weekdays.
Hotels: in district.
Lunches served except Wed.

L 65   Whitchurch

Tel. Cardiff 60985
Whitchurch, Cardiff CF4 6XD.
3 miles N of Cardiff on A470.
Parkland course.
18 holes, 6220 yds. S.S.S. 70
Visitors welcome except Sat.
Green Fees. Weekdays £6.50 per day (£2.50 with member); weekends £5.00 with member only.
Society Meetings by arrangement.
Hotels: in Cardiff.
Meals served.

L 66   Whitehall

Tel. Abercynon 740245
The Pavilion, Nelson, Treharris, Mid Glam.
M4 to Merthyr. Turn off on roundabout at Abercynon for 800 yds., then take Mountain Rd. for ¼ mile.
Mountain course.
9 holes, 5646 yds. S.S.S. 67
Visitors welcome.
Green Fees. £3.00 (£2.00 with member).
Society Meetings 6 per annum. Must be arranged by Mar. each year.
Hotels: Llechwen Hall; Thorne Hotel; Abercynon Hotel.
Meals served.

M North Wales

M 1   Aberdovey

Tel. Aberdovey (0654) 72210
Aberdovey, Gwynedd LL35 0RT.
On A493, adjoining Aberdovey Station.
Seaside course.
18 holes, 6421 yds. S.S.S. 72
Course redesigned by J. Braid.
Visitors welcome on weekdays.
Green Fees. On application.
Society Meetings weekdays by arrangement.
Hotels: Trefeddian, Aberdovey; Corbett Arms, Tywyn.
Meals served.

M 2   Abergele & Pensarn

Tel. Abergele (0745) 824034
Tan-y-Goppa Rd., Abergele, Clwyd.
On A55 ½ mile W of Abergele.
Parkland course.
18 holes, 6086 yds. S.S.S. 69
Course designed by Hawtree & Son.
Visitors welcome.
Green Fees. Weekdays £5.00 per day; weekends £6.00 per day.
Society Meetings welcome weekdays and Sun.
Hotels: Kinmel Manor, Abergele; Hotel 70°, Old Colwyn.
Meals and bar snacks served.

M 3   Abersoch

Tel. Abersoch 2622
Abersoch, Pwllheli, Gwynedd LL53 7EY.
6 miles from Pwllheli; beyond village turn left into Golf Rd.
Seaside course.
9 holes, 5722 yds. S.S.S. 68
Visitors welcome.
Green Fees. Daily £3.00; weekly £15.00; fortnightly £25.00.
Hotels: Neigwl; Porthtocyn; Riverside Hotel; Harbour Hotel, Abersoch.

M 4   Anglesey

Tel. Rhosneigr (0407) 810219
Station Rd., Rhosneigr, Gwynedd LL64 5QT.
Left off A5 about 8 miles from Holyhead.
Seaside course.
18 holes, 6204 yds. S.S.S. 70
Visitors welcome.

Green Fees. Weekdays £2.90; weekends £4.00; weekly £13.80.
Society Meetings by arrangement.
Hotels: Bay Hotel; Glan Neigr.
Meals served.

M 5   Bala

Tel. Bala (0678) 520359
Penlan, Bala, Gwynedd LL23 7SR.
A494; first right out of Bala towards Dolgellau.
Mountainous course.
10 holes, 7431 yds. S.S.S. 64
Visitors welcome.
Green Fees. Weekdays £2.50 per day; weekends and bank holidays £3.50.
Hotels: Royal White Lion; Fron Dderw Guest House.
Catering for parties only.

M 6   Baron Hill

Tel. Beaumaris 231
Beaumaris, Gwynedd LL58 8YN.
¾ mile from town centre.
Undulating course.
9 holes, 5062 yds. S.S.S. 67
Visitors welcome on weekdays.
Green Fees. Weekdays £3.00 (£2.00 with

member); weekends and bank holidays £4.00 (£2.50 with member).
Hotels: Bulkeley Arms; Bull's Head; White Lion; Liverpool Arms; Bishopgate House.
Full catering in club house.

M 7   Bull Bay

Tel. Amlwch 830 213
Bull Bay, Amlwch, Gwynedd.
Undulating clifftop course.
18 holes, 6175 yds. S.S.S. 70
Visitors welcome.
Green Fees. Weekdays £4.00; weekends £6.00. 20% reduction for parties over 12.
Society Meetings welcome.
Hotels: Dinorben Arms, Amlwch; Trecastell Hotel; Bull Bay Hotel, Bull Bay.
Full catering service.

M 8   Caernarfon

Tel. Caernarfon 3783
Llanfaglan, Caernarfon, Gwynedd.
¾ mile S of Caernarfon, turn for Aber shore, 1 mile.
Parkland course.
18 holes, 6000 yds. S.S.S. 69
Green Fees. £5.00 per day.
Hotels: Royal; Black Boy Hotel.

M 9   Caernarvonshire (Conwy)

Tel. Conwy 2423
The Morfa, Conwy, Gwynedd.
From Conwy, A55 to Bangor, first turn right.
Seaside course.
18 holes, 6656 yds. S.S.S. 73
Visitors welcome if members of recognized club.
Green Fees. Weekdays £5.50; weekends £7.00.
Society Meetings welcome.
Hotels: Ferry Hotel; Deganwy Castle Hotel, Deganwy, Conwy.
Meals served except Tues.

M 10   Clwb Golff Betws-y-Coed

Tel. Betws-y-Coed (069 02) 556
Betws-y-Coed, Gwynedd.
200 yds. from A5 in centre of the village.
Meadowland course.
9 holes, 4740 yds. S.S.S. 63
Visitors welcome
Green Fees. Weekdays £3.00 per day; weekends and bank holidays £5.00.
Society Meetings welcome; fee 50p per player, parties of 12 and over.
Hotels: in Betws-y-Coed.
Light refreshments served.

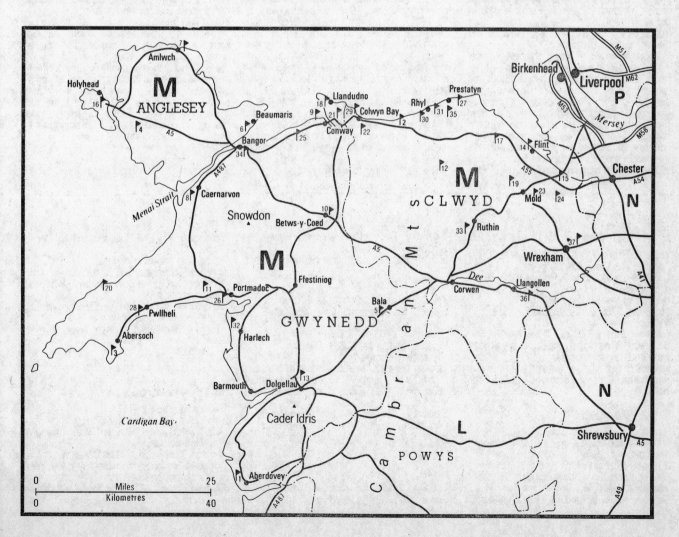

Pilgrimage to Aberdovey

One June morning during the Ladies' championship of 1967, I took the little train from Harlech which, having crossed the quaint old bridge spanning the glorious estuary at Barmouth, slipped southwards to Aberdovey.

Aberdovey, looking out over Cardigan Bay, is the course which Bernard Darwin so often confessed his soul loved best in all the world and I went by train because the great man would have done the same. It was, after all, a pilgrimage and I was determined to treat it as such. But in the beauty of that sunlit morning, everything seemed somehow so familiar as I crossed the track from the station by the clubhouse.

Darwin, by his writing, had done much to bring it to life, and I remembered how the original course had been laid out by one of his uncles, Colonel Ruck from Formby, who in the early 1880's borrowed nine flower pots from a lady in the village and cut nine holes in the marsh to put them in.

There is the story, too, of the first scratch medal in 1893 which Darwin won with a score of 100, and many a tale about the terrors of a blind short hole, 'Cader'. In the early days, the primitive game imported by the good Colonel began much farther from the present site of the clubhouse and the famous 'Cader' did not form part of the course until 1893 when it took more or less the shape that is recognizable today.

The result of lying on a long, narrow strip of land beside the sandhills—which alas, could never be utilised—is that the holes go straight out and straight home, but there are hummocks and undulations everywhere and in ever-changing moods as much variety as could be expected.

The 'Cader', the 3rd, is not so frightening as in the days when, it is said, only a fool or a millionaire took a new ball, but there is challenge enough in the outward half of less than 3000 yards which, after the short 5th, moves inland nearer the railway.

Coming home the holes have rather more feature, and on the evidence of a single round played in a pleasant heat when I was thankful that the greens, protected from the sheep by electric fencing, had been sympathetically watered, are easier to remember.

The subtlety of the drive into the elbow of the dogleg at the 11th matches the glory of the 12th green, a small raised perch in the dunes with the first real view of the sea. The 13th (546 yds) coming back alongside the dunes, is the longest hole while the 14th offers the choice from the tee of attempting a formidable carry or tucking a shot into a tight little corner.

But equally fascinating is the 16th (288 yds) with a tempting drive from a sleepered bunker round the curve of the railway fence towards a green which, from the wrong angle, is difficult to hit even with a pitching club.

The path home is by way of two good fours through flat country of rushes and ditches, and I am glad to say my second to the 18th won an admiring glance from the small group by the clubhouse whom I rapidly joined for very welcome refreshment in the sun.

Later I found that my appraisal of the course had been masked by a general delight at finally filling such a notable gap in my golfing education, but I was glad, all the same, that I had not had to play a medal in a stiff wind when the comparative smallness of the greens and a need to pitch shrewdly would have been accentuated.

Owing to the rather leisurely Cambrian trains, the journey back was split in two and it was evening when I returned to Harlech, the home of the Royal St. David's club, where the course twists backwards and forwards rather more than at Aberdovey.

The first thirteen holes are very different in character from the last five which, plunging more into the sandhills, have decided many a championship, but for all the excellence of the golf, Harlech commands a setting which that evening was at its best. The sun set on a becalmed sea, the peaks of Snowdonia turned black against the sky and the old castle, rearing high above the links, stood guard over all as it has done for centuries. It had been a perfect day.

M 11 Criccieth

Tel. Criccieth (076 671) 2154
Ednyfed Hill, Criccieth, Gwynedd.
A497, 4 miles from Portmadoc; turn right past Memorial Hall, up hill ½ mile.
Undulating meadowland course.
18 holes, 5755 yds. S.S.S. 68
Visitors welcome.
Green Fees. £3.00 (£1.50 with member).
Society Meetings welcome weekdays, weekends by arrangement.
Hotels: Lion; Marine; George IV.
Snacks and light meals served May to Sept. inclusive.

M 12 Denbigh

Henllan Rd., Denbigh, Clwyd.
On the Hellan road, 2 miles from Denbigh.
Meadowland course.
9 holes, 4822 yds. S.S.S. 63
Course designed by J. Stockton.
Visitors welcome.
Green Fees. Weekdays £4.00; weekends £6.00.

Society Meetings welcome weekdays.
Hotels: Bull; Crown.
Meals served on weekdays by arrangement.

M 13 Dolgellau

Tel. Dolgellau (0341) 422603
Pencefn Rd., Dolgellau, Gwynedd LL40.
½ mile from town centre.
Undulating parkland course.
9 holes, 4512 yds. S.S.S. 64
Visitors welcome.
Green Fees. Weekdays £3.00 per day (£1.50 with member); weekends and bank holidays £4.00 per day (£2.00 with member).
Society Meetings by arrangement 2 months in advance.
Hotels: in area.
Teas served.

M 14 Flint

Tel. Flint 2327
Cornist Park, Flint, Clwyd.
About 1 mile from A548 Coast road, turn right at Town Hall, follow signs to Cornist Park.
Undulating parkland course.
9 holes, 6535 yds. S.S.S. 68
Visitors welcome on weekdays, weekends with member only.
Green Fees. Weekdays £2.00; weekends £2.00 with member only.
Hotels: Springfield; Halkyn, Holywell.
Snacks served in evening.

M 15 Hawarden

Tel. Hawarden 531447
Hawarden, Deeside, Clwyd.
A55 first left after Hawarden Station going W.
Parkland course.
9 holes, 5829 yds. S.S.S. 68
Visitors welcome on weekdays, weekends with member only.
Green Fees. £3.00 per round, £2.00 with member.
Hotels: in Chester.

M 16   Holyhead

Tel. Holyhead 3279
Holyhead, Gwynedd LL65 2YG.
Turn left off A5 at Valley, 2 miles.
Seaside course.
18 holes, 6081 yds. S.S.S. 70
Course designed by J. Braid (1912).
Visitors welcome if members of recognized club.
Green Fees. On application to secretary.
Society Meetings welcome.
Hotels: Dormy House.
All catering facilities available.

M 17   Holywell

Tel. Holywell 710040
Brynford, Holywell, Clwyd.
2 miles to left at traffic lights on A55 from Chester at Holywell. Turn right at Brynford, signpost to Pantasaph.
Moorland course.
9 holes, 6234 yds. S.S.S. 70
Visitors welcome on weekdays, weekends with member only.
Green Fees. Weekdays £2.00 (£1.00 with member); weekends £2.50.
Society Meetings by arrangement.
Hotels: Springfield; Halkyn, Holywell; Fielding Arms, Pantasaph; Stamford Gate, Holywell.

M 18   Llandudno

Tel. Llandudno (0492) 76450
Hospital Rd., Llandudno, Gwynedd, LL30 1HU.
A496 to Conway, 1 mile SW of Llandudno Railway.
Seaside course.
18 holes, 6556 yds. S.S.S. 72
Visitors welcome.
Green Fees. Weekdays £5.00 per day; weekends £6.00 per day.
Society Meetings by arrangement.
Hotels: in area.
Meals served by arrangement.

M 19   Mold

Tel. Mold (0352) 740318
Pantymwyn, Mold, Clwyd.
From town centre follow signpost for Gwernaffield, 3 miles.
Undulating course.
18 holes, 5521 yds. S.S.S. 67
Visitors welcome 7 days a week.
Green Fees. Weekdays £3.00; weekends £4.00.
Society Meetings by arrangement.
Hotels: Bryn Awel; Dolphin, Mold.

M 20   Nefyn & District

Tel. Nefyn 720218 (Sec. 720966)
Morfa Nefyn, Pwllheli, Gwynedd LL53 6DA.
1 mile W of Nefyn.
Seaside course.
18 holes, 6335 yds. S.S.S. 71
Visitors welcome.
Green Fees. Weekdays £5.00; weekends £6.00; weekly £20.00.
Society Meetings by arrangement
Hotels: Cecil Court; Nanhorn Arms; Woodlands Hall Hotel.
Full catering except Tues.

M 21   North Wales

Tel. Llandudno (0492) 75325
72 Bryniau Rd., West Shore, Llandudno, Gwynedd LL30 2DZ.
Seaside course.
18 holes, 6132 yds. S.S.S. 69
Visitors welcome if members of recognized club.
Green Fees. Weekdays £5.00 per round, £6.00 per day; weekends £6.00 per round, £7.00 per day; weekly Mon.-Fri. £20.00.
Society Meetings welcome.
Meals served.

M 22   Old Colwyn

Tel. Colwyn Bay (0492) 55581
Woodland Ave., Old Colwyn, Clwyd.
200 yards off A55 in Old Colwyn.
Meadowland course.
9 holes, S.S.S. 66
Visitors welcome.
Green Fees. Weekdays £3.00 per round or day; weekends £4.00 per round or day; weekly £12.00.
Society Meetings by arrangement.
Hotels: Norfolk.
Meals served by arrangement.

M 23   Old Padeswood

Tel. Buckley (0244) 547401
Station Road, Padeswood, nr. Mold, Clwyd.
A5118, 2 miles from Mold, 10 miles from Chester.
Undulating parkland course.
9 holes, 5946 yds. S.S.S. 68
Visitors welcome; restrictions only on competition days.
Green Fees. Weekdays £3.00 (£2.00 with member); weekends and bank holidays £4.00 (£2.50 with member).
Society Meetings catered for (no restrictions).
Hotels: Bryn Awel, Mold.
Meals served by prior arrangement only.

M 24   Padeswood & Buckley

Tel. Buckley (0244) 542537
Station Lane, Padeswood, Mold, Clwyd CH7 4JD.
8 miles W of Chester, 4 miles from Mold on A5118.
Parkland course.
18 holes, 5746 yds. S.S.S. 68
Visitors welcome except Sun.
Green Fees. Weekdays £4.00; Sat. £6.50; weekly Mon.-Sat. £15.00.
Society Meetings welcome weekdays.
Hotels: in Chester, Mold, Wrexham.
Meals served by arrangement.

M 25   Penmaenmawr

Tel. Penmaenmawr (0492) 623330
Cae Maen Pavilion, Penmaenmawr, Gwynedd LL34 6AU.
Midway between Conwy and Penmaenmawr.
Parkland course.
9 holes, 4471 yds. S.S.S. 65
Visitors welcome.
Green Fees. Weekdays £2.50 per day; weekends £4.00 per day; weekly £10.00.
Society Meetings by arrangement.
Hotels: Mountain View; Puffin; Crescent.
Meals by arrangement.

M 26   Porthmadoc

Tel. Porthmadoc 2037
Morfa Bychan, Porthmadoc, Gwynedd.
1½ miles from Porthmadoc.
Undulating seaside course.
18 holes, 5728 yds. S.S.S. 68
Course designed by J. Braid.
Visitors welcome.
Green Fees. Weekdays £4.00 (£2.00 with member); weekends £5.00 (£2.50 with member).
Society Meetings welcome.
Hotels: Tyddyn Llwyn; Royal Sportsman, Porthmadoc.
Lunches served.

M 27   Prestatyn

Tel. Prestatyn 4320
Marine Rd. East, Prestatyn, Clwyd.
A548 coast road from Queensferry, turn right by entrance to Pontins holiday village.
Seaside course.
18 holes, 6517 yds. S.S.S. 72
Visitors welcome.
Green Fees. Weekdays £5.00; weekends and bank holidays £6.00.
Society Meetings welcome.
Hotels: Grand; Royal Victoria; Nant Hall Hotel.
Meals served.

M 28   Pwllheli

Tel. Pwllheli (0758) 2520
Golf Rd., Pwllheli, Gwynedd LL53 5PS.
Turn into Cardiff Rd. in town centre, bear right at first fork.
Undulating seaside course.
18 holes, 6011 yds. S.S.S. 69
First 9 holes designed by T. Morris (1900), second 9 holes by J. Braid (1909).
Visitors welcome.
Green Fees. On application.
Society Meetings welcome except Tues. and Thurs.
Hotels: Crown; Tower.
Meals served except Mon.

M 29   Rhos on Sea

Tel. Llandudno (0492) 49641
Penrhyn Bay, Llandudno, Gwynedd LL30 3PU.
A546 to Llandudno.
Seaside course.
18 holes, 6064 yds. S.S.S. 69.
Visitors welcome.
Green Fees. On application to secretary.
Society Meetings welcome.
Hotels: Accomodation available at clubhouse for 29.
Meals served.

M 30   Rhuddlan

Tel. Rhuddlan (0745) 590217 (Sec. 590675; Pro 590898)
Rhuddlan, Rhyl, Clwyd, LL18 6LB.
3 miles from Rhyl on A525.
Parkland course.
18 holes, 6038 yds. S.S.S. 69
Course designed by F. Hawtree.
Visitors bona fide members of golf clubs welcome with handicap certificate. Ladies have priority on Tues.
Green Fees. Weekdays £4.00 per round,

£5.00 per day; weekends £5.00 per round, £6.50 per day; weekly £16.00.
Hotels: Oriel Hotel, St. Asaph; Westminster, Rhyl.
Coffee, lunch and dinner served.

M 31   Rhyl

Tel. Rhyl (0745) 53171
Coast Rd., Rhyl, Clwyd.
1 mile from station on A548.
Seaside course.
9 holes, 6057 yds. S.S.S. 69
Visitors welcome.
Green Fees. Weekdays £3.00 per day; weekends £4.00.
Society Meetings by arrangement.
Hotels: Westminster; Hotel Marina, Grange.
Bar snacks; lunches served except Mon.

M 32   Royal St. David's

Tel. Harlech (0766) 780361 (Sec. and Pro), 780203 (clubhouse)
Harlech, Gwynedd.
A496.
Seaside course.
18 holes, 6496 yds. S.S.S. 72
Visitors welcome.
Green Fees. Weekdays £6.00 (£3.00 with member); weekends £8.00 (£4.00 with member); weekly £26.00.
Society Meetings welcome, weekends max. 24.
Hotels: St. David's; Castle Hotel; Queens.
Meals served.

M 33   Ruthin-Pwllglas

Tel. Ruthin 2296
Pwllglas, Ruthin, Clwyd.
2½ miles S of Ruthin on A494.
Moorland course.
9 holes, 5300 yds. S.S.S. 66
Visitors welcome on weekdays.
Green Fees. Weekdays £2.50; weekends £3.50.
Society Meetings weekdays by arrangement.
Hotels: Ruthin Castle; Wynnstay; Castle Hotel, Ruthin.

M 34   St. Deiniol

Tel. Bangor (0248) 53098
Bangor, Gwynedd LL57 1PX.
Off A5 on eastern outskirts of Bangor.
Parkland course.
18 holes, 5421 yds. S.S.S. 67
Course designed by J. Braid.
Visitors welcome.
Green Fees. Weekdays £2.00 (£1.50 with member); weekends £3.00 (£1.50 with member).
Society Meetings welcome except Mon.
Hotels: British; Gwynedd; Waverley.
Lunches served except Mon.

M 35   St. Melyd

Tel. Prestatyn 4405
The Paddock, Meliden Rd., Prestatyn, Clwyd.
On A547 between Prestatyn and Meliden.
Undulating meadowland course.
9 holes, 5762 yds. S.S.S. 68
Visitors welcome on weekdays.
Green Fees. Weekdays £4.00 per day;

weekends £5.00 per day.
Society Meetings welcome.
Hotels: Nant Hall; Grand.
Extensive catering facilities.

M 36   Vale of Llangollen

Tel. Llangollen (0978) 860040
Holyhead Rd., Llangollen, Clwyd.
A5 Oswestry to Llangollen, 2 miles before Llangollen on right.
Parkland course.
18 holes, 6330 yds. S.S.S. 70
Visitors welcome.
Green Fees. Weekdays £4.00 (£3.50 with member); weekends £5.00 (£4.50 with member).
Society Meetings by arrangement.
Hotels: Royal; Bryn Howel; Hand; Chain Bridge.
Snacks served; meals by arrangement.

M 37   Wrexham

Tel. Wrexham (0978) 364268 and 261033
Holt Rd., Wrexham, Clwyd LL13 9SB.
A534, ½ mile from Wrexham in Holt direction.
Undulating course.
18 holes, 6057 yds. S.S.S. 69
Course designed by Gadd of Roehampton.
Visitors welcome.
Green Fees. Weekdays £5.00 per round or day; weekends £7.00 per round or day.
Society Meetings welcome Mon. and Fri. only.
Hotels: Crest Motel; Cross Lanes Hotel.
Meals served by arrangement except Thurs.

N Cheshire, Staffordshire, Shropshire, Derbyshire

N 1   Alderley Edge

Tel. Alderley Edge 585583
Brook Lane, Alderley Edge, Ches. SK9 7RU.
12 miles S of Manchester off A34.
Undulating meadowland course.
9 holes, 5840 yds. S.S.S. 68
Visitors welcome if members of recognized club.
Green Fees. Weekdays £4.00; weekends £5.00.
Society Meetings by arrangement.
Hotels: Edge Hotel, Alderley Edge; Cherry's; Harden Park Hotel, Wilmslow.
Snacks served; meals by arrangement.

N 2   Alfreton

Tel. Alfreton 2070
Wingfield Rd., Alfreton, Derbys.
B6024, Matlock road, 1 mile from Alfreton.
Undulating parkland course.
9 holes, 5012 yds. S.S.S. 65
Visitors welcome on weekdays, weekends with member only.
Green Fees. £4.00 (£2.00 with member).
Society Meetings welcome on weekdays.
Hotels: George.
Snacks and lunches served except Mon.

N 3   Allestree Park

Tel. Derby 550616
Allestree, Derby.
2½ miles N of Derby on A6.
Parkland course.
18 holes, 5683 yds. S.S.S. 67
Visitors welcome on weekdays, weekends with reservation.
Green Fees. Weekdays £1.60; weekends £2.20.
Society Meetings welcome on weekdays.
Hotels: in Derby.
Meals served by arrangement.

N 4   Ashbourne

Tel. Ashbourne 42078
Clifton, Ashbourne, Derbys.
On A515 2 miles S of Ashbourne.
Undulating parkland course.
9 holes, 5359 yds. S.S.S. 66
Course designed by F. Pennink & Co.
Visitors welcome.
Green Fees. Weekdays £2.20; weekends £4.00.

Society Meetings welcome (small societies only).
Hotels: Cock Inn, Clifton; Green Man, Ashbourne.
Meals served except Thurs.

N 5 Astbury

Tel. Congleton 2772
Peel Lane, Astbury, Congleton, Ches.
¾ mile off A34 in village.
Parkland course.
18 holes, 6250 yds. S.S.S. 71
Visitors welcome.
Green Fees. Weekdays £5.00 (£2.50 with member); weekends £3.00 with member only.
Society Meetings welcome.
Hotels: Fox Hotel, Rushton Spencer.
Meals served by arrangement.

N 6 Bakewell

Tel. Bakewell 2307
Station Rd., Bakewell, Derbys.
Hilly course.
9 holes, 4738 yds. S.S.S. 64
Visitors welcome.
Green Fees. Weekdays £3.00 (£1.00 with member); weekends £4.00 (£2.00 with member).
Society Meetings welcome.
Hotels: Rutland Arms.
Lunches served by arrangement.

N 7 Beau Desert

Tel. Hednesford 2626
Hazel Slade, Cannock, Staffs. WS12 5Pl.
A51 from Lichfield, left after 5 miles at signpost to Upper Longdon, left at

crossroads after 2 miles. A460 from Cannock, through Hednesford, right at traffic lights, left at next turn.
Undulating moorland course.
18 holes, 6285 yds. S.S.S. 71
Visitors welcome on weekdays, weekends with member only.
Green Fees. £6.50 per round or day (£2.50 with member).
Society Meetings welcome on weekdays.
Hotels: Cedar Tree; Eaton Lodge Hotel, Rugeley.
Meals served Mon. to Fri.

N 8 Birchwood

Tel. Padgate (0925) 818819 (Pro/Manager)
Kelvin Close, Risley, Warrington, Cheshire.
M62 junction 11; follow A574 for

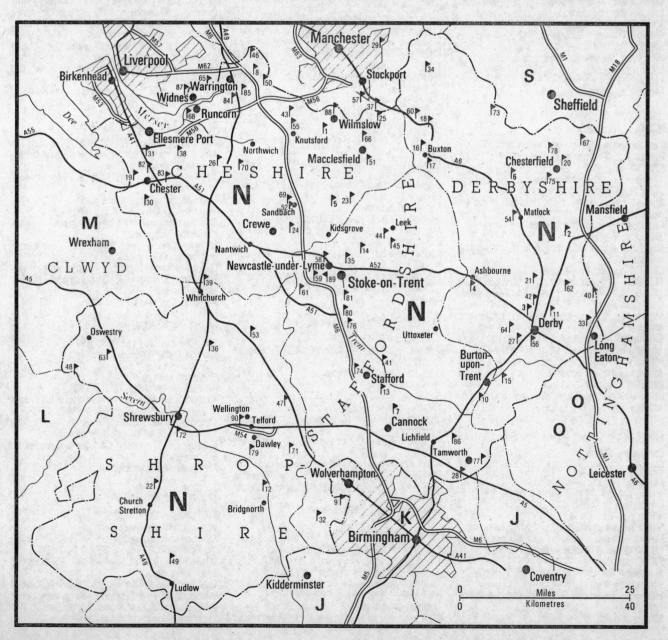

Risley/Birchwood (entrance opposite Data-General).
Recently constructed mature parkland course.
18 holes, 6666 yds. S.S.S. 72
Course designed by T.J.McAuley.
Visitors welcome (restricted times).
Green Fees. Weekdays £3.00; weekends £5.00.
Society Meetings welcome (restricted times).

N 9 Blackhill Wood

Tel. (09077) 892279 (Pro 895015)
Blackhill Wood, Swindon, Dudley, Worcs.
On B4176, 2 miles S of Wolverhampton.
Parkland course.
18 holes, 5954 yds. S.S.S. 69
Course designed by Cotton (C.K.), Pennink, Lawrie and Partners.
Visitors welcome.
Green Fees. Weekdays £2.50; weekends £3.50.
Society Meetings welcome on weekdays by arrangement.
Hotels: Himley Hotel.
Meals and snacks served.

N 10 Branston

Tel. Burton-on-Trent (0283) 43207
Burton Rd., Branston, Burton-on-Trent DE14 3DP.
1 mile from A38. Follow road for Burton-on-Trent and Branston; beyond village take access road to the right through wood to clubhouse.
Wooded meadowland course.
18 holes, 6458 yds. S.S.S. 71
Visitors welcome, but booking necessary at weekends.
Green Fees. Weekdays £4.50 per round (£2.50 with member), £5.50 per day (£3.50 with member); weekends and bank holidays £6.00 per round (£2.50 with member), £7.00 per day (£3.50 with member).
Society Meetings welcome by arrangement on weekdays; special terms.
Hotels: Riverside, Branston; Stanhope Arms, Bretby, Burton-on-Trent; Dog and Partridge, Tutbury.
Lunches and dinners served except Mon. Bar snacks.

N 11 Breadsall Priory Hotel, Golf & Country Club

Tel. 0332 832235
Moor Rd., Morley, Nr. Derby.
1 mile off the A61, 3 miles N of Derby.
Undulating parkland course.
18 holes
Visitors welcome. Book starting time.
Green Fees. Weekdays £5.50 per round; £6.50 per day; weekends £6.50 per round, £7.50 per day.
Society Meetings welcome 7 days by arrangement.
Hotels: Breadsall Priory in grounds of course.
Meals served.

N 12 Bridgnorth

Tel. Bridgnorth (0742) 3315 (Pro 2045)
Stanley Lane, Bridgnorth, Shropshire.
Via town Northgate.
Meadowland course.
18 holes, 6627 yds. S.S.S. 72
Visitors welcome on weekdays, weekends with reservation.
Green Fees. Weekdays £5.00; weekends £8.00.
Society Meetings welcome on weekdays by arrangement.
Hotels: Falcon; Parlours Hall Hotel.
Meals served except Mon.

N 13 Brocton Hall

Tel. Stafford 661485
Brocton, Stafford ST17 0TH.
¼ mile E of A34 from Brocton crossroads.
Parkland course.
18 holes, 6095 yds. S.S.S. 69
Course designed by H. Vardon.
Visitors welcome by arrangement.
Green Fees. Weekdays £6.50; weekends £8.00.
Society Meetings Tues. and Thurs. by arrangement.
Meals served by arrangement (tel. Stafford 660357) except Fri.

N 14 Burslem

Tel. Stoke-on-Trent (0782) 87006
Wood Farm, High Lane, Tunstall, Stoke-on-Trent ST6 7ST.
Hamil Rd. from Burslem, left at High Lane junction, 2 miles.
Moorland course.
11 holes, 5615 yds. S.S.S. 68
Visitors welcome on weekdays if members of recognized club.
Green Fees. £2.50 per day (£1.25 with member).
Hotels: George, Burslem; Grand, Hanley.
Lunches served except Tues.; dinners by arrangement.

N 15 Burton-on-Trent

Tel. Burton 44551
Ashby Rd. East, Burton-on-Trent, Staffs. DE15 0PS.
3 miles from town centre.
Parkland course.
18 holes, 6555 yds. S.S.S. 71
Course designed by Henry Beck.
Visitors welcome with member or with letter of introduction.
Green Fees. Weekdays £6.00; weekends £9.00.
Society Meetings by arrangement.
Hotels: Stanhope Arms, Bretby; Newton Park Hotel, Newton Solney; Midland, Burton-on-Trent.
Meals served by arrangement.

N 16 Buxton & High Peak

Tel. Buxton (0298) 3453
Fairfield, Buxton, Derbys.
1 mile from Buxton station on A6.
Meadowland course.
18 holes, 5913 yds. S.S.S. 68
Visitors welcome.
Green Fees. Weekdays £4.00 per round or day; weekends £5.50.
Society Meetings by arrangement.
Hotels: Hawthorn Farm Guest House; St. Ann's; Palace Hotel, Buxton.
Meals served.

N 17 Cavendish

Tel. Buxton 3494
Gadley Lane, Off Watford Rd., Buxton, Derbys. SK17 6XD.
¾ mile W of town centre, signposted on A53 and A5002.
Undulating parkland/downland course.
18 holes, 5815 yds. S.S.S. 68
Course designed by Dr. Mackenzie.
Visitors welcome on weekdays, weekends with reservation.
Green Fees. Weekdays £4.50 per round or day (£2.00 with member); weekends £6.00 per round or day (£2.50 with member). Members may introduce three visitors on each occasion at reduced rates; juniors half normal rates.
Society Meetings weekdays and weekends by arrangement.
Hotels: Palace Hotel; St. Ann's; Grove; Old Hall Hotel.
Snacks and teas served; meals by arrangement.

N 18 Chapel-en-le-Frith

Tel. Chapel-en-le-Frith (029 881) 2118
The Cockyard, Manchester Rd., Chapel-en-le-Frith, Stockport, Ches.
Midway between Sheffield and Manchester off the A6.
Undulating meadowland course.
18 holes, 6048 yds. S.S.S. 70
Course designed by David Thomas.
Visitors welcome.
Green Fees. Weekdays £3.50; weekends and bank holidays £4.50.
Society Meetings by arrangement.
Hotels: St. Anne's; Buckingham; Palace Hotel, Buxton.
All meals served except Mon.

N 19 Chester

Tel. Chester 671185/675100
Curzon Park, Chester.
1 mile from city centre off A55.
Parkland course.
18 holes, 6270 yds. S.S.S. 70
Visitors welcome on weekdays if members of recognized club.
Green Fees. £5.00.
Society Meetings by arrangement.
Hotels: Chester Curzon; Grosvenor; Blossoms.
Meals served except Mon.

N 20 Chesterfield

Tel. Chesterfield 32035
Walton, Chesterfield, Derbys.
Meadowland course.
18 holes, 6326 yds. S.S.S. 71
Visitors welcome on weekdays, weekends with member only.
Green Fees. Weekdays £5.00 (£2.50 if introduced by and playing with a member); weekends £2.50 with member only.
Lunches served by arrangement.

N 21   Chevin

Tel. Derby 841864
Golf Lane, Duffield, Derbys. DE6 4EE.
On A6 9 miles N of Derby.
Undulating parkland/moorland course.
18 holes, 5966 yds. S.S.S. 69
Visitors welcome on weekdays, weekends with member only.
Green Fees. Weekdays £5.00 per round or day (£2.00 with member); weekends £3.00 per round or day (with member).
Society Meetings by arrangement.
Hotels: Pennine; York; Midland, Derby.
Meals served by arrangement.

N 22   Church Stretton

Tel. Church Stretton (0694) 722281
Links Rd., Church Stretton, Shropshire.
On A49.
Undulating moorland course.
18 holes, 5008 yds. S.S.S. 65
Visitors welcome.
Green Fees. As posted in the clubhouse.
Society Meetings weekdays by arrangement.
Hotels: Sandford; All Stretton Hall Hotel; Denehurst; Longmynd Hotel.
Meals served by arrangement.

N 23   Congleton

Tel. 026-02 3540
Biddulph Rd., Congleton, Ches.
½ mile from Congleton station on main Congleton to Biddulph road A527.
Wooded parkland course.
9 holes, 5080 yds. S.S.S. 64
Visitors welcome if members of recognized club or with member.
Hotels: Lion & Swan; Bulls Head.
Lunches served by arrangement.

N 24   Crewe

Tel. Crewe 584227 and 584099
Fields Rd., Haslington, Crewe, Ches.
Off M6 at Exit 17, 5 miles along A534.
Parkland course.
18 holes, 6046 yds. S.S.S. 69
Green Fees. Weekdays £5.00 per day (Mon.-Fri. only).
Hotels: Crewe Arms; Royal, Crewe.
Lunches served by arrangement.

N 25   Davenport

Tel. 099-67 877321
Worth Hall, Middlewood Rd., Poynton, Stockport, Ches. SK12 1TS.
Off A523, 6 miles S of Stockport.
Undulating parkland course.
18 holes, 6006 yds. S.S.S. 69
Course designed by F. Middleton.
Visitors welcome except Wed. before 5.15 p.m. and Sat. before 5.00 p.m.
Green Fees. £5.00 per day (£3.00 with member).
Society Meetings Tues. and Thurs.
Hotels: Alma Lodge Hotel, Stockport; Macclesfield Arms, Macclesfield.
Snacks served; meals by arrangement.

N 26   Delamere Forest

Tel. Sandiway 882807
Delamere, Northwich, Ches. CW8 2JE.
N off A556 on to B5152, 1¼ miles.
Downland course.
18 holes, 6287 yds. S.S.S. 70
Course designed by Fowler (1910).
Visitors welcome.
Green Fees. Weekdays £6.00 (£1.00 with member); weekends £7.00 (2 balls only) (£1.00 with member).
Society Meetings Tues., Wed. and Thurs.
Hotels: Hartford Hall Hotel, Hartford; Swan, Tarporley; Oaklands Hotel, Weaverham.
Meals served except Fri.

N 27   Derby

Tel. Derby 766462
Sinfin, Derby.
2 miles from town centre.
Parkland course.
18 holes, 6223 yds. S.S.S. 69
Visitors welcome.
Green Fees. Weekdays £1.40 per round; weekends £2.15 per round.
Hotels: Sherwood.
Light meals served.

N 28   Drayton Park

Tel. Tamworth 61451
Drayton Park, Tamworth, Staffs. B78 3TN.
On A4091 2 miles S of Tamworth.
Parkland course.
18 holes, 6414 yds. S.S.S. 71
Course designed by James Braid.
Visitors welcome on weekdays, weekends with member only.
Green Fees. £5.75 per round or day.
Society Meetings Tues. and Thurs. May to Sept. Wide wheel trolleys only.
Hotels: Castle Hotel, Tamworth; Penns Hall Hotel, Sutton Coldfield.
Meals served.

N 29   Dukinfield

Tel. 061-338 2340
Lyne Edge, Dukinfield, Ches. SK16 5DB.
From Ashton Rd., ½ mile then right onto Yew Tree Lane, club 1 mile on right.
Meadowland course.
12 holes, S.S.S. 67
Visitors welcome on weekdays except Wed.
Green Fees. £3.00 (£1.50 with member).
Society Meetings welcome weekdays except Wed.
Meals served.

N 30   Eaton

Tel. Chester 674385
Eccleston, Chester.
3 miles S of Chester.
Parkland course.
18 holes, 6601 yds. S.S.S. 72
Course designed by F.W. Hawtree.
Visitors welcome with letter of introduction.
Green Fees. Weekdays £6.00 (£3.00 with member); weekends £7.00 (£3.50 with member).
Society Meetings welcome on weekdays.

Hotels: Grosvenor, Chester.
Meals served except Mon.

N 31   Ellesmere Port

Tel. 051-399 7689
Chester Rd., Hooton, Wirral, Ches. L66 1QH.
6 miles N of Chester on A41.
Parkland course.
18 holes, 6436 yds. S.S.S. 72
Course designed by F. Pennink.
Visitors welcome.
Green Fees. Weekdays £1.50; weekends and bank holidays £2.00.
Society Meetings welcome on weekdays.
Hotels: Wirral Mercury Motel, Mollington; Woodhey, Little Sutton.
Lunches served.

N 32   Enville

Tel. Kinver 2074
Highgate Common, Enville, Stourbridge, W. Midlands.
Off A458, signpost to Halfpenny Green airport.
Heathland course.
18 holes, 6541 yds. S.S.S. 72
9 holes, 2807 yds. S.S.S. 34
Visitors welcome on weekdays, with reservation, weekends with member only. Handicap certificate required.
Green Fees. £6.90.
Society Meetings Tues. and Fri. by arrangement.
Hotels: Himley House, Himley.
Meals served except Mon.

N 33   Erewash Valley

Tel. Ilkeston 322984
Stanton-by-Dale, Ilkeston, Derbys.
Off A609.
Undulating meadowland/parkland course.
18 holes, 6436 yds. S.S.S. 71
Visitors welcome, with reservation.
Green Fees. Weekdays £5.50 (£2.25 with member); weekends £6.50 (£3.25 with member).
Society Meetings Mon. only, or by arrangement.
Hotels: Post House; Novotel.
Meals served by arrangement except Fri. and Sun.

N 34   Glossop & District

Tel. Glossop 3117
Sheffield Rd., Glossop, Derbys.
Off A57, 1 mile from town centre.
Moorland course.
9 holes, 5723 yds. S.S.S. 68
Visitors welcome.
Green Fees. Weekdays £4.00 (£2.50 with member); weekends £5.00 (£2.50 with member); weekly £10.00.
Hotels: Norfolk Hotel.
Meals served by arrangement.

N 35   Greenway Hall

Tel. Stockton Brook (0782) 503158
Stockton Brook, Stoke-on-Trent, Staffs.
5 miles N of Stoke-on-Trent.
18 holes, 5722 yds. S.S.S. 67
Visitors welcome with members only.

N 36　Hawkstone Park Hotel

Tel. Lee Brockhurst (093 924) 611
Weston, Shrewsbury SY4 5UY.
A49 between Whitchurch and Shrewsbury.
Just off A442, Hodnet to Whitchurch.
Parkland courses.
Hawkstone 18 holes, 6463 yds. S.S.S. 71
Weston 18 holes, 5400 yds. S.S.S. 66
Visitors welcome.
Green Fees. Weekdays £6.00 per day,
weekends £7.00 per day.
Society Meetings welcome; non-resident
day party tariff available.
Meals served.

N 37　Hazel Grove

Tel. 061-483 3217
Stockport, Ches.
18 holes, 6276 yds. S.S.S. 70
Visitors welcome.
Society Meetings welcome Thurs. and
Fri. only.
Lunches served except Mon.

N 38　Helsby

Tel. Helsby 2021
Towers Lane, Helsby, Warrington, Ches.
3 miles from Frodsham on A56, left into
Primrose Lane, right to Towers Lane.
Parkland course.
18 holes, 6220 yds. S.S.S. 70
Visitors welcome on weekdays.
Green Fees. Weekdays £5.00; weekends
£7.00.
Society Meetings welcome on weekdays
except Fri.
Hotels: Old Hall Hotel, Frodsham.

N 39　Hill Valley　*Directory Enquiries 192.*

Tel. Whitchurch 3584
Terrick Rd., Whitchurch, Shropshire.
Off A49, 1 mile from centre of Whitchurch.
Parkland course.
18 holes, 6200 yds. S.S.S. 73
Course designed by P. Alliss, D. Thomas Ltd.
Visitors welcome.
Green Fees. Weekdays £4.00 per day;
weekends £6.00 per day.
Society Meetings welcome.
Hotels: Terrick Hall Hotel.
Meals served.

N 40　Ilkeston Borough

Peewit Municipal Golf Course, West End
Drive, Ilkeston, Derbys.
½ mile W of Ilkeston market place.
Parkland course.
9 holes, 4116 yds. S.S.S. 60
Visitors welcome.
Green Fees. £1.25 per round.
Hotels: Rutland Hotel.

N 41　Ingestre

Tel. Weston 270061
Ingestre, Stafford.
5 miles E of Stafford.
Parkland course.
18 holes, 6367 yds. S.S.S. 70
Course designed by F.W. Hawtree and Co.
Green Fees. On application.
Visitors Details on application to secretary.

N 42　Kedleston Park

Tel. Derby (0332) 840035
Kedleston, Quarndon, Derby DE6 4JD.
A5111 to Kedleston Rd. island, follow signs
to Kedleston Hall.
Parkland course.
18 holes, 6643 yds. S.S.S. 72
Course designed by J.S.F. Morrison.
Visitors welcome.
Green Fees. Weekdays £6.50 per day;
weekends £7.50 per day.
Society Meetings by arrangement six
months in advance.
Hotels: Kedleston Hotel.
Meals served.

N 43　Knutsford

Tel. Knutsford 3355
Mereheath Lane, Knutsford, Ches.
½ mile E of town centre.
Parkland course.
9 holes, 6200 yds. S.S.S. 70
Visitors welcome with reservation or if
playing with member except Tues. and Wed.
afternoon.
Green Fees. Weekdays £5.00 (£1.25 with
member); weekends £8.00 (£1.75 with
member).
Society Meetings by arrangement Mon.
and Thurs. only.
Hotels: in Knutsford.
Meals served by arrangement.

N 44　Leek

Tel. Leek 382226
Birchall, Leek, Staffs. ST13 5RE.
½ mile from Leek on Stone road.
Moorland course.
18 holes, 6229 yds. S.S.S. 70
Course designed by Tom Williamson.
Visitors welcome.
Green Fees. Weekdays £5.00 per round,
£7.00 per day; weekends £10.00.
Society Meetings Mon. and Wed. only.
Hotels: Southbank, Leek; Palace Hotel,
Buxton; Fox Inn, Rushton.
Meals served except Mon.

N 45　Leek Westwood

Tel. Leek (0538) 382651
Newcastle Rd., Wallbridge, Leek, Staffs.
On A53 W of Leek.
Hillside meadowland course.
9 holes, 5488 yds. S.S.S. 67
Visitors welcome on weekdays and Sat.
morning.
Green Fees. £1.50 per day (£1.00 with
member).
Society Meetings by arrangement.
Hotels: Southbank Hotel, Leek.
Limited catering.

N 46　Leigh

Tel. Culcheth 2943 and 3130
Kenyon Hall, Kenyon, Warrington, Ches.
WA3 4BG.
5 mins. from Culcheth village centre.
Parkland course.
18 holes, 5861 yds. S.S.S. 68
Visitors welcome.
Green Fees. Weekdays £5.00 (£1.50 with
member); weekends £6.00 (£1.50).

Society Meetings Tues. only.
Hotels: Greyhound.
Lunches served by arrangement except
Mon.; Dinners served by arrangement except
Mon. and Fri.

N 47　Lilleshall Hall

Tel. Telford 603840
Lilleshall, Newport, Shropshire TF10 9AS.
Off Abbey Rd., Lilleshall.
Meadowland course.
18 holes, 5837 yds. S.S.S. 68
Course designed by H.S. Colt.
Visitors welcome on weekdays.
Green Fees. Weekdays £5.00.
Hotels: Barley Mow; Royal Victoria,
Newport.
Light lunches and teas served.

N 48　Llanymynech

Tel. Llanymynech 830542
Pant, Oswestry, Shropshire.
A483, 5 miles South of Oswestry.
18 holes, 6107 yds. S.S.S. 69
Visitors welcome.
Green Fees. Weekdays £3.50; weekends
£4.50.
Society Meetings by arrangement.
Meals served except Tues.

N 49　Ludlow

Tel. Bromfield (977) 285
Bromfield, Ludlow, Shropshire SY8 2BT.
2 miles N of Ludlow on A49.
Parkland course.
18 holes, 6266 yds. S.S.S. 70
Visitors welcome.
Green Fees. Weekdays £4.60; weekends
£7.00.
Society Meetings welcome on weekdays.
Hotels: Angel; Feathers, Ludlow.
Lunches served except Mon.

N 50　Lymm

Tel. Lymm 5020
Whitbarrow Rd., Lymm, Ches.
5 miles S of Warrington.
Parkland course.
18 holes, 6330 yds. S.S.S. 70
Visitors welcome.
Green Fees. Weekdays £5.00; weekends
and bank holidays £7.00.
Society Meetings Mon. and Wed. by
arrangement.
Hotels: Lymm Hotel; Statham Lodge Hotel.
Meals served by arrangement except Mon.

N 51　Macclesfield

Tel. Macclesfield (0625) 23227 (Sec.
615845)
The Hollins, Macclesfield, Ches.
Off Windmill St., Macclesfield (A527
Macclesfield to Leek).
Moorland course.
12 holes, 6184 yds. S.S.S. 69
Visitors welcome on weekdays except
Thurs., weekends with member only.
Green Fees. Weekdays £3.60; weekends
£4.60 (£2.30 with member).
Society Meetings catered for.
Hotels: Belgrade, Bollington; Flower Pot.
High teas served Wed. and weekends.

N 52 Malkins Bank Municipal

Tel. Sandbach (093 67) 5931
Betchton Rd., Sandbach, Ches.
1½ miles off M6, junction 17.
Parkland course.
18 holes, 6178 yds. S.S.S. 69
Course designed by Hawtree.
Visitors welcome, public course.
Green Fees. Weekdays £2.00; weekends £2.50.
Society Meetings by arrangement.
Hotels: Chimney House.

N 53 Market Drayton

Tel. Market Drayton 2266
Sutton, Market Drayton, Shropshire.
1½ miles S of town.
Undulating meadowland course.
11 holes, 6265 yds. S.S.S. 69
Visitors welcome except Sun. with member only.
Green Fees. Weekdays £4.00; weekends £5.00.
Society Meetings welcome on weekdays, max. 30.
Hotels: Corbet Arms, Market Drayton; Royal Victoria, Newport.
Meals served by arrangement.

N 54 Matlock

Tel. Matlock 2191
Chesterfield Rd., Matlock, Derbys. DE4 5LF.
On Matlock to Chesterfield road, 1½ miles out of Matlock.
Moorland/parkland course.
18 holes, 5865 yds. S.S.S. 69
Visitors welcome on weekdays, weekends with reservation.
Green Fees. Weekdays £4.50 (£2.75 with member); weekends and bank holidays £6.00 (£4.20 with member); weekly £17.50; monthly £35.00.
Society Meetings welcome on weekdays.
Hotels: Matlock, Matlock Bath.
Meals served by arrangement.

N 55 Mere Golf & Country Club

Tel. Bucklow Hill (0565) 830155
Chester Rd., Mere, Knutsford, Ches.
2 miles from Junction 19, M6.
Parkland course.
18 holes, 6659 yds. S.S.S. 72
Course designed by James Braid and George Duncan.
Visitors welcome with reservation.
Green Fees. From £4.25.
Society Meetings by arrangement.
Hotels: Swan, Bucklow Hill; Royal George, Knutsford; Valley Lodge, Wilmslow.
Meals served.

N 56 Mickleover

Tel. Derby (0332) 513339
Uttoxeter Rd., Mickleover, Derby.
A516 3 miles from Derby.
Meadowland course.
18 holes, 5621 yds. S.S.S. 68
Visitors welcome.
Green Fees. Weekdays £5.00; weekends £6.00.
Society Meetings Mon. and Thurs. only.
Hotels: in Derby.

N 57 Mirrlees

Tel. 061-483 2042
Bramhall, Moor Lane, Hazel Grove, Stockport, Ches.
Meadowland course.
9 holes, 6102 yds. S.S.S. 68
Visitors must be accompanied by member.
Green Fees. £1.00 (with member only).
Hotels: in area.

N 58 Newcastle

Tel. Newcastle (0782) 617006
Whitmore Rd., Newcastle under Lyme, Staffs. ST5 2QB.
1½ miles from Newcastle.
Parkland/meadowland course.
18 holes, 6450 yds. S.S.S. 71
Visitors welcome on weekdays, weekends with member only.
Green Fees. Weekdays £5.50 (£2.75 with member); weekends £3.00 with member only.
Society Meetings Mon., Wed. and Thurs.
Hotels: Post House, Newcastle; Clayton Lodge Hotel, Clayton, Newcastle.
Meals served by arrangement except Mon.

N 59 Newcastle under Lyme

Tel. Newcastle (0782) 627596
Keele Rd., Newcastle, Staffs.
Off M6 at junction 15 on to A519, then A525 for 2 miles.
Undulating parkland course.
18 holes, 6301 yds. S.S.S. 70
Course designed by Hawtree & Son.
Visitors welcome with reservation.
Green Fees. Weekdays £1.60 per round; weekends £2.30 per round.
Hotels: Clayton Lodge Hotel; Post House Motel; Borough Arms; Ambassador Hotel.
Meals served.

N 60 New Mills

Tel. New Mills 43485
Shaw Marsh, New Mills, via Stockport, Ches.
Off A6015.
Moorland course.
9 holes, 5924 yds. S.S.S. 68
Visitors welcome on weekdays, weekends with member only.
Green Fees. £4.20 (£1.80 with member).
Society Meetings by arrangement.
Hotels: George, Hayfield.
Meals served except Thurs.

N 61 Onneley

Tel. 0782 750577
Onneley, Nr. Crewe, Cheshire.
A525 1 mile from Woore. Between Woore and Madeley.
Undulating meadowland course.
9 holes, 5816 yds. S.S.S. 68
Visitors welcome on weekdays, Sat. with member only.
Green Fees. £4.00 (£2.00 with member).

N 62 Ormonde Fields

Tel. Ripley (0773) 42987
Nottingham Rd., Codnor, Derbyshire.
A610 towards Ripley.
Undulating.
18 holes, 6007 yds. S.S.S. 69
Visitors welcome on weekdays.
Green Fees. Weekdays £3.50; weekends £4.50.
Society Meetings welcome on weekdays.
Meals served.

N 63 Oswestry

Tel. Queens Head 221
Aston Park, Oswestry, Shropshire.
4 miles SE of Oswestry near junction of A4083 and A5.
Undulating parkland course.
18 holes, 6055 yds. S.S.S. 69
Course designed by James Braid.
Visitors welcome.
Green Fees. Weekdays £5.50 per day; weekends £6.50 per day.
Society Meetings Wed. and Fri. only by arrangement.
Hotels: in Oswestry.
Meals served except Mon.

N 64 Pastures

Tel. Derby (0332) 513921
The Pastures Hospital, Mickleover, Derby.
On A516, 4 miles W of Derby.
Undulating, meadowland course.
9 holes, 4886 yds. S.S.S. 64
Course designed by F. Pennink.
Visitors welcome with member only.
Green Fees. Weekdays £1.00; weekends £2.00.

N 65 Poulton Park

Tel. Padgate (0925) 812034
Dig Lane, Poulton with Fearnhead, Warrington, Ches.
Crab Lane (off A574), 3 miles from Warrington.
Meadowland course.
9 holes, 2702 yds. S.S.S. 66
Visitors welcome on weekdays.
Green Fees. Weekdays £3.00 (£2.00 with member); weekends and bank holidays £4.60 (£2.50 with member).
Society Meetings catered for weekdays.
Meals and bar snacks except Mon.

N 66 Prestbury

Tel. Prestbury (0625) 828241
Macclesfield Rd., Prestbury, Macclesfield, Ches. SK10 4BJ.
2 miles NW of Macclesfield.
Undulating parkland course.
18 holes, 6359 yds. S.S.S. 71
Course designed by Colt and Morrison.
Visitors welcome on weekdays, weekends with member only and letter of introduction.
Green Fees. Weekdays £7.50 (£3.75 with member).
Society Meetings Thurs. only.
Hotels: Belgrade, Kerridge; Mottram Hall, Mottram St. Andrew.
Meals served except Mon.

N 67 Renishaw Park

Tel. Eckington 2044
Renishaw, Sheffield S31 9UZ.
2 miles from Barlborough.
Parkland/meadowland course.
18 holes, 6253 yds. S.S.S. 70
Visitors welcome.

Green Fees. Weekdays £4.00 (£2.25 with member); weekends £5.50 (£3.50).
Society Meetings welcome on weekdays.
Meals served by arrangement except Tues.

N 68 Runcorn

Tel. Runcorn 72093
Clifton Rd., Runcorn, Ches.
Signposted 'The Heath'.
High parkland course.
18 holes, 6012 yds. S.S.S. 69
Visitors welcome.
Green Fees. Weekdays £4.00; weekends and bank holidays £6.00.
Society Meetings by arrangement.
Hotels: Esso; Lord Daresbury.
Meals served by arrangement.

N 69 Sandbach

Tel. Sandbach (09367) 2117
Middlewich Rd., Sandbach, Ches.
1 mile N of Sandbach.
Meadowland course.
9 holes, 5055 yds. S.S.S. 67
Visitors welcome on weekdays except Tues., weekends with member only.
Green Fees. £3.25.
Society Meetings Wed. and Fri. only by arrangement.
Hotels: Grove House Hotel; Saxon Cross Motel.
Meals and snacks served by arrangement except Mon. and Thurs.

N 70 Sandiway

Tel. Sandiway (0606) 883247
Chester Rd., Sandiway, Northwich, Ches. CW8 2DJ.
On A556, 15 miles from Chester, 4 miles from Northwich.
Parkland/woodland course.
18 holes, 6435 yds. S.S.S. 72
Course designed by S. Collins.
Visitors welcome with letter of introduction.
Green Fees. Weekdays £7.00; weekends £8.00.
Society Meetings Tues. by arrangement.
Hotels: Blue Cap, Sandiway; Hartford Hall, Hartford; Woodpecker, Northwich; Oaklands, Weaverham.
Meals served by arrangement (0606) 882606.

N 71 Shifnal

Tel. Telford 460330
Decker Hill, Shifnal, Shropshire TF11 8QL.
B4379 from Shifnal.
Parkland course.
18 holes, 6504 yds. S.S.S. 71
Course designed by J.J.F. Pennink.
Visitors welcome with reservation except Sun.
Green Fees. £5.00.
Society Meetings by arrangement.
Hotels: Park House Hotel; Olde Bell; Jerningham Arms.
Meals served except Mon.

N 72 Shrewsbury

Tel. Bayston Hill 2976/7
Condover, Shropshire.
4 miles SW of Shrewsbury; follow signs for

Condover and golf club.
Meadowland course.
18 holes, 6229 yds. S.S.S. 70
Course designed by Cotton (C.K.), Pennink & Lawrie.
Visitors welcome if members of recognized club.
Green Fees. Weekdays £4.50; weekends £6.00.
Hotels: in Shrewsbury.
Meals served except Mon.

N 73 Sickleholme

Tel. Bamford 306
Bamford, Sheffield S30 2BH.
A625, W of Sheffield.
Undulating course.
18 holes, 6064 yds. S.S.S. 69
Visitors welcome with reservation.
Green Fees. Weekdays £5.50 per round or day; weekends £4.50 per round, £6.50 per day.
Society Meetings by arrangement.
Hotels: Marquis of Granby; Anglers Rest; Rising Sun.
Meals served by arrangement.

N 74 Stafford Castle

Tel. Stafford (0785) 3821
Newport Rd., Stafford.
½ mile from town centre.
Meadowland course.
9 holes, 6462 yds. S.S.S. 71
Visitors welcome.
Green Fees. Weekdays £4.00; weekends £6.00.
Society Meetings welcome weekdays only.
Hotels: in Stafford.
Meals served by arrangement except Mon.

N 75 Stanedge

Tel. Chesterfield 6156
Walton Hay Farm, Walton, Chesterfield, Derbys.
B6015 off A619.
Moorland course.
9 holes, 4934 yds. S.S.S. 64
Visitors welcome on weekdays.
Hotels: Portland, Chesterfield; Red Lion, Stanedge.
Green Fees. £2.00.

N 76 Stone

Tel. Stone 813103
The Filleybrooks, Stone, Staffs. ST15 8PX.
On A34 1 mile N of Stone.
Meadowland course.
9 holes, 6129 yds. S.S.S. 69
Visitors welcome on weekdays, weekends with member only.
Green Fees. Weekdays £6.00 (£2.00 with member).
Society Meetings by arrangement.
Hotels: Crown; Wayfarer; Brooms.
Snacks and meals served by arrangement except Mon.

N 77 Tamworth Municipal

Tel. Tamworth 53850
Eagle Dr., Tamworth, Staffs. B77 4EG.
Off the Tamworth to Polesworth road.

Parkland/meadowland course.
18 holes, 6695 yds. S.S.S. 72
Course designed by Hawtree & Sons.
Visitors welcome.
Green Fees. Weekdays £2.00 per round; weekends £2.30 per round. Reduced rates for juniors and O.A.P.s.
Society Meetings welcome on weekdays, max. 36.

N 78 Tapton Park

Tel. Chesterfield 73887
Murray House, Tapton, Chesterfield, Derbys.
½ mile from Chesterfield station.
Municipal parkland/meadowland course.
18 holes, 6210 yds. S.S.S. 69
Course designed by George Duncan.
Visitors welcome.
Green Fees. Weekdays £1.20 per round; weekends £1.75 per round.
Society Meetings by arrangement.
Hotels: Station; Portland.

N 79 Telford

Tel. Telford (0952) 585642
Great Hay, Sutton Hill, Telford, Shropshire TF7 4DT.
5 miles S of Telford city centre along A442 Bridgnorth road. Turn off at Sutton Hill roundabout.
Undulating parkland course.
18 holes, Championship 7020 yds., Men's medal 6750 yds. S.S.S. 72
Course designed by John Harris.
Visitors welcome; handicap certificate or proof of membership of bona fide club required.
Green Fees. Weekdays from £5.00; weekends from £6.00.
Society Meetings welcome; rates, inclusive of meals, from £11.00 per day.
Hotels: Own hotel with swimming pool, sauna, squash, badminton and snooker.
Full catering.

N 80 Trentham

Tel. Stoke-on-Trent (0782) 658109
14 Barlaston Old Rd., Trentham, Stoke-on-Trent, Staffs. ST4 8HB.
Off A34 S of Newcastle under Lyme.
Parkland course.
18 holes, 6503 yds. S.S.S. 71
Visitors by arrangement.
Green Fees. Weekdays £7.00; weekends £10.00.
Society Meetings by arrangement.
Hotels: Crown, Stone; Clayton Lodge Hotel; Post House Motel, Newcastle under Lyme.
Meals served by arrangement.

N 81 Trentham Park

Tel. Stoke-on-Trent (0782) 658800
Trentham Park, Stoke-on-Trent, Staffs. ST4 8AE.
4 miles S of Newcastle under Lyme on A34; near junction 15 of M6.
Parkland course.
18 holes, 6403 yds. S.S.S. 71
Course designed by Duke of Sutherland.
Visitors welcome on weekdays. Ladies day Tues.
Green Fees. Weekdays £6.00; weekends £8.00.

Society Meetings Wed. and Fri. only.
Hotels: Clayton Lodge Hotel, Newcastle; Post House Motel, Hanchurch; North Staffs Hotel, Stoke.
Meals and teas served except Mon.

N 82   Upton-by-Chester

Tel. Chester 381183
Upton Lane, Upton-by-Chester, Chester CH2 1EE.
Off A41, N of Chester.
Parkland course.
18 holes, 5847 yds. S.S.S. 68
Course designed by J.W. Davies (1934).
Visitors welcome.
Green Fees. Weekdays £5.00 (£2.50 with member); weekends £7.00 (£3.50 with member).
Hotels: in Chester.
Snacks served; meals by arrangement.

N 83   Vicars Cross

Tel. Chester 35174
Tarvin Rd., Littleton, Chester.
On A56 2½ miles E of Chester.
Parkland course.
18 holes, 5857 yds. S.S.S. 68
Visitors welcome.
Green Fees. Weekdays £4.00 per round, £6.00 per day; weekends and bank holidays £5.00 per round, £7.50 per day; half fees with member.
Society Meetings welcome except June.
Hotels: in Chester.
Meals served except Tues.

N 84   Walton Hall

Tel. Warrington 66775
Warrington Rd., Higher Walton, Warrington, Ches. WA4 5LU.
Off A56, 2 miles from Warrington.
Undulating, parkland course.
18 holes, 6647 yds. S.S.S. 72
Course designed by F. Pennink.
Visitors welcome.
Green Fees. Weekdays £1.75; weekends £2.50.
Society Meetings welcome on weekdays.
Hotels: Lord Daresbury, Daresbury; Fir Grove, Warrington.
Lunches served except Mon.

N 85   Warrington

Tel. Warrington (0925) 61775/65431
Hill Warren, London Rd., Appleton, Warrington, Ches. WA4 5HR.
A49 3 miles S of Warrington.
Meadowland course.
18 holes, 6217 yds. S.S.S. 70
Visitors welcome with reservation.
Green Fees. Weekdays £5.50; weekends £7.50.
Society Meetings Wed. only.
Hotels: Old Vicarage, Stretton; Highcliffe Hydro, Appleton.
Meals served by arrangement.

N 86   Whittington Barracks

Tel. Whittington 432212
Tamworth Rd., Lichfield, Staffs. WS14 9PW.
On A51.

Heathland course.
18 holes, 6457 yds. S.S.S. 71
Visitors welcome on weekdays.
Green Fees. £7.00 per day.
Society Meetings by arrangement.
Meals served.

N 87   Widnes

Tel. 051-424 2995
Highfield Rd., Widnes, Ches.
Near town centre.
Parkland course.
18 holes, 5688 yds. S.S.S. 67
Visitors welcome on weekdays, weekends with reservation.
Green Fees. Weekdays £4.00 (£1.60 with member); weekends £5.00 (£1.60 with member).
Society Meetings welcome weekdays except Tues.
Hotels: Hillcrest.
Meals served by arrangement.

N 88   Wilmslow

Tel. Mobberley 2148
Great Warford, Mobberley, Knutsford, Ches. WA16 7AY.
2 miles from Wilmslow on B5085.
Parkland course.
18 holes, 6500 yds. S.S.S. 71
Visitors welcome with reservation and letter of introduction.
Green Fees. From £7.00.
Society Meetings Tues. and Thurs. only by arrangement.
Hotels: Belfry, Handforth; Royal George, Knutsford; Stanneylands; Valley Lodge, Wilmslow.
Meals and teas served by arrangement except Mon.

N 89   Wolstanton

Tel. Newcastle under Lyme (0782) 622413
Dimsdale Old Hall, Hassam Parade, Wolstanton, Newcastle, Staffs. ST5 9DR.
1½ miles NW of Newcastle under Lyme on A34.
Undulating parkland course.
18 holes, 5807 yds. S.S.S. 68
Visitors welcome on weekdays if members of recognized club.
Green Fees. £5.00 per round, £7.00 per day.
Society Meetings by arrangement.
Hotels: Clayton Lodge Hotel, Clayton; Post House, Hanchurch.
Meals served except Fri. Snacks.

N 90   Wrekin

Tel. Telford 44032
Ercall Woods, Telford, Shropshire TF6 5BX.
Undulating parkland course.
18 holes, 5657 yds. S.S.S. 67
Visitors welcome weekdays, weekends with member only.
Green Fees. Weekdays £4.50 (£1.50 with member).
Society Meetings welcome on weekdays.
Hotels: Charlton; Red Lion, Wellington.
Meals served except Mon., ordered in advance.

O Nottinghamshire, Leicestershire, Lincolnshire

O 1   Beeston Fields

Tel. Nottingham (0602) 257062
Beeston Fields, Beeston, Nottingham NG9 3DD.
Off A52, 4 miles W of Nottingham, 4 miles from M1 Exit 25.
Parkland course.
18 holes, 6404 yds. S.S.S. 71
Visitors welcome on weekdays.
Green Fees. Weekdays £6.00 (£2.25 with member); weekends £7.00 (£2.25 with member).
Society Meetings welcome Mon. and Wed.
Hotels: Albany; Post House.
Meals served.

O 2   Belton Park

Tel. Grantham 3355 and 67399
Belton Lane, Londonthorpe Rd, Grantham, Lincs. NG31 9SH.
27 holes, 6412 yds. S.S.S. 71
Visitors welcome.
Green Fees. Weekdays £5.00; weekends £7.50.
Hotels: George; Angel.
Meals served.

O 3   Birstall

Tel. Leicester (0533) 674322
Station Rd., Birstall, Leicester LE4 3BB
2 miles N of town off the A6.
Meadowland course.
18 holes, 6203 yds. S.S.S. 70
Visitors welcome Mon., Wed., Fri.; weekends with member only.
Green Fees. £6.00 (£1.60 with member); weekends £2.50 (with member only).
Society Meetings catered for Wed. and Fri.
Hotels: Rothley Court; Post House, Leicester.
Lunches served except Mon. Evening meals by arrangement.

O 4   Blankney

Tel. Metheringham 20263
Blankney, Lincoln LN4 3AZ.
On B1188, 10 miles SE of Lincoln.
Parkland course.
18 holes, 6232 yds. S.S.S. 70
Visitors welcome weekdays, weekends with reservation.
Green Fees. Weekdays £5.00 (£3.50 with

member); weekends £8.00 (£5.00 with member).
Society Meetings welcome weekdays except Tues.
Hotels: Moor Lodge Hotel, Branston. Meals served except Tues.

O 5 Boston

Tel. Boston (0205) 62306
Cowbridge, Horncastle Rd., Boston, Lincs.
2 miles N of Boston on B1183.
Parkland course.

18 holes, 5764 yds. S.S.S. 68
Visitors welcome.
Green Fees. Weekdays £4.00; weekends £6.00.
Society Meetings by arrangement.
Hotels: New England; White Hart.
Meals served by arrangement except Wed.

O 6 Bulwell Forest

Tel. Nottingham (0602) 278008
Hucknall Rd., Bulwell, Nottingham.
Off A611, 4 miles N of Nottingham, 2 miles from M1 Exit 26.

Undulating moorland course.
18 holes, 5606 yds. S.S.S. 67
Visitors welcome on weekdays, weekends with reservation.
Green Fees. £2.00 per round.
Society Meetings by arrangement.
Hotels: in Nottingham.
Snacks served.

O 7 Burbage Common

Tel. Hinckley (0455) 615124
Leicester Rd., Hinckley, Leics. LE10 2DR.
On A47, one mile NE of Hinckley.

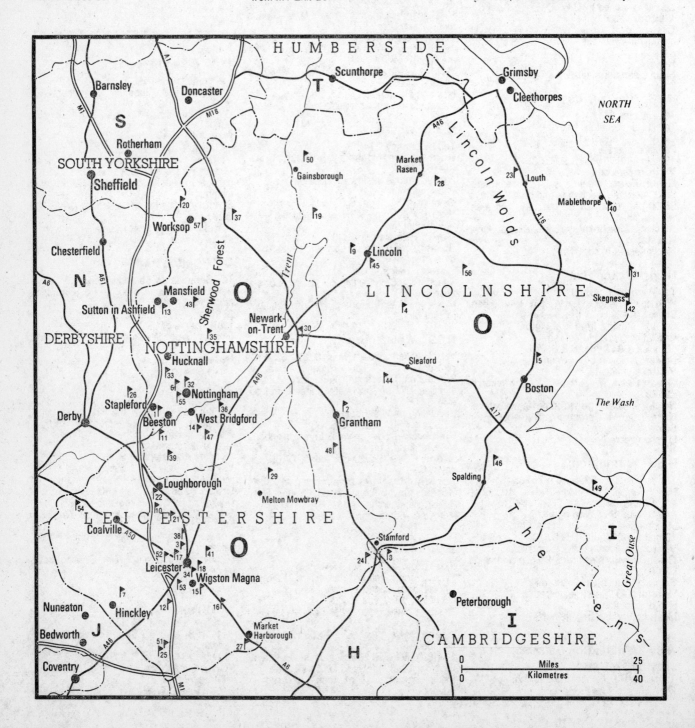

Heathland course.
9 holes, 5845 yds. S.S.S. 68
Visitors welcome on weekdays.
Green Fees. £4.00 (£3.00 with member).
Society Meetings welcome weekdays only.
Hotels: Union Hotel; Sketchley Grange.
Meals served by arrangement.

O 8 Burghley Park

Tel. Stamford (0780) 2100
St. Martins Without, Stamford, Lincs. PE9 3JX.
Leave A1 at roundabout 1 mile S of Stamford; entrance to course on right after ½ mile.
Parkland course.
18 holes, 6095 yds. S.S.S. 69
Visitors welcome on weekdays; weekends (May to Oct.) after 3p.m.
Green Fees. Weekdays £5.00 (£3.00 with member); weekends £5.00 (£4.00 with member).
Society Meetings welcome weekdays only (numbers from 12 to 40).
Hotels: George; Crown, Stamford.
Meals served except Tues.

O 9 Carholme

Tel. Lincoln (0522) 23725 and 38241
Carholme Rd., Lincoln LN1 1SE.
On A57, 1 mile NW of Lincoln city centre.
Parkland course.
18 holes, 5995 yds. S.S.S. 69
Visitors welcome, Sun. after 11.30a.m.
Green Fees. Weekdays £2.50; weekends £3.00.
Society Meetings by arrangement.
Hotels: Eastgate Court; Grand; White Hart.
Snacks and lunches served.

O 10 Charnwood Forest

Tel. Woodhouse Eaves (0533 92) 890259
Breakback Lane, Woodhouse Eaves, Loughborough, Leics.
B591 off A6 at Quorndon, 3 miles SE of Loughborough.
Heathland course.
9 holes, 6200 yds. S.S.S. 70
Course designed by J. Braid.
Visitors welcome if members of recognized club.
Green Fees. Weekdays £4.00; weekends £6.00.
Society Meetings by arrangement.
Hotels: King's Head, Loughborough.
Light meals served by prior arrangement.

O 11 Chilwell Manor

Tel. Nottingham 257050
Meadow Lane, Queens Rd., Chilwell, Nottingham NG9 5AE.
Off A453, 4 miles SW of Nottingham.
Meadowland course.
18 holes, 6345 yds. S.S.S. 70
Visitors welcome, but must play with member between 4.30p.m. and 6.30p.m. weekdays; weekends before 10.30a.m. and between 12.00p.m. and 3.00p.m.
Green Fees. Weekdays £2.50; weekends £5.00.
Society Meetings Wed. only. Limited number.

Hotels: in Nottingham. Strathdon Hotel; Albany Hotel; Bridgford Hotel.
Meals served.

O 12 Cosby

Tel. Leicester 864759
Chapel Lane, Cosby, Leicester.
8 miles SW of Leicester.
Parkland course.
18 holes, 6270 yds. S.S.S. 70
Visitors welcome on weekdays (after 4.00 p.m. with member); weekends with member only.
Green Fees. Weekdays £5.00 per round (£2.00 with member); weekends £2.00 (with member only).
Society Meetings by arrangement.
Meals served by arrangement.

O 13 Coxmoor

Tel. Mansfield 57348
Coxmoor Rd., Sutton-in-Ashfield, Notts.
On A611, 2 miles SW of Mansfield, 5 miles from M1 Exit 27.
Undulating meadowland course.
18 holes, 6501 yds. S.S.S. 72
Visitors welcome.
Green Fees. Weekdays £6.50 per day; weekends and bank holidays £8.50 per day. Half rates with member.
Society Meetings by arrangement.
Meals served by arrangement.

O 14 Edwalton Municipal

Tel. Nottingham 233225
Wellin Lane, Edwalton, West Bridgford, Nottingham. (Correspondence: 57 Trevor Rd., West Bridgford, Nottingham).
Left off A606 from Nottingham at Edwalton Hotel; Wellin Lane 2nd left.
Undulating meadowland course.
Main course 9 holes, 6672 yds. S.S.S. 72 (18 holes)
Par 3 course 9 holes, 1592 yds.
Course designed by J.J.F. Pennink, Cotton (CK), Pennink, Lawrie and Partners.
Visitors welcome.
Green Fees. Main course peak £1.70 (juniors £1.50); off-peak £1.00 (juniors 75p). Par 3 course peak £1.20 (juniors £1.00); off-peak 80p (juniors 50p).
Hotels: Edwalton Hall; Nottingham Knight, Nottingham.
Hot and cold bar snacks available at all times.

O 15 Glen Gorse

Tel. Leicester (0533) 714159
Glen Rd., Oadby, Leics. LE2 4RF.
3 miles SE of Leicester on A6.
Meadowland course.
18 holes, 6486 yds. S.S.S. 71
Visitors welcome on weekdays, weekends with member only.
Green Fees. Weekdays £5.50 (£2.00 with member); weekends £2.00.
Hotels: Grand; Holiday Inn, Leicester; Leicester Moat House, Oadby; The Firs, Great Glen.
Lunches and teas served; evening meals by arrangement except Mon.

O 16 Kibworth

Tel. Kibworth (053753) 2301
Weir Road, Kibworth Beauchamp, Leics. LE8 0LP.
8 miles SE of Leicester on A6.
Meadowland course.
18 holes, 6256 yds. S.S.S. 70
Visitors welcome on weekdays, weekends with member only.
Green Fees. Weekdays £5.20; weekends £2.50.
Society Meetings welcome Wed., Thurs. and Fri. by arrangement.
Hotels: Angel, Market Harborough; Hermitage, Oadby; Coach & Horses, Kibworth.
Meals served except Mon.

O 17 Kirby Muxloe

Tel. Leicester 393457
Station Rd., Kirby Muxloe, Leicester.
On A47, 4 miles W of Leicester, 7 miles from M1 Exit 21.
Parkland course.
18 holes, 6264 yds. S.S.S. 70
Visitors welcome on weekdays, weekends by arrangement.
Green Fees. Weekdays £5.00 per day; weekends £6.00 (Capt. permission only).
Society Meetings Wed., Thur. and Fri. (restricted numbers).
Hotels: Europa Lodge Motel; Holiday Inn; Posthouse.
Meals served except Sun. and Mon., teas served Sun.

O 18 Leicestershire

Tel. Leicester (0533) 738825
Evington Lane, Leicester LE5 6DJ.
2 miles from city centre.
Parkland course.
18 holes, 6335 yds. S.S.S. 70
Visitors welcome.
Green Fees. Weekdays £5.50 (£1.75 with member); weekends £6.50 (£2.25 with member).
Society Meetings welcome weekdays only.
Hotels: in Leicester.
Lunches served except Mon.

O 19 Lincoln

Tel. Torksey (1891) 210
Torksey, Lincoln.
Off A156, 12 miles NW of Lincoln.
Undulating meadowland course.
18 holes, 6354 yds. S.S.S. 70
Visitors welcome with reservation and letter of introduction.
Green Fees. Weekdays £6.00 per day; weekends by appointment only.
Society Meetings weekdays by arrangement.
Hotels: White Hart; Grand, Lincoln.
Meals served by arrangement.

O 20 Lindrick

Tel. Worksop (0909) 5282
Lindrick, Worksop, Notts. S81 8BH.
On A57, 4 miles W of Worksop.
Heathland course.
36 holes, 6613 yds. S.S.S. 72

Visitors welcome on weekdays with reservation.
Green Fees. Weekdays £8.00 per round, £10.00 per day; weekends £12.00 per round or day.
Society Meetings weekdays by arrangement.
Hotels: Ye Olde Bell, Retford; Crown, Bawtry.
Snacks served; meals served by arrangement.

O 21 Lingdale

Tel. Woodhouse Eaves (0509) 890035
Joe Moore's Lane, Woodhouse Eaves, Loughborough, Leics.
On B5330, 6 miles S of Loughborough.
Parkland course.
9 holes, 6644 yds. S.S.S. 72
Visitors welcome. Restricted weekends when club matches in progress.
Green Fees. Weekdays £3.50 (£2.00 with member); weekends £4.50.
Society Meetings weekdays by arrangement.
Hotels: Bull's Head, Quorn; King's Head, Loughborough; Rothley Court, Leicester.
Light lunches and teas served except Mon.; Full lunches by arrangement.

O 22 Longcliffe

Tel. Loughborough 39129
Snell's Nook Lane, Nanpantan, Loughborough, Leics. LE11 3YA.
On B5350, 2 miles SW of Loughborough, 1 mile from M1 Exit 23.
Heathland course.
18 holes, 6453 yds. S.S.S. 71
Visitors welcome on weekdays, weekends with member only.
Green Fees. Weekdays £7.00 (£2.00 with member).
Society Meetings Wed., Thurs. and Fri. by arrangement.
Hotels: King's Head, Loughborough.
Meals served except Mon.

O 23 Louth

Tel. Louth (0507) 2554
Crowtree Lane, Louth, Lincs.
Off A16, 16 miles S of Grimsby.
Undulating parkland course.
18 holes, 5727 yds. S.S.S. 68
Course designed by F. Pennick, C.K. Cotton & Co.
Visitors welcome on weekdays.
Green Fees. Weekdays £4.00; weekends £6.00.
Society Meetings weekdays except Wed.
Hotels: Priory; Masons Arms; King's Head.
Snacks, lunches and evening meals served.
Squash courts.

O 24 Luffenham Heath

Tel. Stamford 720205
Ketton, Stamford, Lincs. PE9 3UU.
On A6121, 6 miles SW of Stamford.
Undulating heathland course.
18 holes, 6382 yds. S.S.S. 70
Course designed by J. Braid.
Visitors welcome with reservation.
Green Fees. Weekdays £6.50; weekends £10.00.

Society Meetings by arrangement.
Hotels: George, Stamford; Cavalier, Collyweston.
Meals served except Tues.

O 25 Lutterworth

Tel. Lutterworth (04555) 2532
Rugby Rd., Lutterworth, Leics.
½ mile from M1 Exit 20 on A4114.
Meadowland course.
15 holes, 5734 yds. S.S.S. 68
Course designed by F.W. Hawtree.
Visitors welcome on weekdays, weekends with member only.
Green Fees. Weekdays £4.50 (with member £3.00).
Society Meetings welcome Mon. and Fri. only.
Hotels: Denbigh Arms.
Meals served.

O 26 Mapperley

Tel. Nottingham (0602) 265611
Plains Rd., Mapperley, Nottingham.
2 miles from city centre.
Meadowland course.
9 holes, 5546 yds. S.S.S. 67; new 18 hole course open for play April 1983.
Visitors welcome.
Green Fees. Weekdays £3.00 (£2.00 with member); weekends £4.00 (£3.00 with member).
Society Meetings welcome weekdays only.
Lunches served by arrangement except Wed.

O 27 Market Harborough

Tel. Market Harborough 63684
Northampton Rd., Market Harborough, Leics.
On A508, 1 mile S of Market Harborough.
Parkland course.
9 holes, 6080 yds. S.S.S. 69
Visitors welcome, weekends with member only.
Green Fees. Weekdays £4.00 (£2.50 with member); weekends £3.50 (with member).
Hotels: Angel; Three Swans.

O 28 Market Rasen & District

Tel. Market Rasen 2319 (Sec.); Pro. & Steward 2416
Legsby Rd., Market Rasen, Lincs.
B1202 off A46, 1 mile S of racecourse.
Undulating heathland course.
18 holes, 6025 yds. S.S.S. 69
Visitors welcome on weekdays if members of recognized club or with member.
Green Fees. £4.25 per round or day (£3.25 with member).
Society Meetings Tues. and Fri. by arrangement.
Hotels: Gordon Arms; Limes Hotel.
Meals served except Mon.

O 29 Melton Mowbray

Tel. Melton Mowbray (0664) 62118
Thorpe Arnold, Melton Mowbray, Leics LE14 3LR.
A607 2 miles NE of Melton Mowbray.
Meadowland course.
9 holes, 6322 yds. S.S.S. 70

Course designed by W. Barfoot (1925).
Visitors welcome on weekdays.
Green Fees. Weekdays £4.00 (£1.50 with member) subsequently £3.00; weekends and bank holidays £5.00 (£2.00 with member) subsequently £4.00.
Society Meetings weekdays by arrangement 4 weeks in advance.
Hotels: Harboro Hotel; George, Melton Mowbray.

O 30 Newark

Tel. Fenton Claypole 282
Kelwick, Coddington, Newark, Notts.
On A17 4 miles E. of Newark.
Parkland course.
18 holes, 6486 yds. S.S.S. 71
Visitors welcome.
Society Meetings Mon., Wed. and Thurs. by arrangement.
Hotels: Robin Hood Hotel, Newark.
Lunches and teas served except Fri.

O 31 North Shore

Tel. Skegness (0754) 3298
North Shore Rd., Skegness, Lincs. PE25 3BG.
1 mile N of town centre.
Parkland and seaside course.
18 holes, 6010 yds. S.S.S. 69
Course designed by J. Braid (1910).
Visitors welcome.
Green Fees. Weekdays £5.00; weekends £6.00.
Society Meetings by arrangement.
Hotels: North Shore.
Meals served.

O 32 Nottingham City

Tel. Nottingham (0602) 278021
Lawton Dr., Bulwell Hall Park, Bulwell, Nottingham.
3 miles NW of city centre.
Parkland course.
18 holes, 6199 yds. S.S.S. 70
Visitors welcome with reservation.
Green Fees. £2.00 per round.
Society Meetings welcome weekdays.
Hotels: in Nottingham.
Lunches and dinners served daily. Sun. by arrangement.

O 33 Nottinghamshire Hollinwell

Tel. Mansfield 753225
Kirkby-in-Ashfield, Notts.
Off A611, 2½ miles from M1 Exit 27.
Woodland, heathland championship course.
18 holes, 7020 yds. S.S.S. 75
Course designed by W. Park, Jun.
Visitors welcome, Sat. with member only.
Booking advisable; handicap certificate required.
Green Fees. Weekdays £8.00; weekends £9.00.
Society Meetings by arrangement Tues.
Hotels: The Swallow.
Meals available every day.

O 34 Oadby

Tel. Leicester (0533) 700215
Leicester Rd., Oadby, Leicester LE2 4AJ.
On A6, 3 miles S. of city centre.

Undulating course.
18 holes, 6213 yds. S.S.S. 70
Visitors welcome.
Green Fees. Weekdays £1.50 per round; weekends £1.85.
Society Meetings by arrangement with Oadby & Wigston Borough Council.
Hotels: Stage Motel, Wigston; Post House, Leicester.
Snacks served; meals by arrangement.

O 35　Oxton

Tel. Nottingham 653545
Oaks Lane, Oxton, Southwell, Notts.
On A614, 9 miles N of Nottingham.
Meadowland course.
18 holes, 6600 yds. S.S.S. 72
Course designed by Cotton (C.K.), Pennink, Lawrie and Partners.
Visitors welcome.
Green Fees. Weekdays £2.50 (reduced fees after 4.00 p.m.); weekends £3.50.
Society Meetings welcome.
Hotels: Savoy, Nottingham.
Meals served.

O 36　Radcliffe-on-Trent

Tel. Radcliffe-on-Trent 3000
Dewberry Lane, Cropwell Rd., Radcliffe-on-Trent, Nottingham NG12 2JH.
Off A52, 7 miles W of Nottingham.
Parkland course.
18 holes, 6413 yds. S.S.S. 71
Course designed by J.F. Pennink.
Visitors welcome. Ladies day Tues.
Green Fees. Weekdays £5.00 (£3.00 with member); weekends £6.50 (£3.75 with member).
Society Meetings by arrangement.
Meals served.

O 37　Retford

Tel. Retford 703733
Ordsall, Retford, Notts.
S off A620.
Woodland course.
9 holes, 6319 yds. S.S.S. 70
Visitors welcome on weekdays.
Green Fees. Weekdays £3.00 (£2.00 with member); weekends £3.00 with member only.
Hotels: West Retford Hotel; Ye Olde Bell Hotel, Barnby Moor.

O 38　Rothley Park

Tel. Sec. Leicester 302809; Club House Leicester 302019
Westfield Lane, Rothley, Leics. LE7 7LH.
Off A6, 6 miles N of Leicester.
Parkland course.
18 holes, 6487 yds. S.S.S. 71
Visitors welcome with handicap.
Green Fees. Weekdays £6.00; weekends £7.00.
Society Meetings welcome.
Hotels: Rothley Court (adjacent).
Meals served.

O 39　Rushcliffe

Tel. East Leake 2209 (Sec. East Leake 2959)
East Leake, Loughborough, Leics.

5 miles S of Nottingham.
Undulating parkland course.
18 holes, 6150 yds. S.S.S. 69
Visitors welcome.
Green Fees. Weekdays £5.00 (£2.50 with member); weekends £7.50 (£5.00 with member).
Society Meetings Fri. by arrangement.
Hotels: Albany, Nottingham.
Meals served except Mon. and Wed.

O 40　Sandilands

Tel. Sutton-on-Sea 41432
Sutton-on-Sea, Mablethorpe, Lincs.
4 miles S of Mablethorpe on coast road.
Seaside course.
18 holes, 5984 yds. S.S.S. 69
Visitors welcome if members of recognized clubs.
Green Fees. Weekdays £3.00 (£2.00 with member); weekends £4.00 (£3.00 with member).
Society Meetings welcome weekdays only.
Hotels: Grange; Links, Sandilands.
Snacks and meals served.

O 41　Scraptoft

Tel. Leicester (0533) 419000
Scraptoft, Leicester.
Off A47 E of Leicester.
Meadowland course.
18 holes, 6247 yds. S.S.S. 69
Visitors welcome on weekdays, weekends with member only.
Society Meetings by arrangement.
Hotels: White House Hotel, Scraptoft.
Meals served.
Green Fees. Weekdays £5.00; weekends £6.00.

O 42　Seacroft

Tel. Skegness (0754) 3020
Seacroft, Skegness, Lincs. PE25 3AU.
A52, A158 to Skegness. 1 mile S of town.
Seaside course.
18 holes, 6478 yds. S.S.S. 71
Visitors welcome.
Green Fees. Weekdays £5.00 per round, £7.00 per day; weekends and bank holidays £6.00 per round, £8.00 per day.
Society Meetings by arrangement.
Hotels: Vine; Links; Crown, Skegness.
Meals and snacks served by arrangement.

O 43　Sherwood Forest

Tel. Mansfield 23327
Eakring Rd., Mansfield, Notts.
On A617 2½ miles SE of town.
Undulating moorland course.
18 holes, 6709 yds. S.S.S. 73
Course designed by J. Braid.
Visitors welcome on weekdays except Tues., weekends by arrangement. Letter of introduction may be requested.
Green Fees. Weekdays £7.00 per round or day; weekends and bank holidays £9.00 per round or day.
Society Meetings by arrangement.
Hotels: Post House; Sandiacre, Nottingham.
Meals served except Mon.

O 44　Sleaford

Tel. South Rauceby 273
South Rauceby, Sleaford, Lincs.
On A153, 3 miles SW of Sleaford.
18 holes, 6290 yds. S.S.S. 70
Visitors welcome.
Green Fees. Weekdays £4.00; weekends £5.00.
Society Meetings welcome weekdays only.
Hotels: Carre Arms; Red Lion; White Hart, Sleaford.
Meals served except Mon.

O 45　Southcliffe & Canwick

Tel. Lincoln (0522) 22166
Canwick Park, Washingborough Rd., Lincoln LN4 1EF.
2 miles from city centre.
Parkland course.
18 holes, 6300 yds. S.S.S. 70
Course designed by F. Hawtree.
Visitors welcome on weekdays.
Green Fees. £3.50 per round or day.
Society Meetings welcome weekdays only.
Hotels: Brierley House Hotel.
Meals served.

O 46　Spalding

Tel. Surfleet (077 585) 386
Surfleet, Spalding, Lincs PE11 4DQ.
Off A16, 4 miles N of Spalding.
Meadowland course.
18 holes, 5847 yds. S.S.S. 68
Visitors welcome.
Green Fees. Weekdays £4.00 (£3.00 with member); weekends £5.50 (£3.50 with member).
Society Meetings Thurs. only.
Hotels: Mermaid Inn, Surfleet; White Hart; Red Lion, Spalding.
Meals served by arrangement except Tues.

O 47　Stanton-on-the-Wolds

Tel. Plumtree (060237) 2044
Stanton-on-the-Wolds, Keyworth, Nottingham.
Off A606 at Blue Star Garage, 8 miles SE of Nottingham.
Meadowland course.
18 holes.
Course designed by T. Williamson.
Visitors welcome on weekdays, weekends with member only.
Green Fees. Weekdays £5.00 per round or day (£3.00 with member); weekends £7.00 (£4.00 with member).
Society Meetings by arrangement in January.
Hotels: Edwalton Hotel.
Meals served by arrangement.

O 48　Stoke Rochford

Tel. Great Ponton (047 683) 275
Stoke Rochford, Grantham, Lincs.
Off A1, 5 miles S of Grantham; entrance at 'Roadhog' motor stop.
Undulating parkland course.
18 holes, 6030 yds. S.S.S. 69
Visitors welcome weekdays, weekends with reservation.

Woodhall—spa and oasis

It is not a particular characteristic of inland courses that they convey the feeling of remoteness that many golfers seek in planning a day's outing or a week's holiday.

It is usually only at the seaside that a real escape can be found from the ever increasing evidence of crowded and hurried times; but Woodhall Spa, in the very heart of the rich agricultural belt of Lincolnshire, is certainly one of the places which comes nearest to proving the exception and, in terms of combining this with golf of high quality, is second to none.

A glance at the sandy fairways, fringed on all sides by heather, broom or silver birch, suggests that it has its origins deep in Surrey or Berkshire—indeed a stranger might well be forgiven for wondering whether he was in Lincolnshire at all—but it needs only a few holes to appreciate that its unexpected nature is a considerable part of its charm and that its high reputation, based on many distinguished opinions, is fully justified.

It is without question one of the finest inland courses in the British Isles, where the English Women's championship, the Women's Home Internationals, the Youths' championship and the Brabazon Trophy have been held and where the English Amateur championship was housed in 1967 for the first time; an occasion that afforded everyone the chance of seeing the smart new extension to the clubhouse and a nine-hole pitch-and-putt course which is a valuable extra amenity. In 1980, the British Women's championship is being held at Woodhall, and in 1981 the Home Internationals.

The course itself has also shown changes—a tightening of the approach to the 6th green and fresh restrictions on the right hand side of the 13th fairway where, so it is said, the slicer had rather too good a time. The hookers no doubt place such a step in the general category of 'improvements' but most people remember Woodhall Spa as plenty hard enough and regard any alterations as a strengthening of a respect that is already firm.

Four excellent par fours make a stern beginning and it may be that the par three that is in prospect at the short 5th will be fully needed at that stage in a medal. Frances Smith, in an outward half of 30 in the final of the English Women's against Elizabeth Price, had the fortune to do it in one, but more often than not some deep, encircling bunkers prove an overwhelming attraction before the player crosses the little railway line to the 500-yard 6th.

The short 8th to a plateau green offers another demanding stroke, as does the second over cross bunkers to the 9th (557 yds), but after starting for home with a drive and pitch to the dogleg 10th at the farthest point of the course, there is no let-up and the second nine, with only one short hole, is a few yards longer than the first.

The 13th can frequently be two woods and the 14th rather more, and though the next three are a good deal shorter, they are no less menacing—the 17th with a wood on the right being a splendid par four of lenient length.

Coming at the end of the round, it has had no small influence on the fate of countless competitions of one sort and another, though mostly, I suspect, as a destroyer; but one man on whom it had the opposite effect was the late Phillip Scrutton who, having been told that he needed 4, 4 to tie for the Brabazon, and carefully corrected his reliable informer to the effect that he meant 3, 4 to win, promptly remained true to his word.

A more than useful putt gave him the three at the 17th and then with his drive a shade too far right at the 18th, he faded a spoon shot round the great tree in a manner that would have drawn a smile from Ben Hogan; the ball finished about ten yards from the flag and the deed was done.

You and I may not be able to do the same but at the first opportunity it is emphatically worth a try.

Green Fees. Weekdays £4.50 per round (£3.00 with member), £6.00 per day (£3.50 with member); weekends after 10.30 a.m. £6.50 per round (£3.50 with member), £8.50 per day (£4.50 with member).
Society Meetings by arrangement.
Hotels: George; Angel & Royal; Kings, Grantham.
Meals served except Mon.

O 49   Sutton Bridge

Tel. Holbeach 350323
New Rd., Sutton Bridge, Spalding, Lincs.
On A17, 10 miles W of King's Lynn.
Parkland course.
9 holes, 5554 yds. S.S.S. 67
Visitors welcome on weekdays.
Green Fees. £5.00.
Hotels: Bridge Hotel.
Lunch and tea served.

O 50   Thonock

Tel. Gainsborough 3088
Thonock, Gainsborough, Lincs.
1 mile E of town centre.
Parkland course.
18 holes, 5214 yds. S.S.S. 68
Visitors welcome.

Green Fees. £3.50 per day (£2.00 with member).
Society Meetings welcome weekdays.
Meals served except Tues.

O 51   Ullesthorpe

Tel. Lutterworth (045 55) 209150
Frolesworth Rd., Ullesthorpe, Lutterworth, Leics.
M1 junction 20 to Lutterworth ½ mile; Lutterworth to Ullesthorpe 4 miles. M6 junction 1 to A5 3 miles; A5 High Cross to Ullesthorpe 3 miles.
Meadowland course.
18 holes, 6200 yds. S.S.S. 70
Visitors welcome.
Green Fees. Weekdays £4.00; weekends £5.00.
Society Meetings welcome; £3.50 per player for small parties, special rates for large groups.
Full catering facilities. Games room; swimming pool.

O 52   Western Park

Tel. Leicester (0533) 872339
Scudamore Rd., Braunstone Frith, Leicester LE3 1UQ.

Off A47, 2 miles W of city centre.
Parkland course.
18 holes, 6843 yds. S.S.S. 73
Course designed by F.W. Hawtree.
Visitors welcome on weekdays, weekends with reservation.
Green Fees. Weekdays £1.90; weekends £2.30.
Hotels: Europa Lodge; Post House.
Meals served.

O 53   Whetstone Park

Tel. Leicester 862399
Cambridge Rd., Cosby, Leics.
At S boundary of Leicester.
9 holes, 3005 yds. S.S.S. 69
Green Fees. Weekdays £1.50; weekends £2.00.

O 54   Willesley Park

Tel. Ashby-de-la-Zouch (0530) 414596
Tamworth Rd., Ashby-de-la-Zouch, Leics. LE6 5PF.
On A453, 1 mile S of Ashby-de-la-Zouch.
Undulating moorland, parkland course.
18 holes, 6310 yds. S.S.S. 70
Visitors welcome if members of recognized club.

Green Fees. Weekdays £6.00 per round, £8.00 per day; weekends and bank holidays £7.00 per round, £9.00 per day.
Society Meetings Wed. Thurs. and Fri. March to October.
Hotels: Royal; Measham Inn; Cedars.
Meals served except Mon.

O 55   Wollaton Park

Tel. Nottingham (0602) 787574
Wollaton Park, Wollaton, Nottingham.
Middleton Boulevard (ring road), off A52 W of Nottingham.
Parkland course.
18 holes, 6540 yds. S.S.S. 71
Course designed by Tom Williamson.
Visitors welcome.
Green Fees. Weekdays £5.25 per round, £7.60 per day; weekends £7.00 per round, £11.00 per day.
Society Meetings Tues. and Fri. by arrangement.
Hotels: Post House, Sandiacre; Albany; Savoy, Nottingham.
Lunches, high teas and grills served by arrangement except Mon.

O 56   Woodhall Spa

Tel. Woodhall Spa (0526) 52511
Woodhall Spa, Lincs LN10 6PU.
On B1191, 6 miles SW of Horncastle, 20 miles SE of Lincoln, 16 miles NE of Sleaford.
Moorland course.
18 holes, 6866 yds. S.S.S. 73
Course designed by Col. S.V. Hotchkin M.C.
Visitors welcome by arrangement.
Green Fees. Weekdays £5.50 per round, £7.50 per day; weekends £6.50 per round, £8.00 per day.
Society Meetings welcome weekdays except Tues., weekends max. 40.
Hotels: Golf Hotel; Petwood; Dover House; Spa Hotel.
Snacks, lunches and high teas served except Tues.

O 57   Worksop

Tel. Worksop 472696
Windmill Lane, Worksop, Notts. S80 2SQ.
SE of Worksop, 7 miles from M1 Exit 30.
Parkland course.
18 holes, 6444 yds. S.S.S. 71
Visitors welcome with reservation.
Green Fees. Weekdays £5.00; weekends £6.00.
Society Meetings welcome.
Hotels: Fourways, Blyth; Old Bell, Barnby Moor.
Meals served by arrangement.

P Merseyside

P 1   Allerton Municipal

Tel. 051-428 1046
Allerton, Liverpool 18.
Renshaw St. from city centre by way of Hardman St. then upper Parliament St. to Smithdown Rd. Follow, to Allerton Rd.
Undulating parkland course.
18 holes, 5081 yds. S.S.S. 65
Visitors welcome on weekdays, weekends with reservation.

Green Fees. 9 hole course £1.30; 18 hole course £1.80.
Hotels: in Liverpool.
Snacks served.

P 2   Arrowe Park Municipal

Tel. 051-677 1527
Arrowe Park, Birkenhead, Ches.
Mersey Tunnel into Borough Rd., then Woodchurch Rd.
Wooded parkland course.
18 holes, 6435 yds. S.S.S. 71
Visitors welcome.
Green Fees. £1.10 all week; juniors 55p.

P 3   Bidston

Tel. 051-638 3412
Scoresby Rd., Leasowe, Wirral, Merseyside L46 1QQ.
A551 from Wallasey, ½ mile.
Parkland course.
18 holes, S.S.S. 70
Visitors welcome on weekdays.
Green Fees. £3.75 per round.
Society Meetings by arrangement.
Hotels: Hotel St. Hilary, Wallasey.
Light meals served; lunches by arrangement.

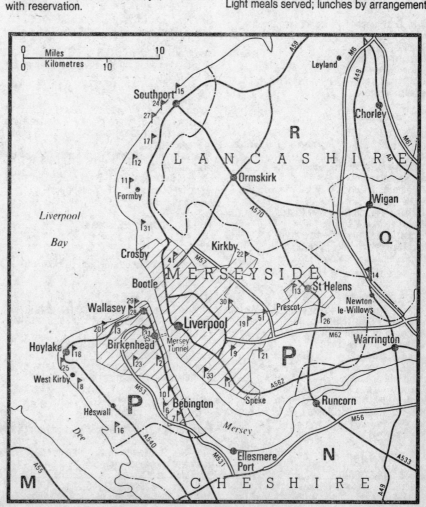

P 4   Bootle

Tel. 051-928 6196
Dunnings Bridge Rd., Bootle, Merseyside L30 2PP.
A565 5 miles from Liverpool.
Seaside course.
18 holes, 6362 yds. S.S.S. 70
Course designed by F. Stephens.
Visitors welcome.
Green Fees. Weekdays £1.65 per round; weekends £2.20.
Society Meetings by arrangement.
Hotels: Park Hotel, Netherton.
Snacks served.

P 5   Bowring

Tel. 051-489 1901
Bowring Park, Roby Rd., Huyton, Liverpool L36 4HD.
4¼ miles from city centre.
Parkland course.
9 holes, 5578 yds. S.S.S. 66
Visitors welcome.
Green Fees. £1.80.
Meals served to members and their guests only.

P 6   Brackenwood

Tel. 051-608 3093
Bracken Lane, Bebington, Wirral, Merseyside.
Off M56 at junction 4, signposted.
Parkland course.
18 holes, 6131 yds. S.S.S. 69
Visitors welcome.
Green Fees. £1.80.
Society Meetings by arrangement.
Hotels: in area.

P 7   Bromborough

Tel. 051-334 2155
Raby Hall Rd., Bromborough, Wirral, Merseyside L63 0NW.
1 mile from Bromborough station.
Parkland course.
White course 18 holes, 6569 yds. S.S.S. 72
Yellow course 6253 yds. S.S.S. 71
Visitors welcome on weekdays.
Green Fees. £5.00.
Society Meetings Wed. only.
Hotels: Dibbinsdale, Bromborough.
Snacks and lunches served.

P 8   Caldy

Tel. 051-625 5660
Links Hey Rd., West Kirby, Wirral, Merseyside L48 1NB.
1½ miles S of West Kirby.
Parkland/seaside course.
18 holes, 6642 yds. S.S.S. 73
Visitors welcome on weekdays, weekends with members only.
Green Fees. £7.00 (£5.50 after 2 p.m.).
Society Meetings welcome on Thurs.
Hotels: Stanley, Hoylake; Dee, West Kirby; Victoria, Heswall.
Meals served.

P 9   Childwall

Tel. 051-487 0654
Naylors Rd., Gateacre, Liverpool L27 2YB.
Via M62 about 1 mile from Huyton exit.
Parkland course.
18 holes, 6413 yds. S.S.S. 71
Visitors welcome with reservation.
Green Fees. Weekdays £5.75; weekends £7.50.
Society Meetings by arrangement in writing. £5.10 per player for groups of over 25 members.
Hotels: Gateacre Hall Hotel, Halewood Road.
Snacks served; meals by arrangement.

P 10   Eastham Lodge

Tel. 051-327 1483
Ferry Rd., Eastham, Wirral, Merseyside L62 0AP.
On A41 6 miles from Birkenhead.
Parkland course.
9 holes, 5830 yds. S.S.S. 68
Course designed by Hawtree & Son.
Visitors welcome on weekdays with letter of introduction, weekends with member only.
Green Fees. £3.25 per day (£1.75 with member).
Society Meetings Mon. and Tues. only.
Hotels: Dresden, Bromborough; Mercury, Great Sutton.
Lunches, snacks and teas served.

P 11   Formby

Tel. Formby 72164
Golf Rd., Freshfield, Liverpool L37 1LQ.
1 mile W of A565 by Freshfield Station.
Seaside course.
18 holes, 6700 yds. S.S.S. 73
Course designed by W. Park. Alterations by H. Colt.
Visitors welcome with letter of introduction, or reservation.
Green Fees. Weekdays £9.00 per round or day (£3.25 with member); weekends £10.00 per round or day (£3.75 with member).
Society Meetings Tues. and Thurs. by arrangement.
Hotels: Treetops, Southport Old Rd. Accommodation for 10 in clubhouse.
Meals served.

P 12   Formby Ladies

Tel. Formby 73493
Golf Rd., Formby L37 1LQ.
Six miles S of Southport, off A565.
Seaside course.
18 holes, 5374 yds. S.S.S. 71
Visitors welcome.
Green Fees. Weekdays £6.00 (£1.50 with member); weekends £7.00 (£2.00 with member).
Society Meetings welcome.
Hotels: in Southport.
Light lunches and afternoon teas served; full lunches by arrangement.

P 13   Grange Park

Tel. St. Helens 22980
Prescot Rd., St. Helens, Merseyside WA10 3AD.
On A58. 2 miles from St. Helens Town Hall towards Liverpool.
Parkland course.
18 holes, 6429 yds. S.S.S. 71
Visitors welcome if members of recognized club, preferably by introduction.
Green Fees. Weekdays £5.50 (£3.00 with member); weekends and bank holidays £7.50 (£4.00 with member).
Society Meetings by arrangement.
Hotels: Fleece Hotel.
Lunches and dinners served.

P 14   Haydock Park

Tel. Newton-le-Willows 4389
Golborne Park, Newton-le-Willows, Merseyside.
M6.
Parkland course.
18 holes, 6000 yds. S.S.S. 69
Visitors welcome on weekdays except Tues., weekends with member only.
Green Fees. Weekdays £4.60 per round; £6.90 per day.
Meals served except Mon. and Thurs.

P 15   Hesketh

Tel. Southport (0704) 36897
Cockle Dick's Lane, Off Cambridge Rd., Southport, Merseyside PR9 9QQ.
1 mile N of town centre.
Seaside course.
18 holes, 6468 yds. S.S.S. 72
Visitors welcome.
Green Fees. Weekdays £5.00 per round, £7.00 per day; weekends £8.50 per round or day.
Society Meetings welcome.
Hotels: in Southport.
Meals served except Mon.

P 16   Heswall

Tel. 051-342 1237
Cottage Lane, Heswall, Wirral, Merseyside L60 8PB.
Meadowland course.
18 holes, 6420 yds. S.S.S. 72
Visitors welcome Mon., Thurs. morning, Fri. and weekends.
Green Fees. Weekdays £5.50 (£1.75 with member); weekends £6.50 (£2.50 with member).
Meals served by arrangement.

P 17   Hillside

Tel. Southport 67169
Hastings Rd., Southport, Merseyside.
By Hillside station, S of town.
Seaside course.
18 holes, 6850 yds. S.S.S. 74
Visitors welcome on weekdays except Tues. a.m., weekends after 3.30 p.m.
Green Fees. Weekdays £9.00; weekends £11.00.
Society Meetings by arrangement.
Hotels: Bold; Royal; Clifton; Prince of Wales.
Meals served except Fri.

P 18   Hoylake

Tel. 051-632 2956
Carr Lane, Hoylake, Wirral, Merseyside.
Off M53 10 miles SW of Liverpool.
Parkland course.
18 holes, 6312 yds. S.S.S. 70
Course designed by J. Braid.
Visitors welcome.

Green Fees. £1.10.
Society Meetings welcome.
Hotels: Stanley; King's Gap, Hoylake.
Meals served at Cafe.

P 19   Huyton & Prescot

Tel. 051-489 3948
Hurst Park, Huyton Lane, Huyton, Liverpool.
7 miles from Liverpool on M57.
Parkland course.
18 holes, 5732 yds. S.S.S. 68
Visitors welcome on weekdays, weekends
with member only.
Society Meetings welcome on weekdays.

P 20   Leasowe

Tel. 051-677 5852
Moreton, Wirral, Merseyside L46 3RD.
1 mile W of Wallasey village.
Seaside course.
18 holes, 6204 yds. S.S.S. 70
Visitors welcome on weekdays, Sun. with
member only.
Green Fees. Weekdays £3.50 (£2.50 with
member); Sat. £5.00 (£2.50 with member);
Sun. £2.50 with member only.
Society Meetings Weekdays by
arrangement except Mon. and Tues.
Meals served by arrangement (1 week in
advance).

P 21   Lee Park

Tel. 051-487 3882
Chidwall Valley Rd., Liverpool L27 3YA.
B5171 off A562.
Parkland course.
18 holes, 5938 yds. S.S.S. 69
Visitors welcome with reservation.
Green Fees. Weekdays £5.00 (£2.50 with
member); weekend £6.00 (£3.50 with
member).
Society Meetings welcome.
Hotels: Adelphi; Bradford, Liverpool.

P 22   Liverpool Municipal

Tel. 051-546 5435
Ingoe Lane, Kirkby, Merseyside.
On M62.
Meadowland.
18 holes, 6588 yds. S.S.S. 71
Course designed by J. Large.
Visitors welcome on weekdays, weekends
with reservation 1 week in advance.
Green Fees. £1.30 per round.
Hotels: in Liverpool.
Meals served.

P 23   Prenton

Tel. 051-608 1053
Golf Links Rd., Prenton, Birkenhead, Ches.
Off A552. Exit 3 M53.
Undulating meadowland course.
18 holes, 6379 yds. S.S.S. 71
Course designed by Hawtree & Son.
Visitors welcome with reservation.
Green Fees. Weekdays £5.00 per day;
weekends £7.25 per day.
Society Meetings Wed. only.
Hotels: Riverhill Hotel, Oxton, Birkenhead.
Meals served.

P 24   Royal Birkdale

Tel. Southport 67920
Southport, Merseyside.
Seaside course.
18 holes, 6711 yds. S.S.S. 73
Visitors welcome with letter of introduction.
Society Meetings welcome.
Hotels: in Southport.
Meals served.

P 25   Royal Liverpool

Tel. 051-632 3101
Meols Dr., Hoylake, Wirral, Merseyside.
Off A553, 10 miles W of Liverpool.
Seaside course.
18 holes, 6737 yds. S.S.S. 74
Visitors welcome with letter of introduction.
Green Fees. Weekdays £8.50 (£3.75 with
member); weekends £10.00 (£4.75 with
member).
Society Meetings welcome on weekdays.
Hotels: Green Lodge; Kings Gap, Hoylake;
Dee, West Kirby; Adelphi, Liverpool.
Lunches served except Mon. and Tues.

P 26   Sherdley Park

Tel. Marshalls Cross (0744) 813149
Elton Head Rd., St. Helens, Merseyside.
2 miles from town centre on Warrington road.
Undulating parkland course.
18 holes, 5941 yds. S.S.S. 69
Visitors welcome.
Green Fees. Weekdays £1.35; weekends
£1.70.
Hotels: Fleece Hotel.
Snacks served.

P 27   Southport & Ainsdale

Tel. Southport (0704) 78000
Bradshaw Lane, Liverpool Rd., Ainsdale,
Southport, Merseyside PR8 3LG.
3 miles S of Southport on A565.
Seaside course.
18 holes, 6615 yds. S.S.S. 73
Course designed by J. Braid.
Visitors welcome on weekdays.
Green Fees. Weekdays £8.50 (£2.00 with
member); weekends £11.00 (£3.00 with
member).
Society Meetings welcome weekdays
only.
Hotels: Prince of Wales; Royal; Clifton;
Scarisbrick, Southport.
Meals served except Mon.

P 28   Wallasey

Tel. 051-639 3700
Bayswater Rd., Wallasey, Merseyside L45
8LA.
From Liverpool take Wallasey tunnel and
follow New Brighton signs at exit. From the
Wirral take New Brighton exit of M53 and
follow New Brighton signs into Bayswater Rd.
18 holes, 6607 yds. S.S.S. 73
Course designed by Tom Morris Snr.
Visitors welcome with reservation if
members of recognized club.
Green Fees. Weekdays £6.00 per round
or day; weekends £7.00 per round or day.
Society Meetings by arrangement.
Hotels: Belvidere; The Grove.
Meals served except Mon.

P 29   Warren Park

Tel. 051-639 5730
Grove Rd., Wallasey, Merseyside.
9 holes, 2957 yds. S.S.S. 34
Visitors welcome.
Green Fees. Weekdays 80p per 18 holes,
juniors 30p; weekends £1.00 per 18 holes.

P 30   West Derby

Tel. 051-228 3420/1540
Yew Tree Lane, Liverpool L12 9HQ.
Parkland course.
18 holes, 6322 yds. S.S.S. 70
Visitors welcome on weekdays, weekends
with member only.
Green Fees. Weekdays £4.50 (£2.25 with
member); weekends £6.50 (£2.75 with
member).
Society Meetings by prior arrangement.
Snacks; light meals served.

P 31   West Lancashire

Tel. 051-924 1076
Hall Rd. West, Blundellsands, Liverpool L23
8SI.
5 miles from centre of Liverpool.
Seaside course.
18 holes, 6756 yds. S.S.S. 73
Visitors welcome on weekdays except
Tues. when Ladies have priority until 4.00
p.m.
Green Fees. Weekdays £7.00 per day
(£3.00 with member); weekends £9.00
(£4.00 with member).
Society Meetings weekdays by
arrangement except Mon.
Hotels: Blundellsands Hotel, Blundellsands;
Royal, Seaforth.
Lunches served except Mon.; evening meals
served Sat. by arrangement.

P 32   Wirral Ladies'

Tel. 051-652 1255
Bidston Rd., Oxton, Birkenhead, Ches. L43
6TS.
On A41.
Heathland course.
Gents 18 holes, 5156 yds. S.S.S. 66,
Ladies 4744 yds. S.S.S. 68
Visitors welcome with letter of introduction
(after 11 a.m. on Sun.).
Green Fees. Weekdays £3.20; weekends
£4.25; weekly £11.00; monthly £33.00.
Hotels: Bowler Hat Hotel; Riverhill Hotel,
Oxton.
Meals served by arrangement.

P 33   Woolton

Tel. 051-486 1601
Doe Park, Speke Rd., Woolton, Liverpool
L25 7TZ.
6 miles from city centre.
Parkland course.
18 holes, 5789 yds. S.S.S. 68
Visitors welcome.
Green Fees. Weekdays £4.03; weekends
£5.75.
Society Meetings by arrangement.
Hotels: in Liverpool.
Lunches served except Mon. and Fri.

Q *Greater Manchester*

Q 1 Acre Gate

Tel. 061-748 1226
Pennybridge Lane, Flixton, Manchester M3 3DN.
Turn into Pennybridge Lane from Flixton Rd. Parkland.
15 holes, 3935 yds. S.S.S. 53
Green Fees. Weekdays £1.50, juniors 75p; weekends £2.00; season ticket residents of Trafford 50p, non-residents 60p.

Q 2 Altrincham

Tel. 061-928 0761 (for booking)
Stockport Rd., Timperley, Altrincham, Ches. WA15.
On A560 1 mile E of Altrincham.
Undulating meadowland course.
18 holes, 6196 yds. S.S.S. 69
Visitors welcome with reservation.
Green Fees. Weekdays £1.80, juniors and O.A.P.s 90p until 5.00 p.m.; weekends £2.50.
Hotels: Cresta Court; Woodlands, Altrincham.

Q 3 Ashton-in-Makerfield

Tel. Ashton-in-Makerfield (0942) 727267
Garswood Park, Liverpool Rd., Ashton-in-Makerfield, Wigan WN4 9AN.
5 minutes from M6.
Parkland course.
9 holes, 6190 yds. S.S.S. 69
Course designed by F.W. Hawtree.
Visitors welcome on weekdays, weekends with member only.
Green Fees. Weekdays £5.00.
Hotels: Cranberry; Post House.

Q 4 Ashton on Mersey

Tel. 061-973 3220
Church Lane, Sale, Ches. M33 5QQ.
2 miles from Sale station.
Parkland course.
9 holes, 6202 yds. S.S.S. 70
Visitors welcome on weekdays, weekends with member only.
Green Fees. £4.00 (£2.00 with member).
Snacks and lunches served.

Q 5 Ashton-under-Lyne

Tel. 061-330 1537
Kings Rd., Higher Hurst, Ashton-under-Lyne, Lancs.
2 miles from town centre.
Moorland course.
18 holes, 6031 yds. S.S.S. 69
Visitors welcome on weekdays, weekends with member only.
Green Fees. Weekdays £4.00 (£2.00 with member); weekends £4.00 (with member only).
Society Meetings weekdays by arrangement.
Hotels: York House, Ashton-under-Lyne.
Meals served except Mon.

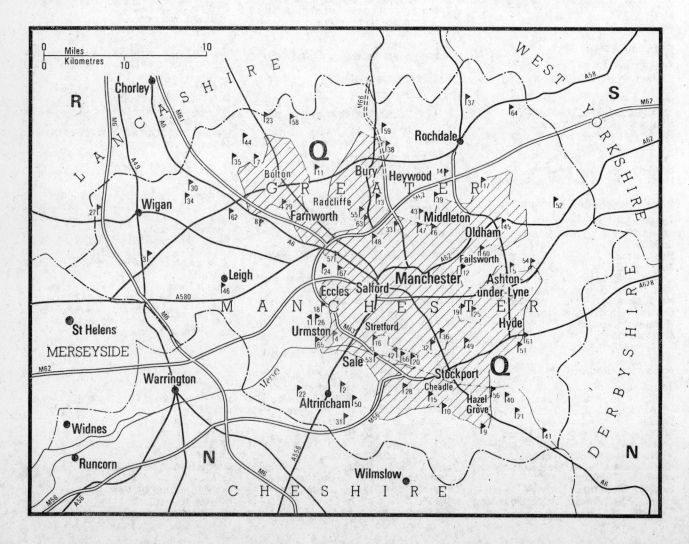

Q 6 Blackley

Tel. 061-643 2980
Victoria Ave. East, Manchester M9 2HW.
Parkland course.
18 holes, 6237 yds. S.S.S. 70
Visitors welcome.
Lunches served by arrangement except Mon.
Green Fees. £3.20; Societies £2.70.

Q 7 Bolton

Tel. Bolton 43067
Lostock Park, Chorley New Rd., Bolton,
Lancs. BL6 4AJ.
Off main road midway between Bolton and
Horwich. Exit 6 M61.
Parkland course.
18 holes, 6215 yds. S.S.S. 70
Visitors welcome with reservation.
Green Fees. Weekdays except Wed.
£7.00; Wed., bank holidays and weekends
£9.00.
Society Meetings welcome Mon., Thurs.
and Fri.
Hotels: Crest Motel, Bolton; Swallow Field,
Horwich.
Lunches and evening meals served except
Sun.

Q 8 Brackley

Tel. 061-790 6076
Bullows Rd., Little Hulton, Worsley,
Manchester.
9 miles from Manchester on A6; turn right at
White Lion Hotel into Highfield Rd., left into
Captain Fold Rd., left into Bullows Rd.
Parkland course.
9 holes, S.S.S. 69
Visitors welcome.
Green Fees. 9 holes weekdays 80p;
weekends and bank holidays £1.15.
Society Meetings welcome.
Hotels: Crest Motel, Bolton; Wendover,
Monton.
No catering facilities at club.

Q 9 Bramall Park

Tel. 061-485 3119
Manor Rd., Bramhall, Stockport, Ches.
8 miles S of Manchester. A6 to Bramhall
Lane then A5102 to Carrwood Rd.
Parkland course.
18 holes, 6214 yds. S.S.S. 70
Visitors welcome on weekdays with letter
of introduction.
Green Fees. Weekdays £5.00; weekends
£6.00.
Society Meetings Tues. only.
Hotels: Alma Lodge Hotel, Stockport;
Belfry, Handforth.
Meals served except Fri.

Q 10 Bramhall

Tel. 061-439 4057
Ladythorn Rd., Bramhall, Stockport, Ches.
SK7 2EY.
Via Bramhall Lane South and Ladythorn Rd.
Parkland course.
18 holes, 6245 yds. S.S.S. 70
Visitors welcome.
Green Fees. Weekdays £5.00 (£2.50 with
member); weekends £7.00 (£3.50 with
member).

Society Meetings Wed. only.
Hotels: Bramhall Moat House Hotel.
Meals served by arrangement.

Q 11 Breightmet

Tel. Bolton 27381
Red Bridge, Ainsworth, Bolton, Lancs.
Main road to Bury, turn left at Empire Rd.,
about 3 miles.
Parkland course.
9 holes, 6400 yds. S.S.S. 71
Visitors welcome with reservation.
Green Fees. Weekdays £3.00 (£1.50 with
member); weekends £5.00 (£2.00 with
member).
Society Meetings by arrangement.
Hotels: Pack Horse, Bolton.
Light meals served except Mon.

Q 12 Brookdale

Tel. 061-681 4534
Ashbridge,   Woodhouses,   Failsworth,
Manchester.
5 miles N of Manchester.
Parkland, meadowland course.
18 holes, 6040 yds. S.S.S. 68
Visitors welcome except Sun.
Green Fees. Weekdays £3.00 (£1.50 with
member); weekends £4.00 (£2.00 with
member).
Society Meetings by arrangement 1
month in advance.
Hotels: Belgrade Hotel, Oldham.
Meals served by arrangement.

Q 13 Bury

Tel. 061-766 4897
Unsworth Hall, Blackford Bridge, Bury,
Lancs. BL9 9TJ.
A56 from Manchester to Bury, 7 miles N of
Manchester.
Undulating course.
18 holes, 5935 yds. S.S.S. 69
Visitors welcome.
Green Fees. Weekdays £4.00 (£2.00 with
member); weekends £5.00 (£3.00 with
member); plus V.A.T.
Society Meetings welcome weekdays
only.
Meals and snacks served except Mon.

Q 14 Castle Hawk

Tel. Rochdale (0706) 40841
Heywood Rd., Castleton, Rochdale, Gtr
Manchester.
Leave Rochdale on Castleton road. In
Castleton turn right directly before railway
station; follow road through to Heywood Rd.
(dirt track), fork left after 100 yds.
Meadowland course.
18 holes, 3158 yds. S.S.S. 56
Course designed by E. Jones.
Visitors welcome except Sun. morning.
Green Fees. Weekdays £1.50; weekends
£3.50.
Society Meetings welcome except Sun.
morning.
Bar snacks; cold buffet.

Q 15 Cheadle

Tel. 061-428 2160
Cheadle Rd., Cheadle, Ches.

1 mile S of Cheadle village.
Undulating parkland course.
9 holes, 5000 yds. S.S.S. 64
Visitors welcome if members of a golf club.
Green Fees. £4.00 (£2.00 with member).
Meals by arrangement.

Q 16 Chorlton-cum-Hardy

Tel. 061-881 3139, Sec. 881 5830, Pro. 881
9911
Barlow Hall, Barlow Hall Rd., Manchester
M21 2JJ.
4 miles S of Manchester on A5103.
Parkland course.
18 holes, 5978 yds. S.S.S. 69
Visitors welcome.
Green Fees. Weekdays £6.00; weekends
£9.00.
Society Meetings by arrangement.
Hotels: Post House, Northenden.
Lunches and dinners served by arrangement.

Q 17 Crompton & Royton

Tel. 061-624 2154
Highbarn, Royton, Oldham, Lancs. OL2 6RW.
Off A627 at Royton Town Hall clock.
Moorland course.
18 holes, 6187 yds. S.S.S. 69
Visitors welcome.
Green Fees. Weekdays £4.50 (£2.30 with
member); ladies and juniors £2.30 (£1.15
with member); weekends £7.00 (£4.60 with
member); ladies and juniors £5.75 (£2.30
with member).
Society   Meetings   welcome   by
arrangement.
Hotels: Belgrade Hotel, Oldham.

Q 18 Davyhulme Park

Tel. 061-748 2856
Gleneagles   Rd.,   Davyhulme,   Urmston,
Manchester.
1 mile from M62/M63.
Parkland course.
18 holes, 6224 yds. S.S.S. 69
Visitors welcome if members of recognized
club.
Green Fees. Weekdays £5.00; weekends
£7.00.
Society Meetings by arrangement.
Hotels: Lymm Hotel, Lymm.
Meals served by arrangement except Mon.
and Thurs.

Q 19 Denton

Tel. 061-336 3218
Manchester Rd., Denton, Lancs. M34 2NU.
A57, 5 miles from Piccadilly.
Parkland course.
18 holes, 6290 yds. S.S.S. 70
Course redesigned by B. Allen.
Visitors welcome if members of recognized
club.
Green Fees. Weekdays £5.00 (£2.00 with
member); weekends £6.00 (£2.50 with
member); plus V.A.T.
Society Meetings welcome weekdays
only.
Hotels: Portland, Manchester; York House
Hotel, Ashton-under-Lyne.
Meals served except Mon., Thurs. afternoon
when snacks are available.

Q 20 Didsbury

Tel. 061-998 2743
Ford Lane, Northenden, Manchester 22.
Just off M56, near Northenden Church.
Parkland course.
18 holes, 6230 yds. S.S.S. 70
Visitors welcome.
Green Fees. Weekdays £5.50; weekends
£7.00.
Society Meetings by arrangement.
Hotels: Post House.
Meals served by arrangement.

Q 21 Disley

Tel. Disley 2071
Jackson's Edge, Disley, Stockport, Ches.
A6, 6 miles from Stockport.
Moorland/meadowland course.
18 holes, 5950 yds. S.S.S. 69
Visitors welcome.
Green Fees. Weekdays £5.00 (£2.75 with
member); weekends £7.50 (£3.75 with
member).
Society Meetings weekdays except
Thurs.
Hotels: Rams Head.
Meals served except Mon.

Q 22 Dunham Forest Golf & Country Club

Tel. 061-928 2605
Oldfield Lane, Altrincham, Ches. WA14 0TY.
About 9 miles S of Manchester on A56.
Parkland course.
18 holes, 6636 yds. S.S.S. 72
Visitors welcome.
Green Fees. Weekdays £8.00 (£4.00 with
member); weekends £10.00 (£5.00 with
member).
Society Meetings welcome.
Hotels: Bowdon Hotel; Alpine, Bowdon.
Meals served except Fri.

Q 23 Dunscar

Tel. Bolton (0204) 53321
Longworth Lane, Bromley Cross, Bolton,
Lancs.
3 miles N of Bolton, on A666 Blackburn road.
Moorland course.
18 holes, 5992 yds. S.S.S. 69
Visitors welcome.
Green Fees. On application to secretary.
Society Meetings welcome weekdays
only.
Hotels: Egerton House Hotel; Last Drop
Village Hotel.
Lunches served except Mon.

Q 24 Ellesmere

Tel. 061-790 2122, 790 8591 (Pro.)
Old Clough Lane, Worsley, Manchester.
A580, E Lancs. road, adjacent to M62
bridges; 5 miles from city centre.
Undulating parkland course.
18 holes, 5957 yds. S.S.S. 69
Visitors welcome on weekdays except at
competition times.
Green Fees. Weekdays £5.00 (£2.00 with
member); weekends £6.00 (£2.50 with
member).
Society Meetings welcome weekdays
before 2.30 p.m. except competition days.
Meals served by arrangement.

Q 25 Fairfield Golf & Sailing Club

Tel. 061-370 1641
Booth Rd., Audenshaw, Manchester M34
5GA.
A635, 6 miles from city centre.
Meadowland course.
18 holes, 5600 yds. S.S.S. 68
Visitors welcome on weekdays, weekends
with reservation.
Green Fees. Weekdays £3.50; weekends
£4.50.
Society Meetings welcome weekdays
only.
Hotels: Trough House Hotel.
Meals served by arrangement.

Q 26 Flixton

Tel. 061-748 2116
Church Rd., Flixton, Urmston, Manchester.
5 miles from Manchester.
Parkland course.
9 holes, 6441 yds. S.S.S. 71
Visitors welcome.
Green Fees. Weekdays £4.00 per day
(£2.00 with member); weekends £6.00 per
day (£3.00 with member).
Society Meetings welcome weekdays
only except Wed. (Ladies Day).
Meals served except Tues.

Q 27 Gathurst

Tel. Appley Bridge 2861
62 Miles Lane, Shevington, Wigan, Lancs.
WN6 8EW.
1 mile S of junction 27 of the M6.
Parkland course.
9 holes, 2308 yds. S.S.S. 70
Visitors welcome on weekdays except
Wed. with member or with reservation.
Green Fees. £2.88 (£1.15 with member).
Society Meetings welcome weekdays
except Wed. by arrangement.
Hotels: Almond Brook Motor Inn, Standish;
Cassinelli's.
Meals served except Mon.

Q 28 Gatley

Tel. 061-437 2091
Waterfall Farm, Styal Rd., Gatley, Cheadle,
Ches. SK8 4JY.
1 mile from Gatley village.
Meadowland course.
9 holes, 5934 yds. S.S.S. 68
Visitors welcome with member only.
Green Fees. £2.25.
Society Meetings by arrangement.
Hotels: Belfry, Handforth; Excelsior,
Ringway.
Meals served by arrangement except Mon.

Q 29 Great Lever & Farnworth

Tel. Bolton 62582
Lever Edge Lane, Bolton BL3 3EN.
1½ miles from town centre.
Meadowland course.
18 holes, 5859 yds. S.S.S. 69
Visitors welcome.
Green Fees. Weekdays £2.75; weekends
£4.00.
Society Meetings welcome.
Hotels: in Bolton.
Meals served by arrangement

Q 30 Haigh Hall

Tel. Wigan (0942) 831107
Haigh Hall Country Park, Haigh, Wigan,
Lancs.
Off B5238 or B5239, 6 miles NE of Wigan.
Undulating parkland.
18 holes, 6423 yds. S.S.S. 71
Visitors welcome.
Green Fees. Weekdays £1.80 per round,
£2.50 per day; weekends £2.50.
Hotels: Grand; Brocket Arms.
Meals served.

Q 31 Hale

Tel. 061-980 4225
Rappax Rd., Hale, Altrincham, Ches.
2 miles SE of Altrincham.
Undulating parkland course.
9 holes, 5241 yds. S.S.S. 68
Visitors welcome; Sat. and Sun. with
member only.
Green Fees. £6.00 (£2.00 with member).
Hotels: Ashley, Hale; Bowdon Hotel,
Bowdon.
Meals served by arrangement except Tues.

Q 32 Heaton Moor

Tel. 061-432 2134
Heaton Mersey, Stockport, Ches. SK4 3NX.
2 miles from Stockport.
Parkland course.
18 holes, 5876 yds. S.S.S. 68
Visitors welcome.
Green Fees. Weekdays £5.00 per day
(£2.60 with member); weekends £7.20 per
day (£3.00 with member).
Meals served except Mon.

Q 33 Heaton Park Municipal

Tel. 061-773 1085
Heaton Park, Manchester.
Leave M62 at Exit 19, right at A576, 200
yards on right.
Undulating parkland course.
18 holes, 5900 yds. S.S.S. 68
Course designed by J. H. Taylor.
Visitors welcome.
Green Fees. Weekdays £1.30; weekends
and bank holidays £1.70.

Q 34 Hindley Hall

Tel. Wigan 55991
Hall Lane, Hindley, Wigan, Lancs. WN2 2SQ.
Via A58 and Ladies Lane to Hall Lane, or
M61 junction 6 A6 to Dicconson Lane to Hall
Lane.
Parkland course.
18 holes, 5821 yds. S.S.S. 68
Course designed by Wigan Coal & Iron Co.
Visitors welcome if members of recognized
club.
Green Fees. £5.00 (£1.50 with member).
Society Meetings by arrangement.
Hotels: Grand; Brocket, Wigan.
Meals served by arrangement except Mon.,
and Fri. after 2p.m.

Q 35 Horwich

Tel. Horwich 66980
Victoria Rd., Horwich, Bolton, Lancs.
Undulating moorland course.
9 holes, 5404 yds. S.S.S. 67

Visitors welcome with member.
Green Fees. £2.00.
Society Meetings by arrangement.
Meals served by arrangement.

Q 36   Houldsworth

Tel. 061-224 5055
Wingate House, Higher Levenshulme, Manchester M19 3JW.
A6 midway between Manchester and Stockport.
Meadowland course.
18 holes, 6078 yds. S.S.S. 69
Visitors welcome on weekdays.
Green Fees. Weekdays £2.00; weekends £4.00.
Society Meetings welcome on weekdays except Mon.
Hotels: in area.
Meals served except Mon.

Q 37   Lobden

Tel. Whitworth 3228
Whitworth, Rochdale, Lancs.
½ mile from centre of village.
Moorland course.
9 holes, 5770 yds. S.S.S. 68
Visitors welcome on weekdays.
Green Fees. Weekdays £2.00; weekends £4.00.
Society Meetings welcome Mon. and Fri.
Hotels: in Rochdale.
Meals served by arrangement.

Q 38   Lowes Park

Tel. 061-764 1231
Hill Top, Walmersley, Bury, Lancs.
2 miles NE of Bury.
Moorland course.
9 holes, 6043 yds S.S.S. 69
Visitors welcome on weekdays, weekends with member only.
Green Fees. Weekdays £3.45 (£1.15 with member).
Society Meetings by arrangement.
Hotels: Woolfield House Hotel, Bury.
Meals served by arrangement.

Q 39   Manchester

Tel. 061-643 3202 (Sec.), 643 2638 (Pro.)
Hopwood Cottage, Middleton, Manchester M24 2QP.
Leave M62 at junction 19 for A6046 to Middleton; at T junction (A664) turn left, club ½ mile on left.
Moorland course.
18 holes, 6453 yds. S.S.S. 72
Visitors welcome.
Green Fees. Weekdays £6.00 (£3.25 with member), juniors £2.50 (£1.75 with member); weekends £7.50 (£3.25 with member). Juniors not permitted at weekends.
Society Meetings welcome weekdays except Fri. afternoon.
Hotels: Midway, Castleton; Wellington, Rochdale; Bower, Chadderton.
Meals served except Thurs., when snacks are available.

Q 40   Marple

Tel. 061-427 2311
Hawk Green, Marple, Stockport, Ches. SK6 7EL.
Off A6 at High Lane for 2 miles, left at Hawk Green.
Parkland/meadowland course.
9 holes, 5564 yds. S.S.S. 67
Visitors welcome on weekdays except Thurs. after 5.00p.m., weekends with member only.
Green Fees. Weekdays £4.00 (£2.00 with member); weekends £4.00 with member.
Hotels: West Towers.
Snacks served; meals by arrangement.

Q 41   Mellor & Townscliffe

Tel. 061-427 2208
Tarden, Mellor, Stockport, Ches.
Off A626. Gibb Lane (opposite Devonshire Arms Hotel).
Undulating parkland/moorland course.
18 holes, 5915 yds. S.S.S. 69
Visitors welcome except before 3.00 p.m. on Sat.
Green Fees. Weekdays £3.00 (£1.50 with member); weekends £5.00 (£2.50 with member).
Society Meetings welcome except Sat.
Hotels: West Towers, Marple; Alma Lodge Hotel, Stockport.
Meals served except Tues.

Q 42   Northenden

Tel. 061-998 4738
Palatine Rd., Manchester 22.
From S M1, M6 and then M56.
Parkland course.
18 holes, 6413 yds. S.S.S. 71
Visitors welcome.
Green Fees. Weekdays £6.00 per day; weekends £7.50.
Society Meetings Tues. and Fri. only.
Hotels: Post House, Northenden.
Meals served except Mon.

Q 43   North Manchester

Tel. 061-643 2941/9033/7094
Old Manchester Rd., Middleton, Manchester M24 4FB.
M6-M66 junction 18 (M62) to Middleton; 1½ miles from motorway end on left.
Undulating, semi-links, moorland course.
18 holes, 6542 yds. S.S.S. 72
Visitors welcome by arrangement.
Green Fees. Weekdays £5.50 (£2.75 with member); weekends £7.50 (£3.75 with member).
Society Meetings welcome on weekdays by arrangement.
Lunches, bar snacks, evening meals served except Tues.

Q 44   Old Links

Tel. Bolton (0204) 42307
Chorley Old Rd., Montserrat, Bolton, Lancs. BL1 5SU.
B6226 off A58 on N side of Bolton.
Moorland course.
18 holes, 6410 yds. S.S.S. 72
Visitors welcome on weekdays.

Green Fees. Weekdays £5.00; weekends and bank holidays £6.00.
Society Meetings welcome weekdays only.
Hotels: Pack Horse; Crest Motel, Bolton.
Meals and snacks served by arrangement except Mon.

Q 45   Oldham

Tel. 061-624 4986
Lees New Rd., Oldham.
Moorland parkland course.
18 holes, 4944 yds. S.S.S. 65
Visitors welcome.
Green Fees. Weekdays £2.50; weekends £3.50.

Q 46   Pennington

Pennington Country Park, St. Helens Rd., Leigh, Greater Manchester.
A572 1 mile SW of town centre; 2 miles NE of junction of A580 (E Lancs road) and A572.
Parkland course.
9 holes, 3104 yds. S.S.S. 35
Visitors welcome.
Green Fees. Weekdays 90p per round, weekends £1.25 per round; juniors weekdays until 6.00 p.m. except Wed. 65p.

Q 47   Pike Fold

Tel. 061-740 1136
Cooper Lane, Blackley, Manchester M9.
4 miles N of city centre off Rochdale Road.
Undulating course.
9 holes, 5789 yds. S.S.S. 68
Course designed by E.W. Phillips.
Visitors welcome on weekdays, weekends with member only.
Green Fees. Weekdays £4.00 (£2.00 with member); weekends £5.00 (£3.00 with member).
Society Meetings welcome weekdays only.
Hotels: Assheton Arms; Wilton Arms, Middleton.
Snacks served; lunches and dinners by arrangement except Thurs.

Q 48   Prestwich

Tel. 061-773 2544
Hilton Lane, Prestwich, Manchester M25 8SD.
On A6044 ¼ mile W of junction with A56.
Parkland course.
18 holes, 4712 yds. S.S.S. 63
Visitors welcome.
Green Fees. Weekdays £3.50 (£2.25 with member); weekends £5.50 (£4.00 with member).
Society Meetings welcome weekdays only.
Hotels: Hazeldean.
Lunches served except Mon.

Q 49   Reddish Vale

Tel. 061-480 2359
Southcliffe Rd., Reddish, Stockport, Ches.
1½ miles N of Stockport, off Reddish Rd.
Undulating course.
18 holes, 6048 yds. S.S.S. 69
Course designed by Dr.A. Mackenzie.
Visitors welcome on weekdays.
Green Fees. £5.00.

Society Meetings welcome on weekdays by arrangement.
Hotels: Alma Lodge Hotel; Belgrade, Stockport.
Meals served.

Q 50 Ringway

Tel. 061-980 2630
Hale Mount, Hale Barns, Altrincham, Ches. WA15 8SW.
8 miles S of Manchester, off M56.
Parkland course.
18 holes, 6421 yds. S.S.S. 71
Visitors welcome.
Green Fees. Weekdays £6.50 (£2.50 with member); weekends £10.00 (£2.50).
Society Meetings Thurs. only.
Hotels: Ashley; Portofino; Cresta, Altrincham.
Meals served.

Q 51 Romiley

Tel. 061-430 2392
Goosehouse Green, Romiley, Stockport, Ches. SK6 4LJ.
B6104 off A560.
Undulating parkland course.
18 holes, 6371 yds. S.S.S. 70
Visitors welcome except Thurs.
Green Fees. Weekdays £5.00; weekends and bank holidays £7.00.
Society Meetings by arrangement.
Meals served except Mon.

Q 52 Saddleworth

Tel. Saddleworth (04577) 2059, 3653 (Pro.)
Mountain Ash, Uppermill, Oldham, Lancs.
5 miles from Oldham signposted off A670 Ashton to Huddersfield.
Moorland course.
18 holes, 5954 yds. S.S.S. 69
Visitors welcome.
Green Fees. Weekdays £3.50 per day (£1.50 with member); weekends £5.00 (£2.50 with member).
Society Meetings by arrangement.
Hotels: Birch Hall Hotel, Lees.
Snacks and meals served except Mon.

Q 53 Sale

Tel. 061-973 1638/3404
Golf Rd., Sale, Ches. M33 2LU.
1 mile from Sale station.
Parkland course.
18 holes, 6351 yds. S.S.S. 70
Visitors welcome.
Green Fees. Weekdays £6.00; weekends £8.00.
Hotels: in Manchester.
Lunches and snacks served except Mon.

Q 54 Stamford

Tel. Mossley 2126
Huddersfield Rd., Stalybridge, Ches. SK15 3ET.
1½ miles from town centre.
Moorland course.
18 holes.
Visitors welcome.
Green Fees. Weekdays £3.00; weekends £5.00.

Society Meetings by arrangement.
Meals served except Mon.

Q 55 Stand

Tel. 061-766 2388
The Dales, Ashbourne Grove, Whitefield, Manchester.
1 mile N of M62 Exit 17.
18 holes, 6411 yds. S.S.S. 71
Visitors welcome.
Meals served by arrangement except Mon.

Q 56 Stockport

Tel. 061-427 2001
Offerton Rd., Offerton, Stockport, Ches. SK2 3HL.
A6 to Hazel Grove, 1 mile along Torkington Rd.
Parkland course.
18 holes, 6319 yds. S.S.S. 71
Visitors welcome on weekdays.
Green Fees. £6.00.
Society Meetings Wed. and Thurs. only by arrangement.
Hotels: Alma Lodge Hotel, Stockport.
Meals served except Mon.

Q 57 Swinton Park

Tel. 061-794 0861/1785
East Lancashire Rd., Swinton, Manchester M27 1LX.
On Manchester to Liverpool road, A580, 6 miles from Manchester.
Parkland course.
18 holes, 6610 yds. S.S.S. 72
Course designed by J. Braid.
Visitors welcome on weekdays, weekends with member only.
Green Fees. £6.00.
Hotels: in Manchester.
Meals served except Mon.

Q 58 Turton

Tel. Turton (0204) 852235
Wood End Farm, Bromley Cross, Bolton, Lancs.
A666 3½ miles N of Bolton.
Moorland course.
9 holes, 5805 yds. S.S.S. 68
Visitors welcome on weekdays, weekends restricted.
Green Fees. Weekdays £3.00 (£1.00 with member), weekends £4.00 (£1.00 with member).
Society Meetings welcome weekdays only.
Hotels: Last Drop, Bromley Cross.
Lunches served except Mon.

Q 59 Walmersley

Tel. 061-764 1429
Garretts Close, Walmersley, Bury, Lancs.
A56 3 miles N of town centre.
Moorland, hillside course.
9 holes, 6114 yds. S.S.S. 70
Visitors welcome on weekdays, weekends with reservation.
Green Fees. £3.50 per day.
Society Meetings welcome weekdays only.
Hotels: in Bury.
Snacks; meals served except Mon.

Q 60 Werneth (Oldham)

Tel. 061-624 1190
Green Lane, Garden Suburbs, Oldham, Lancs.
Undulating course.
18 holes, 5375 yds. S.S.S. 66
Visitors welcome on weekdays, weekends with member only.
Green Fees. £4.00; weekly £15.00.
Meals served.

Q 61 Werneth Low

Tel. 061-368 2503
Werneth Low, Hyde, Ches.
2 miles from Hyde via Joel Lane, Gee Cross.
Undulating moorland course.
9 holes, 5734 yds. S.S.S. 68
Visitors welcome, Sun. with member only.
Green Fees. Weekdays £4.75 per day (£1.75 with member); Sat. £6.00 per day (£2.00 with member); Sun. £2.00 per day.
Society Meetings by arrangement 4 weeks in advance.
Snacks served except Wed.

Q 62 Westhoughton

Tel. Westhoughton (0942) 811085
Long Island, Westhoughton, Bolton, Lancs.
4 miles SW of Bolton on A58.
Meadowland course.
9 holes, 5834 yds. S.S.S. 67
Visitors welcome on weekdays.
Green Fees. £2.70 (75p with member).
Society Meetings by arrangement.
Hotels: Mercury Motel.

Q 63 Whitefield

Tel. 061-766 2904
Higher Lane, Whitefield, Manchester M25 7EZ.
Leave M62 at Exit 17, take Radcliffe road for ½ mile.
Parkland course.
18 holes, 6300 yds. S.S.S. 70
Visitors welcome.
Green Fees. Weekdays £5.00 (£2.50 with member); weekends £5.00 with member.
Society Meetings by arrangement.
Lunches served; dinner served except Mon.

Q 64 Whittaker

Tel. Littleborough (0706) 78310
Littleborough, Lancs.
1½ miles from town centre.
Moorland course.
9 holes, 5632 yds. S.S.S. 67
Visitors welcome except Sun.
Green Fees. £2.00.
Society Meetings welcome weekdays only.
Hotels: Dearnley Cottage Hotel.

Q 65 William Wroe

Tel. 061-748 8680
Penny Bridge Lane, Flixton, Manchester 31.
M63, Exit 4, B5124, then B5158 to Flixton Rd.
Parkland course.
15 holes, 3935 yds. S.S.S. 54
Visitors welcome on weekdays, weekends and bank holidays with reservation; book Fri. for Sat., Sat. for Sun.

Green Fees. Weekdays £1.80, O.A.P.s and juniors 90p before 5.00 p.m.; weekends £2.50.

Q 66 Withington

Tel. 061-445 9544
Palatine Rd., West Didsbury, Manchester M20 8UD.
15 minutes from centre of Manchester.
Parkland course.
18 holes, 6336 yds. S.S.S. 70
Visitors welcome.
Green Fees. Weekdays £4.75 per round, £6.50 per day; weekends £6.50 per round, £8.50 per day.
Society Meetings by arrangement.
Hotels: Post House, Northenden; Riverside Hotel, West Didsbury.
Snacks served except Mon.; lunches and evening meals served by arrangement.

Q 67 Worsley

Tel. 061-789 4202
Monton Green, Monton, Eccles, Greater Manchester M30 8AP.
1 mile from junction of M62 and M63.
Woodland, parkland course.
18 holes, 6217 yds. S.S.S. 70
Visitors welcome with member or letter of introduction.
Green Fees. Weekdays £6.00 (£2.00 with member); weekends £8.00 (£3.50 with member).
Society Meetings welcome Mon., Wed. and Thurs.
Hotels: Wendover Hotel, Monton.
Snacks, lunches and evening meals served.

R Lancashire, Isle of Man

R 1 Accrington & District

Tel. Accrington 32734
New Barn Farm, West End, Oswaldtwistle, Accrington, Lancs.
On A679 2½ miles from Blackburn.
Moorland course.
18 holes, 5863 yds. S.S.S. 68
Visitors welcome.
Society Meetings welcome.
Lunches served.

R 2 Ashton & Lea

Tel. Preston (0772) 726480
Tudor Ave., Lea, Preston, Lancs. PR4 0XA.
Off A584 4 miles W of Preston.
Meadowland course.
18 holes, 6286 yds. S.S.S. 70
Visitors welcome except Thurs. with reservation.
Green Fees. Weekdays £4.50 per day (£2.25 with member); weekends £5.50 per day (£2.75 with member).
Society Meetings weekdays except Thurs. by arrangement.
Hotels: Crest Hotel; Tickled Trout; County Hotel.
Meals served by arrangement.

R 3 Bacup

Tel. Bacup 3170
Bankside Lane, Bacup, Lancs.
Off A671, 7 miles N of Rochdale.
Moorland course.
9 holes, 5656 yds. S.S.S. 67
Visitors welcome with reservation if members of recognized club.
Green Fees. Weekdays £1.50; weekends £2.00.
Hotels: Market Hotel.
Meals served by arrangement.

R 4 Baxenden & District

Tel. Accrington 34555
Top o' th' Meadow, Baxenden, Accrington, Lancs.
Off A680 via Langford St., 2 miles SE of Accrington.
Moorland course.
9 holes, 5740 yds. S.S.S. 68
Visitors welcome.
Green Fees. Weekdays £3.00 (£1.50 with member); weekends £4.00 (£2.00 with member).
Meals served by arrangement except Thurs.

R 5 Beacon Country Park

Tel. Up Holland (0695) 622700
Beacon Park Centre, Beacon Lane, Dalton, Lancs. WN8 7RU.
M6 junction 26, signposted for Liverpool/Skelmersdale/Southport; M58 junction 5, signposted for Up Holland.
Public hillside/parkland course.
18 holes, 5996 yds. S.S.S. 69
Course designed by D. Steel, Cotton Pennink Lawrie & Partners.
Visitors welcome.
Green Fees. Weekdays £2.00 (juniors and O.A.P.s £1.00); weekends and bank holidays £3.00
Hotels: Briars Hall, Lathom; Lindley, Parbold; Holland Hall Country Club; Balcony Inn, Skelmersdale.
Bar snacks available.

R 6 Bentham

Tel. Bentham (0468) 61018
Robin Lane, Bentham, Nr. Lancaster LA2 7LF.
Midway between Lancaster and Settle on B6480 13 miles E of M6 Junction 34.
Undulating meadowland course with magnificent views.
9 holes, 5850 yds. S.S.S. 69
Visitors welcome.
Green Fees. Weekdays £2.50 per day; weekends £3.50.
Society Meetings welcome.
Hotels: Black Bull, Bentham; Bridge Hotel, Ingleton.
Meals available at club.

R 7 Blackburn

Tel. Blackburn (0254) 51122
Beardwood Brow, Blackburn, Lancs. BB2 7AX.
W of town.
Undulating course.
18 holes, 6099 yds. S.S.S. 70
Visitors welcome on weekdays.
Green Fees. Weekdays £4.00; weekends £5.00.
Society Meetings welcome weekdays only.
Hotels: Saxon Inn Motor Hotel.
Meals served except Mon.

R 8 Blackpool North Shore

Tel. Blackpool (0253) 52054
Devonshire Rd., Blackpool, Lancs. FY2 0RD.
On A587, N of Blackpool.
Undulating meadowland course.
18 holes, 6440 yds. S.S.S. 71
Visitors welcome.
Green Fees. Weekdays £6.50; weekends £7.50.
Society Meetings welcome weekdays except Thurs.
Hotels: Imperial; Savoy.
Meals served.

R 9 Blackpool - Stanley Park

Tel. Blackpool 33960
North Park Dr., Blackpool, Lancs.
Undulating parkland course.
18 holes, 6192 yds. S.S.S. 69
Course designed by Dr. Mackenzie.

Visitors welcome.
Green Fees. Weekdays £2.15; weekends £3.15; weekly £14.50.
Hotels: in Blackpool.

R 10 Burnley

Tel. Burnley 21045
Glen View, Burnley.
Off A56 to Glen View Rd., 300 yards on turn right.
Moorland course.
18 holes, 5891 yds. S.S.S. 69
Visitors welcome except Sat.
Green Fees. Weekdays £3.45 (£2.30 with member); weekends £4.60 (£3.45 with member).
Society Meetings welcome on weekdays and Sun.
Hotels: Keirby; Sparrow Hawk.
Meals served except Mon. and Wed.

R 11 Castletown

Tel. Castletown (0624 82) 2201
Fort Island, Castletown, Isle of Man.
1½ miles E of Castletown.
Seaside course.
18 holes, 6804 yds. S.S.S. 73
Course designed by MacKenzie Ross.
Visitors welcome.
Green Fees. Weekdays £3.75; weekends £4.00; weekly £17.00.
Society Meetings by arrangement.
Hotels: Castletown Golf Links Hotel, Fort Island.
Meals served Apr. 1st to Oct. 18th.

R 12 Chorley

Tel. Adlington 480263
Hall o'th' Hill, Heath Charnock, Chorley
Off A6, 2 miles S of Chorley.
Moorland course.
18 holes, 6317 yds. S.S.S. 70
Course designed by J.A. Steer (1925).
Visitors welcome on weekdays with reservation.
Green Fees. Weekdays £4.50 per day; weekends £6.50.
Society Meetings weekdays by arrangement.
Hotels: Royal Oak, Chorley; Pines, Clayton-le-Woods; M6 Motel, Charnock Richard.
Lunches served; meals by arrangement.

R 13 Clitheroe

Tel. Clitheroe 22618
Clitheroe, Lancs BB7 1PP.
Off A59, 2 miles S of Clitheroe.
Parkland course.
18 holes, 6311 yds. S.S.S. 71
Course designed by J. Braid.
Visitors welcome.
Green Fees. Weekdays £5.00; weekends £6.00.

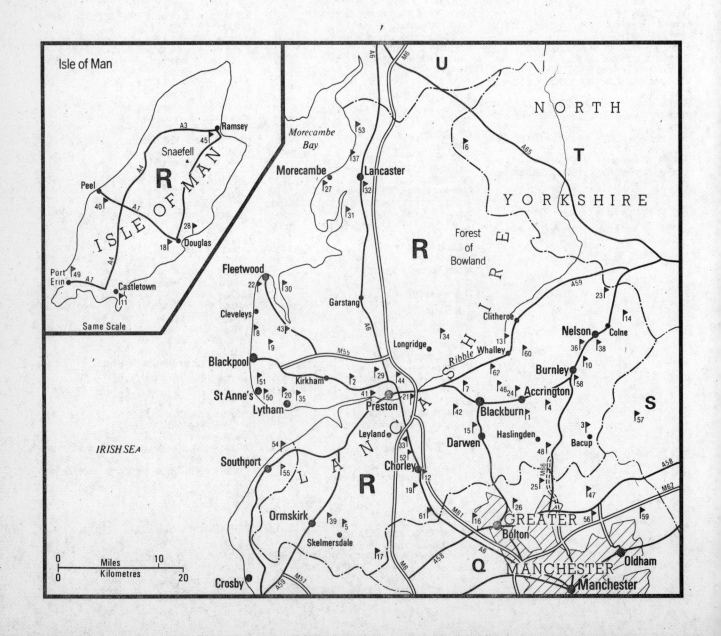

Society Meetings welcome.
Hotels: Roefield Hotel, Clitheroe; Stirk House Hotel, Gisburn.
Meals served except Fri.

R 14   Colne

Tel. Colne 863391
Law Farm, Skipton Old Rd., Colne, Lancs.
1½ miles from A56 through Colne.
Moorland course.
9 holes, 5850 yds. S.S.S. 68
Visitors welcome.
Green Fees. Weekdays £4.00 per day (£2.00 with member); weekends and bank holidays £5.00 per day (£2.50 with member); weekly £15.00.
Meals served except Mon.

R 15   Darwen

Tel. Darwen 71287
Winter Hill, Darwen, Lancs.
18 holes, 5672 yds. S.S.S. 68
Green Fees. Weekdays £3.45 (£2.30 with member); weekends £4.60 (£3.45 with member).

R 16   Deane

Tel. Bolton 61944
Off Junction Rd., Deane, Bolton, Lancs.
Parkland course.
18 holes, 5511 yds. S.S.S. 67
Visitors welcome.
Society Meetings weekdays except Wed.
Hotels: Pack Horse; Crest Motel, Bolton.
Lunches served.

R 17   Dean Wood

Tel. Up Holland 622219 (Sec.)
Lafford Lane, Up Holland, Skelmersdale, Lancs. WN8 0QZ.
M6 Exit 26. A577 5 miles W of Wigan.
Undulating parkland course.
18 holes, 6097 yds. S.S.S. 70
Visitors welcome on weekdays, weekends with member only.
Green Fees. Weekdays £5.75; weekends £6.90.
Society Meetings Mon. and Thurs. (preferably Thurs.).
Hotels: Holland Hall Country Club; Brocket Arms, Wigan; Cassinelli's Motel.
Meals served.

R 18   Douglas Municipal

Tel. Douglas (0624) 5952
Pulrose, Douglas, Isle of Man.
1 mile from town centre.
Parkland course.
18 holes, 5859 yds. S.S.S. 69
Course designed by Dr. McKenzie.
Visitors welcome.
Green Fees. £1.55 per round, £2.50 per day; weekly £6.75.
Hotels: in Douglas.
Light meals served.

R 19   Duxbury Park

Tel. Chorley (025 72) 65380
Wigan Lane, Chorley, Lancs.
Off A6, 1 mile S of Chorley.
Parkland course.
18 holes, 6270 yds. S.S.S. 70

Course designed by Hawtree & Son.
Green Fees. Weekdays £2.00; weekends £3.00.
Hotels: Royal Oak; Hartwood Hotel.

R 20   Fairhaven

Tel. Lytham 736741/736976
Lytham Hall Park, Ansdell, Lytham St. Annes, Lancs. FY8 4JU.
On B5261 2 miles from Lytham.
Seaside course.
18 holes, 6885 yds. S.S.S. 73
Visitors welcome on weekdays.
Green Fees. Weekdays £6.50; weekends £7.50.
Society Meetings welcome weekdays only.
Hotels: Clifton Arms, Lytham; Dalmeny Hotel; Princes Hotel, St. Annes-on-Sea.
Meals served except Mon.

R 21   Fishwick Hall

Tel. Preston (0772) 798300
Glenluce Dr., Farringdon Park, Preston, Lancs. PR1 5TB.
Leave M6 at Samlesbury, exit 31, come on to A59, cross river Ribble bridge, Glenluce Dr. first turning on left.
Undulating meadowland course.
18 holes, 6186 yds. S.S.S. 69
Visitors welcome.
Green Fees. Weekdays £3.00 (£1.50 with member); weekends and bank holidays £5.00 (£2.50 with member).
Society Meetings by arrangement.
Hotels: Crest; Tickled Trout.
Meals served by arrangement.

R 22   Fleetwood

Tel. Fleetwood 3661
Princes Way, Fleetwood, Lancs. FY7 8AF.
On A587, 7 miles N of Blackpool.
Seaside course.
18 holes, 6324 yds. S.S.S. 71
Course designed by J.A. Steer.
Visitors welcome. Ladies' day Tues.
Green Fees. Weekdays £6.50; weekends £8.00.
Hotels: North Euston Hotel; Mount Hotel; Boston Hotel; Southbrook Hotel.
Meals served except Thurs.

R 23   Ghyll

Tel. Earby 2466
Barnoldswick, Colne, Lancs.
Off A56, 1 mile from Barnoldswick.
Parkland course.
9 holes, 5706 yds. S.S.S. 68
Visitors welcome.
Green Fees. (per day or part day) £3.00 (£2.00 with member); weekends and bank holidays £4.00 (£2.00 with member).
Hotels: Manor House Hotel, Thornton-in-Craven.

R 24   Green Haworth

Tel. Accrington 37580
Green Haworth, Accrington, Lancs.
2 miles from town centre.
Moorland course.
9 holes, 5470 yds. S.S.S. 67
Visitors welcome.
Green Fees. Weekdays £2.00 (£1.50 with

member); weekends £3.00 (£2.00 with member).
Society Meetings welcome by prior arrangement.
Hotels: Commercial Hotel, Accrington.
Meals served.

R 25   Greenmount

Tel. Tottington 3712
Greenhaigh Fold Farm, Greenmount, Bury, Lancs.
Parkland course.
9 holes, 4915 yds. S.S.S. 64
Visitors welcome with member only.
Lunches served except Thurs.

R 26   Harwood

Tel. Bolton 22878
Roading Brook Rd., Bolton, Lancs.
B6391 off A666.
Parkland course.
9 holes, 5925 yds. S.S.S. 69
Visitors welcome.
Green Fees. £4.00.
Society Meetings welcome.
Hotels: Pack Horse.

R 28   Howstrake

Tel. Douglas (0624) 24299
Groudle Rd., Onchan, Isle of Man.
On A11, 2 miles NE of Douglas.
Undulating seaside course.
18 holes, 5900 yds. S.S.S. 66
Visitors welcome.
Green Fees. £1.20 per round, £1.20 per day.
Hotels: Howstrake Hotel; Majestic.

R 27   Heysham

Tel. Pro. Heysham 52000
Trumacar Park, Heysham, Morecambe, Lancs. LA3 3JH.
Off A589, 3 miles S of Morecambe on Middleton road.
Undulating meadowland course.
18 holes, 6224 yds. S.S.S. 69
Course designed by S. Herd.
Visitors welcome if members of recognized club.
Green Fees. Weekdays £5.00; weekends £7.00.
Hotels: in Morecambe.
Meals served.

R 29   Ingol Golf & Squash Club

Tel. Preston (0772) 864752
Ingol, Preston, Lancs.
On A6 to Preston. Turn first right down Lightfoot Lane, take second turn on left and first left again.
Undulating meadowland course.
18 holes, 6560 yds. S.S.S. 71
Course designed by Cotton (C.K.), Pennink, Lawrie & Partners.
Visitors welcome.
Green Fees. On application to Secretary.
Society Meetings by arrangement.
Hotels: Eurocrest Hotel; Tickled Trout, Preston.
Meals served.

R 30   Knott End

Tel. Knott End 810576
Wyreside, Knott End-on-Sea, Blackpool, Lancs. FY6 0AA.
Follow signs for Knott End or Pilling from A6 or take pedestrian ferry from Fleetwood.
Undulating meadowland course.
18 holes, 5852 yds.
Visitors welcome weekdays, weekends by invitation.
Green Fees. Weekdays £4.00; weekends £5.00; weekly £20.00.
Society Meetings welcome weekdays, max. 40.
Hotels: Bourne Arms, Knott End.
Catering facilities except Tues.

R 31   Lancaster Golf & Country Club

Tel. Galgate (0524) 751247
Ashton Hall, Ashton-with-Stodday, Lancaster LA2 0AJ.
3 miles S of Lancaster on A588. Leave M6 northbound at exit 33, southbound exit 34.
Undulating parkland course.
18 holes, 6444 yds. S.S.S. 72
Visitors welcome.
Green Fees. Weekdays and weekends £7.00 per day or round.
Society Meetings considered on weekdays.
Hotels: Accommodation available for 18 at clubhouse.
Meals served.

R 32   Lansil

Tel. Lancaster (0524) 2016
Caton Rd., Lancaster LA1 3PD.
On A683, 2 miles E of Lancaster ½ mile W of junction 34 on M6.
Parkland course.
9 holes, 5608 yds. S.S.S. 67
Visitors welcome on weekdays, weekends after 1p.m.
Green Fees. Weekdays £3.50; weekends £5.00.
Hotels: King's Arms.
Snacks served.

R 33   Leyland 21359

Wigan Rd., Leyland, Lancs.
Off A49, ½ mile from M6 exit 28.
Meadowland course.
18 holes, 5980 yds. S.S.S. 69
Visitors welcome on weekdays.
Green Fees. £5.00 (£1.50 with member).
Society Meetings welcome weekdays only.
Hotels: Hartwood Hall Hotel, Chorley; Park Hall Hotel, Charnock Richard.
Lunches and teas served except Mon.

R 34   Longridge

Tel. Longridge 3291/3799
Fell Barn, Jeffrey Hill, Longridge, Preston, Lancs.
8 miles NE of Preston.
Moorland course.
18 holes, 5735 yds. S.S.S. 68
Visitors welcome.
Green Fees. Weekdays £3.50 (£2.25 with

member); weekends £4.50 (£3.00 with member).
Society Meetings by arrangement.
Meals served except Mon.

R 35   Lytham Green Drive

Tel. Lytham (0253) 737390
Ballam Rd., Lytham St. Annes, Lancs. FY8 4LE.
1 mile from Lytham Square.
Parkland course.
18 holes, 5827 yds. S.S.S. 68
Visitors welcome.
Green Fees. Weekdays £6.25; weekends £7.25.
Society Meetings welcome, weekdays max. 50; weekends max. 20.
Hotels: in Lytham St. Annes.
Meals served except Tues. when bar snacks are available.

R 36   Marsden Park

Tel. Nelson 67525
Townhouse Rd., Nelson, Lancs.
Off A56, 8 miles N of Burnley.
Undulating meadowland course.
18 holes, 5806 yds. S.S.S. 68
Course designed by C.K. Cotton & Co. and F.W. Hawtree.
Visitors welcome.
Green Fees. Weekdays 85p, juniors 43p; weekends £1.20.
Hotels: Great Marsden Hotel.
Snacks served.

R 37   Morecambe

Tel. Morecambe 412841
Bare, Morecambe, Lancs. LA4 6AJ.
5 miles from A6 at Carnforth.
Seaside course.
18 holes, 5766 yds. S.S.S. 68
Visitors welcome.
Green Fees. Weekdays £5.00 per day; weekends £6.00 per day.
Society Meetings by arrangement.
Hotels: in Morecambe.
Meals served.

R 38   Nelson

Tel. Nelson 64583
Marsden Heights, Brierfield, Nelson, Lancs.
2 miles NE of Burnley.
Moorland course.
18 holes, 5866 yds. S.S.S. 68
Visitors welcome except on Sat. and Thurs. afternoon.
Green Fees. Weekdays £5.50 (£2.50 with member); weekends £6.50 (£3.00 with member).
Society Meetings welcome Mon., Wed. and Fri.
Hotels: Crest, Burnley.
Meals served except Mon.

R 39   Ormskirk

Tel. Ormskirk 72112
Cranes Lane, Lathom, Ormskirk, Lancs. L40 5UJ.
From M6 to M58; leave at junction 3; right on to B5240, left on to A577 to Ormskirk, right at Halton Castle Inn, right at next road junction.

Parkland course.
18 holes, 6327 yds. S.S.S. 70
Course designed by H.H. Hilton Esq.
Visitors welcome with reservation.
Green Fees. Weekdays except Wed. £6.50 per round or day; weekends and Wed. £7.50 per round or day.
Society Meetings by arrangement.
Hotels: Briars Hall Hotel, Lathom.
Meals served by arrangement except Mon.

R 40   Peel

Tel. Peel 2227
Rheast Lane, Peel, Isle of Man.
On A1, signposted on outskirts of Peel, coming from Douglas.
Moorland course.
18 holes, 5747 yds. S.S.S. 68
Course designed by J. Braid.
Visitors welcome.
Green Fees. Weekdays £2.88 (£2.30 with member), parties of 8 or more £2.30 per person; weekends £3.45 (£2.88 with member), parties of 8 or more £2.88 per person.
Society Meetings welcome.
Snacks served; meals by arrangement.

R 41   Penwortham

Tel. Preston (0772) 743207
Blundell Lane, Penwortham, Preston PR1 0AX.
Off A59 at Penwortham traffic lights 1½ miles W of Preston.
Parkland course.
18 holes, 6085 yds. S.S.S. 69
Visitors welcome except weekends during season.
Green Fees. Weekdays £4.60 (£2.00 with member); weekends £6.90 (£3.10 with member); weekly £16.00.
Society Meetings welcome on weekdays by arrangement.
Hotels: in Preston.
Lunches and evening meals served except Mon.

R 42   Pleasington

Tel. Blackburn (0254) 22177
Pleasington, Blackburn, Lancs. BB2 5JF.
3 miles from Blackburn off A674.
Undulating parkland, moorland course.
18 holes, 6445 yds. S.S.S. 71
Visitors welcome on weekdays.
Green Fees. Weekdays £6.00; weekends £7.00.
Society Meetings welcome weekdays only.
Hotels: Saxon, Blackburn; Pines, Clayton-le-woods.
Meals served.

R 43   Poulton-le-Fylde

Tel. Poulton-le-Fylde (0253) 899357
Myrtle Farm, Breck Rd., Poulton-le-Fylde, Lancs.
2 minutes from Poulton town centre via Breck Rd.
Municipal meadowland course.
9 holes
Visitors welcome.

Green Fees. 9 holes weekdays £1.20; weekends £1.60.
Hotels: River Wyre.
No catering facilities.

R 44   Preston

Tel. Preston (0772) 700011
Fulwood Old Hall, Fulwood Hall Lane, Fulwood, Preston, Lancs. PR2 4DD.
N of Preston off Watling Street Rd.
Undulating course.
18 holes, 6249 yds. S.S.S. 70
Visitors welcome.
Green Fees. Weekdays £6.50; weekends £8.00.
Society Meetings by arrangement.
Hotels: Barton Grange Hotel, Barton; Crest Hotel, Preston.

R 45   Ramsey

Tel. Ramsey (0624) 812244
Brookfield, Ramsey, Isle of Man.
5 minutes' walk from town centre.
Parkland course.
18 holes, 6019 yds. S.S.S. 69
Course designed by J. Braid.
Visitors welcome.
Green Fees. Weekdays £3.50; weekends £4.50.
Hotels: Viking; Grand Island Hotel; Queens; Beach Hotel.
Lunches served daily.

R 46   Rishton

Tel. Great Harwood 884442
Eachill Links, Rishton, Blackburn, Lancs.
Adjacent to Rishton railway station.
Moorland course.
9 holes, 6012 yds. S.S.S. 69
Visitors welcome on weekdays, weekends with member only.
Green Fees. Weekdays £4.00 (£1.50 with member); weekends £1.50 (with member only).
Hotels: Dunkenhalgh Hotel, Clayton-le-Moors.

R 47   Rochdale (1888) Private

Tel. Rochdale 46024
Edenfield Rd., Bagslate, Rochdale.
3 miles from M62 Exit 20.
Parkland course.
18 holes, 5981 yds. S.S.S. 69
Visitors welcome with reservation.
Green Fees. Weekdays £5.00; weekends £6.00.
Society Meetings by arrangement.
Hotels: Broadfield, Rochdale; Midway, Castleton, Rochdale.
Meals served by arrangement.

R 48   Rossendale

Tel. Rossendale 3056
Ewood Lane Head, Haslingden, Rossendale, Lancs. BB4 6LH.
7 miles N of Bury near end of M66, Haslingden exit.
Meadowland course.
18 holes, 6262 yds. S.S.S. 70
Visitors welcome on weekdays, Sat. with member only, Sun. if members of recognized club.

Green Fees. Weekdays £4.00 (£2.00 with member); weekends and bank holidays £6.00 (£2.00 with member).
Society Meetings by arrangement.
Hotels: Queen's, Rawtenstall.
Meals served except Mon.

R 49   Rowany

Tel. 834108
Rowany Dr., Port Erin, Isle of Man.
Off Promenade.
Seaside course.
18 holes, 5813 yds. S.S.S. 68
Visitors welcome.
Green Fees. Weekdays £3.50 per day; weekends £3.75 per day.

R 50   Royal Lytham & St. Annes

Tel. St. Annes 724206/7
Links Gate, St. Annes on Sea, Lancs. FY8 3LQ.
1 mile from centre of St. Annes.
Seaside course.
18 holes, 6673 yds. S.S.S. 73
Visitors welcome weekdays with letter of introduction.
Green Fees. £8.00 per round, £11.00 per day.
Society Meetings by arrangement.
Hotels: in area.
Meals served.

R 51   St. Annes Old Links

Tel. St. Annes (0253) 723597
Highbury Rd., St. Annes on Sea, Lancs. FY8 2LD.
A584 through Lytham and St. Annes along Clifton Dr. ½ mile through traffic lights in St. Annes towards Blackpool. Highbury Rd. is right at next traffic lights.
Seaside course.
18 holes, 6616 yds. S.S.S. 72
Visitors welcome.
Green Fees. Weekdays £7.00 (£2.50 with member); weekends £10.00 (£3.00 with member); weekly £30.00.
Society Meetings welcome on weekdays.
Hotels: St. Ives Hotel; Hotel Glendower; Fernlea Hotel.
Lunches, dinners and snacks served.

R 52   Shaw Hill

Tel. Chorley 65930
Whittle-le-Woods, Chorley, Lancs.
On A6, 1½ miles N of Chorley.
Parkland course.
18 holes, 6139 yds. S.S.S. 69
Visitors welcome on weekdays.
Green Fees. £6.50 per day.
Hotels: Pines, Clayton-le-Woods.
Meals served except Mon.

R 53   Silverdale

Tel. Silverdale 300
Silverdale, Carnforth, Lancs.
M6 to Carnforth, Silverdale 5 miles.
Undulating course.
9 holes, 5256 yds. S.S.S. 67
Visitors welcome.
Green Fees. Weekdays £3.50 (£2.50 with member); weekends £4.50 (£3.00 with member).

Society Meetings welcome weekdays only.
Hotels: in Silverdale.

R 54   Southport Municipal

Tel. Southport 35286
Park Rd. West, Southport, Merseyside.
N end of promenade.
Seaside course.
18 holes, 5939 yds. S.S.S. 70
Visitors welcome.
Green Fees. Weekdays £1.20, Juniors 55p, 35p after 7p.m.; weekends £1.75.
Society Meetings by arrangement.
Hotels: in Southport.
Meals served.

R 55   Southport Old Links

Tel. Southport 28207
Moss Lane, Southport, Merseyside.
2 miles from town centre.
Seaside course.
9 holes, S.S.S. 71
Visitors welcome.
Green Fees. Weekdays £2.50; weekends £4.00.
Society Meetings by arrangement.
Meals served by arrangement.

R 56   Springfield Park

Tel. Rochdale 49801
Marland, Rochdale, Lancs.
3 miles from M62.
18 holes, 5981 yds. S.S.S. 65
Visitors welcome.

R 57   Todmorden

Tel. Todmorden 2986
Rive Rocks, Cross Stone Rd., Todmorden, Lancs.
½ mile from town centre.
Moorland course.
9 holes, 5800 yds. S.S.S. 68
Visitors welcome.
Green Fees. Weekdays £3.00 (£1.50 with member); weekends £5.00 (£2.50 with member).
Society Meetings welcome weekdays only.
Hotels: Queen's.
Meals served except Wed.

R 58   Towneley

Tel. Burnley (0282) 38473
Towneley Park, Todmorden Rd., Burnley, Lancs.
1½ miles E of town centre.
Parkland course.
18 holes, 5840 yds. S.S.S. 68
Visitors welcome.
Green Fees. Weekdays 70p; weekends 90p.
Hotels: Keirby Hotel.

R 59   Tunshill

Tel. Rochdale 342095
Miln Row, Rochdale, Lancs.
Moorland course.
9 holes, 5812 yds. S.S.S. 68
Visitors welcome.
Society Meetings by arrangement.

Green Fees. Weekdays £2.00 (£1.50 with member); weekends £2.50 (£2.00 with member).

R 60   Whalley

Tel. Whalley (025482) 2236
Portfield Lane, Whalley, Blackburn, Lancs.
Off A680, 1 mile S of Whalley.
Parkland course.
9 holes, 5809 yds. S.S.S. 69
Visitors welcome.
Green Fees. Weekdays £3.00 (£1.50 with member); weekends £5.00 (£2.50 with member).
Society Meetings by arrangement.
Hotels: Dunkenhalgh, Clayton-le-Moors; Saxon Inn, Blackburn.
Lunches, high teas and dinners served.

R 61   Wigan

Tel. Standish 421360
Arley Hall, Haigh, Wigan, Lancs. WN1 2UH.
On B5239, 2 miles N of Wigan.
Parkland course.
9 holes, 6198 yds. S.S.S. 69

R 62   Wilpshire

Tel. Blackburn (0254) 48260
Whalley Rd., Wilpshire, Blackburn, Lancs.
On A666, 4 miles N of Blackburn.
Moorland course.
18 holes, 5362 yds. S.S.S. 68
Visitors welcome.
Green Fees. Weekdays £5.50; weekends £7.00.
Society Meetings by arrangement.
Hotels: Saxon Inn, Blackburn; Dunkenhalgh, Clayton-le-Moors.
Meals served every day.

S *West Yorkshire, South Yorkshire*

S 1   Abbeydale

Tel. Sheffield 360763
Twentywell Lane, Dore, Sheffield S17 4QA.
Off A621 Sheffield to Baslow road at Dore & Totley station.
Parkland course.
18 holes, 6368 yds. S.S.S. 70
Visitors welcome.
Green Fees. £5.00 to £9.00. Half rates if playing with member.
Society Meetings Tues. and Fri. by arrangement.
Hotels: Grosvenor House Hotel.
Meals served except Mon.

S 2   Alwoodley

Tel. Leeds (0532) 681680
Wigton Lane, Alwoodley, Leeds 17.
5 miles N of Leeds on A61.
Moorland course.
18 holes, 6755 yds. S.S.S. 72
Course designed by Dr. A. Mackenzie.
Visitors welcome except 12.30 to 1.30 p.m.
Green Fees. Weekdays £10.00 per day; weekends £12.00 per day.
Society Meetings by arrangement.
Snacks served; meals served except Fri.

S 3   Baildon

Tel. Shipley (0274) 584266
Moorgate, Baildon, Shipley, W. Yorks. BD17 5PP.
5 miles NW of Bradford.
Moorland course.
18 holes, 6178 yds. S.S.S. 69
Visitors welcome.
Green Fees. Weekdays £3.25 (£2.25 with member); weekends £4.50 (£3.00 with member).
Society Meetings by arrangement.
Hotels: in Bradford and Bingley.
Meals served except Mon.

S 4   Barnsley

Tel. Barnsley 382856
Wakefield Rd., Staincross, Nr. Barnsley, S. Yorks.
On A61 3 miles from Barnsley.
Undulating meadowland course.
18 holes, 6020 yds. S.S.S. 69
Visitors welcome on weekdays, weekends with reservation.
Green Fees. Weekdays £1.75 per round; weekends £2.25 per round.
Hotels: Royal; Ardsley House Hotel; Queens Hotel.
Lunches and teas served except Tues.

S 5   Beauchief Municipal

Tel. Sheffield 360648
Abbey Lane, Beauchief, Sheffield.
Parkland course.
18 holes, 5470 yds. S.S.S. 67
Green Fees. Weekdays £1.50, juniors 70p; weekends £1.40.
Hotels: Beauchief Hotel.
Lunches served; snacks only on Tues.

S 6   Ben Rhydding

Tel. Ilkley 608759
High Wood, Ben Rhydding, Ilkley, W. Yorks.
Moorland course.
9 holes, 4264 yds. S.S.S. 62
Visitors welcome except Sun. a.m.
Hotels: Wheatley, Ben Rhydding; Craiglands; Troutbeck, Ilkley.

S 7   Bingley

Tel. Bradford 562506
St. Ives Mansion, St. Ives Estate, Bingley, W. Yorks.
Off B6429, 8 miles NW of Bradford city centre.
Parkland, moorland course.
18 holes, 6405 yds. S.S.S. 71
Visitors welcome.
Green Fees. Weekdays £2.60 per round; weekends £5.00 per round.
Society Meetings Tues. Wed. and Thurs.
Hotels: Bankfield, Bingley.
Meals served except Mon.

S 8   Birley Wood

Tel. Sheffield (0742) 656440 (Steward). 390099 (Pro.)
Birley Lane, Sheffield 12.
6 miles from M1; at junction 30 take A616 to Eckington for 4 miles. Course is approx. 1½ miles after Mosbrough.
Meadowland course.
18 holes, 6257 yds. S.S.S. 70
Visitors welcome except before 10 a.m. at weekends.
Green Fees. Weekdays £3.50 per round (£1.75 with member); weekends £5.50 per round (£3.00 with member).
Society Meetings welcome, preferably midweek; occasional weekends if booked well in advance.
Hotels: Sitwell Arms, Renishaw; Mosbrough Hall, Mosbrough.
Bar snacks; restaurant.

S 9   Bradford

Tel. Guiseley (0943) 75570
Hawksworth Lane, Guiseley, Leeds LS20 8NP.
3½ miles from Shipley.
Moorland/meadowland course.
18 holes, 6259 yds. S.S.S. 70
Visitors welcome.
Green Fees. Weekdays £6.00 (£3.00 with member); weekends £8.50 (£4.25 with member).
Society Meetings welcome on weekdays.
Hotels: in Ilkley.
Meals served except Mon.

S 10   Bradford Moor

Tel. Bradford (0274) 638313
Scarr Hall, Pollard Lane, Bradford 2, W.
Yorks.
2 miles from Bradford.
Undulating meadowland course.
9 holes, 5838 yds. S.S.S. 68
Visitors welcome.
Green Fees. Weekdays £2.50 before
4.00p.m., £3.50 after 4.00p.m. (£1.50 with
member); weekends £4.50 (£2.50 with
member).
Society Meetings welcome on weekdays.
Hotels: Baron Hotel.
Meals served by arrangement.

S 11   Branshaw

Tel. Haworth 43235
Branshaw Moor, Keighley, W. Yorks.
On B6143 2 miles SW of Keighley.
Moorland course.

18 holes, 5790 yds. S.S.S. 68
Visitors welcome.
Society Meetings by arrangement 4
weeks in advance.
Hotels: Fleece Inn, Oakworth; Black Bull,
Haworth.
Lunches served except Mon.

S 12   City of Wakefield

Tel. Wakefield 74316
Lupset Park, Horbury Rd., Wakefield, W.
Yorks.
Off M1 at exit 39.
Parkland course.
18 holes, 6423 yds. S.S.S. 71
Visitors welcome.
Green Fees. Weekdays £1.75; weekends
and bank holidays £3.44.
Society Meetings by arrangement.
Hotels: Swallow; Albany.
Meals served.

S 13   Clayton

Tel. Bradford (0274) 880047
Thornton View Rd., Clayton, Bradford. W.
Yorks. BD14 6JX.
On A647 SW of Bradford.
Meadowland course.
9 holes, 4853 yds. S.S.S. 64
Visitors welcome except Sun.
Green Fees. Weekdays £2.00; weekends
£4.00.
Hotels: Victoria; Norfolk Gardens Hotel,
Bradford.
Limited catering.

S 14   Cleckheaton & District

Tel. Cleckheaton (0274) 877851
Bradford Rd., Cleckheaton, W. Yorks.
1½ miles N of Bradford on M62, interchange
26 then 100 yds on A638.
Meadowland course.
18 holes, 5829 yds. S.S.S. 68

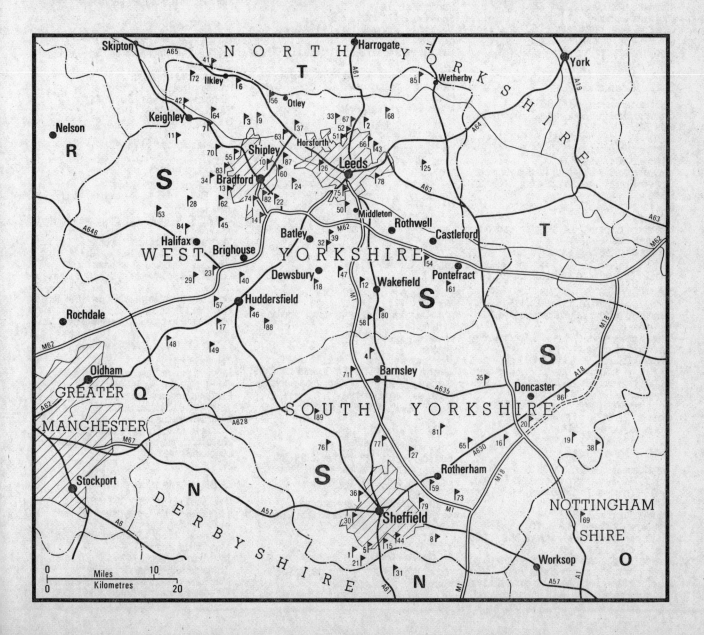

Visitors welcome.
Green Fees. Weekdays £5.00 per round or day; weekends £7.00 per round or day.
Society Meetings welcome.
Hotels: Novo Hotel, Bradford.
Meals served.

S 15   Concord Park

Tel. Sheffield 613605
Shiregreen Lane, Sheffield S5.
Firth Park up Bellhouse Rd. to Concord Park Sports Centre.
Undulating parkland.
18 holes, 4174 yds. S.S.S. 60
Visitors welcome.

S 16   Crookhill Park Municipal

Tel. Rotherham 862974
Conisbrough, Doncaster, S. Yorks.
7 miles W of Doncaster.
Parkland course.
18 holes, 5846 yds. S.S.S. 68
Visitors welcome.
Green Fees. Weekdays £1.50, juniors and O.A.P.s 75p; weekends £2.25.
Society Meetings welcome.
Bar snacks; cafeteria.

S 17   Crosland Heath

Tel. Huddersfield (0484) 653216
Crosland Heath, Huddersfield, W. Yorks. HD4 7AF.
3 miles W of Huddersfield.
Heathland course.
18 holes, 6017 yds. S.S.S. 70
Visitors welcome except Wed. afternoon.
Green Fees. Weekdays £4.00; weekends £6.00.
Society Meetings welcome by arrangement.
Hotels: George; Dryclough; Ladbroke Mercury, Huddersfield.
Full catering facilities except Tues.

S 18   Dewsbury District

Tel. Mirfield (0924) 492399
Sands Lane, Mirfield, W. Yorks. WF14 8HJ.
Undulating parkland, heathland course.
18 holes, 6256 yds. S.S.S. 70
Course designed by Alliss and Thomas.
Visitors welcome.
Green Fees. Weekdays £4.00 per round or day (£1.50 with member); weekends £6.00 per round or day (£2.50 with member).
Society Meetings by arrangement.
Hotels: Black Bull; Flowerpot Inn.
Meals served except Mon.

S 19   Doncaster

Tel. Doncaster (0302) 868316
Bawtry Rd., Bessacarr, Doncaster, S. Yorks.
On A638 5 miles S of Doncaster, 4 miles N of Bawtry.
Moorland course.
18 holes, 6293 yds. S.S.S. 70
Visitors welcome on weekdays, after 11.00 a.m. at weekends.
Green Fees. Weekdays £4.00 per day; weekends £5.00 per day; plus V.A.T.
Society Meetings welcome on weekdays.
Hotels: Punch's; The Old Bell, Barnby Moor.
Snacks and meals served by arrangement.

S 20   Doncaster Town Moor

Tel. Doncaster (0302) 55286
Neatherd's House, Belle Vue, Doncaster, S. Yorks. DN4 5HV.
1 mile S of town centre on A638, clubhouse next to airport entrance.
Meadowland course.
18 holes, 6100 yds. S.S.S. 69
Visitors welcome, after 11.30a.m. on Sun.
Green Fees. Weekdays £3.00 (£1.50 with member); weekends £4.00 (£2.00 with member).
Society Meetings by arrangement with Secretary.
Hotels: Danum; Punch's; Balmoral.
Lunches and bar snacks served except Mon.

S 21   Dore & Totley

Tel. Bradway (0742) 360492
Bradway Rd., Sheffield, S17 4PR.
S of Sheffield off A61.
Parkland course.
18 holes, 6301 yds. S.S.S. 70
Visitors welcome on weekdays with reservation.
Green Fees. £5.00 per round, £7.00 per day.
Society Meetings by arrangement.
Hotels: Hallam Tower Hotel; Grosvenor House Hotel.
Meals served except Mon.

S 22   East Bierley

Tel. Bradford 681023
South View Rd., East Bierley, Bradford, W. Yorks.
3 miles SE of Bradford on Wakefield/Heckmondwike road.
Undulating semi-moorland course.
9 holes, 5800 yds. S.S.S. 63
Snacks served; meals by arrangement except Thurs.

S 23   Elland

Tel. Elland (04227) 2505
Hammerstones Leach Lane, Elland, W. Yorks.
1½ miles from centre of town leaving by Victoria Rd.
Undulating parkland course.
9 holes.
Visitors welcome on weekdays.
Green Fees. £3.00 (£1.50 with member).
Society Meetings welcome on weekdays.
Hotels: Mercury Hotel.
Meals served on weekdays.

S 24   Fulneck

Tel. Pudsey (0532) 565191
Fulneck, Pudsey, W. Yorks. LS28 8NT.
Midway between Leeds and Bradford.
Undulating parkland course.
9 holes, 5470 yds. S.S.S. 67
Visitors welcome on weekdays.
Green Fees. Weekdays £3.00 (£1.50 with member).

S 25   Garforth

Tel. Garforth (0532) 863308
Garforth, Leeds LS25 2DS.
6½ miles E of Leeds on A63, then left on to A642.

Parkland course.
18 holes, 6296 yds. S.S.S. 70
Visitors welcome; weekends and bank holidays with member only.
Green Fees. Weekdays £6.00; weekends £7.00.
Society Meetings welcome on weekdays.
Hotels: Windmill, Seacroft; Mercury Motel, Garforth.
Meals served.

S 26   Gott's Park

Tel. Leeds (0532) 638232
Armley Ridge Rd., Leeds LS12 2QX.
About 3 miles W of city centre.
Parkland course.
18 holes, 4449 yds. S.S.S. 62
Visitors welcome on weekdays.
Green Fees. Weekdays £1.35; Sun. £1.80.
Hotels: in Leeds.
Light lunches and teas served.

S 27   Grange Park

Tel. Rotherham (0709) 559497
Grange Park, Upper Wortley Rd., Rotherham, S. Yorks.
On A629, M1 exit 35.
Parkland/meadowland course.
18 holes, 6425 yds. S.S.S. 71
Visitors welcome.
Green Fees. Weekdays 95p; weekends £1.30.
Hotels: Brecon, Moorgate.

S 28   Halifax

Tel. Halifax (0422) 244171
Bob Hall, Union Lane, Ogden, Halifax, W. Yorks.
On A629 4 miles out of Halifax towards Keighley.
Moorland championship course.
18 holes, 6034 yds. S.S.S. 70
Visitors welcome at all times.
Green Fees. Weekdays £3.00; weekends £5.00.
Society Meetings welcome at all times.
Hotels: White Swan, Halifax.
Meals served by arrangement except Mon.

S 29   Halifax Bradley Hall

Tel. Elland 4108
Holywell Green, Halifax, W. Yorks.
On B6112, 3 miles S of Halifax.
Parkland, moorland course.
18 holes, 6101 yds. S.S.S. 69
Visitors welcome.
Society Meetings by arrangement.
Hotels: White Swan; Old Cock, Halifax.
Lunches served.

S 30   Hallamshire

Tel. Sheffield (0742) 302153
Redmires Rd., Sandygate, Sheffield S10 4LA.
3 miles W of Sheffield just off A57 Manchester road.
Moorland course.
18 holes, 6396 yds. S.S.S. 71
Visitors welcome with letter of introduction.
Green Fees. Weekdays £6.00 per round or day; weekends £8.00 per round or day.

Society Meetings by arrangement.
Hotels: Hallam Tower Hotel, Broomhill.
Meals served by arrangement except Tues.

S 31   Hallowes

Tel. Dronfield 413734
Hallowes Lane, Dronfield, Sheffield S18 6UA.
6 miles S of Sheffield on A61; local signposts in Dronfield.
Moorland course.
18 holes, 6302 yds. S.S.S. 70
Course designed by A. Mitchell and G. Duncan.
Visitors welcome weekdays, weekends and bank holidays with member only.
Green Fees. £6.00 per round; £8.00 per day.
Hotels: in Sheffield and Chesterfield.
Meals served by arrangement, tel. 410394.

S 32   Hanging Heaton

Tel. Dewsbury 461606
White Cross Rd., Dewsbury, W. Yorks. WF12 7HJ.
½ mile from town centre.
Meadowland course.
9 holes, 2917 yds. S.S.S. 68
Visitors welcome except Sun. morning.
Green Fees. Weekdays £3.00 (£2.00 with member); weekends £5.00 (£2.00 with member).
Hotels: Little Saddle.
Snacks and meals served by arrangement.

S 33   Headingley

Tel. Leeds (0532) 673052
Back Church Lane, Adel, Leeds LS16 8DW.
About 5 miles from city centre on A660.
Moorland / parkland course.
18 holes, 6238 yds. S.S.S. 70
Visitors welcome.
Green Fees. Weekdays £6.00; weekends £9.00.
Society Meetings welcome on weekdays.
Hotels: Parkway Hotel, Posthouse.
Meals served on weekdays except Fri.

S 34   Headley

Tel. Bradford 833348
Lower Kipping Lane, Thornton, Bradford, W. Yorks. BD13 3JT.
On B6145, 3½ miles W of Bradford.
Undulating moorland course.
9 holes, 5010 yds. S.S.S. 64
Visitors welcome Mon. to Sat.
Green Fees. Weekdays £2.00 (£1.00 with member); weekends £4.00 (£2.00 with member).
Society Meetings by arrangement.
Hotels: Bankfield, Bingley.

S 35   Hickleton

Tel. Rotherham 892496
Hickleton, Doncaster, S. Yorks.
7 miles out of Doncaster on A635 to Barnsley.
Undulating meadowland course.
18 holes, 6361 yds. S.S.S. 70
Course designed by Huggett, Coles & Dyer.
Visitors welcome if members of recognized club.
Green Fees. Weekdays £3.00 (£1.00 with

member); weekends £4.00 (£2.00 with member).
Society Meetings welcome on weekdays.
Hotels: in Doncaster.
Meals served by arrangement except Mon.

S 36   Hillsborough

Tel. Sheffield (0742) 349151
Worrall Rd., Sheffield S6 4BE.
Moorland / parkland course.
18 holes, 6192 yds. S.S.S. 69
Course designed by Tom Williamson (1920).
Visitors welcome.
Green Fees. Weekdays £5.00 per round (£3.50 per round, £4.25 per day with member); weekends £7.25 per round (£4.25 per round, £5.00 per day with member).
Society Meetings welcome on weekdays.
Hotels: Kenwood; Rutland.
Meals served by arrangement.

S 37   Horsforth

Tel. Leeds 586819 (Sec.), 585200 (Pro.)
Layton Rise, Layton Rd., Horsforth, Leeds.
NW of Leeds on A65 to Ilkley.
Moorland course.
18 holes, 6070 yds. S.S.S. 69
Visitors welcome.
Green Fees. Weekdays £5.00 per round or day (£2.50 with member); weekends £6.50 per round or day (£3.25 with member).
Society Meetings welcome on weekdays except Mon. £1.00 reduction for 16 or more.
Hotels: Post House, Bramhope; also in Leeds and Bradford.
Bar snacks and lunches served except Mon.; evening meals by arrangement. Supper licence available.

S 38   Hoveringham

Tel. (0302) 710841
Cross Lane, Austerfield, S. Yorks.
Off A614, 4 miles N of Bawtry.
Moorland course.
18 holes, 6824 yds. S.S.S. 73
Course designed by E. & M. Baker Ltd.
Visitors welcome.
Green Fees. Weekdays £2.30 (£1.70 with member); weekends £2.70 (£1.70 with member).
Society Meetings welcome.
Hotels: Crown, Bawtry.
Snacks served.

S 39   Howley Hall

Tel. Batley 472432
Scotchman Lane, Morley, LS27 0NX.
7 miles from Leeds.
Meadowland course.
18 holes, 6446 yds. S.S.S. 71
Visitors welcome.
Green Fees. Weekdays £4.00 per round (£3.00 with member), £6.00 per day (£4.00 with member).
Society Meetings welcome on weekdays.
Meals served except Mon.

S 40   Huddersfield

Tel. Huddersfield 26203 (Sec.), 26463 (Pro.)
Fixby   Hall,   Lightridge   Rd.,   Fixby,

Huddersfield, W. Yorks. HD2 2EP.
A64 from Huddersfield to Bradley Bar roundabout, left into Fixby Rd. for 1 mile, left into Lightridge Rd., ½ mile.
Parkland course.
18 holes, 6424 yds. S.S.S. 71
Visitors welcome if members of recognized club.
Green Fees. Weekdays £6.50 (£2.50 with member); weekends £7.50 (£3.00 with member).
Society Meetings by arrangement.
Hotels: Saxon Inn; George, Huddersfield.
Meals served except Mon.

S 41   Ilkley

Tel. Ilkley 600214
Myddleton, Ilkley, W. Yorks. LS29 0BE.
A65 from Leeds.
Parkland / meadowland course.
18 holes, 6249 yds. S.S.S. 70
Visitors welcome.
Green Fees. Weekdays £7.00 per round or day; weekends and bank holidays £10.00 per round or day.
Society Meetings by arrangement.
Hotels: Craiglands; Crescent; Trout Beck.
Meals served by arrangement.

S 42   Keighley

Tel. Keighley 604778
Howden Park, Utley, Keighley, W. Yorks. BD20 6DH.
1 mile NW of Keighley on the Skipton road.
Parkland course.
18 holes, 6134 yds. S.S.S. 70
Visitors welcome.
Green Fees. Weekdays £5.00 per round or day; weekends and bank holidays £7.50 per round or day.
Society Meetings welcome on weekdays by arrangement.
Hotels: Victoria, Keighley; Bankfield, Bingley.
Meals served.

S 43   Leeds

Tel. Leeds (0532) 658775
Elmete Lane, Leeds LS8 2LJ.
A58 4 miles from Leeds.
Parkland course.
18 holes, 6084 yds. S.S.S. 69
Visitors welcome.
Green Fees. Weekdays £6.00 per day, £4.50 per round; weekends £8.50 per day (£5.00 after 3.30 p.m.).
Society Meetings by arrangement.
Hotels: in Leeds.
Meals served except Mon.

S 44   Lees Hall

Tel. Sheffield (0742) 54402
Hemsworth Rd., Norton, Sheffield S8 8LL.
3½ miles S of city centre.
Parkland / meadowland course.
18 holes, 6090 yds. S.S.S. 69
Course designed by Alex Herd (1911).
Visitors welcome except Sun. morning.
Ladies' day Wed.
Green Fees. Weekdays £4.40 per round, £5.50 per day; weekends and bank holidays £5.50 per round.
Society Meetings by arrangement.

Hotels: Hallam Towers Hotel; Grosvenor; Kenwood.
Lunches and teas served except Tues; dinners by arrangement.

S 45   Lightcliffe

Tel. Halifax (0422) 22459
Knowle Top Rd., Lightcliffe, Halifax, W. Yorks.
4 miles E of Halifax on A58.
Undulating heathland course.
9 holes, 5868 yds. S.S.S. 68
Visitors welcome except 11.30-4.30 on Wed. (ladies' day).
Green Fees. Weekdays £4.00 (£2.00 with member); weekends £7.00 (£3.00 with member).
Society Meetings by arrangement.
Hotels: White Swan, Halifax; Ladbroke Mercury, Elland.
Snacks served; meals by arrangement except Fri.

S 46   Longley Park

Tel. Huddersfield 22304
Off Somerset Rd., Huddersfield, W. Yorks.
¼ mile from town centre.
Undulating parkland course.
9 holes, 5324 yds. S.S.S. 65
Visitors welcome.
Green Fees. Weekdays £2.50; weekends £4.50.
Society Meetings by arrangement.
Hotels: George; Ladbroke Mercury.
Meals served.

S 47   Low Laithes

Tel. Ossett 27 3275
Parkmill Lane, Flushdyke, Ossett, W. Yorks.
Off the Batley to Wakefield road 1 mile from Wakefield; ½ mile from M1 junction 40.
Parkland course.
18 holes, 6431 yds. S.S.S. 71
Visitors welcome.
Green Fees. Weekdays £4.00; weekends £6.00.
Society Meetings by arrangement.
Hotels: Albany, Wakefield.
Meals served except Thurs.

S 48   Marsden

Tel. Marsden (0484) 844 253
Hemplow, Marsden, Huddersfield, W. Yorks.
8 miles out of Huddersfield on A64 to Manchester.
Moorland course.
9 holes, 5702 yds. S.S.S. 68
Visitors welcome.
Green Fees. Weekdays £2.75 (£1.25 with member); weekends £4.50 (£1.75).
Society Meetings by arrangement.
Hotels: Dirker Roods, Meltham.
Meals served by arrangement.

S 49   Meltham

Tel. Huddersfield (0484) 850227
Thick Hollins Hall, Meltham, Huddersfield, W. Yorks. HD7 3DQ.
4 miles S of Huddersfield.
Moorland/parkland course.
18 holes, 6201 yds. S.S.S. 70
Visitors welcome.
Green Fees. Weekdays £5.00 (£1.50 with member); weekends £7.00 (£2.50 with member).
Society Meetings Mon., Thurs. and Sun. by arrangement.
Hotels: Durker Roods.
Meals served by arrangement.

S 50   Middleton Park

Tel. Leeds 700449
Town St., Middleton, Leeds LS10 3TN.
3 miles S of city centre.
Parkland course.
18 holes, 5233 yds. S.S.S. 65

S 51   Moor Allerton

Tel. Leeds (0532) 661154/5
Coal Rd., Leeds LS17 9NH.
Off A61 from Leeds at Alwoodley Gates (city boundary); turn right, proceed to T-junction, turn left, first right, first left.
Undulating parkland course.
27 holes, 6677 yds. S.S.S. 74
Course designed by Robert Trent Jones.
Visitors welcome on weekdays.
Green Fees. Weekdays £6.50.
Society Meetings welcome on weekdays.
Hotels: Harewood Arms, Harewood; Post House, Bramhope; St. George's, Harrogate; Dragonara, Leeds.
Meals served by arrangement except Fri.

S 52   Moortown

Tel. Leeds (0532) 681682
Harrogate Rd., Alwoodley, Leeds LS17 7DB.
4 miles from centre of Leeds on A61 to Harrogate.
Moorland/parkland course.
18 holes, 6606 yds. S.S.S. 72
Course designed by Dr. Mackenzie.
Visitors welcome on weekdays, weekends with reservation.
Green Fees. Weekdays £5.50 per round, £6.50 per day; weekends £7.50 per round or day.
Society Meetings welcome on weekdays.
Hotels: Post House, Bramhope; Harewood Arms, Harewood; Parkway, Leeds.
Snacks served on Mon.; lunches served Tues. to Sun.; evening meals served Tues. to Sat.

S 53   Mount Skip

Tel. Hebden Bridge 2896
Great Mount, Wadsworth, Hebden Bridge, W. Yorks. HX7 8PH.
1 mile N of Hebden Bridge.
Moorland course.
9 holes, 2579 yds. S.S.S. 65
Visitors welcome.
Green Fees. Weekdays £2.00 per round or day (£1.00 with member); weekends £3.00 per round or day (£1.50).
Hotels: White Lion Inn; Nutclough House, Hebden Bridge.
Snacks served; meals by arrangement except Mon.

S 54   Normanton

Tel. Wakefield 892943
Snydale Rd., Snydale, Normanton, W. Yorks.
Off M62 1 mile from town centre.
Undulating course.
9 holes, 5284 yds. S.S.S. 66

Visitors welcome Mon. to Sat.
Green Fees. Weekdays £2.50; Sat. £4.00.
Society Meetings welcome on weekdays.
Hotels: Parklands, Wakefield; North Eastern, Castleford.
Snacks served.

S 55   Northcliffe (Shipley)

Tel. Bradford 584085
High Bank Lane, Moorhead, Shipley, W. Yorks. BD18 4LJ.
From Bradford Bingley-Keighley road to Saltaire roundabout, first left up Moorhead Lane for 1 mile.
Parkland course.
18 holes, 6025 yds. S.S.S. 69
Visitors welcome.
Green Fees. Weekdays £4.50 (£2.00 with member); weekends and bank holidays £6.50 (£3.00 with member).
Hotels: Belvedere, Bradford; Bankfield, Shipley.
Snacks served; meals by arrangement except Mon.

S 56   Otley

Tel. Otley 2081
West Busk Lane, Otley, W. Yorks.
On Otley to Bradford road.
Meadowland course.
18 holes, 6229 yds. S.S.S. 70
Visitors welcome.
Green Fees. Apr. to Oct.: weekdays £5.00 per round or day; weekends £6.00 per round or day. Nov. to Mar.: weekdays £3.00 per round or day, weekends £3.50 per round or day.
Society Meetings weekdays by arrangement.
Hotels: Post House, Bramhope.
Meals served except Mon.

S 57   Outlane

Tel. Elland 74762
Slack Lane, Outlane, Huddersfield, W. Yorks.
On A640 Huddersfield to Rochdale road.
Moorland course.
18 holes, 5590 yds. S.S.S. 67
Visitors welcome.
Green Fees. Weekdays £2.00 (£1.25 with member); weekends £4.00 (£2.00).
Hotels: Pennine President.
Meals served.

S 58   Painthorpe House Country Club

Tel. Wakefield 272351
Painthorpe Lane, Crigglestone, Wakefield, W. Yorks.
1 mile from exit 39 on M1.
Undulating meadowland course.
9 holes, 4008 yds. S.S.S. 60
Visitors welcome on weekdays.
Green Fees. Weekdays £1.00.
Society Meetings by arrangement.
Hotels: Swallow; Parklands, Wakefield.
Meals served.

S 59   Phoenix

Tel. Rotherham 63864
Brinsworth, Rotherham, S. Yorks.
Exit 34 on M1 on to Bawtry road for 2 miles.

Undulating meadowland course.
18 holes, 6041 yds. S.S.S. 69
Visitors welcome on weekdays if members of recognized club, weekends with member only.
Green Fees. Weekdays £4.00 per day (£1.50 with member); weekends and bank holidays £2.00 (with member only).
Hotels: Brentwood; Brecon, Moorgate; Limes, Rotherham.
Lunches and afternoon teas served.

S 60   Phoenix Park

Tel. Bradford 667573
Phoenix Park, Thornbury, Bradford 3, W. Yorks.
Near Thornbury roundabout.
9 holes, 4955 yds. S.S.S. 64
Green Fees. Weekdays £2.50; weekends £3.50.

S 61   Pontefract & District

Tel. Pontefract (0977) 72241
Park Lane, Pontefract, W. Yorks. WF8 4QS.
From Pontefract on A639 then on to B6134.
Parkland course.
18 holes, 6257 yds. S.S.S. 70
Visitors welcome.
Green Fees. Weekdays £5.00 (£2.50 with member); weekends £6.50 (£3.25 with member).
Society Meetings welcome on weekdays.
Hotels: Wentbridge House Hotel, Wentbridge.
Lunches served except Mon.

S 62   Queensbury

Tel. Bradford (0274) 882155
Brighouse Rd., Queensbury, Bradford, W. Yorks. BD13 1QF.
4 miles from Bradford on A647.
Undulating parkland course.
9 holes, 5102 yds. S.S.S. 65
Visitors welcome.
Green Fees. Weekdays £3.00 (£1.50 with member); weekends £5.00 (£2.50).
Society Meetings by arrangement.
Hotels: Norfolk Gardens, Bradford; White Swan, Halifax.
Meals served except Mon.

S 63   Rawdon Golf & Lawn Tennis Club

Tel. Rawdon (0532) 506040
Buckstone Dr., Rawdon, Leeds LS19 6BD.
On A65 6 miles from Leeds.
Undulating parkland course.
9 holes, 5902 yds. S.S.S. 68
Visitors welcome on weekdays.
Green Fees. Weekdays £3.00 (£1.50 with member).
Society Meetings welcome on weekdays.
Hotels: Robin Hood, Yeadon.
Lunches served except Mon.

S 64   Riddlesden

Tel. Keighley (0535) 602148
Howden Rough, Elamwood Rd., Riddlesden, Keighley, W. Yorks. BD20 5QN.
A650 Keighley to Bradford road, left into Bar Lane, left into Scott Lane for 2 miles.
18 holes, 4140 yds. S.S.S. 61
Visitors welcome.

Green Fees. Weekdays £1.50 per round or per day, O.A.P.'s 75p; weekends £3.00 per round or per day.
Society Meetings by arrangement.
Hotels: Beeches, Keighley.
Light lunches served; meals by arrangement.

S 65   Rotherham

Tel. Rotherham 850466, Pro. 850480
Thrybergh Park, Thrybergh, Rotherham, S. Yorks.
On Sheffield to Doncaster road 3 miles from Rotherham.
Parkland course.
18 holes, 6324 yds. S.S.S. 70
Visitors welcome with reservation.
Green Fees. Weekdays £6.00; weekends £8.50.
Society Meetings by arrangement.
Hotels: Elton, Bramley; Brentwood; Brecon, Rotherham.
Meals served.

S 66   Roundhay

Tel. Leeds 662695
Park Lane, Roundhay, Leeds 8.
4 miles N of city centre.
Parkland course.
9 holes, 5390 yds. S.S.S. 66
Visitors welcome.
Green Fees. £1.55 per round; Sun. £1.80.
Hotels: Parc Mont.
Snacks served at weekends.

S 67   Sand Moor

Tel. Leeds (0532) 685180
Alwoodley Lane, Leeds LS17 7DD.
Off A61 5 miles from Leeds.
Undulating parkland / moorland course.
18 holes, 6423 yds. S.S.S. 71
Visitors welcome.
Green Fees. Weekdays £7.00 (£3.00 with member); weekends £10.00.
Society Meetings weekdays by arrangement.
Hotels: Post House, Bramhope; Harewood Arms, Harewood; Parkway, Leeds.
Meals served except Mon. when snacks are served.

S 68   Scarcroft

Tel. Thorner (0532) 892263
Syke Lane, Leeds LS14 3BQ.
On A58 7 miles from Leeds.
Parkland course.
18 holes, 6426 yds. S.S.S. 71
Visitors welcome.
Green Fees. Weekdays £6.00 per round, £7.50 per day (£3.00 with member); weekends £9.00 (£3.00 with member).
Society Meetings welcome on weekdays.
Hotels: New Inn.
Lunches served except Mon.

S 69   Serlby Park

Tel. Ranskill (9182) 268
Serlby, Doncaster, S. Yorks. DN10 6BA.
12 miles S of Doncaster.
Parkland course.
9 holes, 5325 yds. S.S.S. 66
Visitors welcome with member only.

S 70   Shipley

Tel. Bradford 563212
Beckfoot, Bingley, W. Yorks. BD16 1LX.
Off A650 5 miles from Bradford.
Parkland / meadowland course.
18 holes, 6300 yds. S.S.S. 70
Visitors welcome.
Green Fees. Mon. to Sat. £5.00 per round or day (£2.50 with member); Sun. £8.00 per round or day (£4.00 with member).
Society Meetings welcome on weekdays.
Hotels: Bankfield, Bingley.
Meals served except Mon.

S 71   Silkstone

Tel. Barnsley 79 8328
Field Head, Silkstone, Barnsley, S. Yorks.
Off M1 at exit 37, A628 towards Manchester for 1 mile.
Undulating course.
18 holes, 5601 yds. S.S.S. 67
Visitors welcome on weekdays, weekends with member only.
Green Fees. Weekdays £5.00 (£2.50 with member).
Society Meetings by arrangement.
Hotels: Queens, Barnsley; Ardsley House, Ardsley.
Meals served except Fri.

S 72   Silsden

Tel. Steeton 52998
High Brunthwaite, Silsden, Keighley, W. Yorks.
5 miles N of Keighley.
Meadowland course.
9 holes, 4532 yds. S.S.S. 62
Visitors welcome.
Green Fees. Weekdays £2.00, weekends £3.50.

S 73   Sitwell Park

Tel. Rotherham 92 63046
Shrogs Wood Rd., Rotherham, S. Yorks. S60 4BY.
Off A631 E of Rotherham.
Parkland course.
18 holes, S.S.S. 70
Visitors welcome.
Green Fees. Weekdays £5.00; weekends £6.00.
Society Meetings by arrangement.
Hotels: Hind; Cutlers.
Meals served except Tues.

S 74   South Bradford

Tel. Bradford 679195
Pearson Rd., Odsal, Bradford 6, W. Yorks.
Leave M606 along Rooley Ave. to Odsal roundabout.
Undulating meadowland course.
9 holes, 6100 yds. S.S.S. 69
Visitors welcome.
Society Meetings welcome on weekdays.
Hotels: Norfolk Gardens.
Lunches served except Mon.

S 75   South Leeds

Tel. Leeds (0532) 700479
Gipsy Lane, Beeston Park, Ring Rd., Leeds LS11 5TU.
4 miles from Leeds.
Parkland course.

18 holes, 5865 yds. S.S.S. 68
Visitors welcome on weekdays, weekends with member only.
Green Fees. Weekdays £5.00 per day (£3.00 with member); weekends £4.00 per day (with member only).
Society Meetings welcome Mon., Wed. and Thurs.
Hotels: in Leeds.
Snacks and meals served.

S 76 Stocksbridge & District

Tel. Stocksbridge (0472) 882003
Royd Lane, Townend, Deepcar, Sheffield S30 5RZ.
7 miles from Sheffield on main Sheffield to Manchester road.
Moorland course.
15 holes, 4501 yds. S.S.S. 64
Visitors welcome.
Green Fees. Weekdays £4.50; weekends £5.50.
Meals served by arrangement.

S 77 Tankersley Park

Tel. Ecclesfield (0742 15) 4247
High Green, Sheffield S30 4LG.
1 mile off A6135 N of Chapeltown.
Parkland course.
18 holes, 6241 yds. S.S.S. 70
Visitors welcome on weekdays, weekends with member only.
Green Fees. Weekdays £4.50 per round (£2.00 with a member); £6.00 per day.
Society Meetings by arrangement, min. 20.
Lunches served except Mon.

S 78 Temple Newsam

Tel. Leeds (0532) 645624, Pro. 647362
Temple Newsam Rd., Leeds LS15 0LN.
On A63. In easy reach of Leeds city centre on Selby road, or from A1, junction at Boot and Shoe Inn.
2 Parkland courses
(1) 18 holes, 6448 yds. S.S.S. 71
(2) 18 holes, 6299 yds. S.S.S. 70
Visitors welcome.
Green Fees. Weekdays £1.55; Sun. £1.80.
Society Meetings by arrangement.
Hotels: Selby Fork Hotel, S. Milford; Manston, Cross Gates; Mercury Motor Inn, Garforth Bridge.

S 79 Tinsley Park

Tel. Sheffield (0742) 42237
Darnall, Sheffield 9.
On A6102.
Woodland course.
18 holes, 6112 yds. S.S.S. 69
Course designed by F. Hawtree.
Visitors welcome.
Green Fees. £1.40 per round.
Meals served by arrangement.

S 80 Wakefield

Tel. Wakefield (0924) 255104
Woodthorpe Lane, Sandal, Wakefield, W. Yorks.
3 miles S of Wakefield on Barnsley road.
Parkland course.
18 holes, 6609 yds. S.S.S. 72
Visitors welcome.

Green Fees. Weekdays £6.00 per round or day (£3.00 with member); weekends £7.00 (£3.50 with member).
Society Meetings Wed., Thurs. and Fri. by arrangement.
Hotels: Swallow, Wakefield.
Meals served by arrangement except Mon.

S 81 Wath

Tel. Rotherham 872149
Abdy, Blackamoor, Rotherham, S. Yorks. S62 7SJ.
Off A633 in Wath, 7 miles N of Rotherham.
Meadowland course.
9 holes, S.S.S. 67
Visitors welcome on weekdays, weekends with member only.
Green Fees. £3.00 per day (£2.00 with member).
Society Meetings welcome by prior arrangement.
Evening meals served by arrangement.

S 82 West Bowling

Tel. Bradford (0274) 24449
Newall Hall, Rooley Lane, Bradford, W. Yorks.
Junction of Bradford ring road and M606.
Meadowland course.
18 holes, 5769 yds. S.S.S. 68
Visitors welcome.
Green Fees. Weekdays £4.50 (£2.25 with member); weekends and bank holidays £8.00 (£4.00 with member).
Society Meetings welcome on weekdays.
Hotels: Novotel, S. Bradford.
Lunches served except Mon.

S 83 West Bradford

Tel. Bradford (0274) 427671
Chellow Grange, Haworth Rd., Bradford 9, W. Yorks.
B6144 4 miles from Bradford.
Meadowland course.
18 holes, 5752 yds. S.S.S. 68
Visitors welcome.
Green Fees. Weekdays £5.18 per round or day (£2.88 with member); weekends £7.48 per round or day (£5.18 with member).
Society Meetings welcome on weekdays.
Hotels: Bankfield, Bingley.
Meals served by arrangement except Mon.

S 84 West End

Tel. Halifax (0422) 53608
Highroad Well, Halifax, W. Yorks.
2½ miles from town centre.
Moorland course.
18 holes, 5489 metres Par 68
Visitors welcome.
Green Fees. Weekdays £4.25 (£2.00 with member); weekends £5.50 (£2.25 with member).
Society Meetings by arrangement.
Hotels: White Swan, Princess.
Meals served except Mon.

S 85 Wetherby

Tel. Wetherby 62527 (Club)
Linton Lane, Wetherby, W. Yorks.
Off A1 at Wetherby.
Parkland course.
18 holes, 6244 yds. S.S.S. 70

Visitors welcome except Tues. and Sat.
Green Fees. Weekdays £5.00 per round, £7.00 per day; weekends £10.00 per round or day.
Society Meetings Wed., Thurs. and Fri.
Hotels: Angel.
No catering on Mon.

S 86 Wheatley

Tel. Doncaster 831655
Armthorpe Rd., Doncaster, S. Yorks.
E off A18.
Parkland course.
18 holes, 6343 yds. S.S.S. 70
Course designed by George Duncan.
Visitors welcome.
Green Fees. Weekdays £4.50 per round (£2.00 with member); weekends £6.50 per round (£3.00 with member).
Society Meetings welcome on weekdays.
Hotels: Punch's; Danum; Earl of Doncaster.
Meals served except Tues.

S 87 Woodhall Hills

Tel. Pudsey (0532) 564771
Calverley, Pudsey, W. Yorks.
A647 to Pudsey roundabout then Calverley road for 1 mile.
Meadowland course.
18 holes, 6227 yds. S.S.S. 70
Visitors welcome after 2.30 p.m. on Sat. and 10.30 a.m. on Sun.
Green Fees. Weekdays £4.00 per round (£2.25 with member); weekends £6.50 per round (£3.50 with member).
Society Meetings by arrangement bronze, silver, gold days. Contact D.N. Brunyard (Pro.) 562857.
Hotels: Norfolk Gardens; Victoria, Bradford; Merrion, Leeds; Post House, Bramhope.
Snacks, lunches and teas served except Mon.; evening meals served Thurs. to Sun. (Tues. and Wed. by arrangement).

S 88 Woodsome Hall

Tel. Kirkburton 2971
Fenay Bridge, Huddersfield, W. Yorks. HD8 0LQ.
3 miles from Huddersfield on Sheffield road A624.
Parkland course.
18 holes, 6036 yds. S.S.S. 69
Visitors welcome except Tues. (ladies' day).
Green Fees. Weekdays £6.00 per round or day; weekends £7.00 per round or day.
Society Meetings welcome on weekdays except Tues.
Hotels: George; Ladbroke Mercury, Huddersfield.
Meals served except Mon.

S 89 Wortley

Tel. Sheffield 882139
Wortley, Sheffield.
2 miles off M1 at exit 36.
Parkland course.
18 holes, 5925 yds. S.S.S. 68
Visitors welcome.
Green Fees. Weekdays £4.00 per round, £5.00 per day; weekends £6.00.
Society Meetings Wed. only by arrangement.
Meals served by arrangement.

T North Yorkshire, Humberside

T 1   Bedale

Tel. Bedale 2568
Leyburn Rd., Bedale, N. Yorks.
A684 300 yards N of Bedale Church.
Parkland course.
18 holes, 5780 yds. S.S.S. 68
Visitors welcome.
Green Fees. Weekdays £3.50; weekends £4.50.
Society Meetings weekdays by arrangement.
Hotels: Kings Head.

T 2   Beverley & East Riding

Tel. Beverley (0482) 867190
Ante-Mill, Westwood, Beverley, N. Humberside HU17.
1½ miles from town centre.
Parkland course.
18 holes, 5937 yds. S.S.S. 68
Visitors welcome on weekdays, weekends with reservation.
Green Fees. Weekdays £3.00 per round or day; weekends £4.50. Reduced rates if playing with member.
Society Meetings by arrangement, max. 40.
Hotels: Beverley Arms; Kings Head.
Meals served by arrangement.

T 3   Boothferry

Spaldington Lane, Spaldington, Goole, N. Humberside.
A63 towards Howden then B1228 to Bubwith for 2 miles; signposted.
Meadowland course.
18 holes, 6593 yds. S.S.S. 72
Course designed by D.M.A. Steel, Cotton (CK), Pennink, Lawrie & Partners.
Visitors welcome.
Green Fees. Weekdays £2.50 per round, £4.00 per day; weekends and bank holidays £3.75 per round, £6.00 per day.
Society Meetings welcome on weekdays.

Hotels: Wellington; Bowmans; Kilpin Country Club, Howden.
Lunches served daily.

T 4   Bridlington

Tel. Bridlington (0262) 72092
Belvedere, Bridlington, N. Humberside.
1½ miles S of Bridlington station.
Seaside course.
18 holes, 6356 yds. S.S.S. 70
Visitors welcome.
Green Fees. Weekdays £2.50 per round; weekends £3.00 per round.
Society Meetings welcome.
Hotels: Spa; Monarch.
Meals served.

T 5   Brough

Tel. Hull (0482) 667374
Cave Rd., Brough, N. Humberside HU15 1HB.
10 miles W. of Hull off A63.
Parkland course.
18 holes, 6153 yds. S.S.S. 69
Visitors welcome on weekdays except Wed.
Green Fees. Weekdays £6.00 (£3.00 with member).
Hotels: Cave Castle, South Cave; Crest Motel, North Ferriby.
Snacks served.

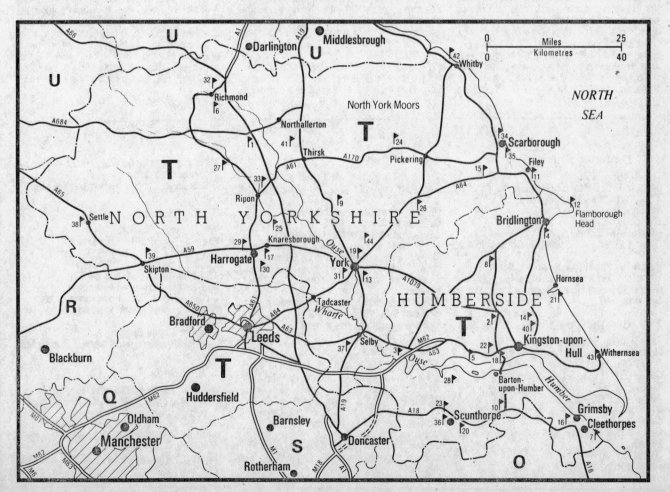

Historic Ganton

Ganton first came to be widely known when Harry Vardon was appointed professional five years after the club was founded in 1891. It was there that he played the second half of his great match with Willie Park in 1899, adding to the small lead gained at North Berwick and later overpowering him; but Ganton has never lived in the past and over the years many historic moments have carried on these early traditions.

The club has played host to English Amateur and Women's championships at various intervals. It is the only inland course that has housed the Amateur. It saw the last appearance of 'The Babe' in Britain, the last match between England and France, and, in 1949, was the scene of America's strong recovery in the Ryder Cup under the non-playing captaincy of Ben Hogan, whose future then was still uncertain after his terrible road accident.

But perhaps Ganton's best recommendation is that it has provided countless hundreds of no particular golfing fame with days in a rich pastoral setting that are remembered longer than most. It is a place to which people look forward to returning —a sure indication of its quality—and no wonder.

To begin with, it is a course of sand, fir trees and gorse, light to the tread and an ideal basis for fairways and greens. This fact has often led it to be likened to seaside golf, but it has a very definite character of its own.

If a good score is to be achieved, not on the scale of Michael Bonallack's phenomenal 61 in the English championship final of 1968, it seems to me essential to lay the foundations on the first five holes which 'Dutch' Harrison once played in five threes against Max Faulkner. True, there is an early awareness of the dreaded gorse that is scattered in fair profusion throughout, but the last four holes before the turn, going back and forth, are very demanding, the 9th, with the Scarborough Road awaiting the bad slicer, having a length of more than 500 yards.

The 10th, in the same direction, is a deceptive short hole into the corner, but the 11th brings us back with an excellent par four to more central parts by the refreshment hut and introduces us to the dogleg 12th which has been much stretched and rearranged since it was said a long time ago 'a tee shot consisted of a mashie shot, played mountains high into the air in order to clear the tops of a row of tall trees'.

One can imagine the discussion that this hole and its various versions have provoked in its time, but one is as glad of a four today as one is of a five at the next. The 14th with its carry over a strategically sited bunker, offers the chance of a three, but that is just as well because the finish is unusually severe and has played a notable part in the destiny of many a championship, not least the Amateur in 1964.

The 15th, a splendid two-shotter, takes us up towards the old church and the little cricket ground opposite, where one hopes many a Yorkshire hero once played, and after following the driveway back down the 16th, there is the 17th where threes can be so valuable and yet so difficult to achieve.

It makes a fine 17th hole at any time but Ganton probably keeps its best and most dramatic until last. The drive must be hit well to the right to avoid being stymied by a menacing clump of firs and to open up the narrow entrance for a longish second across the road.

Many a card lies in shreds before the green is reached, but there are compensations, and for many the pleasures of Ganton are just beginning. York ham and Ganton cake await and if, for some reason, one's playing of the last hole falls below expectation, these delights and the Yorkshire hospitality that follows, I dare wager, will not.

T 6 Catterick Garrison

Tel. 074883 3268
Leyburn Rd., Catterick Garrison, N. Yorks.
A1 to Catterick village, 4 miles.
Parkland/moorland course.
18 holes, 6336 yds. S.S.S. 70
Visitors welcome.
Green Fees. Weekdays £5.00; weekends £6.50.
Society Meetings by arrangement.
Hotels: Bridge House Hotel; Angel, Catterick; Kings Head, Richmond.
Meals served.

T 7 Cleethorpes

Tel. Grimsby 814060
North Sea Lane, Cleethorpes, S. Humberside DN35 0PN.
Off A1031, 1 mile S of Cleethorpes.
Seaside course.
18 holes, 6015 yds. S.S.S. 69
Visitors welcome if members of recognized club.
Green Fees. Weekdays £4.60; weekends £6.90.
Hotels: Kingsway Hotel.
Meals served.

T 8 Driffield

Tel. Driffield (0377) 43116
Sunderlandwick, Driffield, N. Humberside.
1 mile S of Driffield on A164.
Undulating meadowland course.
9 holes, 6202 yds. S.S.S. 70
Course designed by C. H. Websdale.
Visitors welcome, no parties at weekend.
Green Fees. Weekdays £3.00 per round or day (£2.00 with member); weekends £4.00 per round or day (£3.00 with member).
Society Meetings by arrangement.
Hotels: Bell Hotel, Driffield.
Meals served by arrangement.

T 9 Easingwold

Tel. Easingwold 21486
Stillington Rd., Easingwold, York YO6 3ET.
A19 1 mile from Easingwold.
Parkland course.
18 holes, 6269 yds. S.S.S. 70
Course designed by Hawtree & Son.
Visitors welcome.
Green Fees. Weekdays £5.50 (£2.50 with member); weekends £8.50 (£4.00 with member).

Society Meetings welcome on weekdays.
Hotels: George.
Snacks and lunches served except Mon.

T 10 Elsham

Tel. Barnetby 688382
Elsham, Brigg, S. Humberside.
A15 3 miles N of Brigg.
Parkland course.
18 holes, 6250 yds. S.S.S. 70
Visitors welcome on weekdays.
Green Fees. £6.00 per round or day.
Society Meetings welcome Mon. Tues. and Wed.
Hotels: Angel, Brigg.
Lunches, evening meals served except Mon.

T 11 Filey

Tel. Scarborough 513293
Filey, N. Yorks. YO14 9BQ.
S end of town.
Seaside course.
18 holes, 6025 yds. S.S.S. 69
Visitors welcome.
Green Fees. Weekdays £5.00; weekends £6.50.

Society Meetings welcome.
Hotels: Hylands; White Lodge Hotel.
Meals served.

T 12 Flamborough Head

Tel. Flamborough 333
Flamborough, Bridlington, N. Humberside.
5 miles NE of Bridlington on B1255.
Undulating seaside course.
18 holes, 5404 yds. S.S.S. 66
Visitors welcome.
Green Fees. Weekdays £4.00 (£2.35 with member); weekends £5.75 (£2.35 with member); weekly £17.25.
Society Meetings welcome.
Meals served except Mon. and Fri.

T 13 Fulford

Tel. Fulford (0904) 413579
Heslington Lane, Heslington, York YO1 5DY.
Off A19, 2 miles from city centre.
18 holes, 6779 yds. S.S.S. 72
Course designed by Dr. Mackenzie.
Visitors by arrangement only.
Green Fees. Weekdays £7.00; weekends £9.00.
Hotels: in York.
Lunches served except Mon.; high teas served except Mon. and Fri.

T 14 Ganstead Park

Tel. Hull 811280
Longdales Lane, Coniston, Hull, N. Humberside HU11 4LB.
Approx. 4 miles E of Hull.
Meadowland course.
9 holes, 5816 yds. S.S.S. 68
Course designed by Ted Eltherington.
Visitors welcome on weekdays.
Green Fees. Weekdays £2.50 (£2.00 with member); weekends £5.00 (£3.50 with member).
Society Meetings welcome on weekdays.
Hotels: numerous in Hull and Beverley.
Lunches, dinners, bar snacks served except Mon.

T 15 Ganton

Tel. Sherburn 329
Ganton, Scarborough, N. Yorks. YO12 4PB.
9 miles from Scarborough on A64.
18 holes, 6693 yds. S.S.S. 73
Visitors welcome with reservation and handicap certificate.
Green Fees. Weekdays £9.00 per day; weekends £12.00 per day.
Society Meetings welcome on weekdays.
Hotels: Greyhound, Ganton; Coachman Inn, Snainton; Foxholm, Ebberston.
Lunches and teas served.

T 16 Grimsby

Tel. Grimsby (0472) 42823, 42630 (Sec.)
Littlecoates Rd., Grimsby, S. Humberside DN34 4LU.
1 mile W of town centre.
Parkland course.
18 holes, 6066 yds. S.S.S. 69
Visitors welcome with reservation if members of recognized club. Ladies' afternoon Tues. Ladies not permitted Sat. p.m. or Sun. a.m.

Green Fees. Weekdays £5.00; weekends £6.50. Half if guest of member and living more than 15 miles away.
Society Meetings weekdays by arrangement.
Hotels: Humber Royal; Crest Motel.
Snacks and afternoon teas served; high teas by arrangement; lunches by arrangement except Wed. and Sat.

T 17 Harrogate

Tel. Harrogate 862999
Forest Lane Head, Starbeck, Harrogate, N. Yorks. HG2 7TF.
2 miles from Harrogate on A59 Knaresborough road.
Parkland course.
18 holes, 6204 yds. S.S.S. 70
Course designed by 'Sandy' Herd (1897).
Visitors welcome except Sat.
Green Fees. Weekdays £5.50 per round (£2.75 with member), £6.50 per day (£3.25 with member); weekends £8.00 per round or day (£4.00 with member).
Society Meetings welcome on weekdays, weekends by arrangement.
Hotels: in Harrogate.
Light lunches and teas served; full lunches and dinners by arrangement.

T 18 Hessle

Tel. Hull (0842) 650171
Westfield Rd., Raywell, Cottingham, N. Humberside HU16 5YL.
Off A164 at Eppleworth Rd., 1 mile from Raywell.
Undulating meadowland course.
18 holes, 6527 yds. S.S.S. 71
Course designed by Allis & Thomas.
Visitors welcome, ladies' day Tues.
Green Fees. Weekdays £4.00 per round, £6.00 per day; weekends £2.50 with member only.
Society Meetings by arrangement.
Hotels: Grange Park Hotel; Eden, Willerby.
Meals served by arrangement except Mon.

T 19 Heworth

Tel. York (0904) 24204
Muncaster House, Muncastergate, York.
1½ miles from city centre on A64.
Meadowland/parkland course.
11 holes, 6078 yds. S.S.S. 69
Visitors welcome except Sun. morning.
Green Fees. Weekdays £5.00 per day (£2.00 with member); weekends and bank holidays £6.00 per day (£3.00 with member).

T 20 Holme Hall

Tel. Scunthorpe (0724) 89090 or 62078
Holme Lane, Battesford, Scunthorpe, S. Humberside DN16 3RF.
2 miles SE of Scunthorpe.
Parkland course.
18 holes, 6429 yds. S.S.S. 71
Visitors welcome on weekdays.
Green Fees. £5.00 (£3.00 with member).
Society Meetings weekdays by arrangement.
Hotels: Wortley; Royal; Bridge Hotel.
Meals served except Fri.

T 21 Hornsea

Tel. Hornsea (04012) 2020
Rolston Rd., Hornsea, N. Humberside HU18 1XE.
In Hornsea follow signs to Hornsea Pottery Ltd.
Meadowland/seaside course.
18 holes, 6461 yds. S.S.S. 71
Visitors welcome.
Green Fees. Weekdays £3.25 per round, £4.25 per day; Sat. £5.00 per round or day; Sun. £5.25 per round or day.
Society Meetings welcome on weekdays.
Meals served except Fri.

T 22 Hull

Tel. Hull (0482) 653026
The Hall, Packman Lane, Kirkella, Hull HU10 7TJ.
Off A164, 5 miles W of Hull.
Parkland course.
18 holes, 6242 yds. S.S.S. 70
Visitors welcome weekdays, weekends with member only.
Green Fees. Weekdays £6.00 (£3.00 with member); weekends £3.00 with member only.
Society Meetings weekdays by arrangement.
Hotels: Grange Park Hotel, Willerby Manor Hotel, Willerby.
Meals served by arrangement.

T 23 Kingsway

Tel. Scunthorpe 840945
Kingsway, Scunthorpe, S. Humberside.
S of A18 between Berkeley and Queensway roundabouts.
Undulating parkland course.
9 holes, 3830 yds. S.S.S. 59
Visitors welcome.
Green Fees. Weekdays 80p, juniors and O.A.P.s 35p; weekends and bank holidays £1.00, juniors and O.A.P.s 40p.
Hotels: Royal; Priory; Wortley.

T 24 Kirkbymoorside

Manor Vale, Kirkbymoorside, York.
On A170, 7 miles W. of Pickering.
Parkland course.
18 holes, 5760 yds. S.S.S. 68
Green Fees. Weekdays £3.00; weekends £4.00.
Hotels: Black Swan; King's Head; George and Dragon; White Horse.

T 25 Knaresborough

Tel. Harrogate 863219
Boroughbridge Rd., Knaresborough, N Yorks.
1½ miles from Knaresborough.
Parkland course.
18 holes, 6117 yds. S.S.S. 70
Visitors welcome.
Green Fees. Weekdays £4.50 per round, £5.50 per day; weekends £6.50 per round or day.
Society Meetings by arrangement.
Hotels: Dower House Hotel.
Meals served.

T 26 Malton & Norton

Tel. Malton (0653) 2959
Norton, Malton, N. Yorks. YO17.
A64 from Scarborough.
Undulating parkland course.
18 holes, 6401 yds. S.S.S. 71
Course designed by Hawtree & Son.
Visitors welcome.
Green Fees. Weekdays £4.60 per day;
weekends and bank holidays £6.90 per day.
Society Meetings weekdays by arrangement except Thurs.
Hotels: Talbot; Green Man; Wentworth Arms; Crown.
Meals served except Mon.

T 27 Masham

Tel. Masham 379
Masham, Ripon, N. Yorks.
8 miles NW of Ripon.
Parkland course.
9 holes, 5000 yds. S.S.S. 64
Visitors welcome on weekdays, weekends with member only.
Green Fees. £3.00 per round or day (£2.00 with member).
Hotels: Kings Head.

T 28 Normanby Hall

Tel. Scunthorpe 62141 Extn 444
c/o Leisure & Recreation Dept, Scunthorpe Borough Council, Civic Centre, Scunthorpe.
The club is 5 miles N of Scunthorpe adjacent to Normanby Hall.
Parkland course.
18 holes, 6521 yds. S.S.S. 70
Course designed by F.W. Hawtree & Son.
Visitors welcome except when course is closed for major competitions (5 times a year).
Green Fees. Weekdays £2.00; weekends and bank holidays £3.50.
Society Meetings welcome on weekdays by arrangement.
Hotels: Wortley; Royal; Berkeley; Crosby.
Catering facilities.

T 29 Oakdale

Tel. Harrogate (0423) 502806, 67162 (Sec.)
Oakdale, Off Kent Rd., Harrogate, N. Yorks. HG1 2LN.
Off A61 from Harrogate at Kent Rd.
Parkland course.
18 holes, 6291 yds. S.S.S. 70
Course designed by Dr. Mackenzie.
Visitors welcome.
Green Fees. Weekdays £4.50 per round, £5.50 per day (£2.00 with member); weekends £6.00 per round or day.
Society Meetings welcome on weekdays.
Full catering service except Mon.

T 30 Pannal

Tel. Harrogate (0423) 871641, 872620 (Sec.), 872620 (Pro.)
Follifoot Rd., Pannal, Harrogate, N. Yorks. HG3 1ES.
2 miles S of Harrogate on A61 (Leeds road).
Moorland/parkland championship course.
18 holes, 6573 yds. S.S.S. 71
Visitors welcome on weekdays.

Green Fees. Weekdays £7.00 per round, £8.50 per day.
Society Meetings Tues., Wed., Thurs. p.m. by arrangement.
Hotels: Prospect; Old Swan; Majestic; St. George; Crown, Harrogate.
Meals served to order.

T 31 Pike Hills

Tel. York (0904) 66566
Copmanthorpe, York.
3 miles W of York on A64.
Parkland course.
18 holes, 6048 yds. S.S.S. 69
Visitors welcome on weekdays until 4.30 p.m., after 4.30 p.m. with member only; weekends with member only.
Green Fees. £5.00 per day.
Society Meetings welcome on weekdays.
Hotels: Chase; Abbey Park Hotel; Elm Bank Hotel; Royal Station, York.
Meals served.

T 32 Richmond

Tel. Richmond 2457
Bend Hagg, Richmond, N. Yorks.
A1 to Scotch Corner then A6108 for 4 miles.
Parkland course.
18 holes, 5704 yds. S.S.S. 68
Course designed by J. F. Pennink.
Visitors welcome on weekdays.
Green Fees. Weekdays £4.00; weekends £5.00.
Society Meetings welcome on weekdays.
Hotels: Kings Head; Fleece; Terrace House.
Meals served.

T 33 Ripon City

Tel. Ripon 3640 (clubhouse), 700411 (Pro.)
Palace Rd., Ripon, N. Yorks. HG4 3HH.
1 mile along A6108 towards Leyburn.
Parkland course.
9 holes, 5752 yds. .S.S.S. 68
Visitors welcome.
Green Fees. Weekdays £3.50 per day; weekends and bank holidays £6.00 per day.
Society Meetings by arrangement.
Hotels: Spa; Unicorn.
Lunch (notice required) and tea served daily except Thurs.

T 34 Scarborough North Cliff

Tel. Scarborough (0723) 60786
North Cliff Ave., Burmiston Rd., Scarborough, N. Yorks. YO12 6PP.
2 miles from town centre on coastal road to Whitby.
Meadowland/parkland course.
18 holes, 6284 yds. S.S.S. 71
Course designed by James Braid.
Visitors welcome.
Green Fees. Weekdays £5.00; weekends £7.00; plus V.A.T.
Society Meetings by arrangement.
Hotels: Scalby Manor Hotel; Brierdene.
Snacks, lunches and high teas served.

T 35 Scarborough South Cliff

Tel. Scarborough (0723) 60522, 74737 (Sec.)
Deepdale Ave., Scarborough, N. Yorks. YO11 2UE.
1 mile S of town centre.
Undulating parkland seaside course.
18 holes, 5863 yds. S.S.S. 68
Course designed by Dr. Mackenzie.
Visitors welcome.
Green Fees. Weekdays £5.50; weekends £7.00.
Society Meetings by arrangement.
Hotels: St. Nicholas; Scarborough Grand; Scarborough Royal.
Lunches and high teas served.

T 36 Scunthorpe

Tel. Scunthorpe 842913
Ashby Decoy, Burringham Rd., Ashby, Scunthorpe, S. Humberside DN17 2AB.
Adjoining Mallard Hotel, Burringham Rd.
Parkland course.
18 holes, 6201 yds. S.S.S. 71
Visitors welcome on weekdays.
Green Fees. £6.00 per round or day. Reduced rates for Society meetings.
Society Meetings weekdays by arrangement.
Hotels: Berkeley; Priory.
Meals served by arrangement.

T 37 Selby

Tel. Gateforth 622
Brayton Barff, Brayton, Selby, N. Yorks.
2 miles from Selby.
Undulating course.
18 holes, 6225 yds. S.S.S. 70
Visitors welcome if members of recognized club or with member.
Green Fees. Weekdays £4.50 per round (£2.50 with member); weekends £7.00 (£2.50 with member).
Society Meetings Wed., Thurs. and Fri. only.
Hotels: Lonsborough; George.
Meals served by arrangement.

T 38 Settle

Giggleswick, Settle, N. Yorks.
Off A65, 1 mile N of Settle.
Parkland course.
9 holes, 4590 yds. S.S.S. 64
Visitors welcome.
Green Fees. Weekdays £1.00; weekends £1.50.
Society Meetings welcome.
Hotels: Black Horse; Royal Oak, Settle.

T 39 Skipton

Tel. Skipton (0756) 3257
Grassington Rd., Skipton, N. Yorks. BD23 1IL.
1 mile from town centre on B6265.
Parkland/moorland course.
18 holes, 6191 yds. S.S.S. 70
Visitors welcome.
Green Fees. Weekdays £4.00 (£2.00 with member); weekends £6.00 (£3.00 with member). Juniors under 19 50% reductions.

Society Meetings by arrangement.
Hotels: Black Horse; Tam House Hotel; Midland Hotel.
Meals served except Mon.

T 40 Sutton Park

Tel. Hull 74242
Saltshouse Rd., Hull.
A165 from city centre, left at roundabout.
Parkland course.
18 holes, 6400 yds. S.S.S. 70
Course designed by L. Herrington.
Visitors welcome.
Green Fees. Weekdays 75p; weekends 95p.
Meals served by arrangement.

T 41 Thirsk & Northallerton

Tel. Thirsk (0845) 22170
Northallerton Rd., Thirsk, N. Yorks.
On A168, 2 miles N of Thirsk.
Meadowland course.
9 holes, 6150 yds. S.S.S. 70
Visitors welcome.
Green Fees. Weekdays £3.00; weekends £5.00.
Hotels: Three Tuns; Fleece.
Snacks served by arrangement except Tues.

T 42 Whitby

Tel. Whitby 602768, 600660 (Sec.)
Low Straggleton, Whitby, N. Yorks.
Adjoining Whitby to Sandsend road.
Seaside course.
18 holes, 5710 yds. S.S.S. 67
Visitors welcome.
Green Fees. Weekdays £4.00 per day; weekends, £5.00 per day; plus V.A.T.
Hotels: in Whitby.
Snacks served; meals by arrangement.

T 43 Withernsea

Chestnut Ave., Withernsea, N. Humberside.
18 miles E of Hull.
Seaside course.
9 holes, 5112 yds. S.S.S. 65
Visitors welcome on weekdays.
Green Fees. On application to Secretary.

T 44 York

Tel. York (0904) 490304
Strensall, York.
6 miles NE of York.
Moorland/parkland course.
18 holes, 6225 yds. S.S.S. 70
Course designed by J. H. Taylor.
Visitors welcome.
Green Fees. Weekdays £5.50 (£2.00 with member); weekends £7.00 (£2.50 with member).
Society Meetings welcome.
Hotels: in York.
Meals served.

U Cumbria, Northumberland, Durham, Tyne & Wear, Cleveland

U 1 Allendale

Tel. Allendale (043 483) 412
Thornley Gate, Allendale, Hexham, Northumberland NE47 9LQ.
11 miles from Hexham.
Meadowland course.
9 holes, 4408 yds. S.S.S. 61
Visitors welcome.
Green Fees. Weekdays £2.00; weekends £2.50 (£2.00 with member).
Society Meetings welcome.
Hotels: Ashlea.

U 2 Alnmouth

Tel. Alnmouth 231
Foxton Hall, Alnmouth, Nr. Alnwick, Northumberland NE66 3BE.
Off A1068, 4 miles E of Alnwick.
Parkland, seaside course.
18 holes, 6414 yds. S.S.S. 71
Course designed by P. Mackenzie Ross.
Visitors welcome on weekdays except Fri., weekends with reservation.
Green Fees. Weekdays £4.40 per round, £6.30 per day; weekends £6.30 per round, £8.85 per day.
Society Meetings by arrangement.
Hotels: White Swan, Alnwick; Schooner, Alnmouth; Dormy House at Club.
Meals served.

U 3 Alnmouth Village

Tel. Alnmouth 370
Marine Rd., Alnmouth, Northumberland.
Off A1068, 5 miles SE of Alnwick.
Seaside course.
9 holes, 6100 yds. S.S.S. 70
Visitors welcome.
Green Fees. Weekdays £2.00; weekends £2.50.
Society Meetings by arrangement.
Hotels: Schooner.
Meals served by arrangement except Wed.

U 4 Alnwick

Swansfield Park, Alnwick, Northumberland.
Bridge St. to top of Swansfield Park Rd.
Parkland course.
9 holes, 5500 yds. S.S.S. 66
Visitors welcome.
Green Fees. Weekdays £2.00 (£1.00 with member); weekends and bank holidays £3.00 (£1.50 with member).
Hotels: Hotspur; White Swan.

U 5 Alston Moor

Tel. Alston (049 83) 675
Hermitage, Alston, Cumbria.
2 miles from Alston on B6277.
Undulating moorland course.
9 holes, 4930 yds. S.S.S. 64
Visitors welcome.
Green Fees. Weekdays £2.00 (£1.50 with member); weekends £3.00 (£2.00 with member).
Society Meetings by arrangement.
Hotels: Hillcrest; Cumberland; Blue Bell; Low Byre; Lovelady Shield; Victoria.

U 6 Appleby

Tel. Appleby 51432
Brackenber Moor, Appleby, Cumbria CA16 6LP.
2 miles S of Appleby on A66.
Moorland course.
18 holes, 5914 yds. S.S.S. 68
Visitors welcome.
Green Fees. Weekdays £2.50; weekends £3.60; weekly £12.50.
Society Meetings by arrangement.
Hotels: Tufton Arms; Courtfield; Royal Oak; Appleby Manor.
Meals served by arrangement.

U 7 Arcot Hall

Tel. Wideopen (089 426) 2794
Dudley, Cramlington, Northumberland NE23 7QP.
1 mile E of A1, 10 miles N of Newcastle.
Parkland course.
18 holes, 6256 yds. S.S.S. 70
Course designed by James Braid.
Visitors welcome with reservation.
Green Fees. Weekdays £6.00 (£4.00 with member); weekends £7.00 (£5.00 with member).
Society Meetings welcome Tues. and Thurs.
Hotels: Holiday Inn, Seaton Burn.
Meals served except Mon.

U 8 Backworth Collieries

Tel. Shiremoor 681048
The Hall, Backworth, Shiremoor, Tyne & Wear.
Off A108, 15 miles NE of Newcastle. Leave Tyne Tunnel road at Killingworth slip road; turn off at Backworth.
Parkland course.
9 holes, 5733 yds. S.S.S. 68
Visitors welcome on weekdays, Tues., Wed. and Thurs. after 5.00 p.m. with member only; Sat. after 4.00 p.m.; Sun after 12.00 noon.
Green Fees. Weekdays £3.45 (£2.30 with member); weekends £4.60 (£3.45 with member).
Meals served by arrangement.

U 9 Bamburgh Castle

Tel. Bamburgh 378
The Wynding, Bamburgh, Northumberland NE69 7DE.
7 miles from Belford off A1.
Seaside course.
18 holes, 5495 yds. S.S.S. 67
Visitors welcome with reservation.

Green Fees. Weekdays £4.50; weekends £6.50.
Hotels: Lord Crewe Arms; Victoria, Bamburgh; Blue Bell, Belford.
Lunches and teas served except Tues.

U 10 Barnard Castle

Tel. Barnard Castle (0833) 37237
Harmire, Barnard Castle, Co. Durham.
On B6278, 1½ miles N of Barnard Castle.
Parkland, meadowland course.
18 holes, 5838 yds. S.S.S. 68
Visitors welcome on weekdays, weekends with reservation.

Green Fees. Weekdays £4.00 per round or day; weekends £6.00 per round or day.
Society Meetings welcome.
Hotels: King's Head; Montalbo; Morritt Arms.
Meals served except Mon. and Fri.

U 11 Barrow

Tel. Barrow (0229) 25444
Rakesmoor, Hawcoat, Barrow-in-Furness.
A590 into Barrow. Turn right at first traffic lights (Hawcoat Lane) 1 mile.
Meadowland course.
18 holes, 6209 yds. S.S.S. 70

Visitors welcome.
Green Fees. £3.50 per day (£2.50 with member).
Society Meetings welcome, max. 40.
Hotels: Victoria Park Hotel; White House Hotel.
Meals served by arrangement.

U 12 Beamish Park

Tel. Stanley 93 32552
Beamish Park, Stanley, Co. Durham.
From Stanley follow signs to Beamish Museum.
Parkland course.

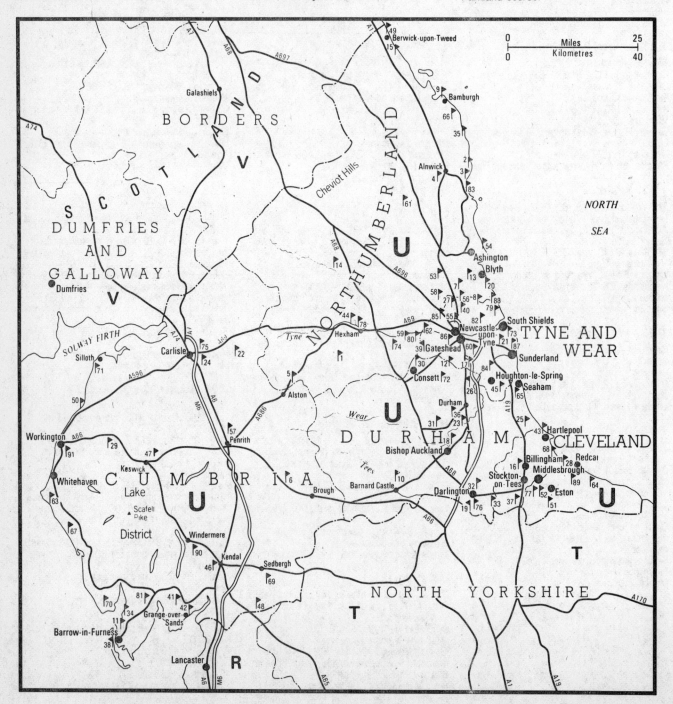

18 holes, 6050 yds. S.S.S. 70
Course designed by Henry Cotton.
Visitors welcome if members of recognized clubs.
Green Fees. Weekdays £3.00; weekends £5.00.
Society Meetings by arrangement.
Meals served by arrangement.

U 13   Bedlingtonshire

Tel. Bedlington (0670) 822457
Acorn Bank, Bedlington, Northumberland.
½ mile W of Bedlington on A1068.
Parkland course.
18 holes, 7000 yds. S.S.S. 73
Course designed by Cotton, (C.K.) Pennink, Lawrie and Partners.
Visitors welcome weekdays 9.00 a.m. to 6.00 p.m., weekends 12.00 noon onwards.
Green Fees. Weekdays £3.00 per round (£2.00 with member), £5.00 per day (£3.00 with member); weekends and bank holidays £3.50 per round (£2.50 with member), £6.60 per day (£3.60 with member).
Society Meetings welcome on weekdays.
Hotels: Red Lion; Ridge Farm, Bedlington; Ridley Arms, Stannington.
Lunches served except Sun; evening meals served on Fri. and Sat.

U 14   Bellingham

Bellingham, Hexham, Northumberland.
Off B6320, 16 miles NE of Hexham. Easy access from A68.
Meadowland course.
9 holes, 5226 yds. S.S.S. 66
Visitors welcome.
Green Fees. £2.00 per day, £1.00 after 5.30 p.m.
Hotels: in area.

U 15   Berwick-upon-Tweed

Tel. Ancroft 87256
Goswick, Ancroft, Berwick-upon-Tweed.
Off A1, 8 miles S of Berwick.
Seaside course.
18 holes, 6411 yds. S.S.S. 71
Course designed by James Braid.
Visitors welcome.
Green Fees. Weekdays £4.00 (£2.00 with member); weekends £7.00 (£2.00 with member).
Society Meetings welcome on weekdays, weekends by arrangement.
Hotels: King's Arms; Castle Hotel; Ravenshome, Berwick; Tilmouth, Cornhill-on-Tweed.
Meals served except Mon.

U 16   Billingham

Tel. Stockton 554494
Sandy Lane, Billingham, Cleveland TS22 5NA.
Off A19 near town centre.
Undulating meadowland course.
18 holes, 6420 yds. S.S.S. 71
Visitors welcome on weekdays, weekends after 10.00 a.m.
Green Fees. Weekdays £4.50; weekends £5.50.
Society Meetings by arrangement.
Hotels: Billingham Arms.
Meals served.

U 17   Birtley

Tel. Birtley 402207
Portobello Rd., Birtley, Co. Durham.
A6127 off A1, 6 miles S of Newcastle.
Parkland course.
9 holes, 5580 yds. S.S.S. 67
Visitors welcome with member only.
Hotels: Post House, Washington; Coach and Horses, Birtley.

U 18   Bishop Auckland

Tel. Bishop Auckland 602198
High Plains, Bishop Auckland, Co. Durham.
On A689, 1 mile E of Bishop Auckland.
Parkland course.
18 holes, 6340 yds. S.S.S. 71
Visitors welcome.
Green Fees. Weekdays £4.00; weekends £6.00.
Society Meetings welcome weekdays only.
Hotels: Queen's Head; Park Head, Bishop Auckland; Eden Arms, Rushyford; Durham Crest Motel, Durham.
Meals served.

U 19   Blackwell Grange

Tel. Darlington (0325) 4464
Blackwell, Darlington, Co. Durham.
On A66, 1 mile S of Darlington.
Parkland course.
18 holes, 5680 yds. S.S.S. 67
Visitors welcome.
Green Fees. Weekdays £4.00; weekends £5.00.
Society Meetings by arrangement.
Hotels: Europa Lodge; Croft Spa Hunting Lodge.
Lunches served by arrangement.

U 20   A) Blyth Old Course

Tel. Blyth 2356
Old Club House, Newsham, Blyth, Northumberland.
On coast, 10 miles NE of Newcastle.
Meadowland course.
12 holes, 5768 yds. S.S.S. 67
Visitors welcome. Juniors must be accompanied by senior member or visitor.
Green Fees. Weekdays £2.50 (£2.00 with member), juniors £1.25 (weekends restricted).
Society Meetings by arrangement.
Hotels: Steamboat Hotel, Blyth.
Light meals served by arrangement.

U 20   B) Blyth New Course

Tel. Blyth 67728
New Club House, New Delaval, Blyth.
10 miles NE of Newcastle.
18 holes, 6000 yds. S.S.S. 71
Visitors welcome on weekdays, weekends with member only.
Green Fees. £4.00 (£2.50 with member).
Society Meetings by arrangement.
Meals served by arrangement.

U 21   Boldon

Tel. Boldon 364182
Dipe Lane, East Boldon, Tyne & Wear NE36 0PQ.
On A184, 3 miles NW of Sunderland.
Meadowland course.

18 holes, 6434 yds. S.S.S. 71
Visitors welcome on weekdays, weekends restricted.
Green Fees. Weekdays £4.50 (£3.50 with member); weekends £5.50 (£3.50 with member).
Society Meetings by arrangement.
Hotels: Seaburn, Roker, Sunderland.
Meals served by arrangement.

U 22   Brampton

Tel. Brampton 2255
Brampton, Cumbria.
On B6413, 2 miles S of Brampton, 9 miles E of Carlisle.
Heathland course.
18 holes, 6426 yds. S.S.S. 71
Visitors welcome.
Green Fees. Weekdays £3.00 (£2.00 with member); weekends £4.00 (£2.00 with member or after 4p.m.) weekly £10.00.
Society Meetings welcome.
Hotels: White Lion; Howard Arms.
Lunches served.

U 23   Brancepeth Castle

Tel. Durham 780075
The Club House, Brancepeth, Co. Durham DH7 8EA.
6½ miles from Durham City on A690 Durham-Crook road; turn left at Brancepeth village crossroads.
Parkland undulating course.
18 holes, 6300 yds. S.S.S. 71
Course designed by H.S. Colt.
Visitors welcome on weekdays, weekends with member only.
Green Fees. Weekdays £6.50 (£3.50 with member); weekends £4.50 with member only.
Society Meetings weekdays by arrangement.
Hotels: The Royal County; The Three Tuns; The Crest Motel.
Meals and snacks served by arrangement.

U 24   Carlisle

Tel. Scotby (303) 022872
Aglionby, Carlisle, Cumbria CA4 8AG.
Off A69, 3 miles E of Carlisle, 1 mile from M6 exit 43.
Parkland course.
18 holes, 6099 yds. S.S.S. 70
Course designed by M.M. Monie and McKenzie Ross.
Visitors welcome.
Green Fees. Weekdays £5.00 (£3.00 with member); weekends £6.25 (£3.75 with member).
Society Meetings welcome Wed. and Fri.
Hotels: Crown & Mitre, Carlisle; Killoran, Wetheral; Crest Motel, Kingstown; Crosby Lodge, Crosby on Eden.
Lunches and high teas served except Mon.

U 25   Castle Eden and Peterlee

Tel. Castle Eden 220
Castle Eden, Hartlepool, Cleveland TS27 4SS.
Off A19, 11 miles S of Sunderland.
Parkland course.
18 holes, 6329 yds. S.S.S. 71
Course designed by Henry Cotton.
Visitors welcome.

Green Fees. Weekdays £5.00 per day; weekends and bank holidays £6.00 per day; weekly £26.00.
Hotels: Hardwick Hotel, Hesleden, Hartlepool; Norseman, Peterlee.
Meals served by arrangement.

U 26 Chester-le-Street

Tel. Chester-le-Street 883218
Lumley Park, Chester-le-Street, Co. Durham DH3 4NS.
Off A1 adjacent to Lumley Castle, 1½ miles S of Chester-le-Street.
Parkland course.
18 holes, 6224 yds. S.S.S. 70
Visitors welcome.
Green Fees. Weekdays £4.00 (£3.00 with member); weekends £5.00 (£4.00 with member).
Hotels: Lumley Castle Hotel; Lambton Arms.
Light meals served.

U 27 City of Newcastle

Tel. Gosforth 851775
Three Mile Bridge, Great North Road, Gosforth, Newcastle upon Tyne NE3 2DR.
On A1 3 miles N of Newcastle.
Meadowland course.
18 holes, 6454 yds. S.S.S. 71
Visitors welcome.
Green Fees. Weekdays £5.00; weekends £7.00.
Society Meetings by arrangement.
Hotels: Gosforth Park Hotel; Airport Hotel.
Meals served except Mon.

U 28 Cleveland

Tel. Redcar (0642) 483693, 471798 (Sec.), 483462 (Pro.)
Coatham, Redcar, Cleveland TS10 1BT.
From A174 to A1042 to Coatham.
Seaside links championship course.
18 holes, 6698 yds. S.S.S. 72
Visitors welcome if members of recognized club.
Green Fees. Weekdays £4.60 per round or day (£2.30 with member); weekends £6.90 (£3.45 with member).
Society Meetings welcome on weekdays only.
Hotels: Hotel Royal York, Redcar.
Full catering daily, limited Mon.

U 29 Cockermouth

Tel. Bass Lake 223
Embleton, Cockermouth, Cumbria CA13 9SG.
4 miles E of Cockermouth on A66 (old road).
Fell land course.
18 holes, 5467 yds. S.S.S. 67
Visitors welcome if members of recognized club with own clubs.
Green Fees Weekdays £4.00 (£2.00 with member); weekends and bank holidays £5.00 (£3.00 with member).
Society Meetings by arrangement.
Hotels: Derwent Water; Armathwaite Hall Hotel; Pheasant Hotel.
Meals served by arrangement except Mon. and Tues

U 30 Consett & District

Tel. Consett (0207) 502186
Elmfield Rd., Consett, Co. Durham DH8 5NN.
A691 12 miles NW of Durham. 3 miles A68.
Undulating parkland, moorland course.
18 holes, 6001 yds. S.S.S. 70
Visitors welcome.
Green Fees. Weekdays £4.00 per day (£2.50 with member); weekends £5.50 per day (£3.50 with member).
Society Meetings welcome weekdays and Sun. by arrangement.
Hotels: Crown & Cross Swords, Shotley Bridge; Braes Hotel, Consett.
Full menu at all times.

U 31 Crook

Tel. Crook (038 882) 2429
The Clubhouse, Low Jobs Hill, Crook, Co. Durham DL15 9AA.
On A690, 7 miles SW of Durham.
Undulating meadowland course.
18 holes, 6057 yds. S.S.S. 69
Visitors welcome.
Green Fees. Weekdays £2.50 (£2.00 with member); weekends £3.50 (£2.50 with member).
Society Meetings weekdays by arrangement.
Hotels: Uplands Hotel, Crook.
Meals served by arrangement.

U 32 Darlington

Tel. Darlington (0325) 63936
Haughton Grange, Darlington, Co. Durham.
Off B1256 at N of town.
Parkland course.
18 holes, 6272 yds. S.S.S. 71
Course designed by Dr. McKenzie.
Visitors welcome.
Green Fees. Weekdays £4.50; weekends £5.50 (£3.50 with member).
Society Meetings welcome weekdays only.
Hotels: The King's Head, Darlington.
Bar snacks served; meals by arrangement.

U 33 Dinsdale Spa

Tel. Dinsdale 332222
Middleton-St.-George, Darlington, Co. Durham DL2 1DW.
5 miles SE of Darlington.
Meadowland course.
18 holes, 6044 yds. S.S.S. 69
Visitors welcome on weekdays.
Green Fees. £4.50 (£3.50 with member).
Society Meetings Wed., Thurs. and Fri
Hotels: Devonport, Middleton-on-Row; Croft Spa, Croft.
Meals served except Mon.

U 34 Dunnerholme

Tel. Dalton-in-Furness 62675
Askam-in-Furness, Cumbria.
A590 to Dalton then A595 for 3 miles N.
Seaside course.
10 holes, 6101 yds. S.S.S. 69
Visitors welcome.
Green Fees. Weekdays £2.00; weekends and bank holidays £3.00.
Society Meetings welcome.

Hotels: Wellington; Clarence House, Dalton-in-Furness.
Meals served on Sun.

U 35 Dunstanburgh

Tel. Embleton 672
Embleton, Alnwick, Northumberland.
Off A1, 8 miles NE of Alnwick.
Seaside course.
18 holes, 6308 yds. S.S.S. 70
Visitors welcome.
Green Fees. Weekdays £3.50; weekends £5.00.
Hotels: Dunstanburgh Castle, Embleton.
Meals served by arrangement.

U 36 Durham City

Tel. Durham (0385) 780069
Littleburn, Langley Moor, Durham DH7 8HL.
Off A690 2 miles SW of Durham City.
Meadowland, parkland course.
18 holes, 6070 yds. S.S.S. 69
Visitors welcome.
Green Fees. Weekdays £3.00 (£1.50 with member); weekends £4.00 (£2.00 with member); plus V.A.T.
Society Meetings by arrangement.
Hotels: Royal County; Three Tuns; Redhills, Durham City.
Lunches, snacks, high teas served. Evening meals served Tues., Fri. and Sat.

U 37 Eaglescliffe

Tel. Eaglescliffe 780098
Yarm Rd., Eaglescliffe, Stockton-on-Tees, Cleveland.
2 miles N of Yarm.
Undulating course.
18 holes, 6242 yds. S.S.S. 71
Course designed by J. Braid and H. Cotton.
Visitors welcome weekdays only.
Green Fees. Weekdays £5.00 (£3.00 with member); weekends £7.00 (£4.00 with member).
Society Meetings weekdays only.
Hotels: The Grange, Stockton-on-Tees; Post House, Thornaby-on-Tees; Parkmore, Eaglescliffe.
Meals served by arrangement except Mon.

U 38 Furness

Tel. Barrow-in-Furness (0229) 41232
Central Dr., Walney Island, Barrow-in-Furness, Cumbria LA14 3LN.
A590 to Barrow, across bridge to Walney Island.
Seaside course.
18 holes, 6400 yds. S.S.S. 70
Visitors welcome.
Green Fees. Weekdays £3.00; weekends £4.00.
Society Meetings welcome.
Hotels: Victoria Park Hotel; Imperial, Barrow.
Meals served by arrangement.

U 39 Garesfield

Tel. Ebchester (0207) 661378
Chopwell, Newcastle upon Tyne NE17 7AP.
A694 to Rowlands Gill, follow signs to Chopwell, 10 miles SW of Newcastle.
Undulating parkland course.

18 holes, 6809 yds. S.S.S. 73
Visitors welcome.
Green Fees. Weekdays £4.00 (£2.50 with member); weekends and bank holidays £6.00 (£3.00 with member).
Society Meetings welcome.
Hotels: In Newcastle upon Tyne.
Meals served by arrangement.

U 40   Gosforth

Tel. Gosforth 853495
Broadway East, Gosforth, Newcastle upon Tyne NE3 5ER.
On A1 3 miles N of city centre.
Parkland course.
36 holes, 5980 yds. S.S.S. 69
Green Fees. Weekdays £5.00 per day; weekends £8.00 per day.
Society Meetings by arrangement.
Hotels: Gosforth Park Hotel, Newcastle.
Snacks, lunches and high teas served except Mon.

U 41   Grange Fell

Tel. Grange-over-Sands (04484) 2536
Fell Rd., Grange-over-Sands, Cumbria LA11 6AH.
Off A590, 14 miles SW of Kendal 1 mile from town centre.
Downland course.
9 holes, 5278 yds. S.S.S. 66
Visitors welcome.
Green Fees. Weekdays £2.50; weekends £4.00; weekly (Mon. to Fri.) £9.00.
Society Meetings welcome, max. 40.
Hotels: Netherwood; Grange; Greyrigge.
Limited catering.

U 42   Grange-over-Sands

Tel. Grange-over-Sands (04484) 3180
Meathop Rd., Grange-over-Sands, Cumbria LA11 6QX.
Off A590, 14 miles SW of Kendal.
Parkland course.
18 holes, 5616 yds. S.S.S. 68
Visitors welcome.
Green Fees. Weekdays £2.00; weekends £3.00.
Society Meetings welcome.
Hotels: Grange; Netherwood; Commodore; Cumbria Grand.
Snacks served; high teas by arrangement.

U 43   Hartlepool

Tel. Hartlepool (0429) 74398
Hart Warren, Hartlepool, Cleveland.
King Oswy Dr., off A1086 at N end of town.
Seaside course.
18 holes, 5998 yds. S.S.S. 69
Visitors welcome if members of recognized clubs.
Green Fees. Weekdays £5.00 (£3.00 with member); weekends £6.50 (£4.00 with member); weekly £20.00.
Hotels: Grand, Hartlepool; Staincliffe Hotel, Seaton Carew.
Meals by arrangement except Mon.

U 44   Hexham

Tel. Hexham (0434) 3072
Spital Park, Hexham, Northumberland NE46 3RZ.

On A69, 1 mile W of Hexham town centre.
Parkland course.
18 holes, 6228 yds. S.S.S. 70
Course designed by C. F. Cotton.
Visitors welcome.
Green Fees. Weekdays £4.50; weekends £5.50.
Society Meetings by arrangement except Sun.
Hotels: Beaumont, Hexham; George, Chollerford.
Meals served except Fri.

U 45   Houghton-le-Spring

Tel. Houghton-le-Spring 841198
Copt Hill, Houghton-le-Spring, Tyne & Wear DH5 8LE.
On A1085, 1½ miles from Houghton-le-Spring.
Undulating meadowland course.
18 holes, 6213 yds. S.S.S. 70
Visitors welcome on weekdays, weekends with member only.
Green Fees. Weekdays £4.00 (£3.00 with member); weekends and bank holidays £5.00 with member only.
Society Meetings weekdays by arrangement.
Hotels: Ramside, Durham; White Lion, Houghton-le-Spring.
Meals served by arrangement.

U 46   Kendal

Tel. Kendal (0539) 24079
The Heights, Kendal, Cumbria.
To Kendal via M6 and A6; signposted to club.
Undulating course.
18 holes, 5483 yds. S.S.S. 67
Visitors welcome.
Green Fees. Weekdays £2.75 (£1.50 with member); weekends £4.00 (£2.50 with member).
Society Meetings welcome.
Hotels: Kendal; Woolpack.
Meals served except Mon.

U 47   Keswick

Tel. Keswick (0596) 72147 or Threlkeld (059 683) 324
Threlkeld Hall, Keswick, Cumbria CA12.
4 miles E of Keswick on A66.
Moorland course, partly tree-lined.
10 holes, 3200 yds. S.S.S. 67
Course designed by Eric Brown.
Visitors welcome, except competition days.
Green Fees. Weekdays £2.50 per day; weekends and bank holidays £3.50 per day.
Society Meetings will be welcomed as facilities improve.
Hotels: White Horse Inn, Scales. Many hotels and guesthouses in area offer free midweek golf on this course.
Catering facilities.

U 48   Kirkby Lonsdale

Casterton Rd., Kirkby Lonsdale, Cumbria 5NL 24Y.
A683 (Sedbergh road) off A65 ½mile. 15 miles SE of Kendal.
Meadowland course.
9 holes, 4028 yds. S.S.S. 60
Visitors welcome.
Green Fees. £1.00.
Hotels: Pheasant, Casterton; Royal, Kirkby.

U 49   Magdalene Fields

Berwick-upon-Tweed.
5 minutes' walk from town centre.
Seaside course (parkland fairways).
18 holes, 6551 yds. S.S.S. 71
Green Fees. Adults £2.50 per day, juniors £1.25 per day; adults weekly £14.00; season ticket £45.00.
Hotels: Kings Arms; Ravensholme Guest House, Berwick.

U 50   Maryport

Tel. Maryport 2605
Bank End, Maryport, Cumbria.
On B5300 off A596, 1½ miles N of Maryport.
Seaside course.
11 holes, 6216 yds. S.S.S. 71
Visitors welcome.
Green Fees. Weekdays £3.00; weekends £5.00.
Hotels: Waverley; Sandpiper.

U 51   Middlesbrough

Tel. Middlesbrough (0642) 316430
Brass Castle Lane, Marton, Middlesbrough, Cleveland.
On A172 5 miles S of Middlesbrough.
Undulating parkland course.
18 holes, 6106 yds. S.S.S. 69
Visitors welcome with letter of introduction or with reservation.
Green Fees. Weekdays £6.00 per day; weekends £10.00 per day.
Society Meetings Wed. before 2.30p.m., Thurs. and Fri.
Hotels: Marton Country Club; Post House.
Meals served; full catering.

U 52   Middlesbrough Municipal

Ladgate Lane, Middlesbrough, Cleveland.
3 miles from Middlesbrough.
Undulating parkland course.
18 holes, 6500 yds. S.S.S. 72
Visitors welcome.
Green Fees. Weekdays £1.75 per round, juniors & O.A.P.s £1.25 per round; weekends £2.50 per round.
Society Meetings by arrangement.
Hotels: Marton Country Club, Marton; Bluebell, Acklam; Post House, Teesside.
Meals served.

U 53   Morpeth

Tel. Morpeth 512065
The Common, Morpeth, Northumberland NE61 2BT.
On A197, 1 mile S of Morpeth.
Undulating course.
18 holes, 6222 yds. S.S.S. 70
Visitors welcome.
Green Fees. Weekdays £5.50 (£3.00 with member); weekends and bank holidays £7.00 (£3.75 with member); weekly £20.00; fortnightly £30.00.
Society Meetings Wed., Thurs., Fri. only.
Hotels: Queen's Head.
Meals served by arrangement except Mon., Tues.

U 54 Newbiggin-by-the-Sea

Tel. Newbiggin 344
Newbiggin-by-the-Sea, Northumberland.
On A197, 9 miles E of Morpeth.
Seaside course.
18 holes, 6444 yds. S.S.S. 71
Visitors welcome.
Green Fees. Weekdays £3.50; weekends
£5.50; weekly £14.00.
Society Meetings by arrangement.
Hotels: In Newbiggin-by-the-Sea.
Meals served by arrangement.

U 55 Newcastle United

Tel. Newcastle upon Tyne 864693
60 Ponteland Road, Cowgate, Newcastle
upon Tyne, Northumberland.
1 mile N of city centre.
Moorland course.
18 holes, 6490 yds. S.S.S. 71
Visitors welcome except at weekends.
Green Fees. Weekdays £4.60.

U 56 Northumberland

Tel. Wideopen (089 426) 2009/2498
High Gosforth Park, Newcastle upon Tyne
NE3 5HT.
Just off A1, 4 miles N of city centre.
Heathland, parkland course.
18 holes, 6640 yds. S.S.S. 72
Visitors welcome with member or letter of
introduction; weekends with reservation.
Green Fees. £7.00 per round, £9.00 per
day.
Hotels: Gosforth Park Hotel adjacent to
club.
Lunches served except Mon; dinners except
Sun. and Mon. in summer, Wed. and Sat. only
in winter.

U 57 Penrith

Tel. Penrith 62217
Salkeld Rd., Penrith, Cumbria CA11 8SG.
1 mile NE of Penrith, ⅓ mile from A6.
Parkland course.
18 holes, 6026 yds. S.S.S. 69
Visitors welcome if members of a
recognized club.
Green Fees. Weekdays £4.00 per day;
weekends £5.00 per day.
Hotels: Edenhall; George; Abbotsford.
Meals served except Mon. and Tues.

U 58 Ponteland

Tel. Ponteland 22689
53 Bell Villas, Ponteland, Newcastle upon
Tyne, NE20 9BD.
On A696, 5 miles NW of Newcastle, 1 mile
beyond airport.
Parkland course.
18 holes, 6518 yds. S.S.S. 71
Visitors welcome on weekdays.
Green Fees. Weekdays £7.00 (£2.30 with
member).
Society Meetings by arrangement.
Hotels: Airport Hotel, Woolsington.
Lunches and dinners served by arrangement.

U 59 Prudhoe

Tel. Prudhoe 32466
Eastwood Park, Prudhoe, Northumberland.
On A695, 10 miles W of Newcastle.
Parkland course.
18 holes, 5507 yds. S.S.S. 67
Visitors welcome on weekdays.
Green Fees. £5.00.
Society Meetings weekdays by
arrangement.
Hotels: Duke of Wellington; Riding Mill.
Meals served.

U 60 Ravensworth

Tel. Low Fell (0632) 872843
Moss Heaps, Wrekenton, Gateshead, Tyne &
Wear NE9 7UU.
Off A1, 2 miles S of Gateshead.
Moorland, parkland course.
18 holes, 5872 yds. S.S.S. 68
Visitors welcome.
Green Fees. Weekdays £4.00 (£2.50 with
member); weekends £5.00 (£3.50 with
member); plus V.A.T.
Society Meetings by arrangement.
Hotels: Five Bridges; Springfield,
Gateshead.
Meals served by arrangement.

U 61 Rothbury

Tel. Rothbury 20718
Race Course, Rothbury, Morpeth,
Northumberland NE65 7UB.
Off A697, 15 miles NE of Morpeth.
Meadowland course.
9 holes, 5586 yds. S.S.S. 67
Visitors welcome.
Green Fees. Weekdays £1.50 per day;
weekends £3.00 per day; season, gents
£15.00, ladies £9.00.
Society Meetings by arrangement.
Hotels: Queen's Head; Coquetvale; Nole
House.

U 62 Ryton

Tel. Ryton 3737
Dr. Stanners, Clara-vale, Ryton, Tyne &
Wear.
Off A695, 7 miles W of Newcastle.
Parkland course.
9 holes, 2969 yds. S.S.S. 69
Visitors welcome weekdays, weekends
with member only.
Green Fees. £3.00 (£2.00 with member).
Society Meetings by arrangement.

U 63 St. Bees

Tel. St. Bees 695
St. Bees, Cumbria.
On B5345, 4 miles S of Whitehaven.
Seaside course.
9 holes, 5026 yds. S.S.S. 64
Visitors welcome.
Green Fees. Weekdays £2.00; weekends
£3.00.
Hotels: Seacote; Manor House Hotel; Albert
Hotel; Queens Hotel.

U 64 Saltburn-by-Sea

Tel. Guisborough 22812
Guisborough Rd., Hob Hill, Saltburn-by-Sea,
Cleveland TS12 1NJ.
1 mile from centre of Saltburn on B1268.
Undulating meadowland course.

18 holes, 5803 yds. S.S.S. 68
Visitors welcome if members of recognized
club.
Green Fees. Weekdays £4.50 per day;
weekends £6.00 per day.
Society Meetings by arrangement.
Snacks served on Mon.; meals by
arrangement Tues. to Sun.

U 65 Seaham

Tel. Seaham 812354
Shrewsbury St., Dawdon, Seaham, Co.
Durham.
Off A19, 6 miles S of Sunderland.
Undulating meadowland course.
18 holes, 5969 yds. S.S.S. 69
Visitors welcome on weekdays, weekends
with member only.
Green Fees. Weekdays £4.00 per day
(£2.50 with member); weekends £5.00
(£4.00 with member).
Society Meetings by arrangement.
Hotels: Sea View Hotel.
Meals served.

U 66 Seahouses

Breadnell Rd., Seahouses, Northumberland
NE68 7YT.
Seaside course.
18 holes, 5370 yds. S.S.S. 68
Visitors welcome.
Green Fees. Weekdays £2.00 per day;
weekends £3.50.
Society Meetings welcome.
Hotels: Bamburgh Castle Hotel, Bamburgh.

U 67 Seascale

Tel. Seascale 28202
The Banks, Seascale, Cumbria CA20 1QH.
B5344 off A595, 12 miles S of Whitehaven.
Seaside course.
18 holes, 6307 yds. S.S.S. 70
Course designed by Willie Campbell.
Visitors welcome on weekdays, weekends
by arrangement.
Green Fees. Weekdays £5.00; weekends
£6.00.
Society Meetings by arrangement.
Hotels: Scawfell; Wansfell; Calder House;
Seafield.
Meals served except Tues.

U 68 Seaton Carew

Tel. Hartlepool (0429) 66249
Tees Rd., Seaton Carew, Hartlepool,
Cleveland TS25 1DE.
Off A689, 3 miles S of Hartlepool.
Seaside links course.
Old Course 18 holes, 6613 yds. S.S.S. 72
New Course 18 holes, 6876 yds. S.S.S. 73
Visitors welcome.
Green Fees. Weekdays £5.00; weekends
£7.00.
Society Meetings welcome. Special rates
for parties of 12 or more.
Hotels: Seaton; Marine; Staincliffe.
Meals served.

U 69 Sedbergh

The Riggs, Sedbergh, Cumbria.
5 miles E of M6 exit 37, ½ mile S of town.
Undulating moorland course.

Silloth—Cumbrian retreat

The radio by my bedside issued the usual flow of gale warnings, a suggestion of snow in Scotland and the threat of rain farther south. November is, of course, not a month when a golfer normally expects to explore and a special journey to Cumberland was therefore something of a risk, but whatever the meteorological state of the rest of Britain may have been, Carlisle was fine and a much delayed visit to Silloth-on-Solway was, after all, blessed with sun.

It is perhaps because Silloth is not on a direct route to anywhere, nestling un-suspectedly on the southern shores of the Solway Firth, that it is not more widely known. But its quiet position is undoubtedly its greatest charm and once the form of the long, low clubhouse has greeted one opposite the giant flour mill and the quaint harbour that serves it, it is quickly evident that it is a course of exceptionally natural qualities and of a class fit for a championship.

The small band of Carlisle businessmen made an inspired decision when they founded the Carlisle and Silloth Golf Club in 1892 (now known as the Silloth-on-Solway Golf Club), for the exacting duneland, beset with heather, gorse and all manner of golfing evils, needed no real architectural genius. It was, as General Moncrieff said of Westward Ho!, 'designed by Providence'.

Much of the club's early fame was spread by the rare talents of Cecil Leitch, daughter of the local doctor, and her four sisters who seem to have been very nearly as good and

who, in their teens, formed the basis of the local team. Legend has it that they alighted one day from the coach for a match at some club in the Borders where their presence was presumed to be in the roles of caddies; that is, until each had won a match. Silloth had scored a resounding success and their male hosts were left a picture of embarrassed con-fusion.

The club's link with Cecil Leitch, four times British Women's champion, is certainly one that has prompted many a journey to these parts, but such nostalgia is far from the only reason and before hitting a single stroke, the prospect from the 1st tee of interesting undulations and glorious Cumberland turf is so enticing that it is easy to understand why men with no Cumbrian traces in their voices speak longingly of it.

Here is a traditional seaside links of subtlety, entertainment and distinction, not perhaps long by modern transatlantic stan-dards but quite demanding enough in a prevailing wind that blows up the Firth to test the imagination of those seeking to master it. A reflection of its quality is gathered from its staging of the 1976 British Women's championship.

As ever by the sea, command of flight is essential in perfecting the second to a lovely plateau green at the 3rd, in finding the 4th where nature spurns the use of bunkers, or in achieving a five at the long 5th which sweeps majestically away along the sands. The 7th is a fine, old-fashioned, slightly blind hole with

its green in a dell and the 9th, one of four admirable short holes, can vary alarmingly according to the wind.

The farthest point has now been reached and the 10th, an attractive dogleg, where the hope of a three more often than not brings the reality of a five, starts the turn for home, but in a strong north-easterly wind that is not uncommon in the winter, the longer inward half offers no relief.

Exciting strokes, such as the second at the 13th between two prominent heathery banks to a green perched on a precarious shoulder against the skyline, continue to abound and one would never be entirely at ease in a scoring competition until the 14th, back parallel with the 13th, has been safely passed.

By then, ambition and hope may have been destroyed and the places most familiar may be those unprescribed and unrecommended parts in the midst of the impenetrable bordering country—a colourful picture none the less when in full bloom. Yet for all that, there is much compensation in the thought of trying again and in the beauty of more distant surroundings.

The lakeland hills to the south; to the north the pleasant green fields beyond the outline of the old town, and away across the shining Firth, Southerness—another golfing delight of the Solway—and the lowland peaks of Scotland. Silloth's appeal is endless.

---

9 holes, 2200 yds. S.S.S. 61 (for 18 holes)
Visitors welcome.
Green Fees. 50p per day; weekly £2.00. Half rates for juniors.
Hotels: Bull Hotel.

U 70   Silecroft

Silecroft, Millom, Cumbria LA18 4AG.
8 miles N of Broughton in Furness at junction of A595 and A5093. Through village towards shore; turn left before caravan site.
Seaside course.
9 holes, 5627 yds. S.S.S. 66
Visitors welcome on weekdays.
Green Fees. Weekdays £1.50 per day; weekends £2.00 per day.
Hotels: Miners Arms.

U 71   Silloth on Solway

Tel. Silloth 31179/31304
Silloth, Carlisle, Cumbria CA4 4DG.
B5302 off A596 at Wigton, 18 miles W of Carlisle.
Undulating seaside course.
18 holes, 6343 yds. S.S.S. 70
Visitors welcome.
Green Fees. Weekdays £4.50 (£3.00 with member); weekends £6.50 per day (£5.00 with member); weekly (Mon. to Fri.) £15.00; juniors half the above rates.
Hotels: Golf; Queen's; Skinburness.
Meals served by arrangement.

U 72   South Moor

Tel. Stanley 32848
The Middles, Craghead, Stanley, Co. Durham.

On B6313, 1½ miles SE of Stanley.
Moorland course.
18 holes, 6445 yds. S.S.S. 71
Visitors welcome.
Green Fees. Weekdays £4.00 per day (£1.50 per round with member); weekends £5.00 per day (£2.00 per round with member); weekly £15.00; fortnightly £20.00.
Society Meetings welcome.
Lunches served except Mon.

U 73   South Shields

Tel. South Shields 568942
Hillcrest, Cleadon Hills, South Shields, Tyne & Wear.
A19, turn off at Quarry Lane, near Cleadon Chimney.
Seaside course.

18 holes, 6264 yds. S.S.S. 70
Visitors welcome.
Green Fees. Weekdays £4.00 (£2.50 with member); weekends £6.00 (£3.00 with member).
Society Meetings Thurs. by arrangement.
Hotels: Sea Hotel; New Crown; Marsden Inn.
Meals served by arrangement.

U 74 Stocksfield

Tel. Stocksfield 3101 (clubhouse), 3041 (office)
New Ridley Rd., Stocksfield, Northumberland NE43 7RE.
Off A695, 1 mile S of Stocksfield.
Parkland, woodland course.
18 holes, 6052 yds. S.S.S. 70
Course designed by Cotton (C.K.), Pennink, Lawrie and Partners.
Visitors welcome.
Green Fees. Weekdays £3.00 (£2.00 with member); weekends £5.00 (£2.00 with member).
Society Meetings welcome weekdays, weekends by arrangement.
Hotels: Angel, Corbridge; Royal; Beaumont; County, Hexham.
Snacks served; meals by arrangement.

U 75 Stony Holme

St. Aidans Road, Carlisle.
Off A69.
Meadowland course.
9 holes, 3003 yds. S.S.S. 69
Course designed by Frank Pennink of Cotton (C.K.), Pennink, Lawrie and Partners.
Visitors welcome.
Green Fees. 75p per round, juniors and O.A.P.s 50p.
Meals served.

U 76 Stressholme

Tel. Darlington 61002
Snipe Lane, Darlington, Co. Durham.
Off Grange Rd., Darlington.
Parkland course.
18 holes, 6511 yds. S.S.S. 71
Course designed by Cotton (C.K.), Pennink, Lawrie and Partners.
Visitors welcome.
Green Fees. Weekdays £2.40 per round; weekends £3.25 per round; practice ground 60p.
Hotels: Europa Lodge Hotel.

U 77 Teesside

Tel. Stockton (0642) 66249
Acklam Rd., Thornaby, Stockton, Cleveland.
Off A19 S of Stockton at Thornaby/Acklam interchange.
Meadowland course.
18 holes, 6472 yds. S.S.S. 71
Course designed by C. Robertson (1901/8); altered 1980.
Visitors welcome; weekends after 11 a.m.
Green Fees. Weekdays £4.00 (£3.00 with member); weekends £7.50 (£5.00 with member).
Hotels: Swallow, Stockton; Golden Eagle, Thornaby; Dragonara, Middlesbrough.
Full catering except Mon.

U 78 Tynedale

Tyne Green, Hexham, Northumberland.
½ mile from town centre next to river Tyne.
Meadowland course.
9 holes, 5706 yds. S.S.S. 68
Visitors welcome.
Green Fees. Weekdays £1.50 per day; weekends and bank holidays £2.00 per day.
Hotels: Beaumont; County; Royal.

U 79 Tynemouth

Tel. North Shields 574578
Spital Dene, Tynemouth, North Shields, Tyne & Wear NE30 2ER.
On A1058, 7 miles E of Newcastle.
Parkland, meadowland course.
18 holes, 6283 yds. S.S.S. 70
Visitors welcome.
Green Fees. Weekdays £5.50 (£3.00 with member); weekends £6.50 (£3.50 with member).
Hotels: Park Hotel; Grand.
Lunches and snacks served except Mon.

U 80 Tyneside

Tel. Ryton-on-Tyne (089 422) 2742
Westfield Lane, Ryton, Tyne & Wear.
On A695, 6 miles W of Newcastle.
Meadowland course.
18 holes, 6029 yds. S.S.S. 69
Course designed by H.S. Colt.
Visitors welcome.
Green Fees. Weekdays £4.00; weekends £6.00.
Society Meetings by arrangement.
Hotels: Ryton Country Club, Ryton; Hedgefield, Blaydon.
Meals served.

U 81 Ulverston

Tel. Ulverston (0229) 52824
Bardsea Park, Ulverston, Cumbria LA12 9QJ.
On A5087, 2 miles S of Ulverston.
Undulating parkland course.
18 holes, 6092 yds. S.S.S. 69
Course designed by W.H. Colt (1909/10).
Visitors welcome weekdays before 5p.m. if members of recognized club. Parties by arrangement.
Green Fees. Weekdays £4.80 (£2.50 with member); weekends £6.50 (£3.50 with member).
Society Meetings by arrangement.
Hotels: Fisherman's Arms, Baycliffe; Farmer's Arms, Lowick; Lonsdale House, Ulverston.
Lunches and snacks served except Mon. Dinners by arrangement.

U 82 Wallsend

Tel. Wallsend 621973
Biggles Main, Wallsend, Tyne & Wear.
Off A1058, turn N at Wallsend boundary.
Parkland course.
18 holes, 6601 yds. S.S.S. 72
Course designed by G. Snowball.
Visitors welcome.
Green Fees. Weekdays £3.85 (£2.75 with member), juniors £2.05 (£1.40 with

member); weekends and bank holidays £6.85 (£4.60 with member), juniors £3.40 (£2.25 with member).
Hotels: Europa.

U 83 Warkworth

Tel. Warkworth 596
Warkworth, Morpeth, Northumberland.
Off A1068, 14 miles NE of Morpeth.
Seaside course.
9 holes, 5817 yds. S.S.S. 68
Visitors welcome.
Hotels: Warkworth House Hotel.

U 84 Wearside

Tel. Hylton 2518
Coxgreen, Sunderland, Tyne & Wear SR4 9JT.
2 miles W of Sunderland on A183.
Meadowland, parkland course.
18 holes, 6315 yds. S.S.S. 70
Visitors welcome with reservation if members of recognized club.
Green Fees. Weekdays £4.50 (£3.00 with member); weekends £6.00 (£3.00 with member).
Society Meetings welcome weekdays except evenings.
Hotels: Post House, Washington; Mowbray Park, Sunderland.
Meals served.

U 85 Westerhope

Tel. Newcastle (0632) 869125
Whorlton Grange, Westerhope, Newcastle upon Tyne NE5 1PP.
5 miles W of Newcastle; airport road for 3 miles then follow signs to Westerhope.
Parkland course.
18 holes, 6407 yds. S.S.S. 71
Visitors welcome.
Green Fees. Weekdays £5.50 (£3.50 with member); weekends £6.50 (£4.00 with member).
Society Meetings welcome weekdays only.
Hotels: Denton; Airport Hotel; Gosforth Park Hotel.
Lunches and high teas served except Mon.

U 86 Whickham

Tel. Whickham 887309
Hollinside Park, Whickham, Newcastle upon Tyne NE16 5BA.
5 miles SW of Newcastle.
Undulating parkland course.
18 holes, 6076 yds. S.S.S. 69
Visitors welcome.
Green Fees. Weekdays £5.00; weekends £7.50.
Society Meetings by arrangement.
Hotels: Springfield, Gateshead.
Lunches and teas served.

U 87 Whitburn

Tel. Whitburn 292144
Lizard Lane, South Shields, Tyne & Wear NE34 7AF.
Off Sunderland to South Shields coast road.
Parkland course.
18 holes, 6027 yds. S.S.S. 69
Visitors welcome.

Green Fees. Weekdays £4.00 (£3.00 with member); weekends £7.00 (£5.00 with member).
Society Meetings weekdays by arrangement.
Hotels: Seaburn Hotel; Roker Hotel, Sunderland.
Meals served before 6.00p.m. by arrangement.

U 88 Whitley Bay

Tel. Whitley Bay (089 44) 20180
Claremont Rd., Whitley Bay, Tyne & Wear NE26 3UF.
On A183, 10 miles NE of Newcastle.
Undulating seaside course.
18 holes, 6712 yds. S.S.S. 72
Visitors welcome on weekdays.
Green Fees. Weekdays £6.00 (£3.00 with member); weekends £4.50 with member only.
Society Meetings welcome on weekdays.
Hotels: in Whitley Bay.
Meals served by arrangement except Mon.

U 89 Wilton

Tel. Easton Grange 465265
Wilton Castle, Redcar, Cleveland TS10 4QY.
Off A174, 6 miles E of Middlesbrough.
Parkland course.
18 holes, 6068 yds. S.S.S. 69
Visitors welcome except Sat. and weekday evenings.
Green Fees. Weekdays £5.00 (£2.80 with member).
Hotels: Queen, Saltburn; Marton Country Club, Middlesbrough.
Snack lunches served except Sun.

U 90 Windermere

Tel. Windermere (096 62) 3123
Cleabarrow, Windermere, Cumbria LA23 3NB.
1½ miles E of Bowness-on-Windermere on B5284.
Undulating parkland course.
18 holes, 4940 yds. S.S.S. 65
Visitors welcome.
Green Fees. Weekdays £5.00 (£2.50 with member); weekends £6.50 (£3.25 with member).
Society Meetings by arrangement.
Hotels: many nearby.
Meals served except Mon.

U 91 Workington

Tel. Workington 3460
Branthwaite Rd., Workington, Cumbria CA14 NW.
Off A595, 1 mile E of Workington.
Undulating meadowland course.
18 holes, 6250 yds. S.S.S. 70
Course designed by James Braid.
Visitors welcome, parties with reservation.
Green Fees. Weekdays £5.00 (£2.60 with member); weekends £6.20 (£4.00 with member).
Society Meetings weekdays by arrangement.
Hotels: Westland Hotel.
Meals served except Mon.

V Lothians, Borders, Dumfries & Galloway

V 1 Baberton

Tel. 031-441 2511
Baberton Ave., Juniper Green, Edinburgh EH14 5DU.
Parkland course.
18 holes, 6140 yds. S.S.S. 69
Visitors welcome with member only.
Green Fees. On application to Secretary.
Society Meetings by arrangement.
Meals served by arrangement.

V 2 Bathgate

Tel. Bathgate 52232; Secretary, 630505
Edinburgh Rd., Bathgate, W. Lothian.
400 yards from Post Office.
Moorland course.
18 holes, 6300 yds. S.S.S. 70
Visitors welcome.
Green Fees. Weekdays £4.00; weekends £6.00.
Society Meetings by arrangement.
Hotels: Golden Circle; Dreadnought.
Meals served by arrangement.

V 3 Braids United

Tel. 031-447 3327
Braid Hills Approach, Edinburgh EH10.
A702 from city centre.
Hillside courses.
(1) 18 holes, 5731 yds. S.S.S. 68
(2) 18 holes, 4832 yds. S.S.S. 63
Visitors welcome except Sun.
Green Fees. £1.80 per round.
Hotels: Braid Hills Hotel.

V 4 Broomieknowe

Tel. 031-663 9317
Golf Course Rd., Bonnyrigg, Midlothian.
7 miles SE of Edinburgh. A7 to Eskbank roundabout, 1 mile.
Parkland/meadowland course.
18 holes, 6046 yds. S.S.S. 69
Course designed by Ben Sayers.
Visitors welcome.
Green Fees. Weekdays £4.00 per round, £6.00 per day; weekends £5.50 per round.
Society Meetings welcome on weekdays.
Hotels: Melville Castle Hotel; Derry Motel, Eskbank; Dalhousie Castle Hotel, Bonnyrigg.
Meals served except Mon.

V 5 Bruntsfield Links

Tel. 031-336 2006
Barnton Ave., Edinburgh EH4 6JH.
Off A90 to Davidson's Mains.
Parkland course.
18 holes, 6402 yds. S.S.S. 71
Course designed by James Braid.
Visitors welcome with member or letter of introduction.
Green Fees. £6.00 per round, £7.00 per day; weekends £8.00.
Society Meetings by arrangement.
Hotels: Barnton; Eurocrest; Learmonth; Queensway.
Meals served.

V 6 Carrickvale

Tel. 031-337 1932
Carrick Knowe Municipal Golf Course, Glendevon Park, Edinburgh EH12 5VZ.
18 holes, 6299 yds. S.S.S. 70

V 7 Castle Douglas

Tel. Castle Douglas 2801
Abercromby Rd., Castle Douglas, Kirkcudbrightshire.
Parkland course.
9 holes, 5408 yds. S.S.S. 66
Visitors welcome except after 4.30 p.m. on Tues. and Thurs.
Green Fees. £2.00 per round or day.
Hotels: in Castle Douglas.

V 8 Colvend

Sandyhills, Dalbeattie, Kirkcudbrightshire DG5 4LN.
Off A710, 5 miles SE of Dalbeattie.
Hilly seaside course.
9 holes, 4206 yds. S.S.S. 61
Visitors welcome.
Green Fees. £2.00 per day.
Society Meetings by arrangement.

V 9 Craigmillar Park

Tel. 031-667 2837
Observatory Rd., Edinburgh EH9 3HG.
A702 from city centre, left at Morningside to Blackford station.
Parkland course.
18 holes, 5775 yds. S.S.S. 68
Visitors welcome.
Green Fees. On application to secretary.
Society Meetings by arrangement.
Hotels: Oratava Hotel.
Meals served.

V 10 Dalmahoy Country Club

Tel. 031-333 1845
Kirknewton, Midlothian EH27 8EB.
7 miles W of Edinburgh on A71.
Parkland courses.
East 18 holes, 6664 yds. S.S.S. 72
West 18 holes, 5212 yds. S.S.S. 66
Course designed by James Braid.
Visitors welcome.
Green Fees. Tel. 031-333 2055/1436.
Society Meetings by arrangement.
Hotels: Dalmahoy House Hotel and Country Club; Dalmahoy Hotel.
Meals served and full accommodation available.

V 11 Duddingston

Tel. 031-661 7688
Duddingston Rd. West, Edinburgh EH15 3QD.
A1 from Edinburgh to Duddingston crossroads, turn right.
Parkland course.
18 holes, 6647 yds. S.S.S. 72
Visitors welcome.
Green Fees. Weekdays £4.60 per round, £6.90 per day; weekends £6.90 per round.
Society Meetings by arrangement.
Hotels: Lady Nairne; Duddingston House Motel.
Meals served by arrangement.

V 12 Dumfries & County

Tel. Dumfries (0387) 3585
Nunfield, Dumfries D91 1JX.
1 mile out of Dumfries on Edinburgh road.
Parkland course.
18 holes, 5884 yds. S.S.S. 68

Visitors welcome.
Green Fees. Weekdays £5.00 (£1.25 with member); weekends £7.00 (£1.50 with member).
Society Meetings by arrangement.
Hotels: Station; County; Cairndale.
Meals served.

V 13 Dumfries & Galloway

Tel. Dumfries (0387) 3582
Laurieston Ave., Dumfries DG2 7NY.
On A75 W of Dumfries.
Parkland course.
18 holes, 5782 yds. S.S.S. 68
Visitors welcome.
Green Fees. Weekdays £4.00; weekends £6.00; reduced fees Nov.-March.
Society Meetings welcome on weekdays except Fri.
Hotels: Cairndale; County; Dalston.
Full catering except Mon.

V 14 Dunbar

Tel. Dunbar 62317
East Links, Dunbar, E. Lothian EH42 1LT.
On seaside at E end of Dunbar, 30 miles E of Edinburgh.
Seaside course.
18 holes, 6441 yds. S.S.S. 71
Visitors welcome on weekdays, not before 10.15 a.m. or between 12.00 noon and 2.30 p.m. at weekends.
Green Fees. Weekdays £5.50 (£1.00 with member); weekends £7.50 (£2.00 with member).
Society Meetings welcome.
Morning coffees, lunches, snacks and high teas served (last orders 6 p.m.).

V 15 Duns

Tel. Duns 2794
Secretary, 8 Trinity Park, Duns, Berwickshire.

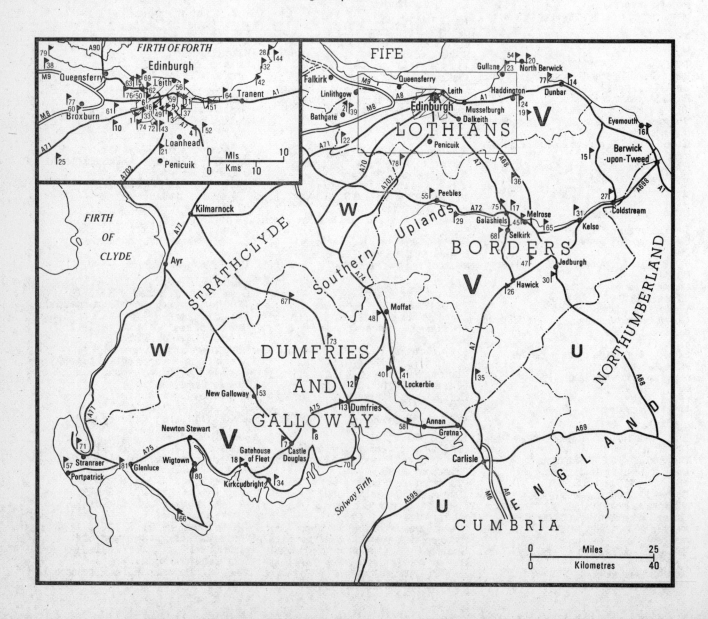

Four links in one

Whenever the question of a centre for a golfing holiday is raised, Gullane in East Lothian is always one of the first that comes to my mind. If anyone feels so inclined, and has the strength and fitness to match, he can play in delightful surroundings on seven different courses in one day.

More likely, however, he will prefer to take a more leisurely look at each or simply stay and sample those absolutely at his doorstep—Luffness New, and the three Gullanes which lie on the other side of Gullane Hill from Muirfield.

Everyone has courses for which he feels unreasoning affection, and Luffness and Gullane No. 1 are unquestionably two of mine. The incomparable stretch of country on which they stand was introduced to me by a kind uncle during my time at school in Edinburgh when a day at Luffness really was an escape from the problems of Plato and Pythagoras; and my earliest recollections are of gloriously smooth, fast putting greens, a blind short hole across a quarry—and a magnificent lunch.

The short hole, at the point where the main road curves sharply for North Berwick, has long since been given a more straightforward approach, but in attempting to qualify for the 1966 Open championship, held jointly at Luffness and Gullane No. 1, I was glad to see that the course, the greens and the lunch had lost none of their appeal.

To my mind the best holes are those from the 8th onwards down nearer Aberlady Bay, where a sense of peace and beauty is complete and the golfer cannot fail to enjoy himself. On a calm day, the demands made upon him are not all that severe, but it is most important to keep straight.

From Luffness it is perfectly possible to hit a ball across the other two Gullane courses—neither of which suffers by comparison with its celebrated neighbour—to Gullane No.1, and to a stranger the four may at first be indistinguishable from each other. In character they have much in common but the starts at Gullane are a little more mountainous.

However, when the view is as magnificent as it is from the third tee, or even better from the seventh tee on Gullane No. 1, it is worth enduring any climb.

It is one of the great sights in the whole world of golf and except in grey, wet and windswept conditions, the Firth of Forth and its golden sands, the distant outline of Edinburgh and the two Forth Bridges, the green fields of Fife and an assortment of boats slipping out to sea past the Bass Rock, can distract one's thoughts from the golf which at this stage is gaining in challenge.

The 7th, rather like the 8th at Luffness, offers an inviting drive down the hill; the 8th gives the chance of a three and the 9th is an engaging short hole where the eye wanders again across the popular beach to the less exposed setting of Muirfield; but then there are three very fine long holes with which to start the homeward half, the 11th and 12th being particularly satisfying to play well, if one can forget the view.

Another testing short hole in a crosswind follows, and two more long holes which can make or mar a medal round. These take us gradually back up the slope to the short 16th along the crest and, in sight of home, we prepare for the final descent to the clubhouse, outside which the legendary Babe Zaharias was once presented with the British Women's Championship Trophy.

That was thirty years ago, but happily little has changed in the meantime; the starter's bell on the first tee is still a welcome sound; the little village street down which so many famous names have stepped has lost none of its charm, and golfers from all parts still converge upon Gullane, Luffness and the many other courses along that coast because they know the quality and fun of the golf never disappoint.

About 1 mile W of Duns off A6105.
Moorland course.
9 holes, 5754 yds. S.S.S. 68
Visitors welcome.
Green Fees. Weekdays £2.00 per round or day; weekends £3.00 per round or day.
Licensed clubhouse.

V 16 Eyemouth

Tel. Eyemouth 50551
Gunsgreen House, Eyemouth, Berwickshire.
Off A1, 8 miles N of Berwick upon Tweed.
Seaside course.
9 holes, 5028 m. S.S.S. 67
Visitors welcome.
Green Fees. Weekdays £2.00; weekends £3.00.
Meals served by Steward on request.

V 17 Galashiels

Tel. Galashiels 3724
Ladhope Recreation Ground, Galashiels, Selkirkshire.
Hill course.
18 holes, 5309 yds. S.S.S. 67
Green Fees. Weekdays £1.25; Sun. £1.50; juveniles 60p; school children 30p.
Hotels: Maxwell; Royal; Douglas; Waverley.

V 18 Gatehouse

Gatehouse of Fleet, Castle Douglas, Kirkcudbrightshire.
On A75, 19 miles SW of Castle Douglas.
Undulating course.
9 holes, 4798 yds. S.S.S. 63
Visitors welcome.
Green Fees. Weekdays £1.00; weekends £1.50, juniors weekdays 50p; weekends £1.00.
Society Meetings by arrangement.
Hotels: Murray Arms Hotel; Cally Hotel; Anworth Hotel; Angel Hotel; Bank O'Fleet Guest House.

V 19 Gifford

Tel. Gifford 267
Cawdor Cottage, Station Rd., Gifford, E. Lothian EH41 4OL.
4½ miles S of Haddington.
Meadowland.
9 holes, 6138 yds. S.S.S. 69
Visitors welcome except Sun. after 12 noon, Wed. after 4.00 p.m. and 3rd Tues. of each month after 4.00 p.m.
Green Fees. Weekdays £2.50 per day; weekends £2.50 per 18 holes.

Society Meetings weekdays by arrangement.
Hotels: Tweeddale Arms; Goblin Ha' Hotel, Gifford.

V 20 Glen

Tel. N. Berwick (0620) 2111
Tantallon Terr., N. Berwick, E. Lothian.
On A198, 1 mile E of station, 23 miles E of Edinburgh.
Seaside course.
18 holes, 6079 yds. S.S.S. 69
Course designed by MacKenzie Ross.
Visitors welcome.
Society Meetings by arrangement.
Meals served by arrangement.

V 21 Glencorse

Tel. Penicuik (0968) 77177
Milton Bridge, Penicuik, Midlothian.
On A701, 9 miles S of Edinburgh.
Parkland course.
18 holes, 5205 yds. S.S.S. 66
Visitors welcome on weekdays, weekends with reservation.
Green Fees. Weekdays £3.00 per round, £4.00 per day; weekends £4.50 per round or day.

Society Meetings weekdays by arrangement.
Hotels: in S. Edinburgh.
Snacks, lunches and high teas served.

V 22 Greenburn

Tel. Fauldhouse 70292 (clubhouse), 70883 (secretary)
Bridge St, Fauldhouse, W. Lothian.
Midway between Glasgow and Edinburgh.
Turn off M8 at Whitburn, 3 miles.
Moorland course.
18 holes, 6203 yds. S.S.S. 70
Visitors welcome.
Green Fees. Weekdays £3.00 (£1.00 with member); weekends £6.00.
Meals served by arrangement at weekends.

V 23 Gullane

Tel. Gullane (0620) 84 2255
Gullane, E. Lothian EH31 2BB.
on A198, 18 miles E of Edinburgh.
Seaside downland courses.
 (1) 18 holes, 6479 yds. S.S.S. 71
 (2) 18 holes, 6127 yds. S.S.S. 69
 (3) 18 holes, 5012 yds. S.S.S. 64
Visitors welcome.
Green Fees. No. 1 course: weekdays £7.00 per round, £10.00 per day; weekends £9.00 per round, £13.00 per day. No. 2 course: weekdays £4.00 per round, £6.00 per day; weekends £5.00 per round, £7.00 per day. No. 3 course: weekdays £3.00 per round, £4.00 per day; weekends £4.00 per round, £5.00 per day.
Society Meetings by arrangement.
Hotels: Queens; Mallard; Bissets; Golf Inn; Marine (North Berwick).
Meals served except Mon.

V 24 Haddington

Tel. Haddington 3627
Amisfield Park, Haddington, E. Lothian.
17 miles E of Edinburgh on A1.
Parkland course.
18 holes, 6122 yds. S.S.S. 69
Visitors welcome with reservation.
Green Fees. Weekdays £2.70 per round, £4.00 per day; weekends £3.50 per round, £5.50 per day.
Hotels: George.
Meals served.

V 25 Harburn

Tel. West Calder 871256 (members) & 871131 (secretary)
Harburn, West Calder, West Lothian.
2 miles south of West Calder.
Undulating moorland course.
18 holes, 5829 yds. S.S.S. 68
Visitors welcome.
Green Fees. Weekdays £3.50 per round, £4.50 per day; weekends £6.00 per day.
Hotels: West End Hotel, West Calder; Golden Circle, Bathgate.
Lunches and high teas served by arrangement.

V 26 Hawick

Tel. Hawick (0450) 2293
Vertish Hill, Hawick.
On A7.
Hillside course.

18 holes, 5980 yds. S.S.S. 69
Visitors welcome.
Green Fees. Weekdays £4.00; weekends £5.00.
Hotels: in Hawick.
Meals served by arrangement.

V 27 Hirsel

Hirsel, Coldstream, Berwickshire.
On A697, halfway between Newcastle and Edinburgh.
Undulating parkland course.
9 holes, 5656 yds. S.S.S. 67
Visitors welcome.
Green Fees. Weekdays £2.50; weekends £3.50.
Society Meetings by arrangement.
Hotels: Majicado; Castle; Newcastle Arms.
Snacks served at weekends; meals by arrangement.

V 28 Honourable Company of Edinburgh Golfers

Tel. Gullane (0620) 84 2123
Muirfield, Gullane, E. Lothian EH31 2EG.
On A198, 5 miles W of North Berwick.
Links course.
18 holes, 6601 yds.
Visitors welcome if introduced by a member or prior arrangement through own golf club secretary.
Green Fees. Weekdays £8.00 per round, £12.00 per day; weekends £10.00 per round, £15.00 per day.
Society Meetings limited, by arrangement.
Hotels: Marine, North Berwick; Queens; Bissets; Greywalls; Gullane; Open Arms; Dirleton.
Lunches served except Thurs.
No clubhouse facilities for ladies.

V 29 Innerleithen

Leithen Water, Innerleithen, Peeblesshire.
1½ miles from Innerleithen. Off A72, 8 miles SE of Peebles.
Moorland course.
9 holes, 5806 yds. S.S.S. 68
Visitors welcome.
Green Fees. Weekdays £1.00; weekends £1.50.
Society Meetings by arrangement 1 month in advance.
Hotels: Traquair Arms; Leithen.
Meals served by arrangement.

V 30 Jedburgh

Tel. Jedburgh 3587
Dunion Rd., Jedburgh, Roxburghshire.
1 mile W of town centre via Castlegate.
Parkland course.
9 holes, 5492 yds. S.S.S. 67
Visitors welcome.
Green Fees. Weekdays £2.00; weekends £3.00.
Hotels: Glenbank.

V 31 Kelso

Berrymoss, Kelso, Roxburghshire TD5 7LT.
N of Kelso.
Parkland course.
9 holes, 6700 yds. S.S.S. 69
Course designed by James Braid.

Visitors welcome on weekdays.
Green Fees. £1.50 per round, £2.00 per day.
Hotels: Woodside; Ednam House Hotel; Queens Head; House O'Hill Hotel.
An extension to 18 holes is being undertaken at present. Hoped that play will commence April/May 1980.

V 32 Kilspindie

Tel. Aberlady (08757) 216 & 358
Aberlady, E. Lothian.
15 miles E of Edinburgh on A198.
Seaside course.
18 holes, 5423 yds. S.S.S. 66
Visitors welcome.
Green Fees. Weekdays £3.00 per round, £4.75 per day; weekends £4.00 per round, £6.00 per day.
Society Meetings by arrangement.
Hotels: in Aberlady, Gullane and North Berwick.
Meals served.

V 33 Kingsknowe

Tel. 031-441 1145
Lanark Rd., Edinburgh EH14 2JD.
On A71 W of Edinburgh.
Parkland course.
18 holes, 5966 yds. S.S.S. 69
Course designed by James Braid.
Visitors welcome.
Green Fees. Weekdays £3.50 per round, £5.50 per day; weekends £5.00 per round, £8.00 per day.
Society Meetings by arrangement.
Hotels: Hailes Hotel, Wester Hailes.
Meals served.

V 34 Kirkcudbright

Stirling Cres., Kirkcudbright.
Signposted on main road into town.
Undulating parkland course.
18 holes, 5386 yds. S.S.S. 66
Visitors welcome.
Green Fees. Weekdays £3.00; weekends £3.00; weekly £10.00.
Hotels: Royal; Selkirk Arms; Mayfield; Arden House.

V 35 Langholm

Whitaside, Langholm, Dumfriesshire.
Off A7 midway between Carlisle and Hawick.
Undulating hillside course.
9 holes, 5246 yds. S.S.S. 66
Visitors welcome.
Green Fees. £2.00 per round or day.
Society Meetings by arrangement.
Hotels: Eskdale; Crown, Langholm.

V 36 Lauder

Tel. Lauder (05782) 381
Lauder, Berwickshire TD2.
Off A68, 29 miles SE of Edinburgh.
Moorland course.
9 holes, 6002 yds. S.S.S. 70
Visitors welcome.
Green Fees. Mon. to Sat. £1.75 per round; Sun. £2.25; reductions for children and O.A.P.s.
Society Meetings welcome.
Hotels: Black Bull; Eagle; Lauderdale; Loanside.

V 37   Liberton

Tel. 031-664 8580
Kingston Grange, Gilmerton Rd., Edinburgh EH16 5UJ.
On A7 S of Edinburgh.
Parkland course.
18 holes, 5299 yds. S.S.S. 66
Visitors welcome except after 5p.m. on Mon., Wed. and Fri.
Green Fees. Weekdays £4.00 per round, £6.00 per day; weekends £6.00 per round, £8.00 per day. Reduced rates if playing with member.
Society Meetings by arrangement.
Hotels: in Craigmillar Park.
Snacks and meals served by arrangement.

V 38   Linlithgow

Tel. Linlithgow 2585
Braehead, Linlithgow.
Off A706 S of Linlithgow.
Parkland course.
18 holes, S.S.S. 68
Visitors welcome except Sat. before 4.00 p.m.
Green Fees. Weekdays £2.75 per round, £4.00 per day; weekends £4.00 per round, £5.00 per day.
Hotels: West Port; Star & Garter.
Meals served.

V 39   Livingston Golf & Country Club

Tel. Livingston 38843
Carmondean, Livingston, West Lothian EH54 8PG.
Leave M8 at Livingston interchange, follow signposts to Knightsridge, club signposted from there.
Undulating parkland course.
18 holes, 6795 yds. S.S.S. 72
Course designed by Charles Lawrie of Cotton (C.K.), Pennink, Lawrie and Partners.
Visitors welcome.
Green Fees. Livingston residents weekdays £2.50, weekends £4.00; non-Livingston residents weekdays £4.00, weekends £5.50.
Society Meetings welcome except during club competitions.
Hotels: Houston House Hotel, Uphall; Golden Circle Hotel, Bathgate.
Snacks, lunches, high teas served. Basket suppers served Sun. evening.

V 40   Lochmaben

Tel. Lochmaben 552
Castehill Gate, Lochmaben, By Lockerbie, Dumfriesshire.
On A709, 8 miles NE of Dumfries.
Parkland course.
9 holes, 5414 yds. S.S.S. 66
Visitors welcome except after 5.00 p.m.
Green Fees. Weekdays £3.00 per round; weekends £4.50 per round. Reduced rates if playing with member.
Society Meetings by arrangement.
Hotels: Balcastle; Kings Arms; Crown.

V 41   Lockerbie

Tel. Lockerbie 3363
Corrie Rd., Lockerbie, Dumfriesshire.
13 miles E of Dumfries.
Inland course.
9 holes, 5228 yds. S.S.S. 66
Green Fees. Mon.-Sat. £3.00 per day; Sun. £4.00; half-price with member; weekly £12.00.

V 42   Longniddry

Tel. Longniddry 52141
Longniddry, E. Lothian EH32 0NL.
15 miles E of Edinburgh. Off A1 at Wallyford roundabout on to A198.
Seaside, parkland course.
18 holes, 6240 yds. S.S.S. 70
Visitors welcome.
Green Fees. Weekdays £5.00 per round, £7.50 per day; weekends £10.00.
Society Meetings by arrangement.
Hotels: Kilspindie House Hotel, Aberlady; Queens, Gullane; Marine, North Berwick.
Catering available.

V 43   Lothianburn

Tel. 031-445 2206
Biggar Rd., Edinburgh EH10 7DU.
On A702 S of Edinburgh.
18 holes, 5750 yds. S.S.S. 69
Meals served by arrangement.

V 44   Luffness New

Tel. Gullane (0620) 84 3114
Aberlady, E. Lothian EH32 0QA.
17 miles E of Edinburgh, 1 mile from Gullane
Links Course.
Seaside course.
18 holes, 6085 yds. S.S.S. 69
Visitors welcome by introduction of member or by prior arrangement through own club.
Green Fees. On application.
Hotels: Kilspindie House, Aberlady; Bissets; Queens; Mallard, Gullane.
Catering available except Mon.

V 45   Melrose

Dingleton, Melrose, Roxburghshire.
½ mile S of town centre.
Parkland course.
9 holes, 5464 yds. S.S.S. 68
Visitors welcome.
Green Fees. Weekdays £3.00; weekends £4.00.
Hotels: Burts; George and Abbotsford; Waverley Castle; Bon Accord; Kings Hotel.

V 46   Merchants of Edinburgh

Tel. 031-447 1219
Craighill Gdns., Edinburgh EH10 5PY.
S side of city.
Hillside course.
18 holes, 4936 yds. S.S.S. 65
Visitors welcome with member only. Applications to play the course accepted from guests at the hotels nominated below.
Green Fees. £3.00 per round, £5.00 per day.
Hotels: Braids; Gillsland.
Meals served by arrangement.

V 47   Minto

Tel. Hawick (0450) 2267, weekends 3569
Minto,   Hawick,   Roxburghshire.
Correspondence to Treasurer, 19 Buccleuch St., Hawick.
Near Denholm, Hawick.
Parkland course.
18 holes, 5459 yds. S.S.S. 68
Visitors welcome.
Green Fees. Weekdays £2.50; weekends £3.00.
Society Meetings by arrangement.
Hotels: Crown; Kirklands; Mansfield Park; Elm House, Hawick.

V 48   Moffat

Tel. Moffat 20020
Coateshill, Moffat, Dumfriesshire DG10 9SB.
On A701 between Beattock and Moffat.
Hillside course.
18 holes, 5218 yds. S.S.S. 66
Course designed by Ben Sayers.
Visitors welcome except after 2.00 p.m. on Wed. April to September.
Green Fees. Weekdays £3.00 per round (juniors £1.00), £4.50 per day (juniors £1.25); weekends £5.50 per day (juniors £1.25); weekly £19.00 (juniors £5.00 with adult); fortnightly (for juniors with adult) £8.50; 5-day ticket (Mon.-Fri.), £12.00.
Society Meetings by arrangement.
Hotels: in Moffat.
Snacks, lunches and high teas served by arrangement.

V 49   Mortonhall

Tel. 031-447 6974
Braid Rd., Edinburgh EH10 6PB.
Off A702. 2 miles S of city.
Moorland course.
18 holes, 6548 yds. S.S.S. 71
Visitors welcome.
Green Fees. Weekdays £5.00 per round, £7.00 per day; weekends £6.00 per round, £8.00 per day.
Society Meetings welcome on weekdays.
Hotels: Braid Hills Hotel.
Lunches and teas served except Mon.

V 50   Murrayfield

Tel. 031-337 3478
Murrayfield Rd., Edinburgh EH12 6EU.
2 miles W of city centre on A8.
Parkland course.
18 holes, 5739 yds. S.S.S. 68
Visitors welcome on weekdays with letter of introduction.
Green Fees. Weekdays £4.50 per round, £6.50 per day.
Society Meetings Tues., Wed. and Thurs. only.
Hotels: Ellersly House Hotel; Murrayfield; Post House.
Meals served except Sun.

V 51   Musselburgh

Tel. 031-665 2005
Monktonhall, Musselburgh, E. Lothian.
1 mile S off A1.
Parkland course.
18 holes, 6800 yds. S.S.S. 72
Course designed by James Braid.
Visitors welcome except 8.00a.m. to 10.00 a.m. at weekends.
Green Fees. Weekdays £3.25 per round, £4.50 per day; weekends £6.50 per day.
Hotels: Ravelston; Woodside; Pittencrieff.
Meals served except Tues.

V 52   Newbattle

Tel. 031-663 2123
Abbey Rd., Dalkeith, Midlothian.
A7 to Eskbank roundabout, then B703.
Parkland course.
18 holes, 6012 yds. S.S.S. 69
Visitors welcome on weekdays by introduction.
Green Fees. £4.00 per round, £5.00 per day.
Society Meetings welcome on weekdays.
Hotels: Motel Derry; Lugton Inn.
Coffees, lunches and high teas served except Mon.

V 53   New Galloway

Tel. New Galloway 239
New Galloway, Castle Douglas, Kirkcudbrightshire DG7 3RP.
Off A713 Ayr to Castle Douglas road 13 miles from Castle Douglas, at S end of village.
Undulating course, fine views.
9 holes, 5300 yds. S.S.S. 66
Visitors welcome.
Green Fees. Weekdays £2.00; weekends £2.00.
Hotels: Kenmure Arms; Kenbridge; Cross Keys Inn, New Galloway.

V 54   North Berwick

Tel. North Berwick (0620) 2135
Beach Rd., North Berwick, E. Lothian EH39 4BB.
23 miles E of Edinburgh on A198.
Seaside course.
18 holes, 6317 yds. S.S.S. 70
Visitors welcome.
Green Fees. Weekdays £4.00 per round, £5.75 per day; weekends £5.75 per round, £8.00 per day.
Society Meetings welcome.
Hotels: Marine; Nether Abbey.
Meals served by arrangement except Thurs.

V 55   Peebles

Tel. Peebles (0721) 20197
Kirkland St., Peebles EH45 8EU.
A701 to Leadburn junction, then A703.
Undulating parkland course.
18 holes, 6137 yds. S.S.S. 69
Visitors welcome.
Green Fees. Weekdays £3.00 per round, £4.00 per day; weekends £4.00 per round, £6.00 per day.
Society Meetings by arrangement with J.P. Armstrong, Superintendent of Parks, District Offices, Rosetta Rd., Peebles EH45 8HG Tel. Peebles 20153.
Hotels: in Peebles.
Meals served 11.30 a.m. to 2.30 p.m. and 5.00 p.m. to 8.00 p.m.

V 56   Portobello

Tel. 031-669 4361
Stanley St., Portobello, Edinburgh EH15.
E from Edinburgh on A1 to Milton Rd.
Parkland course.
9 holes, 2419 yds. S.S.S. 32
Visitors welcome except Sun.
Green Fees. 80p.
Hotels: Kings Manor Hotel; Lady Nairne.

V 57   Portpatrick (Dunskey)

Tel. Portpatrick (0776) 81273
Portpatrick, Stranraer, Wigtownshire DG9 8TB.
On A77, 7 miles SW of Stranraer.
Seaside course.
18 holes, 5644 yds. S.S.S. 67
Visitors welcome.
Green Fees. Weekdays £4.00 (60p with member); weekends £5.00 (60p with member); weekly £14.00; fortnightly £20.00.
Society Meetings by arrangement.
Hotels: Portpatrick Hotel; Fernhill; Roslin; Crown; Rickwood.
Meals served except Mon.

V 58   Powfoot

Tel. Cummertrees 227
Cummertrees, Annan, Dumfriesshire.
3 miles W of Annan off B724.
Seaside course.
18 holes, 6283 yds. S.S.S. 70
Course designed by James Braid.
Visitors welcome on weekdays.
Green Fees. Weekdays £5.50 per round or day; weekends £7.00 per round or day; five day ticket (Mon.-Fri.) £20.00.
Society Meetings welcome on weekdays only by arrangement.
Hotels: Powfoot Golf; Richmond, Cummertrees.
Lunches and teas by arrangement except Fri.

V 59   Prestonfield

Tel. 031-667 1273 / 9665
6 Priestfield Rd. North, Edinburgh 16.
18 holes, 6216 yds. S.S.S. 70
Visitors welcome on weekdays; weekends by arrangement with professional (Tel. 031-667 8597).
Green Fees. Weekdays £4.50 per round, £6.50 per day; weekends £6.00 per round, £8.00 per day.

V 60   Pumpherston

Tel. Livingston (0506) 32869
Drumshoreland Rd., Pumpherston, Livingston, West Lothian EH53 0LF.
M8 to Livingston, 2½ miles from turn-off.
Meadowland course.
9 holes, 5110 yds. S.S.S. 65
Course designed by club committee.
Visitors by introduction only.
Green Fees. Weekdays £1.50 (concessionary 50p); weekends £3.00 (concessionary £1.00).
Society Meetings restricted.
Hotels: Houston House, Uphall.
Snacks served.

V 61   Ratho Park

Tel. 031-333 1252
Ratho, Midlothian EH28 8NX.
6 miles W of centre of Edinburgh off A8 or A71.
Parkland course.
18 holes, 6028 yds. S.S.S. 69
Course designed by James Braid.
Visitors welcome.
Green Fees. Weekdays £4.25 per round, £6.00 per day; weekends £8.00.

Society Meetings welcome Tues. to Thurs.
Hotels: in Edinburgh.
Meals served except Fri.

V 62   Ravelston

Tel. 031-332 3486
Ravelston Dykes Rd., Blackhall, Edinburgh EH4 3NZ.
Off A90 Queensferry Rd. at Blackhall.
Parkland course.
9 holes, 5200 yds. S.S.S. 66
Course designed by James Braid.
Visitors with members preferred.
Green Fees. £3.00 per day.
Hotels: Barnton Hotel; Eurocrest.
Light meals served.

V 63   Royal Burgess Golfing Society of Edinburgh

Tel. 031-339 2075
Whitehouse Rd., Barnton, Edinburgh EH4 6BY.
6 miles from city centre towards Forth Road Bridge.
Parkland course.
18 holes, 6604 yds. S.S.S. 72
Course designed by James Braid.
Visitors welcome with letter of introduction.
Green Fees. Weekdays £9.00 per round or day; weekends £11.00 per round or day.
Hotels: Barnton Hotel; Esso Motel.
Lunches served.

V 64   Royal Musselburgh

Tel. Prestonpans 810 276
Prestongrange House, Prestonpans, E. Lothian.
On A198 1 mile from Wallyford roundabout on North Berwick road.
Parkland course.
18 holes, 6207 yds. S.S.S. 70
Course designed by James Braid.
Visitors welcome.
Green Fees. Weekdays £4.00 per round; weekends £5.00 per round.
Hotels: in Edinburgh.
Meals served by arrangement except Tues.

V 65   St. Boswells

Tel. St. Boswells 2359
St. Boswells, Roxburghshire TD6 0AT.
Off A68 at St. Boswells, ¼ mile along side of River Tweed.
Parkland course.
9 holes, 5054 yds. S.S.S. 65
Course designed by Park of Musselburgh (1899), redesigned by Shade of Duddingston (1956).
Visitors welcome.
Green Fees. Weekdays £1.00 per round or day; weekends £2.00 per round or day.
Hotels: Dryburgh Abbey; Buccleuch.

V 66   St. Medan

Tel. Port William 358
St. Medan, Monreith, Port William, Wigtownshire DG8 8NJ.
On A747, 24 miles SE of Stranraer.
Seaside moorland course.
9 holes, 4554 yds. S.S.S. 62
Visitors welcome.
Green Fees. Weekdays £2.00 per round;

Mon.-Sat., £3.00 per day; Sun., £3.50.
Hotels: Eagle; Monreith Arms, Port William.
Lunches and high teas served by arrangement at clubhouse (April-Sept.).

V 67   Sanquhar

Tel. Sanquhar 577 (clubhouse), 287 (Secretary)
Euchan Golf Course, Sanquhar, Dumfriesshire.
On A76 midway between Dumfries and Kilmarnock.
Undulating moorland course, fine views.
9 holes, 5630 yds. S.S.S. 68
Visitors welcome.
Green Fees. Weekdays £1.50 per day; Sat. £2.00 per day; Sun. £2.50 per day; weekly £7.50.
Hotels: Nithsdale; Glendyre; Blackaddic; Mennock Foot.
Society Meetings welcome, by arrangement, especially on Saturdays.
Catering at clubhouse arranged for visiting parties if ordered in advance.

V 68   Selkirk

Tel. Selkirk 20621
Selkirk Hills, Selkirk TD7 5AB.
1 mile S of Selkirk on A7, c 300 yds. past 'Little Chef'.
Hillside heathland course.
9 holes, 5560 yds. S.S.S. 67
Visitors welcome.
Green Fees. Weekdays £2.50 per round or day; weekends £4.00 per round or day.
Hotels: Woodburn; Heatherlie Glen; Fleece.

V 69   Silverknowes

Tel. 031-336 5359
Silverknowes Parkway, Edinburgh EH4 5ET.
18 holes, 6210 yds. S.S.S. 70
Visitors welcome.

V 70   Southerness

Tel. Kirkbean 677
Southerness, Dumfries DG2 8AZ.
Off A710, 15 miles S of Dumfries.
Links course.
18 holes, 6548 yds. S.S.S. 72
Course designed by Mackenzie Ross.
Visitors welcome.
Green Fees. Weekdays £5.00; weekends £7.00; weekly £20.00.
Society Meetings by arrangement.
Hotels: Cavens House, Kirkbean, Dumfries.
Meals served except Wed.

V 71   Stranraer

Tel. 0776-87 245
Creachmore, Stranraer, Wigtownshire DG9 0LF.
On A718 3 miles N of Stranraer.
Parkland course.
18 holes, 6300 yds. S.S.S. 71
Course designed by James Braid.
Visitors welcome.
Green Fees. Weekdays £4.63; weekends £6.61; weekly £23.80.
Hotels: North West Castle Hotel; George, Stranraer.
Meals served.

V 72   Swanston

Tel. 031-445 2239
Swanston Rd., Edinburgh EH10.
5 miles from W end of city.
Hillside course.
18 holes, 4825 yds. S.S.S. 64
Visitors welcome.
Green Fees. On application to secretary.
Hotels: in Edinburgh.
Snacks served.

V 73   Thornhill

Tel. Thornhill 30546
Thornhill, Dumfriesshire.
Off A76, 14 miles N of Dumfries.
Undulating course.
18 holes, S.S.S. 70
Visitors welcome without reservation.
Green Fees. Weekdays £3.00 per day; weekends £5.00 per day.
Hotels: Buccleuch & Queensberry Hotel; George.
Snacks and light meals served by arrangement.

V 74   Torphin Hill

Tel. 031-441 1100
Torphin Rd., Edinburgh EH13 0PG.
SW of Colinton.
Hillside course.
18 holes, 5020 yds. S.S.S. 66
Visitors welcome on weekdays before 5.00 p.m.
Green Fees. Weekdays £2.50 per day.
Society Meetings weekdays by arrangement.
Bar snacks and meals served.

V 75   Torwoodlee

Tel. Galashiels 2260
Galashiels, Selkirkshire.
On A7 NW of Galashiels.
Parkland course.
9 holes, 5720 yds. S.S.S. 68
Visitors welcome.
Green Fees. Mon. to Sat. £2.50 per round or day (£1.00 with member); Sun. £4.00 per day (£1.00 with member).
Society Meetings welcome on weekdays.
Hotels: Royal; Douglas; Maxwell.
Meals served by arrangement.

V 76   Turnhouse

Tel. 031-334 1014
Turnhouse Rd., Edinburgh EH12 0AD.
On B9080 W of city.
Parkland/moorland course.
18 holes, 6171 yds. S.S.S. 69
Course designed by Jas. Braid.
Visitors welcome with member or letter of introduction.
Green Fees. £3.00 per round, £4.75 per day.
Hotels: Royal Scot; Post House.
Meals served.

V 77   Uphall

Tel. Broxburn 856404
Uphall, W. Lothian.
Off M8, 14 miles W of Edinburgh.
Meadowland course
18 holes, 6250 yds S.S.S. 68
Visitors welcome.

Green Fees. Weekdays £4.00; weekends £5.00.
Society Meetings by arrangement.
Hotels: Houston House Hotel, Uphall; Golden Circle, Bathgate.
Meals served by arrangement.

V 78   West Linton

Tel. West Linton (09686) 463
West Linton, Peeblesshire.
On A702, 17 miles SW of Edinburgh.
Moorland course.
18 holes, 5955 yds. S.S.S. 69
Visitors welcome.
Green Fees. Weekdays £3.00; weekends £6.00.
Society Meetings by arrangement.
Hotels: Linton Arms; Pantiles; Raemartin.
Meals served except Tues.

V 79   West Lothian

Tel. Boness (050 682) 2330
Airngath Hill, Boness, West Lothian.
18 holes.
Visitors welcome.
Green Fees. Weekdays £5.00 per day; weekends £6.00 per day.
Society Meetings by arrangement.

V 80   Wigtown & Bladnoch

Wigtown, Wigtownshire.
On A714, 7 miles S of Newton Stewart, 200 yards S of town square.
Parkland course.
9 holes, 5424 yds. S.S.S. 67
Visitors welcome.
Green Fees. Weekdays £1.50 per round or day; weekends £2.50 (half rates with member). Half rates after 6p.m.
Hotels: Fordbank; Galloway.

V 81   Wigtownshire County

Glenluce, Newton Stewart, Wigtownshire DG8 0QN.
On A75, 8 miles E of Stranraer, 2 miles W of Glenluce.
Seaside course.
9 holes, 5716 yds. S.S.S. 68
Visitors welcome.
Green Fees. Weekdays £2.50, juniors £1.25; weekends £3.00, juniors £1.50; weekly £12.00; juniors £6.00; fortnightly £25.00, juniors £12.50;any day after 6 p.m. £1.25.
Hotels: Judges Keep; Kelvin; Crown Inn; Kings Arms, Glenluce, Auld Kings Arms.
Meals served by arrangement.

V 82   Winterfield

Tel. Dunbar (0368) 62280
North Rd., Dunbar, E. Lothian.
W side of Dunbar.
Seaside course.
18 holes, 5035 yds. S.S.S. 65
Visitors welcome.
Green Fees. Weekdays £2.50 per round, £3.00 per day; weekends £3.00 per round, £5.00 per day; weekly (Mon. to Fri.) £10.00.
Society Meetings welcome.
Hotels: in Dunbar.
Meals served except Thurs.

W *Strathclyde*

W 1 Airdrie

Tel. Airdrie 62195
Rochsoles, Airdrie, Lanarkshire.
From Airdrie Cross to Glenmavis.
Parkland course.
18 holes, 6004 yds. S.S.S. 69
Course designed by James Braid.
Visitors welcome with reservation.
Green Fees. £3.45 per round, £5.75 per day.
Hotels: Tudor Hotel, Airdrie.
Meals served.

W 2 Alexandra Park

Tel. 041-554 1204
Alexandra Park, Alexandra Parade, Glasgow G31 3SE.
9 holes, 2281 yds.
Green Fees. Weekdays adults 35p, juniors 18p, O.A.P.s free; weekends adults, juniors and O.A.P.s 59p.

W 3 Annanhill

Tel. Kilmarnock (0563) 21644
Irvine Rd., Kilmarnock KA3 1DW.
Off main Kilmarnock to Irvine road.
Parkland course.
18 holes, 6269 yds. S.S.S. 70
Course designed by J. McLean.
Visitors welcome on weekdays, weekends with reservation.
Green Fees. Weekdays £2.90 per day; weekends £3.90 per day.
Society Meetings welcome by arrangement.
Hotels: Howard Park Hotel; Ross Hotel.
Lunches served by arrangement.

W 4 Ardeer

Tel. Stevenston (0294) 64542
Greenhead, Stevenston, Ayrshire KA20 6LB.
1 mile E of the A78.
Undulating course.
18 holes, 6640 yds. S.S.S. 72
Course designed by Stutt Ltd.
Visitors welcome.
Green Fees. Weekdays £4.00; weekends £6.00.
Society Meetings welcome weekdays; 25% discount for parties of 12 or more.
Hotels: Hayocks, Stevenston; Redburn, Irvine.
Meals served except Thurs.

W 5 Ayr Belleisle

Tel. Alloway 41258
Doonfoot Rd., Ayr, Ayrshire.
1¼ miles from town centre.
Undulating parkland course.
18 holes, 6540 (or 6022) yds. S.S.S. 71 (or 69)
Course designed by James Braid.
Visitors welcome.
Green Fees. Weekdays £2.50 per round, £3.30 per day; weekends £5.00 per day.
Society Meetings by arrangement except Wed. and Sat.
Hotels: in Ayr.
Meals served.

W 6 Ayr Dalmilling (Municipal)

Tel. Ayr (0292) 263893
Westwood Ave., Ayr.
Approx. 2 miles from town centre on NE boundary, A77.
Meadowland course.
18 holes, 5401 yds. S.S.S. 66
Visitors welcome
Green Fees. Weekdays £2.00 per round, £2.60 per day; weekends £2.50 per round, £4.00 per day.
Society Meetings welcome.
Hotels: Braehead Hotel, Whitletts.
Lunches and high teas served.

W 7 Ayr Seafield

Tel. Alloway 41258
Doonfoot Rd., Ayr, Ayrshire.
1¼ miles from town centre.
Seaside course.
18 holes, 5244 (or 4889) yds. S.S.S. 66 (or 64)
Course designed by James Braid.
Visitors welcome.
Green Fees. Weekdays £1.75 per round, £2.30 per day; weekends £3.50 per day.
Society Meetings by arrangement except Wed. and Sat.
Hotels: in Ayr.
Meals served.

W 8 Ballochmyle

Tel. Mauchline 50469
Mauchline, Ayrshire.
A76 Kilmarnock to Dumfries road, 1 mile S of Mauchline.
18 holes, 5847 yds. S.S.S. 69
Visitors welcome on weekdays and Sun.
Hotels: Royal, Dumfries Arms, Cumnock; Sinclair Arms, Auchinleck.
Meals served.

W 9 Balmore

Tel. Balmore 240
Balmore, Torrance, Stirlingshire.
A803 then A807 from Glasgow.
Parkland course.
18 holes, S.S.S. 66
Course designed by James Braid.
Visitors welcome with member only.
Green Fees. £6.00 per round or day.
Hotels: Black Bull, Milngavie.
Meals served.

W 10 Barshaw

Tel. 041-889 2908
Barshaw Park, Glasgow Rd., Paisley, Renfrewshire.
5 miles from central Glasgow, ½ mile from Paisley Cross.
Meadowland course.
18 holes, 5669 yds. S.S.S. 67
Visitors welcome.
Green Fees. £1.20 per round.
Hotels: Brabloch; Normandy; Glynhill, Renfrew.
No catering facilities at club.

W 11 Bearsden

Tel. 041-942 2351
Thorn Rd., Bearsden, Glasgow.
1 mile from Bearsden Cross.
Parkland course.
9 holes, 5977 yds. S.S.S. 70
Visitors welcome with member only.
Green Fees. Weekdays £1.00; weekends £2.00.
Hotels: Burnbrae, Bearsden; Cameron House Hotel, Hardgate.
Meals served.

W 12 Beith

Tel. Beith 3166
Beith, Ayrshire.
On A737 Paisley to Kilwinning road.
Moorland course.
9 holes, 5488 yds. S.S.S. 67
Visitors welcome except Sat. or after 4.00 p.m. on weekdays.
Green Fees. £2.00.
Snacks served; meals by arrangement.

W 13 Biggar

Tel. Biggar (0899) 20816
Broughton Rd., Biggar.
18 holes, 5258 yds. S.S.S. 66
Visitors welcome.
Green Fees. Weekdays £1.75 per day; weekends £3.00 per day.
Society Meetings by arrangement.

W 14 Bishopbriggs

Tel. 041-772 1810
Brackenbrae Ave., Bishopbriggs, Glasgow G64.
Undulating parkland course.
18 holes, 6041 yds. S.S.S. 69
Visitors welcome with member.
Green Fees. Mon. to Sat. £1.00; Sun. £1.50; visiting party £5.75 per day.
Hotels: in Glasgow.
Meals served by arrangement.

W 15 Blairbeth

Tel. 041-634 3355
Burnside, Rutherglen, Glasgow.
2 miles S of Rutherglen via Stonelaw Rd.
Parkland course.
18 holes, 5448 yds. S.S.S. 67
Visitors welcome with member only.
Green Fees. Weekdays £1.00; weekends £2.00.
Hotels: Mill Hotel, Rutherglen.
Meals served except Tues.

W 16 Blairmore & Strone

c/o Mrs M. Torrance, Heatherbloom, Strone, Dunoon.
A880, off A815.
Undulating course.
9 holes, 4208 yds. S.S.S. 62
Course designed by James Braid.

Visitors welcome.
Green Fees. £1.00 per round or day.
Hotels: Kilmun Hotel, Kilmun; Argyll Hotel, Strone.

W 17 Bonnyton

Tel. 041-560 2781
Eaglesham, Renfrewshire.
On S side of Glasgow via Clarkston.
Moorland course.
18 holes, 6248 yds. S.S.S. 70; also 9 hole course.
Visitors welcome with member only.
Green Fees. £3.50 per round.
Society Meetings by arrangement.
Hotels: Eglinton Arms.
Dining room and bar facilities available.

W 18 Bothwell Castle

Tel. Bothwell 85 3177
Blantyre Rd., Bothwell, Lanarkshire.
On A74, 3 miles N of Hamilton.
Meadowland course.
18 holes, 6456 yds. S.S.S. 71
Visitors welcome with member only.
Green Fees. Introduced 58p, courtesy granted by Committee £6.00.
Hotels: Silvertrees; Cricklewood.

W 19 Brodick

Tel. Brodick (0770) 2349
Brodick, Isle of Arran.
½ mile from Brodick pier.
Seaside course.
18 holes, 4404 yds. S.S.S. 62
Visitors welcome.
Green Fees. £3.00 per day.
Society Meetings by arrangement.
Hotels: Kingsley; Ormidale; Glenartney; Ennismor.

W 20 Calderbraes

Tel. Uddingston 3425
Roundknowe Rd., Uddingston, Glasgow.
9 holes, 5032 yds. S.S.S. 67
Green Fees. Weekdays 50p; weekends £1.00 introduced with member only.
Hotels: Mount Vernon Hotel; Coach House Hotel.
Meals served.

W 21 Caldwell

Tel. 041-248 7495
Uplawmoor, Glasgow.
Parkland course.
18 holes.
Course designed by T. Fernie.
Visitors welcome with member.
Green Fees. Mon. to Sat. 75p per round, £1.00 per day; Sun. £2.00; parties £5.00 per day.
Meals served.

W 22 Cambuslang

Tel. 041-641 3130
Westburn, Cambuslang, Glasgow.
½ mile from station.
9 holes, 6146 yds. S.S.S. 69
Visitors welcome with member only.

W 23 Campsie

Tel. 041-310 244
Crow Rd., Lennoxtown, Glasgow G65 7HU.
B822 on outskirts of Lennoxtown.
Undulating course.
9 holes, 5020 yds. S.S.S. 66
Visitors weekdays only.
Green Fees. £2.00 per day.
Hotels: Lennox Arms; Campsie Glen.

W 24 Caprington

Tel. Kilmarnock 21915
Ayr Rd., Kilmarnock KA1 4UW.
S of Kilmarnock on Ayr road.
Parkland course.
18 holes, S.S.S. 68
Visitors welcome.
Green Fees. Weekdays £1.80; weekends £3.00.
Hotels: Golden Sheaf Hotel.

W 25 Cardross

Tel. Cardross (038 984) 213
Cardross, Dumbarton G82 5LB.
On A814, 4 miles W of Dumbarton.
Parkland course.
18 holes, 6466 yds. S.S.S. 71
Course designed by Willie Fernie.
Visitors welcome on weekdays before 4.30 p.m., weekends with member only.
Green Fees. £8.00 per day.
Society Meetings by arrangement.
Hotels: Muirholm, Cardross; Queen's, Helensburgh.
Meals served.

W 26 Carluke

Tel. Carluke 71070
Mauldsue   Rd.,   Hallcraig,   Carluke, Lanarkshire.
Signposted at Carluke Cross traffic lights.
Parkland course.
18 holes, 5807 yds. S.S.S. 68
Visitors welcome on weekdays before 4.30 p.m.
Green Fees. £5.00.
Hotels: Crown, Carluke.
Meals served by arrangement except Thurs.

W 27 Carnwath

Tel. Carnwath 251
1 Main St., Carnwath, Lanarkshire ML11 8HH.
On A70, 7 miles from Lanark.
Undulating course.
18 holes, 5823 yds. S.S.S. 68
Visitors welcome.
Green Fees. Weekdays £4.00; Sun. £6.00.
Society Meetings welcome.
Meals served.

W 28 Carradale

Tel. Carradale (058 33) 624
Carradale, Campbeltown, Argyll PA28 6QX.
25 miles from Tarbert, 15 miles from Campbeltown. A83 to Tarbert; 4 miles beyond Tarbert take B8001, B842 and B879.
Seaside/parkland course with scenic views.
9 holes, 2493 yds. S.S.S. 63

Visitors welcome, no introduction necessary.
Green Fees. Weekdays and Sat. 1 round £1.50, per day £3.00; Sun. 1 round £2.00, per day £4.00. Weekly, fortnightly and monthly tickets available.
Society Meetings welcome.
Hotels: Carradale Hotel; Ash Bank Hotel.

W 29 Cathcart Castle

Tel. 041-638 0082
Mearns Rd., Clarkston, Glasgow G76.
On A77, 7 miles from Glasgow.
Undulating parkland course.
18 holes, 5818 yds. S.S.S. 68
Visitors welcome with member only.
Green Fees. On application to Secretary.
Society Meetings by arrangement.
Hotels: Redhurst, Giffnock; MacDonald, Giffnock.
Meals served.

W 30 Cathkin Braes

Tel. 041-634 4007
Cathkin Rd., Carmunnock, Glasgow.
5 miles SE of Glasgow.
Undulating moorland course.
18 holes, 6266 yds. S.S.S. 71
Visitors welcome with member only.
Green Fees. £6.00 per round, £8.00 per day.
Society Meetings by arrangement.
Hotels: in Glasgow or East Kilbride.
Meals served except Mon.

W 31 Cawder

Tel. 041-772 7101
Cadder Estate, Bishopbriggs, Glasgow G64.
On A803 N of Glasgow.
Parkland course.
Keir 18 holes, 5885 yds. S.S.S. 68
Cawder 18 holes, 6307 yds. S.S.S. 71
Course designed by James Braid.
Visitors welcome with member, parties by arrangement.
Green Fees. Party £7.50 per day.
Hotels: Stepps Hotel; Campsie Hotel.
Meals served.

W 32 Clober

Tel. 041-956 1685
Craigton Rd., Milngavie, Dunbartonshire G62 7HP.
7 miles N of Glasgow.
Parkland course.
18 holes, 5100 yds. S.S.S. 65
Visitors welcome on weekdays before 4.30 p.m.
Green Fees. £2.50 per round or day.
Society Meetings by arrangement.
Hotels: Black Bull; Burnbrae.
Meals served except Mon.

W 33 Clydebank & District

Tel. Duntocher 73289
Hardgate, Clydebank, Dunbartonshire G81 5QY.
8 miles NW of Glasgow via Great Western Rd.
Parkland course.
18 holes, 5825 yds. S.S.S. 68

Visitors welcome on weekdays, weekends with member only.
Green Fees. £3.00 per day; weekly £6.00.
Hotels: Cameron House Hotel; Boulevard; Pine Trees; Radnor.
Meals served.

W 34   Clydebank Overtoun (Dalmuir)

Tel. 041-952 6372
Dalmuir Park, Dalmuir, Clydebank, Dunbartonshire G81.
7 miles NW of Glasgow.
Parkland course.
18 holes, 5286 yds. S.S.S. 65
Visitors welcome.
Green Fees. Mon. to Sat. £1.30; Sun. and bank holidays £1.50.
Hotels: Radnor; Boulevard.
Meals served.

W 35   Cochrane Castle

Tel. Johnstone 20146
Craigston, Johnstone, Renfrewshire.
Moorland/parkland course.
18 holes, 6173 yds. S.S.S. 69
Hotels: Lyndhurst Hotel, Johnstone.
Meals and bar snacks served.

W 36   Colville Park

Tel. Motherwell 63017
New Jerviston House, Motherwell.
1¼ miles N of Motherwell on A723.
Parkland course.
18 holes, 6209 yds. S.S.S. 70
Course designed by James Braid.
Visitors welcome with member only.
Green Fees. £4.60 per round or day (70p with member).
Society Meetings welcome on weekdays.
Hotels: Garrion Hotel.
Meals served.

W 37   Corrie

Corrie, Brodick, Isle of Arran.
On A841.
Seaside course.
9 holes, 3896 yds. S.S.S. 61
Visitors welcome.
Green Fees. £1.00 per day; weekly £5.00; fortnightly £6.00; monthly £7.00.
Hotels: Corrie Hotel.

W 38   Cowal

Tel. Dunoon (0369) 2216
Ardenslate Rd., Dunoon, Argyll PA23 8LT.
NE Dunoon.
Moorland course.
18 holes, 6251 yds. S.S.S. 70
Course designed by James Braid.
Visitors welcome.
Green Fees. Mon. to Sat. £3.50; Sun. £5.75; weekly £16.00.
Society Meetings welcome on weekdays, weekends by arrangement.

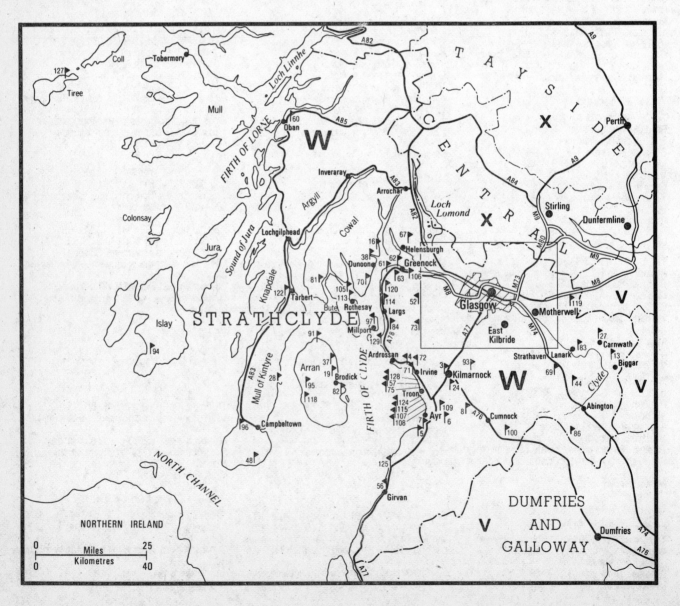

131

STRATHCLYDE

Hotels: Cedars, Dunoon; Rosscairn, Kirn.
Meals served by arrangement except Mon.

W 39 Cowglen

Tel. 041-632 0556
Barrhead Rd., Glasgow G43.
Parkland course.
18 holes, 6033 yds. S.S.S. 69
Visitors welcome with member only.
Hotels: Newlands Hotel.
Lunches served by arrangement.

W 40 Crow Wood

Tel. 041-779 2011
Garnkirk Estate, Muirhead, Chryston, Glasgow G69 9JF.
1 mile N of Stepps on A80.
Parkland course.
18 holes, 6209 yds. S.S.S. 70
Course designed by James Braid.
Visitors with member only.
Society Meetings welcome on weekdays.
Hotels: Crow Wood Road House Hotel; Garfield.
Meals served except Mon.

W 41 Deaconsbank

Tel. 041-638 8919
Stewarton Rd., Thornliebank, Glasgow G46 7UY.
Undulating parkland course.
18 holes, 4600 yds. S.S.S. 63
Course designed by James Braid.
Visitors welcome.
Green Fees. On application to Secretary.
Society Meetings by arrangement.
Hotels: MacDonald, Eastwood Toll; Trade Winds; Avion, Thornliebank; Orchard Park, Giffnock.
Snacks served.

W 42 Dougalston

Tel. 041-956 5750
Strathblane Rd., Milngavie, Glasgow.
On A81 from Glasgow.
Parkland course, tree-lined.
18 holes, 6673 yds. S.S.S. 71
Course designed by Cdr. John Harris.
Visitors welcome.
Green Fees. Weekdays £2.50 per round, £3.50 per day; weekends £3.00 per round, £4.00 per day.
Society Meetings welcome.
Hotels: Burnbrae; Black Bull, Milngavie.
Full catering service daily.

W 43 Douglas Park

Tel. 041-942 2220
Hillfoot, Bearsden, Glasgow.
Adjacent to station; shares Railway road entrance.
18 holes, 5957 yds. S.S.S. 68
Visitors welcome with member only.
Society Meetings Mon., Wed. and Fri. only.
Meals served by arrangement.

W 44 Douglas Water

Rigside, Lanark.
7 miles SW of Lanark on A70 2 miles E of A74.
9 holes, 2916 yds. S.S.S. 69

W 45 Drumpellier

Tel. Coatbridge 24139
Drumpellier, Coatbridge ML5 1RX.
1 mile from Coatbridge.
Parkland course.
18 holes, 6117 yds. S.S.S. 70
Visitors welcome weekdays with letter of introduction.
Green Fees. £7.00 per day.
Hotels: Coatbridge Hotel; Georgian.
Meals served.

W 46 Dullatur

Tel. Cumbernauld 23230
Dullatur, Glasgow G68 0AQ.
2 miles N of Cumbernauld off A80.
Parkland course.
18 holes, 6229 yds. S.S.S. 70
Course designed by James Braid.
Visitors welcome on weekdays.
Green Fees. £5.00 per round or day (£1.00 with member); plus V.A.T.
Society Meetings weekdays by arrangement.
Meals served except Wed.

W 47 Dumbarton

Tel. Dumbarton 32830
Broadmeadow, Dumbarton, Dunbartonshire G82 2BQ.
15 miles NW of Glasgow.
Meadowland course.
18 holes, 5913 yds. S.S.S. 69
Visitors welcome on weekdays.
Green Fees. £4.00 per day.
Hotels: Dumbuck Hotel; Dumbarton Hotel.
Meals served.

W 48 Dunaverty

Southend, Campbeltown, Argyll PA28 6RF.
On B842, 10 miles S of Campbeltown.
Undulating seaside course.
18 holes, 4597 yds. S.S.S. 63
Visitors welcome.
Green Fees. £1.30 per round, £2.00 per day; weekly £8.00.
Hotels: Keil Hotel.
Snacks served.

W 49 Easter Moffat

Tel. Caldercruix 289
Plains, by Airdrie, Lanarkshire.
On A89, 3 miles E of Airdrie.
Parkland, moorland course.
18 holes, 6221 yds. S.S.S. 70
Visitors welcome on weekdays 9a.m.-3.30p.m.; parties from recognized golfing societies.
Green Fees. £4.00 per round, £6.00 per day.
Hotels: Tudor, Airdrie; Eastercroft, Caldercruix.
Meals served.

W 50 East Kilbride

Tel. East Kilbride 20913
Nerston, East Kilbride, Glasgow.
Meadowland course.
18 holes, 6419 yds. S.S.S. 71
Visitors welcome on weekdays with reservation, weekends with member only.
Hotels: Stuart Hotel; Bruce Hotel, East Kilbride.
Lunches served.

W 51 East Renfrewshire

Tel. Loganswell 256
Pilmuir, Newton Mearns, Glasgow.

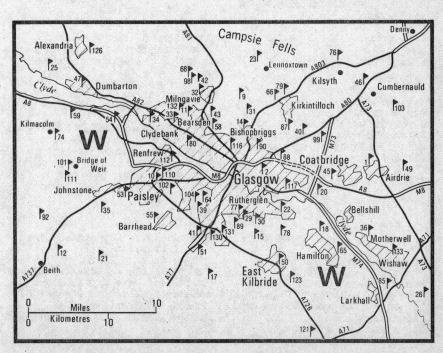

18 holes, 6097 yds. S.S.S. 70
Visitors welcome with member.
Green Fees. 1 round £6.00; 2 rounds £8.00

W 52   Eastwood

Tel. Loganswell (035 55) 261 & 280 Sec.
Muirshield, Loganswell, Newton Mearns, Glasgow G77.
10 miles S of Glasgow on A77.
Undulating moorland course.
18 holes, 5886 yds. S.S.S. 68
Course designed by Theodore Moone.
Visitors welcome with member only.
Green Fees. £6.00.
Society Meetings by arrangement.
Hotels: Macdonald; Redhurst; Tinto Firs.
Meals served except Thurs. afternoon and Mon.

W 53   Elderslie

Tel. Johnstone 22835 & 23956
63 Main Rd., Elderslie, Renfrewshire PA5 9AZ.
On A737 9 miles W of Glasgow, midway between Johnstone and Paisley.
18 holes, 6004 yds. S.S.S. 69
Visitors welcome with member, parties by arrangement.
Green Fees. £4.00 per round, £5.75 per day; reduced rates with member.
Hotels: in area.
Lunches served by arrangement.

W 54   Erskine

Tel. Bishopton 2302
Bishopton, Renfrewshire PA7 5PH.
N of M8. Leave M8 at Erskine Bridge toll barrier and turn left along B815 for 1½ miles.
Parkland course.
18 holes, 6287 yds. S.S.S. 70
Visitors welcome if introduced by or playing with member.
Hotels: Bishopton Hotel.
Meals served to members' guests only.

W 55   Fereneze

Tel. 041-881 1519
Fereneze Ave., Barrhead, Glasgow.
9 miles SW of Glasgow.
Moorland course.
18 holes, 5821 yds. S.S.S. 68
Visitors welcome with member only.
Society Meetings by arrangement 4-6 weeks in advance.
Hotels: Dalmeny Park Hotel.
Lunches served by arrangement except Mon.

W 56   Girvan

Tel. Girvan 0465 4272
Golf Course Rd., Girvan, Ayrshire KA26 9HW.
Seaside meadowland course.
18 holes, 5078 yds. S.S.S. 65
Visitors welcome.
Green Fees. Weekdays £1.35 per round, £1.80 per day; weekends £1.80 per round, £2.65 per day.
Society Meetings welcome.
Meals served by arrangement except Tues.

W 57   Glasgow

Tel. Irvine (0294) 311347
Gailes, Irvine, Ayrshire.
1 mile S of Irvine on road to Troon.
Seaside course.
18 holes, 6432 yds. S.S.S. 71
Visitors welcome on weekdays with letter of introduction.
Green Fees. £7.50 per day.
Society Meetings by arrangement with Secretary at Glasgow Golf Club, Killermont, Bearsden, Glasgow.
Hotels: in Troon and Ayr.
Lunches and high teas served.

W 58   Glasgow

Tel. 041-942 2011
Killermont, Bearsden, Glasgow G61 2TW.
6 miles NW of Glasgow.
Parkland course.
18 holes, 5960 yds. S.S.S. 69
Visitors welcome with member only.
Meals served.

W 59   Gleddoch Golf & Country Club

Tel. Langbank (0475 54) 304
Gleddoch Golf and Country Club, Langbank, Renfrewshire PA14 6YE.
M8 W from Glasgow.
Parkland moorland course.
18 holes, 6236 yds. S.S.S. 71
Course designed by J. Hamilton Stutt.
Visitors welcome on weekdays, weekends with member only.
Green Fees. Weekdays £5.75 per day; weekends £8.00 per day.
Society Meetings welcome weekdays, weekends restricted.
Meals served.

W 60   Glencruitten

Tel. Oban (0631) 2868
Glencruitten Rd., Oban, Argyll.
½ mile from station on A816, fork left on road signposted 'Glencruitten' and continue for 1 mile.
Undulating meadowland course.
18 holes, 4416 yds. S.S.S. 63
Course designed by James Braid.
Visitors welcome.
Green Fees. Weekdays £3.00; weekends £4.00; reduced rates with member.
Society Meetings by arrangement.
Hotels: Rowantree.
Meals served by arrangement.

W 61   Gourock

Tel. Gourock 31001
Cowal View, Gourock.
2 miles W of station above Yacht Club.
Moorland course.
18 holes, 6492 yds. S.S.S. 71
Visitors welcome with letter of introduction.
Green Fees. Weekdays £5.00 per day; weekends £6.00 per day; weekly £16.00; fortnightly £28.00; monthly £40.00.
Hotels: Gantock; Castle Levan Hotel; Queen's.
Meals served.

W 62   Greenock

Tel. Greenock (0475) 20793
Forsyth Street, Greenock, Renfrewshire PA16 8RE.
Undulating parkland, moorland course.
27 holes, 5883 yds. S.S.S. 68
Course designed by J. Braid.
Visitors welcome on weekdays and Sun.
Green Fees. Weekdays £5.00 per round or day; weekends £6.00; weekly £12.00; monthly £32.00.
Society Meetings welcome on weekdays.
Hotels: Tontine.
Meals served except Thurs.

W 63   Greenock Whinhill

Tel. Greenock (0475) 24694
Beith Rd., Greenock, Renfrewshire.
23 miles W of Glasgow via M8.
Moorland course.
18 holes, 5454 yds. S.S.S. 68
Visitors welcome.
Green Fees. 85p per round.
Hotels: Tontine.

W 64   Haggs Castle

Tel. 041-427 0480
70 Dumbreck Rd., Glasgow G41 4SN.
Along Paisley Rd. West to Dumbreck Rd.
Turn left, course is ¾ mile on right.
Parkland course.
18 holes, 6464 yds. S.S.S. 72
Course redesigned by Peter Alliss, Dave Thomas Ltd.
Visitors welcome with member, parties by arrangement.
Green Fees. Visiting parties £6.00 per round, £10.00 per day.
Hotels: Bellahouston Hotel.
Meals served.

W 65   Hamilton

Tel. 24751
Riccarton, Ferniegair, Hamilton, Lanarkshire.
Off A74 between Larkhall and Hamilton.
Parkland course.
18 holes, 6264 yds. S.S.S. 70
Course designed by James Braid.
Visitors welcome with member or with reservation.
Green Fees. £4.60 per round, £8.05 per day.
Society Meetings by arrangement.
Hotels: Commercial; Avonbridge; Royal, Hamilton.
Meals served.

W 66   Hayston

Tel. 041-776 1244
Campsie Rd., Kirkintilloch, Glasgow G66 1RN.
12 miles NE of Glasgow.
Undulating course.
18 holes, 6042 yds. S.S.S. 69
Course designed by James Braid.
Visitors welcome on weekdays before 4.30 p.m. with letter of introduction, weekends with member only.
Green Fees. £4.00 per round, £6.00 per day.

Society Meetings Thurs. only.
Hotels: Campsie Glen Hotel, Campsie Glen. Meals served until 6 p.m., after 6 p.m. by arrangement.

W 67   Helensburgh

Tel. Helensburgh (0436) 4173
25 Abercromby St., Helensburgh, Dunbartonshire.
Abercromby St. off Sinclair St.
Moorland course.
18 holes, 5966 yds. S.S.S. 69
Course designed by Tom Morris.
Visitors welcome on weekdays, weekends with member only.
Green Fees. £4.50 per round, £6.00 per day.
Society Meetings welcome.
Hotels: Queen's; Cairndhu; Lomond Castle. Meals served by arrangement.

W 68   Hilton Park

Tel. 041-959 4657 (Sec.)
Stockiemuir Rd., Milngavie, Glasgow G62 7HB.
4 miles from Bearsden on Drymen road.
Moorland course.
Allander 18 holes, 5409 yds. S.S.S. 69
Hilton 18 holes, 6021 yds. S.S.S. 70
Visitors welcome weekdays only.
Green Fees. 1 round £4.00, 2 rounds £6.00; plus V.A.T.
Society Meetings by arrangement.
Hotels: Black Bull, Milngavie; Buchanan Arms, Drymen; Kirkhouse Inn, Strathblane. Full catering service except Mon.

W 69   Hollandbush

Tel. Lesmahagow 3484
Acretophead, Lesmahagow, Lanarkshire.
Off A74 between Lesmahagow and Coalburn.
Parkland course.
18 holes, 6110 yds. S.S.S. 70
Visitors welcome.
Green Fees. Weekdays £1.75; weekends £3.50.
Hotels: Commercial, Lesmahagow; Station, Coalburn.
Lunches and teas served.

W 70   Innellan

Tel. 0369-3546
Craigard, Royal Cres., Dunoon.
4 miles S of Dunoon.
Seaside course.
9 holes, 4878 yds. S.S.S. 63
Visitors welcome.
Green Fees. £2.00 per day.
Hotels: Royal.
Meals and bar service.

W 71   Irvine

Tel. Irvine (0294) 78139
Bogside, Irvine, Ayrshire.
N of Prestwick Airport on coast road.
Seaside course.
18 holes, 6454 yds. S.S.S. 71
Visitors welcome with member.
Green Fees. £5.00 per round, £8.00 per day.

Society Meetings Mon., Tues. and Thurs. only.
Hotels: in Troon.
Meals served.

W 72   Irvine Ravenspark

Tel. Irvine (0294) 79550
Kidsneuk, Irvine, Ayrshire.
On A78 midway between Irvine and Kilwinning.
Meadowland course.
18 holes, 6439 yds. S.S.S. 71
Course designed by J. Walker.
Visitors welcome.
Green Fees. Weekdays 60p per round; weekends £1.00 per round.
Hotels: Redburn; Kings Arms; Grange; Eglinton Arms.
Meals served except Tues. and Thurs.

W 73   Kilbirnie Place

Tel. Kilbirnie 3398
Largs Rd., Kilbirnie, Ayrshire KA6 7EU.
On A760, 8 miles W of Largs.
Parkland course.
18 holes, 5617 yds. S.S.S. 67
Visitors welcome except Sat.
Green Fees. Weekdays £3.00; Sun. £5.00; 50p if playing with member.
Hotels: Milton.

W 74   Kilmacolm

Tel. Kilmacolm (050 587) 2139
Kilmacolm, Renfrewshire.
A761.
Moorland course.
18 holes, 5890 yds. S.S.S. 68
Visitors welcome on weekdays, weekends with member.
Green Fees. £6.50 per day.
Lunches served except Mon.

W 75   Kilmarnock (Barassie)

Tel. Troon (0292) 313920/311077
Hillhouse Rd., Barassie, Troon, Ayrshire KA10 6SY.
On A78 2 miles N of Troon. 100 yards from Barassie station.
Seaside course.
18 holes, 6451 yds. S.S.S. 71
Course designed by John Allan (1894), redesigned by Theodore Moone (1931).
Visitors welcome on weekdays except Wed. with member or letter of introduction; Wed. and weekends with member only.
Green Fees. £6.00 per round or day.
Society Meetings Tues. and Thurs. by arrangement.
Hotels: Tower, Barassie; Sun Court; Marine, Troon.
Meals served.

W 76   Kilsyth Lennox

Tel. Kilsyth 822190
Tak-Ma-Doon Rd., Kilsyth, Glasgow G65.
On A803, 12 miles from Glasgow.
Moorland course.
9 holes, 5834 yds. S.S.S. 69
Visitors welcome on weekdays, weekends after 4 p.m.

Green Fees. £3.00 (£1.00 with member).
Hotels: Coachman.
Meals served.

W 77   Kings Park

Croftfoot Ave., Croftfoot, Glasgow.
Municipal course.
9 holes, 2056 yds. S.S.S. 64

W 78   Kirkhill

Tel. 041-641 3083
Greenlees Rd., Cambuslang, Glasgow.
18 holes, 5854 yds. S.S.S. 69
Visitors welcome if introduced by member.

W 79   Kirkintilloch

Tel. 041-776 1256
Todhill, Campsie Rd., Kirkintilloch, Glasgow G66 1RN.
1 mile from town.
Parkland course.
18 holes, 5269 yds. S.S.S. 66
Visitors with members only.
Hotels: Campsie Glen Hotel, Campsie Glen; Kincaid House Hotel, Milton of Campsie.
Lunches served.

W 80   Knightswood

Tel. 041-959 2131
Lincoln Ave., Glasgow G13.
4 miles W of city centre.
Meadowland course.
9 holes, 5434 yds. S.S.S. 66
Visitors welcome.
Green Fees. Weekdays 75p; weekends £1.00.

W 81   Kyles of Bute

Tel. Tighnabruaich (070 081) 355 (Sec.)
Kames, Tighnabruaich, Argyll.
By car ferry Gourock-Dunoon, then A815, B836 to Glendaruel and A8003 to Kames; or from A83 Glasgow-Inveraray by A815 to Strachur, A886 to Glendaruel and A8003 to Kames.
Moorland seaside course with scenic views.
9 holes, 2379 yds. S.S.S. 34
Visitors welcome at all times.
Green Fees. Day ticket adult and intermediate £1.00, juniors 50p; weekly ticket adult £6.00, intermediate £4.50, juniors £2.50.
Society Meetings welcome by arrangement.
Hotels: Kames; Royal, Tighnabruaich; Kilfinan Hotel, Kilfinan, Kames Hotel, Kames. No catering facilities at club.

W 82   Lamlash

Tel. Lamlash 296
Lamlash, Brodick, Isle of Arran.
A841, ferry from Ardrossan to Brodick. 3 miles from South Pier.
Undulating heathland course.
18 holes, 4860 yds. S.S.S. 63
Visitors welcome.
Meals served during summer only.

W 83   Lanark

Tel. Lanark (0555) 3219
The Moor, Lanark, Lanarkshire.

Machrie's many splendours

Machrie's charm lies in its out of the way setting. Lapped on one side by the Atlantic and separated from the mainland by a sea voyage (or a short aeroplane hop from Glasgow), its delights are little known.

They are certainly not as well known as they deserve to be, because the course is in the very best tradition of seaside links. However, by developing its assets a little more than in the past, the Island of Islay is putting itself far more on the map; and, without wishing to spoil a way of life by causing a golfing invasion to its shores, the recommendation for its golf is based on happy personal experience that it would be churlish not to pass on.

After years of acting as co-tenants to grazing sheep and cattle, golfers now owe something of a transformation to the owners of Bowmore Distillery who bought the course and hotel, and have added a cluster of cottages alongside which are an ideal base for whatever form of holiday you seek on Islay.

It is a wide choice but, as golfers have supported the distillers' product ever since man first took three putts, there is a delicious aptness about the change. However, Machrie's new look is not confined to new management. It has six new holes which add enormously to its rating as a test of golf.

Some of the eccentricities that grew up before there was much in the way of machinery or golf course architects have been reduced; gone are one or two, though not all, of the blind shots into crater greens— a type of hole not so favourably looked upon as it once was; and in their place have arisen a new 2nd, 10th, 11th, 12th, 13th and 14th that offer, in distillers' language, a smoother blend.

The 1st, a gentle opener, has an inviting drive from a raised tee, but the 2nd quickly gets down to the real golfing business. The first of the alterations, it is a swinging dogleg to the left, the dogleg taking the form of a fast flowing brook with plans for extending the hole to a par 5.

Anyone with thoughts of getting home in two will need a strong nerve as well as two good shots, although the 3rd and 4th are less stern. The 5th is a fine short hole and the 6th typical of Machrie's natural blessings with a drive to the left providing the correct approach and view of a green in a dell.

In its early days in the last century, the drive at the 7th over a vast sandhill was rather more formidable than it is now; all the same, it can still strike fear at the beginning of a stretch of three holes, all par fours, which follow the line of a glorious sandy beach. These emphasize the remoteness and the beauty and that, unlike many famous

seaside courses, here is the opportunity to really see the sea.

The 10th tee is a notable example even if it is no time to be distracted. A marvellous natural short hole at the furthest limit of the course marks the introduction to the new golfing country; this is nicely demanding but, at the same time, there is a pleasant scenic change to the hills and lonely peat moors.

The 11th requires a strong second to a long green with a heathery drop to the left and the not so short par 3 12th is even tougher. The main feature of the 13th, a par 5 bending left, is the amphitheatre in which the green is situated, while the 14th is perhaps the hardest of all the par fours. A long drive is necessary for the proper view of the flag outlined against the skyline.

After a spell where stout hitting is essential, the last four holes are not quite as severe; nevertheless, the need for good judgement is paramount and, against any sort of wind, the 16th and 18th, in particular, can pose much greater problems. However, if your score doesn't turn out quite the way you planned (how many do?), there are ample consolations.

There is no shortage of spirituous assistance to help forget the bad round—and celebrate the good—and the atmosphere of the Club and hotel, as of the island as a whole, is wonderfully friendly and informal.

Signposted at bus station. Turn left into Whitelees Rd. for ½ mile.
Moorland course.
18 holes, 6425 yds. S.S.S. 71
Visitors welcome on weekdays before 4.30 p.m. by telephoning Pro. (Lanark 61456).
Green Fees. £5.75 per round, £8.05 per day.
Society Meetings Mon. and Tues.
Hotels: Cartland Bridge Hotel, Lanark; Tinto; Hartree, Biggar.
Full catering by arrangement.

W 84 Largs

Tel. Largs (0475) 673594
Irvine Rd., Largs, Ayrshire KA30 8EU.
On A78 1 mile S of town centre.
Parkland course.
18 holes, 6257 yds. S.S.S. 70
Visitors welcome with reservation.
Green Fees. Weekdays £4.50 per round, £6.00 per day; weekends £4.50 per round, £6.00 per day, £4.30 after 4.00 p.m.
Society Meetings Tues. and Thurs. only.
Hotels: in Largs.
Meals served.

W 85 Larkhall

Tel. Larkhall 881113
Burnhead Rd., Larkhall, Lanarkshire.
SW on B7019.
9 holes, 6236 yds. S.S.S. 70
Green Fees. 65p per 9 holes.

W 86 Leadhills

Leadhills, Abington, Lanarkshire.
From Leadhills follow lane at side of Hopetoun Arms for 300 yds.
High moorland/mountain course.
9 holes, 1946 yds. S.S.S. 32
Visitors welcome.
Green Fees. Adult £1.00 per day, juniors 50p per day.
Society Meetings not catered for.
Hotels: Abington Hotel, Abington.
No catering facilities at club.

W 87 Lenzie

Tel. 041-776 1535
19 Crosshill Rd., Lenzie, Glasgow G66 5DA.
6½ miles from Glasgow, ½ mile from Lenzie station.
Parkland, moorland course.

18 holes, 5982 yds. S.S.S. 69
Visitors welcome with member only.
Green Fees. Weekdays 60p; weekends £1.50.
Society Meetings weekdays except Mon. by arrangement.
Meals served except Mon.

W 88 Lethamhill

Tel. 041-770 6220
Cumbernauld Rd., Glasgow G33 1AH.
On A80 adjacent to Hogganfield Loch.
Municipal course.
18 holes, 6073 yds. S.S.S. 69
Green Fees. Weekdays 69p; weekends 96p.
Tea room at club April to September.

W 89 Linn Park

Tel. 041-637 5871
Simshill Rd., Glasgow G44.
Off M74 S of Glasgow.
Parkland course.
18 holes, 4832 yds. S.S.S. 63
Visitors welcome.
Green Fees. On application to Secretary.
Snacks served 10 a.m. to 4 p.m.

Traditional delights of Machrihanish

Machrihanish belongs to a world of its own. It has peace, remoteness and beauty, a pace to life that is appealingly unhurried, and a golf course which, if you respect the traditions of British seaside links, is a minor classic.

Situated on the west coast of the Mull of Kintyre, the narrow peninsula of Argyll that is a feature of the famous view from Turnberry, it is the sort of place that makes exiled Scotsmen think of home. To most golfers, however, Machrihanish is no more than an unmistakably Scottish name, a dot on the map 130 circuitous miles from Glasgow, or more conveniently, half an hour in a box-like plane from Abbotsinch.

In the days before and after World War 1, the area around Campbeltown, for all its fame as one of the most socially acceptable golfing resorts in Scotland, appealed to a wider world for the number of distilleries then operating; golf has, however, outlasted most of the distilleries and Machrihanish still commands great affection in the hearts of those who have been there.

From the moment that you tee up by the professional's shop, wondering how much of the sandy bay you dare cut off, the prospects are invigorating. Even without the thought that there is nothing but ocean to the west between the first tee and Long Island, there can be few better opening drives in the world, a fact proudly extolled and preserved by a notice to non-golfers which reads; 'Danger. First tee above, please move farther along the beach.' But after the Machrihanish Burn and the shot over the crest to the 2nd green have been negotiated, the true duneland character of the fine outward half is quickly apparent.

Although Machrihanish has housed the Scottish Women's and Scottish Professional championships, it is really more of a holiday course with a combination of challenge and surroundings rare even in a country where spectacular golf abounds. As with so many of our old established seaside courses— Machrihanish, founded as the Kintyre Club, is almost a century old—the course goes out and back, but following the curve of the great bay just enough to ensure that the wind is not constantly in one's face or on one's back.

If the first two holes give a wonderful impression of the setting, they do not penetrate the dune country to which the delightful 3rd hole introduces us and in which the next five holes are firmly set. These dunes are the true heart of Machrihanish.

The 3rd, with its rolling fairway and the sea beyond, has an inviting second shot; the short 4th (115 yds), with its small plateau green, demands both touch and judgment; and the drive to the 5th, an excellent left-hand dogleg, leaves little room for error.

The 6th is another good drive over a central ridge; the 7th poses a good, old-fashioned second over a high sandhill, and the 8th needs a well-hit second to an elevated green.

The greens, though generally large, owe little to the hand of man and are thoroughly in keeping with a course whose founders would still happily recognise it. The one exception perhaps is the background to the 9th where the guidepost is mixed up with the landing lights for the airport.

The airport, despite having the second longest runway in Europe, also has just about the smallest terminal building and only a couple of flights a day from Glasgow. There is, none the less, a welcome informality about it; you can chat to the pilot, make your own coffee or inspect the boxes of lobsters bound for Billingsgate. There is no bar, no stream of inaudible announcements and no interminable wait for your baggage. If you want a drink, you bring your own—but that embraces another undeniable charm of a place to which the golf course contributes greatly.

The homeward half of the course shows how quickly the character of the terrain can change as you move inland. The journey back to the row of houses by the clubhouse which look out on the ever changing moods of the ocean is quite a contrast, but there is nothing much wrong with the 10th and 12th, the two par fives. The 11th and 15th greens make elusive targets even without a wind; the 13th green is subtly raised at the front and there is the unusual feature of successive short holes, the 15th and 16th.

Cypress Point, Royal Jersey, West Sussex and Sandy Lodge are other courses which come to mind with this same characteristic but, if (theoretically at any rate) the short holes should help the score, the 17th is full of danger.

With out of bounds along the left, the fairway is alarmingly narrow but elsewhere there is plenty of opportunity to open the shoulders and, if one overall comment is how little Machrihanish resorts to bunkers, it is true to say that it doesn't need them. Nature is its great defence.

W 90 Littlehill

Tel. 041-772 1916
Auchinairn Rd., Bishopbriggs, Glasgow.
3 miles N of city centre.
Parkland course.
18 holes, 6199 yds. S.S.S. 69
Visitors welcome; municipal course.
Green Fees. Weekdays £1.10; weekends £1.40.
Hotels: in area.
Meals and snacks available.

W 91 Lochranza

Tel. Lochranza 273
Lochranza, Brodick, Isle of Arran.
9 holes, 3580 yds.

W 92 Lochwinnoch

Tel. Lochwinnoch 842153
Burnfoot Rd., Lochwinnoch.
Off A760, 10 miles from Paisley.
Undulating parkland course.
18 holes, 6223 yds. S.S.S. 70
Visitors welcome on weekdays before 6 p.m., weekends with member only.
Green Fees. £5.00 (£1.00 with member).
Society Meetings welcome on weekdays.
Hotels: Mossend.

W 93 Loudoun Gowf Club

Tel. Galston 820551
Galston, Ayrshire.
Parkland course.
18 holes, 5820 vds. S.S.S. 68

Green Fees. £5.75.
Lunches and high teas served by arrangement.

W 94 Machrie

Tel. Port Ellen (0496) 2310
Machrie Hotel, Port Ellen, Isle of Islay, Argyll PA42 7AN.
By plane from Glasgow or ferry from Kennacraig. On A846 S of airfield.
Seaside course.
18 holes, 6095 yds. S.S.S. 69
Course designed by Willie Campbell (1891).
Visitors welcome.
Green Fees. £2.50 per round, £3.00 per day.
Society Meetings by arrangement.
Hotels: Machrie Hotel.
Meals served in hotel.

Prestwick — home of the Open Championship

Whenever there is talk of low scoring with all the various aids of modern equipment, it is always salutary to remember the total of 149 with which young Tom Morris won the third of his victories in the Open championship belt and so made it his own. It was for three rounds of Prestwick's 12-hole course in 1870, and forms perhaps the most famous chapter in the history of a club where tradition and romance are thickly clustered.

Regrettably nowadays, championships and major tournaments are out of fashion there, mainly because of the difficulties of crowd control, and opportunities to revisit and recall great days long ago thus grow fewer; but it still ought to be part of every golfer's education to play at Prestwick, the original home of the Open championship.

Happily little has changed in over a century, and ordinary golfers whose ideas are not too much influenced by modern architectural principles will be delighted to see as good a stretch of natural golfing country as there is to be found, with sand-hills, cavernous bunkers, a rushing burn, railway and a measure of blind shots.

There are many great holes in golf in which railways play a sinister part, but the first hole at Prestwick is, for my money, quite the best. I can think of no more pleasant way of waiting for a train than on the station platform on the other side of the grey wall, watching as player after player, stiff and nervous, puts his anti-slice mechanism into action.

The slice is the main crime at this hole of medium length, where the railway runs the entire length, but in efforts to avoid the dreaded fate the hook can prove almost equally disastrous. There is, in short, no substitute for courage and even if John Ball performed the hole in three at the 37th in the Amateur final in 1899, a four will make most people's day. At least we don't have to play it three times!

Some relief is found—though not much against a stiff wind—at the short 2nd, but by this time the menacing sleepered Cardinal bunker is in sight at the 3rd and some knowledge of the countless distinguished catches it has made, Braid included, may induce another somewhat more humble one. Provided one is not too ambitious, one ought to clear it with a decent second and be in range of the green, but then follow the distractions of the Pow Burn at the 4th, eating along the right hand side of the fairway, and the large sandhill that has to be cleared in order to reach the green at the short 5th.

The next five holes, the first four of which form a little inland loop close to the airport, do not contain anything like the same special features—though the 10th is a fine hole where it is advisable not to top your drive—but when the course turns for home along the sea out by the short 11th, the character changes again.

The 12th, 13th and 14th, the 13th with a testing second to an unusually shaped green, bring us back to the shadow of the old clubhouse and finally there is the famous loop which is yet another distinctive feature of Prestwick. The 15th, 16th and 18th all offer the definite chance of a three—as long as one makes up one's mind how to play the 15th and can negotiate a treacherous putting surface—but the 17th, one of the finest blind holes in the world, is considerably more formidable and proof that not all holes of this nature are bad and chancy.

In the days of the hickory and the gutty, the 2nd, over the top of the mountainous grassy hill with an attracting bunker beyond, must have been positively alarming and even today nobody is likely to be entirely happy in a scoring competition until it is behind him.

That surely is a tribute that the spirit of the past lives on at Prestwick, and in a world that is forever changing, what an infinite blessing it provides.

W 95   Machrie Bay

Tel. Machrie 258
Machrie, Brodick, Isle of Arran.
9 holes, 2082 yds. S.S.S. 62
Visitors welcome except Sun.
Green Fees. 60p per round; £1.00 per day.

W 96   Machrihanish

Tel. Machrihanish 213
Machrihanish, Campbeltown, Argyll.
5 miles from Campbeltown.
Seaside course.
18 holes, 6228 yds. S.S.S. 70
Course designed by Tom Morris.
Visitors welcome.
Green Fees. Weekdays £4.00 per round, £5.00 per day; weekends £6.00 per day; weekly £20.00; fortnightly £30.00.
Hotels: Ardair Guesthouse, Ardbay Guesthouse, Machrihanish; Argyll Arms; Ardshiel; White Hart; Royal, Campbeltown.
Meals served by arrangement.

W 97   Millport

Tel. Millport 311
Golf Rd., Millport, Isle of Cumbrae.
Seaside moorland course.
18 holes, 5831 yds. S.S.S. 68
Visitors welcome.
Green Fees. Weekdays £3.00 per round, £4.50 per day; weekends £3.50 per round, £5.00 per day.
Society Meetings welcome except July and Aug.
Meals served.

W 98   Milngavie

Tel. 041-956 1619
Laighpark, Milngavie, Glasgow.
Off A809, 6 miles N of Glasgow.
Moorland course.
18 holes, 5818 yds. S.S.S. 68
Course designed by Auchterlonie brothers.
Visitors welcome with member, parties by arrangement.
Green Fees. £6.50 per day.
Hotels: Black Bull, Milngavie.
Meals served by arrangement.

W 99   Mount Ellen

Tel. Glenboig 2277
Gartcosh, Lanarkshire.
Johnston Rd. at British Steel Corporation Works.
Meadowland course.
18 holes, 5525 yds. S.S.S. 67
Visitors welcome with member, parties weekdays by arrangement.
Green Fees. On application to Secretary.
Hotels: Crow Wood, Stepps; Golden Eagle, Cumbernauld.
Meals served.

W 100   New Cumnock

Lochill, New Cumnock, Ayrshire.
On A7, W of New Cumnock.
9 holes, 4730 yds. S.S.S. 63
Visitors welcome.
Green Fees. Weekdays £1.00; weekends £1.50.
Hotels: Crown.

W 101   Old Course Ranfurly

Tel. Bridge of Weir 613612
Bridge of Weir, Renfrewshire.

On A761.
Moorland course.
18 holes, 6266 yds. S.S.S. 70
Visitors welcome on weekdays with reservation, weekends with member only.
Green Fees. On application to Secretary.
Society Meetings welcome weekdays by arrangement.
Hotels: Gryfe Hotel.
Lunches served.

W 102 Paisley

Tel. 041-884 2292
Braehead, Paisley PA2 8TZ.
From Paisley Cross, by Causeyside St., Neilston Rd., then right to Glenburn Housing Estate, then left at roundabout and straight up the hill.
Moorland course.
18 holes, 6405 yds. S.S.S. 71
Visitors welcome with member, parties by arrangement.
Green Fees. £4.00 per round, £6.00 per day.
Hotels: Brabloch; Watermill; Silver Thread, Paisley; Excelsior, Glasgow Airport.
Snacks served; meals by arrangement.

W 103 Palacerigg

Tel. Cumbernauld (023 67) 34969
Palacerigg Country Park, Cumbernauld, Glasgow.
A80 Glasgow-Stirling, A8011 Cumbernauld; follow AA signs to Country Park.
Parkland/moorland course (Cumbernauld Municipal course).
36 holes, 6500 yds. S.S.S. 71
Course designed by R. Kyle M.B.E.
Visitors to clubhouse by arrangement with Secretary.
Green Fees. Weekdays £2.40; weekends and bank holidays £3.00.
Society Meetings by arrangement.
Hotels: Park; Cladham, Falkirk.
Catering by arrangement with Secretary/Steward.

W 104 Pollok

Tel. 041-632 4351
90 Barrhead Rd., Glasgow G43.
On A736, 4 miles S of city centre.
Parkland course.
18 holes, 6257 yds. S.S.S. 70
Visitors welcome with member or letter of introduction.
Green Fees. £6.00 per round, £9.00 per day.
Society Meetings Mon. and Wed. by arrangement 6 months in advance.
Hotels: Macdonald; Tinto Firs.
Meals served.

W 105 Port Bannatyne

Bannatyne Mains Rd., Port Bannatyne, Bute.
2 miles N of Rothesay.
Undulating moorland course.
18 holes, 4654 yds. S.S.S. 63
Visitors welcome.
Green Fees. 85p per round.
Hotels: Mount Clare; Crown.
Meals served.

W 106 Port Glasgow

Tel. Port Glasgow (0475) 41563
Devol Farm Industrial Estate, Port Glasgow, Renfrewshire.
Undulating course.
18 holes, 5712 yds. S.S.S. 69
Visitors welcome on weekdays.
Green Fees. £2.00 per round, £3.00 per day.
Society Meetings by arrangement.

W 107 Prestwick

Tel. Prestwick 77404
Links Rd., Prestwick, Ayrshire KA9 1QG.
1 mile from Prestwick Airport adjacent to Prestwick station.
Seaside course.
18 holes, 6544 yds. S.S.S. 72
Visitors welcome by arrangement except Sat.
Green Fees. £9.50 per day, £6.00 after 4.00 p.m.
Society Meetings welcome except Sat.
Hotels: Caledonian, Ayr; Links; Queens, Prestwick; Marine, Troon.
Lunches served.

W 108 Prestwick St. Cuthbert

Tel. Prestwick (0292) 77107
East Rd., Prestwick, Ayrshire KA9 2SX.
Off main Ayr to Prestwick road at Bellevue Rd.
Parkland course.
18 holes, 6470 yds. S.S.S. 71
Course designed by Stutt Ltd.
Visitors welcome on weekdays, weekends with member only.
Green Fees. £3.00 per round, £4.00 per day; weekly £12.00; quarterly £28.00.
Society Meetings by arrangement.
Hotels: St. Nicholas; Golden Lion.
Meals served.

W 109 Prestwick St. Nicholas

Tel. Prestwick (0292) 77608
Grangemuir Rd., Prestwick KA9 1SN.
Off A79.
Seaside course.
18 holes, S.S.S. 68
Visitors welcome weekdays with letter of introduction.
Green Fees. £6.50 per day.
Society Meetings by arrangement Tues. and Thurs., by Nov.
Hotels: Links; St. Nicholas; Park; Queens.
Meals served.

W 110 Ralston

Tel. 041-882 1349
Strathmore Ave., Ralston, Paisley, Renfrewshire.
Parkland course.
18 holes, 6100 yds. S.S.S. 69
Visitors organized parties only.

W 111 Ranfurly Castle

Tel. Bridge of Weir 612609
Golf Rd., Bridge of Weir, Renfrewshire.
Undulating moorland course.
18 holes, 6284 yds. S.S.S. 70

Society Meetings by arrangement.
Hotels: Gryfe Arms, Bridge of Weir.
Lunches served by arrangement.

W 112 Renfrew

Tel. 041-886 6692
Blythswood Estate, Inchinnan Rd., Renfrew, Renfrewshire.
Off A8 to Greenock. Common entrance with Normandy Hotel.
Parkland course.
18 holes, 6850 yds. S.S.S. 73
Visitors welcome on weekdays with letter of introduction.
Green Fees. £6.00 per day.
Society Meetings welcome on weekdays except Mon.
Hotels: Normandy Airport Hotel, Renfrew; Excelsior, Glasgow Airport.
Meals served except Mon.

W 113 Rothesay

Tel. Rothesay (0700) 3012
Canada Hill, Rothesay, Bute.
Undulating course.
18 holes, 5370 yds. S.S.S. 67
Course designed by James Braid.
Visitors welcome.
Green Fees. £1.20 per round.
Hotels: Glenburn; Foley House Hotel.
Meals served.

W 114 Routenburn

Tel. Largs 673230
Largs, Ayrshire KA30 9AH.
1 mile N of Largs.
Moorland course.
18 holes, 5588 yds. S.S.S. 67
Course designed by James Braid.
Visitors welcome.
Green Fees. On application to Secretary.
Hotels: Springfield; Queens; St. Helens.
Morning coffees, lunches and high teas served by arrangement.

W 115 Royal Troon

Tel. Troon (0292) 311555
Craigend Rd., Troon, Ayrshire KA10 6EP.
3 miles from Prestwick Airport.
Seaside courses.
(Old) 18 holes, 6649 yds. S.S.S. 71
(Portland) 18 holes, 6274 yds. S.S.S. 70
Visitors to Old course welcome on weekdays after 9.30 a.m. and Sun. after 10.30 a.m. Ladies welcome Mon., Wed. and Fri. Visitors to Portland course welcome.
Green Fees. Old course £10.00; Portland course £7.50.
Society Meetings weekdays by arrangement.
Hotels: Marine; Sun Court; Craiglea; Piersland.
Lunches and high teas served.

W 116 Ruchill

Tel. 041-946 8604
Brassey St., Glasgow G20.
Parkland course.
9 holes, 4378 yds. S.S.S. 61
Visitors welcome.
Green Fees. Mon. to Fri. 60p per 9 holes; weekends 85p per 9 holes.

Contrasting splendour of Turnberry and Gleneagles

Shortly after the war if one looked down from the terrace of Turnberry Hotel the prospect for the golfer was forlorn. The two lovely courses, the Ailsa and the Arran, were still being used as the runways of an airfield and, to the layman at any rate, appeared to have suffered a fate worse than death. It needed an imaginative eye and an optimistic mind to visualise their restoration, but through the skill of Mackenzie Ross and the creative work of a fleet of bulldozers—all too often regarded as monsters of destruction—Turnberry was miraculously reborn.

Thereafter its re-establishment was rapid. By housing the Amateur championship, the Walker Cup, the Home Internationals, the match-play championship, the Braemar 7 club tournament and the now defunct match between the amateurs and professionals—all within the space of a few years—the Ailsa course won itself the reputation of being as stern and fair a test as there is to be found in Britain; and the Arran that of the ideal companion. Now it has held a triumphant Open championship and the final acclaim has been accorded it.

If one had to play a round for one's life, which heaven forbid, Turnberry is the classic example of a course where the good shot is rewarded and the bad punished; but the magic of Turnberry lies as much in the grandeur of its surroundings as in the splendour of its golf. Many an exile has imagined himself gazing out on Ailsa Craig, the dark peaks of Arran across the Firth of Clyde and the flatter form of the Mull of Kintyre, and wished he could be walking down the hotel steps with a bag of clubs over his shoulder. But not all Turnberry's beauty is distant or remote and the special thrill of the golf is emphasised by holes such as the 4th, 9th and 10th which bring the golfer into alarmingly close touch with the shore. To stand on the back tee at the 9th one summer evening as the oystercatchers search for their supper, the wavelets tease the rocks and the lighthouse reflects itself in a golden sunset over Arran, is to me perhaps the greatest delight that the many hundreds of British courses have to offer.

As the symbol of seaside golf, it is an important part of our national heritage; but golf in Scotland is full of contrast and, if Turnberry is a noted example of a championship links, Gleneagles, a few miles southwest of Perth, is without doubt the most famous of Scotland's courses inland.

To the countless Americans who flock there each summer, it is the course that comes most easily to mind because it has a unique quality that is at once memorable. For them the luxury of the most famous hotel in the land is an obvious aid to enjoyment, but fulfilment of golfing expectation is only a short step away and on the first tee of either the King's or Queen's the prospect is inspiring.

I often marvel at the insight of the men who first conceived the idea of building courses and hotels at Turnberry, Gleneagles and Moretonhampstead, for they bestowed the game and the British Transport Hotels, who now own them, with mighty assets.

From tees that are for the most part elevated, the golf at Gleneagles is full of inviting drives to heather-lined fairways and there is a succession of delightful second shots to be played from the superb, moorland turf. On a quiet day the play is far from alarming, although against a background of mountain, glen and moor, the problem of clubbing is considerable and it is not surprising that the local caddies are usually better at it than you. In a wind, however, things are very different and the good striker, as he deserves, comes into his own. But always at Gleneagles the golfer has the lasting consolation of the call of the grouse, the partridge, the pheasant, the geese, the duck, the snipe and the woodcock. In a majestic setting that epitomises the glories of Scotland, Gleneagles' motto 'High above the High' is wonderfully apt.

W 117 Sandyhills

Tel. 041-778 1179
Sandyhills Rd., Sandyhills, Glasgow G32 9NA.
3 miles E of city centre.
Undulating parkland course.
18 holes, 6253 yds. S.S.S. 70
Visitors welcome with member only.
Green Fees. £4.00 per round, £6.00 per day.
Society Meetings by arrangement.

W 118 Shiskine

Tel. Shiskine 226
Blackwaterfoot, Isle of Arran, Bute.
12 miles from Brodick.
Seaside course.
12 holes, 2977 yds. S.S.S. 42
Visitors welcome.
Green Fees. £1.75 per round, £2.50 per day, weekly £11.50, fortnightly £17.25, monthly £20.70.
Hotels: Kinloch; Rock.
Meals served during summer.

W 119 Shotts

Tel. Shotts 20431, 22658 (Pro.), 20403 (Sec.)
Blairhead, Shotts, Lanarkshire.
1½ miles off A8, midway between Glasgow and Edinburgh.
Moorland, parkland course.
18 holes, 6125 yds. S.S.S. 70
Visitors welcome, with reservation.
Green Fees. Weekdays £4.60; weekends £5.75.
Society Meetings weekdays.
Catering facilities.

W 120 Skelmorlie

Tel. Wemyss Bay (0475) 520152
Skelmorlie, Ayrshire PA17 5AL.
1 mile from Wemyss Bay station.
Parkland, moorland course.
13 holes, 5104 yds. S.S.S. 65
Visitors welcome except Sat. from Mar. to Oct.
Green Fees. Weekdays £3.00 per day; weekends £5.00.
Society Meetings welcome except Sat.

Hotels: Manor Park Hotel; Heywood Hotel; Wemyss Bay Hotel.
Lunches, dinners and teas served.

W 121 Strathaven

Tel. Strathaven (0357) 20539
Glasgow Rd., Strathaven, Lanarkshire.
On A726, 5 miles from M74 junction 2.
Parkland course.
18 holes, 6225 yds. S.S.S. 70
Course extension designed by J.R. Stutt Ltd.
Visitors welcome on weekdays before 4.30 p.m.
Green Fees. £4.00 per round, £7.00 per day; plus V.A.T.
Hotels: Strathaven.
Meals served except Thurs.

W 122 Tarbert

Tel. Tarbert (08802) 565
Tarbert, Argyll PA29 6TZ.
On B8024, 1 mile W of Tarbert.
Moorland course.
9 holes, 4460 yds. S.S.S. 64
Visitors welcome.
Green Fees. £2.00 per day; weekly £5.00.

Hotels: West Loch Hotel; Tarbert Hotel; Stonefield Castle Hotel.
Licensed clubhouse open evenings.

W 123   Torrance House

Tel. East Kilbride 33451
Strathaven Rd., East Kilbride, Glasgow G75 0QZ.
On A726 on outskirts of East Kilbride.
Parkland course.
18 holes, 6403 yds. S.S.S. 71
Course designed by Hawtree and Sons.
Visitors welcome.
Green Fees. £2.35 per round. Booking system April to October (telephone East Kilbride 48638).
Hotels: Stuart; Bruce; Torrance; Crutherland.
Lunches served.

W 124   Troon Municipal

Tel. (0292) 312 464
Harling Dr., Troon, Ayrshire KA10 6NE.
On A759.
Seaside courses.
3 courses, Lochgreen 18 holes, 6765 yds. Darley 18 holes, 6327 yds. Fullarton 18 holes, 4784 yds.
Visitors welcome, Sat. with reservation until 3.00 p.m. for Lochgreen and Darley courses.
Green Fees. Lochgreen and Darley, weekdays £2.50 per round, £3.30 per day; weekends £5.00 per day; Fullarton weekdays £1.75 per round, £2.30 per day; weekends £3.50 per day. Prices subject to review.
Hotels: South Beach Hotel; Craiglea Hotel; Ardneil Hotel.
Lunches, snacks and high teas served.

W 125   Turnberry Hotel Courses

Tel. Turnberry (06553) 202
Turnberry Hotel, Turnberry, Ayrshire KA26 9LT.
Off A77 from Glasgow just before Girvan.
Seaside courses.
Ailsa 18 holes, 6384 yds. S.S.S. 69
Arran 18 holes, 6276 yds. S.S.S. 69
Course designed by Mackenzie Ross.
Visitors welcome.
Green Fees. Residents £7.50 per day, non-residents £6.50-£13.00 per day.
Society Meetings welcome.
Hotels: Turnberry Hotel; Dormy House.
Morning coffees, lunches and high teas served.

W 126   Vale of Leven

Tel. Alexandria 52531
Northfield Course, Bonfield, Alexandria, Dunbartonshire.
Off A82 at Bonhill.
Moorland course.
18 holes, 5155 yds. S.S.S. 65
Visitors welcome April to September except Sat.
Society Meetings welcome except Sat.
Hotels: Griffen Hotel, Alexandria; Balloch Hotel; Loch Lomond Hotel, Balloch.
Meals served.

W 127   Vaul

Scarinish, Isle of Tiree, Argyll.
Seaside course.
9 holes, 6246 yds. S.S.S. 70
Visitors welcome except Sun.
Green Fees. £2.00 per day; juniors £1.00; weekly £8.00, juniors £2.00; fortnightly £12.00, juniors £2.00.
Hotels: Lodge Hotel, Gott Bay; Scarinish Hotel, Scarinish.

W 128   Western Gailes

Tel. 041-332 1754
Gailes, Irvine, Ayrshire KA11 5AB.
On A78 3 miles N of Troon.
Seaside course.
18 holes, 6763 yds. S.S.S. 72
Visitors welcome on weekdays except Thurs. with letter of introduction.
Green Fees. £6.50.
Society Meetings by arrangement with J.A. Clement, 182 Bath St., Glasgow at above tel. no.
Hotels: in Troon.
Meals served.

W 129   West Kilbride

Tel. West Kilbride 823128
Fullerton Dr., Seamill, West Kilbride, Ayrshire KA23 9LQ.
35 miles from Glasgow off Largs to Irvine road.
Seaside course.
18 holes, 6325 yds. S.S.S. 70
Visitors welcome on weekdays.
Green Fees. £7.00 per day; weekly £25.00; fortnightly £35.00; monthly £40.00.
Society Meetings Tues. and Thurs. only by arrangement. No societies June, July, August.
Hotels: Seamill Hydro; Ardenlee; Galleon Inn; Inverclyde.
Meals served by arrangement.

W 130   Whitecraigs

Tel. 041-639 1681
72 Ayr Rd., Giffnock, Glasgow G77 6SW.
On A77, 9 miles S of Glasgow.
Undulating parkland course.
18 holes, 6230 yds. S.S.S. 70
Course designed by Wm. Fernie.
Green Fees. £6.00 per round, £8.00 per day.
Society Meetings Wed. March to October.
Hotels: Macdonald, Eastwood Toll.
Meals served except Mon.

W 131   Williamwood

Tel. 041-637 1783
Clarkston Rd., Netherlee, Glasgow G44.
5 miles S of Glasgow.
Wooded parkland course.
18 holes, 5808 yds. S.S.S. 68
Course designed by James Braid.
Visitors by introduction only.
Green Fees. By arrangement.
Society Meetings weekdays by arrangement.
Hotels: Macdonald, Giffnock; Redhurst, Clarkston.
Lunches and evening meals served.

W 132   Windyhill

Tel. 041-942 2349
Windyhill, Bearsden, Glasgow.
Off Duntocher Road.
18 holes, 6230 yds. S.S.S. 70
Visitors welcome on weekdays.
Green Fees. £5.50 per day.
Society Meetings by arrangement.

W 133   Wishaw

Tel. Wishaw 72869
55 Cleland Road, Wishaw, Lanarkshire.
15 miles SW of Glasgow.
Parkland course.
18 holes, 6134 yds. S.S.S. 69
Course designed by James Braid.
Visitors welcome on weekdays before 4.00 p.m. and Sun. after 11.00 a.m.
Green Fees. Weekdays £4.50 per day; weekends £6.00 per day.
Society Meetings by arrangement.
Hotels: Crown; Commercial, Wishaw; Popinjay, Rosebank.
Meals served except Mon. and Wed.

X Tayside, Central Region, Fife

X 1 Aberdour

Tel. Aberdour (0383) 860256 (professional/starter), 860688 (clubhouse) Seaside Pl., Aberdour, Fife.
On A92, 4 miles E of N side of Forth Bridge.
Parkland course.
18 holes, 4431 yds. S.S.S. 62
Visitors welcome.
Green Fees. Weekdays £3.00 per round, £4.00 per day.
Society Meetings by arrangement.
Hotels: Woodside Hotel; Aberdour Hotel.
Meals served.

X 2 Aberfeldy

Tel. 088 72 535
Taybridge Rd., Aberfeldy, Perthshire.
On A827 SW of Pitlochry.
Parkland course.
9 holes, 5400 yds. S.S.S. 67
Visitors welcome.
Green Fees. Weekdays and weekends £3.00.
Society Meetings by arrangement.
Hotels: Breadalbane; Station.
Bar snacks.

X 3 Aberfoyle

Tel. Aberfoyle 493
Braeval, Aberfoyle, Stirling.
On A81, 25 miles N of Glasgow.
Hillside course.
12 holes, 5040 yds. S.S.S. 65
Visitors welcome.
Green Fees. £2.00.
Society Meetings welcome.
Hotels: in Aberfoyle.
Lunches served by arrangement.
Meals served except Mon. and Tues.

X 4 Alloa

Tel. Alloa (0259) 722745
Schawpark, Sauchie, Clackmannanshire FK10 3AX.
On A908, 1 mile N of Alloa.
Parkland course.
36 holes, 6240 yds. S.S.S. 70
Visitors welcome.
Green Fees. On application to secretary.
Society Meetings welcome weekdays by arrangement.
Hotels: Endrick; Dunmar.
Meals served.

X 5 Alva

Beauclerc St., Alva, Clackmannanshire.
On A91, 3 miles N of Alloa.
Undulating course.
9 holes, 4574 yds. S.S.S. 64
Visitors welcome.
Green Fees. Weekdays 50p per day; weekends £1.00.

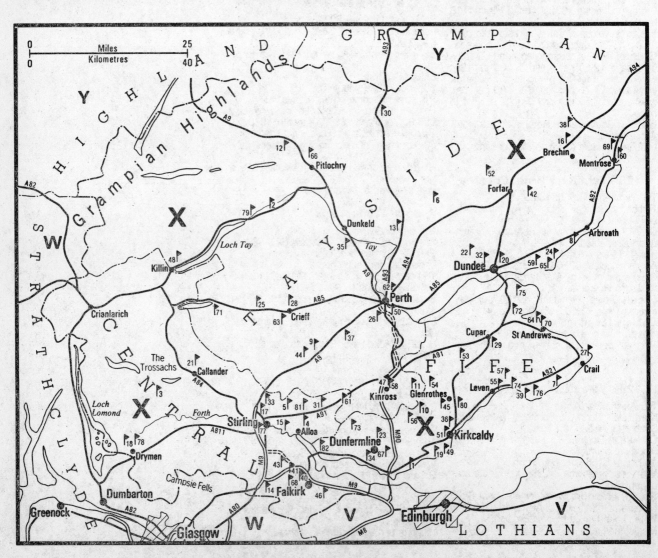

Hotels: Johnstone Arms; Alva Glen Hotel. New clubhouse with bar.

X 6　Alyth

Tel. Alyth 2268
Pitcrocknie, Alyth, Perthshire.
A926 or A927 to Alyth, 16 miles NW of Dundee.
Parkland, moorland course.
18 holes, 6226 yds. S.S.S. 70
Visitors welcome with reservation.
Green Fees. Weekdays £4.50 per day; weekends £6.00 per day.
Society Meetings by written application.
Hotels: Alyth Hotel, Alyth; Lands of Loyal, Alyth; Kings of Kinloch, Meigle.
Meals served.

X 7　Anstruther

Tel. Anstruther (0333) 310387
Marsfield, Anstruther, Fife.
10 miles S of St. Andrews by A959.
Seaside course.
9 holes, 4504 yds. S.S.S. 63
Visitors welcome.
Green Fees. Weekdays £1.60; weekends £2.50; weekly £10.00.
Hotels: Craws Nest; The Smugglers Inn; Royal.
Bar etc.

X 8　Arbroath

Tel. Arbroath 72272, 72069 (Arbroath Artisan Golf Club), 75837 (professional/starter)
Elliot, Arbroath, Angus.
On A92, 2 miles S of Arbroath.
Seaside course.
18 holes, 6078 yds. S.S.S. 69
Visitors welcome.
Green Fees. Weekdays £2.75 per round, £4.00 per day; weekends £4.00 per round, £6.00 per day.
Hotels: in Arbroath.
Meals by arrangement, max. 50.

X 9　Auchterarder

Tel. Auchterarder 2804
Orchil Rd., Auchterarder, Perthshire.
Off A9 to SW of town, approx. 400 yds. up A824.
Parkland course.
18 holes, 5712 yds. S.S.S. 68
Visitors welcome.
Green Fees. Weekdays £3.50; weekends £5.00.
Hotels: Ruthven Tower; Crown; Queen's; Golf.
Meals served by arrangement.

X 10　Auchterderran

Woodend Rd., Cardenden, Fife KY5 0NH.
On A910, 7 miles W of Kirkcaldy.
Moorland course.
9 holes, 5400 yds. S.S.S. 66
Visitors welcome.
Green Fees. Weekdays 75p; weekends £1.00.

X 11　Bishopshire

Kinnesswood, Kinross.
M90, turn off at Kinross on to the A911 Glenrothes road.

Undulating course.
9 holes, 4600 yds. S.S.S. 63
Visitors welcome.
Green Fees. Weekdays £1.00; weekends £1.50.
Society Meetings welcome.
Hotels: Lomond.

X 12　Blair Atholl

Blair Atholl, Pitlochry, Perthshire.
On A9, 7 miles N of Pitlochry.
9 holes, 2859 yds. S.S.S. 69
Visitors welcome.
Green Fees. Mon.-Sat. £2.30; Sun. £3.45; weekly £11.50.
Full clubhouse facilities.

X 13　Blairgowrie

Tel. Blairgowrie (0250) 2383
Rosemount, Blairgowrie, Perthshire PH10 6LG.
A93 from Perth.
Moorland course.
18 holes, 6581 yds. S.S.S. 71
18 holes, 6865 yds. S.S.S. 73
Visitors welcome. Wed. and weekends restricted.
Green Fees. On application to Secretary.
Society Meetings by arrangement.
Meals served.

X 14　Bonnybridge

Tel. Bonnybridge 2645
Larbert Rd., Bonnybridge, Stirlingshire.
On B816, 3 miles W of Falkirk.
Undulating moorland course.
9 holes, 6060 yds. S.S.S. 69
Visitors welcome with reservation.
Green Fees. On application to secretary.
Society Meetings welcome on weekdays.
Hotels: Norwood.
Meals served.

X 15　Braehead

Tel. Alloa 722078
Cambus, Alloa, Clackmannanshire.
2 miles W of Alloa on A907.
18 holes, 6162 yds. S.S.S. 69
Visitors and parties welcome.
Green Fees. Weekdays £3.00 per round, £4.00 per day; weekends £4.00 per round, £6.00 per day.

X 16　Brechin

Tel. Brechin 2383
Trinity, Brechin, Angus.
On A94, 1 mile N of Brechin.
Parkland, meadowland course.
18 holes, 5245 yds. S.S.S. 66
Course designed by James Braid.
Visitors welcome.
Green Fees. Weekdays £2.05 per round, £2.70 per day; weekends £2.40 per round, £3.45 per day.
Society Meetings welcome.
Hotels: Northern Hotel, Brechin.
Meals served by arrangement.

X 17　Bridge of Allan

Tel. Bridge of Allan 832332
Pendreich Rd., Sunnylaw, Bridge of Allan, Stirling.

3 miles N of Stirling. At river in Bridge of Allan turn up hill to golf course - signposted.
Undulating parkland course.
9 holes, 4932 yds. S.S.S. 65
Visitors welcome except Sat. during summer.
Green Fees. Weekdays £2.00; weekends £3.00.
Society Meetings by arrangement.
Hotels: Royal; Queen's, Bridge of Allan.
Meals served by arrangement.

X 18　Buchanan Castle

Tel. Drymen (036 06) 60307
Drymen, Glasgow.
Off A809, 17 miles NW of Glasgow.
Parkland course.
18 holes, 6032 yds. S.S.S. 69
Course designed by James Braid.
Visitors welcome with reservation.
Green Fees. Men £7.00 per round, Ladies £6.00 per round.
Society Meetings Thurs. only.
Hotels: Buchanan Arms; Winnock.
Meals served by arrangement.

X 19　Burntisland House

Tel. Burntisland (0592) 873247
Dodhead, Burntisland, Fife KY3 9EL.
On B923, ½ mile E of Burntisland.
Undulating parkland course.
18 holes, 5871 yds. S.S.S. 68
Visitors welcome.
Green Fees. Weekdays £3.00 per round, £4.00 per day; weekends £4.50 per round, £6.50 per day.
Society Meetings welcome by arrangement with secretary.
Hotels: Greenmount; Kingwood; Milton; Leonard.
Full catering facilities.

X 20　Caird Park

Tel. Dundee (0382) 453606
Mains Loan, Dundee.
Kingsway, on N edge of city.
Parkland course.
18 holes, 6303 yds. S.S.S. 70
Visitors welcome.
Green Fees. £2.50 per round.

X 21　Callander

Tel. Callander (0877) 30259 Sec.; 30090 Clubhouse; 30301 Bookings Sec.
Aveland Rd., Callander, Perthshire.
¼ mile from town centre.
Moorland, parkland course.
18 holes, 5204 yds. S.S.S. 66
Visitors welcome on weekdays, Sats. with reservation.
Green Fees. Weekdays £3.00 per round, £4.00 per 2 rounds; weekends £6.00 per day; weekly £20.00.
Society Meetings by arrangement with Bookings Sec.
Hotels: in Callander.
Meals served; bar.

X 22　Camperdown

Tel. Dundee 645450 (club facilities), 23141 ext. 414 (course bookings), 645457 (starter)
Camperdown Park, Dundee DD2.

Coupar Angus Rd. at Kingsway junction.
Parkland course.
18 holes, 6561 yds. S.S.S. 72
Visitors welcome, 2 rounds Mon. to Fri., 1 round Sat. or Sun. Bookings from Parks Dept., 17 Kings St., Dundee.
Green Fees. £3.00 per day (Mar.-Oct.); £2.00 per day (Nov.-Feb.); booking fee 20p per golfer.
Society Meetings welcome on weekdays.
Hotels: Taypark Hotel.
Meals by arrangement except Tues. a.m.

X 23   Canmore

Tel. Dunfermline 24969
Venturefair, Dunfermline, Fife.
On A823 1 mile N of Dunfermline.
Undulating parkland course.
18 holes, 5474 yds. S.S.S. 66
Visitors welcome.
Green Fees. Weekdays £2.15 per round, £4.00 per day; weekends £5.00 per round or day.
Society Meetings welcome weekdays by arrangement.
Hotels: King Malcolm, Dunfermline.
Meals served by arrangement.

X 24   Carnoustie

Tel. Carnoustie (0241) 53249
Links Parade, Carnoustie, Angus DD7 6AP.
On A630, 12 miles E of Dundee.
Seaside courses.
Championship 18 holes, 6809 yds. S.S.S. 74
Burnside 18 holes, 5935 yds. S.S.S. 69
Buddon Links 18 holes, 6445 yds. S.S.S. 71
Visitors welcome with reservation.
Green Fees. Championship weekdays £5.50; weekends £6.50; Burnside weekdays £3.50; weekends £4.50; Buddon Links weekdays £2.50, weekends £3.00.
Hotels: Brax; Glencoe; Bruce; Station.

X 25   Comrie

Comrie, Perthshire.
On A85, 6 miles W of Crieff.
Highland course.
9 holes, 5962 yds. S.S.S. 69
Visitors welcome.
Green Fees. Weekdays £2.00; weekends £3.00.
Society Meetings by arrangement.
Hotels: Comrie; Royal; Ancaster.

X 26   Craigie Hill

Tel. Perth 24377
Cherrybank, Perth.
On Glasgow road at W end of town.
Undulating course.
18 holes, 5379 yds. S.S.S. 66
Course designed by J. Anderson.
Visitors welcome.
Green Fees. Weekdays £4.03; weekends £6.90.
Hotels: in Perth.
Meals served.

X 27   Crail Golfing Society

Tel. Crail 033 35 278 or 686
Balcomie Clubhouse, Fifeness, Crail, KY10 3XN.
10 miles SE of St. Andrews.
Seaside links course.

18 holes, 5749 yds. S.S.S. 68
Visitors welcome.
Green Fees. Weekdays £3.50 per round, £5.00 per day; weekends £6.00.
Society Meetings on written application to Secretary. No parties during July or August.
Hotels: Golf; Marine; Croma; Balcomie Links; East Neuk.
Meals served.

X 28   Crieff

Tel. Crieff (0764) 2909
Perth Rd., Crieff, Perthshire PH7 3LR.
On A85 NE of Crieff, towards Perth.
Undulating parkland courses.
18 holes, 5818 m.
9 holes, 2632 m.
Visitors welcome with reservation.
Green Fees. 18 holes weekdays £3.50 per round, weekends £5.00 per round; 9 holes weekdays £2.50 per round, weekends £3.50 per round.
Society Meetings by arrangement.
Hotels: Arduthie; Murray Park Hotel; Crieff Hydro.
Lunches, bar snacks; high teas served by arrangement.

X 29   Cupar

Tel. Cupar 53549
Hill Tarvit, Cupar, Fife.
Off A91, 10 miles W of St. Andrews.
9 holes, 5074 yds. S.S.S. 65
Visitors welcome.
Hotels: Royal; Station.
Green Fees. Weekdays £1.75 per round, £2.30 per day (juniors 35p per day); weekends £2.30 per round, £3.45 per day (juniors 65p per round).

X 30   Dalmunzie

Tel. Glenshee (025085) 224
Glenshee, Blairgowrie, Perthshire PH10 7QG.
A93 beside hotel, 22 miles N of Blairgowrie.
Undulating course.
9 holes, 2110 yds. S.S.S. 62
Visitors welcome.
Green Fees. £1.50 per 9 holes, £3.00 per day; weekly £10.00.
Hotels: Dalmunzie Hotel.

X 31   Dollar

Tel. Dollar 2400
Brewlands House, Dollar, Clackmannanshire.
On A91, 13 miles E of Stirling.
Hillside course.
18 holes, 5144 yds. S.S.S. 66
Visitors welcome on weekdays, weekends with member only.
Green Fees. £3.50 per round or day; weekly £12.00.
Meals served.

X 32   Downfield

Tel. Downfield (0382) 825595
Turnberry Ave., Dundee DD2 3QP.
Via Kingsway, A923 and Harrison Rd.
Parkland course.
18 holes, 6916 yds. S.S.S. 73
Visitors welcome on weekdays, weekends with member only, reservation advised.

Green Fees. £4.75 per round, £7.00 per day.
Hotels: Angus; Queen's; Swallow.
Meals served.

X 33   Dunblane

Tel. Dunblane 822343
Perth Rd., Dunblane, Perthshire.
On A9.
Parkland course.
18 holes, 5876 yds. S.S.S. 68
Visitors welcome on weekdays.
Green Fees. £3.00 per round, £5.00 per day.
Hotels: Dunblane Hydro; Stirling Arms.
Meals served by arrangement.

X 34   Dunfermline

Tel. Dunfermline (0383) 23534
Pitfirrane, Crossford, Dunfermline, Fife.
Leave M90 at junction 3; A907 to Dunfermline.
Parkland course.
18 holes, 6244 yds. S.S.S. 70
Visitors welcome with reservation.
Green Fees. £4.00 per round, £6.00 per day.
Society Meetings by arrangement.
Hotels: Pitfirrane Arms; Keavil House, Crossford; King Malcolm, Dunfermline; Halfway House, Kingseat.
Meals served except Thurs.

X 35   Dunkeld & Birnam

Tel. Dunkeld 524
Fungarth, Dunkeld, Perthshire.
2 miles N of Dunkeld on Blairgowrie road.
Undulating moorland course.
9 holes, 2632 yds. S.S.S. 66
Visitors welcome.
Green Fees. Weekdays £1.00; Sat. £1.50; Sun. £2.00.
Society Meetings by arrangement.
Hotels: Royal; Atholl; Tayside, Dunkeld.
Meals served by arrangement.

X 36   Dunnikier Park

Tel. Kirkcaldy (0592) 61599
Dunnikier Way, Kirkcaldy, Fife.
N boundary of town.
Parkland course.
18 holes, 6601 yds. S.S.S. 72
Visitors welcome.
Green Fees. Weekdays £1.65 per round; weekends £2.50 per round.
Society Meetings welcome on weekdays, weekends at 10.00 a.m. and 3.00 p.m., max. 30.
Hotels: Dunnikier House Hotel.

X 37   Dunning

Tel. Dunning 398
Rollo Park, Dunning, Perth.
Off A9, 9 miles SW of Perth.
Parkland course.
9 holes, 4836 yds. S.S.S. 64
Green Fees. Weekdays £1.50; weekends £2.00.
Hotels: Dunning; Kirk Style; Thorntree; Kippen House.

Up periscopes at Elie

Although St. Andrews naturally enough dwarfs them all, there are several other courses throughout Fife which offer some splendidly enjoyable golf.

These include Leven, Lundin Links, up the coast from Kirkcaldy, Ladybank, Scotscraig, the Balcomie Links at Crail—one of the six or seven oldest clubs in the world—and finally Elie, a comfortable drive south through green fields from St. Andrews.

Many were the times that I visited Elie as a boy to stay with friends in a house overlooking the 5th green, and I have always thought of it as having a distinct atmosphere only to be found in golfing towns in Scotland; but it was many years before I actually hit a stroke over the course, and came to realise what I had missed.

Elie was a Danish settlement centuries ago, but the golfing historians recognize it as the birthplace of James Braid, who thus sowed the seeds of his distinguished career on its pleasant stretch of linksland; a recommendation in itself.

No clear indication exists as to when golf was first played there, but there seems little doubt that over twenty-seven acres of the present course there was activity for well over 100 years before the Golf House Club

was founded in 1875, each hole following the engaging custom of the time of having a name of its own.

The clubhouse stands at the top of a narrow, walled lane and after the starter in his little green hut has seen that the way is clear by means of his submarine periscope, the round begins with a blind drive over the crest of a hill which looks away towards a rich, agricultural setting inland.

At first the ground may seem somewhat lacking in the character expected at the seaside, and the opening holes which take us out past a row of houses at Earlsferry, frequently the unintended target of the golfers, are not remarkable, but this is because there is a growing impatience to see the sea and once one has carried over the brow of the 6th fairway, Elie's full charm is apparent.

The 9th, with the wind off the sea, is out of reach in two, and a well-judged pitch is needed down a little slope to the green; the 10th (275 yds) has an inviting drive in spite of not having a sight of the green by the water's edge, where the view on a good day shows North Berwick and Muirfield across the Firth of Forth; and the 11th (Sea Hole),

easily the shorter of the two par threes, is full of menace.

A big drive from the back tee at the 12th (Bents) must cut the corner of the rocky beach, and then there is the 13th (Croupie) the best of all the holes, out into the corner near MacDuff's cave under the shadow of a grey mountainous cliff. The drive here is relatively straightforward but the second in a crosswind is a most demanding stroke to a raised angled green, capable of accommodating two or three cricket pitches end to end.

With its several sloping greens, many awkward drives and frequent blind shots, Elie provides enormous fun for family holiday golf and is rightly most popular in this respect, but such a description does it less than justice.

The bulk of the Scottish professionals found it far from easy during their championship; the Scottish women's championship has been held there twice since the war, and the good amateur invariably finds the task of breaking 70 rather more than he can manage. In short, it combines the best of both worlds and, like all seaside courses, is rarely the same two days running—an added part of its appeal.

X 38   Edzell

Tel. Edzell 235
Edzell, Angus.
On B966, 6 miles N of Brechin.
Parkland course.
18 holes, 6299 yds. S.S.S. 70
Visitors welcome.
Green Fees. Weekdays £4.00 per round, £6.00 per day; weekends £7.00 per round or day.
Society Meetings by arrangement.
Hotels: Glenesk; Central Hotel; Panmure Arms.
Meals and morning coffee served by arrangement.

X 39   Elie

Tel. Elie 330301
Elie, Fife KY9 1AS.
10 miles from St. Andrews.
Seaside course.
18 holes, 6253 yds. S.S.S. 70
Visitors welcome.
Green Fees. Weekdays £4.00; weekends £5.00.
Society Meetings welcome weekdays only.
Hotels: Golf; New Queens.
Lunches and teas served.

X 40   Falkirk

Tel. Falkirk 23457
Stirling Rd., Falkirk, Stirlingshire.
On A9, 1½ miles W of Falkirk town centre.
Parkland course.
18 holes, 6090 yds. S.S.S. 69
Visitors welcome on weekdays up to 4.00 p.m.
Society Meetings welcome weekdays by prior arrangement with Hon. Secretary.
Meals served.

X 41   Falkirk Tryst

Tel. Larbert 2415
86 Burnhead Rd., Larbert, Stirlingshire FK5 4BD.
4 miles from Falkirk, ¾ mile from Larbert station.
Moorland course.
18 holes, 6037 yds. S.S.S. 69
Visitors welcome weekdays except Wed.; Wed., Sat. and Sun. with member only.
Green Fees. £3.50 per round, £5.00 per day; with member Mon. to Sat. 80p; Sun. £1.20.
Society Meetings Tues. and Thurs. only.
Hotels: Plough, Stenhousemuir; Station, Larbert.

X 42   Forfar

Tel. Forfar 62120, professional 65683
Cunninghill, Arbroath Rd., Forfar, Angus DD8 2RL.
1½ miles E of Forfar on A932.
Undulating moorland, woodland course.
18 holes, 5537 m. S.S.S. 69
Visitors welcome.
Green Fees. Weekdays £3.50; weekends £6.00 (V.A.T. additional).
Society Meetings by arrangement.
Hotels: Royal; County; Queen's; Benholme.
Meals served.

X 43   Glenbervie

Tel. Larbert 2605
Stirling Rd., Larbert, Stirlingshire FK5 4SJ.
On A9 between Falkirk and Stirling.
Parkland course.
18 holes, 6423 yds. S.S.S. 71
Course designed by James Braid.
Visitors welcome on weekdays.
Green Fees. £6.00 per round, £10.00 per 2 rounds.
Society Meetings by arrangement.
Hotels: Airth Castle; Powfoulis; Park.
Meals served by arrangement with clubmistress.

X 44   Gleneagles Hotel

Tel. Auchterarder (07646) 2231 (hotel reservations), 3543 (golf reservations)
Telex 76105
Auchterarder, Perthshire PH3 1NE.
Off A9, 16 miles SW of Perth.
Moorland courses.
King's 18 holes, 6503 yds. S.S.S. 71
Queen's 18 holes, 6278 yds. S.S.S. 70
Prince's 18 holes, 4678 yds. S.S.S. 64
Glendevon 18 holes, 5763 yds. S.S.S. 68
King's and Queen's designed by James Braid.
Visitors welcome. Advance booking advisable either by telephone or in writing - for the attention of the Golf Reservations Office, Gleneagles Hotel Golf Courses, Auchterarder, Perthshire.
Green Fees. On application to Golf Reservations Office.
Meals served in Dormy House Restaurant, open all year round.
Society Meetings by arrangement.
Hotels: Gleneagles Hotel.

X 45   Glenrothes

Tel. Glenrothes (0592) 758686
Golf Course Rd., Glenrothes.
West end of Glenrothes.
Undulating parkland course.
18 holes, 6449 yds. S.S.S. 71
Course designed by J.R. Stutt.
Visitors welcome.
Green Fees. Weekdays £1.65 per round; weekends £2.50 per round.
Society Meetings welcome except Sat.
Hotels: Rothes Arms.
Meals served by arrangement.

X 46   Grangemouth Municipal

Tel. Polmont (0324) 711500
Polmonthill, Falkirk, Stirlingshire, Scotland.
M9 junction 4, follow signpost at roundabout to Polmonthill.
Parkland course.
18 holes, 6339 yds. S.S.S. 71
Visitors welcome.
Green Fees. Weekdays £1.75 per round, £2.50 per day; weekends £2.25 per round, £3.00 per day.
Society Meetings by arrangement.
Hotels: Inchrya Grange Hotel, Polmont.
Coffee, lunches and high teas served by arrangement 24 hours in advance.

X 47   Green Hotel

Tel. Kinross (0577) 63467
Green Hotel, Kinross KY13 7AS.
On M90 between Edinburgh and Perth.
Parkland course.
18 holes, 6086 yds. S.S.S. 70
Visitors welcome.
Green Fees. Weekdays £2.50 per round, £3.60 per day; weekends £6.20 per day.
Society Meetings by arrangement.
Hotels: Green Hotel.
Meals served.

X 48   Killin

Tel. Killin (056 72) 312
The Golf Course, Killin, Perthshire.
1 mile from village on A827 Aberfeldy road.
Parkland course.
9 holes, 2508 yds. S.S.S. 65
Visitors welcome.
Green Fees. Weekdays £2.50; weekends £3.00; weekly excluding Sat. or Sun. £10.00.
Society Meetings welcome Apr., May, Sept., Oct.
Hotels: Bridge of Lochay; Killin Hotel, Killin; Lochearnhead Hotel, Lochearnhead.
Lunches and bar snacks served.

X 49   Kinghorn

Tel. Kinghorn 890345, secretary 890373
MacDuff Cres., Kinghorn, Fife.
3 minutes from railway station.
Undulating seaside, parkland course.
18 holes, 5216 yds. S.S.S. 67
Visitors welcome.
Green Fees. Weekdays £1.65 per round; weekends £2.50 per round.
Hotels: Carlin Craig; Kinghorn Hotel.
Parties catered for by arrangement.

X 50   King James VI

Tel. Perth 25170 & 32460
Moncreiffe Island, Perth PH2 8NR.
On River Tay in centre of city.
Inland course.
18 holes, 6037 yds. S.S.S. 69
Green Fees. Weekdays £3.50 per round, £5.00 per day; weekends £7.00 per day.
Hotels: Salutation Hotel; Royal George.
Lunches served by arrangement.

X 51   Kirkcaldy

Tel. Kirkcaldy (0592) 60370
Balwearie, Kirkcaldy, Fife.
On A92 at W end of town.
Parkland course.
18 holes, 5960 yds. S.S.S. 69
Visitors welcome.
Green Fees. Weekdays £3.50 per round, £4.50 per day; weekends £4.50 per round, £5.50 per day; £1.50 if playing with member.
Society Meetings by arrangement.
Hotels: Station; Ollerton; Royal Albert, Kirkcaldy.
Morning coffees, lunches and high teas served.

X 52   Kirriemuir Players'

Tel. Kirriemuir 2144
Kirriemuir, Angus.
1 mile N of town centre.
Moorland, meadowland course.
18 holes, 5521 yds. S.S.S. 67
Visitors welcome on weekdays, weekends with member only.
Green Fees. £4.50 per day.
Society Meetings weekends by arrangement.
Hotels: Ogilvy Arms; Airlie Arms, Kirriemuir; Dykehead, Cortachy.
Meals served by arrangement.

X 53   Ladybank

Tel. Ladybank 30320
Annsmuir, Ladybank, Fife KY7 7LE.
Main Edinburgh-Dundee road 6 miles from Cupar.
Moorland course.
18 holes, 6665 yds. S.S.S. 72
Course designed by Tom Morris Sen. (1879).

Visitors welcome.
Green Fees. Weekdays £4.50 per round, £6.50 per day; weekends £6.00 per round, £8.00 per day.
Society Meetings by arrangement.
Hotels: Fernie Castle Hotel, Letham, Ladybank.
Lunches, bar snacks, high teas and suppers served.

X 54   Leslie

Balsillie, Leslie, Fife.
Undulating course.
9 holes, 4670 yds. S.S.S. 63
Hotels: Greenside Hotel; Rothes Oak Hotel; Station.

X 55   Leven Golfing Society

Tel. Leven (033 32) 26096
Links Rd., Leven, Fife KY8 4PX.
9 miles NE of Kirkcaldy on coast road.
Seaside course.
18 holes, 6425 yds. S.S.S. 71
Visitors welcome on weekdays with reservation.
Green Fees. Weekdays £3.50 per round (£1.75 with member), £5.00 per day (£2.50 with member); weekends £4.60 per round (£2.30 with member), £6.90 per day (£3.45 with member).
Hotels: Caledonian; Beach; Morven Guest House.
Meals served by arrangement.

X 56   Lochgelly

Tel. Lochgelly 780174
Cartmore Rd., Lochgelly, Fife.
On A910, 2 miles NE of Cowdenbeath.
Parkland course.
18 holes, 5394 yds. S.S.S. 66
Visitors welcome on weekdays.
Green Fees. On application to secretary.
Society Meetings welcome weekdays only.
Hotels: Queens Arms.

X 57   Lundin

Tel. Lundin Links 320202
Golf Rd., Lundin Links, Fife KY8 6BA.
On A915, 3 miles NE of Leven.
Seaside course.
18 holes, 6377 yds. S.S.S. 71
Visitors welcome Mon. to Sat.; Sun. with member only, Sats. outwith competition times.
Green Fees. £5.00 per round, £7.50 per day; weekly £20.00; fortnightly £30.00.
Hotels: Beach Hotel; Lundin Links Hotel; Old Manor.
Meals served by arrangement except Mon.

X 58   Milnathort

Lumbenny, Milnathort, Kinross.
Off M90, 1½ miles N of Kinross.
9 holes, 5918 yds. S.S.S. 68
Visitors welcome.
Green Fees. Weekdays £1.25 per day; Sat. £2.00 per day; Sun. £2.50 per day.
Society Meetings by arrangement.
Hotels: Royal; Thistle, Milnathort.

X 59   Monifieth Links

Tel. Monifieth 2678
Princes St., Monifieth, Angus.
Secretary Mr. Ian F. Baxter, 5 The Fairway,
Monifieth, Dundee DD5 4TL.
On A930, 7 miles E of Dundee.
Seaside courses.
Medal 18 holes, 6657 yds. S.S.S. 72
Ashludie 18 holes, 5123 yds. S.S.S. 66
Visitors welcome on weekdays, Sun. with
reservation.
Green Fees. Medal course weekdays
£4.60 per round, Sun. £5.60 per round;
£8.00 per day; weekly £18.00. Ashludie
course weekdays £3.00, Sun. £3.40; £6.50
per day; weekly £12.00.
Society Meetings weekdays by
arrangement.
Hotels: Panmure; Monifieth; Royal; Milton
House.
Meals served by arrangement with club
stewards, Monifieth G.C.; Broughty G.C.;
Grange, Dundee G.C.

X 60   Montrose Mercantile

Tel. Montrose 2408
East Links, Montrose, Angus DD10 8SW.
Off A92, 1 mile from town centre.
Seaside courses.
Medal 18 holes, 6410 yds. S.S.S. 71
Broomfield 18 holes, 4863 yds. S.S.S. 63
Visitors welcome.
Green Fees. Medal Mon. to Sat. £1.50
(juniors 75p); Sun. £2.50 (juniors 75p).
Broomfield Mon. to Sat. £1.10 (juniors 50p);
Sun. £1.50 (juniors 75p). All fees under
review.
Society Meetings by arrangement with
Mr. J. McPherson, Town Buildings, High St.,
Montrose.
Hotels: in Montrose.
Meals served by arrangement except Thurs.

X 61   Muckhart

Tel. Muckhart (025981) 423
Drumburn, Muckhart, Dollar, Clackmannan-
shire.
Off A91, 14 miles E of Stirling.
Moorland course.
18 holes, 6112 yds. S.S.S. 70
Visitors welcome.
Green Fees. Weekdays £4.50 per day;
weekends £5.50 per day.
Society Meetings welcome.
Hotel: Rumbling Bridge Hotel.
Meals served.

X 62   Murrayshall

Tel. Perth (0738) 51173 (secretary),
52784 (professional)
Murrayshall, Scone, Perth PH2 7PH.
A94, 2 miles from Perth.
Undulating parkland course.
18 holes, 6416 yds. S.S.S. 71
Course designed by Hamilton Stutt.
Visitors welcome.
Green Fees. Weekdays £3.50 per round,
£5.00 per day; weekends £5.00 per round,
£8.00 per day.
Society Meetings welcome weekdays
and Suns. with advance booking.
Hotels: Murrayshall House Golf; Wheel Inn
Motel, Scone; Salutation, Perth.
Coffee, club lunches and high teas served.

X 63   Muthill

Peat Rd., Muthill, Perthshire PH7.
On A822, 3 miles S of Crieff.
Parkland course.
9 holes, 4742 yds. S.S.S. 63
Visitors welcome with reservation.
Green Fees. Weekdays £1.50; weekends
£2.00; 1st Oct. to 31st Mar. £1.50.
Hotels: Drummond Arms; Commercial.

X 64   New

Tel. St. Andrews (0334) 73426
3-6 Gibson Pl., St. Andrews, Fife KY16 PJE.
Seaside courses.
Visitors welcome.
Hotels: in St. Andrews.
Lunches served.

X 65   Panmure

Tel. Carnoustie (0241) 53120
Barry, Carnoustie, Angus.
Off A930, 2 miles W of Carnoustie.
Seaside course.
18 holes, 6301 yds. S.S.S. 70
Visitors welcome except Sat.
Green Fees. Weekdays £6.50; Sun.
£7.50.
Society Meetings by arrangement.
Hotel: Bruce, Carnoustie.
Snacks served; meals except Mon.

X 66   Pitlochry

Tel. Pitlochry (0796) 2114
Pitlochry Estates Office, Pitlochry, Perthshire
PH16 5QY.
Follow signs from Larchwood Rd., Pitlochry.
Undulating course.
18 holes, 5811 yds. S.S.S. 68
Course designed by Major Cecil Hutchison.
Visitors welcome.
Green Fees. Weekdays £4.00; weekends
£6.00.
Society Meetings by arrangement.
Hotels: in Pitlochry.
Meals served.

X 67   Pitreavie (Dunfermline)

Tel. Dunfermline (0383) 22591
Queensferry Rd., Dunfermline, Fife.
S of town, off M90.
Parkland course.
18 holes, 6770 yds. S.S.S. 69
Visitors welcome.
Green Fees. Weekdays £3.45; weekends
£7.00 (75p with member).
Society Meetings welcome.
Hotel: King Malcolm.
Full catering facilities.

X 68   Polmont

Tel. Polmont 711277
Manuelrigg, Maddiston, Falkirk, Stirlingshire
FK2 0HR.
On B805, 4 miles W of Falkirk.
Undulating course.
9 holes, 6014 yds. S.S.S. 69
Visitors welcome.
Green Fees. Weekdays £1.50; Sat.
£2.00; Sun. £2.50.
Society Meetings welcome.
Hotels: Inchyra Grange; Polmont Bank
Hotel, Polmont.
Meals served.

X 69   Royal Albert

Tel. Montrose 2376
Dorward Rd., Montrose, Angus.
Seaside courses.
Auxiliary 18 holes, 4863 yds. S.S.S. 66
Medal 18 holes, 6442 yds. S.S.S. 71
Hotels: Park Hotel; Corner House Hotel.
Lunches served.

X 70   A) St. Andrews Eden Course

Tel. St. Andrews (0334) 74296
Golf Pl., St. Andrews, Fife KY16 9JA.
From Edinburgh over Forth Road Bridge,
take A91 just before end of motorway
beyond Kinross.
Seaside course.
18 holes, 5971 yds. S.S.S. 69
Visitors welcome.
Green Fees. Weekdays £2.50; weekends
£3.50; weekly £12.00.
Society Meetings by arrangement.
Hotels: in St. Andrews.

X 70   B) St. Andrews Jubilee Course

Tel. St. Andrews (0334) 73938
Golf Pl., St. Andrews, Fife KY16 9JA.
From Edinburgh over Forth Road Bridge,
take A91 just before end of motorway
beyond Kinross.
Seaside course.
18 holes, 6284 yds. S.S.S. 70
Visitors welcome.
Green Fees. Weekdays £2.00; weekends
£3.00; weekly £12.00.
Society Meetings by arrangement.
Hotels: in St. Andrews.

X 70   C) St. Andrews New Course

Tel. St. Andrews (0334) 73938
Golf Pl., St. Andrews, Fife KY16 9JA.
From Edinburgh over Forth Road Bridge,
take A91 just before end of motorway
beyond Kinross.
Seaside course.
18 holes, 6604 yds. S.S.S. 72
Visitors welcome.
Green Fees. Weekdays £3.00; weekends
£4.00; weekly £12.00.
Society Meetings by arrangement.
Hotels: in St. Andrews.

X 70   D) St. Andrews Old Course

Tel. St. Andrews (0334) 73393
Golf Pl., St. Andrews, Fife KY16 9JA.
From Edinburgh over Forth Road Bridge,
take A91 just before end of motorway
beyond Kinross.
Seaside course.
18 holes, 6578 yds. S.S.S. 72
Visitors welcome except Sun.
Green Fees. Weekdays £6.00; Sat.
£7.00.
Society Meetings by arrangement.
Hotels: in St. Andrews.

X 71   St. Fillans

Tel. St. Fillans 312
St. Fillans, Perthshire.
On A85 between Lochearnhead and Comrie.
Parkland course.
9 holes, 2556 yds. S.S.S. 65
Visitors welcome.

Green Fees. Weekdays £1.50; juniors £1.00; weekends £2.50; weekly £8.00.
Hotels: Drummond Arms; Four Seasons, St. Fillans; Lochearnhead Hotel, Marie Stuart, Hansewood; Lochearnhead.
Snacks served.

X 72   St. Michaels

Tel. Leuchars 365
Leuchars, Fife.
On A919, 6 miles N of St. Andrews.
9 holes, 5510 yds. S.S.S. 67

X 73   Saline

Tel. Saline 591
Kinneddar Hill, Saline, Fife.
4 miles NW of Dunfermline.
Undulating course.
9 holes, 5192 yds. S.S.S. 65
Visitors welcome (some restrictions on competition days).
Green Fees. Weekdays £1.25; weekends and holidays £2.00.

X 74   Scoonie

Municipal Golf Course, Leven, Fife.
10 miles SW of St. Andrews.
Parkland course.
18 holes, 5500 yds. S.S.S. 66
Visitors Weekdays £1.60, juniors 60p; weekends £2.50, juniors £1.00.
Hotels: Caledonian; Beach Hotel.

X 75   Scotscraig

Tel. Tayport (082 65) 2515
Golf Rd., Tayport, Fife DD6 9DZ.
On B946 3 miles from S end of Tay Road Bridge.
Seaside course.
18 holes, 6477 yds. S.S.S. 71
Visitors welcome.
Green Fees. Weekdays £4.50 per round, £6.50 per day; weekends £5.50 per round, £7.50 per day; weekly £20.00.
Society Meetings by arrangement.
Hotels: Sandford Hill, Wormit; Seymour Hotel, Newport-on-Tay.
Meals served except Tues.

X 76   Sports Club

Tel. Elie 330955
Elie, Fife KY9 1AG.
10 miles S of St. Andrews.
Seaside course.
9 holes, 5800 yds. S.S.S. 66
Visitors welcome.
Green Fees. £2.00.
Hotels: Golf; Queens.
Meals served.

X 77   Stirling

Tel. Stirling 3801, professional 71490
Queens Rd., Stirling FK8 2QY.
Off ring road, situated in Kings Park.
Undulating parkland course.
18 holes, 6458 yds. S.S.S. 71
Course designed by Tom Morris (1892).
Visitors welcome on weekdays and Sun. afternoon.
Green Fees. Weekdays £3.50 per round, £5.50 per day; weekends £7.00.

Society Meetings weekdays by arrangement.
Hotels: Garfield; Golden Lion; Station.
Meals served except Fri.

X 78   Strathendrick

Drymen, Glasgow.
On A811 19 miles N of Glasgow.
Undulating course.
9 holes, 5063 yds. S.S.S. 65
Visitors welcome if accompanied by member.
Hotels: Buchanan Arms; Winnock.

X 79   Taymouth Castle

Tel. Kenmore 228
Kenmore, Aberfeldy, Perthshire.
On A827, 6 miles SW of Aberfeldy.
Parkland course.
18 holes, 6066 yds. S.S.S. 69
Visitors welcome.
Green Fees. Weekdays £4.00 per day; weekends £6.60 per day.
Society Meetings welcome except July, Aug and Sept.
Hotels: Kenmore Hotel (preferential green fees for residents).
Licensed restaurant.

X 80   Thornton

Tel. Glenrothes (0592) 771111
Thornton, Fife KY1 4DW.
Off A92, 2 miles S of Glenrothes.
Parkland course.
18 holes, 6358 yds. S.S.S. 70
Visitors welcome.
Green Fees. Weekdays £3.00 per day; weekends £4.00 per round, £5.00 per day.
Society Meetings welcome.
Hotels: Thornton; Crown.
Meals served.

X 81   Tillicoultry

Tel. Tillicoultry 741
Alva Rd., Tillicoultry, Clackmannanshire.
On A91 9 miles E of Stirling.
Parkland course.
9 holes, 5100 yds. S.S.S. 65
Visitors welcome.
Green Fees. Weekdays £1.50 per day; weekends £3.00 per day.
Society Meetings welcome (Sun. after 2 p.m.).
Hotels: Bridge Hotel.
Snacks served.

X 82   Tulliallan

Tel. Kincardine 30396
Alloa Rd., Kincardine, Alloa, Clackmannanshire.
On A908, 1 mile N of Kincardine Bridge.
Parkland course.
18 holes, 5982 yds. S.S.S. 69
Visitors welcome.
Green Fees. Weekdays £3.00 per round, £5.00 per day; weekends £5.00 per round, £8.00 per day.
Society Meetings welcome except Sat.
Hotels: Commercial.
Morning coffee, high teas, snacks and lunches served.

Y Highlands, Grampian

Y 1   Abernethy

Tel. Nethybridge (047 982) 204 (Sec.)
Rothiemoon, Nethybridge, Inverness-shire PH25 3DD.
Turn off A9 10 miles N of Aviemore onto A95, then via Boat of Garten to B970.
Moorland course.
9 holes, 2484 yds. S.S.S. 66
Visitors welcome weekdays and Sun.
Green Fees. £2.00 per day; weekly £10.00 (juniors half-price).
Society Meetings by arrangement.
Hotels: Nethybridge; Mountview.
Light refreshments.

Y 2   Aboyne

Tel. Aboyne 2328
Aboyne, Aberdeenshire.
At E end of village turn N from A93 onto Golf Rd.
Parkland, heathland course.
18 holes, 5304 yds. S.S.S. 66
Visitors welcome.
Green Fees. Weekdays £3.00 per round, £4.00 per day; weekends £5.00; weekly £20.00; fortnightly £30.00.
Society Meetings welcome except Sun.
Hotels: Huntly Arms; Balnacoil.
Meals served by arrangement.

Y 3   Alness

Royal Bank; Alness, Ross-shire.
On A9, 10 miles N of Dingwall.
Parkland course.
9 holes, 4718 yds. S.S.S. 63
Visitors welcome.
Green Fees. Mon. to Sat. £1.00; Sun. £1.50; weekly (Mon. to Sat.) £4.00.
Hotels: Station, Alness; Novar Arms, Evanton.

Y 4   Askernish

Tel. (087 84) 277
Daliburgh, Isle of South Uist, Western Isles.
On A865, 2 miles N of Daliburgh.
Seaside course.
18 holes, 5141 yds. S.S.S. 67
Course designed by Tom Morris.
Visitors welcome.
Green Fees. £1.00 per day; weekly £4.50.

Hotels: Lochboisdale Hotel, Lochboisdale; Borrodale Hotel, Daliburgh; Golf Holidays, Loch 'an' Eilean Holiday Homes, Askernish.

Y 5 Auchenblae

Tel. Auchenblae 527
Auchenblae, Laurencekirk, Kincardineshire.
2 miles off A94 at Fordoun.
Parkland course.
9 holes, 4158 yds. S.S.S. 33
Visitors welcome.
Green Fees. £1.00 per day; Sun. £1.50.
Hotels: Drumtochty Arms; Thistle Inn.

Y 6 Ballater

Tel. Ballater (033 82) 567 (secretary), 658 (professional)
Ballater, Aberdeenshire AB3 5QX.
A93 on Deeside, 40 miles W of Aberdeen.
Flat inland course.
18 holes, 6106 yds. S.S.S. 69
Visitors welcome.
Green Fees. Weekdays £3.45 per day; Sat. or Sun. £4.60; weekly £14.50; fortnightly £26.00; season £34.50.
Hotels: Westbank; Craigard; Glen Lui; Deeside; Coach House; Darroch Learg; Ravenswood.
Meals served.

Y 7 Balnagask

Tel. Aberdeen 23456
Dept. of Leisure & Recreation, St. Nicholas House, Broad St., Aberdeen AB9 1XJ.

2 miles SE of city centre.
Undulating seaside course.
18 holes, 5984 yds. S.S.S. 69
Course designed by Hawtree & Son.
Visitors welcome.
Green Fees. Mon. to Sat. £2.10 per round; Sun. £3.10.
Hotels: in area.

Y 8 Banchory

Tel. Banchory 2365
Kinneskie, Banchory, Kincardineshire AB3 3TA.
18 miles W of Aberdeen on N Deeside Rd.
Parkland course.
18 holes, 5271 yds. S.S.S. 66
Visitors welcome.
Green Fees. Weekdays £4.00; weekends £5.00.
Society Meetings welcome.
Hotels: Tornacoil; Burnett Arms; Banchory Lodge.
Meals served.

Y 9 Boat of Garten

Tel. Boat of Garten (047 983) 282
Boat of Garten, Inverness-shire PH24 3BU.
Off A9, 6 miles N of Aviemore. In Boat of Garten take first right past Boat Hotel.
Undulating parkland course.
18 holes, 5637 yds. S.S.S. 68
Course designed by James Braid.
Visitors welcome.
Green Fees. Weekdays £3.00; weekends

£3.50; after 5 p.m. £2.00; weekly £14.00; fortnightly £21.00. Reserved tee times at weekends.
Society Meetings by arrangement.
Hotels: Boat; Craigard.
Snacks and light lunches served.

Y 10 Bon Accord

Tel. Aberdeen 633464
19 Gulf Rd., Aberdeen.
Seaside course.
18 holes, 6683 yds. S.S.S. 71
Visitors welcome.

Y 11 Braemar

Tel. Braemar (033 83) 618
Braemar, Aberdeenshire AB3 2XX.
¾ mile from centre of village, signposted.
Undulating moorland course.
18 holes, 5011 yds. S.S.S. 64
Visitors welcome.
Green Fees. Weekdays £1.80 per round, £3.00 per day; weekends £2.30 per round, £4.00 per day; weekly £13.80.
Society Meetings welcome, max. 40.
Hotels: Fife Arms; Invercauld Arms.

Y 12 Brora

Tel. Brora 417
Golf Rd., Brora, Sutherland KW6.
Off A9, 78 miles N of Inverness.
Seaside course.
18 holes, 6110 yds. S.S.S. 69
Course designed by James Braid.

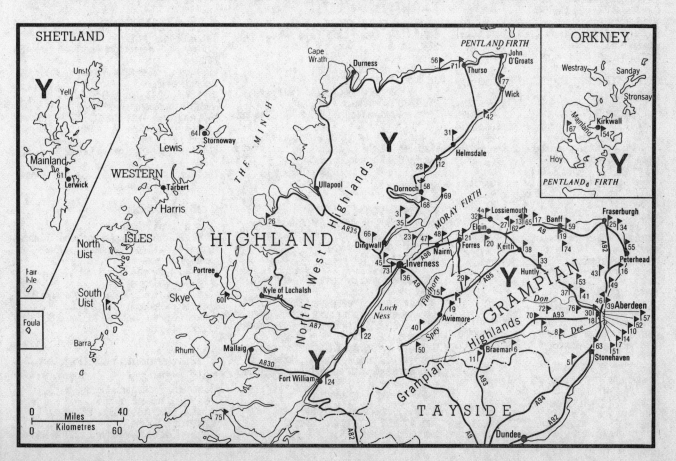

Visitors welcome.
Green Fees. £3.00 per day; weekly £13.50; fortnightly £21.00; 3 weeks £25.00; monthly £30.00.
Society Meetings by arrangement.
Hotels: Links; Royal Marine; Bayview; Braes; Sutherland Arms Hotel.

Y 13   Buckpool

Tel. Buckie 32236
Barrhill Rd., Buckie, Banffshire AB5 1DU.
½ mile off A98 at W end of Buckie.
Seaside course.
18 holes, 6276 yds. S.S.S. 70
Visitors welcome.
Green Fees. Weekdays £2.00 per day; weekends £3.00 per day.
Hotels: St. Andrews; Marine; Commercial; Cluny.

Y 14   Caledonian

Tel. Aberdeen 632443
King's Links, Aberdeen.
18 holes, 6316 yds. S.S.S. 70
Visitors welcome.
Green Fees. Weekdays £1.60; Sun. £2.40.

Y 15   Carrbridge

Tel. Carrbridge (047 694) 674
Inverness Rd., Carrbridge, Inverness-shire PH23 3AV.
Off A9, 14 miles N of Aviemore.
Moor and meadowland course.
9 holes, 2600 yds. Par 36
Visitors welcome.
Green Fees. £1.00 per day (juniors 50p); weekly £5.00.
Hotels: Carrbridge; Rowenlea; Struan.

Y 16   Cruden Bay Golf & Country Club

Tel. Cruden Bay 285
Aulton Rd., Cruden Bay, Aberdeenshire AB4 7NN.
23 miles N of Aberdeen, by A92 then A975.
Seaside course.
18 holes, 6373 yds. S.S.S. 71
Visitors welcome except before 10.30a.m. on Sun. and 12.00 to 2.30 Sat. & Sun.
Green Fees. Weekdays £3.50; Sat. £5.00; Sun. £6.00; weekly £20.00; fortnightly £28.00.
Society Meetings welcome weekdays only.
Hotels: Red House; Kilmarnock Arms.
Meals served.

Y 17   Cullen

Tel. Cullen (0542) 40685
The Links, Cullen, Buckie, Banffshire. All correspondence to Secretary Mr J. Douglas, 103 Seatown, Cullen, Buckie, Banffshire AB5 2SN.
A98.
Seaside course.
18 holes, 4610 yds. S.S.S. 62
Course designed by Neaves (1905).
Visitors welcome.
Green Fees. Weekdays £2.00; weekends £2.50; weekly £7.50.
Society Meetings by arrangement.

Hotels: Royal Oak; Cullen Bay; Three Kings; Grant Arms, Cullen; Waverley; Seafield Arms.
Snacks served by arrangement June to Sept.

Y 18   Deeside

Tel. Aberdeen (0224) 47697
Bieldside, Aberdeenshire.
4 miles W of Aberdeen on A93 N Deeside Rd.
Parkland course.
18 holes, S.S.S. 69
Visitors welcome with letter of introduction.
Green Fees. Weekdays £6.00; weekends £8.00.
Society Meetings by arrangement.
Hotels: in Aberdeen.
Meals served by arrangement.

Y 19   Duff House Royal

Tel. Banff (026 12) 2062, professional 2075
Barnyards, Duff House, Banff AB4 3SX.
2 minutes from town centre.
Parkland course.
18 holes, 6161 yds. S.S.S. 69
Course designed by McKenzie.
Visitors welcome.
Green Fees. Weekdays £2.50 per round, £3.50 per day; weekends £3.50 per round, £4.00 per day.
Society Meetings by arrangement.
Hotels: Banff Springs; Fife Arms; County; Fife Lodge.
Meals served.

Y 20   Elgin

Tel. Elgin (0343) 2338
Hardhillock, Birnie Rd., Elgin, Moray N30 3SX.
One mile S of Elgin off A96.
Moorland, parkland course.
18 holes, 6421 yds. S.S.S. 71
Course designed by Capt. McHardy.
Visitors welcome.
Green Fees. Weekdays £4.00; weekends £5.00.
Society Meetings by arrangement.
Hotels: Eight Acres; St. Leonards; Sunninghill; Torr House, Elgin.
Meals served by arrangement.

Y 21   Forres

Tel. Forres 72949 & 72261
Muiryshade, Edgehill Rd., Forres, Moray.
1 mile S of A96 by Tolbooth St., St. Leonards Rd. and Edgehill Rd.
Undulating parkland.
18 holes, 6141 yds. S.S.S. 69
Course designed by James Braid (1912).
Visitors welcome.
Green Fees. Weekdays £2.00 per day; weekends £2.20 per round; weekly (Mon. to Fri.) £6.60; fortnightly (excluding weekends) £11.00.
Society Meetings welcome on weekdays.
Hotels: Ramnee Hotel; Park Hotel.
Bar snacks served; meals by arrangement.

Y 22   Fort Augustus

Fort Augustus, Inverness-shire.
Turn off A82 at W end of village.
Moorland course.
9 holes, 2577 yds. S.S.S. 66

Visitors welcome.
Green Fees. June to September £1.00 per round or day; weekly £4.00. Oct. to May 50p per round or day; weekly £2.00.
Society Meetings welcome.
Hotels: Lovat Arms; Inchnacardoch; Braes; Caledonian.

Y 23   Fortrose and Rosemarkie

Tel. Fortrose 20529
Fortrose, Ross-shire.
Cross Kessock bridge by A9 from Inverness and follow signposts to Fortrose.
Seaside course.
18 holes, 5894 yds. S.S.S. 69
Visitors welcome.
Green Fees. Mon. to Sat. £3.75 per day; Sun. £4.30 per day.
Hotels: Marine, Rosemarkie.
Snacks served during summer.

Y 24   Fort William

Tel. Fort William (0397) 4464
Torlundy, Fort William, Inverness-shire.
On A82, 2½ miles from Fort William.
Undulating moorland course.
18 holes.
Course designed by Stutt Ltd.
Visitors welcome.
Green Fees. £3.00 per day.
Society Meetings welcome.
Hotels: Inverlochy Castle Hotel; Milton; Alexandra; Grand, Fort William.
Meals served.

Y 25   Fraserburgh

Tel. Fraserburgh 2287
Corbie Hill, Fraserburgh, Aberdeenshire AB4 5RJ.
On A92 40 miles from Aberdeen.
Seaside course.
18 holes, 6217 yds. S.S.S. 70
Visitors welcome.
Green Fees. Weekdays £3.00 (£1.50 with member); weekends £4.00 (£2.00 with member).
Society Meetings welcome weekdays only.
Hotels: Royal; Alexandra; Saltoun Arms.
Meals served by order.

Y 26   Gairloch

Gairloch, Ross-shire.
A832, 30 miles from Achnasheen, 60 miles from Dingwall, 74 miles from Inverness.
Seaside course.
9 holes, 4186 yds. S.S.S. 63
Visitors welcome.
Green Fees. £2.00 per day; weekly £8.00.
Hotels: Gairloch; Creag Mor; Gairloch Sands; Myrtle Bank; Old Inn; Shieldaig Lodge, Millcroft.

Y 27   Garmouth and Kingston

Tel. Spey Bay 388
Garmouth, Fochabers, Moray.
Off A96, 8 miles E of Elgin.
9 holes, 5285 yds. S.S.S. 65
Visitors welcome.
Green Fees. Weekdays £1.50; weekends £2.00.

Y 28 Golspie

Tel. Golspie (04083) 266
Ferry Rd., Golspie, Sutherland.
First right in Golspie off A9 from Inverness.
Seaside course.
18 holes, 5852 yds. S.S.S. 68
Visitors welcome.
Green Fees. £3.50 per day; weekly
£15.00; fortnightly £25.00.
Society Meetings by arrangement.
Hotels: Golf Links; Sutherland Arms; Ben
Bhraggie.
Snacks served in summer.

Y 29 Grantown-on-Spey

Tel. Grantown-on-Spey (0479) 2079
Grantown-on-Spey, Morayshire.
12 miles N of Aviemore.
Woodland, moorland course.
18 holes, 5745 yds. S.S.S. 67
Visitors welcome.
Green Fees. Weekdays £3.00; weekends
£3.50.
Society Meetings by arrangement.
Hotels: in Grantown-on-Spey and Aviemore.
Meals served by arrangement.

Y 30 Hazlehead

Tel. Aberdeen 23456
Dept. of Leisure & Recreation, St. Nicholas
House, Broad St., Aberdeen AB9 1XJ.
4 miles NW of city centre.
Moorland course.
18 holes, 6205 yds. S.S.S. 70
Visitors welcome.
Green Fees. Mon. to Sat. £2.10 per round;
Sun. £3.10.
Hotels: in area.

Y 31 Helmsdale

Helmsdale, Sutherland.
Turn left at Bridge Hotel, take A897 for 350
yards.
Undulating course.
9 holes, 1845 yds. S.S.S. 31
Visitors welcome.
Green Fees. £1.00 per day; weekly £3.50;
monthly £5.00.

Y 32 Hopeman

Hopeman, Elgin, Morayshire.
9 miles N of Elgin.
9 holes, 4930 yds. S.S.S. 63
Visitors welcome.
Hotels: Station; Neuk Hotel.
Green Fees. Weekdays £2.50, juniors
£1.25; weekends £3.00, juniors £1.50;
weekly £13.00.

Y 33 Huntly

Tel. Huntly (0466) 2643
The Cooper Park, Huntly, Aberdeenshire.
On A96, ½ mile from town centre.
Parkland course.
18 holes, 5538 yds. S.S.S. 67
Visitors welcome.
Green Fees. Weekdays £2.50; weekends
£3.50.
Society Meetings Mon., Tues., Fri, Sat.
and Sun.

Hotels: Castle Hotel; Hill Hotel; Gordon
Arms; Huntly.
Meals served by arrangement.

Y 34 Inverallochy

45 Main St., Cairnbulg, Aberdeenshire AB4
5YJ.
5 miles from Fraserburgh on Cairnbulg road.
Seaside course.
18 holes, 5107 yds. S.S.S. 65
Course designed by James Gibb.
Visitors welcome.
Green Fees. On application to secretary.
Society Meetings by arrangement.
Hotels: Tufted Duck, St. Combs.

Y 35 Invergordon

Tel. Invergordon 852116
Cromlet Dr., Invergordon, Ross-shire.
Parkland course.
9 holes, 3014 yds. S.S.S. 69
Course designed by Fraser Middleton.
Visitors welcome.
Green Fees. Weekdays £1.00; weekends
£1.50.
Hotels: Marine; Viewfirth.
Snacks served.

Y 36 Inverness

Tel. Inverness 33422
Culcabock, Inverness.
Inland course.
18 holes, 6176 yds. S.S.S. 69
Visitors welcome on weekdays.
Green Fees. Weekdays £4.00.
Hotels: Station; Caledonian; Royal;
Kingsmills.
Lunches served by arrangement.

Y 37 Inverurie

Tel. Inverurie 20207
Davah Wood, Blackhall Rd., Inverurie,
Aberdeenshire.
15 miles NW of Aberdeen on A96.
Moorland, parkland course.
18 holes, 5722 yds. S.S.S. 68
Course designed by John Stutt Ltd.
Visitors welcome.
Green Fees. Weekdays £3.50; weekends
£5.00.
Society Meetings by arrangement.
Hotels: Gordon Arms; Kintore Arms.
Meals served by arrangement.

Y 38 Keith

Tel. Keith 2496
Fife-Keith, Keith, Banffshire.
½ mile off A96 on Dufftown Road.
Undulating parkland course.
18 holes, 5745 yds. S.S.S. 68
Visitors welcome.
Green Fees. Weekdays £2.00 per day;
weekends £3.00 per day.
Society Meetings welcome.
Hotels: Gordon Arms; Royal & Seafield.
Meals served for society meetings only.

Y 39 Kings Links

Tel. Aberdeen 23456
Dept. of Leisure & Recreation, St. Nicholas
House, Broad St., Aberdeen AB9 1XJ.

E of city centre.
Seaside course.
18 holes, 6494 yds. S.S.S. 71
Visitors welcome.
Green Fees. Mon. to Sat. £2.10 per round;
Sun. £3.10.
Hotels: in area.

Y 40 Kingussie

Tel. Kingussie 374
Gynack Rd., Kingussie, Inverness-shire PH21
1LR.
¼ mile off A9 at Kingussie.
Undulating, parkland course.
18 holes, 5468 yds. S.S.S. 67
Course designed by Harry Vardon.
Visitors welcome.
Green Fees. Weekdays £3.00 per round,
£4.00 per day; weekends £5.00; weekly
£20.00.
Society Meetings by arrangement.
Hotels: Duke of Gordon; Royal; Star;
Silverfjord.
Snacks served; meals for societies by
arrangement.

Y 41 Kintore

Tel. Kintore 631
Kintore, Inverurie, Aberdeenshire.
Off A96, 12 miles N of Aberdeen.
Parkland course.
9 holes, 5240 yds. S.S.S. 66
Visitors welcome.
Green Fees. Weekdays £2.50 per day;
evening round and juniors' day ticket £1.50;
weekends £3.00 per day, evening round
£2.00.
Society Meetings welcome on weekdays.
Hotels: Kintore Arms; Crown; Torryburn.

Y 42 Lybster

Main St., Lybster, Caithness.
13 miles S of Wick on A9; signposts on A9
and in village Main St.
Seaside, moorland course.
9 holes, 1764 yds. S.S.S. 62
Visitors welcome.
Green Fees. £1.00 per day, £4.00 per
week; pay at Post Office, Main St., Lybster.
Hotels: Portland Arms; Bayview;
Commercial.

Y 43 McDonald

Tel. Ellon 20576
Ellon, Aberdeenshire.
A92 to Ellon, 1 mile on A948.
Parkland course.
18 holes, 5984 yds. S.S.S. 69
Visitors welcome.
Green Fees. Weekdays £2.50; weekends
£4.00.
Hotels: in Ellon.

Y 44 Moray

Tel. Lossiemouth 2018
Stotfield Rd., Lossiemouth, Moray.
A941 from Elgin.
Seaside course.
18 holes, 6643 yds. S.S.S. 72
18 holes, 6258 yds. S.S.S. 71
Visitors welcome.
Green Fees. Old Moray weekdays £3.50.

Kingussie's peaks of excellence

Kingussie is a classic example of a course of character and charm in an incomparable Highland setting, although its challenge is sporting rather than overwhelmingly severe. However, its 5,468 yards sound modest enough until a scratch golfer remembers that he is supposed to go round in 67. That, as those who have tried will tell you, is far easier said than done.

The variation of contour and its susceptibility to the wind ensure that success lies in a combination of power and control, but it is, above all, a glorious place to play, and those on their way between Perth and Inverness, or holidaying locally, will find a round immensely stimulating.

Tucked away on an elevated perch above the town, a sense of escape is immediate. Beauty beckons from every direction and the new, enlarged clubhouse keeps a friendly welcome, but the 1st hole, 230 yards to a half hidden green, is anything but friendly. It is as tough an opening stroke as you will find.

Not that there is any relief at the excellent 2nd, 426 yards, where a fine drive still leaves plenty to do. The 3rd, a gentler par 4, is parallel like the 4th but they could never be said to be dull. The 4th, in fact, aptly named The Fort, has all the characteristics of a par 5, its main defence being the sharp approach to an unusually raised green which rarely sees anyone home in two.

It is a subtle way of making the ascent to higher ground and of introducing the contrast of the 5th and 6th which are very much easier if the drives are well positioned and very much harder if they are not. From the 6th the panorama unfurls with mountains, near and far, dominating the scene. There is something inspiring about playing against the backcloth of mountains and, at Kingussie, there is the constant reminder of how fortunate golf is in the variety of its surroundings.

There is also something inspiring about short holes to a green below you and the 7th is just such a picture hole. Kingussie twice has successive short holes but the 7th and 8th could hardly be more different. The 8th has a blind shot over a heathery ridge to a tiny green but the 9th has everyone opening their shoulders again; and very necessary, too.

For years, the 10th, another par 3, has turned away on to a green high above the tee but recently there has been talk of a change; a change both of direction and height to a green with the rare feature of being bordered by juniper bushes.

If many of the holes receive their character from the rise and fall of the ground, the 11th, 12th and 13th do not have that advantage except for the drive from the 11th. The

fairway looks inviting from a high tee and it is not at all easy to judge the second shots at either the 12th or 13th.

The same is true of the 14th, 432 yards, whose main threat is an out of bounds wall along the left and a green at the top of a slope that is difficult to hit. The 15th, 105 yards, across the fast flowing Gynack, might be thought to be some relief but it can be as tantalizing as the 16th which, almost twice as long, quite definitely cannot be trifled with.

On paper, Kingussie's last four holes are not formidable. They average only about 240 yards, but the 17th, 383 yards, is made by a cluster of lichen-covered birch trees on the left of another inviting drive; and the 18th can be make or break.

282 yards, it automatically raises hopes of a birdie. Strong men can drive its green with the clubhouse beyond; and what better way to finish a round? However, from a new back tee, there is a longish carry along the river bank and several ways of turning a prospective birdie into disaster.

Triumph or disaster, the final judgement will be the same: a hearty vote of confidence in the course, as strong as the urge to return; for here, in summer, when the northern twilight holds the night at bay, there is enough golf to satisfy the fittest and strongest.

---

per day, weekends £5.50 per day, weekly £18.00; New Moray £2.00 per day.
Society Meetings welcome on weekdays.
Hotels: Stotfield; Laverockbank; Huntly House; Skerry Brae.
Meals served by arrangement.

Y 45   Muir-of-Ord

Muir-of-Ord, Ross and Cromarty.
A9, 15 miles N of Inverness.
Moorland, parkland course.
18 holes, 5022 yds. S.S.S. 65
Visitors welcome.
Green Fees. Weekdays £2.00; weekends £3.00.
Society Meetings catered for.
Hotels: Ord Arms; Tarradale; Ord House; Fairmile Inn; Station.
Snacks and light meals served by arrangement.

Y 46   Murcar

Tel. Aberdeen (0224) 704354
Murcar, Bridge of Don, Aberdeen AB2 8BD.
4 miles from Aberdeen on Peterhead road (A92).
Seaside course.
18 holes, 6219 yds. S.S.S. 70
Visitors welcome.
Green Fees. Weekdays £6.00 per day; weekends £7.50 per day.
Hotels: Northern; Tree Tops; Amatola.
Meals served.

Y 47   Nairn

Tel. Nairn (0667) 53208
Seabank Rd., Nairn IV12 4HB.
1 mile N of A96, W of Nairn, signposted in town.
Seaside course.
18 holes, 6462 yds. S.S.S. 71
Visitors welcome.

Green Fees. Weekdays £5.50; weekends £6.50; weekly £25.00.
Society Meetings weekdays by arrangement.
Hotels: Newton; Golf View; Royal Marine; Altonburn.
Meals served April to October.

Y 48   Nairn Dunbar

Tel. Nairn (066 75) 52741
Lochloy Rd., Nairn.
On A96, ½ mile E of town.
Seaside course.
18 holes, 6471 yds. S.S.S. 71
Visitors welcome.
Green Fees. Weekdays £2.00; weekends £2.50.
Society Meetings welcome on weekdays.
Hotels: in Nairn.

Y 49 Newburgh-on-Ythan

Tel. Newburgh 648
Newburgh-on-Ythan, Ellon, Aberdeenshire AB4 0BL.
On A975, 12 miles N of Aberdeen.
Seaside course.
9 holes, 6340 yds. S.S.S. 70
Visitors welcome.
Green Fees. Weekdays and weekends £3.00; weekly £15.00.
Hotels: Udny Arms; Ythan Hotel, Newburgh-on-Ythan.

Y 50 Newtonmore

Tel. Newtonmore 328
Golf Course Rd., Newtonmore, Inverness-shire PH20 1AT.
Turn off at school from S, at Balavil Hotel from N.
Moorland course.
18 holes, 5890 yds. S.S.S. 68
Course designed by A. Mackenzie and James Braid.
Visitors welcome.
Green Fees. £3.00 per day; weekly £12.00.
Society Meetings by arrangement.
Meals served by arrangement.

Y 51 Nigg Bay

Tel. Aberdeen 871286
St. Fitticks Rd., Balnagask, Aberdeen.
Seaside course.
18 holes, 5984 yds. S.S.S. 69
Visitors welcome.
Green Fees. Mon. to Sat. £1.60; Sun. £2.30.
Society Meetings by arrangement.
Hotels: Gloucester Hotel.

Y 52 Northern Aberdeen

Tel. Aberdeen 21440
Golf Rd., Kings Links, Aberdeen.
18 holes, 6700 yds. S.S.S. 72
Visitors welcome.
Lunches served.

Y 53 Oldmeldrum

Tel. Oldmeldrum 339
Oldmeldrum, Aberdeenshire.
Heathland course.
9 holes, 2567 yds. S.S.S. 65
Hotels: Meldrum House Hotel; Meldrum Arms.

Y 54 Orkney

Grainbank, Kirkwall, Orkney.
½ mile W of Kirkwall.
Parkland course.
18 holes, 5406 yds. S.S.S. 68
Visitors welcome.
Green Fees. £2.00 per day; weekly £6.00; monthly £14.00.
Hotels: Kirkwall; Ayr; Queen's; Royal, Kirkwall.

Y 55 Peterhead

Tel. Peterhead 2149
Craigewan Links, Peterhead, Aberdeenshire.
A92 and A975, 30 miles N of Aberdeen.
Seaside course.

18 holes, 6070 yds. S.S.S. 69
Visitors welcome.
Green Fees. Weekdays £2.50; weekends £5.00.
Society Meetings welcome on weekdays.
Hotels: Palace Hotel.
Snacks served; meals by arrangement.

Y 56 Reay

Tel. Reay (084 781) 288
Reay, Caithness.
11 miles W of Thurso.
Seaside course.
18 holes, 5876 yds. S.S.S. 68
Visitors welcome.
Green Fees. Weekdays £2.00 per day; weekends £2.50 per day.
Hotels: Pentland; Royal; Weigh Inn, Thurso.

Y 57 Royal Aberdeen

Tel. Balgownie 702571
Balgownie, Bridge of Don, Aberdeen AB2 8AT.
2 miles N of Aberdeen on A92.
Seaside course.
18 holes, 6404 yds. S.S.S. 71 (also 9 hole course).
Visitors welcome with letter of introduction.
Green Fees. Weekdays £6.00 per round, £8.00 per day; weekends £8.00 per round, £10.00 per day.
Hotels: Northern Hotel, Aberdeen.
Meals served by arrangement.

Y 58 Royal Dornoch

Tel. Dornoch 219
Golf Rd., Dornoch, Sutherland IV25 3LW.
B949 off A9 from Inverness.
Championship links course.
18 holes, 6533 yds. S.S.S. 72
Course designed by Tom Morris Sen.
Visitors welcome.
Green Fees. £6.00 per day, £4.75 per round after 11.00 a.m.; weekly £24.00; fortnightly £35.00. (Under 16s half-price.)
Society Meetings by arrangement (except July and Aug.).
Hotels: Royal Golf Hotel; Dornoch Hotel; Castle Hotel; Burghfield Hotel.
Adjacent airstrip for light aircraft.
Catering facilities except Mon.

Y 59 Royal Tarlair

Tel. Macduff 32897
Buchan St., Macduff, Banffshire AB4 1UX.
On A98, 48 miles from Aberdeen.
Seaside course.
18 holes, 5866 yds. S.S.S. 68
Visitors welcome.
Green Fees. Apr.-Oct. adults weekdays £2.00 per day; weekends £3.00 per day; juniors weekdays £1.00 per day; weekends £1.50 per day. Nov.-Mar. adults £1.50 per day; juniors 50p per day. Holiday fees weekly, adults £10.00; juniors £4.00. Husband & wife weekly £15.00; fortnightly £25.00.
Hotels: Fife Arms; Deveron House, Macduff; Banff Springs; County, Banff.
Meals served; parties by arrangement.

Y 60 Sconser

Tel. Portree 2364
Sconser, Isle of Skye.
Midway between Broadford and Portree.
Meadowland course.
9 holes, 2522 yds. S.S.S. 63
Visitors welcome.
Green Fees. £1.50 per day; £5.00 per week.
Hotels: Sconser Lodge; Sligachan.
Meals and bar snacks served.

Y 61 Shetland

Tel. Gott 369
Dale Golf Course, Shetland.
N road from Lerwick, 3 miles.
Undulating moorland course.
18 holes, 5900 yds. S.S.S. 71
Course designed by F.M. Middleton.
Visitors welcome.
Green Fees. Weekdays £3.00; weekends £4.00.
Society Meetings welcome weekdays only.
Hotels: Lerwick Hotel; Grand; Queens; Kvelsdro, Lerwick; Scalloway Hotel, Scalloway.

Y 62 Spey Bay

Tel. Fochabers 820424
Spey Bay Hotel, Spey Bay, Fochabers, Morayshire.
Turn off A96 near Spey Bridge, Fochabers; follow B9104 for 5 miles.
Seaside links course.
18 holes, 6059 yds. S.S.S. 69
Visitors welcome.
Green Fees. £2.00 per round (£1.75 with member), £3.00 per day (£2.25 with member); weekly £14.00; country member £30.75.
Society Meetings by prior arrangement.
Hotels: Spey Bay Hotel.
Meals served.

Y 63 Stonehaven

Tel. Aberdeen (0224) 62124
Cowie, Stonehaven, Kincardineshire AB3 2RH.
On A92, 1 mile N of Stonehaven.
Seaside, meadowland course.
18 holes, 5103 yds. S.S.S. 65
Course designed by George Duncan.
Visitors welcome.
Green Fees. Weekdays £3.00; weekends £5.00; juniors half adult fees.
Society Meetings welcome weekdays before 4p.m. and Sun. 10.30a.m. to 11.30a.m.
Hotels: Royal; Commodore; Belvidere; Alexandra; St. Leonards; Heugh.
Meals served.

Y 64 Stornoway

Tel. Stornoway (0851) 2240
Castle Grounds, Stornoway, Isle of Lewis.
5 minutes' walk from town centre.
Parkland, moorland course.
18 holes, 5120 yds. S.S.S. 66
Visitors welcome except Sun.

A perfect highland interlude

For many years the name of Dornoch meant no more to me than the fact that, in my early school days, I shared a desk with a boy who lived there. Like all good young Scotsmen he played golf, and often used to speak of his course, adding with a typical youthful boast that I ought to go and see it for myself.

I never took him very seriously because I knew from the atlas that Dornoch was 620 miles from home, in the far north of Scotland, and there was no reason to justify a trip. But, as time passed, more and more people confirmed what he had said, and as I listened one day at St. Andrews to an enthusiastic description by Billy Joe Patton of a recent visit he had made, on the firm recommendation of his Walker Cup captain, Dick Tufts, I decided that I must go after all at the first opportunity.

Shortly afterwards, ambition was at last fulfilled. It was a perfect Highland interlude, and for three days my partner and I were caught in Dornoch's enchanting spell, playing round after round with an eagerness that is rare on a new course. Here was a traditional links, set amid gentle dune country, never out of sight or sound of the sea, and untouched by the centuries.

According to local records, golf was played at Dornoch as early as 1616, which would make it, according to some authorities, the second oldest golfing nursery in the world after St. Andrews. In 1628 King Charles I granted a royal charter to the burgh, but it was not until 1877 that the Royal Dornoch Golf Club was founded and old Tom Morris was commissioned to come up from St. Andrews to lay out nine holes.

Another nine were added and, shortly after the turn of the century, they were transformed into a championship links by John Sutherland, who for over fifty years was club secretary.

Dornoch is perhaps not widely known as a championship test because its remoteness makes it impractical for such occasions, but it is still held to be one of the outstanding courses in the world by men close to the heart of the game. The announcement that the 1980 Home Internationals were to be played there, three years after the Club's centenary, brought pleasure to everyone.

In the warmth of a friendly hotel, with the long northern twilight lingering outside, we tried our conclusions each evening and became more than ever convinced that the course had an unmistakable quality of greatness. Such things are purely a matter of opinion, but in the light of any analysis it would be hard to think of a course that ranks above it as a pure test of golf or one that is more enjoyable to play.

In half a gale, a full gale, and, on the final morning, in the most perfect conditions imaginable, we experienced unusual contrasts, but each time the course proved itself fair, challenging and rewarding for every class of player. Even now the holes stay firmly in the memory and I can see again the long, gradual curve at two levels of the first eight moving out to the point towards Embo where the 9th fairway turns for home along the shore.

The thrill of the drive from the 3rd tee to a narrow fairway on a shelf below; the pitch to the pulpit green at the 5th; the splendour of four superb short holes and the succession of good shots that are demanded from the turn if a score is not to get out of hand—that is the essence of Dornoch.

The tees are angled and the course slightly crescent shaped, so that the wind is not constantly in one's face or on one's back, and the greens are so guarded or raised as to ensure that the ill-judged and ill-conceived second or approach is unlikely to succeed even from turf where the lies are seldom less than good.

The 12th (500 yds) is a classic of its length and the 14th, 'Foxy', an admirable illustration of a hole where bunkers need have no place, the second to a plateau green depending entirely on the placing of the drive.

These were one's special impressions, but when all thoughts of golf were forgotten, the matchless beauty of the setting remained. The massive, brooding hills of Sutherland, the golden stretch of sand that borders the huge sweep of the Dornoch Firth, and the lighthouse on its lonely distant point, gave an added inspiration that made the world at large seem a thousand miles away and the visitor glad in his heart that he had come.

Green Fees. £2.50 per day (50p with member); weekly £10.00.
Hotels: Royal; Caberfeidh; Acres.
Meals served by arrangement.

Y 65   Strathlene

Tel. Buckie (0542) 31798
Buckie, Banffshire AB5 2DJ.
On A942, 2 miles E of Buckie harbour. From main Banff to Inverness road take turning to Strathlene 3 miles E of Buckie road sign.
Undulating seaside course.
18 holes, 5957 yds. S.S.S. 69
Course designed by George E. Smith.
Visitors welcome.
Green Fees. Weekdays £1.00 per round, £1.50 per day; weekends £1.50 per round, £2.00 per day.
Society Meetings welcome on weekdays, weekends by arrangement.

Hotels: Strathlene House; Arradoul House; Cluny; Marine.
Snacks served; meals for parties by arrangement.

Y 66   Strathpeffer Spa

Tel. Strathpeffer (099 72) 219
Strathpeffer, Ross-shire.
Signposted: ¼ mile N of village square, 5 miles from Dingwall.
Undulating course.
18 holes, 4813 yds. S.S.S. 65
Visitors welcome except Sat. 8.00-10.00a.m., Thurs. and Fri. 4.00p.m.-7.30p.m.
Green Fees. Weekdays £1.50 per round (with member only); £3.00 per day; weekly £11.50 (Mon.-Fri.).
Society Meetings by arrangement.
Hotels: MacKay's; Richmond; Highland; Ben Wyvis.
Meals served except Mon.

Y 67   Stromness

Tel. Stromness 850245
Ness, Stromness, Orkney.
Seaside course.
18 holes, 4822 yds. S.S.S. 64
Visitors welcome.
Green Fees. £2.00 per round or day, May to Oct.
Hotels: Stromness; Oakleigh; Braes; Royal, Stromness; Ferry Inn.

Y 68   Tain

Tel. Tain 2314
Tain, Ross-shire.
A9, ½ mile from town centre.
seaside, moorland course.
18 holes, 6207 yds. S.S.S. 70
Course designed by Tom Morris
Visitors welcome.

Green Fees. £3.50 per day; weekly £14.00; country membership £15.00 (over 50 miles by road), £25.00 (under 50 miles by road).
Hotels: Royal; Mansfield House; Morangie House; Castle Styles Motel, Tain.
Morning coffees served; lunches except Mon.

Y 69 Tarbat

Tel. Portmahomack (086 287) 519
Portmahomack, Ross-shire.
B9165 off A9, 7 miles E of Tain.
Seaside course.
9 holes, 4656 yds. S.S.S. 63
Course designed by J. Sutherland (1909).
Visitors welcome except Sun.
Green Fees. £1.00 per day; weekly £4.00.
Hotels: Caledonian; Castle Hotel.

Y 70 Tarland

Tel. Tarland (033 981) 413
Tarland, Aboyne, Aberdeenshire AB3 4YL.
On A974, 31 miles W of Aberdeen and 11 miles NE of Ballater.
Meadowland course.
9 holes, 5812 yds. S.S.S. 68
Visitors welcome.
Green Fees. Weekdays £2.00 per day; weekends £2.50; weekly £8.00; fortnightly £14.00.
Hotels: Commercial; Aberdeen Arms, Tarland.
Snacks, lunches and teas served.

Y 71 Thurso

Tel. Thurso (0847) 3807
Newlands of Geise, Thurso, Caithness.
2 miles W of station.
Parkland course.
18 holes, 5841 yds. S.S.S. 69
Visitors welcome.
Green Fees. Weekdays £2.00; weekends £2.50 (half-price if introduced by member).
Society Meetings by arrangement.
Hotels: Pentland; Royal Thurso; Weigh Inn Motel.
Meals served.

Y 72 Torphins

Tel. Torphins (033 982) 493
26 Beltie Rd., Torphins, by Banchory, Grampian AB3 4JT.
22 miles W of Aberdeen on A980; NW corner of village.
Undulating heathland course.
9 holes, 2330 yds. S.S.S. 63
Visitors welcome.
Society Meetings welcome.
Hotels: Learney Arms; Macbeth Arms, Lumphanan.

Y 73 Torvean

Tel. Inverness 33450
Glenurquhart Rd., Inverness.
On A82 1 mile W of city centre.
18 holes, 4628 yds. S.S.S. 63
Hotels: Loch Ness House Hotel.

Y 74 Turriff

Tel. Turriff (08882) 2745
Rosehall, Turriff, Aberdeenshire AB5 7HD.

On B9024, 1 mile from Turriff.
Parkland course.
18 holes, 5808 yds. S.S.S. 68
Visitors welcome.
Green Fees. Weekdays £2.50 per round, £3.00 per day; weekends £3.00 per round, £4.00 per day; weekly £10.00; fortnightly £15.00.
Society Meetings welcome.
Hotels: Union Hotel, Turriff.

Y 75 Western Isles

Tobermory, Isle of Mull.
9 holes, 4736 yds. S.S.S. 64
Green Fees. £1.50 per day; weekly £5.00; fortnightly £8.50; monthly £12.00.

Y 76 Westhill

Westhill, Skene, Aberdeenshire.
Turn right off A944 at Westhill, 5 miles from Aberdeen; straight on for 1 mile.
Parkland, moorland course.
18 holes, 6211 yds. S.S.S. 70
Course designed by Charles Laurie of Cotton (CK), Pennink, Laurie & Partners.
Visitors welcome except Sat.
Green Fees. Weekdays £3.00; weekends and holidays £5.00.
Society Meetings welcome except Sat.
Hotels: Westhill Inn.
Catering facilities open 1982.

Y 77 Wick

Tel. Wick 2726
Reiss, Wick, Caithness KW1 4RW.
3 miles N of Wick on John O'Groats road.
Seaside course.
18 holes, 5846 yds. S.S.S. 69
Visitors welcome.
Green Fees. £2.00 per day; weekly £9.00; fortnightly £12.00.
Hotels: Mackay's; Rosebank; Station; Mercury Motor Inn, Wick.

Z Northern Ireland

Z 1 Ardglass

Tel. Ardglass 841219
Ardglass, Co. Down.
On B176, 6 miles from Downpatrick.
Seaside course.
18 holes, 5980 yds. S.S.S. 68
Visitors welcome.
Green Fees. Weekdays £2.90; weekends £5.75.
Society Meetings by arrangement.
Hotels: Downs; Arms.
Meals served by arrangement.

Z 2 Ballycastle

Tel. Ballycastle 62536
Cushendall Rd., Ballycastle.
A26. N of Ballymena branch off onto A44.
Undulating parkland, seaside course.
18 holes, 5906 yds. S.S.S. 68
Visitors welcome.
Green Fees. Weekdays £3.00; weekends £4.50. Weekly and monthly tickets available.
Society Meetings by arrangement except July and August.
Hotels: Antrim Arms; Hillsea.
Meals served by arrangement.

Z 3 Ballyclare

Tel. Ballyclare 22696
25 Springfield Rd., Ballyclare, Co. Antrim.
14 miles N of Belfast.
Parkland course.
9 holes, 6708 yds. S.S.S. 71
Course designed by P. Alliss and Co.
Visitors welcome weekdays before 4.00 p.m.
Green Fees. On application to Secretary.
Society Meetings welcome weekdays before 4.00 p.m.
Hotels: Chimney Corner, Newtownabbey.
Meals served.

Z 4 Ballymena

Tel. Broughshane 861207
Broughshane Rd., Ballymena, Co. Antrim.
2½ miles E of town on A42 to Broughshane and Carnlough.
Parkland course.
18 holes, 5683 yds. S.S.S. 67
Visitors welcome.
Green Fees. Weekdays £4.50; weekends £7.00.

Society Meetings welcome except Sat.
Hotels: Adair Arms Hotel; Leighinmohr House Hotel; Tullyglass House Hotel.

Z 5 Balmoral

Tel. Belfast (0232) 668514
Lisburn Rd., Belfast BT9 66X.
S of Belfast.
Parkland course.
18 holes, 6210 yds. S.S.S. 69
Visitors welcome.
Green Fees. Weekdays £5.00; weekends £6.50.
Society Meetings by arrangement.
Hotels: in Belfast.
Meals served.

Z 6 Banbridge

Tel. Banbridge 22342
Huntly Rd., Banbridge, Co. Down BT32 3UR.
25 miles SW of Belfast.
Parkland course.
12 holes, 5879 yds. S.S.S. 68

Visitors welcome.
Green Fees. Weekdays £3.00; weekends £4.00.
Society Meetings by arrangement.
Hotels: Belmont; Downshire; Banville.

Z 7 Bangor

Tel. Bangor 3922
Broadway, Bangor, Co. Down BT20 4RB.
On A2, 14 miles E of Belfast.
Parkland course.
18 holes, 6450 yds. S.S.S. 71
Visitors welcome except Tues. if members of recognized club.
Green Fees. Weekdays £3.50 (£2.50 with member); weekends £5.00 (£3.00 with member); parties £2.90.
Society Meetings welcome Mon., Wed. and Fri.
Hotels: Royal.
Meals served.

Z 8 Belvoir Park

Tel. Belfast (0232) 643693 and 641159
Church Rd., Newtown Breda, Belfast BT8 4AN.
By Ormeau Rd., 3 miles from city centre.
Parkland course.
18 holes, 6439 yds. S.S.S. 71
Course designed by H.S. Colt.
Visitors welcome.
Green Fees. Weekdays £4.50 (£2.50 with member); weekends £6.50 (£4.00 with member).
Society Meetings by arrangement.
Hotels: in Belfast.
Meals served.

Z 9 Bushfoot

Tel. Bushmills 317
Portballintrae, Bushmills, Co. Antrim.
6 miles E of Portrush.
Seaside course.
9 holes, 5572 yds. S.S.S. 67

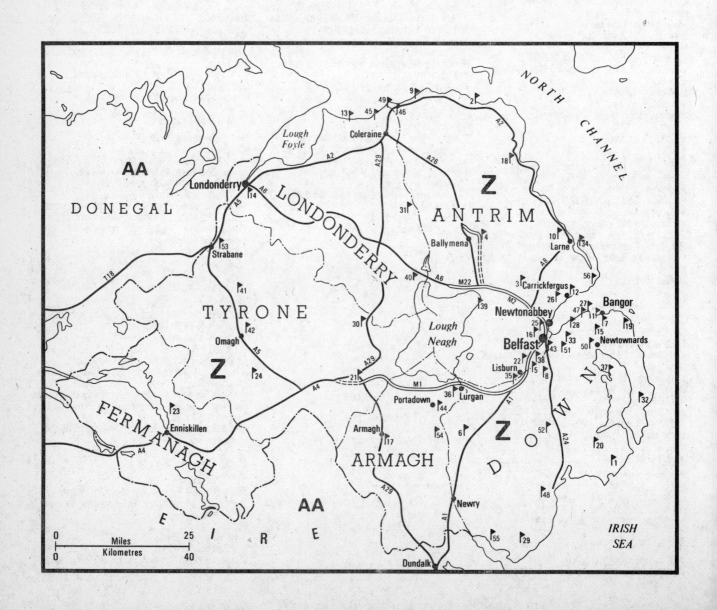

Course designed by Commander Harris.
Visitors welcome.
Green Fees. Weekdays £3.00; weekends £4.00.
Hotels: Bayview; Beach Hotel.
Snacks served.

Z 10   Cairndhu

Tel. Ballygally 324
192 Coast Rd., Ballygally, Larne, Co. Antrim.
On A2, 4 miles N of Larne.
Parkland course.
18 holes, 6112 yds. S.S.S. 69
Visitors welcome.
Green Fees. Weekdays £4.00; weekends £6.00.
Society Meetings welcome except Sat.
Hotels: Ballygally Castle Hotel; Half-Way House, Ballygally; Drumnagreagh, Glenarm.
Meals served except Mon.

Z 11   Carnalea

Tel. Bangor 65004
Station Rd., Bangor, Co. Down BT19 1EZ.
Near Crawfordsburn, 2 miles E of Bangor.
Seaside course.
18 holes, 5564 yds. S.S.S. 66
Course designed by James Braid.
Visitors welcome on weekdays.
Green Fees. Weekdays £2.85 (£2.00 with member); weekends £5.00 (£3.00 with member).
Society Meetings welcome on weekdays.
Hotels: Crawfordsburn Inn, Crawfordsburn; Royal, Bangor.
Meals served.

Z 12   Carrickfergus

Tel. Carrickfergus 63713
North Rd., Carrickfergus BT38 8LP.
Off A2, 9 miles NE of Belfast.
Parkland, meadowland course.
18 holes, 5759 yds. S.S.S. 67
Visitors welcome on weekdays and Sun.
Green Fees. Weekdays £3.45 (£2.30 with member); weekends £5.75 (£3.45 with member).
Society Meetings welcome on weekdays before 4.30 p.m.
Hotels: Coast Road Hotel, Carrickfergus; Edenmore; Glenavna, Newtownabbey.
Meals served.

Z 13   Castlerock

Tel. Castlerock (026 584) 314
Circular Rd., Castlerock, Co. Londonderry.
On A2, 6 miles W of Coleraine.
Seaside course.
18 holes, 6568 yds. S.S.S. 72
Course designed by Ben Sayers.
Visitors welcome on weekdays.
Green Fees. Weekdays £4.00 (£2.50 with member); weekends £6.00 (£4.00 with member).
Society Meetings welcome on weekdays except July and August.
Hotels: Golf Hotel.
Snacks and high teas served.

Z 14   City of Derry

Tel. Londonderry 42610
49 Victoria Rd., Prehen, Londonderry.
18 holes, 6764 yds. Par 73

Green Fees. Weekdays £3.50; weekends £4.00; 50p reduction for visitors if playing with member.

Z 15   Clandeboye

Tel. Bangor 65767
Tower Rd., Conlig, Newtownards.
On A20, 2 miles from Bangor into Conlig village.
Ava: moorland, meadowland course. Dufferin: parkland, woodland course.
Ava: 18 holes, 5634 yds. S.S.S. 67
Dufferin: 18 holes, 6000 to 7000 yds. S.S.S. 70 to 73
Courses designed by W.R. Robinson, and Peter Alliss, Dave Thomas and Co.
Visitors welcome.
Green Fees. Ava: weekdays men £4.00 (£2.00 with member), ladies: £2.50 (£1.50 with member); weekends men £5.00 (£2.50 with member), ladies £4.00 (£2.50 with member). Dufferin: weekdays men £5.00 (£2.50 with member), ladies £3.50 (£2.00 with member); weekends men £7.00 (£3.50 with member).
Society Meetings welcome Mon., Tues., Wed. and Fri. before 4.30 p.m.
Hotels: Royal, Bangor; Culloden, Craigavad; Crawfordsburn Inn, Crawfordsburn; Strangford Arms, Newtonards.
Meals served.

Z 16   Cliftonville

Tel. Belfast (0232) 744158
Westland Rd., Belfast BT14 6NH.
Meadowland course.
9 holes, 6204 yds. S.S.S. 69
Visitors welcome on weekdays and Sun.
Green Fees. Mon. to Fri. £3.50; Sun. and bank holidays £4.50.
Society Meetings by arrangement.
Hotels: Landsdowne Court; Chester Park Hotel.
Meals served by arrangement.

Z 17   County Armagh

Tel. Armagh (0861) 522501
Demesne, Newry Rd., Armagh.
40 miles SW of Belfast. Off Newry road, ½ mile from city centre.
Parkland course.
18 holes, 6043 yds. S.S.S. 69
Visitors welcome.
Green Fees. Weekdays £2.50; weekends £4.00.
Society Meetings by arrangement.
Hotels: Drumsill House Hotel; Charlemont Arms Hotel.
Meals served by arrangement.

Z 18   Cushendall

Tel. Cushendall (026 672) 318
Cushendall, Ballymena, Co. Antrim.
On A2, N of Belfast.
Undulating seaside course.
9 holes, 4678 yds. S.S.S. 62
Visitors welcome, no ladies Sun. morning.
Green Fees. Weekdays £2.00; weekends £3.00; weekly Mon.-Fri. £8.00; monthly £20.00.
Society Meetings weekdays by arrangement.
Hotels: Glenariffe Inn, Waterfoot; Thornlea, Cushendall; McBrides, Cushendun.

Z 19   Donaghadee

Tel. Donaghadee 883624 & 882519
Warren Rd., Donaghadee, Co Down.
On A2, 18 miles E of Belfast.
Undulating seaside course.
18 holes, 6090 yds. S.S.S. 69
Visitors welcome.
Green Fees. Weekdays men £2.50, ladies £1.50; weekends £4.00.
Society Meetings welcome.
Hotels: Imperial; New Mount Royal; Dunallen; Copelands.
Meals served.

Z 20   Downpatrick

Tel. Downpatrick 2152
Saul Rd., Downpatrick, Co. Down BT30 6PA.
A24 and A7 SE of Belfast 23 miles.
Parkland course.
18 holes, 5823 yds. S.S.S. 68
Visitors welcome.
Green Fees. Weekdays £3.00 (£2.00 with member); weekends £5.00 (£3.00 with member).
Society Meetings by arrangement; special discounts on Sat.
Hotels: Denvir's Hotel; Abbey Lodge Hotel.
Meals served.

Z 21   Dungannon

Tel. Dungannon 22098
Dungannon, Co. Tyrone.
½ mile out of town on Donaghmore Rd.
Parkland course.
18 holes, 5818 yds. S.S.S. 68
Visitors welcome.
Green Fees. Weekdays £2.00 (£1.50 with member or society outing); weekends £4.00 (£3.00 with member or society outing).
Society Meetings welcome.
Hotels: Inn on the Park; Dunowen.
Lunches served by arrangement.

Z 22   Dunmurry

Tel. Belfast (0232) 621402 & 610834
Upper Dunmurry Lane, Dunmurry, Belfast BT17 0QD.
On A1, 4 miles from Belfast.
Undulating parkland course.
18 holes, 5972 yds. S.S.S. 68
Visitors welcome on weekdays, weekends with member only.
Green Fees. Weekdays £3.00 (£2.50 with member); weekends £4.00. Reduced rates for more than 12 players.
Society Meetings welcome Mon. Tues. and Thurs.
Hotels: Beechlawn, Dunmurry; Woodlands, Lisburn.
Meals served except Mon.

Z 23   Enniskillen

Tel. Enniskillen (0365) 22900
Castle Coole, Enniskillen, Co. Fermanagh.
1 mile from Enniskillen.
Parkland course.
9 holes, 5990 yds. S.S.S. 69
Visitors welcome.
Green Fees. £2.00 per day.
Society Meetings welcome.
Hotels: Killyhevlin; Manor House Hotel; Railway Hotel; Fort Lodge Hotel.

Z 24   Fintona

Tel. Fintona (036562) 480
Ecclesville, Demesne, Fintona, Co. Tyrone.
8 miles S of Omagh, 75 miles W of Belfast.
Parkland course.
9 holes, 6250 yds. S.S.S. 70
Visitors welcome.
Green Fees. £1.50 per day (£1.00 with member).
Hotels: Knocknamoe Castle Hotel; Royal Arms, Omagh.

Z 25   Fortwilliam

Tel. Belfast (0232) 771770
Downview Ave., Belfast B15 4EZ.
On A2, 3 miles N of Belfast.
Meadowland course.
18 holes, 5846 yds. S.S.S. 68
Visitors welcome.
Green Fees. Weekdays £3.10; weekends £5.00.
Hotels: Landsdowne Court.
Meals served.

Z 26   Greenisland

Tel. Whiteabbey 62236
78 Upper Rd., Greenisland, Co. Antrim BT38 8RW.
9 holes, 5034 yds. S.S.S. 69
Visitors welcome except Sat.
Green Fees. Weekdays £3.00; Sun. £4.00.
Hotels: Edenmore; Glenavna.
Meals available.

Z 27   Helen's Bay

Tel. Helen's Bay 852601
Helen's Bay, Bangor, Co. Down.
Off A2, 9 miles E of Belfast.
Seaside course.
9 holes, 5638 yds. S.S.S. 66
Visitors welcome on weekdays and Sun., Sat. with member only.
Green Fees. Weekdays £4.00; Sun. £5.00.
Society Meetings by arrangement, max. 40.
Hotels: Crawfordsburn Inn, Crawfordsburn.
Meals served except Sun. after 2.00 p.m.

Z 28   Holywood

Tel. Holywood 2138
Demesne Rd., Holywood, Co. Down.
On A2, 6 miles E of Belfast.
Undulating course.
18 holes, 5743 yds. S.S.S. 67
Visitors welcome.
Green Fees. Weekdays £3.00; weekends £4.50.
Society Meetings welcome.
Hotels: Culloden.
Meals served except Mon.

Z 29   Kilkeel

Tel. Kilkeel 62296
Ballyardle, Kilkeel, Newry, Co. Down.
On A2, 46 miles S of Belfast.
Parkland course.
9 holes, 6030 yds. S.S.S. 69
Course designed by Lord Justice Babington.
Visitors welcome.

Green Fees. Weekdays £2.50; weekends and bank holidays £3.50.
Society Meetings welcome except during July and August.
Hotels: Royal; Cranfield House; Kilmoey Arms, Kilkeel.
Meals served except Mon.

Z 30   Killymoon

Tel. Cookstown (064 872) 62254
Killymoon Rd., Cookstown, Co. Tyrone.
Off A29 at S end of town.
Parkland course.
18 holes, 5629 yds. S.S.S. 68
Course designed by F. W. Hawtree.
Visitors welcome except Sat.
Green Fees. Weekdays £3.50; weekends £5.00.
Society Meetings welcome on weekdays.
Hotels: Glenavon; Royal; Greenvale.
Meals served.

Z 31   Kilrea

Tel. Kilrea 721
Drumagarner Rd., Kilrea, Co. Londonderry BT51 5TB.
½ mile out of Kilrea on Maghera Rd.
Undulating course.
9 holes, 4400 yds. S.S.S. 60
Visitors welcome except Sun.
Green Fees. Weekdays £1.50; weekends £2.00.
Hotels: Mercers Arms Hotel, Kilrea.

Z 32   Kirkistown Castle

Tel. Portavogie 233
Cloughy, Newtownards, Co. Down.
A20 from Belfast to Kircubbin, then B173 to Cloughy.
Seaside course.
18 holes, 6176 yds. S.S.S. 70
Course designed by James Braid.
Visitors welcome.
Green Fees. Weekdays men £2.50, ladies £2.00; Sat. men £5.00, ladies £3.00; Sun. men £6.00, ladies £3.00.
Society Meetings welcome except July and August.
Hotels: Road House Hotel, Cloughy; Portaferry Hotel, Portaferry; Strangford, Newtownards.
Snacks and meals served.

Z 33   The Knock

Tel. Dundonald (023 18) 2249 & 3251
Summerfield, Upper Newtownards Rd., Dundonald, Belfast BT16 0QX.
On A20, 4 miles E of city centre.
Parkland course.
18 holes, 6372 yds. S.S.S. 70
Visitors welcome.
Green Fees. Weekdays £4.00 per day (£3.00 with member); weekends £7.00 per day (£3.00 with member).
Society Meetings Mon. and Thurs. only.
Hotels: Stormont Hotel, Belfast.
Meals served except Sun.

Z 34   Larne

Tel. Islandmagee (096 035) 228
Ferris Bay Rd., Islandmagee, Larne B40 3RT.

By ferry from Larne or round Larne Lough by road.
Seaside meadowland course.
9 holes, 6114 yds. S.S.S. 69
Course designed by G. L. Bailey (1894).
Visitors welcome weekdays, Sat. after 5.30 p.m. and Sun.
Green Fees. Weekdays £2.00 (£1.50 with member); weekends £3.00 (£2.00 with member).
Society Meetings welcome on weekdays.
Hotels: Kings Arms; Laharna, Larne; Dolphin, Whitehead.
Snacks and light meals served by arrangement.

Z 35   Lisburn

Tel. Lisburn (023 82) 2186
Blaris Lodge, Eglantine Rd., Lisburn.
M1 and A1 from Belfast to Hillsborough, 3 miles from Lisburn station.
Parkland course.
18 holes, 6556 yds. S.S.S. 71
Course designed by F. W. Hawtree.
Visitors welcome.
Green Fees. Weekdays men £3.00, ladies £2.00, juniors £1.50; weekends men £4.00, ladies £3.00, juniors 75p. Rates halved with member.
Society Meetings by arrangement.
Hotels: Woodlands, Lisburn; White Gables, Hillsborough.
Meals served.

Z 36   Lurgan

Tel. Lurgan (076 282) 22087
The Demesne, Lurgan, Craigavon BT67 9BN.
M1 or A3 from Belfast, ½ mile from station.
Parkland course.
18 holes, 6286 yds. S.S.S. 69
Visitors welcome except Sat.
Green Fees. Weekdays £4.00 (£2.50 with member); Sun. £5.00 (£3.50 with member).
Society Meetings by arrangement except Sat.
Hotels: Country Club Inn.
Meals served; lunches and late meals by arrangement.

Z 37   Mahee Island

Tel. Killinghy 234
Mahee Island, Comber, Newtownards. Co. Down.
Off A22 14 miles SE of Belfast.
Seaside course.
9 holes, 5580 yds. S.S.S. 67
Visitors welcome.
Green Fees. Weekdays £2.50 (£1.50 with member); weekends £4.00 (£2.00 with member).
Hotels: in Belfast.
Meals served by arrangement.

Z 38   Malone

Tel. Belfast (0232) 612758
240 Upper Malone Rd., Dunmurry, Belfast BT17 9LB.
On M1, 5 miles SW of Belfast.
Parkland course.
18 holes, 6186 yds. S.S.S. 69
9 holes, 5790 yds. S.S.S. 68
Course designed by F. W. Hawtree.

Visitors welcome except Sat. before 5.00 p.m.
Green Fees. 18-hole course weekdays £4.50 per day; weekends £7.00 per day. 9-hole course weekdays £1.70 per day; weekends £3.00 per day.
Society Meetings Mon. and Thurs. only.
Hotels: Conway.
Meals served.

Z 39 Massereene

Tel. Antrim 2096, 3293
Lough Rd., Antrim, Co. Antrim.
1 mile S of town, 3½ miles from Aldergrove Airport.
Undulating, parkland course.
18 holes, 6287 yds. S.S.S. 70
Visitors welcome.
Green Fees. Weekdays £3.50 (£2.00 with member); weekends £5.50 (£3.50 with member), half fees after 5.00 p.m. Sat. and Sun. April-Nov.
Society Meetings by arrangement.
Hotels: Deerpark Hotel; Dunadry Inn.
Meals served.

Z 40 Moyola Park

Tel. Castledawson (064 885) 392 or 468
Shanemullagh, Castledawson, Co. Derry BT45 8AF.
Parkland course.
18 holes, 6456 yds. S.S.S. 71
Course designed by Don Patterson.
Visitors welcome.
Green Fees. Weekdays £2.50; weekends and bank holidays £4.00.
Society Meetings welcome.
Hotels: Moyola Lodge; Arches, Magherafelt.
Full catering facilities.

Z 41 Newtownstewart

Tel. Newtownstewart 61466
Baronscourt, Newtownstewart, Co. Tyrone.
On B84, 2 miles W of Newtownstewart.
Undulating parkland course.
18 holes, 5936 yds. S.S.S. 68
Course redesigned by F. Pennink.
Visitors welcome.
Green Fees. £2.00 per day; weekly £7.50; monthly £15.00.
Society Meetings by arrangement.
Hotels: Royal Arms; Silver Birches; Knocknamoe Castle Hotel, Omagh; Inter County, Lifford; Fir Trees Lodge, Strabane.

Z 42 Omagh

Tel. Omagh 3160
Dublin Rd., Omagh, Co. Tyrone.
On A5 in outskirts of Omagh.
Undulating meadowland course.
9 holes, 5576 yds. S.S.S. 66
Visitors welcome except Sat.
Green Fees. £2.00 per day; £7.50 per week.
Society Meetings welcome on weekdays.
Hotels: Royal Arms; Knocknamoe Castle Hotel; Silver Birch.
Bar snacks served.

Z 43 Ormeau

Tel. Belfast (0232) 641069
Ravenhill Rd., Belfast BT6.

2 miles from city centre.
Parkland course.
9 holes, S.S.S. 64
Visitors welcome Mon. to Sat.
Green Fees. Weekdays £2.20; Sat. £3.00.
Hotels: Europa.

Z 44 Portadown

Tel. Portadown (0762) 35356
Carrickblacker, Gilford Rd., Portadown, Co. Armagh BT63 5LF.
On A50, 3 miles SE of Portadown.
Parkland, meadowland course.
18 holes, 6199 yds. S.S.S. 70
Visitors welcome on weekdays, weekends with reservation.
Green Fees. Weekdays £3.00 (£2.00 with member); weekends £5.00 (£3.00 with member).
Society Meetings by arrangement.
Hotels: Seagoe, Portadown; Country Club Inn, Lurgan; Banville, Banbridge.
Meals served by arrangement.

Z 45 Portstewart

Tel. Portstewart 2015
117 Strand Rd., Portstewart, Co. Londonderry BT55 7PG.
4 miles W of Portrush.
Seaside course.
18 holes, 6784 yds. S.S.S. 72
Visitors welcome.
Green Fees. Weekdays £4.00; weekends £6.50 (£3.80 with member).
Society Meetings weekdays by arrangement.
Hotels: Strand; Edgewater; Carrig-Na-Cule.
Meals served by arrangement, tel. 2015.

Z 46 Rathmore

Tel. Rathmore 2285
Bushmills Rd., Portrush, Co. Antrim.
Seaside course.
Play over Royal Portrush Dunluce course, 9-hole course and Valley course.
Visitors welcome.
Green Fees. Weekdays £3.50 (£2.00 after 4.00 p.m.); weekends £6.00.
Society Meetings welcome weekdays only.
Lunches served except Mon.

Z 47 Royal Belfast

Tel. Holywood (02317) 2165
Station Rd., Craigavad, Holywood, Co. Down BT18 0BP.
Off A2, 2 miles E of Holywood.
Parkland course.
18 holes, 6225 yds. S.S.S. 70
Course designed by H. S. Colt.
Visitors welcome with letter of introduction.
Green Fees. Weekdays £5.00 (£2.50 with member); weekends £7.50 (£4.00 with member).
Society Meetings weekdays by arrangement.
Hotels: Culloden.
Meals served; dinner except Sun.

Z 48 Royal Co. Down

Tel. Newcastle (039 67) 23314
Newcastle, Co. Down BT33 0AN.
On A2, 30 miles S of Belfast.
Seaside courses.
No. 1 18 holes, 6969 yds. S.S.S. 73
No. 2 18 holes, 4100 yds. S.S.S. 60
Course designed by Tom Morris.
Visitors welcome, introduction needed for use of clubhouse.
Green Fees. No. 1 course weekdays £6.00; weekends £8.00. No. 2 course weekdays £3.50; weekends £4.00.
Society Meetings by arrangement.
Hotels: Slieve Donard; Brook Cottage; Burrendale.
Lunches and teas served.

Z 49 Royal Portrush

Tel. Portrush (0265) 822311
Bushmills Rd., Portrush, Co. Antrim BT56 8JQ.
On A29, 4 miles N of Coleraine.
Seaside courses.
Dunluce 18 holes, 6812 yds. S.S.S. 73
Valley 18 holes, 6177 yds. S.S.S. 69
Skerries 9 holes, 2374 yds.
Courses designed by H.S. Colt.
Visitors welcome.
Green Fees. Dunluce: weekdays £5.00 (£3.00 with member and after 4.30 p.m. June-August); weekends and bank holidays £8.00 (£4.00 with member and after 4.30 p.m. June-August); weekly (7 days) £30.00; weekly (5 days) £18.00. Valley: weekdays £3.50 (£2.50 with member), £2.00 after 4 p.m.; weekends and bank holidays £6.00 (£3.00 with member); weekly (7 days) £20.00; weekly (5 days) £12.00. Skerries: 60p per round. Putting: 15p per round.
Society Meetings welcome on weekdays.
Hotels: Skerry-Bhan; Eglinton; Beach, Port Ballintrae; Carrig-Na-Cule, Portstewart.
Meals served except Mon.

Z 50 Scrabo

Tel. Newtownards 812355, 815048 (Sec.)
Scrabo Rd., Newtownards, Co. Down.
Off A20, 10 miles E of Belfast.
Undulating course.
18 holes, 6079 yds. S.S.S. 69
Visitors welcome.
Green Fees. Weekdays £3.00 (£2.00 with member); weekends £5.00 (£3.50 with member).
Society Meetings welcome on weekdays.
Hotels: Strangford Arms.
Meals served at weekends; weekdays by arrangement in advance.

Z 51 Shandon Park

Tel. Belfast 793730
73 Shandon Park, Belfast BT5 6NY.
Parkland course.
18 holes, 6248 yds. S.S.S. 69
Visitors welcome.
Green Fees. Weekdays £4.00 (£2.25 with member); ladies £2.00 (£1.25 with member); weekends £6.00 (£3.25 with member); ladies £3.00 (£1.75 with member); societies £3.00.

Paradise here cost only £4

If you are lucky enough to play golf on Northern Ireland's two great courses, Royal County Down and Royal Portrush, somebody, sooner or later, is bound to ask you which you prefer.

Rather like being asked whether Bobby Jones was a better player than Hogan, or Hobbs a better batsman than Bradman, it is a provocative question which is not easily answered, but one fact upon which nearly everyone is agreed is that both rank among the eight best courses in Great Britain and Eire, and no golfer visiting those parts for the first time should play the one and not the other.

Without any disrespect to Portrush, my own slight preference is for County Down at Newcastle, because its setting under the shadow of the Mountains of Mourne is so majestic and inspiring that nobody could fail to be moved by it. There is something special about playing with a backcloth of mountains, and invariably that is a stranger's first comment, but if Newcastle had found itself surrounded by industry and not a quiet seaside town, the qualities of its course would still be outstanding.

It lies, in fact, on a narrow strip of dune country on the edge of Dundrum Bay and with its fine, natural features, forms the severest of championship tests. There is an unusually high premium on long, straight driving and no end of challenging strokes to well protected greens.

Originally, Tom Morris was commissioned to develop a course from the sandhills in 1889 at a cost not to exceed £4, and though there have since been a few changes and an increase in the budget, its character has changed little; but for all its exacting length, Newcastle can be enjoyed as much for holidays as a home for championships or the Curtis Cup.

The first three holes along the shore make a stern beginning; then comes a classic par four, the 5th, and at intervals according to one's fancy, more holes that stick in the memory and linger in the mind before one reaches them again. For the average handicap man there are alternative tees but a sight should be had at least once from the very back and, if the prospect is at first alarming, the thought that many great men have felt equally weak at the knees will make even the sixes and sevens a little more worthwhile than is usually the case.

Not that Portrush offers any more relief. It, too, lies in the midst of some marvellous natural golfing country away to the north, and with the wind blowing in from the Atlantic and the rough in full bloom, good scoring is no light matter.

Bernard Darwin, on seeing it for the first time, wrote that the redesigner of the old course, H. S. Colt, had built himself a monument more enduring than brass and it undoubtedly provides as thorough an examination of the golfer's skill as could be imagined, but it is also a place of remote beauty, and as soon as it comes into view around a curve in the coast road from Antrim, the urge to take a closer look is overwhelming.

I particularly like the 5th with its green by the water's edge looking away towards the Giant's Causeway, and the magnificent one-shot 6th that follows. Then, later on, there are holes aptly termed 'Calamity Corner' and 'Purgatory', and all the time, to spur one on, the reminder of the last British victory in the Open by Max Faulkner in 1951 or of the summer's day in 1960 when Joe Carr, perhaps the best-known and most-loved figure in all Ireland, stood 10 up and 10 to play in the final of the Amateur Championship.

These were the supreme moments in the lives of two players who in the worlds of amateur and professional golf, have provided more colour and entertainment than any of their contemporaries. For them, Portrush must have a warm place in their hearts, and no wonder.

Hotels: Stormont Hotel; Cavalier Hotel; Drumkeen Hotel, Belfast.

Z 52   Spa

Tel. Ballynahinch (0238) 562365
20 Grove Rd., Ballynahinch, Co. Down.
On A24, 12 miles S of Belfast.
Parkland course.
9 holes, 6310 yds. S.S.S. 69
Course designed by R. R. Bell and A. Mathers.
Visitors welcome except Sat.
Green Fees. On application to Secretary.
Society Meetings by arrangement except Sat.
Hotels: White Horse; Millbrook Lodge Hotel.

Z 53   Strabane

Tel. Strabane 2271
Ballycolman, Strabane, Co. Tyrone BT82 9PH.
Undulating parkland course.
18 holes, 4675 metres S.S.S. 69
Green Fees. Weekdays £1.50; weekends £2.00.
Hotels: Fir-Trees Lodge, Strabane; Inter County, Lifford.

Z 54   Tandragee

Tel. Tandragee 840 727
Markethill Rd., Tandragee, Co. Armagh.
On A27, 4 miles from Portadown.
Parkland course.
18 holes, 6023 yds. S.S.S. 69
Course designed by Hawtree and Son.
Visitors welcome.
Green Fees. Weekdays £1.50 (£1.00 with member); weekends £2.50 (£1.50 with member).
Society Meetings by arrangement.
Hotels: Seagoe, Portadown; Bannville, Gilford.
Meals for societies served by arrangement.

Z 55   Warrenpoint

Tel. Warrenpoint 3695
Lower Dromore Rd., Warrenpoint, Co. Down.
On A2, ½ mile W of Warrenpoint.
Undulating parkland course.
18 holes, 5628 metres S.S.S. 69
Visitors welcome.
Green Fees. Weekdays £3.00 (£1.50 with member); weekends and public holidays £6.00 (£3.00 with member).
Society Meetings by arrangement.
Hotels: Crown; Rostrevor; Ballyedmond.
Meals served.

Z 56   Whitehead

Tel. Whitehead 2792
McCrae's Brae, Whitehead, Co. Antrim.
On A2, 16 miles NE of Belfast.
Undulating parkland course.
18 holes, 6403 yds. S.S.S. 71
Course designed by A. B. Armstrong.
Visitors welcome except Sat.
Society Meetings by arrangement.
Hotels: Royal George; Dolphin.
Meals served by arrangement.

AA North Eire

AA 1 Achill Island

Achill Island, Co. Mayo.
9 holes, 5240 yds. S.S.S. 66
Green Fees. £1.00 per day.
Open Oct.-Apr.

AA 2 Ardee

Tel. Ardee (041) 53227
Town Parks, Ardee, Co. Louth.
½ mile from N end of town.
Meadowland course.
9 holes, 3034 yds. S.S.S. 67
Visitors welcome.
Green Fees. Weekdays £3.00; weekends £4.00.
Society Meetings Mon., Wed. and Sat. only.
Hotels: Brophys, Ardee; Grove, Dunleer.

AA 3 Athenry

Tel. 091-84466
Athenry, Co. Galway.
13 miles from Galway.
Parkland course.
9 holes, 5448 yds. S.S.S. 66
Visitors welcome.
Green Fees. £2.00 per day.
Society Meetings welcome.
Hotels: Western; Hanberry's.

AA 4 Athlone

Tel. Athlone (0902) 2073
Hodson Bay, Athlone, Co. Westmeath.
3½ miles NW of Athlone.
Undulating parkland course.
18 holes, 5946 yds. S.S.S. 68
Visitors welcome.
Green Fees. Weekdays £3.00 (£1.50 with member); Sat. £4.00 (£2.00 with member).
Society Meetings welcome on weekdays.
Hotels: Prince of Wales; Royal; Shamrock Lodge Hotel; Hodson Bay Hotel, Athlone.
Meals served by arrangement.

AA 5 Balbriggan

Tel. Dublin 412173
Blackhall, Balbriggan, Co. Dublin.
From city centre along Northern road, between Swords and Balbriggan.
Meadowland course.
9 holes, 5952 yds. S.S.S. 70
Visitors welcome on weekdays with reservation.
Green Fees. Weekdays £3.00 per day; weekends £4.00; £1.50 for not more than three playing with member, all days.
Society Meetings by arrangement.
Hotels: Grand; Balrothery Inn.

AA 6 Ballaghaderreen

Tel. Ballaghaderreen 43
Ballaghaderreen, Co. Roscommon.
2 miles from Ballaghaderreen.
Moorland course.
9 holes, 2884 yds. S.S.S. 65
Course designed by P. Skerritt.
Visitors welcome.
Green Fees. £1.00 per day.
Society Meetings welcome.
Hotels: Western Hotel; Louch Gara.
Meals served to Societies only.

AA 7 Ballina

Tel. 096-21050
Mosgrove, Ballina, Co. Mayo.
1 mile E of town.
Parkland course.
9 holes, 5668 yds. S.S.S. 65
Visitors welcome.
Green Fees. £2.00 per day.
Society Meetings welcome on weekdays.
Hotels: Downhill; Moy; Bartra House; Hurst; Beleck Castle.

AA 8 Ballinamore

Tel. Ballinamore 163 or 187
Creevy, Ballinamore, Co. Leitrim.
1 mile from town centre.
Rolling parkland course.
9 holes, 5736 yds. S.S.S. 67
Visitors welcome.
Green Fees. £1.50 per day; weekly £7.50 (no charge to residents of hotels listed below).
Society Meetings welcome.
Hotels: Sliabh An Iarainn; Commercial.

AA 9 Ballinasloe

Tel. Ballinasloe 2126
Ballinasloe, Co. Galway.
T4, 2 miles from town.
Parkland course.
9 holes, 5804 yds. S.S.S. 67
Visitors welcome.
Green Fees. £2.00 per day.
Society Meetings welcome.
Hotels: Hayden's Hotel; East County.

AA 10 Ballinrobe

Tel. Ballinrobe 52 & 500
Ballinrobe, Co. Mayo.
Parkland course.
9 holes, 5762 yds. S.S.S. 66
Visitors welcome.
Green Fees. £1.00 per day.
Society Meetings welcome.
Hotels; Valkenburg; Lakeland; Ashford Castle Hotel; Ryan's Cong.

AA 11 Ballybofey & Stranorlar

Tel. Ballybofey 93
Ballybofey, Lifford, Co. Donegal.
12 miles W of Strabane on T18.
18 holes, 5825 yds. S.S.S. 67
Course designed by E. Hackett.
Visitors welcome except Tues. after 6.00p.m.
Green Fees. £3.00.
Society Meetings welcome.
Hotels: Kee's, Stranorlar; Jackson's, Ballybofey.

AA 12 Ballyhawnis

Tel. Ballyhawnis 14
Coolnaha, Ballyhawnis, Co. Mayo.
2½ miles out of Ballyhawnis on Sligo road.
Parkland course.
9 holes, 5852 yds. S.S.S. 68
Visitors welcome.
Green Fees. £2.00 per day; £10.00 per week.
Hotels: Central Hotel.

AA 13 Ballyliffin

Tel. Clonmany 19
Clonmany, Lifford, Co. Donegal.
25 miles from Derry.
Seaside course.
18 holes, 6611 yds. S.S.S. 71
Visitors welcome.
Green Fees. £2.00.
Society Meetings welcome on weekdays.
Hotels: Strand; Ballyliffin Hotel; Ballyliffin.

AA 14 Bellmullet

Tel. Bellmullet 44
Bellmullet, Co. Mayo.
Seaside course.
9 holes, 5658 yds. S.S.S. 67
Visitors welcome.
Hotels: Western Strands Hotel.

AA 15 Belturbet

Tel. Belturbet 2287
Erne Hill, Belturbet, Co. Cavan.
Beside town on Cavan road.
Parkland course.
9 holes, 5122 yds. S.S.S. 65
Visitors welcome.
Society Meetings by arrangement.
Hotels: Seven Horseshoes Hotel.

AA 16 Blacklion

Tel. Blacklion 24
Toam, Blacklion, Co. Cavan.
10 miles S of Enniskillen.
Undulating meadowland course.
9 holes, 6140 yds. S.S.S. 67
Course designed by E. Hackett.
Visitors welcome.
Green Fees. Weekdays £1.00 per day; weekends £1.50; weekly £5.00.
Society Meetings welcome.
Hotels: McNean House.

AA 17 Boyle

Boyle, Co. Roscommon.
1½ miles from Boyle on Roscommon road.
Parkland course.
9 holes, 5312 yds. S.S.S. 65
Visitors welcome.
Green Fees. £2.00.
Hotels: Forest Park Hotel; Royal.

AA 18 Buncrana

Tel. Buncrana 116
Buncrana, Co. Donegal.
9 holes, 4040 yds. S.S.S. 61

AA 19 Bundoran

Tel. Bundoran (072) 41302
Bundoran, Co. Donegal.
Undulating seaside course.
18 holes, 6265 yds. S.S.S. 69
Course designed by H. Vardon.
Visitors welcome.
Green Fees. Weekdays £3.00; weekends £4.00.
Society Meetings by arrangement.
Hotels: Great Northern.
Meals served.

AA 20 Carrickmines

Tel. Dublin 895676
Carrickmines, Co. Dublin.
T43 S from Dublin, left at Sandyford, 7 miles from Dublin.
9 holes, 6026 yds. S.S.S. 69
Visitors welcome. Sat. and bank holidays with member only.
Green Fees. Weekdays £3.00 (£1.00 with member); Sun. £4.00.

AA 21 Carrick-on-Shannon

Tel. Carrick-on-Shannon 157
Carrick-on-Shannon, Co. Leitrim.
3 miles from station on Sligo road.
Undulating parkland course.
9 holes, S.S.S. 67
Visitors welcome.
Green Fees. £2.00 per day; weekly £8.00; fortnightly £12.00; monthly £20.00.
Society Meetings welcome except Sun. by arrangement 5 weeks in advance.
Hotels: Bush Hotel; County Hotel; Cartown House Hotel.
Snacks served; meals by arrangement.

AA 22 Castle

Tel. Dublin (01) 904207
Woodside Dr., Rathfarnham, Dublin 14.
About 4 miles from city centre.
Parkland course.
18 holes, 6183 yds. S.S.S. 68
Course designed by H.S. Colt.
Visitors welcome on weekdays.
Green Fees. Weekdays £3.50 (£1.50 with member); weekly £9.00.
Society Meetings weekdays by arrangement.
Hotels: in Dublin.
Meals served.

AA 23 Castlebar

Tel. Castlebar (094) 21649
Rocklands, Castlebar, Co. Mayo.
Inland course.
9 holes, 2948 yds. S.S.S. 66
Visitors welcome.
Green Fees. £2.00 per day.
Hotels: Breaffy House Hotel; Traveller's Friend; Welcome Inn; Imperial.

AA 24 Castlerea

Tel. Castlerea 68
Castlerea, Co. Roscommon.
Parkland course.
9 holes, 5466 yds. S.S.S. 66
Visitors welcome.
Green Fees. £2.00 per day.
Hotels: Tully's; Three Counties.

AA 25 Claremorris

Tel. Claremorris 094 71527
Claremorris, Co. Mayo.
Parkland course.
9 holes, 5338 yds. S.S.S. 66
Visitors welcome.
Green Fees. £2.00 per day.
Hotels: Central Hotel; Western Hotel.
Lunches and snacks served by arrangement.

AA 26 Clones

Tel. Scotshouse 17
Hilton Park, Clones, Co. Monaghan.
3 miles S of Clones.
Parkland course.
9 holes, 5260 yds. S.S.S. 66
Visitors welcome.
Green Fees. On application to Secretary.
Society Meetings by arrangement.
Hotels: Creighton; Lennard Arms; Hibernian.
Snacks served after 2 p.m.; light meals by arrangement.

AA 27 Clontarf

Tel. Dublin (01) 332669
Malahide Rd., Dublin 3.
NE of city centre 3 miles on main road to Malahide.
Parkland course.
18 holes, 5894 yds. S.S.S. 67
Visitors welcome on weekdays.
Green Fees. Weekdays £6.00.
Society Meetings by arrangement.
Hotels: Clare Manor; Skylon; Hollybrook.
Meals served.

AA 28 Connemara

Tel. Ballyconneely 5 Clifden 29
Ballyconneely, Clifden, Ballyconneely.
Via Galway, Clifden, Ballyconneely.
Seaside links course.
18 holes, Medal 6754 yds. S.S.S. 71 par 72
Championships 7107 yds. S.S.S. 72
Course designed by Edward Hackett.
Visitors welcome.
Society Meetings welcome. Reduced fees for parties of 20 or over.
Hotels: Roch Glen; Atlantic Coast, Clifden.
Snacks served.

AA 29 Corballis

Tel. Dublin 450583
Donabate, Co. Dublin (Dublin Co. Council, Parks Dept.).
T1 N from Dublin, right down L91, 2 miles beyond Swords.
Seaside links.
18 holes, 5200 yds. S.S.S. 62
Visitors welcome. Open to the public.
Society Meetings welcome except Sun.

AA 30 County Cavan

Tel. Cavan (049) 31283
Aranmore House, Drumelis, Co. Cavan.
2 miles from Cavan off Cavan to Killashandra road.
18 holes, 5972 yds. S.S.S. 69
Visitors welcome.
Green Fees. On application to Secretary.

Society Meetings Mon. and Sat. only.
Hotels: Farnham Arms; Lakeland, Cavan.
Light meals served by arrangement.

AA 31 County Longford

Tel. Glack (043) 6310
Glack, Longford.
Off Dublin to Sligo road (N4) E of town, signposted.
Undulating course.
18 holes, 6028 yds. S.S.S. 67
Course designed by E. Hackett.
Visitors welcome.
Green Fees. £2.00.
Society Meetings welcome.
Hotels: Annally; Longford Arms, Longford.
Snacks served.

AA 32 County Louth

Tel. Drogheda (041) 22329
Baltray, Drogheda, Co. Louth.
Seaside course.
18 holes, 6852 yds. S.S.S. 72
Course designed by T. Simpson.
Visitors welcome.
Green Fees. Weekdays £3.00; weekends £5.00.
Meals served.

AA 33 County Sligo

Tel. 071 77186, Secretary 77134
Rosses Point, Co. Sligo.
5 miles from Sligo.
Seaside course.
18 holes, 6354 yds. S.S.S. 70
Course designed by Colt and Allison.
Visitors welcome.
Green Fees. Weekdays £4.00 per day; weekends £6.00.
Hotels: Yeats Country Ryan Hotel: Ballincar House Hotel.
Meals served.

AA 34 Donabate

Tel. Dublin (01) 450335
Donabate, Co. Dublin.
1st right 1 mile N of Swords on Dublin-Belfast road.
Parkland course.
Medal 18 holes, 6187 yds. S.S.S. 67
Forward 18 holes, 5847 yds. S.S.S. 66
Visitors welcome on weekdays.
Green Fees. On application to Secretary.
Society Meetings welcome Tues. and Thurs. only.
Hotels: Crofton Airport Hotel.
Meals served Wed. and weekends, or by arrangement.

AA 35 Donegal

Tel. Ballintra 54
Murvagh, Laghey P.O., Co. Donegal.
Off T18, 7 miles S of Donegal.
Undulating seaside course.
18 holes, 6701 yds. S.S.S. 72
Course designed by E. Hackett.
Visitors welcome.
Green Fees. Weekdays £3.00 per day; weekends £4.00 per day.
Society Meetings welcome.
Hotels: Central Hotel; Abbey; National, Donegal; Sand House Hotel, Rossnowlagh.
Snacks served, meals by arrangement.

AA 36 Dun Laoghaire

Tel. Dublin (01) 803916, Professional
801694
Eglinton Park, Dun Laoghaire, Co. Dublin.
Off Tivoli Rd.
Parkland course.
18 holes, S.S.S. 68
Visitors welcome.
Green Fees. Weekdays £6.00; weekends
£7.50.
Hotels: Royal Marine.
Meals served.

AA 37 Dundalk

Tel. (042) 32731
Blackrock, Dundalk, Co. Louth.
Off T1, 3 miles S of Dundalk, on Dundalk Bay.
Parkland course.
18 holes, 6435 yds. S.S.S. 69
Course designed by Golf Construction Ltd.
Visitors welcome.
Green Fees. Weekdays £4.00; weekends
£5.00.
Society Meetings by arrangement.
Hotels: Ballymascanlon House Hotel;
Imperial; Derryhale; Fairways, Dundalk.
Meals served by arrangement.

AA 38 Dunfanaghy

Tel. Dunfanaghy 7
Dunfanaghy, Letterkenny, Co. Donegal.
23 miles from Letterkenny.
Seaside course.
18 holes, 5230 yds. S.S.S. 65
Visitors welcome.
Green Fees. 75p per day.
Hotels: Arnold's; Carrig Rua; Pier; Port-na-
Blagh, Shandon.

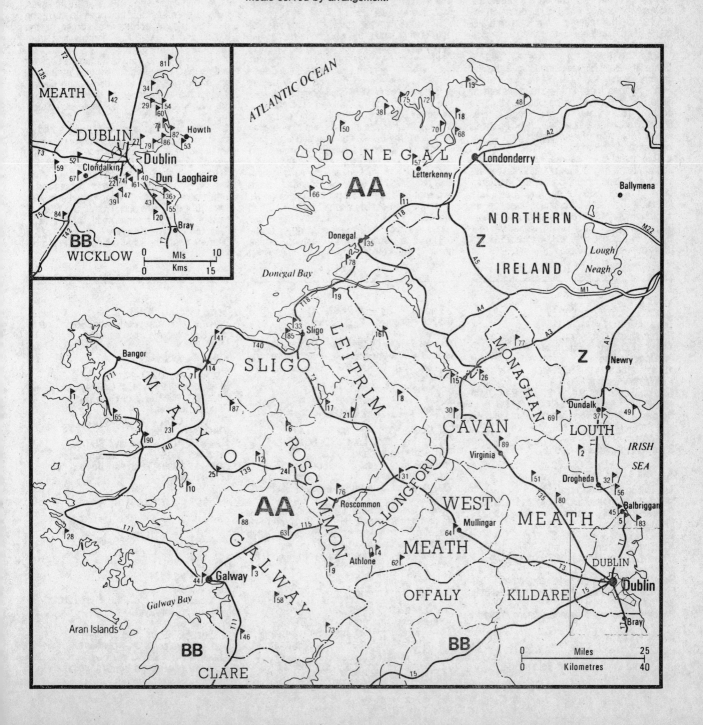

Rosses Point—in a different world

Long before the road through the green Glencar valley slips gently down into Sligo, there is an awareness that golf at Rosses Point offers something very special. Rosses Point, the home of the County Sligo club, lies a few miles beyond the old town, but what makes it a name noted throughout Ireland and most of the golfing world is not so much the quality of the course—which is magnificent—as the majesty of its setting—which is unsurpassed.

Away to the north across an inlet to Drumcliff, Ben Bulben stands guard over country where the poet Yeats lies buried; twin estuaries meet in the broad waters of Sligo Bay; the coastline beyond Knocknarea edges from view through vast acres uninhabited, undeveloped and unspoilt; and all around a feeling of remoteness and peace inspires and distracts.

This mood is, of course, not always constant and the annual Easter gathering for the West of Ireland championship speaks more often of winds, storms and rain. But I was fortunate that my introduction was on an afternoon of stillness and sunshine, and that I had as my guide Cecil Ewing, something of a legend in those parts, who was born in the hotel opposite the club.

Though he then devoted most of his time to his role as British and Irish selector, much of the old flair remained and it was easy to see how this massive, kindly figure, with narrow stance and short swing, was such a formidable golfer, capable of hitting the ball low and straight through Atlantic gales when few others could stand.

The first two are not particularly memorable golfing holes, the second in fact taking us up quite a slope, but it is worth climbing Everest for the view from the third tee with the whole superb panorama suddenly unfurled. Now the course has really begun, and there is a series of challenging strokes—varying according to the wind—which takes us out at a lower level nearer the sea.

The 5th offers an inviting drive to a fairway far below, the 6th demands a subtle second over a hidden dip in front of the green, and the 7th, turning inland, provides a testing second over a stream guarding the green. The outward half ends with another grand two-shot hole and a short 9th along a ridge, but to me the best lies ahead from the 10th to the 16th, where the golf through miniature dunes is typical of a great seaside course.

The 10th, following the estuary which flows down towards the little church at Drumcliff, is a beautiful hole; the 11th, back up to the 9th green, is a stiff four against the prevailing wind, and the 12th (495 yds), round the curve of the bay, frequently costs five or more. But the 14th, from an elevated tee, has perhaps the greatest appeal, with a drive that must be well placed to miss bunkers on either hand and open up the green for the second across the corner of the beach and its surrounds encroaching from the right.

The drive at the 15th is through a shallow valley; the 17th takes us half way up the hill again and the 18th, with its second played against the background of Knocknarea and the distant outline of Sligo itself, completes the ascent.

Golf is over, but enjoyment lingers and in my case—and I am sure in yours—was extended over a glass or three in the clubhouse. Outside the evening sun cast its shadow on the whole tranquil scene that inspired so much of Yeats's verse and I remembered that my day had begun amid the bustle of London Airport. Golf in the west of Ireland, as it is farther south at Lahinch, Ballybunion and Killarney, is part of a different world and what a blessing it is to be sure.

AA 39 Edmonstown

Tel. Dublin (01) 907461
Rathfarnham, Dublin 14.
T42 S of Dublin, Rathfarnham, 1 mile.
Parkland course.
18 holes, 5897 yds. S.S.S. 69
Visitors welcome, Sun. after 12.00 a.m.
Green Fees. Weekdays £3.00 (£1.50 with member); weekends £4.00 (£2.00).
Society Meetings welcome weekdays and Sat. mornings.
Hotels: in Dublin.
Snacks and meals served.

AA 40 Elm Park

Tel. Dublin (01) 693438
Nutley Lane House, Donnybrook, Dublin 4.
2 miles from city centre.
Parkland course.
18 holes, 5448 yds. S.S.S. 67
Visitors welcome.
Green Fees. Weekdays £6.00 (£2.00 with member); weekends £9.00 (£2.50).
Society Meetings by arrangement.
Hotels: Montrose; Tara Towers; Burlington; South County.
Snacks; Lunches; teas and dinners served.

AA 41 Enniscrone

Enniscrone, Co. Sligo.
½ mile from Enniscrone on Ballinu Rd.
Seaside course

18 holes, 6334 yds. S.S.S. 70
Course designed by E. Hackett.
Visitors welcome.
Green Fees. On application to Secretary.
Society Meetings welcome.
Hotels: Castle Arms; Benbulben; Atlantic; Marine.
Bar snacks served.

AA 42 Forrest Little

Tel. Dublin (01) 401763
Forest Rd., Cloghran, Co. Dublin.
Parkland meadowland course.
18 holes, 6271 yds. S.S.S. 68
Course designed by Hawtree.
Visitors welcome on weekdays, weekends after 5.30p.m.
Green Fees. £5.00 (£2.00 with member). No green fees after 2 p.m. on Wed. and Fri.
Hotels: Dublin International Hotel, Dublin Airport; Crofton Airport Hotel.
Snacks; evening meals served; lunch by arrangement.

AA 43 Foxrock

Tel. Dublin (01) 893992
Torquay Rd., Foxrock, Co. Dublin.
T7 S, turn right just past Stillorgan on to Leopardstown Rd. then left into Torquay Rd.
Parkland course.
9 holes, 6308 yds. S.S.S. 68
Visitors welcome.

Green Fees. £3.00.
Hotels: Montrose; Burlington; South County.
Meals served by arrangement.

AA 44 Galway

Tel. Galway (091) 22169.
Blackrock, Galway, Co. Galway.
On L100, 2 miles W of Galway.
Parkland course.
18 holes, 6193 yds. S.S.S. 69
Visitors welcome.
Green Fees. Weekdays £5.00.
Society Meetings by arrangement.
Hotels: several in immediate vicinity.
Meals served.

AA 45 Gormanston

Tel. Balbriggan 412203 (01)
Gormanston, Co. Meath.
9 holes, 3956 yds. S.S.S. 58

AA 46 Gort

Tel. Gort 204
Gort, Co. Galway.
On County Road No. 363 Gort-Tubber, 24 miles S. of Galway.
Parkland course.
9 holes, 5380 yds. S.S.S. 65
Visitors welcome on weekdays.
Green Fees. £1.50 per day.
Society Meetings by arrangement.
Hotels: Glynns; Sullivan's.

AA 47   Grange

Tel. Dublin 907889
Rathfarnham, Dublin 16.
On bus route 47 and 47b.
Parkland course.
18 holes, 6036 yds. S.S.S. 69
Visitors welcome with reservation.
Green Fees. Weekdays £5.00.
Hotels: Montrose; Intercontinental.
Lunches served, evening meals served
summer till 10.00 p.m., winter till 8.00 p.m.

AA 48   Greencastle

Tel. Greencastle 13
Greencastle, Moville, Co. Donegal.
On L85, 23 miles NE of Londonderry.
Seaside course.
9 holes, S.S.S. 65
Visitors welcome.
Green Fees. Weekdays £2.00; weekends
£3.00.
Society Meetings by arrangement.
Hotels: Castle Inn, Greencastle; Foyle;
Keaveney's, Moville; New Lark Hotel.
Meals served.

AA 49   Greenore

Tel. 042 73212
Greenore, Co. Louth.
Seaside course.
18 holes, 6100 yds. S.S.S. 68
Visitors welcome.
Hotels: Fairways; Ballymascanlon; Road
House Hotel.
Lunches served except Mon.

AA 50   Gweedore

Tel. Bunbeg 64
Derrybeg, Letterkenny, Co. Donegal.
L82 from Letterkenny or T72 from Donegal.
Seaside course.
9 holes, 2700 yds. S.S.S. 66
Visitors welcome.
Hotels: Derry Beg; Seaview; Gweedure.
Lunches served.

AA 51   Headfort

Tel. Ceannannas Mor 146
Kells, Co. Meath.
On T35, 40 miles NW of Dublin.
Parkland course.
18 holes, 6319 yds. S.S.S. 69
Visitors welcome.
Green Fees. Weekdays £4.00; weekends
£5.00.
Society Meetings welcome Mon. to Sat.
Hotels: Headfort Arms, Kells; Kirwan Arms,
Athboy; Ardboyne, Navan.
Snacks served.

AA 52   Hermitage

Tel. Dublin 265049/264549
Lucan, Co. Dublin.
T3 W from Dublin, 7 miles.
Parkland course.
18 holes, 6300 yds. S.S.S. 70
Visitors welcome.
Green Fees. Weekdays £6.00; weekends
£8.00.
Society Meetings by arrangement.
Hotels: Ashling Hotel, Dublin.
Meals served.

AA 53   Howth

Tel. Dublin (01) 323055
Carrickbrack Rd., Sutton, Dublin.
1½ miles from Sutton Cross.
Undulating moorland course.
18 holes, 5994 yds. S.S.S. 68
Course designed by J. Braid.
Visitors welcome. Ladies' day Wed.
Green Fees. Weekdays £4.00 (£2.00 with
member); weekends £3.00 with member
only.
Society Meetings by arrangement.
Hotels: Marine; Howth Lodge.
Meals served weekends only.

AA 54   Island

Tel. Dublin 450595 (clubhouse), 452205
(Secretary)
Corballis, Donabate, Co. Dublin.
From Dublin leave T1 approx. 1 mile beyond
Swords, then L91 for 3 miles, right turn to
Corballis.
Seaside course.
18 holes, 6203 yds. S.S.S. 70
Visitors welcome.
Lunches served.

AA 55   Killiney

Tel. Dublin (01) 851983
Killiney, Co. Dublin.
7 miles S of Dublin.
Parkland course.
9 holes, 6318 yds. S.S.S. 68
Visitors welcome on weekdays except
Thurs. which is ladies' day.
Green Fees. Weekdays £5.00.
Hotels: Killiney Court; Fitzpatrick's Castle
Hotel.
Lunches and teas served by arrangement.

AA 56   Laytown and Bettystown

Tel. Drogheda 27534
Bettystown, Co. Meath.
On L125, off T1, 28 miles N of Dublin.
Undulating seaside course.
18 holes, 6254 yds. S.S.S. 69
Visitors welcome.
Green Fees. Weekdays £4.00 (£2.00 with
member); weekends £5.00 (£2.50 with
member).
Society Meetings by arrangement.
Hotels: Neptune; Village Hotel; Ros-na-Rec;
Boyne Valley.
Meals served.

AA 57   Letterkenny

Tel. Letterkenny 144
Barnhill, Letterkenny, Co. Donegal.
On T72, 2 miles N of Letterkenny.
Parkland course.
18 holes, 6299 yds. S.S.S. 69
Course designed by E. Hackett.
Visitors welcome.
Green Fees. £2.00 per day.
Society Meetings welcome.
Hotels: Ballyraine; Three Ways;
Gallagher's; McCarry's.
Snacks served; meals by arrangement.

AA 58   Loughrea

Tel. Galway (091) 41049
Loughrea, Co. Galway.

On L11, 1 mile N of Loughrea.
Meadowland course.
9 holes, 5798 yds. S.S.S. 66
Visitors welcome.
Green Fees. Weekdays £1.50; weekends
£2.00.
Society Meetings Mon. to Sat. by
arrangement.
Hotels: in area.

AA 59   Lucan

Tel. Dublin 280246
Lucan, Co. Dublin.
9 holes, 5876 yds. S.S.S. 67
Visitors welcome; restricted after 6p.m.
and weekends.
Hotels: Spa Hotel.

AA 60   Malahide

Tel. Dublin (01) 450248
Malahide, Co. Dublin.
8 miles S of Dublin.
Parkland course.
9 holes, 5568 yds. S.S.S. 65
Course designed by N. Hone.
Visitors welcome.
Green Fees. On application to Secretary.
Society Meetings by arrangement.
Hotels: Grand; Royal Stuart.
Minimal catering.

AA 61   Milltown

Tel. Dublin 977060
Milltown, Dublin 14.
T7 3½ miles S of city.
Parkland course.
Visitors welcome except Sat.
Society Meetings by arrangement.
Hotels: Many in vicinity.
Lunches served.

AA 62   Moate

Tel. 0902 31271
Moate, Co. Westmeath.
On T4, 8 miles E of Athlone.
Parkland course.
9 holes, 5348 yds. S.S.S. 65
Visitors welcome.
Green Fees. On application to Secretary.
Society Meetings welcome Mon. to Sat.
Hotels: Grand; Killcleagh Park Hotel.
Bar snacks served by arrangement.

AA 63   Mount Bellew

Tel. 0905 9259
Shankill, Mount Bellew, Co. Galway.
On T4, 28 miles E of Galway.
Parkland course.
9 holes, 5492 yds. S.S.S. 65
Visitors welcome.
Green Fees. On application to Secretary.
Society Meetings welcome.
Hotels: Hayden's, Ballinasloe; Imperial,
Tuam; St. Annes Guest House, Mount Bellew.
Meals served by arrangement.

AA 64   Mullingar

Tel. 044 8366
Belvedere, Mullingar, Co. Westmeath.
3 miles S of Mullingar.
Parkland course.
18 holes, 6370 yds. S.S.S. 70

Course designed by James Braid.
Visitors welcome.
Green Fees. On application to Secretary.
Society Meetings welcome on weekdays.
Hotels: Greville Arms; Lake County Hotel;
Broders Hotel.
Meals served.

AA 65 Mulrany

Tel. Mulrany 3
Mulrany, Westport, Co. Mayo.
On T71, 21 miles W of Castlebar.
Undulating seaside course.
9 holes, 6380 yds. S.S.S. 69
Course designed by E. Hackett.
Visitors welcome.
Green Fees. £1.00 per day.
Society Meetings by arrangement.
Hotels: Great Southern, Mulrany; Newport
House Hotel, Newport; Achill Sound Hotel,
Achill Sound.

AA 66 Narin & Portnoo

Tel. Clooney 21
Portnoo, Co. Donegal.
8 miles W of Glenties via T72 and L81.
Seaside course.
18 holes, 5700 yds. S.S.S. 68
Visitors welcome.
Green Fees. £2.00 per day.
Society Meetings by arrangement.
Hotels: Lake House Hotel; Portnoo Hotel;
Nesbitt Arms; Highlands Hotel.

AA 67 Newlands

Tel. Dublin 593157
Clondalkin, Co. Dublin.
6 miles from city centre on main Southern
Cork road.
Parkland course.
18 holes, 6188 yds. S.S.S. 69
Course designed by J. Braid.
Visitors welcome on weekdays.
Green Fees. £5.50.
Society Meetings welcome.
Hotels: Green Isle Hotel.
Meals served.

AA 68 North West

Tel. Buncrana 12
Lisfannon, Fahan, Co. Donegal.
12 miles from Derry on main Buncrana road.
Seaside course.
18 holes, 5928 yds. S.S.S. 67
Visitors welcome.
Green Fees. Weekdays £2.50 (£2.00 with
member); weekends £3.50 (£3.00 with
member).
Society Meetings catered for on
weekdays and at weekends by prior
arrangement.
Hotels: Roneragh House, Fahan; White
Strand Motor Inn; Lough Swilly, Buncrana.

AA 69 Nuremore

Tel. 042 614
Nuremore, Carrickmacross, Co. Monaghan.
50 miles from Dublin on main Dublin to Derry
road.
Meadowland course.
9 holes, 5943 yds. S.S.S. 68
Visitors welcome

Green Fees. On application to Secretary.
Society Meetings welcome.
Hotels: Nuremore Hotel.
Meals served.

AA 70 Otway

Rathmullan, Co. Donegal.
On the Western shore of Loch Swilly.
Seaside course.
9 holes, 4134 yds. S.S.S. 60
Visitors welcome.
Hotels: Fort Royal; Rathmullan House; Pier
Hotel.

AA 71 Portmarnock

Tel. Dublin (01) 323082
Portmarnock, Co. Dublin.
3 miles E of Dublin Airport.
Seaside course.
27 holes, 7097 yds. S.S.S. 74
Course designed by Ross & Pickman.
Visitors welcome on weekdays if members
of recognized club, weekends with
reservation.
Green Fees. Weekdays (Men) £8.00;
weekends (Men) £10.00; weekdays
(Ladies) £3.00.
Society Meetings parties welcome
weekday mornings except Wed.
Hotels: Marine, Sutton; Grand, Malahide.
Meals served weekdays.

AA 72 Portsalon

Tel. Portsalon 11
Portsalon, Co. Donegal.
Main road from Letterkenny (L78).
Seaside course.
18 holes, 5522 yds. S.S.S. 67
Visitors welcome.
Green Fees. £3.00 per day.
Hotels: Portsalon.

AA 73 Portumna

Tel. Portumna 59
Portumna, Co. Galway.
On T4, NW shore of Lough Derg.
Woodland parkland course.
9 holes, 5801 yds. S.S.S. 68
Course designed by W O'Brien, redesigned
by E. Hackett.
Visitors welcome, except after 12.00 a.m.
Sun.
Green Fees. On application to Secretary.
Society Meetings welcome except Sun.
Hotels: Westpark Hotel.
Meals served by arrangement.

AA 74 Rathfarnham

Tel. Dublin 905201
Newtown, Rathfarnham, Dublin 16.
T42 and L94 S, 6 miles from city centre.
Parkland course.
9 holes, 6304 yds. S.S.S. 69
Visitors welcome on weekdays.
Society Meetings welcome by
arrangement.
Lunches served by arrangement.

AA 75 Rosapenna

Tel. Downings 4
Downings Co. Donegal.
22 miles from Letterkenny.

Seaside course.
18 holes, 6254 yds. S.S.S. 70
Course designed by T. Morris 1893.
Visitors welcome.
Green Fees. Weekdays £2.00; weekends
£2.25.
Society Meetings by arrangement.
Hotels: Rosapenna Golf Hotel.
Meals served.

AA 76 Roscommon

Tel. 0903 6283
Mote Park, Roscommon, Co. Roscommon.
On T15, 96 miles W of Dublin.
Meadowland course.
9 holes, 6340 yds. S.S.S. 70
Visitors welcome.
Green Fees. On application to Secretary.
Society Meetings by arrangement.
Hotels: Abbey; Royal.

AA 77 Rossmore

Tel. 047 81316
Rossmore Park, Monaghan.
3 miles from town centre.
Undulating course.
9 holes, 5750 yds. S.S.S. 68
Visitors welcome.
Green Fees. Weekdays £2.00; weekends
£3.00; weekly £10.00; monthly £20.00.
Hotels: Westerna; Hotel Hillgrove; Four
Seasons, Monaghan.
Meals served.

AA 78 Rossnowlagh

Tel. Bundoran (072) 65343
Sand House Hotel, Rossnowlagh, Co.
Donegal.
Seaside course.
9 holes.
Visitors welcome only during holiday
season.
Green Fees. 60p per day.
Hotels: Sand House Hotel.
Lunches served.

AA 79 Royal Dublin

Tel. Dublin (01) 336346
Bull Island, Dollymount, Dublin 3.
3 miles NE of city centre.
Championship links.
18 holes, 6795 yds. S.S.S. 72
Visitors welcome except Sat.
Green Fees. Weekdays £7.50; Sun.
£10.00.
Society Meetings by arrangement.
Hotels: Royal Marine; Howth Lodge.
Meals served.

AA 80 Royal Tara

Tel. Navan (046) 25244
Bellinter, Navan, Co. Meath.
Off Dublin/Navan road.
Parkland course.
18 holes, 6356 yds. S.S.S. 69
Visitors welcome.
Green Fees. Weekdays £3.00; weekends
£4.00.
Society Meetings welcome weekdays
and Sat. mornings.
Hotels: Beechmount; Russell Arms;
Ardboyne, Navan.
Meals served.

AA 81 Rush

Tel. Dublin (01) 437548
Rush, Co. Dublin.
T1 to Lusk, then L96, 16 miles from Dublin.
Seaside course.
9 holes, 3084 yds. S.S.S. 69
Visitors welcome on weekdays.
Green Fees. £4.00.
Society Meetings welcome weekdays
and Sat. mornings.
Hotels: Holmpatrick, Skerries.
Meals served by arrangement.

AA 82 St. Anne's

Tel. Dublin (01) 332797 / 336471
Bull Island, Clontarf, Dublin 5.
4 miles from Dublin.
Seaside course.
9 holes, 6104 yds. S.S.S. 67
Visitors welcome on weekdays.
Green Fees. £5.00 (£2.50 with member).
Society Meetings by arrangement.
Hotels: in Dublin.
Meals served by arrangement.

AA 83 Skerries

Tel. Dublin (01) 491204 / 491567
Hacketstown, Skerries, Co. Dublin.
Signposted from town of Skerries.
Parkland course.
18 holes, 6298 yds. S.S.S. 69
Visitors welcome.
Green Fees. Weekdays £4.00 (£2.50 with
member); weekends £6.00 (£3.00 with
member).
Hotels: Holmpatrick; Skerries.
Meals served.

AA 84 Slade Valley

Tel. 01-582207
Brittas, Co. Dublin.
NW side of Dublin Mountains. Via Naas road
and through Saggart village for 1½ miles, or
off Blessington road 1 mile.
Undulating parkland course.
18 holes, 5995 yds. S.S.S. 68
Course designed by W. Sullivan and D.
O'Brien.
Visitors welcome most days; ladies' day
Tues.
Green Fees. Weekdays £4.00 (£2.00 with
member); weekends £5.00 (£3.00 with
member).
Society Meetings welcome; dates
available most weekdays and weekend
mornings.
Hotels: Green Isle; Cill Dara, Naas Road.
Meals available most evenings.

AA 85 Strandhill

Tel. Sligo (071) 78188
Strandhill, Co. Sligo.
5 miles W of town.
Seaside course.
18 holes, 5600 yds. S.S.S. 66
Visitors welcome.
Green Fees. Weekdays £2.00; weekends
£3.00.
Society Meetings by arrangement.
Hotels: Kincora; Baymount; Sancta Maria;
Ocean View.
Snacks served.

AA 86 Sutton

Tel. Dublin (01) 323013
Cush Point, Sutton, Dublin 13.
7 miles NE of city centre.
Seaside course.
9 holes, 5522 yds. S.S.S. 65
Visitors welcome except Tues. and Sat.
between 1.00 and 5.00 p.m.
Green Fees. Weekdays £3.00; weekends
£5.00.
Society Meetings by arrangement.
Hotels: Marine, Sutton; Claremont; Royal,
Howth.
Meals served by arrangement.

AA 87 Swinford

Brabazon Park, Swinford, Co. Mayo.
Parkland course.
9 holes, 5220 yds. S.S.S. 66
Visitors welcome.
Green Fees. £1.00 per day; weekly £4.00.
Hotels: O'Connor's, Swinford; Westways,
Kiltimagh.

AA 88 Tuam

Tel. Tuam (0903) 24354
Barnacurragh, Tuam, Co. Galway.
2 miles from Tuam on the Athenry road.
Parkland course.
9 holes, 3033 yds. S.S.S. 67
Course designed by E. Hackett.
Visitors welcome.
Green Fees. On application to Secretary.
Society Meetings welcome except Sun.
Hotels: Imperial; Hermitage, Tuam.

AA 89 Virginia

Tel. Virginia 35
Virginia, Co. Cavan.
50 miles N of Dublin on Dublin to Cavan road.
Parkland course.
9 holes, 4282 yds. S.S.S. 61
Course designed by Hession & Gallacher
(Rooskey) Ltd.
Visitors welcome except on Thurs. after
6.00 p.m. and Sun. between 3.00 p.m. and
6.30 p.m.
Green Fees. Weekdays £1.00; weekends
£1.50.
Society Meetings welcome.
Hotels: Park Hotel.
Meals served.

AA 90 Westport

Tel. Westport 547
Carrowholly, Westport, Co. Mayo.
2 miles from Westport.
Parkland course.
18 holes, 6706 yds. S.S.S. 71
Course designed by Hawtry & Sons.
Visitors welcome.
Green Fees. Weekdays £4.00 (£2.00 with
member); weekends £5.00 (£2.50 with
member).
Society Meetings welcome.
Hotels: Clew Bay; Castlecourt; Ryan; Hotel
Westport.
Snacks and meals served.

BB South Eire

BB 1 Abbey Leix

Abbey Leix, Co. Leix.
60 miles S of Dublin, ¼ mile off main Dublin-
Cork road.
Parkland course.
9 holes, 5790 yds. S.S.S. 67
Hotels: Hibernian Hotel; Devesci Arms
Hotel.
Green Fees. £2.00 per day; weekly
£10.00.

BB 2 Adare Manor

Tel. Adare (061) 94204, Sec. 54513
Adare, Co. Limerick.
10 miles from Limerick on Killarney road.
Parkland course.
9 holes, 5430 yds. S.S.S. 65
Visitors welcome.
Green Fees. £4.00.
Society Meetings welcome on weekdays.
Hotels: Dunraven Arms.
Snacks served; lunches by arrangement.

BB 3 Arklow

Tel. Arklow (0402) 2492
Abbeylands, Arklow, Co. Wicklow.
½ mile from Arklow.
Seaside course.
18 holes, 5963 yds. S.S.S. 68
Course designed by Hawtree and Taylor.
Visitors welcome except Sun.
Green Fees. Weekdays £3.00; weekends
£4.00; weekly £10.00.
Society Meetings welcome except Sun.
Hotels: Royal; Bridge; Arklow Bay Hotel;
Hoynes.
Meals served by arrangement.

BB 4 Athy

Tel. Athy 21455
Geraldine, Athy, Co. Kildare.
On T6, 2 miles N of Athy.
Undulating grassland course.
9 holes, 6200 yds. S.S.S. 68
Visitors welcome.
Hotels: Leinster Arms, Athy; Kilkea Castle
Hotel, Castledemont.
Meals served by arrangement for groups
only.

BB 5 Ballybunion

Tel. Ballybunion (068) 27146.
Sandhill Rd., Ballybunion, Co. Kerry

9 miles from Listowel on L106.
Seaside course.
18 holes, 6500 yds. S.S.S. 71
Visitors welcome.
Green Fees. £5.00 per day; weekly
£20.00; monthly £30.00.
Society Meetings welcome.
Hotels: Marine; Castle Hotel; Central Hotel.
Snacks and meals served 11.00a.m. to
9.00p.m.

BB 6   Baltinglass

Tel. Baltinglass 52
Baltinglass, Co. Wicklow.
38 miles S of Dublin.
Parkland course.
9 holes, 3026 yds. S.S.S. 68
Visitors welcome.
Green Fees. £2.00 per day.
Society Meetings by arrangement.
Hotels: Downshire, Blessington; Royal,
Carlow.
Meals served by arrangement.

BB 7   Bandon

Tel. Bandon (023) 41111, Pro. 42224
Castlebernard, Bandon, Co. Cork.

Signposted from Bandon.
Parkland course.
18 holes, 6101 yds. S.S.S. 68
Course designed by Cotton (C.K.), Pennink
& Lawrie.
Visitors welcome.
Green Fees. Weekdays £3.00 (£2.00 with
member); weekends £4.00 (£2.00 with
member).
Society Meetings welcome.
Hotels: Munster Arms.
Full catering facilities.

BB 8   Berehaven

Tel. Castletown Bear 24
Berehaven, Castletown Bear, Co. Cork.
9 holes, 4950 yds. S.S.S. 64

BB 9   Birr

Tel. Birr 82
The Glenns, Birr, Co. Offaly.
About 2 miles from Birr.
Undulating course.
18 holes, 6216 yds. S.S.S. 68
Visitors welcome.
Green Fees. Weekdays £1.50; weekends
£2.00.

Society Meetings by arrangement.
Hotels: County Arms; Dooly's; Egans.
Snacks served.

BB 10   Blainroe

Tel. Wicklow (0404) 2675
Blainroe, Co. Wicklow
3 miles S of Wicklow on coast road.
Coastal parkland course.
18 holes, 6681 yds. S.S.S. 72
Course designed by F.W. Hawtree & Sons.
Visitors welcome daily, weekly, monthly.
Green Fees. On application.
Society Meetings welcome. Special rates
available on application.
Hotels: in Wicklow and Arklow.
Full catering available.

BB 11   Borris

Tel. Carlow (0503) 73143
New Ross Rd., Carlow.
On Carlow to Waterford road.
Parkland course.
9 holes, 6004 yds. S.S.S. 68
Course designed by Col. J.H. Curry.
Visitors welcome.

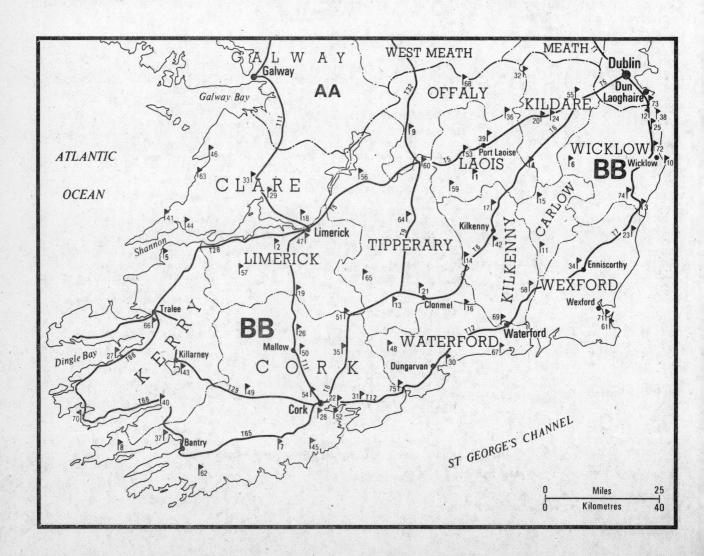

Green Fees. Weekdays £2.00; Sun. and public holidays £3.00.
Society Meetings Mon. to Sat. by arrangement.
Hotels: New Park Hotel, Kilkenny; Royal; Carlow Lodge Hotel, Carlow; Idrone, Borris.
Meals served by arrangement.

BB 12   Bray

Tel. Bray 862092
Bray, Co. Wicklow.
L29 from Dublin, 12 miles.
Parkland course.
9 holes, 6398 yds. S.S.S. 68
Visitors welcome weekends after 5.00 p.m.
Hotels: Royal Starlight; Mellifont, Bray.
Lunches served by arrangement.

BB 13   Cahir Park

Tel. Cahir 474
Kilcommon, Cahir, Co. Tipperary.
On Dublin to Cork road.
Parkland course.
9 holes, 6262 yds. S.S.S. 68
Course designed by E. Hackett.
Visitors welcome.
Green Fees. On application to Secretary.
Society Meetings welcome Mon. to Sat.
Hotels: Cahir House Hotel; Kilcoran Lodge Hotel.
Snacks served.

BB 14   Callan

Tel. Callan (056) 25136
Geraldine, Callan, Co. Kilkenny.
10 miles SW of Kilkenny.
Undulating meadowland course.
9 holes, 5656 yds. S.S.S. 66
Course designed by P. Mahon.
Visitors welcome.
Green Fees. On application to Secretary.
Society Meetings welcome except Sun.
Hotels: in Kilkenny.
Meals served by arrangement.

BB 15   Carlow

Tel. Carlow (0503) 31695; Sec. (0503) 42599
Deer Park, Carlow, Co. Carlow.
1 mile from station.
Parkland course.
18 holes, 6521 yds. S.S.S. 70
Course designed by Simpson.
Visitors welcome.
Green Fees. Weekdays £3.00; weekends £6.00.
Hotels: Royal; Oaklands; Lodge Hotel Carlow; Kilkea Castle.
Catering on premises.

BB 16   Carrick-on-Suir

Tel. Carrick-on-Suir 47
Garavoone, Carrick-on-Suir, Co. Tipperary.
16 miles W of Waterford.
Parkland/moorland course.
9 holes, 6176 yds. S.S.S. 68
Course designed by E. Hackett.
Visitors welcome.
Green Fees. £1.50 per day.
Society Meetings welcome except Sun.
Hotels: Tinvane; Bessborough Arms.
Snacks served.

BB 17   Castlecomer

Tel. 056 41258
Castlecomer, Co. Kilkenny.
9 holes, 6824 yds. S.S.S. 70
Visitors welcome.
Green Fees. Weekdays £2.00; weekends £3.00.

BB 18   Castleroy

Tel. Limerick (061) 45261
Castleroy, Limerick.
2 miles from Limerick off Limerick to Dublin road.
Undulating parkland course.
18 holes, 6089 yds. S.S.S. 68
Course designed by Maj. Ronnie Deakin.
Visitors welcome Mon. to Sat.
Green Fees. £4.00 per day.
Society Meetings by arrangement.
Hotels: Parkway Motel.
Meals served.

BB 19   Charleville

Tel. Charleville (063) 257
Smiths Rd., Charleville, Co. Cork.
On Limerick to Cork road 20 miles from Limerick.
Parkland course.
18 holes, 6380 yds. S.S.S. 71
Visitors welcome on weekdays.
Green Fees. On application to Secretary.
Society Meetings Sat. only.
Hotels: Imperial; Deer Park Hotel.
Meals served for Society Meetings only.

BB 20   Cill Dara

Tel. Kildare (045) 21433
Kildare, Co. Kildare.
1 mile E of Kildare.
Moorland course.
9 holes, 6196 yds. S.S.S. 66
Visitors welcome.
Green Fees. Weekdays £2.00 per day; weekends £3.00 per day.
Society Meetings by arrangement.
Hotels: Derby House Hotel, Kildare; Hotel Kaedeen, Newbridge.
Meals served by arrangement.

BB 21   Clonmel

Tel. Clonmel (052) 21138
Mountain Rd., Clonmel, Co. Tipperary.
3 miles SE of Clonmel.
Meadowland course.
18 holes, 6330 yds. S.S.S. 69
Course designed by E. Hackett.
Visitors welcome.
Green Fees. Weekdays £2.00; weekends £3.00.
Society Meetings by arrangement.
Hotels: Clonmel Arms.
Meals served.

BB 22   Cork

Tel. Cork (021) 953451, 953037, 953263
Little Island, Co. Cork.
5 miles E of Cork.
Parkland course.
Medal 18 holes, 6362 yds. S.S.S. 69
Championship 18 holes, 6635 yds. S.S.S. 71
Course designed by David Brown,

redesigned by Cotton, Pennink & Lawrie.
Visitors welcome.
Green Fees. Weekdays £5.00 (£3.00 with member); weekends £6.00 (£3.00 with member).
Society Meetings welcome.
Hotels: Silver Springs; Tivoli; Metropole, Cork; Ashbourne House, Glounthane.
Meals served.

BB 23   Courtown

Tel. Gorey (055) 25166
Kiltennel, Gorey, Co. Wexford.
3½ miles from Gorey.
Parkland course.
18 holes, 6398 yds. S.S.S. 69
Course designed by Harris and Cotton.
Visitors welcome.
Green Fees. Weekdays £3.00; weekends £4.00.
Society Meetings welcome except June to August.
Hotels: in Courtown.
Meals served.

BB 24   Curragh

Tel. Curragh (045) 41238
Curragh, Co. Kildare.
Undulating parkland course.
18 holes, 6564 yds. S.S.S. 70
Visitors welcome.
Green Fees. Weekdays £3.00; weekends £5.00.
Society Meetings by arrangement.
Hotels: Keadeen; Lumville House Hotel; Jockey Hall Hotel; Rockingham Hotel.
Snacks served.

BB 25   Delgany

Tel. Dublin (01) 874645, 874536
Delgany, Co. Wicklow.
Off T7, 15 miles S of Dublin.
Parkland course.
18 holes, 5937 yds. S.S.S. 67
Visitors welcome.
Green Fees. Weekdays £3.00; weekends £6.00.
Society Meetings by arrangement.
Hotels: Delgany Inn; Wicklow Arms; Horse and Hounds; Glenview.
Meals served except Mon.

BB 26   Doneraile

Tel. Doneraile (022) 24137
Doneraile, Co. Cork.
Off T11, 28 miles N of Cork, 9 miles from Mallow.
Parkland course.
9 holes, 5528 yds. S.S.S. 66
Visitors welcome.
Green Fees. £2.00.
Society Meetings welcome.
Hotels: Central Hotel; Hibernian, Mallow; Deerpark, Charleville.
Meals served.

BB 27   Dooks

Tel. Glenbeigh 5
Glenbeigh, Co. Kerry.
Off T66, 8 miles W of Killorglin.
Seaside course.
18 holes, 5694 yds. S.S.S. 66

Visitors welcome.
Green Fees. Apr. to Oct. £2.50 per day; weekly £12.00; Nov. to Mar. £1.50 per day.
Society Meetings welcome.
Hotels: Towers; Glenbeigh Hotel; Falcon Inn; Bianconi.

BB 28   Douglas

Tel. Cork (021) 291086, 295297
Douglas, Co. Cork.
2½ miles S of Cork city centre.
Parkland course.
18 holes, 6270 yds. S.S.S. 69
Visitors welcome on weekdays except Tues., weekend afternoons with reservation.
Green Fees. Weekdays £5.00; weekends £6.00.
Society Meetings by arrangement.
Hotels: Imperial; Jury's; Hotel Metropole, Cork.
Meals served.

BB 29   Dromoland Castle

Tel. 061 71144, Telex 26854
Newmarket-on-Fergus, Co. Clare.
On T11, 18 miles NW of Limerick.
Parkland course.
9 holes.
Course designed by B.E. Wiggington.
Visitors welcome April to October.
Green Fees. £2.50 per day.
Society Meetings welcome.
Hotels: Dromoland Castle Hotel; Clare Inn.
Meals served.

BB 30   Dungarvan

Tel. 058 41605
Ballinacourty, Dungarvan, Co. Waterford.
On T63, 3½ miles E of Dungarvan.
Meadowland course.
9 holes, 6332 yds. S.S.S. 68
Course designed by E. Hackett.
Visitors welcome.
Green Fees. Weekdays £1.50 per day (£1.00 with member); weekends £2.00 (£1.00 with member).
Society Meetings by arrangement.
Hotels: Ocean View Hotel.
Light meals served by arrangement.

BB 31   East Cork

Tel. Cork (021) 631687
Gortacrue, Midleton, Co. Cork.
1 mile N of Midleton; signposted.
Meadowland course.
18 holes, 5700 yds. S.S.S. 66
Visitors welcome.
Green Fees. £2.50 per day.
Society Meetings welcome, 2 months' notice required.
Lunches served; snacks all day.

BB 32   Edenderry

Tel. Edenderry (0405) 31072
Edenderry, Co. Offaly.
On T41, 30 miles W of Dublin.
Parkland, moorland course.
9 holes, 5771 yds. S.S.S. 67
Course designed by Travers.
Visitors welcome on weekdays, Sat. with reservation.

Green Fees. Weekdays £1.00; weekends £2.00.
Society Meetings Sat. only.
Meals served on Sat. for societies only.

BB 33   Ennis

Tel. Ennis (065) 21070
Drumbiggle, Ennis, Co. Clare.
1 mile W of Ennis.
Parkland course.
18 holes, 5890 yds. S.S.S. 66
Visitors welcome.
Green Fees. On application to Secretary.
Society Meetings by arrangement.
Hotels: West Country Inn; Queens; Old Ground; Auburn Lodge Hotel.
Snacks served; meals by arrangement.

BB 34   Enniscorthy

Tel. Enniscorthy (054) 2191
Knock Marshall, Enniscorthy, Co. Wexford.
On T7, 75 miles S of Dublin.
Parkland course.
9 holes, 6278 yds. S.S.S. 68
Visitors welcome on weekdays.
Green Fees. Weekdays £1.50; weekends £2.00.
Society Meetings welcome on weekdays.
Hotels: Murphy-Floods, Enniscorthy; Talbot; White's, Wexford.
Catering limited.

BB 35   Fermoy

Tel. (025) 31472
Fermoy, Co. Cork.
On T6, 20 miles NE of Cork.
Heathland course.
18 holes, 6200 yds. S.S.S. 67
Course designed by Commander Harris.
Visitors welcome.
Green Fees. £2.00 per day (£1.50 with member).
Society Meetings by arrangement.
Hotels: Grand; Royal.
Meals served by arrangement.

BB 36   Garryhinch

Tel. Portarlington (0502) 23115
Portarlington, Co. Offaly.
6 miles from Monasterevin.
Parkland course.
9 holes, 5598 yds. S.S.S. 66
Visitors welcome.
Green Fees. On application to Secretary.
Society Meetings welcome except Sun.
Hotels: Montague, Portlaoise; Hazel, Monasterevin.
Meals served by arrangement. Meals for societies to be booked 1 week in advance.

BB 37   Glengarriff

Glengarriff, Co. Cork.
On T65, 55 miles W of Cork.
Undulating parkland course.
18 holes, 6250 yds. S.S.S. 61
Visitors welcome.
Green Fees. £2.50 per day.
Hotels: Mountain View Hotel; Golf Links; Casey's; Eccles Hotel.
Snacks served.

BB 38   Greystones

Tel. Dublin (01) 874136
Greystones, Co. Wicklow.
On L29, 15 miles S of Dublin.
Parkland course.
18 holes, 5921 yds. S.S.S. 67
Visitors welcome on weekdays. Ladies' day Thurs.
Green Fees. £5.00 per day.
Hotels: La Touche; Woodlands.
Meals served by arrangement.

BB 39   Heath

Tel. Portlaoise (0502) 26533
The Heath, Portlaoise, Co. Laois.
On T5, 4 miles NE of Portlaoise.
Moorland course.
18 holes, 6125 yds. S.S.S. 68
Visitors welcome.
Green Fees. On application to Secretary.
Society Meetings welcome.
Hotels: Killeshin; Montague Motel; Cappakeel.
Meals served for parties by arrangement.

BB 40   Kenmare

Tel. (064) 41291
Kenmare, Co. Kerry.
On T65, 20 miles S of Killarney.
Seaside course.
9 holes, S.S.S. 62
Visitors welcome.
Green Fees. £3.00 per day.
Society Meetings welcome.
Hotels: Kenmare Bay Hotel; Riversdale House Hotel; Park Hotel.

BB 41   Kilkee

Tel. Kilkee 48
East End, Kilkee, Co. Clare.
On T41, 57 miles W of Limerick.
Meadowland seaside course.
9 holes, 5970 yds. S.S.S. 68
Visitors welcome.
Green Fees. £1.50 per day.
Society Meetings welcome.
Hotels: in Kilkee.

BB 42   Kilkenny

Tel. Kilkenny (056) 22125
Glendine, Kilkenny, Co. Kilkenny.
2 miles N of town off Castlecomer Rd.
Parkland course.
18 holes, 6359 yds. S.S.S. 69
Visitors welcome except Sat. after 11.30a.m.
Green Fees. Weekdays £4.00; weekends £5.00.
Society Meetings by arrangement.
Hotels: New Park Hotel; Rose Hill Hotel; Spring Hill Hotel; Clubhouse Hotel.
Meals served by arrangement.

BB 43   Killarney

Tel. 064 31034
Mahony's Point, Killarney, Co. Kerry.
On T29, 3 miles E of Killarney.
Undulating lakeside courses.
Killeen 18 holes, 6893 yds. S.S.S. 73
Mahony's Point 18 holes, 6734 yds. S.S.S. 72

Course designed by Sir Guy Campbell.
Visitors welcome.
Green Fees. £5.00 per day; weekly £24.00.
Society Meetings welcome.
Hotels: in area.
Snacks served; meals except Mon.

BB 44 Kilrush

Tel. Kilrush 138
Parknamoney, Kilrush, Co. Clare.
On T41, 1 mile NE of Kilrush.
Meadowland course.
9 holes, 5478 yds. S.S.S. 66
Visitors welcome.
Green Fees. £2.00 per day (juniors £1.00); weekly £10.00 (juniors £5.00); fortnightly £14.00 (juniors £7.00).
Society Meetings by arrangement.
Hotels: Riverside Hotel, Kilrush.

BB 45 Kinsale

Tel. Cork (021) 72197
Ringnanean, Belgooly, Co. Cork.
On L42, 14 miles S of Cork.
Moorland riverside course.
9 holes, 2790 yds. S.S.S. 65
Visitors welcome on weekdays, weekends with reservation.
Green Fees. £3.00 per day; weekly £10.00.
Society Meetings by arrangement.
Hotels: in Kinsale.

BB 46 Lahinch

Tel. Lahinch 3
Lahinch, Co. Clare.
On T69, 20 miles W of Ennis (Shannon 30 miles).
Seaside course.
Old 18 holes, 6500 yds. S.S.S. 70
New 18 holes, 5400 yds. S.S.S. 66
Course designed by Tom Morris Sen.; redesigned by Dr. A. McKenzie.
Visitors welcome.
Green Fees. Old course £5.00 per day; weekly £25.00. New course £3.00 per day; weekly £15.00.
Society Meetings by arrangement.
Hotels: Aberdeen Hotel; Atlantic Hotel; Santa Maria; Claremont; Falls Hotel, Ennistrymin; Liscannor Hotel, Liscannor.
Meals served.

BB 47 Limerick

Tel. Limerick 44083
Ballyclough, Limerick.
On T11, 4 miles S of Limerick.
Parkland course.
18 holes, 6355 yds. S.S.S. 69
Course designed by James Braid.
Visitors welcome on weekdays, weekends by arrangement.
Green Fees. £4.00 per day.
Hotels: Hanratty's; Cruises; Jury's; Ryan's Ardhu; Limerick Inn; Parkway Motel.
Meals served by arrangement.

BB 48 Lismore

Tel. 058 54026
Lismore, Co. Waterford.
On T30, 35 miles NE of Cork.

Parkland course.
9 holes, 5460 yds. S.S.S. 66
Course designed by E. Hackett.
Visitors welcome.
Green Fees. £2.00 per day.
Society Meetings welcome except Sun.
Hotels: Keaneland; Ballyrafter House Hotel.

BB 49 Macroom

Tel. Macroom 72
Lackaduv, Macroom, Co. Cork.
On T29, 24 miles W of Cork.
Parkland, meadowland course.
9 holes, 5935 yds. S.S.S. 67
Visitors welcome.
Green Fees. £3.00 per day.
Society Meetings welcome.
Hotels: Castle Hotel; Victoria.

BB 50 Mallow

Tel. Mallow (022) 21145
Mallow, Co. Cork.
On T11, 21 miles N of Cork.
Parkland course.
18 holes, 6700 yds. S.S.S. 71
Visitors welcome.
Green Fees. Weekdays £2.50 per day; weekends £3.00.
Society Meetings by arrangement.
Hotels: Central Hotel; Hibernian; Langueville House Hotel.
Limited accommodation in clubhouse. Meals served.

BB 51 Mitchelstown

Tel. (025) 24072
Gurrane, Mitchelstown, Co. Cork.
On T6, ½ mile from Michelstown.
Undulating parkland course.
9 holes, 5474 yds. S.S.S. 66
Visitors welcome.
Green Fees. £2.00 per day.
Society Meetings welcome.
Hotels: Royal; Kilcoran Lodge Hotel; Glauca Maura Inn.

BB 52 Monkstown

Tel. Cork (021) 841225 (Pro.), 841376 (Sec.)
Parkgarriffe, Monkstown, Co. Cork.
On L68, 7 miles S of Cork.
Parkland course.
18 holes, 5654 yds. S.S.S. 68
Visitors welcome on weekdays.
Green Fees. Weekdays £4.00 per day (£3.00 with member); weekends £5.00 (£3.00 with member).
Society Meetings welcome on weekdays.
Hotels: Norwood Court, Rochestown; Club Hotel, Glenbrook.
Meals served except Mon.

BB 53 Mountrath

Mountrath, Co. Laoise.
8 miles from Portlaoise on main Dublin-Limerick road.
9 holes, 5196 yds. S.S.S. 65
Visitors welcome.
Hotels: Pathe Hotel, Roscrea; Killeshin; Kelly's; County, Portlaoise.

BB 54 Muskerry

Tel. Muskerry (021) 85297, 85104
Carrigrohane, Co. Cork.
7 miles W of city centre.
Undulating parkland course.
18 holes, 6315 yds. S.S.S. 70
Visitors welcome on weekdays.
Green Fees. £4.00 per day.
Society Meetings welcome weekdays only.
Hotels: in Cork.
Snacks served.

BB 55 Naas

Tel. 045 97509
Kardiffstown, Sallins, Naas, Co. Kildare.
Leave dual carriageway at Johnstown Village and take link road N of carriageway to Sallins.
18 holes, 6233 yds. S.S.S. 68
Visitors welcome.
Green Fees. £3.50.
Society Meetings welcome Mon. Wed. and Fri.
Hotels: Lawlor's; Osberstown House Hotel; Cill Dara; Town House; Osta John Devoy.

BB 56 Nenagh

Tel. Nenagh (067) 31476
Nenagh, Co. Tipperary.
3½ miles from Nenagh, signposted.
Inland course.
18 holes, 6006 yds. S.S.S. 67
Course designed by E. Hackett.
Visitors welcome.
Green Fees. Weekdays £2.00; weekends £3.00.
Society Meetings by arrangement.
Hotels: O'Meara's; Ormonde.
Meals served by arrangement.

BB 57 Newcastle West

Tel. Newcastle West 76
Newcastle West, Co. Limerick.
1 mile from town on road to Cork.
Meadowland course.
9 holes, 5400 yds. S.S.S. 65
Visitors welcome.
Green Fees. On application to Secretary.
Society Meetings by arrangement.
Hotels: River Room Motel; Devon Hotel; Central Hotel.

BB 58 New Ross

Tel. New Ross (051) 21433
Tinneranny, New Ross, Co. Wexford.
1 mile W of New Ross.
Meadowland course.
9 holes, 6080 yds. S.S.S. 68
Visitors welcome.
Green Fees. £1.50 per day.
Society Meetings welcome.
Hotels: Five Counties Hotel; Royal Hotel.
Meals served.

BB 59 Rathdowney

Rathdowney, Portlaoise, Co. Leix.
9 holes, 6416 yds. S.S.S. 66
Visitors welcome.
Hotels: Central, Rathdowney.

BB 60   Roscrea

Tel. Roscrea (0505) 21130
Dublin Rd., Roscrea, Co. Tipperary.
2 miles from town centre.
Parkland course.
9 holes, 6059 yds. S.S.S. 68
Visitors welcome.
Green Fees. £2.00.
Hotels: Pathe; Tower; Rackett Hall.

BB 61   Rosslare

Tel. 053 32113
Rosslare, Co. Wexford.
Seaside course.
Blue course: 18 holes, 6495 yds.
White course: 18 holes, 6066 yds.
Visitors welcome.
Green Fees. Weekdays £4.00; weekends
£5.00 per day; weekly £18.00.
Hotels: Strand; Iona; Golf; Cedars.
Lunches served.

BB 62   Skibbereen

Tel. Skibbereen (028) 21227
Skibbereen, Co. Cork.
Off T65, 47 miles SW of Cork.
Moorland course.
9 holes, 5890 yds. S.S.S. 67
Visitors welcome.
Green Fees. £3.00 per day, £15.00 per
week.
Society Meetings welcome.
Hotels: West Cork; Eldon; Lissard House.

BB 63   Spanish Point

Spanish Point, Miltown Malbay, Co. Clare.
2 miles from Miltown Malbay on sea front.
9 holes, 3044 yds. S.S.S. 54
Visitors welcome.
Hotels: Central Hotel, Miltown Malbay.

BB 64   Thurles

Tel. Thurles (0504) 21983
Turtulla, Thurles, Co. Tipperary.
1½ miles from town centre on Cork road.
Parkland course.
18 holes, 6300 yds. S.S.S. 69
Visitors welcome.
Green Fees. £3.50 per day.
Society Meetings welcome.
Hotels: Anner; Haye's.
Meals served.

BB 65   Tipperary

Tel. 062 51119
Rathanny, Tipperary.
1 mile from town.
Parkland course.
9 holes, 6054 yds. S.S.S. 68
Visitors welcome except Mon.
Green Fees. On application to Secretary.
Society Meetings by arrangement.
Hotels: Glen; Royal; Aherlow House Hotel,
Tipperary.

BB 66   Tralee

Tel. Tralee 21150, Sec. 22406
Mount Hawk, Tralee, Co. Kerry.
T68 from Limerick.
Parkland course.
9 holes, 6086 yds. S.S.S. 68
Visitors welcome.
Green Fees. £3.00 per day.
Society Meetings welcome.
Hotels: in Tralee.
Lunches and snacks served.

BB 67   Tramore

Tel. Tramore (051) 81247
Newtown Hill, Tramore, Co. Waterford.
Via Waterford, 1 mile beyond Tramore.
Parkland course.
18 holes, 6408 yds. S.S.S. 70
Course designed by Tibbett (1936/7).
Visitors welcome.
Green Fees. Weekdays £4.50; weekends
£6.00.
Society Meetings by arrangement.
Hotels: Majestic; Grand; Sea View Hotel.
Meals served except Mon.

BB 68   Tullamore

Tel. Tullamore (0506) 21439
Brookfield, Tullamore, Co. Offaly.
2 miles SW of town, T41 from Dublin.
Parkland course.
18 holes, 6254 yds. S.S.S. 69
Course designed by J. Braid.
Visitors welcome.
Green Fees. Weekdays £3.00; weekends
£5.00.
Society Meetings by arrangement.
Hotels: Haye's Hotel; Bridge House,
Tullamore.
Meals served.

BB 69   Waterford

Tel. Waterford (051) 74182 & 76748
Newrath, Waterford.
½ mile from city centre.
Parkland course.
18 holes, 6185 yds. S.S.S. 68
Course designed by J. Braid.
Visitors welcome on weekdays.
Green Fees. Weekdays £2.00 (£1.50 with
member); weekends £2.50 (£2.00 with
member).
Society Meetings welcome weekdays
and Sat. morning between 11a.m. and
12.30p.m.
Hotels: Ardree; Metropole; Bridge Hotel;
Tower Hotel; Dooleys Hotel.
Meals served except Fri.

BB 70   Waterville

Tel. Waterville (066) 23100, Telex 28246
Waterville Lake Hotel, Waterville, Ring of
Kerry.
18 holes, 7146 yds. S.S.S. 74
Visitors welcome.

BB 71   Wexford

Tel. Wexford 053 22238
Wexford, Co. Wexford.
Parkland course.
9 holes, 6108 yds. S.S.S. 68
Visitors welcome.
Hotels: Talbot; White's, Wexford; Kelly's
Strand, Rosslare.

BB 72   Wicklow

Dunbur Rd., Wicklow, Co. Wicklow.
On L29, 32 miles S of Dublin.
Undulating seaside course.
Visitors welcome.
Green Fees. Weekdays £4.00; weekends
£5.00 (half rates when playing with
member).
Hotels: Grand; Strabreaga.
Limited catering.

BB 73   Woodbrook

Tel. Dublin (01) 821343
Bray, Co. Wicklow.
N11, 11 miles S of Dublin.
Parkland course.
18 holes, 6499 yds. S.S.S. 71
Visitors welcome.
Green Fees. Weekdays £5.00; weekends
£8.50.
Hotels: Killiney Castle Hotel.
Meals served.

BB 74   Woodenbridge

Tel. Arklow (0402) 5202
Arklow, Co. Wicklow.
On T7, 45 miles S of Dublin.
Parkland course.
9 holes, S.S.S. 66
Visitors welcome except Sat.
Green Fees. Weekdays £4.00 (£3.00 with
member); weekends £5.00 (£4.00 with
member).
Hotels: Woodenbridge Hotel; Valley Hotel;
Valeview Hotel.
Limited catering.

BB 75   Youghal

Tel. 024 2787
Knockaverry, Youghal, Co. Cork.
30 miles from Cork, 48 miles from Waterford
on N25 Cork/Waterford road.
18 holes, 6067 yds. S.S.S. 69
Visitors welcome.
Hotels: Hilltop Hotel; Walter Raleigh Hotel;
Motor Inn; Monatrea House Hotel.

Index